# MANAGING LOCAL GOVERNMENT SERVICES

## A PRACTICAL GUIDE

A completely revised and updated version of *Managing Small Cities and Counties*

**Edited by Carl W. Stenberg and Susan Lipman Austin**

Published by ICMA in cooperation with the Institute of Government, School of Government, University of North Carolina at Chapel Hill

ICMA is the premier local government leadership and management organization. Its mission is to create excellence in local governance by developing and advocating professional management of local government worldwide. ICMA provides member support; publications, data, and information; peer and results-oriented assistance; and training and professional development to more than 8,200 city, town, and county experts and other individuals throughout the world.

Established in 1931, the Institute of Government provides training, advisory, and research services to public officials and others interested in the operation of state and local government in North Carolina. The Institute and the university's Master of Public Administration Program are the core activities of the School of Government at The University of North Carolina at Chapel Hill. For more information about the School, the Institute, and the MPA program, visit the Web site (www.sog.unc.edu) or call 919-966-5381.

Library of Congress Cataloging-in-Publication Data

Managing local government services : a practical guide / edited by Carl W. Stenberg and Susan Lipman Austin.
    p. cm.
 "A completely revised and updated version of Managing small cities and counties."
 Includes bibliographical references and index.
 ISBN-13: 978-0-87325-709-5 (alk. paper)
 ISBN-10: 0-87326-709-5 (alk. paper)
 1. Municipal services—United States—Management. I. Stenberg, Carl W. II. Austin, Susan Lipman. III. International City/County Management Association. IV. Managing small cities and counties.
 HD4605.M25 2007
 363.6068--dc22

2006039422

Design: Charles E. Mountain

Printed in the United States of America

2013 2012 2011 2010 2009 2008 2007 2006

5 4 3 2 1

# Contents

**Sidebars and figures highlighting local governments**

*Meeting the Challenge of Change*

### The Clerk

### Budgeting and Financial Management

### Human Resource Management

### Emergency Management

### Police Services

### Fire and Other Emergency Services

### Service Delivery Alternatives

*A Manager's Toolbox*

Note: Unless otherwise noted, all populations shown in sidebars are July 2005 estimates from the U.S. Bureau of the Census.

# Foreword

*M*anaging Local Government Services is the third edition of ICMA's popular *Managing Small Cities and Counties: A Practical Guide*, developed and ably guided through its first two editions by James M. Banovetz, professor emeritus, Northern Illinois University.

For the third edition, Carl W. Stenberg and Susan Lipman Austin of the School of Government at the University of North Carolina at Chapel Hill assembled a team of practitioners and academics to refocus and update the text in a number of areas. The first chapter, by way of introduction, places local government management firmly in the context of "governance": the web of relationships that surrounds local program planning and service delivery. This chapter outlines demographic, economic, technological, and cultural trends that affect the management of service delivery.

A new chapter on alternative methods of service delivery addresses public-private options as well as intergovernmental service delivery approaches, and a new chapter on community development recognizes this increasingly important focus of management and service delivery. A new closing chapter presents the reader with "A Manager's Toolbox," five management practices that are fast becoming the standard for professional local government management. Other chapters cover the legal context in which cities and counties operate, and the basic management functions and core services that were covered in earlier editions.

Why the name change? The short answer is that the volume you hold in your hand has been, for two decades, ICMA's only text on the complete spectrum of services that the local government manager must make sure are provided. All local governments budget and plan, manage people to get work done, protect the health and safety of the community and its residents, promote economic growth, maintain the infrastructure, and work to uphold and improve the quality of life for all residents. The requirements for these basic services, defined and addressed in this book, are the same—although the level of demand may be higher in larger places.

*Managing Local Government Services* continues to highlight the problems and experience of managers in small communities, because most local government managers serve in small cities and counties. Managers in many small cities and counties do not have the staff or the financial resources to introduce and maintain a full spectrum of sophisticated services. Many of these managers must personally see to everything from purchasing to tree removal. Many feel that change is more difficult in a small place. This book addresses the special concerns of local governments with limited resources and closes every chapter with a set of questions designed for managers of small communities.

With this revision, *Managing Local Government Services* also recognizes its relevance to local governmental units of all sizes and its function as the comprehensive text on the subject. Focused on services, this new text is a companion to *The Effective Local Government Manager*, which addresses the tasks and roles of the manager-leader.

As communities continue to evolve in a world that is growing smaller, more competitive, more informed, and more conscious of environmental uncertainty, *Managing Local Government Services* will be a touchstone for the aspiring as well as the experienced local government manager. ICMA is pleased to publish this practical guide to the core work of the profession.

Robert J. O'Neill Jr.
Executive Director
ICMA

# *Preface*

This book has been written for local government professionals who lead and manage cities and counties and who are responsible for the efficient, effective, and equitable administration of services to citizens. It should be especially helpful to new or entry-level managers and those in smaller communities, to enable them to grasp the scope and complexity of local services and to appreciate the challenges and opportunities of governance.

A central theme of the book is that local managers operate in an increasingly complex environment, which involves building both a professional organization within their city or county and a capacity to engage with intergovernmental and intersectoral networks that are critical to successful problem-solving and service delivery. The knowledge, skills, and competencies needed to do so are wide-ranging, and call upon the manager to engage in organizational and community leadership.

The sixteen chapters have been organized to give the reader a broader and deeper perspective on the dynamic world of local government services. Our goal has been to produce a highly practical book that provides a "one-stop" overview of common organization, best practices, and challenging issues regarding management of core local services. Each chapter has been reviewed by a team of practitioners and academicians for accuracy, relevance, and state-of-the-art treatment.

A book like this involves contributions of many people. Susan Lipman Austin, project director at the University of North Carolina (UNC) at Chapel Hill Institute of Government, joined with me to co-edit this edition. She was particularly adept at managing communications and paper flows between the editors, authors, and reviewers and keeping the production of chapters on track. Christine Ulrich, ICMA's editorial director, provided valuable ideas and insights regarding topics, author selection, advisor recruitment, and substantive content. Jane Cotnoir, senior editor at ICMA, skillfully edited each of the chapters. We are indebted to the diverse team of authors who agreed to contribute their time and talent to the project. Finally, we would like to express our appreciation to Dean Michael Smith and our colleagues at the School of Government for their encouragement and support throughout this project.

We worked with an outstanding group of practitioner and academic advisors who read chapters from the second edition and suggested changes and additions in coverage of topics, reviewed chapter outlines for the third edition for content and continuity, and commented on the preliminary and final drafts of the chapters. We are indebted to the following members of the advisory board for their help ensuring that the project goals were met: Mike Abels, city manager, DeLand, Florida; Arthur Anselene, director of parks and recreation, Herndon, Virginia; Carol Bloodworth, city administrator (retired), Maize, Kansas; Frayda Bluestein, professor of public law and government, UNC–Chapel Hill; Barbara Blumenfield, regional vice president, ICMA Executive Board, and former city administrator of Oak Creek, Wisconsin; Jon Bormet, director, International Resource Cities Program; Octavio Chavez, resident advisor, ICMA-Mexico; Leon Churchill, managing director, Reading, Pennsylvania; Carla Dicandia, recreation supervisor, Saddleback Valley Unified School District, Mission Viejo, California; Rex Facer, assistant professor of public management, Brigham Young University; Daniel Fitzpatrick, city manager, Peekskill, New York; Joyce Forbes, village clerk, Riverdale, Illinois; Candace Goode Vick, associate professor of parks, recreation, and tourism management, North Carolina State University; Charles Gossett, professor of political science, California State Polytechnic University; Rod Gould, city manager, Poway, California; John Granito, special advisor, Management Partners Inc., Cincinnati, Ohio; John M. Greiner, senior management and budget specialist, Montgomery County, Maryland; David Habecker, assistant fire chief, Flossmoor, Illinois; Harry Hayes, local government project director, University of Georgia; Mike Johnson, city administrator, Marshall, Minnesota; Wendy Kellogg, associate professor of urban planning and environmental studies, Cleveland State University; Roger Kemp, author, consultant, and former manager of cities in California, New Jersey, and Connecticut; David Kilbane, village administrator, Round Lake Beach, Illinois; Kurt Kimball, city manager, Grand Rapids, Michigan; Greg Kuhn, senior associate, Northern Illinois University; Bob LaSala, city manager, Lancaster, California; Mark Levin, city administrator, Maryland Heights, Missouri; David Limardi, city manager, Highland Park, Illinois; J. Thomas McCarty, county administrator, Eau Claire County, Wisconsin; David McEntire, associate professor of emergency administration and planning, University of North Texas; Jonathan Q. Morgan, assistant professor of public administration and government, UNC–Chapel Hill; William Nelson, city manager, Dowagiac, Michigan; Brian Nickerson, associate professor of public administration, Pace University; David Niklaus, adjunct faculty, Southern Maine Community College; William C. Rivenbark, associate professor of public administration and government, UNC–Chapel Hill; Bruce Romer, chief administrative officer, Montgomery County, Maryland; John Rukavina, director of public safety, Wake County, North Carolina; John W. Swain, professor of public administration, Governors State University; Dave Timmons, city manager, Port Townsend, Washington; Victor Vasquez, assistant city manager, Grand Rapids, Michigan; Kenneth Vittum, town manager, Pearisburg, Virginia; and Gail Weniger, township manager, Warwick, Pennsylvania.

James M. Banovetz, editor of the first two editions, dedicated the book to local government leaders, who must anticipate and adapt to the challenge of change; develop goals and objectives for their communities; and manage the programs and services to achieve their vision. We too salute these leaders, to whom Americans have entrusted the quality of life in their communities, and dedicate the third edition to them.

Carl W. Stenberg
Chapel Hill, North Carolina

# Meeting the Challenge of Change

## Carl W. Stenberg

How cities and counties can adapt to the new economy and the information age is a key topic of debate among government reformers, public officials, civic groups, and students of local government. Increasingly, boundaries between local governments are blurring, responsibilities for service delivery are being shared, and partnerships and collaborative approaches across jurisdictions and sectors are becoming common. Citizens expect local governments to be entrepreneurial and equitable, as well as efficient and effective. And professional local government managers find themselves working as community leaders and change agents.

It wasn't always this way. Historically, cities and counties were responsible for basic services to support their communities, such as public safety, libraries, public utilities, public works, and cemeteries. Counties acted as arms of state government in unincorporated areas, and townships served citizens in rural areas in twenty states. Public education was provided by school districts, which were usually separate from general-purpose local governments. In most cases, these functions were predominantly or exclusively local, in the sense that their performance entailed little or no collaboration with other local jurisdictions or units, receipt of external funds, or regulation by state and federal authorities.

During the twentieth century, as our nation's population grew and became more urbanized, a new set of services was added to local government responsibilities. These services included land use planning, zoning and subdivision control, urban renewal, housing, parks and recreation, and public health and welfare. Over the past sixty years, local services have continued to expand and diversify. Joining the mix of city and county responsibilities have been animal control, job training, juvenile and senior centers, meals-on-wheels, community and economic development, emergency preparedness, leisure services, and environmental protection. Special districts have sprung up to finance and manage discrete services, such as flood control, water supply, and fire protection.

As Figure 1–1 illustrates, the expansion and diversification of responsibilities at the local level led to new layers of local government superimposed on the existing government structure. This trend also produced five troubling conditions: proliferation in the number of general and special-purpose local units; lack of uniformity in local government boundaries; service coordination problems; voter confusion and apathy; and high taxes and local government spending.

### Figure 1-1  New kinds of local government

New kinds of local government were superimposed on the existing government structure in response to changing local concerns and needs for services.

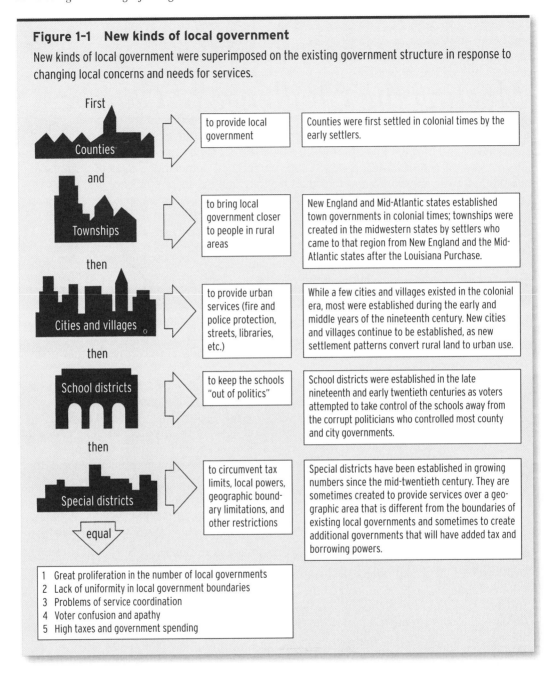

First

Counties

| | |
|---|---|
| to provide local government | Counties were first settled in colonial times by the early settlers. |

and

Townships

| | |
|---|---|
| to bring local government closer to people in rural areas | New England and Mid-Atlantic states established town governments in colonial times; townships were created in the midwestern states by settlers who came to that region from New England and the Mid-Atlantic states after the Louisiana Purchase. |

then

Cities and villages

| | |
|---|---|
| to provide urban services (fire and police protection, streets, libraries, etc.) | While a few cities and villages existed in the colonial era, most were established during the early and middle years of the nineteenth century. New cities and villages continue to be established, as new settlement patterns convert rural land to urban use. |

then

School districts

| | |
|---|---|
| to keep the schools "out of politics" | School districts were established in the late nineteenth and early twentieth centuries as voters attempted to take control of the schools away from the corrupt politicians who controlled most county and city governments. |

then

Special districts

| | |
|---|---|
| to circumvent tax limits, local powers, geographic boundary limitations, and other restrictions | Special districts have been established in growing numbers since the mid-twentieth century. They are sometimes created to provide services over a geographic area that is different from the boundaries of existing local governments and sometimes to create additional governments that will have added tax and borrowing powers. |

equal

1  Great proliferation in the number of local governments
2  Lack of uniformity in local government boundaries
3  Problems of service coordination
4  Voter confusion and apathy
5  High taxes and government spending

Reformers today criticize the irrational pattern of local governmental units; the excessive number of small jurisdictions performing a limited range of duties; the costly duplication of functions; the parochial orientations of local leaders; and the lack of coordination between special districts, school districts, and general-purpose local units. They also express concerns about limitations on the time and expertise of part-time elected officials and governing bodies, and about antiquated budgetary, personnel, and procurement rules under which many local governments operate. In their view, many communities are not prepared to tackle complex and costly problems that spill across local boundary lines, and are unable to take timely collective and authoritative remedial actions. These constraints make it difficult to provide the quality of life needed to attract and retain businesses and taxpayers in the competitive global economy of the twenty-first century.

Others argue the virtues of a government that is close to the citizen—virtues such as accessibility and affordability, the need for local autonomy and control, and the cost-effectiveness of voluntary leadership. They contend that democratic values of responsiveness and fairness are more important than technocratic values of efficiency and effectiveness. Moreover, they point out that while local government structure and operations may not meet ideal standards, in most places they work satisfactorily in delivering services demanded by the public at prices (i.e., taxes and fees) that citizens are willing to pay. Part-time elected officials, served by professional managers and their staff, rather than professional politicians are the appropriate leaders of grassroots community governments because they are close to both the problems and the citizens.[1]

> *Given the strong political and public support for maintaining the structural, functional, and financial status quo, how can local governments continue to provide the level of services expected by their citizens in a rapidly changing world?*

As is often the case in such debates, the real truth lies somewhere between the extremes. But the question remains relevant: given the strong political and public support for maintaining the structural, functional, and financial status quo in many communities, how can local governments continue to provide the level of services expected by their citizens in a rapidly changing world?

One thing is certain: these trends were accompanied by the need for greater professionalism in local government as the scope and complexity of services grew. Two major forms of professional management became popular: the council-manager form and the administrator form. In the *council-manager form*, the mayor and council appoint a chief executive officer, who serves at the council's pleasure and has full responsibility for the day-to-day administrative operations of the government. Managers see themselves as facilitators, playing key roles in policy development and implementation. However, they have neither a vote nor a veto in council meetings. In the *administrator form*, either the mayor or the mayor and council appoint a chief administrative officer, who serves at the pleasure of the appointing authority. Administrators' powers vary: they may have limited authority or have powers identical to those of a manager. Administrators see themselves as coordinators, implementing policy under the leadership of the chief elected official.

This chapter discusses the contemporary context for managing local services. It explains how the rules of the game have been changing in recent years. It also identifies trends driving the management of local service delivery now and in the future, and it reviews a range of intergovernmental responses. Finally, it reviews the key roles and related knowledge, skills, and abilities required of twenty-first-century city and county managers.

## The contemporary context: How the rules of the game have changed

The contemporary context for local government service delivery and management has been shaped by powerful ideological and political forces and trends. These forces and trends have generated discussion and debate over the role of government in American society, the size and scope of governmental activities, and the cost of government. They have also had profound impacts on the rules of the game in at least four areas: the role of citizens, the values and views of elected officials, the manager's roles and responsibilities, and the ways in which local governments conduct their business.

### New roles for citizens

Citizens tend to have two enduring attitudes about local government. First, most citizens think their local government is more trustworthy and efficient than the state or national government; accordingly, they want the local government to be allowed to identify local needs, set priorities, and find the most suitable ways to address problems.[2] Second, although they want quality services, many citizens resist tax increases to pay for improvements or new services. In short, they want more for less.

To meet the challenges of managing and budgeting in this environment, some critics of government began suggesting in the early 1990s that public managers "reinvent" government and its relationship with citizens.

Citizens have always been the *owners* of government in that they elect, give legitimacy to, and hold accountable councils and boards and, through these governing bodies, professional managers and staff. Citizens also have traditionally been considered *clients* of local agencies, such as health and human services departments. Those who promote reinventing government call upon public managers to also treat citizens as *customers* and *coproducers*.

Those who describe citizens as customers see the local government system as a marketplace that offers choices among multiple jurisdictions. In this view, citizens "vote with their feet," moving from one jurisdiction to another in search of services they desire at tax and fee rates they are willing to pay. For example, interdistrict school choice plans pioneered by Minnesota gave parents educational options beyond the neighborhood public school and put pressure on schools from which students were being transferred to improve their performance.

Within individual local governments, the idea that citizens are customers encourages managers to abandon one-size-fits-all approaches and customize or tailor such services as

---

**Volunteers teach community preparedness in Westminster, Colorado**

The city of Westminster, Colorado (pop. 105,084), has developed a community preparedness program in which community volunteers teach other citizens what to do during various emergencies. Program costs to employ a part-time coordinator and print community preparedness booklets and other information are funded by a grant from the U.S. Department of Homeland Security. Volunteer teachers participate in a four-hour training session and meet monthly to discuss their experiences. Organizations in the city can request training on a variety of topics, and the city usually sends out two volunteers for each session, as well as a community preparedness program coordinator or the city's emergency coordinator.

police patrol and solid-waste collection to the preferences of various neighborhoods. All local personnel are expected to have a strong customer-service orientation and attitudes comparable to private sector companies recognized nationally for excellence in this area.[3]

As coproducers, citizens take part in providing a wide range of local services—from Neighborhood Watch police programs, to volunteer fire departments, to citizen advisory boards, to planning departments, to faith-based organizations in human services. The common factor is professional managers working alongside amateur citizens.

Treating citizens as customers creates performance pressures on managers to deliver a service at competitive levels of quality and cost satisfaction; treating them as coproducers requires managers to put aside "we know best" and "we-they" attitudes. Both of these dimensions of the citizen's role potentially expand the manager's accountability beyond the governing body to include the larger community.

Finally, citizens care more about the quality and cost of services than about which unit provides the services. Most citizens do not understand or appreciate the wide range of special and general-purpose local units that exists across the country. They look to the professional manager and governing body of the community to ensure that their expectations are met, even though service provision might involve cooperation with other localities or might be contracted out to the private sector, putting responsibility for performance beyond the control of local officials.

## Elected officials' values and views

Within the cultural, legal, and fiscal framework of the local government system, the basic roles of local governing bodies have not changed dramatically: representing citizens and constituents, making policy, overseeing administration, and "doing" politics. But the ways in which these roles are played, as well as the orientations of the officials who serve, have changed in important respects.

> *Partisan politics and single-issue politics reinforce a short-term orientation and incremental approach to policy making by elected officials who do not share a common vision for the community.*

In a representative democracy, elected officials are expected to listen to constituents and seek to address their needs and meet their expectations in ways that are consistent with the core values of the community. As local governments replace nonpartisan with partisan electoral systems, and as more and more municipal council and county board members are elected from districts rather than from the entire jurisdiction,[4] it has become increasingly challenging for these elected officials to find a general will or guiding public interest that can serve as the foundation of policy for the whole community. A growing number of single-issue candidates and antigovernment candidates have also made it harder for elected officials to reach coalitions within the governing body, find common ground, and build consensus. When elected officials cannot reconcile conflicting public values, the result is sometimes political and economic polarization between communities, neighborhoods, and citizens.

In places where this has happened, the policy-making process has changed. Managers may not receive clear or consistent direction on implementation priorities. Candidates who have run successfully against the local government may consider the manager to be part of the problem rather than the solution and may not fully trust—and may even seek to replace—him or her. Incumbents who seek a long-term career in city or county elective office may be reluctant to make unpopular or controversial decisions that could jeopardize their political future, preferring that the manager take the lead.

Partisan politics and single-issue politics reinforce a short-term orientation and incremental approach to policy making by elected officials who do not share a common vision for the community. If the governing body does not agree on strategic goals and objectives, it cannot develop action plans and priorities for programs and budgets. They contribute to growing gaps between professional managers, governing bodies, and citizens that arise from their differing backgrounds, expectations, and competencies.[5] These conditions make it difficult for a governing body to set clear and realistic expectations for the manager—or for itself as a council or board—or to effectively oversee and fairly evaluate administration.

## The manager's roles and responsibilities

As elected officials have become more partisan and more focused on single issues, managers have been drawn into the policy-making process, being asked to do more than provide accurate information and impartial advice. For example, managers are expected to identify and assess options and make recommendations for the governing body to consider. Politics and administration are no longer a dichotomy (if they ever were), and managers and governing bodies share responsibility in the spheres of mission, policy, administration, and management.[6]

Many of the changes described in the last few pages, as well as other developments and trends, have changed the manager's job and sometimes created tension in his or her relationship with elected officials and community leaders. The most important of these factors include (1) antigovernment feelings among the public, leading to distrust of elected and appointed officials and support for local candidates running against the government; (2) unrealistic citizen expectations that they can have more services for less taxes; (3) local elected officials' shift from a trustee role to an activist role, and their corresponding emphasis on constituent service instead of common and cooperative problem solving; (4) the increasing visibility, powers, and political ambitions of mayors; (5) the tendency of local elected officials to focus on implementation and to micromanage administration; (6) governing bodies' pressure on managers to privatize government services; and (7) access to information about local operations that the technology revolution has given citizens

---

### Professional administration in local government

"In the future the legitimacy of professional administrators in local government will be grounded in the tasks of community-building and enabling democracy—in getting things done collectively, while building a sense of inclusion."

Source: John Nalbandian, "Facilitating Community, Enabling Democracy: New Roles for Local Government Managers," *Public Administration Review* 59 (May/June 1999): 189.

and interest groups, enabling them to easily register complaints, monitor performance, and put administration under the spotlight.[7]

As a result of these factors, managers must devote more attention to policy, leadership, and constituent relations in their dealings with governing bodies than they have in the past. Because managers and elected officials need to spend a good deal of time together to forge a partnership for leading and governing their communities, the manager is sometimes viewed as the "sixth council member." Managers and elected officials are mutually dependent and share responsibility for most aspects of local government, yet they need to divide responsibility in order to efficiently, effectively, and equitably provide services and fulfill the expectations of citizens.

## How local governments conduct business

A fourth dimension of the changing rules of the game involves the shift from "government" to "governance." While the focus in the past was on the authority and activity of individual units of government, the focus today is on how governmental units can work with each other and the private and nonprofit sectors to accomplish results that the public wants. A key factor responsible for this shift has been the inability of local governments acting alone to respond to contemporary challenges and to operate in the businesslike, entrepreneurial manner envisioned by governmental critics who want more efficient and effective government.

In most parts of the United States, local government is fragmented. Individual local governments are small in territory and population, and are generally limited with respect to powers and range of responsibilities. The number of governmental units and the relationship between general- and special-purpose units affect efficiency, effectiveness, equity, and economies of scale—core values in service delivery. However, these values collide with other important virtues of the local government system: closeness, responsiveness, smallness, and customization. Reconciling these competing and conflicting values is the job of both elected officials and professional managers. The conflict of values sometimes exacerbates the gap between the elected officials' priorities of building the community and representing citizens, and the professional administrators' desire to modernize the organization and improve local services.[8]

The complexity of local government has come under scrutiny with the recognition that most important public problems can be addressed only by working across jurisdictional and sector boundaries—that is, with other communities, agencies, nonprofit organizations, businesses, citizen groups, and volunteers (see Figure 1–2). The term *governance* describes the reality that governments are only one of the players in local service delivery, albeit a critical player; it refers to "(1) all community interests affected by challenges and necessary to their resolution, not just government institutions, and (2) the collaborative problem-solving mechanisms needed to design timely strategies as well as the government institutions and other service-delivery mechanisms needed to implement them."[9]

The need to manage within and work with a diverse array of horizontal and vertical networks of governmental partners, public-private organizations, and regional and community groups has altered the traditional authority of both managers and governing bodies. The more that these entities have become facilitators, brokers, and networkers, the less they operate in a hierarchical command-and-control model. While their responsibility has grown, their authority has become more shared.[10]

**Figure 1-2 John Q. Citizen's domain**

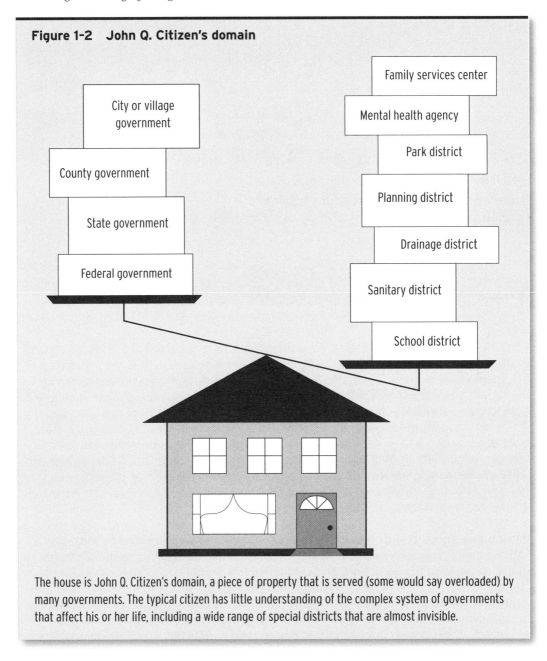

The house is John Q. Citizen's domain, a piece of property that is served (some would say overloaded) by many governments. The typical citizen has little understanding of the complex system of governments that affect his or her life, including a wide range of special districts that are almost invisible.

In summary, all these ideological and political trends have had a profound impact on the work of the manager. Apart from the roles and responsibilities indicated above, the manager increasingly serves as a bridge over sometimes troubled waters. Gaps continue to widen in many communities: between the education and experience of professional full-time managers and that of amateur part-time governing bodies; between the basic roles of elected officials to represent and make policy for the community and those of managers to build organizational capacity to effectively carry out policy; between citizen "more for less," "we want it our way," "just in time," and "quicker, better, cheaper" expectations for service delivery and the need to represent community interests and engage in deliberative decision making; and between the community place-based orientation of elected officials and other local leaders and the boundary-spanning nature of contemporary problem solving and service delivery.[11]

## The global context: External trends that drive local decisions

In addition to the important developments at the local level, at least seven significant national and international trends will drive future city and county decisions: population mobility; demographics; the new economy; technology; environmental quality, resource management, and conservation; privacy and security; and finances. Generalizations about the impacts of these trends on the diverse array of local governments in the United States are risky; nevertheless, it is clear that at one time or another during the next two decades (if not already), managers and elected officials will need to confront the implications of these trends in the decisions they make about local services.[12]

### Population mobility

Americans have long been a mobile population, and the trends cited above have affected local governments. In recent years, many people have moved from older northwestern and midwestern communities to the West and South. Their reasons for doing so include weather conditions, job opportunities, housing costs, and lifestyle preferences. In addition to these regional shifts, some people have been leaving the central cities and older suburbs that ring them and going to new, lower-density suburban or exurban communities, while other people have been attracted by the lifestyle found in smaller cities and rural counties. Some central cities have successfully created neighborhood environments that entice middle- and upper-income affluent couples—often those with no children—into moving to older neighborhoods and renovating housing, but many central cities have become home for disproportionate numbers of poor, minority, and elderly citizens. Their central business districts are hollow shells of once-thriving economic activity, and their physical infrastructure is in disrepair. These conditions lead to a weakened tax base as well as to a disproportionately higher amount of spending for noneducational purposes than is common in the suburbs, making it difficult for central city school systems to be competitive with their neighbors. In many jurisdictions, the school systems are independent of the local government, yet they can be the main factor causing middle- and upper-income families to "vote with their feet" and move to affluent suburbs with better schools. Thus, partnership with the school system is essential if the local government desires to have some control over the community's destiny.

Population shifts include both people and businesses, and the impacts on localities gaining or losing population are significant. In recent years, more than a million acres of farmland have been developed for residential, industrial, or commercial use annually.[13] Residents of new suburban communities bring with them expectations for schools, water and sewer lines, trash collection, streets and highways, and public safety. These expectations, which can strain local capital and operating budgets, are especially challenging if the developments are in unincorporated areas. In some of these new communities, housing costs will be relatively high, which raises issues of affordability and access; in others, the lack of adequate zoning and subdivision controls has produced disorderly development patterns, or sprawl, and has led to traffic congestion, inefficient land use, and environmental problems. Older central cities and suburbs must devote an increasing share of their budgets to repair and replacement of deteriorating infrastructure while responding to the basic service needs of their remaining population, many of whom lack the ability to pay for services through taxes. As they lose population, these older jurisdictions also are losing their political influence in the state legislature and the U.S. Congress to the developing suburbs.

## Demographics

Demographics will shape the destiny of many communities. Two significant demographic trends are the aging of America and immigration. According to the U.S. Bureau of the Census, between 2000 and 2050 the number of people older than age 65 will more than double, while that of adults under 65 will increase by less than 15 percent.[14]

*The aging of America*   The aging of the nation's population will affect communities differently, but all managers and elected officials will need to develop strategies to deal with an older population. For example, health care advances can extend the working lives of city or county employees into their seventies. However, the advantages that come with experience may be offset if these employees cling to old rules of management, or if their employment blocks the advancement of younger professionals. On the other hand, retirement of many in the baby boomer generation, including a substantial number of senior managers, will create gaps in management capacity unless succession planning is in place.

Some local governments are reaching out to the growing number of second-career employees—those who have left careers in the military, police and fire protection, or traditional civil service and potentially have another ten to twenty years to contribute to the local workforce. This effort can be seen in offers of phased retirement, part-time positions, and job rotation arrangements. Similarly, the expanding number of women and "Generation X" workers has been accompanied by requests for on-site day care services, flex-time work schedules, and job sharing to make local government service more attractive and feasible to those who are balancing professional commitments and personal priorities.

Retirees who are healthy and want to contribute on a part-time basis can be tapped to serve on local elected and appointed bodies, as volunteers assisting local agencies, and in other ways as coproducers. For their part, local governments must recognize the desires and needs of retirees when making decisions about public services and amenities, such as libraries, parks and recreation, street and sidewalk design, public parking, "smart home" standards, and health care. In some communities where the number of elderly is expanding while the number of youth is declining, plans will be needed to replace schools with facilities related to wellness, health care, social services, and recreation. Finally, the aging trend could have negative fiscal impacts. The local property tax base could be eroded by the growing number of citizens eligible for homestead exemptions and tax credits to reduce their liability. Depending on the structure of their retirement systems and local contribution history, cities and counties could face increased exposure as retirees choose to draw down their pension benefits.

**The economic impact of North Carolina's Hispanic population**

In January 2006 two professors at the University of North Carolina's Kenan-Flagler Business School released a study of the impact of the Hispanic population on the state's economy. Accounting for 7 percent of the state's total 2004 population and rapidly growing, the "Hispanic population contributes more than $9 billion to the state's economy through its purchases and taxes, while the net cost to the state budget (after Hispanic tax contributions) is an estimated $102 per Hispanic resident for health care, education, and corrections." With 600,013 Hispanics residing in North Carolina, this cost totaled $61,293,126. The total impact of Hispanic spending was estimated to increase to $18 billion by 2009.

Source: John D. Kasarda and James H. Johnson Jr., *The Economic Impact of the Hispanic Population on the State of North Carolina* (Chapel Hill, N.C.: Frank Hawkins Kenan Institute of Private Enterprise, January 2006).

*Immigration*   Immigration is a second factor that will affect local governments. According to the Census Bureau, in 2004 the immigrant proportion of the nation's population stood at record levels, accounting for 34.2 million people, or about 12 percent of the total population. Fifty-three percent of the foreign-born population came from Latin America, and about 25 percent came from Asia. Immigrants come to large cities but also to many small, rural communities. Hispanics in particular are becoming an important component of the workforce in a range of low-tech and high-tech industries, including agriculture, housing and building construction, hotel services, health care, information technology (IT), and local government.[15]

In addition to contributing to the workforce, immigrants add to the cultural diversity of communities. A manager must consider the community's growing diversity in hiring decisions to ensure that the local workforce is representative of the population it serves. Police, corrections, schools, elections, and other local personnel will need cultural diversity training to equip them with the skills needed to interact effectively with their immigrant populations. The council or board will need to hire translators for public meetings, and professional staff will need to recruit personnel who are fluent in foreign languages. Local communications personnel will need to develop literacy programs to help immigrants understand local laws and regulations as well as the benefits and services to which they are entitled, such as health care. Some local agencies, such as police departments, should consider locating substations in immigrant neighborhoods, hiring officers who are bilingual, and holding civilian police academies in foreign languages. Parks and recreation departments can also make important outreach efforts, such as offering soccer tournaments and ethnic festivals.

## The new economy

Not only are major changes occurring in the "look" of communities and the "faces" of the local government workforce, but the new economy has also required public and private leaders to adopt a new worldview. While cities, counties, and states continue to compete with one another to attract and retain business and industry, offering inducements such as an attractive quality of life, low taxes, accessible transportation, affordable labor and raw materials, and financial incentives, the arena for competition is becoming increasingly global.

Globalization is characterized by a cross-national integration of business, government, and individual economic activities, facilitated by technology and information systems.[16] To compete in this environment, local governments must conduct business differently. Many are investing in state-of-the-art Web sites that industrial recruiters can quickly access to determine whether the city or county could potentially meet their needs. Other approaches include sending delegations of elected and appointed local officials, business representatives, and civic and educational leaders on trade missions abroad to develop personal contacts, promote products, and communicate their community's competitive advantages; employing their own economic development staff or hiring consultants to help identify opportunities and position the community to compete; and establishing offices in trade centers in important international locations such as Seoul, Shanghai, Taipei, and Tokyo. While the costs of some of these approaches may be prohibitive for smaller communities, a state-of-the-art Web site is essential for any community that wants to attract business.

*The new economy is based on knowledge and services.*

Why are local governments making these investments? The new economy is based on knowledge and services. Over the past few years, manufacturing, textile, and agricultural jobs have increasingly been sent abroad to countries where production is significantly cheaper than in America, and these jobs have not been replaced; in localities both small and large, rural and urban, abandoned factories and vacated land are commonplace. Advances in communication technology have also enabled companies to outsource a wide array of service jobs to China, India, Mexico, and other countries.

Globalization has had a profound effect on intergovernmental relationships as well. State and local requirements regarding acceptable product content, environmental impacts, recyclability, and the disposability of manufactured products—such as refrigerators, televisions, computers, and automobile emission systems—can raise production costs. Therefore, business interests have increasingly called on Congress to preempt state and local authority and establish a single, stable national standard to ensure international competitiveness.

## Technology

Apart from its influence on globalization, technology has had major and wide-ranging impacts on city halls and county courthouses. As a result of the e-government revolution, appointed and elected officials receive and must respond to large volumes of inquiries, complaints, suggestions, and position papers from individuals and organizations delivered electronically. While access to public officials has been a key factor responsible for the favorable ratings local governments receive in opinion polls, the dramatically increased volume of electronic communications requires a major commitment of public officials' time and energy, since citizens expect prompt response. Moreover, as public documents, e-mail messages are often monitored by the media. Some local officials have Web logs, or "blogs," in which they discuss issues, and citizens use blogs to comment about local affairs and officials.

**Technology brings information to citizens in Lucas County, Ohio**

Lucas County, Ohio (pop. 448,229), provides a variety of business services to its residents through Web-based and GIS applications. For example, residents with computers can access real estate information online that includes tax records, appraisal data, mapping, front structure photos, property sketches, and historical documents. At public kiosks maintained by the county, residents can use a touch screen to access information such as the location of easements or zoning classifications affecting their properties or to print out a map of their neighborhoods. (To see data and maps available online, visit co.lucas.oh.us/AREIS/areismain.asp.)

Source: Based on *The GIS Guide for Local Government Officials* (Redlands, Calif.: ESRI Press, 2005), 85-87.

IT advances have required local governments to make investments in personnel and technology in order to capitalize on cost-effective ways to meet citizen needs, identify and solve problems, and make decisions, as well as to promote their economic competitiveness. Most communities now have a Web site on which they provide key personnel contacts, and a growing number are using their Web sites to provide information about public meetings and enable citizens to pay taxes and fines, register for activities, apply for permits, participate in opinion or satisfaction surveys, renew licenses, or make complaints online. Many localities use data generated by geographic information systems (GIS) to plan capital projects, determine routes for trash collection and policing, and monitor service performance. More and more localities are investing in IT staff to train personnel, keep equipment operational, and identify new technologies to consider for adoption. Some are developing broadband Internet access or "hot spots" for citizens and businesses via fiber or wireless systems, either on their own or jointly with the private sector. And it is not uncommon for governing body members to be given laptop computers so that they can reference reports and technical data during meetings, and communicate with constituents and access meeting agendas and other important documents when away from the office.

## Environmental quality, resource management, and conservation

Reflecting growing environmental awareness, many local governments are adopting resource management policies and implementing them through zoning and land use regulations. A number of communities have adopted "smart growth" ordinances, pushing developers to use available space for residential or commercial infill development, providing disincentives for consumption of green areas and open spaces, and encouraging preservation of wetlands and agricultural lands. Local governing bodies and managers have been challenged to find new ways to use old public buildings in order to conserve open space and promote development in the central business district.

Meanwhile, public concern about the environment continues to have significant effects on local government. Although air and water quality are largely state or interstate responsibilities, local public works officials must ensure the purity of drinking water and the effectiveness of sewer, stormwater runoff, and wastewater treatment systems; they also play major roles in inspecting and enforcing compliance with state and federal laws and regulations. Many cities and counties have adopted voluntary recycling programs or imposed fines for failure to comply with recycling regulations; others have used alternative energy sources in their local vehicles and have retrofitted or constructed government buildings to make them "green" in order to promote energy efficiency. And antismoking campaigns have led many local governments to make public buildings smoke free, while business owners worry that bans on smoking in restaurants and bars will drive customers away and result in revenue and tax losses.

## Privacy and security

As a result of terrorist attacks, natural disasters, and technological advances in data sharing, individual privacy and community security have become steadily increasing concerns for cities and counties. From cleanup following Hurricane Katrina to prevention of a bird flu pandemic, local governments are on the front lines of security: they are the first responders through police, fire, and emergency management preparedness, and they are critical collaborators and partners with state and federal agencies. Local governments also manage prime terrorist targets—airports, ports, water systems, and hospitals—as well as sensitive data housed in GIS and other electronic systems.

While federal and state funds assist local governments with the mounting costs of security, city and county budgets are having to absorb increasing expenses for capital equipment, communications systems, and personnel. Local governments of all sizes need to revisit their policies on public access to infrastructure blueprints, emergency plans, vulnerability assessments, hazardous materials transport routes, and other security-sensitive public documents. Clearly, local governments will need to devote more resources to ongoing planning for preparedness.

## Finances

Recent studies by the U.S. Government Accountability Office, Congressional Budget Office, National Academy of Public Administration, national associations representing local and state officials, and academic experts have concluded that the nation is on a course heading toward a fiscal crisis. In addition to the impacts of the *demographic* trends noted above on the finances of pension systems, more and more retirees will rely on Medicare and Medicaid programs to help meet their health care expenses. Three other "d" words also affect the federal fiscal forecast: *deficits,* which amounted to $331 billion in FY 2005; *debt,* which is projected to increase by $5.3 trillion between 2005 and 2015; and *defense* costs, which will continue to grow as a result of the war in the Middle East and concerns about international terrorism. These mandatory expenditures will constrain federal discretionary spending for the foreseeable future. Between 1963 and 2003, for example, the discretionary portion of the federal budget shrank from 68 percent to 39 percent.[17]

The likely results of the four "d's" will be a reduction in federal spending for many domestic programs and services that are delivered at the local level.[18] To the extent that states ratify rather than replace cuts in federal spending and pass along other reductions in state financial or administrative assistance, local governments will be under pressure to raise taxes and fees or cut services. Lack of political support or consensus for either strategy puts local elected officials and managers in a difficult position. Their options are further limited by federal preemption of revenue sources, especially taxation on Internet transactions, unfunded federal and state mandates, and state constitutional and statutory restrictions on city and county authority to levy new taxes and issue bonds. Similarly, if states fail to modernize their revenue systems to tap into the new economy and technology trends—for instance, by taxing professional services or allowing localities to reduce their dependence on property taxes—their fiscal pressures will rapidly mount as well.

## The web of governance: Who's in charge?

The past four decades witnessed dramatic changes in the roles and relationships of local, state, and national governments in the United States. The interactions between these governments and private profit-making and not-for-profit organizations also underwent

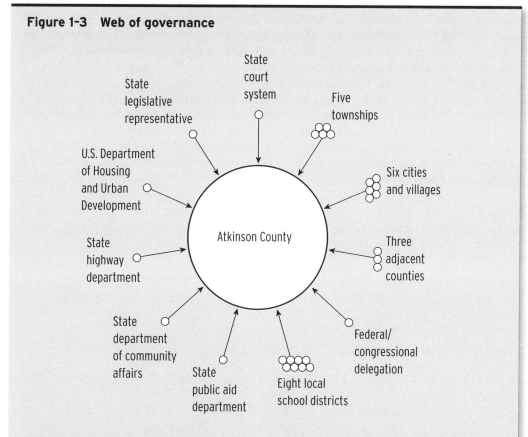

**Figure 1-3  Web of governance**

Many government department and agencies can provide advice and information on questions in intergovernmental management for the chief administrator and department heads. Here is the hypothetical example of Atkinson County, which can draw on legislative, executive, and judicial agencies at all levels of government—from neighboring cities and counties to the regional and national offices of the U.S. Department of Housing and Urban Development in Washington, D.C.

marked shifts. Attention has been focused on the fiscal dimensions of these changes, especially grants-in-aid and tax policy. Equally significant are their regulatory and administrative aspects. Growing intergovernmental and public-private collaboration has created a "web" of governance (see Figure 1–3) and raised basic questions about who is in charge: who is responsible for the delivery of services, the payment for services, and the performance of services? This section reviews recent trends in intergovernmental relations as they relate to local services management.

## Local discretionary authority and regional collaboration

The number and structure of local governmental units vary widely across the country, but the general pattern is a fragmented structure of many small (under 2,500 population) units with overlapping responsibilities and limited boundaries. Meanwhile, it has become difficult to identify purely local problems, over which individual counties, cities, or other general-purpose units exercise control without significant policy, financial, or regulatory involvement of neighboring jurisdictions or state or federal authorities. This is true even for traditional local government functions—such as police and fire protection, libraries, and streets—as well as for school districts, all of which receive state and federal grants accompanied by standards and requirements as conditions of aid.

Between 1952 and 2002, there was a net decline of 29,231 in the number of local units—from 116,756 to 87,525—but fragmentation of local government authority actually increased. During this period, 2,622 new general-purpose municipalities were created (nearly a 16 percent increase, reflecting the continuing suburbanization of the nation), and the number of non-school special districts (most of which provided a single function within a single jurisdiction) grew by 185 percent. (These increases in the number of non-school local units were offset by a nearly 80 percent reduction in the number of school districts.)[19] The constant factor has been the fiscal and administrative independence of both school and non-school districts from cities and counties, contributing to structural and administrative fragmentation.

> *Most local governments try to increase their effectiveness by collaborating with other local governments as well as with the private sector.*

In addition to structural limitations, local government powers are constrained by state constitutions and statutes. Local governments are creations of their state, from which they derive authority over their form of government, functional responsibilities, personnel, and finances. There is wide interstate variation in the extent to which constitutions and statutes grant "home rule," or discretionary authority, to various types of general-purpose local governments. In general, states have been willing to give local governments greater authority over their functional responsibilities, form of government, and personnel policies than over their finances. Legislatures have been less willing to grant home rule to counties than to cities, mainly because of the traditional role that county governments play as administrative arms of their state. Even in states where local governments have been granted broad home rule powers, judges, attorneys general, bond counsels, and legislators have imposed sometimes formidable constraints on the local governments' ability to excerise these powers.[20]

**Working across boundaries in Englewood, Colorado**

The city of Englewood, Colorado (pop. 32,350), owned a closed landfill in what is now the city of Sheridan (pop. 5,483). Englewood opened a golf course on part of the 122-acre site, but the rest of the site was blighted property, used for outdoor storage, auto auctions, and adult businesses. Sheridan acquired this part of the site through a combination of purchase and eminent domain, and the two cities cooperated with a private developer to clean up the site and redevelop it for lease to "big box" and specialty retail stores, restaurants, and a movie theater. The remediation of the site included reconfiguration of the golf course and reestablishment of some wetlands. The site was brought into the state's Voluntary Cleanup Program, which coordinated the developer's planning with the state's water quality program, solid-waste program, and air program, as well as with the state's attorney general and the two cities. During the six-month planning process, all participants met bi-weekly to share newly collected data.

As a result of the fragmentation of local authority and the legal constraints on that authority, it is very difficult for most local governments to respond to boundary-crossing environmental, social, and economic problems on their own. Therefore, most local governments try to increase their effectiveness by collaborating with other local governments as well as with the private sector, and to do so, they have used a variety of collaborative mechanisms. Foremost have been formal and informal interlocal contracts and agreements for the joint provision of services, and mutual assistance pacts between police, fire, and emergency medical service departments. In nearly all cases, these arrangements are made between two governmental units for a single service. A second mechanism, which grew in popularity during the 1990s, has been the privatization of services through contracting with for-profit and nonprofit organizations for the performance of local functions. Local officials have also adopted a variety of fiscal instruments—such as tax increment financing, tax exemptions, revenue bonds, and leasing—in their search for ways to circumvent state restrictions on taxing and spending.[21]

Ironically, the formation of special districts and public authorities, described above as one of the causes of fragmentation, is also one of three major institutional responses to boundary-crossing problems. Two additional institutional responses, also dating back to the 1960s, are the reorganization of "urban" counties and the formation of regional planning and coordinating bodies. All three responses have been implemented with varying degrees of success, and usually in tandem with traditional legal and procedural mechanisms that states have granted cities and counties to enable them to address interlocal matters. Besides contracts and agreements, these mechanisms include negotiated boundary adjustments, extraterritorial powers, annexation, and interlocal functional transfers. Use of these tools, however, has been limited by opposition from citizens and public employees.[22]

***Special districts and public authorities***   Special-purpose local units are popular for such functions as fire protection, housing and community development, water supply, drainage and flood control, and soil and water conservation. Ease of creation, ability to draw boundaries around "problem-sheds," avoidance of debt limits, and a pay-as-you-go approach to finances have been pragmatic inducements to local officials to use this approach. However, special districts have been criticized as being "invisible" governments, in that their boards of directors have a low profile with voters and thus rate poorly on citizen accountability values. Their relative independence from any one local governing body also is a concern. While most special districts provide only a single service to a single jurisdiction, making it difficult for them to undertake comprehensive, coordinated approaches to problems, 9 percent of the 35,052 special districts in existence in 2002 performed more than one function, and 13 percent were areawide (multicounty). About two-thirds of these areawide districts covered two counties.[23]

***The reorganized or "urban" county***   County governments are found in all but two states (Connecticut and Rhode Island), and many of these units have the geographic scope requisite for addressing regional needs or problems and achieving economies of scale. Further, counties can contract with communities within their borders to provide services, thereby reducing their operating and capital costs. However, county governments have at least three limitations. First, they have traditionally served as arms of state government responsible for law enforcement, administration of justice, tax assessment and collection, road maintenance, welfare and social services, and education in unincorporated areas. State constitutions and statutes may restrict counties from expanding their functional scope to address other needs. Second, many counties continue to operate under a commission form of government, in which part-time commissioners or supervisors elected from districts exercise authority and, in some jurisdictions, head departments. Authority is further fragmented by the separate election of the sheriff, treasurer, prosecutor, school superintendent, tax assessor, and other key officials. Third, in some metropolitan areas the geographic scope and governmental powers of a single county are inadequate to deal with regional issues.

States such as California, Florida, Maryland, New York, and Virginia have empowered their counties by authorizing them to perform municipal-type (or "urban") functions and giving them home rule. Led by county executives or chief administrative officers, who are separately elected or appointed by the governing body, these reorganized counties possess the structure, powers, and management capacity to serve as regional governments, especially where their boundaries are coterminous with those of the metropolitan area. The urban county form has not been widely adopted, however, because county boards and state associations of county officials are reluctant to seek empowerment, state legislators are unwilling to support county modernization, and municipal officials are concerned about threats to their authority and autonomy.

***Regional planning and coordinating bodies***   The federal government and some state governments have tried to encourage regional problem-solving approaches. For example, a 1959 amendment to Section 701 of the Housing Act of 1954 authorized federal funds to stimulate formation and support operations of regional planning commissions and councils of governments (COGs)—generally called "regional councils"—under the direction of local elected officials who comprised a majority of their governing body's membership. More than 500 of these multipurpose bodies exist today, even though federal funding has been greatly reduced.

COGs were not intended to provide services, and only a few have taken on this role—usually for constituent local governments rather than directly for citizens. Rather, they were established primarily to

- Collect data and provide information
- Serve as communications vehicles for elected officials from different jurisdictions
- Develop comprehensive land use plans for the region
- Review and comment on proposed local projects based on these plans
- Assist member jurisdictions in preparing grant-in-aid applications and with other technical needs.

Many COGs also play important roles vis-à-vis federal and state agencies. They serve as clearinghouses for grant applications, economic development districts (as designated by the U.S. Department of Commerce), and metropolitan planning organizations (MPOs) for regional transportation. They also facilitate the allocation of federal and state revolving loan funds for wastewater and drinking water facilities and for organizations on aging that provide direct or indirect services to the elderly.[24]

The federal government has also funded the formation of single-purpose areawide bodies for environmental protection, health care, economic development, and other functions. While they are responsible chiefly for planning activities, these entities also perform grant coordination, standard setting, and regulation. They are often separate from regional councils, which contributes to additional structural fragmentation. Currently, the most visible and authoritative of the federally supported regional organizations are air quality districts organized pursuant to the Clean Air Act (1990) and MPOs established under the Intermodal Surface Transportation Efficiency Act, or ISTEA (1991); the Transportation Equity Act for the 21st Century, or TEA-21 (1998); and their successor, the Safe, Accountable, Flexible, Efficient, Transportation Equity Act: A Legacy for Users, or SAFETEA-LU (2005).

During the 1960s and 1970s, many states organized their own areawide planning and development districts to serve state purposes, to meet federal requirements, and to assist localities within their boundaries. Most of these multicounty organizations focused on planning, economic development, and transportation. More recently, in response to resistance from public officials and citizens to the consolidation of governmental units or functions—and at the behest of coalitions of local officials, business executives, chambers of commerce, and civic leaders—some state legislatures have considered bills to provide state financial incentives for regional activities.

**Communities cooperate to handle household hazardous waste in Lewiston, Maine**

The Androscoggin Valley Council of Governments used a grant from the state planning office to build a new environmental depot in Lewiston, Maine (pop. 36,050), for the collection and disposal of household hazardous wastes, services that would be very expensive for individual small towns to handle. Residents of participating towns can obtain a voucher from their town to bring materials to the facility or to participate in scheduled local collections.

Source: avcog.org/whats_new.php?i=65 (accessed September 25, 2006).

## States under the spotlight

The previous section highlighted two important dimensions of the local-state relationship: local discretionary authority and interlocal and regional collaboration, the latter being of particular value to managers of smaller jurisdictions. States significantly affect the management of local services in at least four other areas as well: financial aid, equity, functional reassignments, and relief from mandates.

*Financial aid*   The bulk of state financial assistance is allocated for activities normally beyond the purview of general-purpose local governments: elementary and secondary education and Medicaid. Nevertheless, state financial support is a key component of local budgets for such services as law enforcement and corrections, roads, and social services. States also usually provide localities with discretionary aid, which is not restricted to particular purposes. And in addition to direct assistance, states help localities through indirect means, such as investment, insurance, and purchasing pools and bond banks.

*Equity*   Under their constitutions, states are entrusted to ensure the equitable treatment of their citizens; this means that the quality of public services like education should not depend on the tax wealth of local units. Some states, for example, are working with their local governments to reduce excessive dependence on the property tax (which accounts for about 75 percent of local budgets) because it is regressive; that is, it ignores the ability of the property holder to pay. (For many years, the property tax has been cited as the "worst" or "least fair" tax in public opinion polls.)[25] Remedies include authorizing property tax "circuit breakers" to limit individual liability when property taxes reach a specified level, and providing tax relief for low-income taxpayers.

*Functional reassignments*   A number of states have broadened local home rule authority to facilitate transfer of functional responsibilities, such as libraries, from cities to counties in order to achieve economies of scale. Another strategy has been to assume greater or full state financial and administrative responsibility for functions where a strong statewide interest in uniformity exists or where costs are prohibitive for local governments. Social welfare, courts, mental health, corrections, and transportation are among the major functions experiencing this shift of responsibility.

*Relief from mandates*   Much of the concern among public officials over mandates has been directed to Congress. However, state legislators are as adept as members of Congress at imposing mandates on local government, and they are often as unwilling to compensate for additional costs. Where a statewide interest is apparent, mandates may be warranted; the case is less persuasive where there is strong local interest. In response to concerns about unfunded mandates, several states have passed legislation requiring that fiscal notes estimating the compliance cost be attached to pending legislation that will affect local governments. Some legislatures have provided for state compensation of these costs or for the extension of local revenue-raising authority to do so. A few states have passed laws allowing local governments to refuse to accept or comply with a mandate unless the state provides a means to pay for it.

In these six areas—local discretionary authority, interlocal and regional collaboration, financial aid, equity, functional reassignments, and mandate relief—states and local governments can be partners or adversaries. Especially in difficult fiscal times, it is tempting for state officials to pass along cuts in financial aid, impose unfunded mandates, preempt local authority, and shift functional responsibilities downwards. As political subdivisions, there is not much local governments can do to resist, even in home rule states. But from the standpoint of effective management and delivery of services that cross local boundaries, the development of a strong working relationship is in the best interest of both local leaders and their state counterparts.

## The federal domestic role: Centralization or devolution?

Beginning in the 1960s the federal government's domestic role and responsibilities began to steadily expand. This growth was a reaction to a number of political and ideological factors, including a regulatory "green light" to Congress and federal agencies by the U.S. Supreme Court in its broad interpretations of the commerce clause, the necessary and proper clause, the supremacy clause, and other implied powers provisions of the Constitution; public opinion supportive of a strong national role in such areas as civil rights, environmental quality, public health protection, poverty reduction, occupational safety, and community development; and growth in public interest and special-interest lobby groups that advocated national involvement. It also was a response to concerns about the limited capacity and uneven commitment of localities and states to adequately fund, effectively plan, and equitably administer programs to tackle tough problems like poverty, illiteracy, crime, disease, pollution, and infrastructure deterioration. These factors continue to be relevant, despite concerns about centralization of authority in Washington, D.C. More recently, the demands and pressures of globalization and the new economy have called for the United States to speak with one national voice, not fifty state voices or 22,463 city and county voices, furthering centralization trends. The vehicles for this expansion of the federal government's domestic role have been grants-in-aid, regulations, and preemptions.

*Grants-in-aid*   The national government has used grants-in-aid for five basic purposes:

1. To support ongoing subnational activities
2. To stimulate new services or activities
3. To improve comprehensive planning, financial management, and reporting capabilities
4. To enhance the caliber of personnel
5. To encourage research and innovation.

The number of grant programs has grown steadily between 1960 and 2002 to more than 660 grants totaling $412 billion and accounting for 21.4 percent of local and state budgets. While more than 80 percent of federal aid flows through categorical or conditional grants, the remainder is delivered via eighteen block grants, which, as instruments of devolution and decentralization, give recipients relatively greater flexibility and discretion in tailoring funds to their needs and priorities within a broadly defined public purpose. Three programs that are particularly important to local government—Temporary Assistance for Needy Families, Community Development, and Social Services—are among the twenty largest federal aid programs.[26] Medicaid, the largest and fastest-growing federal program, now accounts for 45 percent of total federal aid. As a result, more federal aid is going to individual citizens and less to cities and counties.

***Regulatory federalism***  Local and state governments are the chief implementers of national policy, through regulations as well as through grant-in-aid programs. Four types of regulatory techniques have been used by the national government:

1. Partial preemptions, where the Congress sets national standards, such as for air and water purity, occupational health and safety, and meat and poultry inspection, and then delegates administrative responsibility for attainment of those standards to local and state governments, but does not necessarily provide additional funding

2. Cross-cutting requirements, where recipients are called upon to demonstrate compliance with conditions that are generally applicable to all federal aid programs regardless of purpose, such as directives to involve citizens in the decision-making process; to engage in comprehensive land use planning; and to ensure that environmental quality standards are met, historic sites are preserved, American products are purchased, and nondiscriminatory practices are followed

3. Crossover sanctions, where failure to comply with requirements in one program, such as the 55-mile-per-hour speed limit on interstate highways or the minimum drinking age of 21, causes a loss of funds in another program (e.g., highway construction)

4. Direct orders, where local and state governments must do (e.g., minimum wage and maximum hour requirements) or refrain from doing (e.g., job discrimination) something under the threat of civil or criminal penalties.[27]

These regulations have affected virtually all aspects of local government programs and have added costs to service delivery that have not been fully recovered. In 1995 Congress passed the Unfunded Mandate Reform Act to reduce the incidence of unfunded mandates and ensure that compliance costs of bills containing federal mandates would be brought to the attention of congressional committees; however, these goals have not been achieved.

***Preemption***  In addition to partial preemptions, where a national minimum standard is established (which states and localities can exceed if they so choose), Congress fully preempted the authority of subnational jurisdictions when it concluded that the nation needs to speak with one voice. An example here is the Internet Tax Nondiscrimination Act, which imposed a moratorium prohibiting local and state governments from levying taxes on Internet sales. The result was an estimated tax revenue loss from e-commerce of $15.5 billion in FY 2003, a loss that is expected to reach between $21.5 billion and $33.7 billion by 2008.[28]

Previously it was noted that the "4 d's"—deficits, debt, demographics, and defense—would significantly reduce the discretionary portion of the federal budget, putting localities and states on a possible fiscal collision course. President Bush's FY 2005–06 budget proposals, which would decrease federal discretionary spending, cut domestic spending, and eliminate deductions for certain state and local taxes, indicate that the national government will continue to seek to "cut, cap, or consolidate" its grant-in-aid program commitments. At the same time, there are no indications that the rate of increase in intergovernmental regulations, mandates, and preemption activities will diminish as the national government's financial role declines; in fact, these constraints are likely to continue to increase, while hopes for turning more authority over to states and localities fade.[29]

## Leading and managing in the twenty-first century

The trends described in this chapter will affect different types and sizes of local governments in different ways, but all cities and counties will be affected. As shown in Figure 1–3, managers will need to recognize and relate to a "web" of other jurisdictions, agencies, and organizations involved in governance. What key knowledge, skills, abilities, and competencies are needed for twenty-first-century city and county managers in this dynamic world of local government?[30]

From the inception of council-manager government, governing bodies have expected their chief executive officer to ensure that city or county operations run smoothly, services are provided efficiently and effectively, and prudent fiscal practices are followed. This expectation continues. Within his or her organization, the manager needs to be a *managerial capacity builder,* applying to local government such contemporary business management practices as workforce and succession planning, job enlargement and work sharing, team building, and mentoring. The manager must demonstrate a *commitment to diversity* in both hiring and service delivery decisions, *loyalty* to those in the organization, and dedication to the *highest ethical standards*, as specified in ICMA's Code of Ethics and local policies. He or she must have a strong moral compass for moving the community forward.

The manager must also be a *process leader* and a *problem solver*, applying his or her expertise, discretionary authority, and creativity to building a high-performing organization to facilitate technical and systemic change. Adept use of such management tools as strategic planning, performance measurement, benchmarking, and program evaluation, as well as technologies like e-government, is essential. The adoption of "lean" practices to reduce production costs by eliminating unnecessary steps that add both time and personnel to service delivery is also useful.

He or she also must be a *skillful communicator* of needs, expectations, and accomplishments, both within and outside of the organization. Moreover, and especially in communities where local government has had a tarnished image, the manager must have strong *marketing and public relations skills* to overcome public skepticism and show how local government works to serve all citizens.

Professionalism and *lifelong learning* are important aspects of these tasks. It is now common for position vacancy announcements for managers, assistant managers, and department heads to require applicants to hold a master's degree. As of 2005, approximately nine hundred managers had successfully completed ICMA's Voluntary Credentialing Program and committed to an additional forty hours of professional development each year in order to retain their credential.

The twenty-first-century manager must be an *educator,* able to close the gap between the experience and knowledge possessed by the manager and department heads and that possessed by elected officials, to orient newly elected governing body members on local operations so they can hit the ground running, and to present complicated information and updates on matters of interest clearly and concisely to busy elected officials. The manager needs to find common ground with the council or board from which to develop a vision for the community, as well as strategies for achieving it over the short and long term.

*Consensus-building, negotiation and mediation,* and *conflict management* skills are critical, especially with governing bodies seeking to serve diverse community groups and

---

### The role of the manager

"As a ... manager, you're really playing the role of trying to make the experiment in democracy work in a local government setting. So that means not only are you doing the normal management things, you're trying to create a community environment in which people feel that they're a part and they're being consulted."

Source: Justin Marlowe and John Nalbandian, "Knowledge Work and Local Government Management: Insights from an Expert," *State and Local Government Review* 37, no. 3 (2005): 254.

---

with individual members who have run on single issues or against incumbents in government. Occasionally the manager has to play the role of *coach*, working with members of the governing body to promote an understanding of issues and public values, build trust, improve its policy-making effectiveness, and strengthen working relationships with the professional staff.

The manager must be a *convener, broker,* and *negotiator of interests* from outside as well as inside the government. Since the successful performance of most important local services requires intergovernmental, private sector, or volunteer engagement, the manager acts as both entrepreneur and the middle person in government-by-contract arrangements. This role involves identifying governance networks and opportunities for engagement, bringing diverse groups together, building coalitions, arranging contracts and agreements, monitoring performance, and ensuring that corrective actions are taken. And here again, the manager is an educator, informing the governing board and professional staff on a wide range of matters, such as community expectations and issues; regional relationships; state and federal grants, mandates, and regulations; statutory, regulatory, and legal requirements; and the limits as well as advantages of privatization. Similarly, in view of citizens' confusion over "who does what" in delivering local services and their sometimes unrealistic expectations about the costs and quality of city or county services, the manager as *educator* must inform the community through Web sites, public meetings, and citizen academies about the roles and responsibilities of the local government and the division of labor between the governing body and the professional staff. Outreach to prospective volunteers is also important.

While local managers should not be expected to play the role of *lobbyist*, in the complex and rapidly changing world of intergovernmental relations, the voice of local government needs to be heard, and the manager is increasingly serving as an *intergovernmental liaison*. Involvement in the work of the state league of municipalities, association of county commissioners, and city and county managers' associations, as well as their counterpart national organizations representing local government interests in Washington, D.C.—the National League of Cities, U.S. Conference of Mayors, National Association of Counties, and ICMA—is an important way for managers to bolster their local officials' efforts to register the needs of their communities and increase opportunities for financial assistance. As professionals, managers must be politically savvy but not politically involved.

All the above-mentioned skills and competencies can be summarized in one word: *leader,* the manager as "someone who goes out and changes things to make things better."[31]

In the contemporary local government environment, sound management knowledge, skills, and abilities are important but will not be sufficient to deal with the political, ideological, intergovernmental, and community-building needs associated with globalization, the new economy, and the information age. As one former manager put it: "As a ... manager, you're really playing the role of trying to make the experiment in democracy work in a local government setting. So that means not only are you doing the normal management things, you're trying to create a community environment in which people feel that they're a part and they're being consulted."[32] Today and in the years to come, the manager must be a *leader,* an *organizational capacity builder,* and a *community change agent.*

## Questions to ask if you manage a small community

Do you provide information about local government organization, operations, and finances to candidates for the council or board, and offer an orientation program for newly elected governing body members?

Do you use governing body retreats as opportunities for members to engage in community visioning, strategic planning, and goal-setting exercises?

Do your local departments periodically conduct citizen/customer satisfaction surveys?

Do your local departments have programs to engage citizens as "coproducers" of services or on advisory bodies?

How much time are you spending with governing body members in working sessions, and what strategies are you using to help build a high-performing governing body?

Have you and your department heads received media relations training?

Does the manager's office have a workforce or succession plan in place for major departments?

What plans have your departments and the governing body made to respond to the impact of changing demographics in your community?

How does your city or county use information technology to inform and engage citizens and to provide online services?

Does your local government have an inventory of contracts and agreements with neighboring communities?

Have you engaged members of the governing body in a discussion of opportunities of and strategies for regional collaboration?

How active are you in the work of ICMA or the state manager's association, and how active are your elected officials in the work of the state municipal league or county commissioners association?

---

**Competencies for managers in the twenty-first century**

Ability to apply contemporary business management practices to local government

Proficient use of management tools and technologies

Communication skills for working with people both within and outside the organization

Capability for educating, information sharing, and closing the "knowledge gap"

Mentoring and coaching

Consensus building, negotiation, mediation, and conflict management

Marketing and public relations

Intergovernmental and sectoral boundary spanning

Understanding of networks and ability to navigate them

Political acumen

---

## Endnotes

1 For more background on these different views, see the following reports by the U.S. Advisory Commission on Intergovernmental Relations' classic Substate Regionalism and the Federalism series: *Regional Decision-Making: New Strategies for Substate Districts* (October 1973); *Regional Governance: Promise and Performance* (May 1973); *The Challenge of Local Governmental Reorganization* (February 1974); and *Governmental Functions and Processes: Local and Areawide* (February 1974).

2 John Kincaid and Richard L. Cole, "Public Opinion on Issues of U.S. Federalism in 2005: End of the Post-2001 Pro-Federal Surge?" *Publius* 35 (Winter 2005): 169–185.

3 David Osborne and Ted Gaebler, *Reinventing Government: How the Entrepreneurial Spirit Is Transforming the Public Sector* (Reading, Mass.: Addison-Wesley Publishing, 1992); David Osborne and Peter Plastrik, *Banishing Bureaucracy: The Five Strategies for Reinventing Government* (Reading, Mass.: Addison-Wesley Publishing, 1997).

4 See H. George Frederickson, Gary A. Johnson, and Curtis Wood, "Type III Cities," in *The Future of Local Government Administration: The Hansell Symposium,* ed. H. George Frederickson and John Nalbandian (Washington, D.C.: ICMA, 2002), 85–97.

5 John Nalbandian, "Professionals and the Conflicting Forces of Administrative Modernization and Civic Engagement," *American Review of Public Administration* 35 (December 2005): 311–326.

6 James H. Svara, "Dichotomy and Duality: Reconceptualizing the Relationship between Policy and Administration in Council-Manager Cities," *Public Administration Review* 45 (January/February 1985): 228.

7 See James H. Svara, "Achieving Effective Community Leadership," in *The Effective Local Government Manager*, 3rd ed., ed. Charldean Newell (Washington, D.C.: ICMA, 2004), 28–32.

8 John Nalbandian, *Professionalism in Local Government* (San Francisco: Jossey-Bass, 1991).

9 William R. Dodge, *Regional Excellence: Governing Together to Compete Globally and Flourish Locally* (Washington, D.C.: National League of Cities, 1996), 38.

10 See H. George Frederickson, "Transcending the Community: Local Leadership in a World of Shared Power," *Public Management* 87 (November 2005): 14; Stephen Goldsmith and William D. Eggers, *Governing by Network: The New Shape of the Public Sector* (Washington, D.C.: Brookings Institution Press, 2004); and Robert Agranoff and Michael McGuire, *Collaborative Public Management: New Strategies for Local Government* (Washington, D.C.: Georgetown University Press, 2003).

11 John Nalbandian, "The Manager as Political Leader: A Challenge to Professionalism?" *Public Management* 82 (March 2000): 7–12.

12 For more in-depth discussion of "change drivers," see Council of State Governments (CSG), *Trends in America: Charting the Course Ahead* (Lexington, Ky: CSG, June 2005); and Mark A. Abramson, Jonathan D. Breul, and John M. Kamensky, *Four Trends Transforming Government* (Washington, D.C.: IBM Center for The Business of Government, Summer 2003).

13 CSG, *Trends in America*, 17.

14 Ibid., 9–11.

15 Ibid., 12–14

16 Ibid., 20.

17 See National Academy of Public Administration, *Ensuring the Future Prosperity of America: Addressing the Fiscal Future* (Washington, D.C.: The Academy, November 2005).

18 President Bush's FY 2005–06 budgets called for the first cuts in domestic spending since 1996. Congress responded with proposed domestic spending reductions ranging from $35 to $50 billion.

19 U.S. Census Bureau, *2002 Census of Governments*, Vol. 1, *Government Organization* (Washington, D.C.: U.S. Government Printing Office, 2002), 13–21.

20 See Carl W. Stenberg, "Structuring Local Government Units and Relationships," in *The Future of Local Government in Michigan: Symposium Proceedings*, ed. Joe Ohren (Ann Arbor: Michigan Municipal League Foundation, 2000), 65–91; Joseph F. Zimmerman, *State-Local Relations: A Partnership Approach*, 2nd ed. (Westport, Conn.: Praeger Publishers, 1995), 1–84; Dale Krane, Platon N. Rigos, and Melvin B. Hill Jr., *Home Rule in America: A Fifty-State Handbook* (Washington, D.C.: Congressional Quarterly Press, 2001).

21 See Alberta M. Sbragia, *Debt Wish: Entrepreneurial Cities, U.S. Federalism, and Economic Development* (Pittsburgh, Pa.: University of Pittsburgh Press, 1996).

22 See Stenberg, "Structuring Local Government Units," 72–74; Dodge, *Regional Excellence*, 243–244; and David B. Walker, "Snow White and the 17 Dwarfs: From Metropolitan Cooperation to Governance," *National Civic Review* 76 (January–February 1987): 14–28.

23 U.S. Census Bureau, *Government Organization*, 13–14.

24 "NARC Regional Council Survey: Some General Characteristics, NARC's 1993/4 Survey," (Washington, D.C.: National Association of Regional Councils, 1995).

25 Kincaid and Cole, "Public Opinion," 175.

26 Carl W. Stenberg, "Reflections on Intergovernmental Re-Balancing: Back to the Future," *The Book of the States 2005* (Lexington, Ky.: CSG, 2005), 35–36.

27 U.S. Advisory Commission on Intergovernmental Relations, *Regulatory Federalism: Policy, Process, Impact and Reform* (Washington, D.C.: U.S. Government Printing Office, February 1984), 97.

28 Donald Bruce and William F. Fox, *State and Local Sales Tax Revenue Losses from E-Commerce: Estimates as of July 2004* (Knoxville, Tenn.: Center for Business and Economic Research, University of Tennessee, September 2004), 4; see also National Academy of Public Administration (NAPA), *Beyond Preemption: Intergovernmental Partnerships to Enhance the New Economy* (Washington, D.C.: NAPA, 2006).

29 John Kincaid, "Trends in Federalism: Continuity, Change and Polarization," *The Book of the States 2004* (Lexington, Ky.: CSG, 2004), 22–23.

30 See Amy Cohen Paul, *Future Challenges, Future Opportunities: The Final Report of the ICMA Future Visions Consortium* (Washington, D.C.: ICMA, 1991); John Nalbandian, "Educating the City Manager of the Future," in *The Future of Local Government Administration: The Hansell Symposium* (see note 4), 253; Camille Cates Barnett and Oscar Rodriquez, "Connections Matter: Using Networks for Improved Performance," *Public Management* 88 (May 2006), 22–25.

31 David Osborne and Peter Hutchinson, *The Price of Government: Getting the Results We Need in an Age of Permanent Fiscal Crisis* (New York: Basic Books, 2004), 307.

32 Justin Marlowe and John Nalbandian, "Knowledge Work and Local Government Management: Insights from an Expert," *State and Local Government Review* 37, no. 3 (2005): 254.

# The Legal Foundations of Local Government

**David R. Berman**

Cities, counties, villages, and towns are dependent on law for their very existence. Such fundamentals as their form of government, minimum standards for services provided, and potential liability from the unauthorized or improper exercise of their official powers are all prescribed in, and limited by, law. This chapter describes the sources of and limits on local authority, and includes a commentary on the role of local attorneys in guiding local governmental legal affairs.

## Sources of local authority

Cities, villages, and in some states boroughs and towns are known in law as state-created municipal corporations. These units generally have more authority and autonomy than other types of local government. Yet, like other units of local government such as counties and special districts, they are the "legal creatures" of their states: that is, states create them, define their authority, determine the possible form of government they may adopt, and may even abolish them. Local governments generally derive their powers from three levels of state law: the state constitution, state statutes, and local or special laws enacted by the state legislature for individual local jurisdictions.

### Dillon's Rule

Consistent with the presumption about the inferior legal status of local governments, courts have commonly applied Dillon's Rule of strict construction, named after the nineteenth-century jurist John F. Dillon, to limit the power of local governments. Said Dillon:

> It is a general and undisputed proposition of law that a municipal corporation possesses and can exercise the following powers, and no others: First, those granted in express words; second, those necessarily or fairly implied in or incident to the powers expressly granted; third, those essential to the accomplishment of declared objects and purposes of the corporation—not simply convenient, but indispensable. Any fair, reasonable doubt concerning the existence of power is resolved by courts against the corporation, and the power is denied.[1]

**Figure 2-1   Sources and limits of local government power**

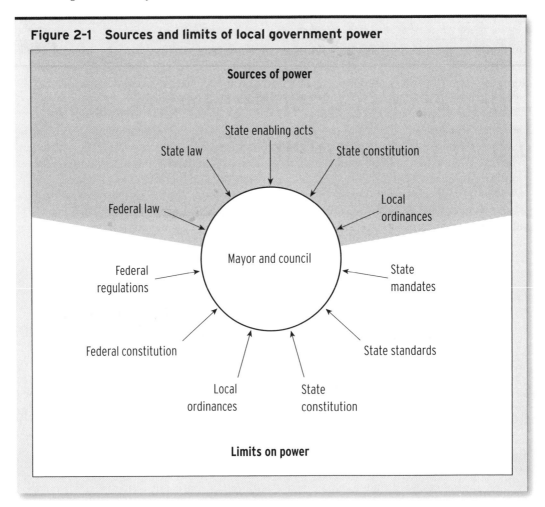

In states that follow Dillon's Rule, local governments (counties as well as municipalities) must obtain specific legislative authority for virtually everything they wish to do, from imposing user fees for trash collection to posting warning signs on frozen ponds. As a result, state legislators are busy passing bills that affect one or a few local governments and are immersed in minor local matters at the expense of policy issues of statewide interest.

In many states, Dillon's Rule has been eroded by judicial rejection of the rule and by state constitutional or statutory provisions that require courts to give a broad interpretation to the powers of local governments. Some courts, though, have been slow to change their approach to construction even when encouraged by the legislature to do so.

## Home rule

To circumvent Dillon's rule, several states allow local governments to obtain home rule. The traditional and most common form of home rule (1) gives local governments that qualify under state constitutional or statutory provisions—for example, a municipality over a certain population size—the right to make decisions without specific grants of authority on local matters; and (2) limits the power of the state to intervene in local matters. In practice, however, courts have found it difficult to distinguish between what is a local matter and what is of statewide concern, and they have usually resolved uncertainties in favor of the state.

Some home rule states authorize local units to carry out any function or exercise any power not expressly forbidden or preempted by the state—in essence, reversing Dillon's Rule. But even in these states, courts have tended to interpret the law to limit municipal action to what they define as a sphere of local affairs,[2] and they often overturn municipal ordinances on the grounds that such ordinances relate to a "statewide" rather than "local" matter.

When it comes to state interference in local affairs, localities are protected to some extent by constitutional prohibitions on special, or local, legislation—that is, acts that affect only a particular local jurisdiction such as a county, city, or town. In some states, however, such laws are common, and there is a strong tradition of giving state legislators a great deal of control over legislation affecting the localities they represent.

## Local ordinances and resolutions

Within the limits set by state law and local charters, local legislative bodies (e.g., city councils, village boards, and county commissions) may enact their own legislation in the form of ordinances or resolutions. Ordinances and resolutions deal with such subjects as zoning, taxes, sale of alcoholic beverages, peddling, traffic control, solid waste, sewers, snow emergency policies, the budget, capital improvements, personnel, and departmental organization. Generally, *ordinances* are viewed as establishing relatively permanent rules or laws for the locality, whereas *resolutions* are not laws but ministerial acts of a special or temporary nature.

---

**Local charters**

Most cities and many counties are governed by charters, which usually prescribe the form of government under which the municipality or county is organized and its powers and responsibilities. There are five types of charters:

1. **Special-act** charters are those granted by the legislature to specifically named local governments.

2. **General-act** charters establish uniform powers and the same form of government for all cities or counties in a state.

3. **Classified general-act** charters classify local governments, often by population, and grant those within each class certain powers and a specific structure.

4. **Optional general-act** charters permit a local government to select and operate under one of several plans provided by general law.

5. **Home rule** charters are drafted, adopted, and amended by the local government, within the limits (which are usually much broader for home rule governments) imposed by the constitution and general laws of the state.

The valid enactment of ordinances or resolutions often requires adherence to specific procedures found in state laws or ordinances that govern such matters as number of public readings, method of voting, majority necessary for passage, and public hearings. When procedures are dictated by state law, they may be considered mandatory by the courts, and failure to follow them can result in the invalidation of an ordinance or resolution.

Unless it is required by law, which is rarely the case, ordinances and resolutions do not have to follow a prescribed form or be codified. Nevertheless, a standard form and codification can result in more orderly, understandable, and accessible ordinances and resolutions, and may reduce or prevent court challenges to them.

## Variations in local discretion

In practice, the level of local discretion varies by region, type of local government unit, and extent of home rule powers.[3] The tradition of local self-government is, for example, stronger in New England than in the southern states, where prohibitions against special legislation never caught on and local bills are common. Throughout the nation, municipalities generally enjoy more discretionary authority and a greater measure of legal protection from state interference than do counties or other units of local government.[4] Unlike municipalities, which are called into being at the direct request—or, at least, with the consent—of the persons composing them, county governments are created by state government acting on its own for its own purposes. Municipalities and counties with home rule generally have more discretion than those without home rule. Local governments of all types, however, generally have more discretionary power in choosing their structures than in choosing what functions they will perform, raising revenues, and making personnel decisions.

## Variations in local functions

The functions and concerns of local government vary from state to state and, within a state, often on the basis of population. Most small to mid-sized municipalities are responsible for public safety, public utilities, public sanitation and health, transportation, and parks and recreation. Some large municipalities, such as New York City, also have responsibility for welfare programs, although this is normally a state and county function.

Council members in large cities spend more time on zoning, planning, and the consideration of executive proposals from the mayor or manager than do council members in small cities and towns. Small-city council members, on the other hand, spend more time reviewing the administration of city functions, answering constituent requests, and keeping track of personnel matters (hirings and firings) than do their counterparts in large cities. Council members in cities of all sizes consider zoning and land use decisions to be the most difficult decisions they face. In terms of citizen complaints, local officials appear most often to hear grievances over dog and other pet control problems (by far the most common complaint), traffic, and rezoning matters.

County governments, in contrast to municipalities, have traditionally functioned as administrative units for state programs in such areas as welfare services, highway construction, education, and the administration of justice. Metropolitan pressures, however, have encouraged several states to give counties, or at least certain categories of counties, home rule charters that allow them to provide many of the services once performed only by municipalities.

Special districts and independent authorities have often been created or authorized to deal with specific problems. Ordinarily, these entities are independent, special-purpose units of government with their own governing bodies, taxing powers, and borrowing authority. Some municipalities and counties may have responsibility for education, but states usually give this function to independent local school districts. Often cities and counties work together through service contracts and agreements and through voluntary regional councils. Numerous states in recent years have encouraged local governments, sometimes under the threat of the loss of state financial aid, to enter agreements through which they share functions and services.

## Forms of local government

With regard to forms of government, as noted in Chapter 1, the chief options for municipalities have been mayor-council and council-manager forms. Counties have traditionally been governed by boards or commissions.

*Mayor-council*  Many jurisdictions have some variation of the mayor-council form, in which there is ordinarily a legislative body called a city council and a separately elected chief executive known as the mayor. The range of the mayor's authority to appoint and remove departmental personnel, prepare a budget for submission to the council, and veto acts of the council vary widely.

*Council-manager*  Another popular model, the council-manager plan, vests the policy-making authority in the elected council and the administration of the community in a professional manager, who is appointed by the council and serves at its pleasure (occasionally under the terms of a written contract). The position of city manager may be part-time or combined with another municipal position in some smaller communities. In small towns, the manager may have only a secretary; in larger ones, he or she may have numerous technically trained people on the immediate staff. The larger the city, the less likely managers are to be involved with daily departmental routines.

*Commission*  A few municipalities have a commission form of government. Elected commissioners serve collectively as the policy-making body and individually as the heads of administrative departments, such as public works and public safety. The mayor is chosen directly by the voters or selected by the commission from within its membership.

*Local town meeting*  In the New England states, there is a strong tradition of local government autonomy and the oldest form of municipal government in the nation: the local town meeting. In its pure form, the local town meeting invites all eligible voters to assemble to discuss community issues and make laws. Today, because of growing populations and the complexity of urban problems, many New England towns have adopted a system whereby representatives from precincts are elected to attend meetings. Many towns have chosen to professionalize their governments by placing responsibility for management in the hands of a town manager, who reports to the board of selectmen.

*County commission*  Historically, county governments have operated under the board or commission form, which vests authority in a board of supervisors or commissioners who are usually elected from the districts. As a rule, the board selects one of its members as presiding officer, whose additional authority is usually limited to presiding over commission meetings. Frequently, board members or committees oversee or head county departments responsible to the commission. Authority is further dispersed among several popularly elected officials, including a sheriff, treasurer, prosecuting attorney, tax assessor, and superintendent of schools. In addition, state or county law may establish numerous independent boards and authorities (e.g., health, hospital, housing, library, and park) to administer various programs at the county level.

*County council-administrator, council-manager, and council–elected executive*   While most counties have the traditional commission form, it has been increasingly popular in urban areas to opt for council-administrator, council-manager, or council–elected executive forms. Under a council-administrator plan, the county council appoints a professional administrator (known as a county manager or chief administrative officer, or by some other title), who has broad authority over personnel, budgeting, and the administration of county departments and agencies. The essential difference between this form and the traditional commission form is the amount of power granted to the administrator.

The council-manager form is similar to the council-administrator form except that the manager in the council-manager form also has authority over hiring and firing.

The council–elected executive form provides for separate legislative and executive branches. The elected executive has administrative powers similar to those of the county manager.

## General restrictions on local authority

In making legislative and administrative decisions, local officials need to be aware of numerous limitations (see Figure 2–1). These include restrictions found in the U.S. Constitution, acts of Congress, rules and regulations developed by administrative agencies, and federal court decisions. A similar set of limitations is found on the state level. Local charters and ordinances provide other restrictions.

### Federal restrictions

The U.S. Constitution limits local governments when it comes to civil rights and liberties and the ability to regulate economic activity. Especially important in the realm of civil rights and liberties is the Fourteenth Amendment to the Constitution (see accompanying sidebar). The due process clause of that amendment generally requires procedural due process, which means that laws must be enforced in a fair manner. The clause may also be used to challenge the constitutionality of a law on the grounds that the law is unfair or unjust, regardless of how it is specifically applied. When such a case arises, the term *substantive due process* is used.

Much of the current debate over the protection of property rights from local regulations—an issue that commonly surfaces with regard to local land use decisions—revolves around the takings clause of the Fifth Amendment. The power of localities to regulate economic activity is also limited by judicial decisions that have given Congress broad power to regulate commerce. When Congress has acted in a lawful manner to regulate commerce, all local laws in conflict must give way. Even in the absence of congressional legislation, courts may invalidate local laws on the grounds that the laws interfere with the flow of interstate commerce.

### The Fourteenth Amendment

The key vehicle for the protection of civil liberties and rights has been the Fourteenth Amendment to the U.S. Constitution, which provides that no state shall "deprive any person of life, liberty, or property, without due process of law; nor deny to any person within its jurisdiction the equal protection of the laws." Over the years, the U.S. Supreme Court has held that the due process clause of this amendment incorporates many of the guarantees found in the Bill of Rights to the Constitution and protects them against state and local action. Thus, today's state and local governments, as well as the national government, function within the limits imposed by the First Amendment's guarantees of freedom of speech, religion, press, and assembly.

Under the equal protection clause of the Fourteenth Amendment, local governments may classify persons or things for the purpose of regulation or carrying out a program, but the classification cannot be unreasonable or arbitrary. In other words, local laws cannot discriminate against people, groups, or businesses unless there is a reasonable basis or justification for the discrimination.

State and local governments also must live up to the constitutional standards, as interpreted by the Supreme Court, of the Fourth, Fifth, Sixth, Seventh, and Eighth Amendments, which largely relate to the rights of those suspected or convicted of a crime.

---

The federal government enforces additional restrictions through often complicated legislation and administrative rules and regulations in policy areas such as air and water quality, solid waste, hazardous waste, transportation standards, labor-management relations, health care, courts, and corrections. Several rules and regulations accompany federal grants-in-aid to localities.

A federal act having a major and continuing influence on local functions and policies is the Civil Rights Act of 1871. Under this law, officials and employees themselves, as well as local governments, can be held liable for constitutional violations arising from official actions or omissions (see "Litigation and Liability" below).

Federal courts hear lawsuits against local governments and their officials on subjects including unequal or terminated public services, employee rights, law enforcement practices, jail conditions, obscenity, and zoning. It is critically important that local officials be aware of relevant federal statutes and court rulings and recognize their potential application to proposed or existing local enactments, policies, and practices.

## State restrictions

States restrict local authority through their constitutions, legislation, mandates, and administrative rules and regulations.

***State constitutions***  Provisions of state constitutions that are not found in detail, if at all, in the U.S. Constitution relate to governmental finance, local government powers, civil service, voting and elections, and regulation of corporations, as well as to public education, health, and welfare programs. The bill of rights found in state constitutions (sometimes called the declaration of rights) contains many of the same rights guaranteed in the federal Bill of Rights. (This duality often gives those whose rights may have been infringed upon the option of taking their case to either state or federal courts, or both if necessary.) State constitutions may also contain guarantees not found in the federal constitution. For instance, twenty-eight states have equal rights provisions in their constitutions similar to the Equal Rights Amendment that was proposed to the U.S. Constitution in 1972 but failed to secure approval. Sometimes state constitutions go beyond the federal constitution in conferring certain rights. For example, whereas the Second Amendment to the U.S. Constitution guarantees that "the right of the people to keep and bear arms shall not be infringed," some state constitutions (e.g., those of Montana and Texas) explicitly authorize the right of individual citizens to bear arms.

> *Some state courts, exercising a "new judicial federalism," base constitutional claims on state constitutions rather than on the federal constitution.*

State court judges tend to go no further than the High Court in protecting constitutional rights. However, some state courts, exercising a "new judicial federalism," base constitutional claims on state constitutions rather than on the federal constitution. For example, state courts in about half the states have found that reliance on the local property tax to finance education discriminates against students in areas where property values are lowest. Much of the law involving governmental regulation of business has also been based on state court interpretations of state constitutions. State courts closely examine local regulations on the basis of state constitutional doctrines relating to equal protection under the laws, due process, and the principles that limit the amount of legislative power that can be delegated to administrative agencies.

**Courts**   State courts have built up an enormous body of case law specifying what local governments can and cannot do. State judges play a major role in determining local authority for taxing, spending, and regulatory powers in general as well as in several policy areas, education, environmental protection, land use planning, and housing. State courts have also prodded state and local units into remedying inequalities in education, housing, and employment opportunities.

**Legislation**   State laws generally dictate optional forms of government. Options may include the powers and duties of officials; incorporation, annexation, and consolidation procedures; land use control and growth management; local elections; merit and retirement systems; financial operations; and open meetings and records. Failure of a local government to comply with state laws invites problems and may nullify a local ordinance or action.

**Mandates**   Along with state directives that they *do* certain things, local governments confront a range of "thou shall not" state directives. Local officials, for example, are continuously on guard against state legislation that would exempt certain businesses from local sales taxes or completely preempt local sales tax authority. Local officials also guard against attempts to preempt their ability to regulate the activities of businesspeople and property owners. As the result of landlords' efforts, for example, thirty-three states now prohibit local governments from adopting rent control measures. Some state laws restrict local ability to pass ordinances regarding tobacco products—such ordinances are often preempted by statewide clean-indoor-air bills—or to impose gun controls. Local governments are also restricted in their ability to require contractors doing business with them to pay their employees a "living wage" exceeding that required by the state or federal government, or to build and operate their own communication infrastructures. Beyond the financial and regulatory areas, prohibitions and preemptions involve everyday local government decisions on personnel and other internal matters. Some states, for example, limit the ability of local governments to set residency requirements for local employees such as police and fire personnel and schoolteachers.

***Administrative rules and regulations***   Much state administrative supervision occurs function by function; for example, a state department of education may implement legislative directives regarding education on the local level. In addition, many state agencies closely monitor the financial activities of local governments.

## Local laws

Local charters may contain a variety of provisions tailored to the desires of a particular locality. Such provisions include how council members are elected (from districts, at-large, or by a combination of the two), eligibility requirements, length of terms, limits on the number of terms, salaries of council members and mayors, procedures for filling vacancies or removing managers, appointive powers of city or county managers, and residency requirements for local government employment. Local laws also address finance, collective bargaining with employee organizations, contracting, and land use planning.

## Specific restrictions on local authority

Some of the most important restrictions on local authority relate to elections, open meetings and open records, land use and annexation, finances, personnel, contracts and franchises, ethical standards, and liability.

### Election laws

General and special local elections must be conducted in accordance with the provisions of state election codes and local charters. Elections in connection with annexations and incorporations and other matters are covered in other laws.

Many communities elect local officials through at-large elections. Others use districts or wards or some combination of the at-large and district system (electing some members at-large and others from districts). No local election system, however, is immune from challenge in court as to its validity. Localities that use wards or districts must grapple with the possibility that districting arrangements are discriminatory to minority groups. On the other hand, an at-large system for local elections may be challenged on the grounds that it dilutes the voting power of minorities and thus violates the national Voting Rights Act.

### Sessions, open meetings, and open records

Regular meetings of local legislatures are held at intervals set by state law or the local legislature's own rules. Generally, a majority of the body constitutes a quorum for the

---

### The Voting Rights Act

The Voting Rights Act of 1965, as amended and extended several times since then by Congress, contains several restrictions on the power of local officials with regard to voting and elections. Provisions added in 1975, for example, require that voter information material and ballots be printed in a language other than English in political jurisdictions in which 5 percent or more of the population is illiterate in English. As implemented, this provision requires more than 500 cities and counties in thirty states to hold elections in more than one language. Another section of the act requires that jurisdictions (cities, counties, or states) with a history of voting discrimination submit proposed changes affecting voting rights (including redistricting or changing county boundaries) to the U.S. Department of Justice (or the U.S. District Court for the District of Columbia) for approval. More recently, the Help America Vote Act of 2002 requires local governments to meet several requirements for voting equipment and election administration.

---

transaction of business; all ordinances, resolutions, and orders for payment of money require a recorded majority vote. In some instances, such as the passage of an emergency measure, a supermajority vote is required.

The frequency of meetings varies by population. In large cities, councils may meet more than once a week; in small cities, regular sessions may take place only once a month. In addition to regular sessions, legislative bodies may meet in adjourned or study sessions or in special sessions often called on an emergency basis.

State open meetings laws generally require all meetings be open to the public. This requirement may also apply to meetings of various local government boards and commissions, depending on their authority and composition. There are, however, numerous exceptions to the rule of openness, such as closed sessions dealing with the purchase or lease of real property, consultation with an attorney, personnel matters, and certain homeland security matters. In some states, localities are required to retain a verbatim record of closed meeting sessions in the form of an audio or video recording.

State public information acts or open records acts generally require that information held by municipal or county governments be released to the public upon a written request. E-mail may be considered a "public record" under state law if it relates to official business. Again, though, the laws typically provide numerous exemptions as to what must be released; officials receiving requests for information (e.g., transcripts of meetings, copies of laws, contracts) need to consult with local counsel before honoring such requests.

## Land use and annexation laws

Courts have long recognized that local governments have broad power to regulate the uses of private property in the interests of public safety, health, and welfare. In recent years, however, property-rights advocates have challenged zoning and other governmental restrictions on the use of private property, contending in state and federal courts that regulations diminish their property values and thus amount to an unconstitutional "taking" of private property without just compensation. Property-rights advocates, realtors, and developers have also pushed for state legislation or voter-approved propositions that would require property owners to be compensated if state or local regulations limit the use of private property (such as billboards).

The power of eminent domain allows local governments to confiscate private property for "public use" if the owner receives "just compensation." In the 2005 ruling of *Kelo v. City of New London* (125 S.Ct. 2655), the U.S. Supreme Court extended the use of eminent domain to purposes of economic development, but it also noted that nothing in its decision prevents states from restricting or banning the use of municipal eminent domain powers. In a more proactive manner, states have become increasingly involved in land use planning, and many require local governments to engage in comprehensive planning.

> *State legislatures have responded to strong political pressure by making it easier for outlying areas to incorporate and thus avoid annexation.*

Through annexation proceedings, a municipality extends its boundaries into unincorporated areas, enabling it to keep its boundaries concurrent with population growth, extend its tax base, and preclude the development of rival governments. Some states give municipalities considerable power to annex contiguous land, and about a dozen states also allow municipalities to veto the incorporation of new municipalities forming outside their boundaries. The general tendency, however, has been to restrict municipalities' freedom to act unilaterally and to increase residents' influence on annexation proceedings through referenda and other means.[5] Most important among the annexation laws have been those granting outlying property owners the sole right of initiating annexation proceedings, and those providing that cities may annex an area only after voters in that area have approved the annexation in a referendum election. In addition to these laws, state legislatures have responded to strong political pressure by making it easier for outlying areas to incorporate and thus avoid annexation.

## Local finances

State governments control nearly all aspects of local financial management: assessment, taxation, indebtedness, budgeting, accounting, auditing, and fiscal reporting.[6] State constitutions and statutes prohibit certain types of local taxes, such as sales and graduated income taxes; they also limit raising property tax rates or assessments beyond certain levels.

More than half the states have tax or expenditure limitations. The amount of total revenue that a local government can raise may be tied to such measures as the growth of personal income, inflation, or population, and all funds raised over the limit have to be refunded to the taxpayers. Some states limit local expenditures by tying them to a growth index. Many states require voter approval for both tax and spending increases above a certain level.

States limit local borrowing by requiring that a local public referendum be held to permit the issuance of bonds, restricting the purposes for which localities may borrow, and/or setting maximum limits on the amount of debt that localities can incur. Debt limits apply to borrowing through general obligation bonds; they are often expressed as a percentage (from 15 to 25 percent) of the value of the property within the jurisdiction, but they may also be stated in specific dollar amounts.

Depending on state law and practices, localities that are faced with mounting debt and an inability to find lenders have the opportunity to declare bankruptcy under the federal bankruptcy code. State laws vary considerably when it comes to local government bankruptcy: some laws deny access at least to certain categories of local governments, some laws allow free access, and some laws impose various types of conditions both before and during bankruptcy.[7]

## Personnel matters

When it comes to hiring, firing, conditions of employment, compensation, and promotion, several federal and state laws, as well as local charters and ordinances, generally prohibit local government discrimination on the basis of such factors as race, sex, sexual preferences, age, religion, national origin, pregnancy, childbirth, and disability; these laws and ordinances also prohibit sexual harassment.

Other laws deal with the ability of local government employees to form, join, and participate in employee organizations for the purposes of collective bargaining. Under state law, local officials may be required to "meet and confer" in good faith with representatives of employee organizations on matters concerning wages, hours, and other terms and conditions of employment. If the parties are unable to reach an agreement, applicable laws may require mediation or further "fact finding," through which an outsider is brought in to break the impasse. Some states permit binding arbitration when parties fail to agree on a mediator or when mediation fails. At the request of the employee organization, an arbitration panel is called in to hear evidence and render a decision that resolves the issues. When an agreement is reached, it is commonly written into a memorandum of understanding, which becomes effective after it has been approved by the governing local legislative body.

## Local contracts and franchises

Localities have no power to contract or to incur any liability unless specifically authorized by state law to do so. Moreover, local governments may have to observe certain formalities or meet certain conditions when entering into contracts. Such conditions might be

- That a contract be authorized by the passage of an ordinance
- That votes authorizing a contract be recorded
- That a contract be in writing
- That a contract involving the expenditure of funds be preceded by an appropriation.

If a contract is beyond the scope of a local government's authority, or if mandatory procedures are not followed or required conditions are not satisfied, a contract can be invalidated. However, a contract usually will not be declared void if mere technical formalities have not been followed, as in the failure of the mayor to sign an ordinance.

Competitive bidding is a common requirement for public works contracts. It may be generally required by state law or municipal ordinance, or for federal or state grants-in-aid, but it is commonly not required on contracts involving the expenditure of relatively small, specifically stated amounts of money. Usually local governments must advertise for sealed bids. State statutes cover such concerns as when and how long advertisements for bids must be published and what information bids must contain. A contract usually must

## Contracts and franchises

In providing various services, local governments have the choice of doing so indirectly by contracting out or directly by performing the activity. There is a long history of contracting with private businesses for such services as trash collection, ambulance dispatch, and street paving. In recent years, this type of contracting has increased. In order to encourage city departments to be competitive with private contractors, some cities allow the departments to compete with private bidders for these services (see Chapter 15).

Local governments also enter into formal contracts and agreements with each other. Three common types of cooperative arrangements are

1. Those in which one governmental unit contracts with another to perform specific services, such as fire protection

2. Those in which two or more governmental units jointly purchase equipment or operate some facility, such as a wastewater treatment plant, under contractual arrangements

3. Those in which two or more governmental units agree to assist one another when the need arises (e.g., a mutual aid pact regarding each other's police force during an emergency).

In general, if a locality is authorized to provide a particular service to its citizens, it may contract with another local government to provide or be provided with that service.

Generally, a franchise is a special privilege—for example, the exclusive authority to construct and operate a public utility—conferred by a government on an individual or corporation. Franchises are also granted by virtue of a government's control of streets, highways, or rights-of-way. For example, the government may collect a percentage of the revenue of a cable television or electric power company in return for permitting that company to run cables or power lines above or below public roads and streets. The government may also exact a flat yearly fee from a taxicab company using community streets. The power of communities to enter into franchise agreements is governed by local charter and state law; thus, local governments must turn to those sources for guidance regarding the extent of their authority and how it may be exercised.

be awarded to the lowest reliable bidder; under its charter, however, a local government may be allowed to enact an ordinance that gives preference to local businesses. A community ordinarily has the power to reject all bids and re-advertise, abandon the project, or perform the work itself.

Through performance-based contracts, the government defines what is to be achieved through a service contract and leaves it to the contractor to determine how this is to be done. While such contracts shift much of the responsibility to the contractor, the locality has a lot of work to do in developing statements that clearly define objectives, in stipulating how the contractor will achieve those objectives, and in monitoring contractor performance.

## Ethical standards

Local officials are subject to state and local laws regarding ethical behavior. A host of judicial decisions and legislation concerns conflicts of interest. The central idea is that public officials should not use their office for private gain. To help prevent this, many

localities require that incoming elected officials disclose certain types of financial information and update this information regularly. Laws also require public officials to disqualify
themselves from participating in decisions that affect their financial interests. Some states
flatly bar local officials or employees from "self-dealing" in local contracts (i.e., benefiting from contracts they have made). Even where no statutes exist, the courts invariably
refuse to uphold public contracts that serve an official's self-interest. Violations can result
in invalidation of the contract, return to the local government of all profits received by
the interested official, removal of the official from office, or criminal prosecution in states
where such an act is a crime.

> *Public officials should not use their office for private gain.*

In addition to the above laws, there are numerous regulations regarding the ability of
public officials to receive gifts (e.g., bans on gifts above a certain amount and requirements of disclosure) and bans on receiving anything of value in exchange for a favorable
decision. These regulations are intended to protect the integrity of the decision-making
process. Other prohibitions, such as on using public resources (e.g., travel expenses, staff
time, and agency equipment) for personal or political purposes, limit the ability of public
officials to take unfair advantage of their offices.

## Litigation and liability

Local officials can expect lawsuits; they are inevitable. There is the possibility of suits
built around a range of general tort and federal civil rights claims involving, for example,
procurements, the awarding of contracts and concessions, zoning and land use actions,
employment discrimination, police misconduct, someone slipping on the sidewalk, or a
decision by the legislative body to go into executive session.

In some states the test of whether a local government's or public official's action can
be the basis for a liability suit is whether the action is discretionary or ministerial. A
*discretionary act* requires the use of personal judgment and does not generally serve as a
basis for governmental liability. A *ministerial act* is one performed in a prescribed manner.
When public officials perform purely ministerial duties required by law and, through mistake or neglect, perform those duties improperly so as to cause injury, they can be made
to pay damages. On the other hand, when officials and employees perform discretionary
acts within the scope of their authority, they are usually immune from personal liability
to anyone injured by their erroneous acts or omissions unless those acts or omissions are
done corruptly, maliciously, willfully, or oppressively. The level of immunity is generally
higher for discretionary acts.

It is important to note that the distinction between discretionary and ministerial acts
is not always discernible, so the question of immunity or liability is not clear-cut for the
courts. Some courts also rely on a "function test": if a community engages in a governmental function, such as the operation of the court system, it will not be liable for claims;
it will be liable, however, if it engages in a proprietary function—that is, one that can be
performed by a private entity. But this distinction is difficult to apply.

Over the years, much of the task of defining the tort liability of local governments has
shifted from the courts to state legislatures. Some legislatures have increased the list of

---

### Steps to reduce personal liability risk

Arrange for the purchase of public official liability insurance to cover all government employees, including elected officials. Be sure that the policy covers exposure to civil rights suits.

Formulate all government administrative policies and procedures in writing; have them reviewed by legal counsel as to legality, including constitutionality; and be sure that they adequately protect the civil rights of government officials and employees as well as of citizens doing business with the government.

Make copies of established government administrative policies and procedures easily available to all officials and employees; immediately train all personnel regarding the intention of those policies and procedures, and the liability inherent in noncompliance with them or in actions that might be interpreted as violating the civil rights of others.

Establish a system for monitoring employees' familiarity and compliance with established policies and procedures.

Increase the level of professionalism in the organization, and be sure that administrative leaders are up-to-date in their understanding of civil rights risk.

During the decision-making process, increase the use of outside experts who can provide guidance in keeping policies and procedures updated and in accord with changing professional legal mandates and requirements.

---

activities for which local governments and their officials and employees have immunity from liability; other legislatures have limited the number of areas in which such personnel are liable. State laws provide considerable protection from the almost paralyzing effect of widespread liability claims. Most states have comprehensive liability laws placing statutory caps on the amount of damages recoverable from local governments and their officials and employees. In addition, many statutes authorize the payment of only compensatory damages, which reflect the actual cost of the injury, and prohibit punitive damages, which are awarded to punish or make an example in order to deter similar conduct in the future.

> *Under federal law, local officials and employees, as well as local governments, can be held liable for constitutional violations arising from official actions.*

States have also passed laws enabling communities to purchase liability or indemnity insurance covering claims based on negligence; contract rights; or violations of civil, constitutional, or common law rights. Laws in many states further authorize communities to provide self-insurance, participate in liability insurance pools, and adopt policies for settling claims and defending themselves against damage actions.

These laws, however, do not protect public officials and employees from lawsuits that charge them with willful, fraudulent, or malicious acts or for crimes involving theft of public property. Moreover, state laws dealing with tort liability have nothing to do with liability for federal civil rights violations. Under federal law, local officials and employees, as well as local governments, can be held liable for constitutional violations arising from official actions.[8]

Local officials need to be aware of liability issues. They should also avoid "litigation paralysis"—that is, they should not pass up the opportunity to make important and necessary decisions benefiting the community simply in order to avoid possible lawsuits.

## The local government attorney

As one authority has put it, "It is difficult to imagine that any municipality could effectively operate very long without the assistance of a local attorney."[9] Most small local governments retain attorneys who are private practitioners to handle their legal work, but a growing number of mid-size governments employ one or more attorneys full time and retain private practitioners for their expertise in particular kinds of cases. In any event, a government must reach a clear understanding with its corporate counsel concerning duties and compensation.

Around the country, municipal attorneys are appointed in different ways—some by the council, some by the mayor, and some by the city manager. Some are independently elected to office. Large cities often have separate criminal and civil law divisions; smaller jurisdictions normally have one office for both functions. Many municipalities receive general or specialized services from the same private firms.

Local government attorneys draft and review ordinances, resolutions, and contracts; advise the government's council or commission and departments on official legal matters and inform them of pertinent changes in the law; attend council or commission meetings; represent the government in court and in settling claims; approve title to property that the government is planning to purchase; and enforce various local codes (see accompanying sidebar). Local attorneys spend much of their time giving legal advice and putting out daily legal "brush fires."

### Attorneys and code enforcement

A largely unsung, but vital, role of the local government attorney is code enforcement. It is primarily through local codes, and especially building codes, that communities protect public safety and welfare.

Local governments are assigned the police power of the state to establish and enforce standards for building construction, housing, sanitation, and other activities affecting the safety, health, and welfare of the community. These standards, as reflected in various codes and ordinances, provide the only visible means for ensuring the orderly development of a community, preventing slums, and safeguarding life and property.

Communities usually pass and then enforce their own building, housing, electrical, and plumbing codes, using national model codes as their basis.

The attorney prepares these codes for legislative consideration and prepares amendments as needed to update the codes. In addition, the attorney provides legal training to those who will enforce the codes and prosecutes those charged with violating the codes.

The in-house local attorney and the private attorney who is retained on a regular basis (with humor in mind, the retained attorney, whether a generalist or specialist, is sometimes referred to as the "out-house" attorney) need general knowledge on a wide variety of matters, an understanding of the dynamics of governmental and political decision making, and the ability to forge effective relations with elected officials even though, in fact, the municipality or county is the attorney's client. One of the strong norms of the local attorney's job is that he or she should be isolated from political pressures; one way to ensure such isolation is by making it clear that the attorney's client is the local government unit rather than particular local officials; that is, the local attorney serves the local unit by telling local officials what the law requires and keeping them within the bounds of legal behavior and activity.

The most common mistake local government officials make is to call their attorney only after they are in trouble. The attorney should be informed of legal problems when they first arise. Legal problems and expenses can be avoided if the attorney's advice is sought during the decision-making process and if the advice is followed. The attorney can also help prevent or reduce problems by conducting training programs on the legal responsibilities of officials and employees, the limits of their authority, and the legal ramifications of improper or unauthorized actions. Establishing a system for keeping officials and employees abreast of relevant legal developments, particularly with regard to personal and governmental liability, is also useful.

## Sources of information

A source of general assistance for local government attorneys is the International Municipal Lawyers Association (IMLA) at 1110 Vermont Avenue, N.W., Suite 200, Washington, DC 20005. Formerly known as the National Institute of Municipal Law Officers (NIMLO), IMLA has been a resource of local government attorneys since 1935. Its Web site, imla.org, has "hot links" to a wide variety of municipal codes, policies, associations, and sources of assistance. Specialized aid is also often available through state leagues of cities or municipal leagues and county associations in various states. Municipal organizations, such as the League of Oregon Cities, have programs especially for smaller cities in their states. In addition, considerable information is commonly available through the municipal law sections of state bar associations.

## The manager/attorney relationship

As a local government manager, it is important to remember that your attorney's *client* is the *city or county, acting through the governing board and staff.*

Just as managers who are ICMA members are bound by the ICMA Code of Ethics, your attorney is required to abide by specific Rules of Professional Conduct, as prescribed by your state bar.

Bear in mind that there is a line separating management and the law. While some managers may use the attorney as a sounding board, it is the manager's role to run the government in accordance with the policies designated by the governing board, and it is the attorney's role to provide legal advice. These roles should be respected by both parties.

In this context it is important for the manager and attorney to establish a collaborative relationship.

> **Questions to ask if you manage a small community**
>
> What are your options as to form of government? Are changes needed in basic structures and procedures?
>
> Are citizens well versed as to what the local government can and cannot do? Should newly elected local officials be oriented regarding their roles and responsibilities?
>
> What procedures are required regarding the enactment of ordinances and resolutions? Must ordinances and resolutions be codified?
>
> Does state law allow your government to annex adjacent property? What are the legal requirements?
>
> May cities and counties in your state contract with one another for the provision of services without state approval? May your locality engage in performance-based contracting?
>
> Is there a "sunshine law" in effect requiring local governments in your state to conduct open meetings? When may they meet in closed session?
>
> Are local elected officials subject to a state-imposed code of ethics? If so, what types of behavior are required and what penalties are provided for?
>
> Are code regulations being consistently enforced?
>
> What constitutional or statutory limitations exist on the amount of property tax that may be levied by local governments in your state? What are the restrictions concerning other revenue sources and going into debt?
>
> What are the restrictions on purchasing? When must bidding be competitive? May your locality engage in cooperative purchasing with other local governments?
>
> Is collective bargaining with public employee representatives authorized? Is binding arbitration provided for?

## Conclusion

The governing responsibilities of local governments, especially smaller ones, have become more numerous and complex in recent years. As residential communities spread into areas once considered "rural," many small governments must cope with the same complicated problems as their larger counterparts—for example, growth management and telecommunications matters. Along with this are increasingly difficult problems with regard to such matters as managing the budget, handling personnel, entering contracts for services, and dealing with litigation. Going about their work, local officials constantly face the challenge of ensuring that their decisions, policies, and procedures will comply with

- State constitutions, laws, and regulations, which generally dictate the powers and duties of local officials and cover such matters as incorporation, annexation, and consolidation procedures; land use control and growth management; local elections; merit and retirement systems; financial operations; and open meetings and records

- State court decisions, which collectively have produced an enormous body of case law specifying what local governments can and cannot do

- The U.S. Constitution, federal statutes, federal regulations, and federal court rulings regarding basic civil rights and liberties and covering such matters as federal grant restrictions, mandates, and preemptions
- Local charters and ordinances, which provide detailed provisions on organizational forms, procedures, responsibilities, and operations.

To meet the challenge posed by this vast array of legal dictates, as well as to prepare for litigation, local officials have come to rely on highly qualified legal assistance. Many legal problems, including the possible nullification of a local action, and much expense can be avoided if local officials seek out and follow a local attorney's advice during the decision-making process. And on a more positive note, sound legal advice clears the air, countering the tendency toward legal paralysis, and helps guide local officials so that they may better serve their communities.

## Endnotes

1   John F. Dillon, *Commentaries on the Law of Municipal Corporations* (Boston: Little, Brown, 1911), 145.

2   Gordon L. Clark, *Judges and the Cities* (Chicago: University of Chicago Press, 1985), 78–79.

3   Joseph F. Zimmerman, *State-Local Relations: A Partnership Approach*, 2nd ed. (New York: Praeger, 1995).

4   Unlike municipalities, which are called into being at the direct request of the people who make them up (or, at least, with their consent), counties are quasi-municipal corporations created by state government for its own purposes. Although some counties have charters that give them a degree of independence, they are primarily administrative units of the state.

5   Jamie L. Palmer and Greg Lindsey, "Classifying State Approaches to Annexation," *State and Local Government Review* 33 (Winter 2001): 60–73.

6   S. C. Wallace, *State Administrative Supervision over Cities in the United States* (New York: Columbia University Press, 1928).

7   Frederick Tung, "After Orange County: Reforming California Municipal Bankruptcy Law," *Hastings Law Journal* 53 (April 2002): 885–929.

8   The most relevant law is the 42 U.S.C. § 1983, the Civil Rights Act of 1871.

9   Ken Smith, "Working with the Municipal Attorney," *Current Municipal Problems* 31 (2004–2005): 448, as cited in the April 2005 issue of *Alabama Municipal Journal*.

# The Clerk

**Drew A. Dolan**

$K$*eeper of the archives, remembrancer, town clerk,* and *city secretary* are all historic terms used to refer to one of the oldest and most common positions in local government: the clerk. The function of "keeper of the archives" dates back to prebiblical times. In ancient Greece, meetings of the governing body began with the "city secretary" reading aloud the documents to be considered and laying a curse on those who sought to deceive the public. In the Book of Acts (Acts 19:21–22, A.D. 58), history records that Paul and his companions were the recipients of the protection of a "town clerk" in Ephesus. A closer relative of today's municipal clerk dates back to 1272 A.D. in England, when a "remembrancer" reminded councilors of what had transpired at previous meetings.

As the early colonists settled in America, they set up forms of local government similar to those with which they were familiar in England. The colonists of Plymouth appointed an official to serve as a recorder of written records, including grants of land, animal regulations, tax collection, and expenditures of the settlement. By the middle of the seventeenth century, clerks had become an integral part of the new communities, recording births, deaths, land and financial transactions, and actions taken at town meetings.

---

### The office of the clerk

In one of the first textbooks on the administration of municipalities, Professor William Bennett Munro stated, "No other office in municipal service has so many contracts. It serves the mayor, the city council, the city manager (when there is one), and all administrative departments without exception. All of them call upon it, almost daily, for some service or information. Its work is not spectacular, but it demands versatility, alertness, accuracy, and no end of patience. The public does not realize how many loose ends of city administration this office pulls together." Munro's description of the clerk is equally accurate today.

Source: William Bennett Munro, *Municipal Administration* (New York: Macmillan, 1934), as cited at iimc.com/about_iimc/History_clerk .shtml.

Today, only the positions of mayor and chairperson of the county governing body are more common than that of clerk. The position of clerk exists in nearly all local governments. At the county level, it is usually filled by election. In cities, towns, and villages, the clerk is likely to be appointed.

Although the position is common, the titles still vary widely: the terms include *clerk-treasurer* in Indiana; *city* and *village clerk* in Illinois; and *clerk–tax collector* in Mississippi. In New Jersey, the terms *municipal clerk, city clerk, borough clerk,* and *township clerk* are used at the municipal level. In New England, the position is commonly known as *town clerk.* The clerk in Texas is often known as the *city secretary;* in Utah the title is commonly *city recorder;* and in Ohio the term *clerk of the commissions* is used. At the county level, the term *county clerk* is most common, but other titles include *clerk to council, clerk to commission,* and *shire clerk.*

## Duties of the clerk

The duties of the clerk are essential and, in many communities, broader than they have been in the past as new technologies, government mandates, and significant professionalization efforts have added new dimensions to the position. The functions of the clerk may be likened to the infrastructure of the community: they are vital to the operation and welfare of the local government organization, but most often they remain unnoticed by the public until a problem arises. For smaller communities especially, the clerk's office often serves as the starting point for inquiries from citizens, businesses, the media, and other public and nonprofit organizations.

The functions of the clerk can be grouped into the following broad categories: central services, records management, election administration, finance administration, licenses and permits, secretariat to the governing body, general administration, and public information.

---

**Typical functions of the clerk and the clerk's office**

While differences in local traditions, state and local laws, population, and the individual skills and personalities of the clerk prevent labeling all clerk positions the same, there are many functions common to those holding that position:

- Maintaining official records, documents, vital statistics, and financial records
- Recording and publishing council or board minutes, ordinances, and resolutions
- Providing information for inquiries from citizens, other departments, and other agencies
- Helping to provide compliance with open meetings and freedom of information requirements
- Facilitating the receipt and processing of bids
- Retaining custody of the official seal of the unit
- Issuing licenses and permits
- Administering elections.

## Central services

Two functions are central to the role of the clerk: preparing the governing body's agenda and providing notification of meetings. These functions are common to all clerks and are typically governed by state statute and local ordinance.

*Agenda preparation* Especially in communities where there is no chief administrative officer, the clerk is commonly the one responsible for preparing the board's or council's agenda. Usually organized to better manage the policy-making process, the agenda outlines the items to be considered at a meeting and establishes the order in which they will be considered. Items placed at the beginning of the agenda, for example, are more likely to receive more extensive discussion than those at the end. Agenda items should contain sufficient information to help the presiding officer, members of the governing body, and the public understand the specific nature of the issue and what action is being sought. Effective agenda preparation can help ensure that a meeting runs smoothly and efficiently.

> *Usually organized to better manage the policy-making process, the agenda outlines the items to be considered at a meeting and establishes the order in which they will be considered.*

In preparing the agenda, the clerk consults with the governing body and the chief administrative officer in communities having such a position. Agenda items may be proposed by members of the governing body, administrative officers, the public, other departments, and other governments. The clerk reviews the actions of previous meetings to determine whether an item should be placed on the agenda as a result of some earlier action, such as a second or third reading of an ordinance, a tabled motion, or a request for reports. The current edition of *Roberts Rules of Order* is commonly used to assist in structuring the agenda and meetings.

In many small communities, agendas are often fairly informal, and the presiding officer uses them merely as a reminder of the issues to be considered. As a community increases in population and the issues faced become more complex, however, the agenda process will become more formalized. In larger communities and where mandated by state government (typically through "open meetings act" legislation), the agenda process will have

---

### The office of the clerk in Bisbee, Arizona

In the city of Bisbee, Arizona (pop. 6,177), the agenda for each regularly scheduled council meeting, or for any special session at which the city is to consider an ordinance, must be available at city hall at least ninety-six hours prior to the meeting. Agendas for other sessions of the council require posting at city hall at least twenty-four hours in advance. Agendas are also to be placed on the city government's cable channel, posted through a link on the office of the city clerk's Web page, and available through e-mail from the clerk's office. In addition, the clerk's office is responsible for posting notices of all city meetings as well as for posting and publishing city ordinances in multiple locations.

Source: City of Bisbee, cityofbisbee.com/ctyclk.html.

---

**Technological efficiency in Lexena, Kansas**

The city of Lenexa, Kansas (pop. 43,434), has adopted a "paperless packet" of information to reduce expenses and increase efficiencies. Through its software package, the city is able to create an electronic document that functions much like the traditional paper documents, but with additional benefits. Supporting documents for agenda items are scanned or converted from e-mails and placed into a pdf format with hypertext links. The packet is then sent to the members of the governing body and made available on the city's Web page. The governing members have found it more convenient to move through the packet, and easier to make notes in the margins and highlight important passages; they are also able to create a comment sheet with links to materials in the document. Through this innovation, the community has saved time, duplication costs, paper costs, and effort.

Source: City of Lexena, ci.lenexa.ks.us/vsnMinutesandAgenda/paperlesspackets.html.

---

rules that establish a precise format, requirements for submitting agenda requests, and mandates for publication or distribution of the agenda at a specified time and place. Many communities also have established rules for citizens or concerned individuals desiring to speak at council or special meetings; increasingly, those individuals are being required to preregister with the clerk's office a set number of days or amount of time before the meeting and are restricted in the time they are allowed for addressing the council. Rules of procedure will also typically place restrictions on both the action that a governing body may take on an issue not listed in the official agenda and the number of council meetings in which an action must be reviewed before it may be taken.

The agenda process has been revolutionized in recent years through the use of computers and various software packages. The clerk's office now has the ability to prepare, disseminate, and record agendas electronically. Many clerks maintain an electronic mailing list of all parties interested in receiving agendas and other materials pertaining to public meetings; post agendas and meeting dates on the community's Web site; and use e-mail to answer any questions regarding the agenda of scheduled meetings.

Some communities have even taken this a step further by going to "paperless" agendas and meetings. The calendars for meetings, agendas for meetings, and information files on agenda items are all processed electronically. Packets of information are transferred electronically to members of the governing body and concerned staff members, and are made available on community Web pages. This process saves considerable expenses on paper, duplicating, and staff assistance in preparing paper packets. Further, it increases the efficiency of disseminating information and maintaining the records of agendas and minutes of meetings.

*Meeting notification*   In addition to preparing the agenda, the clerk is often responsible for posting or publishing the dates and times of meetings of the governing body. The notices must be given in a manner that complies with local laws and regulations as well as the individual state's open meetings act. Notices of all meetings involving local elected officials must be made public through prescribed methods at a specified time in advance of the meeting and must include information on the business to be considered. Open meetings acts will often set guidelines on the level of coverage; notification of the type of meeting to be held (special, irregular, emergency, or closed); and the keeping of the minutes. It is also typically the function of the clerk to compile and maintain mailing lists of those desiring meeting notification (individuals, newspapers, radio stations, etc.) and to prepare the minutes for public inspection within the required timeline of the act.

## Records management

An effective records management program usually begins with the determination of what constitutes a record. Most people understand that documents, letters, and other papers are records, but some are surprised to learn that e-mails, maps, photographs, magnetic tape, and microfilm can also be records. In fact, local government records can include a myriad of different materials and come in many forms. At a basic level, records may be defined as anything produced or received in the official conduct of local government operations.

All clerks are required to keep and maintain records on agendas, minutes, resolutions and ordinances, codes, contracts and agreements, bids, deeds, maps and drawings, births, deaths, marriages, and various licenses. Because the desire to provide historical highlights for anniversary celebrations and genealogical research has spurred citizen interest in older records, the clerk may also be responsible for maintaining various historical records regarding the community, its governing body, and its citizens. In many communities, the preservation and availability of cemetery records, vital statistics, tax rolls, census data, and property transfers are also within the purview of the clerk's office.

*Legal requirements*   The number and type of records kept, the methodology used for storing records, and the accessibility of records vary by community and are often dictated by state statute and local ordinance. Each clerk must reference his or her own state's and community's requirements regarding what types of records are to be kept, how they may be stored, how long they must be kept, who may be given access to each type of record, the time frame within which the records must be made available, and issues of security.

In most states, the county clerk is required by law to file commissions for notary publics, record names adopted by new businesses, issue marriage licenses, and maintain campaign disclosure documents and various kinds of financial statements. The county clerk may also be required to compute the property taxes for the different units of local government, in accordance with the rates allowed by law and the assessed value of residential, commercial, and industrial property within the district. From these data, individual tax bills are prepared.

Certain records are required by law to be kept for specified periods of time. For example, financial records of federal grants often must be made available for audit years after the money has been spent. Moreover, many states impose penalties for the destruction or alteration of specified records. Issues regarding the retention of records are discussed further on in this section.

*Right of privacy vs. freedom of information*   Some records, such as tax returns, employee personnel files, and reports of police investigations, are considered confidential. Allowing access to confidential records by unauthorized persons is often punishable by law; on the other hand, refusing access to most public government documents, files, and records is also a punishable offense. The clerk must constantly stay abreast of legislative changes and judicial mandates regarding access to information.

---

### Managing records in Great Falls, Montana

As posted on the Web site of the city clerk's office in Great Falls, Montana (pop. 56,338),

> Government records are an asset, not a liability. Measures need to be taken to protect them, enhance them, and utilize them to their fullest potential. Merely creating, filing, and storing records in a basement or attic is not enough. Records, which take thousands of man-hours to create, are useless if they cannot be retrieved and used. Poor records management practices result in wasting valuable and scarce tax dollars as the local government purchases unnecessary filing equipment and uses up valuable office space for records. Records management provides for efficiency of time and space, is a money saver and not a frivolous expense.

Source: City of Great Falls, ci.great-falls.mt.us/people_offices/city_clrk/manage.htm (accessed May 9, 2006).

---

Under the 1966 Freedom of Information Act (FOIA), states have provided strict regulations governing accessibility, and the clerk must be aware of all legislation pertaining to the public's right of access to records. Most clerks have easy access to their state's FOIA through the Internet.[1] The act will detail for the clerk such issues as which records must be made available and which are exempt, who is to have access to which records, how records are to be maintained, how requests are to be made and within what time frame they must be responded to, and what fees may be charged. Absent knowledge of what is subject to laws covering right of privacy and those covering freedom of information, clerks expose both themselves and their governments to substantial liability.

*Records storage and accessibility*    Today's clerk must be able to store records efficiently and safely in a timely manner and still make them readily accessible to governing officials, staff, and the public almost instantly. A comprehensive records management program requires that all local government records be identified and inventoried. Inventory worksheets may contain information for each category of record with regard to size, location, series (groups of related records), names, numbers, descriptions, and recommended retention periods. However, the sheer volume of paper records often poses a storage space problem. Moreover, natural and man-made disasters can threaten the safety of records that are stored improperly.

Other challenges entailed in meeting the demands for safe and efficient storage and accessibility include version control, security, privacy, authenticity, and technical obsolescence are all concerns to be addressed in meeting these demands. Clerk offices across the United States and around the world have met these challenges by moving record keeping into the digital age. Using scanning equipment, document imaging software, digital document databases, and client-server architecture, the clerk's office can store records quickly, accurately, and safely, while ensuring that they are easily and quickly accessible. For many clerks, automated records management systems provide a cost-effective alternative to the labor-intensive, time-consuming, and often costly traditional models of record management.

*Records retention*    Following a review of the inventory worksheets cited above, a formalized record retention schedule for each category of records is determined. Record retention schedules govern the disposition of records by prescribing how long, where, and in what form the records are to be kept. The schedules are based on a review of the administrative, legal, fiscal, and historical value of the records. Those records that are not required for day-to-day office use must be transferred to a centralized storage area, where they are to be maintained until destroyed in accordance with the schedules.

States with laws that require local governments to have a records management program usually require that the record retention schedules be approved by a specified state agency. In most states, the office of the secretary of state administers the local records division and regularly advises the clerk regarding document retention and destruction. For example, the retention schedule for communities in Montana is available to all communities on a Web site created by the state.[2] Typically, a clerk may not destroy any document without obtaining written consent.

Many important records—for example, charters, minutes, ordinances, vital statistics, and cemetery records—are scheduled for permanent retention because of their legal or historical value. However, very old records tend to deteriorate physically, especially if abused or neglected, and a scientifically controlled environment may be needed to halt their deterioration. Where local governments are unable to provide such an environment, the documents are placed in the custodial care of state agencies, colleges and universities, regional facilities, libraries, or other institutions experienced in the preservation of documents.

***Recorder of deeds***   In many states, the county clerk will also serve as the recorder of deeds (often titled the *register of deeds),* recording all deeds, mortgages, subdivision plats, attachments, mechanics liens, federal and state tax liens, and statements on personal property. The governing body may also authorize the clerk to maintain a tract index of real estate transactions, including titles to property and mortgage liens held against the property.

The types of documents requiring recording, the methodologies allowed for recording and duplication, certification and seal requirements, and signature and identity authorizations are often set by state statute and supported with local ordinances. Each document is assigned an official document number at the time it is presented for recording. The document is then entered the proper book/computer file and indexed for quick reference and retrieval. The records are generally copied or duplicated for permanence and security.

As with many of the other duties assigned to the clerk's office, the register of deeds function has entered the e-government age. Clerks in many counties have incorporated digital scanning and electronic storage into the recording process. The services provided in this area, descriptions of those services, forms used, and answers to frequently asked questions are made available to citizens and businesses around-the-clock through Web pages.[3]

## Election administration

The administration of elections (federal, state, and local) is a primary function of local governments, and the clerk's office, both city and county, is often responsible for overseeing and coordinating the electoral process. Basic election duties fulfilled by the clerk include voter registration, maintenance of a permanent record of registered voters, issuance and receipt of all candidate petition filings, issuance of official publications relating

**Voter information on the Web in Wasilla, Alaska**

The clerk of Wasilla, Alaska (pop. 8,471), maintains a Web site that informs potential voters of how and where to register to vote. This site also provides notification of vacancies in offices and of upcoming elections, offers filing information to candidates, details where voting is to take place, instructs voters on how to use absentee ballots or vote early, posts election results, and provides an e-mail address for questions.

Source: City of Wasilla, cityofwasilla.com/clerk/absentee.asp.

to elections, appointment and training of election judges, printing and delivery of all necessary election materials, tabulation of results, and canvassing of final election results. The processes and procedures of each of these tasks are specified by federal and state election laws.

Coordinating all the activities involved in the electoral process can be a daunting task. To this task are added concerns over voter registration, problems with ballots and voting machines, and issues of voter fraud. Thus, it is imperative that the clerk regularly monitor changes in federal and state election laws and court decisions concerning elections and voting. As with other areas of responsibility, many clerks' offices have integrated computer and Web-based technologies into the administration of the electoral process.

Leading the challenges facing the clerk's office in the area of election administration is the need to comply with the federal Help America Vote Act of 2002.[4] Under this act, each state must select a single type of voting methodology to be used in all elections carried out in the state. Newer methodologies include touch-screen voting and optical scan voting. Although each state legislature is responsible for selecting that state's methodology, it is up to the clerk's office to implement the new methodology. It is the clerk's responsibility to ensure that training is available for those who will supervise voting and that the methodology is used correctly, and to handle any difficulties that may arise. As further changes and modifications to the electoral process occur, they too will fall to the clerk's office for implementation.

## Finance administration

Most clerks are responsible for some aspect of finance administration; it is not unusual for the clerk to perform functions that range from balancing bank statements to organizing the sale of tax-delinquent properties. Common tasks in this area include accounting, billing, bill collecting, and budgeting. Other such tasks often handled by the clerk's office include tax collection, bid procedures, issuance of bonds, payroll, cash management, and investments. In larger jurisdictions where finance departments exist, the financial responsibility of the clerk is often limited to managing the budget of the clerk's office. However, in many local governments, particularly small ones, the clerk may also serve as the treasurer or finance officer.

Several of the clerk's functions in the area of finance administration may be highly regulated by both state statute and local ordinance. For example, the bid process has become a very structured and regulated process in order to avoid any sense of impropriety. The clerk may be responsible for placing a "notice inviting bids" in local newspapers and trade journals and on the community's Web site. Requirements may also exist regarding the number of days in advance of the opening of the bid that the notice must be published, and the number of times it is to be published.

In addition, the clerk's office may be the recipient of incoming bids, which will come in by mail, United Parcel Service, Federal Express, walk-in, and so on. As the bids come in, they are stamped with the date and time received and remain sealed until the designated date and time of opening. If the clerk's office is also responsible for opening the bids, the clerk will open and read the bids while a fellow staff member records them. The bids are then passed on to the department or individual responsible for evaluating them.

## Licenses and permits

The licenses and permits issued by local governments both regulate services and produce revenues. States typically authorize two types of licenses and permits: the first is granted to any individual or business that meets a basic set of requirements; the second allows the unit of local government some level of discretion in determining who will be issued the license or permit. In the latter case, it is the governing authority or an appointed board that decides whether to issue the license; the clerk usually has very limited discretion.

The requirements that must be met by someone requesting a license vary greatly by type of license. Generally speaking, the greater the potential for impact on or damage to the community and its citizens, the stricter the licensing requirements. In many places, contractors must document their competency, taxicab drivers must have good driving records and adequate insurance, and convicted felons are not allowed to receive alcoholic beverage licenses. If the proper application and fees are submitted and required authorization (if needed) is given, it is generally the duty of the clerk to issue the license.

> *Generally speaking, the greater the potential for impact on or damage to the community and its citizens, the stricter the licensing requirements.*

License fees vary greatly throughout the country. Several states have established uniform business licensing provisions that apply to all local government units. Other states leave the decision to the local government or place a limit on the amount that a local government may charge. Some local governing bodies may try to use the licensing function to prohibit or regulate activities by establishing excessive fees or unreasonable requirements. However, courts have usually held such ordinances to be invalid when challenged.

Typically the clerk is required to make some determination of the facts to ensure compliance with licensing requirements. The clerk may have to verify whether the proposed location of a new business has the proper zoning, and whether certain requirements—such as those for parking spaces, square footage, availability of restrooms, or insurance coverage—have been met. Some licenses require the prior approval of building inspectors, code enforcement officers, fire inspectors, or health officials. If the price of a license is based on the income or gross receipts of a business, the clerk is often empowered to examine the financial records of that business.

---

**License and permit information on the Web in Wauwatosa, Wisconsin**

The city clerk in Wauwatosa, Wisconsin (pop. 46,312), maintains a Web site that provides information on available licenses and permits, including requirements, costs, forms, and an e-mail link. Users of this Web site may obtain information by "clicking" on the type of permit or license in which they are interested:

| **Permits** | **Licenses (continued)** |
|---|---|
| Block party permit | Hotel/motel license |
| Building permit | Jukebox license |
| Fire/safety permit | Massage establishment license |
| Planning and zoning permit | Massage technician license |
| Street occupancy permit | Pinball machine license |
|  | Pool table license |
| **Licenses** | Precious metal and gem dealer license |
| Amusement arcade license | Secondhand dealer license |
| Amusement device license | Secondhand dealer mall license |
| Bed and breakfast license | Service station license |
| Beer and liquor license | Soda water license |
| Bowling lane license | Street vendor license |
| Building, electrical, and plumbing license | Swimming pool license |
| Dance license | Theater license |
| Dog and cat licenses | Tobacco products license |
| Food and restaurant license | Used car dealer license |
| Gun or weapons dealer license | Vending machine license |

Source: City of Wauwatosa, wauwatosa.net/display/router.asp?DocID=691.

---

Many clerks' offices have increased their efficiency and accessibility by putting the licensing service, including applications and payment capabilities, on the local government's Web site, where it is available to citizens and businesses around the clock seven days a week.

## Secretariat to the governing body

The office of the clerk may provide support services to the governing body beyond those already discussed; these services reflect the requirements of the position that are "secretarial" in nature. Thus, in addition to recording and maintaining minutes, ordinances, and resolutions of the governing body, the office of the clerk may research current issues, provide messenger and mail service for the governing body, perform copying and other secretarial services, and sell reports.

As secretariat, the clerk's office assists and advises the governing body with respect to such matters as parliamentary procedure and the relationship of proposed actions to state and federal law. In smaller communities, the governing body further depends on the clerk to supply information concerning changes in state and federal laws and regulations. For many local governments, the clerk's office will also be required to provide similar support to the boards and commissions that assist the governing body.

## General administration

In smaller communities, when there is not a chief administrator to handle the day-to-day duties of government, the clerk may serve as the government's administrative officer. The efficient and effective operation of the community then becomes dependent on a strong working relationship between the governing body and the clerk/administrator. Several of the training and development programs set up by national and state associations of clerks have incorporated components geared toward training in administration and leadership (see the section "Professionalism of the Clerk" beginning on page 60).

When the clerk serves as administrator, his or her duties expand to include such functions as preparing the budget and financial reports, handling payroll, dealing with state and federal grants, accounting, and managing human resources. These functions are carried out with varying degrees of direction and supervision from the governing body—often depending on the experience of the clerk and the level of trust that has developed between the governing body and the clerk.

## Public information

Today it is not uncommon for larger jurisdictions to have a formally designated public information office. For most communities, however, the office of the clerk has traditionally served as the public information center. Inquiries and complaints concerning the unit of government commonly come to the clerk's office. Although the inquiry or complaint may not be directly related to or targeted at the clerk, the clerk will be expected to have an answer or information readily available, obtain the information for the interested party, or refer the matter to the appropriate office or individual.

This role is appropriate for the clerk for several reasons. First, the clerk's office serves as the repository for official records of the jurisdiction, and any inquiry regarding the details of an ordinance, an action of the governing body, or the membership of

**The city clerk's office on the Web in O'Fallon, Illinois**

The Web page of the city clerk's office in O'Fallon, Illinois (pop. 25,155), provides a variety of resources. Through this site, residents and interested individuals can contact the clerk, other city and community officials, and board and committee members; get information on community services; obtain council minutes and agendas; and gain access to various records and documents. The site also provides a list of frequently asked questions and responses. Other links provide information on such issues as election and voter registration, the code of ordinances, business registration and licensing, and employment opportunities, as well as on how to volunteer with the community and how to become an e-mail subscriber.

Source: City of O'Fallon, ofallon.org/Public_Documents/OFallonIL_CityClerk/index.

an appointed board or commission is appropriately submitted to the clerk. Second, the clerk's office is a logical starting point for persons unfamiliar with a particular government. Third, people prefer to deal with individuals whom they know, and since many clerks remain in office through a succession of mayors, council members, city and county managers, and department heads, there tends to be greater continuity in the clerk's office than in most other government offices. As a result, the clerk is usually well known in the community, either personally or by name, and is often the individual who first receives a question or complaint from a concerned citizen.

This service, too, has been affected by advances in technology. Many clerks have taken advantage of the Internet to create easily accessible pages on their communities' Web sites. As shown by the examples given throughout this chapter, these pages provide direct links to services and sources of information offered by the clerk and the community.

## Professionalism of the clerk

As this chapter has shown, a clerk wears many hats. In small communities, the clerk may be the entire government staff. In larger communities with various departments, the clerk's office still will retain responsibility for a broad range of functions. Because of the importance of the office and the technical competence required, a growing emphasis has been placed on professionalization of the clerk. Clerks are increasingly seeking opportunities for professional development, acquiring specialized knowledge and competencies, sharing information, and developing improved methods for discharging their diverse duties.

### Professional training

Among clerks, membership in professional organizations continues to increase, as does the number of clerks seeking certification and participating in training programs. The principal organizations offering professional services to clerks are the International Institute of Municipal Clerks (IIMC) for municipal clerks and the International Association of Clerks, Recorders, Election Officials, and Treasurers (IACREOT) for county clerks. Founded in 1947, IIMC now counts more than 10,000 members in the United States, Canada, and several other countries. IACREOT, founded in 1971, has some 1,600 members throughout the United States and other countries. In addition, state associations of both city and county clerks exist throughout the country. These associations hold annual conferences, provide training and development programs and seminars, publish newsletters, and issue bulletins. Often the city clerks and county clerks meet separately, but training programs for the two are frequently combined.

The primary goal of the IIMC "is to actively promote the continuing education and professional development of Municipal Clerks through extensive education programs, certification, publications, networking, annual conferences and research."[5] On its Web page, the institute provides profiles of and links to its Certified Municipal Clerk (CMC) and Master Municipal Clerk (MMC) programs in North America and Europe.[6] The profiles describe the programs and their requirements, costs, and other pertinent details. Although the specifics of the individual programs may vary (there are forty-four CMC and thirty-one MMC Academy programs), each program meets the specified requirements of the IIMC and may reflect the requirements of state clerk organizations. The programs provide clerks with training in such areas as leadership, interpersonal communications, public relations, and technological innovations. Attainment of CMC or MMC status is based on a number of achievements, including completion of approved academy programs, professionally related higher education courses, and self-study programs, as well as on professional and social contributions. To further reinforce the need for continued professional training, the IIMC instituted a recertification program for CMCs in 2000, which requires annual education or training.

While some state clerk organizations have met with great success in professionalizing the clerk's position, others have had limited success. Nevertheless, the value of such designations as Certified Municipal Clerk and Master Municipal Clerk will continue to be promoted among clerks and local governments as a means of increasing the efficiency and effectiveness of the position, and the achievement of such designations will continue to be synonymous with professionalism in office, ethical behavior, and continuing education and training.

## Ethics and the clerk

Much of what the clerk does is specifically delineated by state statute and local ordinance, and care must be taken to carry out the functions of the position with an eye toward not violating the law. Beyond that imperative, professional organizations such as the IIMC and various state clerk associations insist that the clerk operate in a fashion that protects the integrity of the position and his or her professional reputation. All members of the IIMC

### IIMC Code of Ethics

Believing in freedom throughout the world, allowing increased cooperation between Municipal Clerks and other officials, locally, nationally and internationally, I do hereby subscribe to the following principles and ethics which I affirm will govern my personal conduct as Municipal Clerk:

To uphold constitutional government and the laws of the community;

To so conduct my public and private life as to be an example to my fellow citizens;

To impart to my profession those standards of quality and integrity that the conduct of the affairs of my office shall be above reproach and merit public confidence in our community;

To be ever mindful of my neutrality and impartiality, rendering equal service to all and to extend the same treatment I wish to receive myself;

To record that which is true and preserve that which is entrusted to me as if it were my own; and

To strive constantly to improve the administration of the affairs of my office consistent with applicable laws and through sound management practices to produce continued progress and so fulfill my responsibilities to my community and others.

These things I, as Municipal Clerk, do pledge to do in the interest and purposes for which our government has been established.

Source: International Institute of Municipal Clerks, iimc.com/about_iimc/code_ethics.shtml.

are required to subscribe to the IIMC Code of Ethics, and most state clerk organizations have adopted a code of ethics that reflects the IIMC code. Violation of this code can result in a clerk losing certification from the IIMC or from a state organization to which the clerk belongs.

## The administrator and the clerk

Thousands of jurisdictions across the country require a clerk to carry out the myriad functions discussed in this chapter. In smaller communities that are just beginning the process of incorporation or of formalizing a government structure, the clerk's responsibilities remain broad and varied. However, as political jurisdictions grow in population and furnish more and more services, there is a corresponding growth in specialization. New city and county departments are created, and they often assume a broad range of responsibilities traditionally held by the clerk in the smaller jurisdictions. In such instances, the responsibilities of the clerk will increasingly become those that support the work of the governing body.

As has been shown, the clerk's office provides many services for the local government body that, when done well and in concert with the activities of the organization, serve to increase the efficiency and effectiveness of that body. In today's information-driven society where immediate, accurate, and complete answers are expected, the clerk's ability to answer questions, provide information, and supply the right documents has become not just an expectation but a legal necessity.

Because the office of the clerk is responsible for managing information and providing continuity to local governing processes, the roles of the administrator and the clerk often intersect. Thus, it is imperative for the clerk and the local government administrator to build a positive and professional working relationship. Each position has a significant, integral, and typically mandated role to play in the functioning of the unit of local government, and it is essential that these roles, both formal and informal, be understood by both parties.

> *In today's information-driven society where immediate, accurate, and complete answers are expected, the clerk's ability to answer questions, provide information, and supply the right documents has become not just an expectation but a legal necessity.*

The local government administrator must view the clerk's position with two thoughts in mind. First, the clerk provides integral support services to the efficient functioning of both the governing and operating sides of the local government. On the governing side, this support includes agenda preparation, meetings, ordinances, and the flow of information. On the operating, or administrative, side, it includes record keeping and retention, access to information, licenses and permits, and elections.

Second, the administrator must recognize that the position of clerk typically does not fall within the administrative line of the organizational hierarchy. The clerk will rarely be required to report to the chief administrator. Rather, the relationship between the clerk and the administrator is informal. Thus, to maximize the professional relationship between the two positions, the administrator must cultivate a positive working relationship with open communication channels. Such a relationship can go a long way toward increasing the efficiency and effectiveness of the local government unit.

A negative or stressed relationship may create problems. Should a confrontational relationship emerge between the clerk and the administrator, polarization may occur and an inordinate amount of time may be spent building and protecting power bases. Although neither the clerk nor the administrator is likely to do anything to negatively affect the operation of the local government unit, a mutual distrust may develop over time and the flow of information through the organization will be constrained so that the efficiency and effectiveness of the unit is ultimately diminished.

## Future demands and challenges

The ever-changing landscape of local government has created an increasing number of challenges for the position of clerk. These challenges include

- Changing technologies that alter service demands and methods of delivery
- Demands for greater technological knowledge, skills, and abilities
- An increase in the volume and types of information to be processed and stored
- Compliance with a growing number of state and federal requirements concerning the storage of and access to information, the governance of elections, and agendas and open meetings
- The demand for services twenty-four hours a day, seven days a week
- The growing number of licenses and permits issued by local governments
- A demand for increased professionalism of the office and its activities.

While the clerk's position will continue to grow professionally, guided by a desire to maintain high levels of professional and ethical behavior, the role of the clerk will be determined by how the clerk reacts to the continuing challenges of the twenty-first century. The clerk must be prepared to respond to the unexpected. The impact of man-made or natural disasters on local governments became all too apparent in the first decade of

---

### Questions to ask if you manage a small community

What is the formal relationship between the administrator and the clerk?

What has been the historic relationship between the administrator and the clerk?

What formal and informal roles does the clerk fulfill in the community?

What do the board and council expect from the positions of administrator and clerk?

How might a positive professional relationship be built with the clerk?

How should the administrator react when the role of the clerk appears to "cross over the boundaries" of the administrator's position?

How might the clerk's office help the administrator fulfill the requirements of the administrator's position?

the new century. The clerk, in concert with other municipal or county staff and the governing body, will need to work toward safeguarding the documents and records entrusted to the office and to develop plans to continue to maintain the integrity of the services that the office provides.

## Endnotes

1 The Freedom of Information Center at the University of Missouri–Columbia maintains a Web site that gives access to the FOIAs and open meeting acts of most states; go to foi.missouri.edu/citelist.html.

2 State of Montana Web site, Office of the Secretary of State, Local Record Forms and Retention Schedules, sos.state.mt.us/RMB/Local_Forms.asp.

3 See, for example, the Web site of the clerk of Macomb County, Michigan, which offers citizens and concerned individuals immediate access to information about a variety of topics, including property records: macombcountymi.gov/CLERKSOFFICE/RegisterofDeedsIndex.asp.

4 Help America Vote Act of 2002, available at fec.gov/hava/law_ext.txt.

5 International Institute of Municipal Clerks, home page, iimc.com/index/index.shtml.

6 International Institute of Municipal Clerks, education summary page, iimc.com/Education/Edu_Summary.shtml.

# 4

# Budgeting and Financial Management

**John W. Swain**

L ocal governments reconcile increasing service demands with scarce resources through budgeting and financial management. Budgeting is the process of deciding how to raise and spend money; financial management involves related tasks, including purchasing, keeping records, and managing money. Both functions are subject to many specific legal requirements.

Budgeting and financial management activities serve various purposes:

- *Planning:* Budgets outline a plan for operations and services.
- *Control:* Budgets and financial techniques control what departments can do and how they can do it.
- *Efficiency:* Budgets manage resources.
- *Communication:* Budgets spell out for citizens and others the government's priorities and resource allocation.
- *Accountability:* Through public decision making and reporting on the financial consequences of those decisions, budgets promote accountability.

Budgets are named for the implementation time period (referred to as a fiscal year— e.g., fiscal year 2010), but a fiscal year may span two calendar years (for instance, fiscal year 2010 may run from July 1, 2009, through June 30, 2010). In any given year, the approved budget is usually the local government's most important policy document. Because of the importance of budgeting in defining and controlling government operations, major policy and management innovations are often incorporated into budgeting. (Chapter 16 describes how performance measurement can be related to budgeting.)

The budgeting process includes four stages: preparation, approval, implementation, and audit and review (see Figure 4–1). While the current year's budget is being implemented, the previous year's budget is being audited and preparation for the following year's budget is under way. The specific elements and activities in each stage are the focus of this chapter.

---

### Figure 4-1  Four budget stages and related activities

| Preparation | Approval | Implementation | Audit and review |
|---|---|---|---|
| Revenue estimates | Budget review | Budget administration | Reporting |
| Expenditure estimates | Budget submission | Accounting | Auditing |
| Capital budget | Budget approval | Revenue administration | Review |
| | | Purchasing | |
| | | Treasury management | |
| | | Debt management | |
| | | Risk management | |

---

## Budget preparation

Budget preparation never stops. Individuals gather and interpret information for future budgets while implementing the current budget. Each fiscal year's budget process formally begins with a budget call letter issued to operating agencies by a leading administrative or executive official to prepare expenditure estimates.

In addition to the requisite request for expenditure estimates, a call may set forth policy guidelines as well as technical instructions. Policy guidelines commonly cover service priorities, personnel raises, and estimates of the impact of inflation on prices. Guidelines may be financial (e.g., limit all requests to 98 percent of current expenditures), substantive (e.g., emphasize services related to economic development), or procedural (e.g., clear all capital equipment requests with the manager's office). If the local government has adopted performance budgeting, the call requires that results (outputs or outcomes) be identified and related to expenditure estimates. *Outputs* refer to work done (e.g., streets swept), and *outcomes* refer to the consequences of the work being done (e.g., clean streets). (See Chapter 16 for more discussion of performance budgeting.)

A call may also include particular forms and a calendar spelling out who does what when. The specific forms and information requested vary widely because of state-imposed requirements, local ordinances, and leadership preferences. A budget calendar sets out budget deadlines (see Figure 4–2). State legal requirements determine key dates (e.g., when a proposed budget has to be published), and local officials use these requirements as a framework to create a budget calendar that specifies internal actions and deadlines. State laws require that hearings be held a specified amount of time before a local government formally acts on a proposed budget, but local officials can specify the times and places for hearings.

The actual preparation of the budget involves both revenues and expenditures; these two sides of the budget have to work together. Discussions of major categories of revenues and expenditures follow.

### Revenues

Revenues support expenditures. States authorize their local governments to collect revenues in very specific terms, defining the bases (the sources), the rates applied, and collection processes. A revenue book, described in the sidebar on page 70, helps local

**Figure 4-2   Budget schedule, Pinecrest, Florida**

## Budget Schedule

The Office of the Village Manager and Finance Department are responsible for the development of the annual budget.  As the schedule below details, the budget process begins in early April with the distribution of budget request forms to all departments.  All departments are responsible for compiling budget figures, which are then reviewed and adjusted by the Village Manager during a series of inter-departmental meetings.  The proposed budget document was presented to the Village Council at its July 19, 2005 meeting.

The Village Council must adopt a preliminary millage rate in July for use on the Notice of Proposed Taxes to be mailed to all property owners by August 24, 2005 by the Miami-Dade County Property Appraiser.  In accordance with Florida Statutes, the tentative millage rate is adopted at the first public budget hearing in September and this rate cannot be increased at the second budget hearing. Additionally, the tentative millage rate cannot exceed the preliminary rate adopted by the Council except by re-notifying all affected property owners by mail.

| DATE | RESPONSIBILITY | ACTION REQUIRED |
|---|---|---|
| April 8, 2005 | Village Manager All Department Heads | Budget Request Forms are distributed. |
| April 25, 2005 | Finance Director All Department Heads | Completed Departmental Budget estimates are submitted to the Assistant to the Village Manager. |
| May 2, 2005 | Village Manager Finance Director All Department Heads | Departmental Budget Review meetings begin. |
| May 31, 2005 | Village Manager Finance Director | Preparation of Budget document for presentation to Council. |
| July 1, 2005 | Miami-Dade County Property Appraiser | Certification of Taxable Value is finalized, DR 420. |
| July 19, 2005 | Village Manager Village Council | Village Manager's Proposed Budget is submitted to the Village Council. Discussion of proposed 2005-2006 millage. Adopt resolution setting proposed millage rate for 2005 and setting public hearing dates. (TRIM Notice). |
| August 4, 2005 | Village Manager | Notify the Property Appraiser of Proposed Millage Rate |
| August 24, 2005 | Miami-Dade County Property Appraiser | Notice of Proposed Tax Bill and Public Hearing Dates (TRIM Notice). |
| September 12, 2005 | Village Council Village Manager | First Public Hearing (TRIM) on Tentative Budget and Ad Valorem Tax Rate. |
| September 19, 2005 | Village Council Village Manager | Final Public Hearing to Adopt Budget and Ad Valorem Tax Rate. |
| September 23, 2005 | Village Manager | Deadline for returning final millages to Property Appraiser and Tax Collector. |
| October 21, 2005 | Village Manager | Certify compliance with Florida Statute Chapter 200 to the Florida Department of Revenue. |

Source: Village of Pinecrest, Florida, *2005–2006 Capital and Operating Budget,* 8, at pinecrest-fl.gov/manager/budget.pdf (accessed May 26, 2006).

---

### Revenue book

In general, a local government revenue book lists all legally available revenue measures and all measures that are currently used, with a historical record of the rates and revenues raised. The listing includes administrative details (e.g., what office collects each type of revenue and its due dates), legal limits on rates, and any special circumstances (e.g., tax abatements). From this listing, officials can see what has been done in the past and what might be done to increase revenues in the future.

Revenue books can be started by organizing current and historical revenue records and by securing or developing lists of legal revenue sources. Often, state finance associations can provide such lists.

---

governments deal with revenue concerns. Although practices vary, most local governments rely on intergovernmental aid, property taxes, and charges for the bulk of their revenues.

*Intergovernmental aid*   Intergovernmental aid, which fluctuates as state and federal governments add, expand, change, consolidate, or eliminate specific programs, consists of shared revenues and grants. *Shared revenues* are the portion of specific revenues that higher levels of government collect and share with local governments. Most shared revenues come from the state and are derived from taxes on retail sales, motor fuel, and income.

Federal and state governments also provide project and formula grants. *Project grants* are narrow in scope and are awarded for a specific period of time. The application process for these grants is often competitive. *Formula grants* are broader in scope, generally awarded for ongoing programs, and available to all local governments meeting legally specified criteria.

*Property taxes*   Property taxes have long been the primary source of local government revenue. For most local governments, property taxes are based on real property (i.e., land and things attached to the land). Local governments collect much smaller amounts of revenue from personal property taxes (i.e., taxes on moveable things, mainly registered vehicles).

Property taxes are especially noteworthy in at least three respects. First, local officials administer property taxes and know the exact size of the tax base. Second, local governments decide how much to collect in property taxes—in addition to other revenues—to fund operations, and then they set a tax rate to produce that amount. All other taxes use established (i.e., generally unchanged from year to year) tax rates, and revenue amounts

---

### Property tax bases and rates

Property tax bases are measured in terms of dollars (*ad valorem*, meaning according to value), and the rates are measured in mills (one-thousandths). A mill is one one-thousandth (1/1,000) of a unit or one-tenth of one percent. In practical terms, each mill that is levied costs a property owner one dollar for every thousand dollars of assessed valuation. The millage is the number of mills.

---

### Figure 4-3  Property tax bill for a single-family house in El Portal, Florida, 2005

**Ad valorem taxes by millage authority:**

| Taxing authority | Millage rate per $1,000 of taxable value | Value ($) | Taxes levied ($) |
|---|---|---|---|
| School board | 7.94700 | 24,6831 | 1,961.57 |
| School board debt service | .49100 | 24,6831 | 121.19 |
| Florida inland navigation district | .03850 | 24,6831 | 9.50 |
| South Florida water management district | .59700 | 24,6831 | 147.36 |
| Everglades construction project | .10000 | 24,6831 | 24.68 |
| Children's trust authority | .42880 | 24,6831 | 105.84 |
| Countywide operating | 5.83500 | 24,6831 | 1,440.26 |
| Countywide debt service | .28500 | 24,6831 | 70.35 |
| Library district | .48600 | 24,6831 | 119.96 |
| Fire rescue operating | 2.60900 | 24,6831 | 643.98 |
| Fire rescue debt service | .05200 | 24,6831 | 12.84 |
| Village of El Portal operating | 8.70000 | 24,6831 | 2,147.43 |

Amounts due are subject to change without notice.

Source: Miami–Dade County real estate tax information, available at egvsys.miamidade.gov:1608/wwwserv/ggvt/txcaw09 .dia?folio=1832070490420 (accessed May 26, 2006).

Note: Folio number, owner's name, property address, total value, exemptions, and millage code have been deleted from this table.

result from the size of the tax base. Third, municipalities and counties face the most public criticism about property taxes, despite the fact that school districts typically receive the majority of property tax revenues. Municipal and county officials can respond by showing the rates (percentages) and amounts levied by the local government and the school district (and other taxing entities) on property tax bills (see Figure 4–3).

Property tax critics emphasize the disadvantages of this tax, which include high administrative costs; consistent unpopularity; the difficulty of making accurate property assessments; steep increases in tax bills when property is reassessed too infrequently; the negative impact on development from taxes on increased property values; and the regressive nature of real property taxes, which means that they have a greater impact on the poor and those with fixed incomes.

The advantages of the property tax are that states authorize their use; their traditional status makes them more acceptable; the amount of property makes them broad-based; they are locally administered; and they steadily produce substantial revenues. Many local officials prefer other tax measures; however, states generally retain those measures for themselves. Thus, despite the criticism, property taxes will continue to be used for the foreseeable future.

*Charges*   Local governments collect charges for a wide variety of services and privileges; other common names for charges are user charges, user fees, and license and permit fees.

User charges vary by the amount of service provided, whereas user fees are generally set at one level for each class of users. Services that carry user charges include trash collection and recreational activities and facilities; services that carry fees include dog licenses and health inspections.

Development fees and impact fees constitute a special category of charges that have been growing in importance. Although the use of the terms varies, *development fees* typically cover local government costs that are directly related to the development of particular pieces of property, whereas *impact fees* typically cover indirect costs. Development fees pay for permits, inspections, water and sewer connections, unpaved road maintenance, and stormwater drainage related to particular properties. Impact fees pay for schools, affordable housing, libraries, and parks. These fees allow local governments to collect payments from developers and builders (who in turn pass the fees on) instead of increasing taxes.

Charges help fund and measure services and reduce demand. Increasing charges is easier than increasing taxes. However, charges may cover only a portion of service costs; where there are shortfalls, subsidies to cover them are either intentional or accidental. In some cases, local governments intentionally subsidize services; for example, subsidies for recreational facilities are justified as a means of promoting the physical and social development of youth. Accidental subsidies occur when local governments do not regularly review charges and service costs. Then, taxpayers bear costs that could be reduced by adjusting charges. Reviewing and revising charges every few years is a good practice as it avoids hitting those who pay charges with sudden large increases.

*Sales taxes*    Local governments impose sales taxes on retail goods (general sales tax) or on specific categories of goods and services (selective sales taxes). State and local general retail sales taxes are parallel and are usually state administered. Selective sales taxes are most often levied on public utility services, motor fuels, and nonessential goods and services (e.g., alcoholic beverages, tobacco products, amusements, lodgings, and restaurant meals). Sales tax rates are usually a percentage of the sales transaction; different rates are used for different taxes (e.g., the general sales tax may be set at 0.05 percent while the tax on lodgings may be set at 0.08 percent).

*Business activity taxes*    The use of business activity taxes varies widely among local governments. Such taxes are applied to gross receipts, number of employees, occupations, and inventories. Gross receipts taxes are levied on the total amount of sales revenue taken in by businesses. Employee head taxes are paid by employers on the number of employees that they have. Occupation taxes are levied upon persons engaging in a specific occupation (e.g., pawnbroker or tree surgeon). Inventory taxes are personal property taxes that are applied to businesses.

*Income taxes*    About a fifth of the states allow one or more local governments to levy income taxes. However, the other four-fifths are extremely unlikely to permit their local governments to impose an income tax, and the fifth that do are unlikely to expand that authority to other local governments.

*Minor revenues*    Minor revenue sources include fines and forfeitures, gifts, and special assessments. Fines and forfeitures (seized assets, some of which can be regained for a payment) penalize any wrongdoing, from parking meter violations to drug dealing. Gifts of money, land, land improvements, and buildings occur irregularly. Special assessments are taxes levied against particular parcels of property that benefit from a specific public project (e.g., sidewalks); their purpose is to recoup part of the cost of public improvements.

## Expenditures

Local governments spend resources to provide the services discussed throughout this book. The bulk of local government expenditures is for public works and public safety and for the expenditure categories of personnel (the largest by far) and capital projects. Other expenditure categories are services, supplies, and equipment. Spending varies depending on services provided. For example, not all municipalities and counties are responsible for welfare, education, and parks and recreation services. Typically, police, fire, and public works departments have the largest numbers of employees, and public works projects for streets, roads, buildings, and water and sewer services are quite expensive. Not only are many local services labor-intensive but also some are staffed around-the-clock.

## Estimating revenues and expenditures

Despite the imperfect character of estimates, estimations of revenues and expenditures are essential to budget preparation and approval. Estimating revenues low and expenditures high avoids the problem of running out of money.

***Revenue estimates***   Local governments produce estimates for each revenue source (e.g., property taxes). Central officials (e.g., clerks, finance directors, chief administrators) usually estimate the largest revenues (e.g., intergovernmental aid and taxes), which are collected centrally. Departments that collect charges often estimate those revenues.

Because overly optimistic estimates can result in service cutbacks or year-end deficits, reasonably accurate forecasting of revenues is critical. Expert opinion and trend analysis are two commonly used forecasting techniques.

An expert in revenue forecasting is someone with knowledge or experience concerning a particular revenue source (e.g., the administrator of the animal shelter for dog license fees). *Expert opinion forecasting* involves one or more experts forming an opinion about future events. This type of technique applies especially to intergovernmental aid before it has been approved and to minor revenue sources.

*Trend forecasting* involves making assumptions about how future events will be similar to past events, gathering data, and doing necessary calculations. For example, if one were to assume that the amount of revenue to be collected in the upcoming budget year could be estimated from an average of the amounts generated by a particular source over the past three years, one would gather the three values and calculate an average to make the forecast. Changes in rates, bases, population, or economic conditions can be added to the forecasting process. Some trend forecasting techniques are relatively simple; others use extremely complicated calculations. Many of these techniques are incorporated in computer spreadsheets. Trend analysis works best for predicting values that result from a large number of events (e.g., taxes and charges).

***Expenditure estimates***   Departments prepare expenditure estimates for the next fiscal year in accordance with guidelines in the budget call. Expenditure estimation requires figuring out the specific items required for operations, the appropriate quantities, and the likely prices. Most expenditure items recur year after year. The primary questions to ask are (1) was the current year's estimate adequate? and (2) what changes have occurred or will occur in policies, technology, and service demands?

*Techniques for estimation*    Although local governments use expert opinion and trend analysis techniques in forecasting quantities and prices for expenditure estimates, expert opinion techniques predominate because many expenditure values are uncertain. For some items on which they spend large amounts of money (e.g., gasoline), local governments enter into annual contracts, which change prices regularly. Personnel costs, such as cost-of-living and other raises, are usually determined by the governing body and contract negotiations; any estimates made prior to approval by the governing body may change. A good general rule is to estimate quantities and prices on the high side.

Whichever technique is used, expenditure estimation requires calculating monetary values as part of, or in addition to, forecasting quantities and prices. Personnel expenditures, for example, require many calculations for factors affecting wages, fringe benefits, and other employee-related payments. Other factors for consideration in personnel expenditures may include actions taken by employees and outsiders, such as claims for payment under workmen's compensation, the amount of which can be affected by employee behavior; pension payments, which are based on employee longevity within an organization; health benefit payments, which are determined by the different health plans that employees choose; and pension contribution rates that are calculated and imposed by the states and thus may be unexpectedly high.

*Presentation in budget proposals*    Expenditure estimates can be presented in various ways in budget proposals. Most local governments use lump sum or line-item budgeting formats that show expenditure estimates without specifying what will be done. *Lump sum budgets* simply show a total dollar amount estimated for each department, subunit, or major category of expenditure (personnel or equipment). *Line-item budgets* list what will be purchased, often with quantity and price information (e.g., four police cars at $36,000 each, for $144,000). Line-item budgets are most common.

Other options for presenting the budget include performance, program, and zero-base formats (see accompanying sidebar). Within the context of specific quantitative values, these formats incorporate line-item information into proposals for activities, projects, functions, or outcomes. These three formats support managing for results (or managing to improve performance), but they require a great deal of time for initial training and for gathering and processing the extra information needed to support decisions. When choosing whether to use one of these approaches, local officials need to decide whether the advantages of focusing on results outweigh the demands on time.

Proposed expenditure estimates are often broken out by the following categories: funds, organizational units, function, and objects of expenditure. *Funds* are used to organize financial information (e.g., general fund) by particular kinds of financial activities; local governments record relevant financial events, including approved budget estimates, in a fund. *Organizational units* refer to departments, which usually estimate their own expenditures in the budget preparation process. *Function* refers to such categories as general government, public safety, public works, health/welfare, and culture/recreation. *Objects of*

---

**Performance, program, and zero-base budget formats**

**Performance budgets** show what will be done with resources in terms of departmental functions, activities, and projects (e.g., what will be the expenditures for vehicle repair, trash collection, and the 15th Street resurfacing project). They show services to be performed (outputs) in terms of quantitative measurements. Performance budgeting promotes efficient operations because attention is directed to the cost of what is to be done.

**Program budgets** show what will be achieved or accomplished by programs—sets of organized activities directed to particular goals (e.g., crime solution)—rather than by functions or departments. Even more than performance budgeting, program budgeting focuses attention on goal attainment or effectiveness by predicting specific outcomes (e.g., percentage of crimes solved).

**Zero-base budgets** resemble performance and program budgets in that outputs or outcomes are specified in the budget proposals. However, the budget is divided into decision units, each of which contains a series of ranked decision packages. Each package includes a description of outputs or outcomes, a list of line items, package and line-item costs, and perhaps a justification, and each carries a ranking. Zero-base budget formats present a variety of results that policy makers can choose among when appropriating funding.

---

*expenditure* refer to what is purchased—either line categories (groups of things purchased, such as office supplies) or line items (particular items such as paper clips).

## Capital budgeting

Many local governments devote special attention to capital projects—construction of facilities or land improvements—in a separate budget that shows planned projects for four or more years. Sometimes a multiyear plan of capital projects is called a *capital improvement program*. Local governments plan capital projects carefully because such projects take years to plan and build, last a long time, and cost large sums. Typically, officials consider plans over a period of several years, develop priorities, and arrange for funding. Capital budgeting creates a forum in which to undertake such planning, to relate projects to revenues over a period of years, and to evaluate projects in terms of local priorities. Capital budget spending in the next fiscal year can be incorporated into a proposed budget.

Local governments mostly use borrowing, saving, and intergovernmental aid to pay for capital projects. Borrowing allows communities to raise revenues over a longer period and can make those who benefit from projects pay for them. Saving (pay-as-you-go financing) avoids debt but may delay projects and create inequities between those paying for and those using the facilities.

## Budget approval

The budget approval process begins when department heads submit their estimates. In addition to estimates for revenues and expenditures, the submitted proposal contains actual expenditures for past years and either expenditure information for the current fiscal

---

### Distinguished Budget Presentation Award

To encourage governments to prepare budget documents of the highest quality to meet the needs of decision makers and citizens, the Government Finance Officers Association (GFOA) recognizes local governments meeting specific criteria for budget presentation with its Distinguished Budget Presentation Award. Those criteria include that a budget serves as a policy guide, financial plan, operations guide, and communication device. Currently, 1,067 local governments participate in the award program.

Source: GFOA, gfoa.org/services/awards.shtml#budgetawards; also, gfoa.org/forms/documents/ BudgetCriteriaExplanations.pdf.

---

year to some point in time or a combination of actual and estimated expenditures for the current year; these figures facilitate comparisons among fiscal years. The local manager reviews the budget to make sure that it meets procedural and legal requirements and produces accurate estimates.

Central officials review and perhaps revise the departmental estimates, and then assemble them into comprehensive budget proposals for submission to the governing body and publication for the citizens. The members of the governing body look at the departmental submissions, hear from the chief administrator or executive, listen to the public in and outside of hearings, and deliberate among themselves. This process enables all those involved to review budget estimates and relate them to particular concerns about the kinds and levels of revenue produced, the choice of services provided, and the overall level of expenditures. Balanced budget requirements and tax and expenditure limitations are some of the technical concerns that influence policy choices.

Department heads and some central officials can change budget estimates before they submit them; the governing body gets the last chance to revise estimates; estimates are final when they are approved, unless changes have to be made during a fiscal year. Finally, local officials submit their approved budget estimates to county and state offices. Budget approval often takes the form of a property tax levy ordinance or an appropriations ordinance.

The requirement to publish or otherwise publicize the proposed budget affords citizens the opportunity to review the document. Budget approval matters to citizens because the budget process determines what they pay for and what they get from their local government. Public hearings provide a forum for citizens to express their opinions on the budget to a governing body. How these hearings are announced and portrayed in news stories, however, can influence participation. To increase citizen participation, local officials can present budget hearings as opportunities for citizens to share their views on taxes and services with elected officials as well as for elected officials to hear from their constituents. Citizens can also express their opinions informally as local officials can host meetings, go on radio programs, and interact with citizens in an online budget forum.

## Budget implementation

During the fiscal year, the local government carries out specific financial management activities to ensure the best possible return for each dollar collected and spent. In addition to overall budget administration, the specific activities include accounting, revenue administration, purchasing, treasury management, debt management, and risk management. In each service department and division, the approved budget is the financial blueprint for providing services.

## Overall budget administration

All managers and central officials engage in some aspect of budget administration. First, a central official communicates expenditure authority to department heads, who in turn communicate expenditure authority to division and program managers. Second, a central official communicates responsibility for collecting revenues to the appropriate officials. Third, program managers make sure their programs stay within authorized expenditure levels. Fourth, one or more officials monitor actual revenues and expenditures to determine whether to change budget plans. Fifth, when unexpected events transpire, someone has to prepare revised budget plans to deal with the new circumstances. Sixth, a central finance office or person usually exerts various procedural and substantive expenditure controls. Procedurally, a finance office may review all or some expenditures with respect to whether the budget authorizes them and whether making them would result in exceeding the amount authorized. Substantively, many local governments require special approvals for certain kinds of expenditures (e.g., travel and training).

## Accounting

Accounting systems collect and report financial information in specific categories for budgeting and financial decision-making purposes; the key information categories include funds, account types, balances, accounting bases, and reports. In addition, accounting systems ordinarily have internal controls, which are meant to ensure accuracy and safeguard public resources. When a local government cannot determine what has happened with some money or resources, either the accounting system lacks internal controls or someone has failed to adhere to internal control requirements. Although more than one person should be involved in a local government's accounting and bookkeeping system, someone should be charged with overseeing it. Many local governments use accounting software to facilitate budget administration and control.

*Funds*  Financial records are divided and grouped into funds. Budget documents show revenues and expenditures within each fund. For example, a county road department might budget and account for monies within two funds—a county roads fund and a bridges fund—on the basis of revenue from a property tax specifically levied for those expenditures; at the same time it might also record revenues and expenditures within a state-aid road fund.

There are three fund groups: governmental, proprietary, and fiduciary. *Governmental funds* are used to account for governmental services; specific fund types are general, special revenue, capital projects, debt service, and permanent. Local governments use the general fund, which is usually the largest, to account for most revenue sources and for most general government expenditures. The other governmental funds are used for more specific purposes: special revenue funds are for restricted revenues (e.g., state-aid road fund); a debt service fund holds monies associated with long-term general debt payments and records those payments; capital projects funds record information for specific projects (e.g., a new jail); and permanent funds contain monies that are invested to earn revenues used to pay for particular programs (e.g., a perpetual cemetery care fund).

*Proprietary funds* are used to account for businesslike activities. There are two types of proprietary funds: enterprise funds, which are used when the public is charged for a service provided (e.g., trash hauling), and internal service funds, which are used when one organizational unit (e.g., the motor pool) supplies something to other units that the other units pay for out of their budgets. In both cases, the service is rationed, and users are charged because of the limited amount of resources available. Proprietary funds record revenues and production costs. Costs can be allocated to users on a per-unit basis.

*Fiduciary funds* account for the use and control of money that is being held for use to benefit someone else; those monies are not available for other uses. Here, again, there are two types of funds: agency funds, which record the holding of monies for other parties, and trust funds, which indicate that a trust agreement binds a local government in handling those monies, as is the case in a pension (and other employee benefits) trust fund, an investment trust fund, and a private-purpose trust fund.

In addition to funds, accounting standards require that local governments maintain records of other financial information, including general capital assets, general long-term liabilities, and pension programs. Such information helps officials make budgeting and financial decisions. (See the discussion of the Governmental Accounting Standards Board under "Reports.")

***Account types***   Within each fund, separate accounts of various types are used to record information that is organized by specific transactions. A transaction is any event about which one wants to collect information. The account types are asset, liability, fund balance, estimated revenue, appropriation, revenue, and expenditure:

- Asset accounts are for things owned (e.g., cash).
- Liability accounts show what is owed to others (e.g., bills or loans).
- Fund balance accounts primarily show net balances between other accounts.
- Estimated revenue and appropriation accounts record the approved budget in the accounting system.
- Revenue and expenditure accounts record the amounts of actual collections and spending for the sake of making comparisons with budgeted amounts.

Specific accounts within each of these types vary widely in how they are organized. Revenue accounts are typically organized by revenue source, and expenditure accounts are organized by organizational units and objects of expenditure. Budget-related accounts and the actual revenue and expenditure accounts use the same categories so that budgeted and actual financial actions can be compared easily and accurately (e.g., property tax estimated revenues and property tax revenues accounts). Accounts can be organized for almost any purpose for which information can be collected. For example, to focus attention on the desired outcome of clean streets, a local government might set up an account for all street-sweeping expenditures.

***Balances***   Balances are the amounts recorded in particular accounts. A balance may result from one or a series of transactions in an account, or it may be the difference between the balances of two or more other accounts (e.g., an account balance indicating how much money can still be spent on library books is the difference between the library books appropriations and expenditure account balances).

***Accounting bases*** Bases are the rules about what transactions are recognized as having occurred and when. Accounting systems may use more than one basis. Because situations can appear quite different depending on the basis or bases used, it is essential in dealing with accounting documents, especially accounting reports, to know what those bases are. Local governments use four bases:

- The *cash basis* recognizes transactions when money moves—that is, when it is collected or sent to pay a bill. However, by speeding up or delaying bill payments, the cash basis can be manipulated to produce misleading reports.

- The *accrual basis* records transactions when an obligation is incurred—that is, when a bill is sent, a service rendered, or a good delivered. Accountants prefer the accrual basis because it produces more accurate reports than the cash basis.

- The *modified accrual basis* means that expenditure-related accounts use the accrual basis while most revenue-related accounts use the cash basis; this is because for most governmental revenue sources, actual payments occur without prior information on obligations.

- The *encumbrance basis* shows only expenditure decisions. This basis provides the earliest possible records of spending decisions and facilitates budgetary control.

Accounting standards require that local governments use the modified accrual basis for governmental funds and use the accrual basis for proprietary and fiduciary funds. Some local governments also use the encumbrance basis. And there are some small local governments that use the cash basis, but this basis is generally considered inappropriate.

***Reports*** Most local officials receive regular accounting reports on a monthly or quarterly basis for operational purposes and receive annual reports for budgeting. A report shows balances for a particular point in time or for a time period. Reports vary enormously with respect to the kinds and amounts of information and levels of detail provided. For example, many department heads get a monthly expenditure report that shows departmental expenditures in particular accounts for the previous month, while elected officials may get only a summary report for the same period. In addition, both monthly and summary expenditure reports indicate total expenditures for the fiscal year up to the end of that month, total appropriations, and remaining expenditure authority for the fiscal year. Figure 4–4 is an example of a monthly report, and Figure 4–5 shows selections from a point-in-time report of balances in the asset, liability, and fund balance accounts.

In 1999, with its Statement No. 34, "Basic Financial Statements—and Management's Discussion and Analysis—for State and Local Governments," the Governmental Accounting Standards Board (GASB) significantly changed the way local governments report their finances. Its reforms instituted a call for more information than previously required, including more comprehensive reports and more accrual basis information. GASB later issued two statements requiring and regulating reporting on postemployment benefits other than pensions (e.g., health, dental, and eye insurance for retirees). GASB reporting standards appear likely to continue moving in the direction of fuller disclosure of financial information. GASB-required accounting reports are described further on in the discussion of audits.

**Figure 4-4   Period report for revenues and expenditures, McCall, Idaho**

City of McCall
Revenues with Comparison to Budget
for the two months ending November 30, 2005

General fund

| Account number/name | Period actual ($) | YTD actual ($) | Budget ($) | Variance ($) | Percent |
|---|---|---|---|---|---|
| **Property tax revenue** | | | | | |
| 10-30-010-100.0 Property taxes | 5,397.06 | 7,744.63 | 1,233,526.00 | 1,225,781.37 | 0.6 |
| **Fines revenue** | | | | | |
| 10-30-035-100.0 PD-fines and court costs | 4,458.65 | 9,404.39 | 30,000.00 | 20,595.61 | 31.4 |
| **Parks department** | | | | | |
| Personnel expense | | | | | |
| 10-59-100-110.0 Salaries and wages | 5,794.09 | 11,243.04 | 84,030.00 | 72,786.96 | 13.4 |
| Operating expense | | | | | |
| 10-59-150-240.0 Minor equipment | 60.40 | 260.35 | 21,709.00 | 21,448.65 | 1.2 |
| Total revenue | 210,405.72 | 640,076.22 | 3,390,123.00 | 2,750,046.78 | 18.9 |
| Total expenditures | 277,691.31 | 492,327.00 | 3,390,123.00 | 2,897,796.00 | 14.5 |
| Revenue over expenditures | (67,285.59) | 147,749.22 | .00 | (147,749.22) | 0.0 |

Source: Extracts from City of McCall, at mccall.id.us/government/departments/finance/financials/200511_financials.pdf, 1, 2, 14, and 16 (accessed May 26, 2006).

*Internal controls*   Internal controls safeguard resources and the accuracy of accounting records. These controls involve written rules for systematic procedures, formally assigned responsibilities that are divided among individuals, and regular reviews of accounting-related records (e.g., monthly checking account reports from the bank). Specific examples of such controls include requiring monthly bank account records to be reconciled by someone who has no part in making cash receipts or disbursements; prenumbered accounting forms; checks to make all paykments; and signature approval by one or more responsible officials for certain actions (e.g., checks, payrolls, invoices, purchase orders, and cash deposits). Regular reviews are crucial.

## Revenue administration

Local governments should collect revenues as efficiently as possible. First, they must locate each revenue base and apply a revenue rate to it. Next, they must provide adequate information (e.g., how taxes are calculated, what taxes are owed, and when they must be paid) to those from whom revenues are to be collected. The actual process of collecting money takes time and resources. Local governments must ensure that collection procedures comply with applicable laws. Enforcement efforts are necessary when people do not

---

**Figure 4-5   Point-in-time report of balances, McCall, Idaho**

City of McCall
Balance Sheet
General Fund
September 30, 2004

**Assets**

| | |
|---|---:|
| Cash and cash equivalents | $ 996,826 |
| Investments | 310,389 |
| Receivables | |
| Taxes | 1,248,911 |
| Intergovernmental | 84,070 |
| Accounts | 33,747 |
| Prepaids | 49,067 |
| Total assets | $2,858,010 |

**Liabilities and fund balances**

Liabilities

| | |
|---|---:|
| Accounts payable | $ 59,237 |
| Payroll payable | 56,077 |
| Deferred revenue | 1,243,283 |
| Total liabilities | $1,358,597 |

Fund balances

| | |
|---|---:|
| Total fund balance | $1,499,413 |
| **Total liabilities and fund balance** | $2,858,010 |

Source: City of McCall, at mccall.id.us/government/departments/finance/financials/2004_Audited.pdf, 18 (accessed May 26, 2006).

---

pay willingly. However, taxpayer appeals may be appropriate in some cases (e.g., property values for property taxes).

## Purchasing

The goal of purchasing is to buy the right things at the best possible prices in an appropriate manner. Successful purchasing generally results from centralization, formal regulations, and regular procedures.

Centralizing overall purchasing responsibilities in one office or person saves money through bulk-purchasing price advantages, reduced costs for small purchases, and control over inventories. It also minimizes delayed deliveries and rush orders. Other benefits include systematic inspection of delivered goods for quantity and quality, standard specifications to ensure the suitability of purchases, discouragement of favoritism, encouragement of greater competition among prospective vendors, and less time spent on purchasing by department heads.

## Information technology in budgeting and financial management

Processing budgeting and accounting information by hand is extraordinarily labor-intensive and susceptible to error. Thus, local governments have adopted information technology in budgeting and financial management to facilitate the use of spreadsheets in making calculations, especially for budgeting, and to process accounting information. Spreadsheet calculations reduce labor and errors as accounting software ensures correct machine calculations and eliminates various input errors. Information technology also facilitates the electronic communication of budgeting and accounting information. Spreadsheet calculations can be stored, manipulated, and transmitted electronically. Local governments can even collect many revenues electronically.

Budgeting and financial management routines have been integrated with accounting systems to automate data handling (e.g., payroll, billing, and budgeting). Comprehensive financial management information systems, enterprise resource planning (ERP) systems, and enterprise resource management (ERM) systems make financial data available for a variety of purposes once the data are entered. ERP and ERM systems also integrate other information (e.g., human resource and operational scheduling) with financial information. The advantages of the more comprehensive information systems are error avoidance, lower costs for handling information, and widespread access to information on a timely basis. The disadvantages are high costs and difficulties of implementation. Those disadvantages stem from the lack of standardization of ERP and ERM systems, which in turn is due to differences in legal requirements and practices in various states.

While states regulate local government purchasing, local purchasing regulations can also be helpful. They can guide purchasing procedures and specify such details as the general duties of different officials (especially a purchasing agent), the dollar amount above which competitive bids are required (the bid limit), informal price gathering, conditions under which emergency purchases can be made, and disposal of obsolete equipment and materials. Written purchasing regulations help in preparing specifications, soliciting formal and informal bids, preparing purchase orders, inspecting and testing goods, making payments, complying with conflict-of-interest legislation, and handling exceptions to normal purchasing procedures. State and local governments often require that the governing body approve all bills for purchases before payment.

Cooperative purchasing, in which governments collaborate in making purchases, promises significant savings to small governments in that it allows them to use large-scale bulk purchasing. Local governments organize such efforts among themselves, and states allow local units to take advantage of state-negotiated contracts for certain items.

## Treasury management

Local governments manage their treasuries to maximize advantages and minimize the costs of money flowing into and out of financial accounts during a fiscal year. Having money to pay bills is the first concern. Officials then seek to maximize their returns on short-term investments and on discounts for early payment of bills, and to minimize the costs of short-term debt and financial services. Treasury management requires forecasting cash flows, planning bill paying, investing money not otherwise needed, and borrowing money when appropriate. Local governments benefit from collecting money as soon as reasonably possible and paying money as late as reasonably possible to avoid debt and to benefit from investments and early payment discounts.

States stipulate which investments are legal and in what kinds of financial institutions investments can be made. Short-term investments generate revenue, but managers should only invest money not needed to make payments. Interest-bearing checking accounts provide investment returns while money is available for bill payment. Large amounts of money not needed to pay bills within thirty days should be invested outside of checking accounts to earn more interest. Investment returns can be calculated using this equation: $0.0278 per day per percentage point per $1,000. Generally, investments for longer investment periods and larger amounts earn higher interest rates.

> *Treasury management requires forecasting cash flows, planning bill paying, investing money not otherwise needed, and borrowing money when appropriate.*

Internally pooling money into one or a few bank accounts is also preferred for investment purposes. External pooling is accomplished through state-sponsored or other local government investment pools.

Managers should choose only those short-term investments from which they can obtain their principal safely within a limited time period. That means the investment has to

---

### Electronic purchasing applications

Electronic purchasing applications use the Internet (e-mail, Web pages, or both) to disseminate and acquire information for purchases (informal quotes, formal bids, or proposals). The obvious advantages are quicker and cheaper communications and possibly better price and quality because of a larger pool of potential suppliers.

Three types of electronic purchasing are used. The type used most widely occurs on bid and proposal aggregating Web sites that sell subscriptions for such information to sellers.[1] In the second type, individual local governments or their purchasing pools e-mail or post requests for bids and proposals on their own Web pages and receive information back in the same way.[2] In the third type, a hybrid model developed by Demandstar by Onvia offers access to significant bid information for a specific local government through that government's Web site.[3] Vendors can generally subscribe to get information, buy information for specific cases (e.g., $6.70 for a 67-page document), or seek the information from the local government directly.

1 An example of an online bidding information subscription service for the public sector is Bidnet at bidnet.com.

2 See, for example, the Web site of Fort Worth, Texas, at fortworthgov.org/purchasing/bidsub.htm.

3 See, for example, bid information posted by Elk Grove Village, Illinois, through Onvia Demandstar at demandstar.com/supplier/bids/Bid_Detail.asp?_PU=%2Fsupplier%2Fbids%2Fagency%5Finc%2Fbid%5Flist%2Easp%3F%5FRF%3D1%26f%3Dsearch%26mi%3D544700&LP=BB&BI=111107 (accessed May 25, 2006).

Elk Grove Village also posted a list of things to bid on at demandstar.com/supplier/bids/agency_inc/bid_list.asp?f=search&mi=544700 (accessed May 25, 2006).

involve some kind of a promise to pay (e.g., a certificate of deposit or an account with a financial institution, a U.S. debt instrument, or a short-term investment pool).

Generally, short-term debt should be avoided. Appropriate occasions for using short-term debt to manage cash flow include unexpected revenue shortfalls or larger-than-anticipated expenditure requirements. Local governments sometimes use tax or revenue anticipation notes to borrow funds to bridge a period of time between the demands for regular expenditures and the availability of regular revenues.

A local government can minimize its financial service costs by soliciting bids or by shopping around among financial institutions, usually banks, for the best total package of checking, investing, and borrowing services. Cost differences among services should be examined to make sure that apparent cost savings do not entail extra work for the local government's own employees.

## Debt management

Debt management concerns borrowed money. Managing debt means managing all details associated with borrowing agreements. Making sure that money is available and submitted for repayment is obvious. Other details may include maintaining financial reserves, making reports, and accounting properly for operations.

Local governments should neither shun debt nor use it excessively. In many cases, local governments fail to borrow even when it would be to their advantage to do so; in others, they use debt too casually. Debt burdens should not exceed a local government's ability to repay them. Increasing amounts of either short-term debt or total indebtedness for three consecutive years signals the possibility of excessive debt.

In order to borrow, local governments must make a legally binding commitment to repay, which is either a general or a limited liability obligation. A local government has an unlimited commitment to repay general obligation debt, which can be used only for general governmental purposes. A limited liability obligation debt is most often associated with revenue-generating activities (e.g., utilities); the debt commonly takes the form of revenue bonds, and a borrower is obliged to use only particular revenue sources (e.g., utility revenues) to repay it. Because revenue bonds have a lesser obligation basis and greater risk of default, lenders impose higher interest costs as well as numerous specific requirements (e.g., no free utility service) on them.

*Local governments should neither shun debt nor use it excessively.*

Local governments manage both short- and long-term debt. For both, a proper decision to take on debt requires paying attention to legal authority, proper procedures, financial capacity to repay, and the appropriateness of borrowing. However, where short-term borrowing is usually used to cover a shortage of money and to finance the purchase of assets under the terms of lease-purchase agreements, long-term borrowing is generally used for the purchase of capital assets and involves more money. Borrowing occurs through bidding or negotiation; generally, smaller borrowings are negotiated and larger ones are bid. The amount borrowed, rates, fees, and length of time determine debt costs. Fees and time are relatively more important for short-term debt, and rates are more important for long-term debt.

In many cases, lease-purchase agreements serve the same purposes as debt. They allow local governments to use and eventually own physical assets (e.g., buildings or equipment) and to pay for those assets over an extended time period. The advantages of these agreements are that they allow local officials to avoid both referendum requirements associated with taking on formal debt and limitations imposed on general obligation debt. The disadvantages are that they are more expensive than debt and can be used to hide the true levels of obligations and costs of purchases. It is important to remember that lease-purchase agreements can burden a local government in the same manner as debt.

## Risk management

Risk management means identifying and preventing or minimizing potential losses and liabilities. Identifying risks involves looking for possible accidents, thefts, fires, equipment breakdowns, and liability suits, both from employees and from persons affected by a local government. Once identified, such risks can be classified according to their frequency and severity; this facilitates decision making about strategies for preventing and minimizing them.

High-frequency and high-severity risks should be targeted for reduction through sensible alteration of practices (e.g., training all employees in how to lift things); transferring risks to other parties; and, in rare cases, abandoning an activity.

Once risks have been identified, classified, and minimized, local governments must prepare to pay for the financial consequences of those risks that remain. Insurance is only one way of paying for risks. Other funding practices include paying for minor risks out of current operating revenues, funding a designated risk payment account or fund in which monies are accumulated to pay for larger losses and liabilities, and participating with other governments in a multijurisdictional risk financing pool.

An ongoing risk management program requires regular reviews of the effectiveness of existing policies and constant identification of new risks. Centralization of risk management responsibility in one person or office, formal policy statements, and good record keeping contribute to success in this area.[1]

## Audit and review

After budget implementation ends, budgeting responsibilities continue. Local governments make reports, undertake audits, and review the concluded fiscal year.

### Reports

Local government reports on the concluded fiscal year differ, depending on their purposes and external requirements.

***Basic annual accounting reports***   Basic annual accounting reports display revenues and expenditures by fund, along with estimated revenues and appropriations (the period report) and balances in the asset, liability, and fund balance accounts at the end of the fiscal year (the point-in-time report) (Figures 4–4 and 4–5). These reports, which result from the ordinary operations of an accounting system, provide information for budgeting and financial management decision making and serve as the basis for other reports. Local governments that focus on managing for results report performance results on a fiscal year basis so that these results can be related to financial information.

State governments require most local governments to file audited annual financial reports, the details of which are discussed within the context of audits (see next section). Some local governments produce and issue comprehensive annual financial reports (CAFRs), the form and content of which are prescribed by GASB as well as other organizations. Figure 4–6 shows some headings and individual items listed in the table of contents of one local government's CAFR. Some states also impose other annual reporting requirements (e.g., a list of payments that exceed stipulated amounts).

**Reports for the public**   When communicating with the public, local governments use the basic accounting reports to produce less formal financial reports, sometimes as part of a comprehensive annual report on local government activities. Reports for the public tend to present information in general terms and with respect to major public concerns—those issues that affect citizens' pocketbooks and services. Such reports usually start with revenues and expenditures relative to budgeted amounts, changes in (or unexpected) revenues and expenditures, and the overall financial position of a local government before they get into more detailed information concerning specific funds, departments, services, situations, or accounts. Annual reports that are published on paper or on a Web site can contain as much information as local officials believe the public can use. Brief, general information can be excerpted from the annual report for press releases, television, and radio outlets; longer, more detailed articles can be excerpted for newspapers.

Few management tasks are more challenging than reporting to the public on local government finances. Fund accounting is technical and complicated, and few in the public or media have the background to read and understand annual fund accounting reports. Therefore, managers have to translate fund accounting information so that it makes sense to the public. Key to this effort is using clear starting points that rely on simple terms, direct statements, graphs and charts, and general information about collecting and spending money (see Figure 4–7 on page 88). Then, more detailed information and more complex points can be related to these initial points.

Successful public reporting requires constant attention to clarity. Members of the public are likely to abandon financial reports when they find such reports confusing. Relating financial reports to the locality's "managing for results" program will help the public understand them better.

## Audits

The local government's financial records are usually audited by persons from outside the local government. In many states, local governments hire external auditors. In some states, a state agency audits local governments. Audits are reviews that answer a variety of questions. Audits can be classified as financial, management letter, compliance, economy/ efficiency, and performance/program.

**Financial audits**   Most audits are financial: they involve a review of accounting reports and records to determine whether a local government is using "generally accepted accounting principles" (GAAP) as prescribed by GASB, which members of the accounting profession are required to follow. If a local government's accounting reports and records conform to GAAP, its audit report letter states that its annual financial reports were prepared in accordance with GAAP and that those reports present financial information

**Figure 4-6    Selected entries from the table of contents of a comprehensive annual financial report, St. George, Utah**

City of St. George, Utah
Comprehensive Annual Financial Report
for the fiscal year ended June 30, 2004
Table of Contents

INTRODUCTORY SECTION
  Letter of Transmittal
  GFOA Certificate of Achievement

FINANCIAL SECTION
  Independent Auditor's Report
  Management's Discussion and Analysis
  Basic Financial Statements:
        Government-wide Financial Statements:
              Statement of Net Assets
              Statement of Activities
        Fund Financial Statements:
              Balance Sheet–Governmental Funds
              Statement of Revenues, Expenditures, and Changes in Fund Balances–
                  Governmental Funds
              Reconciliation of the Statement of Revenues, Expenditures, and Changes in
                  Fund Balances of Governmental Funds to the Statement of Activities
        Notes to Financial Statements
  Supplemental Information
        Schedules of Revenues, Expenditures, and Changes in Fund Balances
              Budget and Actual:
              Economic Development–Special Revenue Fund
        Capital Assets Used in the Operation of Governmental Funds:

STATISTICAL SECTION:
  Electric Fund–Statistical Analysis
  Revenues and Other Financing Sources by Source–General Fund
  Property Tax Rate–All Direct and Overlapping Governments
  Computation of Legal Debt Margin
  Computation of Direct and Overlapping Debt
  Demographic Statistics
  Miscellaneous Statistics

CONTINUING DISCLOSURE SECTION:
  Municipal Building Authority Lease Revenue Refunding–1998A

Source: City of St. George at www.sgcity.org/finance/WEBCAFR.pdf (accessed May 26, 2006).

**Figure 4-7   Explaining city expenditures to citizens in Wilmington, North Carolina**

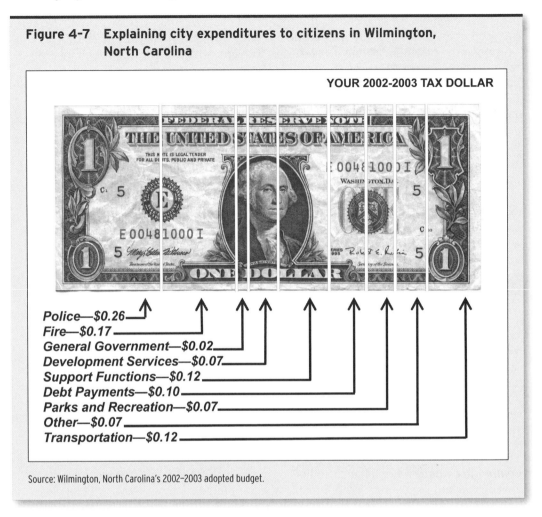

Source: Wilmington, North Carolina's 2002–2003 adopted budget.

correctly; the precise term is "present fairly." If the reports and records do not comply with GAAP, the letter notes specific exceptions or says that the auditor can offer no opinion. Although audit reports use mild terms to indicate noncompliance, such statements tell informed readers very clearly that they cannot rely on the local government's financial reports for accurate information in some or all respects.

As noted earlier, GASB's Statement No. 34 substantially changed local government financial reporting. Among its reforms, it introduced requirements for new information, information categories, terms, and ways of organizing information. New information required includes the degree to which revenue for specific service areas covers costs (e.g., general government activities such as public safety are not expected to generate revenue to cover their costs, but services using enterprise funds, such as water, may be expected to cover their costs). Local governments are also required to report on the value of infrastructure assets, including roads, bridges, water and sewer facilities, and dams. In addition, GASB 34 requires a "Management Discussion and Analysis" that covers two-year trends, major achievements or challenges, and significant changes while also assessing whether financial operations have improved or deteriorated during the reporting period.

Among the new information categories is "Governmental Activities," which incorporates information for all governmental funds with all internal service funds. Among the new terms is "major" funds, which are defined as only those governmental or enterprise funds that meet one of three requirements, with all other funds being considered "minor." The major funds are supposed to draw attention because they are larger portions of local government finances. Without the requirement for individual reports for each fund, most local governments will not provide reports for individual fiduciary, minor governmental, and enterprise funds. Instead, that information will be reported in totals for fiduciary, minor governmental, and minor enterprise funds.

Figures 4–8 and 4–9 provide an example of each of the two government-wide reports— Statement of Net Assets and Statement of Activities—required by GASB 34 for both governmental and business-type activities. In the governmental activities portions, information initially accounted for and reported on using the modified accrual basis for governmental funds (standard accounting system routines) is converted, or transformed, into accrual basis information, after which it is consolidated with internal service fund information. Consolidation involves adding the amounts in the same categories and making adjustments for transactions between funds to avoid misleading values. Enterprise fund information is consolidated to create the business-type activities portions of the two reports.

**Management letters**   Auditors may be asked to produce a management letter, the next most common audit component, in conjunction with the financial audit. A management letter provides an extremely detailed review of internal controls. After purchasing this service for two years in a row, local government officials may be well advised not to invest in this service again unless they change their internal controls, because the letters they receive each year will be remarkably similar. However, if a local government has not had a management letter for more than three or four years, officials should purchase this service.

**Compliance audits**   Compliance audits concern whether local governments have followed laws and regulations in both financial and nonfinancial areas (e.g., federal civil rights laws). Some grants require compliance audits.

**Economy/efficiency and performance/program audits**   Economy/efficiency audits examine whether operational costs have been minimized. Performance/program audits evaluate whether a local government has produced expected or predicted results. Neither of these is common, probably because each one replicates the work of local government management staff.

## Review

Local officials review a fiscal year after the basic annual accounting reports are available, and they ordinarily review the past two or three years of revenue and expenditure information before approving budget estimates for the following year. This review of past years' information helps them to identify challenges and opportunities and to evaluate successes, failures, and ongoing concerns.

Although reviews can deal with the same sort of questions raised in economy/efficiency and performance/program audits, they differ from audits in that they are less formal; they

### Figure 4-8  St. George, Utah: Statement of Net Assets for the year ended June 30, 2004

| | Governmental activities | Business-type activities | Total |
|---|---|---|---|
| **Assets** | | | |
| Cash | $ 38,069,791 | $ 18,800,546 | $ 56,870,336 |
| Restricted cash | | 30,873,290 | 30,873,290 |
| Accounts receivable (net of allowance for doubtful accounts) | 8,656,242 | 5,987,390 | 14,643,632 |
| Inventory | 52,517 | 1,789,550 | 1,842,068 |
| Notes receivable | 595,088 | | 595,088 |
| Internal balances | 2,859,096 | (2,859,096) | |
| Bond discounts | | 2,470,519 | 2,470,519 |
| Prepaid expenses | 313,537 | 2,830 | 316,367 |
| Capital assets (net of depreciation) | | | |
| Land | 18,803,876 | | 18,803,876 |
| Buildings | 15,696,427 | | 15,696,427 |
| Improvements | 29,469,354 | | 29,469,354 |
| Infrastructure | 31,160,769 | | 31,160,769 |
| Machinery & equipment | 5,606,820 | | 5,606,820 |
| Plant, property, and equipment | | 163,131,362 | 163,131,362 |
| Total assets | $ 151,283,517 | $ 220,196,392 | $ 371,479,910 |
| **Liabilities** | | | |
| Accrued liabilities | $ 1,840,356 | $ 7,547,428 | $ 9,387,785 |
| Construction bonds held | 363,654 | | 363,654 |
| Deposits payable | | 997,817 | 997,817 |
| Deferred compensation | 722,811 | | 722,811 |
| Interest payable | 602,029 | | 602,029 |
| Unearned revenues | 2,682,119 | | 2,682,119 |
| Bonds payable: | | | |
| Due within one year | 1,740,000 | 5,099,000 | 6,839,000 |
| Due in more than one year | 27,945,000 | 81,579,986 | 109,524,986 |
| Capital leases: | | | - |
| Due within one year | 248,000 | 618,926 | 866,926 |
| Due in more than one year | 6,488,255 | | 6,488,255 |
| Bond premiums | - | 4,244,519 | 4,244,519 |
| Total liabilities | 42,632,225 | 100,087,676 | 142,719,901 |
| **Net assets** | | | |
| Invested in capital assets, net of related debt | 64,315,991 | 71,588,932 | 135,904,923 |
| Restricted for: | | | |
| Unspent bond proceeds for construction | | 26,112,857 | |
| Debt service | 3,374,791 | 4,760,433 | 8,135,224 |
| Unrestricted | 40,960,510 | 17,646,496 | 58,607,006 |
| Total net assets | $ 108,651,293 | $ 120,108,718 | $ 228,760,009 |

The notes to the financial statements are an integral part of this statement.

Source: City of St. George at sgcity.org/finance/WEBCAFR.pdf, 32 (accessed May 26, 2006).

# Figure 4-9   St. George, Utah: Statement of Activities for the year ended June 30, 2004

| | | Program revenues | | | | | |
| --- | --- | --- | --- | --- | --- | --- | --- |
| | Expenses | Charges for services | Operating grants & contributions | Capital grants & contributions | Net governmental activities | Business-type activities | Total |
| **Governmental activities:** | | | | | | | |
| General government | $ 3,491,260 | $ 2,567,926 | $ - | $ - | $ (923,334) | $ | (923,334) |
| Public safety | 9,520,843 | 1,966,363 | 838,708 | - | (6,715,772) | | (6,715,772) |
| Interest on long-term debt | 1,652,796 | | | | (1,652,796) | | (1,652,796) |
| Total governmental activities | 36,122,509 | 9,546,794 | 7,970,554 | 4,720,122 | (13,885,039) | | (13,885,039) |
| **Business-type activities:** | | | | | | | |
| Water | 8,322,925 | 14,638,893 | | 1,071,866 | | 7,387,834 | 7,387,834 |
| Golf courses | 4,206,536 | 4,241,585 | 17,401 | | | 52,450 | 52,450 |
| Municipal building authority | 440,543 | - | 672,036 | | | 231,493 | 231,493 |
| Total business-type activities | 64,534,946 | 77,909,432 | 695,437 | 1,071,866 | | 15,141,789 | 15,141,789 |
| | | | | | | | |
| **General revenues:** | | | | | | | |
| Taxes: | | | | | | | |
| Property taxes levied for general purposes | | | | | 6,544,523 | | 6,544,523 |
| Property taxes levied for debt service | | | | | 1,779,323 | | 1,779,323 |
| Franchise taxes | | | | | 3,886,551 | | 3,886,551 |
| General sales taxes & highway sales taxes | | | | | 13,584,265 | | 13,584,265 |
| Business licenses | | | | | 409,493 | | 409,493 |
| Investment income | | | | | 844,527 | 395,162 | 1,239,689 |
| Transfers | | | | | 208,470 | (208,470) | - |
| Total general revenues & transfers | | | | | 27,496,135 | 495,727 | 27,991,862 |
| Change in net assets | | | | | 13,611,096 | 15,637,516 | 29,248,612 |
| Net assets - beginning | | | | | 95,040,197 | 104,471,202 | 199,511,399 |
| Net assets - ending | | | | | $ 108,651,293 | $ 120,108,718 | $ 228,760,011 |

The notes to the financial statements are an integral part of this statement.

Source: City of St. George at sgcity.org/finance/WEBCAFR.pdf, 32 (accessed May 26, 2006).

only sometimes result in reports, some of which are not provided to the public; and they are conducted internally and therefore are not regulated by national standards.

Reviews tend to be general evaluations of the overall financial situation of a jurisdiction or department (e.g., "we sure are spending a lot of money on overtime; let's look into that"). Particular values are compared against expectations or opinions on those values; for example, a review of excessively high expenditures for hand tools in a public works department might lead to the discovery that someone was stealing those tools. Reviews also focus on specific operational areas and specific revenues and expenditures, especially those that are unusual, and on problems during implementation, such as low revenues or high expenditures. Local officials conduct reviews as individual reflections on a fiscal year, oral discussions in a meeting, or writing exercises culminating in a report.

*Reviews tend to be general evaluations of the overall financial situation of a jurisdiction or department.*

Reviews that focus on improving results can compare actual results with expected or predicted results, or they can compare actual results from the most recently completed fiscal year with results from one or more previous fiscal years or similar results from one or more other jurisdictions. When actual results are compared with expectations or predictions, discrepancies may indicate errors in those expectations or predictions. When results from one year are compared with those from another year or with results from other jurisdictions, discrepancies are more likely to reflect real differences in the situations; finding the differences may make it possible to make the adjustments needed to improve results.

Performance and program evaluations associated with managing for results are usually tailored to specific concerns because resources available for analysis are limited. Whenever possible, those evaluations should be conducted on a fiscal year basis, including all seasons in order to equalize seasonal variations. Also, financial information is more readily available for fiscal years. Finally, financial resources vary by fiscal year, and such variations should be taken into account.

## Conclusion

The local government manager's role in budgeting and financial management is primarily that of facilitator: the manager is an intermediary between elected officials and department heads. At the same time, though, the manager is the individual with ultimate responsibility for the proper handling of budgeting and financial management. This responsibility involves preparing budget estimates for elected officials; providing options and analysis for deliberations in budget approval; overseeing implementation; and ensuring that reports are issued, auditors get cooperation, and budget reviews are productive. In meeting these responsibilities, the manager has three most important concerns:

- Communicating the overall financial situation, which requires being sufficiently familiar with accounting terminology to be able to translate it into commonsense terms

- Ascertaining that legal requirements are being meet, which requires having a manager or a designee assess local practices against those requirements

- Ensuring that internal controls are being implemented, the key element of which requires having someone independently review the financial processes to make sure they are being handled properly. In fact, all personnel working within any part of a budgeting and financial management system should have some of their work reviewed by other responsible individuals.

Many students of government believe that budgeting and financial management are the most crucial functions of management. It is in budgeting that the ultimate policy decisions are made, priorities are established, resources are allocated, and service levels are determined. It is in financial management—the handling of the public's money—that the local government manager's discharge of what Woodrow Wilson called "the sacred trust" is most evident and most easily monitored. Good financial management often means the difference between good government and mediocre government, between long-term fiscal health and future fiscal crisis. Finally, budgeting and financial management are the tools that enable the manager to meet the public's demands to "do more with less" without increasing either taxes or spending. In short, good budgeting and financial management is essential to good government.

---

### Questions to ask if you manage a small community

Are you paying sufficient attention to internal controls so that no one person handles money and financial information from the beginning to the end of a process?

Do you view budgeting as an opportunity to involve citizens?

Do you make sure that your government complies with relevant laws in this area?

Are you sure that your elected officials and citizens understand your government's financial situation?

Have you systematically reviewed any routine area of financial management in the last year?

Does your community comply with GASB 34 by using the same basic Management Discussion and Analysis report every year?

---

### Competencies for managers in the field of budgeting and finance

Knowledge of fund accounting information categories

Knowledge of internal controls

Knowledge of state laws governing budgeting and financial management practices

Knowledge of specific financial management areas

Ability to explain budgeting and financial management activities and ideas to others

Listening skills for interacting with others on financial matters

---

## Endnotes

1 To stay current in the field of risk management, local governments can refer to the Public Risk Management Association (PRIMA) at primacentral .org

# 5

# Human Resource Management

**Gregory Streib**

Experienced local government managers know that despite the election year rhetoric of political candidates, governments cannot be run exactly like businesses. Government is about societal values as much as it is about efficient service provision, and nowhere is this more true than in the management of human resources. The application of human resource (HR) management techniques in individual circumstances is highly complex. The outcome of a particular situation is affected by the interaction between issues and values, on the one hand, and a wealth of information that may be interpreted in a variety of ways on the other. Government HR management is an inherently political process. This is true because there are political aspects to all types of human interactions, and also because public sector HR processes are linked so tightly to broader societal concerns.

HR management may well be the most critical activity in local government. Most local government services are provided by people, and ensuring that all of them fulfill their responsibilities in an effective manner is what the HR function is all about.

---

### The functions of an HR manager

Developing a job classification system with appropriate compensation levels

Recruiting and selecting employees

Evaluating employee performance

Providing health benefits and pension options

Negotiating and coordinating with employee unions

Determining training needs and providing employee training and career development opportunities

Implementing affirmative action programs and managing diversity programs

Accommodating employees with disabilities

Providing assistance for employees with substance abuse problems or mental health needs

Providing and coordinating nontraditional work assignment options

## Merit as a guiding principle

The merit principle has its roots in a reform movement that flourished in the United States in the late 1800s after President James A. Garfield was assassinated by a dissatisfied patronage seeker. Merit-based HR systems typically possess the following traits:

- Employees are recruited, selected, and promoted on the basis of their relative abilities, knowledge, and skills. Entry-level jobs are open to all qualified applicants.

- Compensation is equitable and adequate.

- Employees are given whatever training is necessary to ensure optimum performance.

- Employees are retained in accordance with the adequacy of their performance, given opportunities to correct inadequate performance, and discharged only when inadequate performance cannot be corrected.

- Fair treatment of applicants and employees is ensured in all aspects of HR administration, without regard to their political affiliation, race, color, national origin, sex, or religious creed, and with proper regard for their privacy and constitutional rights as citizens.

- Employees are ensured protection against political coercion and are prohibited from using their official authority to interfere with, or affect the results of, an election or a nomination for office.

### Civil service systems

In many local governments, merit principles are incorporated into a system of rules and regulations known as a civil service system, although civil service systems can be established without merit as a major consideration. Merit-based HR systems in local governments tend to be associated with other changes, such as adoption of the council-manager form of government. This "reformed" system of government emphasizes the recruitment of professionally trained employees who are insulated from political pressures.

Despite the broad-based success of the reform movement, however, political patronage is an accepted part of HR practices in many large cities and in many counties, where hiring and advancement decisions rest with key political leaders.

### A changing view of merit

The term *merit* can be misleading because it tends to imply a high level of performance. Ironically, in many cases merit principles and civil service regulations have become synonymous with poor performance. Merit principles and civil service regulations were established to prevent political abuse, but today they can also shield poor employees from disciplinary action. As a result, even the term *civil servant* has developed a negative connotation. Not only does excessive protection mar the image of government service, but it also limits management control.

Many local governments have reacted to these problems by increasing management control over the HR function and bypassing civil service regulations in favor of new approaches that reward employee excellence and achievement. Often called simply "merit systems," these new approaches use HR policies to promote higher work quality rather than to insulate workers from political pressures. They seek to restore the traditional meaning of merit and restore public confidence in local government.

# Organizing the human resource function

Organization of the HR function is highly related to concerns for merit and management control. For example, in the past a higher proportion of local governments possessed an independent HR board or civil service commission that had total responsibility for the HR function. Today modern local governments often use one of the following three models:

- A central HR department or a single director with full authority over the HR function
- A central HR department or a single director with an independent HR board or civil service commission with limited functions
- Decentralization of the HR function into individual departments.

The first two approaches are currently the most popular. Decentralization of the HR function to the department level is used only in a limited number of small cities and counties.

The declining emphasis on civil service commissions reflects the desire for greater management control as well as the increasing complexity of the HR function. Managing an HR system in a modern local government requires a trained professional with a thorough knowledge of legal requirements and specialized management tools.

# Position classification

Position classification is a cornerstone of effective management of the HR function in local governments. It organizes essential information about how work is done in the organization so that the information can be used in HR operations. Similar positions are grouped under common job titles according to the type of work performed, the level of difficulty and responsibility involved, and the qualifications required. Position classification should be performed by a trained and experienced person, as it reflects the value placed on different jobs, making classification plans subject to legal challenges.

For classification purposes, every position consists of a group of duties and responsibilities assigned to an employee. A *class* is a group of positions that (1) are similar in duties and responsibilities, (2) require the same qualifications in education and experience, (3) can be filled through similar testing procedures, and (4) can be assigned the same job title and salary range. The description of duties, responsibilities, and qualifications of positions in the class is called the *class specification*. A complete classification system takes in (1) all the classes and class titles that have been established, (2) the specification of each class, and (3) procedures for maintaining the position classification plan.

Properly prepared class specifications are essential for establishing pay scales; recruitment, selection, and promotion procedures; training programs; performance evaluation criteria; and labor-management relations. Class titles and specifications provide a uniform terminology for discussing positions, keeping records, and preparing systematic budget requests for HR services. Class specifications help clarify how positions within the organization relate to one another and provide information needed to compare both internal rates of pay and rates relative to other jurisdictions. In addition, class specifications are useful in compiling HR statistics and conducting management studies.

## Developing a position classification plan

The first step in classifying a position is usually developing a questionnaire that asks employees in great detail about every aspect of their work (see Figure 5–1). The questionnaires are analyzed and used to group positions into common classes. Work audits are later used to verify responses. A preliminary allocation of positions is then made to the appropriate classes, and specifications are written for each class. Each specification should contain

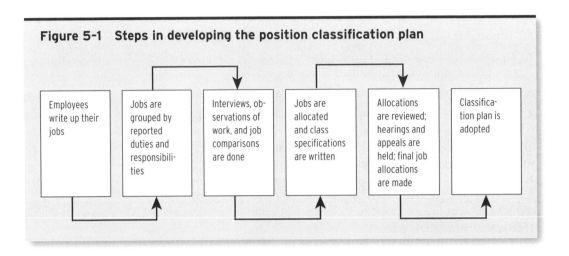

**Figure 5-1   Steps in developing the position classification plan**

| Employees write up their jobs | Jobs are grouped by reported duties and responsibilities | Interviews, observations of work, and job comparisons are done | Jobs are allocated and class specifications are written | Allocations are reviewed; hearings and appeals are held; final job allocations are made | Classification plan is adopted |

## Professional personnel administration

Historically, employees were not highly valued in organizations. The personnel function consisted of collecting time sheets and doing the payroll and, in some cases, administering benefits. Modern organizations now know that the human resource is their greatest commodity, and with this realization, personnel administration has taken on a more comprehensive meaning and become a much more complex task.

Along with time sheets and payroll, HR officers may attend to the issues of compensation, management-employee relations, recruitment, job classification, training, employee evaluation, and policy and procedure administration, among others. Larger organizations may hire specialists in each of these areas; in smaller organizations, the HR officer may not have an in-house staff and may therefore rely on outside consultants to assist with such technical issues as job classification and the evaluation process.

Professional HR officers come from a variety of academic backgrounds. Some universities offer a master's degree in the field. Several professional associations provide training. For example, the Society for Human Resource Management offers the Advanced HR Generalist Program, and the International Society of Certified Benefits Specialists offers a number of training courses and exams, as does the International Foundation of Employee Benefit Plans. State licensing boards, relevant state departments, and county extension services can provide information on other training available.

Complex issues such as terminations, labor negotiations, and compliance with federal legislation such as the Fair Labor Standards Act and the Americans with Disabilities Act often require legal expertise. To be most effective, HR professionals need a combination of education and experience in the field, as well as access to outside consultants and attorneys.

five elements: a descriptive title, a description of the nature of the work, examples of the work, a summary of duties and responsibilities, and a statement of required qualifications.

Meetings are held with department heads and supervisors to discuss the specifications and review the tentative allocation of positions to their respective classes. Any necessary adjustments can be made at this time. Individual positions are allocated to the appropriate classes on the basis of existing duties, responsibilities, and place in the organizational hierarchy. Individual employees are notified of the proposed allocation of their positions and are provided with an opportunity to comment on it. When completed, the classification plan is usually adopted by the elected board either in a separate ordinance or as part of a more comprehensive HR ordinance.

## Implementing the plan

The classification plan also includes rules for its own interpretation and maintenance. Rules cover such issues as the definition of terms, allocation of positions to classes, amendment of classes and class specifications, and procedures for changing HR and financial records to conform with the classification plan. An appeals procedure is essential in order to protect the integrity of the plan, and each employee must be provided an opportunity to appeal his or her job allocation.

No classification plan can be expected to remain static. Class specifications need to be reviewed and revised periodically to ensure that the requirements are job related and do not discriminate against minorities, women, or other protected groups. Periodic reviews also serve to keep management abreast of changes in the nature of the work, the number of positions, the number of employees performing specific duties, and changes in the skills needed by workers. Changes in organizational structure as well as in the scope and level of services provided also affect the classification plan.

HR experts recommend a complete reclassification study every five or six years, supplemented by periodic review of the plan, particularly when revisions of an accompanying pay plan are contemplated. Supervisors should initiate reclassification studies before implementing pay-plan changes in order to avoid paying employees improperly. Whenever employees work outside classifications, morale and liability problems might be expected.

## The broadbanding option

Job classifications can become extremely narrow, as may be apparent when employees with specific types of technical skills are being sought; however, job markets are competitive and fluid. Both the nature of the work and the employment market can change more quickly than any complex position classification plan.

Thus, as an alternative to traditional job classification practices, some local governments are switching to an approach known as *broadbanding*. Broadbanding collapses the pay grades and reduces the number of classifications, giving department heads greater flexibility in how they determine the pay or benefits of their employees. This approach can help support efforts to develop a results-oriented government, and it can also help when recruiting employees who possess hard-to-find skills.

While broadbanding does address some of the problems inherent in traditional HR classification plans, it also creates some new challenges. Since the HR department usually develops pay bands by conducting market surveys, this process can take a long time. Additionally, while broadbanding allows managers to respond more quickly in competitive labor markets, their efforts can attract both internal and external candidates; thus, local government departments might find themselves competing against each other for qualified employees.

## Hiring new employees

Placing a person on the payroll of a local government generally follows a recruitment and selection process that may take only a few days or stretch out over months. Recruitment involves seeking out prospective employees for a job; selection involves choosing a person from the list of applicants to receive a job offer.

Local governments must approach the recruitment and selection process carefully. They also have an obligation to hire scrupulously and to avoid even the appearance of favoritism, nepotism, or discrimination. If they proceed properly, their workforce will be more productive and efficient; if not, the cost in nonperformance and litigation can be enormous.

### Recruitment

Considerable imagination and initiative are needed in developing a recruitment program. Local government recruitment policies must address both basic salary considerations and equal employment opportunities. They also need to define the dimensions of the search for suitable candidates. Will the local government advertise locally, or will it broaden the search to recruit talent throughout the region or the nation? In addition, the individual responsible for recruitment needs to be well acquainted with job requirements; sources of qualified candidates; and the many local, state, and federal laws and regulations governing recruitment and selection.

It is worth noting here that geographic location cannot be used as a selection criterion. For example, successful applicants cannot be required to be residents. A local government can require employees to live within the boundaries of the jurisdiction where they work, but it cannot make their location a job requirement. On the other hand, it is not uncommon for local law to make citizenship a requirement for government employees, especially peace officers.

---

**Friends and neighbors referral program in Springfield, Missouri**

The Friends and Neighbors Program in Springfield, Missouri (pop. 150,298), rewards employees for referring acquaintances for specific job openings. City employees need to fill out an employee referral application form before either the application deadline or the testing deadline for a specific job opening. Employees who refer a successful applicant receive a $500 bonus plus the chance to win other special incentives throughout the year.

At the beginning, only selected positions were eligible for referral, but the program's success caused the city to include all regular positions with a posted vacancy. The city, which employs about 1,600, budgets $21,500 for the program to cover the bonuses, marketing, and special incentives. In February 2004, for example, any referral that met the qualifications for the open position won the employee two movie tickets; also, every ticket winner was entered into a drawing for a $50 gift certificate to a local restaurant. Cost-effective recruitment, high retention rate, high-quality applicants, and employee goodwill are the program's goals, and Springfield believes it's getting its money's worth.

Position descriptions and requests from the hiring agency for specific skills (such as specialized computer skills) are used to prepare a public job announcement. The announcement includes

- The title of the position
- A brief description of duties
- The salary range
- A statement of the minimum education and experience required
- The method of application
- The closing date for filing the application.

Completed announcements are then publicized. A good practice, often required by law, is to post announcements of examinations and job vacancies where employees can see them. Advertisements are usually placed in newspapers and on appropriate Web sites; local governments often have a place on their own Web sites reserved for this purpose. To demonstrate their good-faith effort to avoid discrimination in employment, many governments insert the phrase "Equal Opportunity Employer" into their advertisements.

In the case of professional and technical positions, job advertisements are usually placed in professional journals, newsletters, and periodicals. Organizations such as ICMA, the American Society of Public Administration, the National Association of County Officials, and the National Association of County Administrators display position announcements on their Web sites, include them in e-mail newsletters to members, or operate placement services that bring together employers and potential applicants—for instance, at professional conferences. Local chambers of commerce, trade associations, public and private employment services, and state municipal leagues can also help advertise professional and technical openings.

As applications for the position are received, an effort should be made to keep applicants informed of their status. Applicants who are ineligible should be notified immediately. If there is to be another stage in the recruitment process, such as an examination, all qualified applicants must be notified of the date, time, and place.

### Better recruitment through technology in Medford, Oregon

Up to 80 percent of those who apply for a job with the city of Medford, Oregon (pop. 70,147), complete their job applications online. The city's Web site provides a list of available positions that can be shown by job title or class, city department, and hours. Once the applicant reviews the position descriptions, he or she can choose to apply online or print out and complete a paper version of the application form. The paper and online forms ask the same questions, and applicants can attach their résumés along with the form. After the applicant submits the form, a confirmation of receipt is automatically sent. The city's HR staff can then query the database to receive all applications for a given position. The online job application form, which was designed by a consulting company in close collaboration with the city's HR and technology services departments, enables the city staff to manage a growing number of recruitments and applicants with no increase in its HR staff.

---

### A nontraditional approach to recruitment in Henrico County, Virginia

Some position classifications are difficult to fill and retain for local governments. For Henrico County, Virginia (pop. 280,581), this is often true for equipment operator positions, as the labor pool for these positions tends to be transient and less interested in nontangible compensation (such as benefits, job security, and retirement). In 2002, the county had a large number of vacancies for Equipment Operator I positions in several departments, and traditional recruiting methods were not effective. After soliciting assistance from the departments of public utilities, public works, recreation and parks, and general services, the HR department developed a nontraditional approach to recruiting for this difficult-to-fill classification. In an interdepartmental effort, an Equipment Operator Job Fair was held to attract applicants in the hopes of hiring at least three new equipment operators. The fair was held on a Saturday in the winter, which is a much slower season for this particular labor pool. The day consisted of extensive oral and visual presentations centered on the equipment operator job classification in the county. On-the-spot interviews were conducted, and applicants were offered assistance with completing their employment applications. Since that time, the county has also instituted a career development plan for its Equipment Operator series.

Source: Excerpted and adapted from the National Association of Counties (NACo) Model County Programs, naco.org.

---

## Selection

Any standard used in deciding who is hired can be considered a test. Personal employment history and background information as described on the application form, personal interviews, oral and written examinations, performance tests, evaluations of education and experience, reference checks, physical examinations, and psychological testing are commonly used. Written tests can be particularly useful for evaluating technical knowledge and writing skills. However, most written employment tests do not evaluate a candidate's personal skills, attitudes, or level of motivation, which are the factors that most often affect job performance. Moreover, many argue that written tests disadvantage groups outside of the majority, particularly women and people of color. Background checks, assessment centers, and certain psychological tests are all additional ways to determine which candidate is most likely to succeed.

Several commercial firms design and market a wide variety of HR tests, but a test should not be chosen simply on the basis of a description in a catalog. Because testing is a specialized field, local government officials should always seek expert advice on the preparation and validation of tests; unless the validity of a test has been established, the results are open to legal challenge.

The testing process must be carefully managed so that federal laws on discrimination in hiring are not violated. As noted above, some critics charge that civil service tests are inherently discriminatory because they assume the point of view and values of the white middle-class culture. Other complaints are that these tests may not be job related and that they often are not subjected to objective validation studies. Recent court decisions and rulings by fair employment practice authorities have resulted in a movement to reconsider testing during the selection process.

## Disabilities

The Americans with Disabilities Act of 1990 built upon the principles established by the 1964 Civil Rights Act, which outlawed discrimination on the basis of race, religion, sex, or national origin and extended coverage to individuals with disabilities, including AIDS and cancer patients and recovering substance abusers. Because of the vagueness of the law, however, the full scope of difficulties that may qualify as disabilities is still open to judicial interpretation.

Strictly speaking, the law specifies that an employer must not discriminate against employees with disabilities and must make "reasonable accommodations" to meet their needs. Employees with disabilities need only perform the "essential" functions of a job with reasonable proficiency to be eligible for legal protection. Accommodations that may be necessary to meet their needs include job restructuring; modified work schedules; acquisition of new equipment or devices; and modification of examinations, training materials, and policies. Local governments could be required to provide special computer equipment or readers for the visually impaired, or amplifiers and hearing aids for employees who have difficulty hearing.

## Affirmative action

The passive prohibition of discriminatory practices is insufficient to ensure equal employment opportunities for all. To meet that goal, local governments are often expected to initiate affirmative action programs that include practical plans to be developed and vigorously pursued at every level.

Because many common recruitment techniques tend to be inadequate for minorities, women, and disabled individuals, affirmative action efforts usually require special recruitment techniques to solicit applications from these groups. Techniques that have been used to recruit among minorities include the use of minority newspapers and radio stations, door-to-door recruiting, posters, job fairs, neighborhood bulletins, and cable television. Extensive use can also be made of religious groups, fraternal societies, community action groups, and such organizations as the National Forum for Black Public Administrators, the Urban League, the National Association for the Advancement of Colored People, and the Hispanic Network. Schools, employment and training programs, and employment agencies can also be useful. Groups selected for affirmative action, whether minorities, women, or disabled persons, may require outreach strategies tailored especially for them.

*The passive prohibition of discriminatory practices is insufficient to ensure equal employment opportunities for all.*

Increasing diversity in local government can have far-reaching benefits, enabling the organization to tap into a wealth of new ideas and viewpoints. However, as women and people of color are recruited and become more represented in local governments, managers will need to develop a strategic plan for *managing* this diversity. For example, women often have different scheduling needs than men, and some international employees may have different approaches to work and different communication patterns. The bottom line is that managers must be attuned to all the differences that diversity from affirmative action programs will bring into the organization.

It should also be remembered that efforts to improve employment opportunities for women, minorities, and disabled workers need not conflict with merit system concepts. Outreach recruitment programs, job restructuring to increase job competition among minority applicants, on-the-job training for upward mobility, and similar affirmative action steps are consistent with true merit principles and the pursuit of excellence in employment.

Local governments undertaking an affirmative action program encounter a number of barriers: budget limitations, inadequate numbers of applicants, public resistance, inability of applicants to pass tests (the fairness and relevance of which must be called into question), civil service restrictions, and resistance from employees and employee organizations and supervisors. A firm commitment from top management is necessary to overcome these obstacles.

## Evaluating employee performance

Local governments must be committed to the job success of every employee. A newly hired person cannot be merely turned loose with instructions in one hand and tools in the other. Employees represent a valuable resource; they require proper orientation and training to reach their potential (see Figure 5–2). Local governments must create management systems that provide adequate supervision while encouraging high levels of performance. Correct use of appropriate evaluation tools is critical to this effort.

A local government's performance evaluation system should include a probationary period, the successful completion of which should be determined by a thorough performance evaluation. The first evaluation of a new employee is really part of the selection process: no new employee should be considered fully hired until this initial probationary period has been completed. Once fully hired, the employee should be evaluated again on at least a yearly basis. Conducting regular evaluations gives management a chance to reiterate organizational goals and expectations; it also helps employees develop a better understanding of what constitutes effective performance and of how they can improve their work habits.

---

### Employee evaluation components

Employee evaluation should be a constructive approach to improving employee performance and productivity. Efforts to develop and maintain an effective system should

- Identify employees who are capable of assuming greater responsibilities and deserving of promotion
- Strengthen the selection and training programs
- Determine employee productivity bonuses
- Keep the supervisor aware of employees' job performances
- Assist the supervisor in counseling employees
- Improve communication between management and employees
- Encourage employees to work toward their own self-development.

Performance evaluation should be closely linked to mechanisms for promotion and disciplinary action. An employee whose performance is inadequate should be given constructive criticism; improvement should always be encouraged and recognized. When it cannot be avoided, disciplinary action must be fair, documented, and consistent with laws or labor contracts. Few aspects of a supervisor's job call for more tact, good judgment, common sense, and fairness than handling a disciplinary action (see Figure 5–3 on page 106).

---

**Figure 5-2   Checklist for orientation of new employees**

### New employee checklist
### Full time/full benefits

| | |
|---|---|
| ☐ Job description reviewed | ☐ Village recycling program |
| ☐ Life insurance | ☐ Hours, workweek, weekends |
| ☐ Hospital benefits | ☐ Overtime requirements |
| ☐ W-4 forms | ☐ Job evaluation |
| ☐ Personnel manual and receipt | ☐ Probation period |
| ☐ TB X-ray form | ☐ Pay increases and promotions |
| ☐ ID card | ☐ Vacations/holidays |
| ☐ Demographic | ☐ Unpaid and emergency leave policy |
| ☐ Fingerprint form | ☐ Rest periods |
| ☐ Background check form | ☐ Seniority/job posting |
| ☐ Pay schedule | ☐ Work rules and regulations |
| ☐ Racial diversity | ☐ Discipline procedures |
| ☐ U.S. savings bonds | ☐ Telephone calls |
| ☐ Credit union | ☐ Attendance/punctuality |
| ☐ Immigration form | ☐ Dress code |
| ☐ HIV policy and statement | ☐ Parking information |
| ☐ EAP | ☐ Sexual harassment policy |
| ☐ Personal data form | ☐ Grievance procedure |

### Nonharassment policy

All employees have the right to a work environment free from intimidation and harassment because of their sex, race, age, religion, ethnic origin, handicap, marital status, and military discharge. Any physical, verbal, visual, or sexual harassment is prohibited. Employees should report any complaints to their immediate supervisor, department head, or human resources officer.

I acknowledge that we have discussed all the above.

_____          _____
Employee's Signature/Date                Human Resource Department/Date

**Figure 5-3    Disciplinary action checklist**

**Prior to disciplinary action**

☐ Have expected standards of performance been communicated to the employee?

☐ Is management rule/policy known and properly promulgated to the workforce?

☐ Was a thorough investigation conducted to determine the facts and degree of violation?

☐ Was the employee given an opportunity to respond to the allegations?

☐ Quality of evidence: did the management's "judge" obtain substantial and compelling evidence?

☐ Severity of infraction: is this an infraction that routinely receives oral reprimand for first offense, suspension, or discharge?

**Corrective/progressive discipline**

☐ Is this a first offense?

☐ If so, is the violation serious enough to warrant punishment?

☐ Was the employee counseled or advised regarding continued conduct?

**Fair and uniform application of management rules/policies**

☐ Was discipline applied without discriminatory or preferential treatment?

☐ Was there back-up support from "other cases" within the organization (i.e., were other employees treated the same way for a similar or the same violation)?

☐ Have all published procedures been followed?

No performance evaluation tool is perfect, and supervisors should be sure that the tool being used matches the outcome being sought. For example, one type of performance evaluation might be used in compensation and promotion decisions, while another might be used to determine training needs. Ideally, a supervisor might use more than one type of evaluation tool in order to most fully appraise an employee's work, but local government managers often work in an environment with constrained resources, making this difficult. The widespread practice remains a single performance evaluation over the course of a calendar year.

Caution must be exercised when developing performance evaluation systems because such systems are considered a test under federal guidelines. They are subject to the same validity standards as any procedure used in the employee selection process. A well-designed system can encourage employees to cooperate in pursuing community goals. During the evaluation, the supervisor and employee together can develop job performance objectives that reflect and help attain the broad goals of the government's mission statement and strategic plan.

## Formal methods of evaluation

Different approaches, ranging from the relatively simple to the very complex, are used to evaluate performance. The utility of these approaches and even their legality are threatened by both their subjectivity (an employee's ratings can vary widely depending on who is doing the rating) and their validity (they may not measure job-related performance). The inability to establish the validity of performance evaluation methods could leave local governments vulnerable to legal challenges. At a minimum, then, local governments should make sure that any rating scales in use pertain strictly to job requirements. Also, they should take steps to ensure that all supervisors understand the problems associated with rating scales as well as the importance of objectivity. Ideally, all supervisors should base their ratings upon standards that are uniformly applied to all employees in similar positions.

*Simple methods*   One of the most commonly used techniques involves a multiple-choice format of rating scales and checklists that requires the grader to judge employees on criteria such as punctuality, cooperativeness, dependability, and general job performance. The evaluation forms usually have room for supervisors to elaborate upon checked-off responses. These forms take a minimum amount of time to fill out and are easy to score. However, they often reflect the evaluator's biases, and their validity is therefore particularly prone to challenge.

A related approach that is commonly used is a narrative-based system that calls for a written evaluation of employees and is not structured by specific questions. Written narratives provide more detailed information about employee behaviors than do rating scales

---

### Conducting an employee evaluation

A employee evaluation should compare the employee's performance against stated job requirements and answer the following questions:

- How well did the employee perform the job overall?
- What are his or her strengths?
- What are his or her weaknesses and problems? What seem to be the reasons for them?
- What appears to be the most likely area for development?
- How can the employee bring about the required improvements?
- How can the supervisor help the employee improve?

To serve a constructive and practical purpose, the performance evaluation should

- Be understood and accepted by the employee
- Be the basis for plans to help the employee improve
- Recognize the employee's strengths as well as weaknesses
- Help the employee understand what is expected of him or her and how success will be measured.

The evaluation process should conclude when the supervisor has covered all the points to be made; the employee has had a chance to review those points, respond, and release any existing tensions; a plan of action has been cooperatively developed; and a natural stopping point has been reached. The employee should be reassured of the supervisor's continuing interest in his or her success.

and can be useful for guiding employee behavior. However, the same cautions noted for rating scales still apply. Any written comments about the suitability of employees must clearly relate to their job responsibilities. Also, using only narrative-based evaluation systems makes it difficult to compare employees or to establish groups of employees who are eligible for different levels of pay increase.

*Complex methods*   More sophisticated performance evaluation systems are specifically designed to ensure that all employees are evaluated against carefully developed performance standards. These systems ask for an evaluation of each employee's work in relation to objectives or goals. This "management by objectives" approach is becoming increasingly popular in local government.[1] It seeks to achieve a strong association between the goals and objectives of the employee and the overall goals and objectives of the organization. Such strategic thinking is becoming increasingly important.[2]

## Fairness

Virtually all performance evaluation plans have come under attack as being unfair, impossible, or useless. There is little agreement about the most effective rating system, and even good systems may be used improperly or ignored by local government leaders. Supervisors often assign average or satisfactory ratings to their employees regardless of the employees' performance. Moreover, salary increments often go into effect automatically, regardless of ratings. It is not uncommon for supervisors to file disciplinary charges against employees to whom they have given high performance ratings in the past. These

---

**Employee evaluation problems**

A principal difficulty in employee evaluation is a lack of objectivity. Errors that the supervisor should recognize and try to avoid are

- The tendency to allow a single personality trait to influence judgment on other factors ("the halo effect")
- The tendency to base evaluations on actions in the recent past or on one dramatic incident
- The tendency to translate abilities not used in the current job, potential usefulness, and/or expectations of growth into a higher evaluation than the employee's performance warrants
- The common tendency to rate everyone as average or a little above average.

The following rules can be useful in overcoming the errors listed above:

- Collect and record evidence throughout the entire evaluation period
- Evaluate employees according to their job levels
- Base the evaluation on the employee's actual performance, not on his or her estimated potential
- Do not allow the individual's good or bad performance in one area to influence the total evaluation
- Do not allow personal feelings to dominate the evaluation
- Document the employee's progress and indicate willingness to discuss matters of concern at any time.

## The right to due process

The notion of "fairness" is critical in all personnel activities. In addition to performance evaluation, it is especially critical in disciplinary and termination actions. In such cases, employers must follow due process. The U.S. Supreme Court has ruled that no public employees may be denied a constitutional right, including property rights to their job, without due process. (In response, many local governments have moved to restrict employee rights in their jobs by making employment "at will"–see next section.)

The court has set down the following steps as an articulation of due process:

- Timely advance notice of the action contemplated by the government and reasons for that action
- An opportunity for persons affected by the proposed action to respond through a hearing
- The right to present evidence
- The right to confront adverse witnesses
- The right of cross-examination
- The right to be represented at the hearing by counsel
- The right to have a decision based solely on applicable legal rules and the evidence adduced at the hearing
- The right to an unprejudiced decision maker
- The right to a statement from the decision makers regarding the reasons for the decision.

The government's attorney should always be consulted before any action is taken to discipline or discharge an employee.

charges are often dismissed when an appeals officer sees inconsistent treatment by a supervisor.

The mere existence of a performance evaluation system does not guarantee that the system will be effective; any such system is only as good as the supervisors involved. Adequate training is necessary to ensure that supervisors are able to fulfill their responsibilities. The most comprehensive performance evaluation systems are often those that are the hardest to implement, given an organization's human and financial resource constraints. It is necessary to balance the need to provide comprehensive feedback with these resource limitations in order to provide the best possible performance evaluation system.

## A shifting view of property rights

Over the past ten years, the move toward what some call the "new public management," or "results-oriented" government, has resulted in some states dismantling employees' property interest in their jobs. Whereas most public employees enjoy due process protection for their positions as local government employees (see sidebar on due process), many local governments have moved to "at-will" employment. Employees who work at-will can be terminated without cause or explanation, just as in the private sector, with no legal recourse available. Employers cannot discriminate against groups that are protected by the law, such as older workers, women, or people of color, but as long as motives are not discriminatory, employers no longer have to go through intricate legal channels in order to terminate an employee.

## Employee compensation

No matter how performance evaluations are handled, for employees the bottom line is often pay. Even if they derive more intrinsic awards from their jobs, employees frequently view pay as a sign of their ultimate worth to their employers. Pay levels can be judged in two ways: by internal equity and external equity. Internal equity is based on pay comparisons within an organization; external equity is based on comparisons with employees in other organizations.

Failure to maintain both types of equity can have serious negative implications for the job satisfaction of employees. Disgruntled employees are likely to exhibit diminished performance and are more likely to leave an organization. Simple fairness requires that leaders in local government develop an equitable pay plan (see Figure 5–4); they also must adhere to a number of statutory requirements.

### Legal requirements

Employers create pay inequity when they allow considerations of age, sex, race, and other nonmerit factors to influence individual salary decisions. In response, many legislative and judicial remedies have been developed to ensure that employers observe basic principles of pay equity.

The *Fair Labor Standards Act (FLSA)* was expanded by a 1985 U.S. Supreme Court decision; it was then further modified by the U.S. Department of Labor in 2003 to cover wage and record-keeping practices of local governments. The act requires that all covered employees receive the minimum wage; that employees who make below a certain amount of money receive overtime or "comp time" when they work more than a forty-hour week; and that records of hours worked and wages paid be kept for at least three years for all employees. Maintaining compliance with this law is especially difficult for local govern-

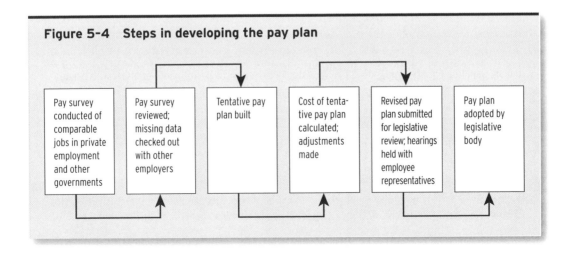

**Figure 5-4    Steps in developing the pay plan**

| Pay survey conducted of comparable jobs in private employment and other governments | Pay survey reviewed; missing data checked out with other employers | Tentative pay plan built | Cost of tentative pay plan calculated; adjustments made | Revised pay plan submitted for legislative review; hearings held with employee representatives | Pay plan adopted by legislative body |

ments because of the irregular work hours of certain employees, such as police officers and firefighters.

Federal laws that forbid employment discrimination also affect compensation practices:

- The *Equal Pay Act of 1962* requires that men and women receive equal pay for equal work that is performed under similar working conditions, but it exempts pay differentials resulting from seniority or merit.

- The *Age Discrimination in Employment Act of 1963* requires employers to give older employees the same pay as younger ones for the same work and prohibits employers from using pension plan provisions to force older employees to take early retirement.

- The *Civil Rights Act of 1964 (Title VII)*, which forbids discrimination based on nonmerit factors, has been interpreted in a number of court cases to require equal pay for comparable jobs. Different jobs can be considered comparable if there are strong similarities in job requirements.

## Linking pay and performance

Many local governments are taking steps to create a stronger link between compensation and employee performance. The goal is to reward top employees and encourage excellence. One popular approach is the use of pay-for-performance plans that offer broad pay ranges for different levels of individual performance. Also, some local governments are offering performance bonuses to individuals or groups who demonstrate noteworthy achievements.

Although the logic of linking pay and performance is compelling, attaining this objective requires overcoming some major barriers. Most important, lean budgets and political considerations may prevent local governments from providing meaningful monetary rewards for all their top performers. Compromises that spread funds too thinly or ignore some deserving employees can do more harm than good.

Another problem is that enhancing the link between pay and performance increases the responsibilities of supervisors because they must decide who gets a pay increase and who is left out. This fact can certainly create conflict between supervisors and their subordinates and possibly between employees who see themselves as competing for monetary rewards.

### Pay for performance in a union setting in Hamilton County, Ohio

In 1996, Hamilton County, Ohio (pop. 806,652), established a pay-for-performance contract with a union bargaining unit. Currently, three bargaining units representing more than half of the county's 1,900 bargaining-unit employees have a pay-for-performance plan. At the end of each annual budget cycle, the county's board of commissioners determines the rates for the following year's merit increases and bonuses. Department heads work with management teams to determine how much of a raise and/or bonus, if any, each employee will receive. All raises and bonuses are based on the results of annual employee evaluations. When bonus dollars are available, some departments also require employees to document the accomplishments that make them deserving of a bonus. The county is attempting to negotiate pay-for-performance contracts with several other bargaining units within the county.

**Pay for performance in Wells, Maine**

The town of Wells, Maine (pop. 10,088), was growing, creating an ever-increasing demand for services. The town could not stop the growth of the municipal labor force, but it could slow its growth through better training and cross training. The town selectmen decided to take nonunion employees off existing step plans, in which everyone received an automatic pay increase, and put them instead on a pay-for-performance plan. This plan looks not only at how well an individual is helping the town achieve its goals, but also at how the individual is improving by meeting his or her own clearly defined goals. Critical to the plan are the goals and objectives set annually by the selectmen, department heads, and the individual employees themselves. The system calls for a strong commitment from management as it relies on a great deal of interaction between management and the employee. And while the system is no more expensive than the old system, it maximizes the use of tax dollars.

Source: Adapted from the National League of Cities (NLC) Examples of Programs for Cities, www2.nlc.org/examples/cknsearchtest. htm, and excerpted from Jo Josephson, "Pay for Performance," *Maine Townsman* 59 (January 1997): 9, available at memun .org/public/publications/townsman/1997/PAYPERFORM.HTM.

Given the problems that may result, local government should not rush to adopt a pay-for-performance program. It is important to have an effective performance evaluation system in place before modifying the compensation system. However, the underlying logic of a pay-for-performance program is consistent with efforts to restore the meaning of merit in government employment.

## Employee benefits

Besides a paycheck, the large majority of local government employees receive a benefits package. Some benefits, such as social security, workmen's compensation, and unemployment compensation, are required by federal law, but other benefits that are typically provided, including health care and pensions, are currently discretionary.

Traditionally in the United States, government employers provided generous benefits plans, particularly when compared with plans offered by private sector organizations. However, civil service reform and concern about rising costs have led to cuts in recent years, resulting in less comprehensive coverage. For example, many government agencies have replaced defined benefit retirement plans with defined contribution plans, which typically save the employer a significant amount of money. Some local governments are making new employees wait six months for full benefits, a trend that has long been common in the private sector but rare among public organizations. Many local governments are also denying part-time and seasonal employees health coverage and other benefits.

### Health benefits

With the high cost of health care, local governments face the difficult dilemma of containing costs while providing a high level of health services. Currently, benefits experts are strongly supporting the concept of "managed care" as the most effective strategy for reducing costs. This strategy requires employers to take an active role in monitoring any activities that can increase health care expenditures. Some local governments have developed extensive "wellness" programs to improve the health of employees by helping them to lose weight, reduce stress, quit smoking, or reduce injuries.

Managed care programs also prompt employees to become more cost-conscious consumers of health care—for example, by requiring employees to share a larger portion of costs through deductibles, coinsurance, or co-payments. Deductibles refer to the initial fixed costs of services that employees are responsible for paying before employer-financed benefits apply. Coinsurance refers to a fixed percentage of health care costs that employees pay above the level of the deductible. Co-payments refer to fixed payments by employees for health care services (e.g., $5 per prescription).

Advocates of managed care also stress the importance of negotiating agreements with health care providers to reduce costs. The idea is for a large employer or a group of cooperating employers to negotiate lower prices for higher volumes of employees. Even a single small jurisdiction may be able to develop mutually beneficial relations with individual physicians. But although developing relationships with what are called "preferred

---

### Employee wellness in Boulder, Colorado

The Employee Wellness Program in Boulder, Colorado (pop. 91,685), decreases instances of injury in the workplace and improves employee fitness levels. Sponsored jointly by the city's human resources department and parks and recreation department, the program offers employees free use of Boulder Reservoir and all city recreation centers, outdoor pools, and drop-in fitness classes. Along with discounts at local vendors, employees receive low-cost health screenings and nutritional consultations, injury prevention and health education workshops, incentive gifts of weight room orientations, and access to both physical and occupational therapists for special needs. Participants undergo a health assessment upon enrollment and at one-year intervals to measure progress. Information regarding the program is available through an employee e-mail group, a newsletter, a calendar of events provided on the city's Web site, and the annual benefit fair/health fair, where employees sign up for their insurance plans. Funding for the program comes through worker's compensation.

Source: Adapted from the National League of Cities (NLC) Examples of Programs for Cities, www2.nlc.org/examples/cknsearchtest .htm, and based on Colorado Municipal League, "How Our Cities and Towns Strive for Wins and Losses," *Colorado Municipalities* 79, no. 6 (December 2003): 21, 23.

---

### The Employee Health Connection in Catawba County, North Carolina

The Employee Health Connection (EHC), a walk-in medical clinic in Catawba County, North Carolina (pop. 151,641), opened in October 2002. It was implemented to enhance and promote employee wellness; reduce health insurance and worker's compensation costs; reduce sick leave usage; provide onsite care for routine illnesses and injuries; offer prevention and early detection of potential health problems; provide services to supplement our wellness and health education program; and offer in-house preemployment medical screenings and drug testing. Since it opened, the clinic has saved thousands of dollars in health and worker's compensation claims.

Source: Excerpted from the National Association of Counties (NACo) Model County Programs, naco.org.

providers" offers the promise of reduced health care costs, such arrangements are often not easy to establish. First, local governments need to acquire access (usually through a third party) to a highly sophisticated database to get the type of information needed to negotiate with providers. Second, they must then find ways to encourage their employees to visit the designated providers for treatment. Because this usually involves switching their family doctors, employees are often not eager to make the change.

Given the complexities of the health care environment, local governments need the help of trained benefits experts. Larger jurisdictions can develop the capacities of their own staffs, but smaller jurisdictions have to choose carefully from among the many third-party services available in the health care market.

## Pension benefits

All employees want to feel that they and their families are financially secure. Pension benefits, generally described in terms of retirement, are meant to provide that security. As with health benefits, however, many local governments are forcing employees to take greater responsibility for achieving this end. There are two typical pension program patterns: defined benefit and defined contribution.

Under traditional *defined benefit* programs, local governments pay benefits to employees or their families upon retirement, disability, or death. Payment amounts are determined by the type of event during a particular period and the length of employment service. Employees frequently, but not always, contribute to funding these programs through payroll deductions. Vesting, whereby employees acquire legal rights to benefits from pension programs, typically comes after a predetermined number of years of service. This practice, along with benefits that are paid at a higher rate for later years of service, tends to reduce employee turnover.

> *Underfunding of pension funds and weak investment performance are making it hard for some local governments to meet their pension obligations.*

A defined benefit pension program has significant administrative burdens. Employers are responsible for designing programs; creating pension funds, which are used to collect and invest monies; determining benefit eligibility; and making payments.

*Defined contribution* programs provide for employee retirement through payments to third parties, who establish retirement investment accounts for each employee. In many cases, employers also provide disability and life insurance. The local government's payments to the third party are based on each employee's salary. Sometimes the employee must contribute as well. The third party administers all aspects of the retirement package. Retirement benefits to the employee depend upon the amount of money contributed to his or her account and the investment performance of the account. The responsibilities of local governments for this kind of retirement program are minimal.

Problems in local pension programs in recent years have created a number of changes. Underfunding of pension funds and weak investment performance are making it hard for some local governments to meet their pension obligations. Employees have often found it difficult or impossible to transfer the money in their accounts to a new pension fund if they change jobs. As a result, employees who are no longer motivated or performing at their peak may remain in an organization solely because they do not wish to lose their benefits.

Common responses to such problems include lowering benefits, increasing employee contributions, striving to improve funding levels and investment performance, and providing portable pension programs that allow employees to retain participation in a pension program when they change employers. Although each of these responses can be managed in the context of defined benefit programs, many local governments have switched to defined contribution programs because they appear to solve most of the problems, especially the employer's responsibilities for managing payments in the future. Of course, employees are then more at risk because they must cover more exigencies themselves.

### New trends in local government benefits

Under the Civil Rights Act of 1964, local governments cannot discriminate in employment against individuals from a series of backgrounds, including women, people of color, older workers, and people with disabilities. However, many local governments are extending these rights by enacting antidiscriminatory laws that are stronger than those suggested by the federal government.

Some local governments are now extending health and retirement benefits to same-sex partners. These actions can help local governments by allowing them to compete more effectively in labor markets and tap into a larger share of the labor pool. This is especially true in areas where same-sex couples are common.

At the same time, as noted previously, local governments are making tough choices about how to reduce the costs of their benefit plans. One sensitive area that has not been mentioned is the provision of health care benefits for retired employees. According to a 2003 ICMA study, this provision is made in the majority of local governments;[3] however, retired employees often pay higher premiums than regular employees. Still, public employers may have been overly generous in their provision of benefits. New rules established by the Governmental Accounting Standards Board will require all cities and counties to declare the costs of their pensions over the next thirty-year period, and this will shine a spotlight on these ballooning costs. Health care benefits and pension plans may change as a result.

## Employee unions

Pressures from employee unions can greatly increase the challenge of managing personnel. The first step in dealing with unions is to develop formal HR policies and rules. Once this task has been completed, the local government is in a much better position to bargain. Should an employee organization be recognized, a number of other steps will become necessary, such as the designation of a bargaining unit, preparations for negotiation, development of a strike contingency plan, and administration of a labor contract.

### The bargaining relationship

In states that have comprehensive labor relations statutes, local government officials must become familiar with the provisions of those statutes. Where state legislation does not exist, local governments should be prepared, if necessary, to adopt an employee relations ordinance that covers all aspects of the bargaining relationship. Such an ordinance generally will recognize the right of employees to join and be represented by a union. Other matters to be covered include

- A procedure for handling grievances
- Rules relating to the activities of the union representatives
- A prohibition of strikes or a specification of conditions under which they are permissible
- A listing of unfair labor practices
- The procedures to be followed in handling an impasse in negotiations.

## The bargaining unit

When an employee organization has demanded recognition or when employees themselves have requested the right to organize, membership in the bargaining unit must be carefully defined. The government must also evaluate the impact of the union's suggested structure on the current management structure and identify positions, usually supervisory and managerial, to be excluded from the unit.

In states with comprehensive labor relations laws covering the public sector, the state agency administering the statute usually is responsible for assisting local governments in determining bargaining units and conducting all aspects of the labor relations program. Where such statutes do not exist, the manager should seek expert advice from other state agencies or local government associations, because it is extremely difficult to change a unit once it has been established. Fragmented bargaining units can impose demands on the employer and make it difficult to keep benefits and working conditions uniform.

After the bargaining unit has been determined, the manager must provide for an election in which affected employees can decide by secret ballot whether they wish to be represented by the unit. Where a state labor relations agency does not exist, assistance with conducting the election may be obtained from the American Arbitration Association or the state mediation service.

Management has a responsibility to participate in the preelection campaign—a responsibility almost always exercised fully in the private sector—to explain to employees the implications of union membership. Although management is prohibited in most states from threatening the loss of jobs or benefits or misrepresenting important facts, it can and should provide factual information. Before getting involved in such an election, however, management should seek and follow expert legal advice to protect itself from accusations of unfair labor practices.

*Labor-management negotiations*   When a local government recognizes an employee organization, the chief administrator must become acquainted with all facets of negotiations. These include a determination of who will serve on the negotiating team, preparation for negotiations, physical arrangements for and scheduling of meetings, evaluation of proposals, methods of preparing counterproposals, strategy and tactics, and preparation of the written agreement.

Often, because of staff limitations, the chief administrator and the local government's legal counsel must assume responsibility for the negotiations. It is often advisable to obtain the assistance of a law firm specializing in labor-management relations.

***Preparing for negotiations***   Direct participation in labor negotiations by members of the governing body is often not advisable. As policy makers, elected officials should limit themselves to determining allowable limits on policies being negotiated and to considering the recommendations of the officials who have been designated to meet with employee representatives on a continuing basis. Senior managers generally play an important role in labor negotiations, especially in smaller cities and counties. Third-party consultants are often involved in larger jurisdictions, but they still operate under the guidance of a senior manager. Of course, the governing body must be provided with regular progress reports regardless of who is involved in the negotiations.

The negotiating team may consist of the chief negotiator, the finance officer, the government attorney, and the official or officials affected by the negotiations. Even a small local government should consider retaining a labor relations consultant if no staff member is skilled in negotiations, because many costly and irreparable mistakes can be made. In a team approach, alternates should be designated so that the negotiating sessions will not be interrupted should a particular member of the team be unavailable.

*Even a small local government should consider retaining a labor relations consultant if no staff member is skilled in negotiations, because many costly and irreparable mistakes can be made.*

Considerable homework is required before negotiations. The negotiator and the negotiating team must determine the management position and work out the tactics they will use. Suggestions should be solicited from supervisors and department heads on matters that might arise during the negotiations. A review of past grievances will also help to determine possible problem areas. Data must be gathered on past and present wages and fringe benefits, recruitment and retention experience, budgets and revenues, and the distribution of employees by classification, work location, and wage. Information on the current HR practices of other local governments in the area is essential.

***Reaching agreement***   Any final agreement must be put into writing. Contract drafting is a vital and complex aspect of collective bargaining. Both union and management should help draft the language of the contract. Contract preparation can be simplified if agreement is reached on the phrasing of each clause during the negotiations. If the municipal attorney or chief administrator has had little or no experience in drafting contracts, a qualified consultant should be retained for this purpose. Mistakes in a first contract will be difficult to rectify in later ones, and a poorly written or ambiguous contract will lead to problems in administration.

Because not all negotiations result in agreement, it is essential that the chief administrator be acquainted with the various alternatives available for resolving disputes—especially mediation, fact finding, and arbitration. Other alternatives include non-stoppage strikes (in which work continues, but at a slower rate), partial strikes, public referendums, votes of union membership on the employer's last offer, and court actions that might lead to injunctions, fines, or penalties. A well-prepared contingency plan for coping with all forms of work actions—including strikes, the spread of "blue flu" (using sick leave to avoid reporting to work) among the uniformed services, speedups or slowdowns, and

**Figure 5-5  Suggested steps in processing employee grievances**

Employee grievance procedure

- ☐ Listen and take notes as necessary
- ☐ Ask questions; get employee's version of events
- ☐ Get additional facts from other sources; verify statements
- ☐ Check records; keep all past records

- ☐ Analyze alternatives
- ☐ Decide who has authority to act
- ☐ Make decision
- ☐ Explain decision
- ☐ Follow up on decision

mass resignations—can minimize the impact of work actions on the community. A plan of this type should be developed well before starting the negotiations.

*Contract administration*   Once a contract has been approved by both sides, the task of contract administration begins. Well-trained and informed supervisors are the key to effective contract administration. Copies of the contract should be distributed to all department heads and supervisors. Orientation sessions to give supervisors a thorough understanding of each provision and how it affects them and their work should also be available. Skillful handling of complaints in the early stages can prevent serious problems from developing during the contract period. Supervisors, whose suggestions can be of great importance in preparing for future negotiating sessions, should be encouraged to keep records of grievances as well as recommendations to revise clauses of the contract that are costly or ambiguous.

The contract generally describes a grievance procedure for resolving questions of interpretation and application. When such procedures are not negotiated as part of the contract, a formalized grievance procedure should be established to clarify and interpret HR policies and practices. Employee participation in the formation of a grievance procedure is essential.

Many grievance procedures consist of three to five steps, including successive reviews, as needed, by the line supervisor, the division head, the department head, and either the HR officer or the representative of the chief administrative officer (see Figure 5–5). Some grievance procedures provide for arbitration of disputes. Many establish grievance committees, consisting of employee and management representatives, to resolve disputes. An employee with a grievance always has the right to choose a representative to be present at any or all stages of the grievance procedure. Careful definition of the channels to be followed and of definite and reasonable time limits ensures prompt consideration and adjustment of grievances.

## Career development and training

Training helps maintain the effectiveness of personnel, ensuring that employee efforts are consistent with established goals and objectives and that employees are able to meet new challenges. A commitment to training expresses a concern for the long-term welfare and productivity of employees serving the community. Training can be expensive in the short run, especially when lost work hours are considered, but failure to provide needed training is even more expensive in the long run, causing both lower productivity and more frequent and costly mistakes. Training can remain cost-effective if maximum use is made of existing organizational resources.

## Determining needs

Training needs can be identified through discussions with supervisors, diagnostic tests, and employee interviews. Department heads and supervisors should always play a prominent role in defining training needs and recommending courses to offer and personnel to be involved.

---

### Developing an effective workforce in Wellington, Florida

The "University" of Wellington, at the village of Wellington, Florida (pop. 53,583), offers village employees a range of educational programs in three sections: Required Training, Required Training for Supervisors and Managers, and A La Carte Options.

Required Training covers new hire orientation, equal opportunity and sexual harassment, drug testing, and Occupational Safety and Health Administration training.

Required Training for Supervisors and Managers includes topics in employment law, leadership skills, and communications, and eight village-specific modules designed and facilitated by village experts on such topics as coaching, counseling, and the disciplinary process; administration, recruiting, and staffing; and risk management and procurement. Forty-five "on demand" self-paced technical training modules are also available.

A La Carte options for 2006 include topics ranging from vehicle safety and heat stress to English as a Second Language, as well as individual elections in such areas as health, financial fitness, and self-directed technical training, all designed to provide personal enrichment and/or job enhancement. Also for the first time, the University of Wellington is offering wellness classes such as yoga and pilates.

---

### Media training class in Stafford County, Virginia

For years, officials in Stafford County, Virginia (pop. 117,874), had operated by a sort of haphazard system to work with the media. Although none of them had received any formal media training, many, if not all, interacted with the media on more than one occasion. Most found their relationship to be awkward and tense, and others attempted to avoid reporters when possible because they simply did not know what to do. Realizing that this approach could have a negative impact on Stafford's public image and detract from the county's high-quality customer service program, the county's public information office developed a short media training program for all directors, assistant directors, and other designated staff to provide tips on building a successful and positive relationship with the media. The training, conducted by the county's public information officer, helps employees understand the media and offers guidelines on writing press releases, conducting an interview, or pitching story ideas. Each attendee also receives a media handbook. The training is provided to individual departments upon request and to new employees during their customer service orientation.

Source: Excerpted from the National Association of Counties (NACo) Model County Programs, naco.org.

With the growing concern for providing equal employment opportunities, training may be used to prepare those with economic and educational disadvantages for permanent types of employment. Training for the disadvantaged involves the improvement of job skills and work habits. Remedial education opportunities can be provided in cooperation with nearby schools and colleges.

In many cases, technological, social, and legislative changes require employees to develop new skills and often underscore the need for in-service retraining programs. For example, special training may help employees improve their computer skills or gain a better understanding of the meaning of sexual harassment. Also, the increasing incidence of labor-management collective bargaining in the public sector has created a need for training in labor relations and negotiation strategies for managers and supervisory personnel.

## Program implementation

From analyses of training needs, objectives can be defined and policies established. Policy decisions need to be made on many matters, including

- Which employees should receive training first
- What balance should be sought between training in administrative skills and in technical skills
- How much time should be devoted to each kind of training
- Whether training should be conducted on or off the job
- Whether leaves of absence should be granted for training
- What the relationship, if any, should be between training and promotion or salary increases
- Whether training should be optional or required
- Whether tuition-refund and education-incentive programs should be developed.

Off-the-job training can involve lectures, conferences, case studies, demonstrations, role playing, field trips, and problem-solving sessions. To meet specific requirements, a program can be tailored from a multitude of approaches. The small local government may find it desirable to initiate a tuition-refund program that encourages employees to take advantage of educational programs offered by community colleges and other institutions.

Training resources and facilities include technical institutes; public schools, colleges, and universities that offer in-service training programs; and professional associations. In cooperation with colleges, state municipal leagues and county associations often offer a variety of training programs for local government officials. University extension divisions and government research bureaus are other valuable sources of employee training programs.

## Other approaches to employee development

The efforts of contemporary local governments to improve employee performance do not end with career development and training. Increasingly, effective local managers are now working in partnership with their employees to find new ways to help them not only improve in their work but also increase their sense of personal fulfillment and satisfaction. The notion is that happy employees who have positive self-images, and who are able

---

**Open communication in Champaign, Illinois**

To encourage open communication, conflict resolution, risk taking, and decision making among employees, the city of Champaign, Illinois (pop. 71,568), formed the safe environment task force. Made up of employees, managers, and department heads, the task force conducted focus groups to solicit employee ideas on how to promote an environment in which employees feel comfortable actively exchanging ideas and concerns. The committee developed recommendations in five areas: fair process to give employees an opportunity to know what is expected of them and why; employee development, including training in communication skills and conflict resolution; recognition for work group and individual accomplishments; relationship building; and accountability to address behaviors that violate safe environment principles. Most of these strategies have been implemented citywide and have become standard operating procedure. For example, when the city's mission and values were updated, the city manager met with every employee group to discuss the proposed values and solicit feedback.

---

to manage stress in their personal lives and balance the demands of home and job effectively, will also be better employees in all respects.

Although the link between these creative approaches and genuine productivity improvements is not clearly established, such efforts may make an important contribution to employee job satisfaction. This can be an important consideration for those local governments that must compete with high-paying private companies for skilled employees.

## Alterations in work requirements

Alterations in work requirements are sometimes allowed to enable employees to achieve a better balance between work and family demands, or simply to enable an individual to achieve more personal satisfaction from the work environment. Such alterations include flex-time, job sharing, job enrichment, telecommuting, and virtually any other arrangement that meets employee needs without unduly burdening the employer. These alterations cannot be applied to all jobs, but they have been productive in a surprising number of different occupations.

*Flex-time*   Flex-time allows employees to change their work schedule. With flex-time, employees may be allowed to come to work earlier or later as long as they are available during designated core hours. Such flexibility can help meet the family demands on single parents or two-career families, or simply enable individuals to schedule more of their working hours during their most productive periods of the day.

Under another flex-time arrangement, employees may work four longer days instead of five regular days each week. Such scheduling has proven to be popular with many employees in nursing and clerical occupations because it enables them to reduce child care and commuting costs.

*Job sharing*   Job sharing is an arrangement in which two employees fulfill the responsibilities of one job. This plan can fit the needs of working parents who have valuable skills but lack the time to meet the requirements of a full-time job. It may also be popular with older workers who want to reduce their work hours but are not ready for retirement.

> ### Telecommuting to fight pollution in Austin, Texas
>
> The city of Austin, Texas (pop. 690,252), encourages its employees to telecommute to reduce traffic congestion and air pollution, especially during "ozone season" (between April 1 and October 1). To work from home, employees must obtain permission from their supervisors, who have the option of granting or denying permission depending on the nature of the employee's work and whether that work can be accomplished from home. Employees whose requests to telecommute are granted take a one-hour class, in which they learn about computer security and how to use software that provides them with remote access to all the data on their office computers. About 15 percent of Austin's employees now work from home an average of one day a week.

*Job enrichment*   Job enrichment is an approach that involves changing the tasks that particular employees perform in order to increase their opportunities for new responsibilities, personal achievement, growth, and advancement. These alterations must be carefully done, however, as they might be viewed as an effort to increase the workload. Employees will become resentful if their workload begins to resemble that of a better-paying job classification.

*Telecommuting*   Some employers have found that both employee satisfaction and productivity can be improved by permitting employees to do some work at home. The arrangement gives employees more control over their home and family. Moreover, when combined with flexible work hours that enable the employee to work during the quiet hours of the day at home, it increases productivity by freeing the employee from the disruptions and interruptions that are a normal part of workplace routine.

## Flexible benefits

Local governments can help employees meet personal or family needs by offering a choice of benefits. In these programs, employees typically take a minimum package of benefits, which may consist of basic life insurance, short-term disability insurance, a week of vacation, and hospital and medical coverage. (In cases in which hospital and medical coverage is required, it can be waived if the employee provides documentation of comparable coverage from another source, such as a spouse's employment.)

Employees are then given an additional level of fringe benefit coverage from which each individual can design a personal program from such options as increased vacation time, more life insurance, dependent health coverage, dental coverage, additional sick or personal leave time, child care assistance, and an investment program. Sometimes employees can choose still more benefits that they can purchase through payroll deductions. Such "cafeteria"-type options tailor job benefits to each individual employee's lifestyle and personal responsibilities, thereby adding to employee job satisfaction without adding to employer costs.

## Employee assistance programs

Some of the toughest decisions facing local managers involve employees whose work performance is suffering because of some type of personal problem. Although managers

---

### Sharing sick leave in Tumwater, Washington

Tumwater, Washington (pop. 13,331), has an ordinance (no. 1375) that allows municipal employees to share sick leave with their fellow employees. Under the ordinance, an employee may receive shared sick leave if he or she suffers from a severe illness, impairment, injury, or physical or mental condition that may necessitate going on leave without pay or being dismissed from city employment. The receiving employee must also have depleted, or be in danger of depleting, all annual leave or sick leave reserves. An employee who chooses to donate sick leave must have at least ten days accrued and may donate no more than 25 percent of his or her accrual balance.

Source: Adapted from the National League of Cities (NLC) Examples of Programs for Cities, www2.nlc.org/examples/cknsearchtest.htm.

---

should be careful when becoming involved in the personal problems of an employee, they should not look the other way when an employee is no longer performing effectively. This is especially true when the problem threatens the safety and security of the public, or when the employee has job security protected by HR rules, a union contract, civil service regulations, or simply a past record of good performance. Employee assistance programs (EAPs) are now common, and they address a wide range of issues.

*Substance abuse*   Because of its destructive effects and because employees go to great lengths to hide this type of problem, even from themselves, drug and alcohol abuse is one of the most difficult personal problems that local managers face.

The first step toward dealing with employee substance abuse is the development of a written policy, communicated to all employees, making it clear that any form of substance abuse is unacceptable. In some cases, a second step may be to develop a drug testing program to enforce the policy. Testing of employees whose job performance may affect public safety (e.g., those who work in public transportation) is generally more accepted than random testing of all employees. However, drug testing is a sensitive and complex issue; managers should act cautiously and should seek both legal advice and guidance from professionals in this field before attempting to institute a program.

> *Testing of employees whose job performance may affect public safety (e.g., those who work in public transportation) is generally more accepted than random testing of all employees.*

Testing can be used as a preemployment screening device, as part of routine physicals, or in cases where there are strong indications that an employee is under the influence of drugs or alcohol. Any efforts in this area should be accompanied by a well-defined, sympathetic yet forceful strategy for dealing with the problem when drug or alcohol abuse is discovered.

Before taking disciplinary action, most employers give troubled employees at least one chance to rehabilitate themselves. EAPs, which offer assessment, professional counseling, referral, treatment, and education, can help employees in this process. Local governments may choose to offer their own EAP or use existing private or public providers.

*Mental health services*  Statistics indicate that over half of all adults now experience some form of mental or emotional illness during their lives, and the increasing tension and stress that have become part of the U.S. lifestyle are making such conditions more common. This means that most employees—even most of the best employees—experience periods on the job when their work suffers from personal problems.

To minimize their losses from such periods, more and more employers, even in small organizations, are now retaining health care professionals to provide employee education and counseling and to diagnose and treat employees needing help. (Diagnostic and treatment costs are typically provided, within limits, by health insurance programs.) Most communities are now served by a nonprofit community mental health center that will provide such services. Private clinical psychologists and psychiatrists can also be employed for this purpose.

### Accommodating employees' family obligations

The movement from one-wage-earner families to two-wage-earner families that has occurred in U.S. society during the last century has generated changes in the labor force and modifications in public and private sector employment practices. For example, some local governments have established day care cooperatives or provided child care subsidies.

The Family and Medical Leave Act of 1993 allows workers to take up to twelve weeks of unpaid leave in any twelve-month period for the birth or adoption of a child, or to care for a sick family member (a child, spouse, or parent). This law applies to government organizations of all sizes (and to private companies with more than fifty employees). While this law was a major advance, it must be remembered that it only offers unpaid leave in most cases. Legislation has since been introduced in a number of states to offer paid leave, but nothing has been passed into federal law.

Continuing employment-related problems confronting families include increased levels of family stress, breakdowns in family communication, inadequate child care options, increasing levels of concern over child development and discipline, and the dissolution of extended family support systems.

Just as the past fifty years have witnessed the expansion of employment opportunities for many citizens, the decades ahead will find increasing attention focused on ways to reconcile work and family life so that existing employment opportunities and worker productivity will support rather than threaten the quality of work and personal life. The approaches to employee development discussed above—and especially such practices as flex-time, job sharing, at-home work assignments, flexible benefits, and counseling programs—exemplify such efforts. The persistent concern over family life, however, suggests that even these tools need both wider application and support from methods not yet devised. Employers will be under increasing pressure in future years to modify their work requirements in ways designed to foster stronger, healthier employee families.

### Conclusion

Excellence in local governance cannot be attained without competent and dedicated administrative staff. Just as the proverbial army can go only as far as its foot soldiers take it, an organization can accomplish only what its staff can produce.

The best and the brightest employees are recruited and retained through a professionally operated HR system consisting of a number of discrete facets, including recruitment and promotion on the basis of merit, regular performance evaluation, competitive salaries and benefits, training to expand skills and encourage personal development, and a well-documented and clearly understood framework of rules and regulations.

HR management has undergone many changes during the last decades of the twentieth century. Unionization has become a fact of life in many communities. Equal opportunity

---

### Questions to ask if you manage a small community

Small-town values are much admired, but they can become a problem as even small governments begin to face big-city problems. Does your community maintain a focus on upholding professional standards, especially when it comes to hiring and firing decisions?

Equity in recruitment and selection is made more difficult by the lack of anonymity of those in the applicant pool. Labor markets are likely to be smaller, with greater interconnectedness between potential employees. Has every possible effort been made to ensure that selection processes are both effective and objective?

Venues for recruiting employees tend to be fewer and more easily identified. In some small communities, word of mouth can be a valuable means of recruitment. Have targeted phone calls and e-mails been used to supplement Web postings and traditional newspaper advertising?

Position classification, in the case of small communities, can easily devolve into an exercise in writing classifications to suit a particular employee's skill set and compensation needs. Are classification decisions reviewed for possible affects on internal pay equity?

Health care benefit costs are rising rapidly. Have all avenues been pursued for providing high-quality, affordable coverage? Have efforts been made to participate in insurance pools developed by state governments, municipal leagues, or other city/county government associations? Every government faces somewhat different issues, and finding the best approach can produce cost savings.

Employee performance evaluation has the potential, in small communities, to become less and less formal. Has an effort been made to follow a predetermined process that is similar for all employees? This will preserve both equity and effectiveness.

If in-house counsel is not available, is a relationship in place with a local attorney who is able to provide advice on employment law issues? Local officials should be careful not to underestimate the relevance and intricacy of employment discrimination and other legal issues.

Has an effort been made to understand the needs of different demographic groups working in the government and residing in the areas, and to ensure that those needs are being met? In small organizations, the relevant areas of diversity are easily identified, and management mechanisms can be tailored to individual needs.

Is merit an integral part of the civil service system? Small local governments are less likely to have a personnel office, which makes it harder to maintain the high level of performance needed for governments to operate effectively. Traditional civil service systems can also have a negative effect by focusing more on protecting employee rights than on incentives. Better integration between management strategies and the personnel system is one approach for addressing this issue.

has become a standard expectation; government staffs now comprise persons of different ethnic groups, races, and sexual orientations.

As staffs evolve, the emphasis on HR management must evolve, too. Not only must opportunities be made equal, but so too must conditions in the workplace. This means that local governments must work proactively to ensure that employees are understanding of and sensitive to diversity and that they strive to make the workplace a pleasant place for all. HR management must also adapt to the changing needs of employees. Workplaces must be made flexible and responsive to a growing variety of needs: they must be accessible to disabled employees, and they must be sensitive to employees' home and family pressures.

In summary, then, the challenges that lay before HR managers are to

- Balance the need to offer managerial flexibility and autonomy with the need to maintain an equitable and consistent hiring process

- Formulate a compensation package, including benefits and retirement options, that can compete for employees with private sector job opportunities

- Determine strategies for managing employees from different backgrounds, using diversity management programs and nontraditional work requirements

- Offer employees a performance appraisal process that is valid and fair and that provides targeted feedback for employee development

- Maintain ongoing career development and training opportunities to keep employees motivated.

The HR function has grown in importance over the last hundred years, and this trend is likely to continue. Pressures to find ways to do more with less are not going to subside, nor will the growth of technological complexity. HR management expertise is an essential skill for any manager seeking a leadership role.

---

### Competencies of the human resource manager

Excellent written and oral communication skills

Effective conflict resolution and negotiation tactics

Good interpersonal skills and ability to build relationships with managers and employees

Knowledge of human resource systems, such as compensation, classification, recruitment, and selection processes

Familiarity with legal issues related to human resources

Sensitivity and discretion with private employee issues, such as drug and alcohol dependency, psychological health issues, and potential legal disputes

## ▨ **Endnotes**

1   Theodore Poister and Gregory Streib, "Municipal Management Tools from 1976 to 1993: An Overview and Update," *Public Productivity and Management Review* 18, no. 2 (1994): 115–125.

2   Gregory Streib and Theodore H. Poister, "The Use of Strategic Planning in Municipal Governments," *The Municipal Year Book 2002* (Washington, D.C.: ICMA, 2002), 18–25.

3   Evelina Moulder, "Local Government Health Care Plans: Customers, Costs, and Options for the Future," *The Municipal Year Book 2004* (Washington, D.C.: ICMA, 2004), 26–34.

# Planning

## Stuart Meck

W here are we now? Where do we want to be in the future? How do we get there? The professional planner asks these questions in a continuous planning process that involves setting goals to address problems and issues; identifying alternative courses of action and gauging the consequences of each; selecting and implementing the alternative that best addresses the goals; and monitoring the chosen course of action to ensure that the goals are met. Put simply, to plan is to apply foresight to action.

That, in theory, is how planning works. In practice, however, the steps of the planning process may be out of sequence, or they may work simultaneously or in small, often uncoordinated increments. All the information needed to evaluate alternatives may not be available, or it may cost more to obtain than the importance of the decision merits. Political factors may eliminate alternatives (such as siting a landfill near a subdivision of expensive homes) before they reach formal consideration. Or the decision maker may decide that a goal is unreachable or needs to be changed.

Cities and counties today face a future made even more complex and ambiguous by an often-contentious political environment. Local officials turn to planning as a mechanism with which to step back from the daily preoccupation with "hot button" issues, to obtain the big picture about their communities, to reach consensus on an approach, and then to chart a desired course. For them, planning is a method of reaching thoughtful and just decisions that result in a better life for all.

## Comprehensive planning

*Comprehensive planning*, as distinguished from functional or strategic planning, refers to the preparation of a document or documents intended to direct a local government's current and future physical, social, and economic development. This planning includes the preparation of a unified physical design—a single integrated schematic—for the public and private development of land, also taking into account the relationship of activities on the land with bodies of water. Comprehensive planning, as it is currently practiced, is a continuing, rather than static, process. The planning documents that are developed are in an ongoing state of evaluation and revision over a specific period, reflecting changes in a community's economic and demographic characteristics as well as changes in the private land market.

*Functional planning* addresses some subsystem of a comprehensive plan, such as utilities (e.g., water, sewers) or transportation. A stormwater management plan, which looks at ways to accommodate runoff from impervious surface cover due to development, is an example of functional planning.

During the 1980s, local governments began to experiment with *strategic planning*, a concept borrowed from the private sector. Corporations prepare strategic plans to change their products, services, and marketing strategies. At the most basic level, the strategic planner analyzes the factors both external to the company (e.g., the general economy, technology, competition, government regulation) and internal (e.g., staffing, marketing, manufacturing processes). In conducting external and internal assessments, the strategic planner identifies the company's strengths, weaknesses, opportunities, and threats (the so-called SWOT analysis). Based on this analysis, corporate planners and executives choose missions, objectives, and strategies that build on strengths, correct weaknesses, take advantage of opportunities, and deal, as best as can be done, with threats.[1]

While local governments do not have all the characteristics of companies, they do have to deal with many of the same generic sets of issues in conducting assessments. Consequently, local government strategic plans tend to focus on internal, operational matters; respond to changes in the political and institutional environment; and deal with matters that overlap with physical planning, such as economic development.

## Why local governments plan

Local governments plan for legal and practical reasons. State enabling legislation may require that local comprehensive plans be prepared before zoning and subdivision controls can be used to regulate land use. Even in the absence of a formal requirement, a plan would be necessary to support development regulations and public investment decisions.

> *Local planning is often the most direct and efficient way to involve the members of the general public.*

The local planning process draws the attention of the local legislative body, appointed boards, and citizens to the community's major development problems and opportunities—whether they be physical, environmental, social, or economic. It offers a chance to look broadly at programs that a local government may initiate regarding housing, economic development, public infrastructure and services, environmental protection, and natural and man-made hazards and to see how they relate to one another. A local comprehensive plan gives elected and appointed officials in particular an opportunity to back off from their preoccupation with pressing, day-to-day issues and to clarify their ideas on the kind of community they are trying to create. At the same time, it represents a "big picture" of the community, one that can be related to the trends and interests of the broader region as well as of the state.

Local planning is often the most direct and efficient way to involve members of the general public in describing the kind of community they want. The process of plan preparation, with its attendant workshops, questionnaires, meetings, and public hearings, permits two-way communications between citizens and local government officials as to a vision of the community and the details of how that vision is to be achieved. In this respect, the plan is "a blueprint of values" that evolves over time.

---

**Planning in action in Denton, Texas**

Planning affects many aspects of community life. For example, ordinances that tell developers what kind of parking they can or must provide help determine community character. Denton, Texas (pop. 104,153), adopted parking standards that prohibit locating large parking lots on the side or in front of buildings and give parking credits to developers who provide on-street parking that is available to the general public. The standards also require pedestrian access along a path or sidewalk.

---

Because it sets out goals and policies for the local government as well as a program of implementation, a local comprehensive plan provides a framework for coordinating governmental action. For example, a plan may propose a new neighborhood park in a developing area. The local government can then coordinate the purchase and development of that park with the construction of a new elementary school.

Finally, local plans are intended to influence decisions of the private sector. A plan sends signals to private developers regarding where development and redevelopment may occur and at what densities and intensities. Thus, the developer knows in general terms what to expect when proposing new projects.[2]

## American city planning: The historical context

Many American cities came into being without substantial comprehensive planning. This type of planning, called "townsite planning" (including colonial planning), was for greenfield property, where the objective was, at bottom, the subdivision of land that a single owner fully controlled for the purpose of selling lots for building.[3]

Several movements affected the emergence of city planning in the United States. For the period from 1893 to 1910, the City Beautiful movement influenced planning in already-built cities, such as Chicago, New York, and San Francisco. This movement grew out of architect/planner Daniel Burnham's plan for the 1893 World's Columbian Exposition in Chicago and its emphasis on civic art. The fair, with its great white classical buildings, grand vistas, ponds, fountains, and flamboyant sculpture, was intended to inspire, uplift, and refine the ideals of the city's people.

*A democratic spirit underlay the establishment of the great public parks, like New York City's Central Park; these were to be the lungs of the city and could be enjoyed by all, not just the wealthy.*

In the early twentieth century, planning was also shaped by the sanitary reform movement. This movement recognized that, if cities were to flourish, they needed to provide a supply of pure water, properly treat and dispose of sewage, install storm drainage facilities, and attend to other public health measures, such as the elimination of privies, to create a healthful, disease-free environment.

A third movement that shaped planning involved the creation of parks commissions and the development of large-scale park systems as a reaction against urban development. Here the emphasis was on creating parks that offered opportunities for exercise and recreation, communing with nature, and contemplation of pastoral beauty. A democratic spirit underlay the establishment of the great public parks, like New York City's Central Park; these were to be the lungs of the city and could be enjoyed by all, not just the wealthy.[4]

Early planning also focused on imposing physical order on the urban community, particularly by eliminating slum housing, secondhand stores, taverns, pool parlors, and the like. Beginning in the second decade of the twentieth century, devices such as zoning were employed to control land use; later, in the 1950s and 1960s, urban renewal programs were created to clear and often rebuild large tracts of blighted areas in central cities. Early planners believed that these efforts—eliminating slums, ensuring homogeneous land use, and providing model tenements, broad streets, impressive civic structures, and large parks—would lead to social order and speed the assimilation of the waves of European immigrants into the mainstream of American life. The city they envisioned would offer the opportunity of a middle-class lifestyle for all.

## Forces shaping contemporary planning

At the outset of the twenty-first century, a different set of forces is shaping contemporary planning in an urban nation. These forces include citizen and state activism; a federal government whose involvement in planning, with a few exceptions, is on the decline; and an ongoing role by the U.S. Supreme Court.

### Citizen activism

Citizen activism at all levels of government has prompted planners to be more flexible and more sensitive to diverse interests. As urban areas have sprawled outward, citizens have

---

**Lakewood, Colorado, reaches out to the Hispanic community**

Although the Hispanic population along the eastern edge of Lakewood, Colorado (pop. 140,671), has been growing rapidly and currently exceeds 20 percent of the city's population, the proportion of Hispanics participating in community meetings and represented on city boards and commissions has been considerably less. To engage the Hispanic community in the planning process, provide its citizens with a solid understanding of community issues, and develop a dialogue between the city and its Hispanic citizens, Lakewood began the Citizen Planning Academy in 2003.

With funding by a grant from the Lutheran Medical Center Foundation, the academy sought to (1) educate members of the community and foster leadership development; and (2) open up the lines of communication, listen to concerns, identify how the city can best serve this growing segment of the community, and find ways for the Hispanic community to become more involved in city issues. In four 3 1/2-hour evening sessions conducted by staff members from the city's Strategic Planning Division, the academy focused on issues pertinent to planning and to Lakewood, including comprehensive planning, economic development, budget, and quality development. Rather than advocate particular solutions, the sessions challenged participants to think about planning from both a broad and a community-based perspective.

Source: Excerpted from "Cities, Towns Take Direct Routes to Citizens," *Colorado Municipalities* (April 2004), 12, available at icma .org/upload/library/2004-08/{061BEC1A-3238-49E0-A1B5-5F5388120520}.pdf (accessed October 28, 2006). Reprinted with permission of the Colorado Municipal League (c) 2004.

sometimes been reluctant to raise taxes to pay for the new infrastructure (roads, bridges, utility lines, parks, and schools) needed to support urban life. Fiscal retrenchment has forced a reconsideration of how to support the infrastructure, support systems, and services required by growth. At the same time, the transformation of the urban and rural landscape into "edge cities"—high-intensity nodes of office and commercial development in suburban and exurban areas—has often spelled the loss of a sense of community, that intangible mixture of shared experiences, activities, and values that bonds residents of an area together.

Lacking an ingrained sense of community, residents may feel alienated from local government or suspicious of its actions or motives. Furthermore, planners are no longer planning only for households that are largely middle-class and consist of two parents and their children (children being the principal conduit through which the traditional family participates in community life through schools and recreational and cultural activities). They now plan for households that consist of poor families, elderly couples, single parents and their children, childless couples, or groups of disabled persons.

Most local governments now have local civic associations or "good government groups" that monitor and participate in local planning decisions. At the regional or the state level, it is common to find nonprofit organizations that attempt to affect planning decisions concerning affordable housing, economic development, land use, and transportation.

**Figure 6-1 Participants in the planning process**

The best response to citizen activism is a planning process that promotes communication among city and county officials, community leaders, neighborhood representatives, and interested persons from the community at large in an effort to reach agreement on community goals and methods of achieving those goals.

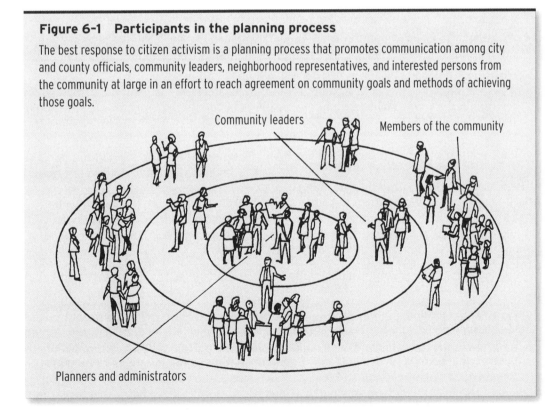

The response to civic activism has been a more open and inclusive planning process in many communities. Today, local plan preparation commonly includes broad-based efforts to involve citizens through visioning exercises, formulation and evaluation of development alternatives, charrettes, public meetings, flyers, and questionnaires to accompany required public hearings (see Figure 6–1). Specially appointed task forces to oversee plan making may supplement the work of the planning commission to give it a broader and deeper representation.

## State activism

A number of states—notably Florida, Maine, New Jersey, Oregon, Rhode Island, Tennessee, Vermont, Washington, and Wisconsin—have adopted programs that demonstrate a more active involvement with local planning and an attempt to manage growth. Among the approaches are the following:

- The infusion of local comprehensive planning with state goals based on the formal review and approval of local plans and regulations to determine whether the plans and regulations reflect those goals.

- An attempt to reduce the consumption of land and make development more compact. An important tool in this regard is urban growth areas, which establish minimum land use density and intensity levels, and ensure an adequate land supply and supporting infrastructure to meet expected growth for periods of up to twenty years. If urban growth areas are employed, the assumptions about how land is to be used, and at what densities and intensities, must be clearly stated and linked to economic and population forecasts.

- An attempt to ensure minimum governmental competence for local planning and land use controls through detailed state statutory and administrative requirements for—and periodic state review of—such plans and regulations.

- The creation of incentives (e.g., higher priorities awarded for state-administered grants) for complying with state goals, and the creation of state-funded programs for the preparation of comprehensive plans.[5]

## The role of the federal government

The federal government's influence on local planning is indirect; it has, in fact, been declining since the 1980s, when the government ceased to provide matching funds for local planning and the construction of wastewater treatment plants. Currently, the federal influence is mostly on funding for transportation planning, which is conducted in urban regions by metropolitan planning organizations (typically regional planning agencies or councils of government) or by state departments of transportation. The federal influence is also felt through the administration of the Community Development Block Grant program, which provides funds for public infrastructure, housing rehabilitation, economic development, fair housing administration, and related activities to benefit low- and moderate-income persons, eliminate slums and blight, and create jobs. And various federal programs support the cleanup and redevelopment of brownfields sites—lands that are, in varying degrees, environmentally contaminated.

Requirements for environmental impact statements and assessments prior to the undertaking of federally funded projects (such as highways), for the designation of sites for the

National Register of Historic Places (administered by the U.S. Department of the Interior), and for the federal protection of endangered species under the federal Endangered Species Act all intersect with local planning. Similarly, decisions to build or expand the federal government's own facilities, or phase them out (as with military bases), affect planning at the local level.

### Constitutional limitations and U.S. Supreme Court decisions

The U.S. Constitution places limitations on the scope of state and local authority. The U.S. Supreme Court upheld the general constitutionality of zoning in 1926,[6] while acknowledging in a 1928 case that zoning could be unconstitutional as applied to a specific piece of property.[7] Planning and land use regulation must comport with the requirements of the Fourteenth Amendment's due process clause, ensuring that procedures are fair and that the goals of planning and the means to accomplish those goals are reasonable, defined as whether the regulation promotes the health, safety, morals, and welfare of the community.[8] In the land use context, the Fourteenth Amendment's equal protection clause raises the question of whether the treatment of the landowner or affected party, when compared with the treatment of other landowners or affected parties, is fair. Courts resolve such disputes using different tests of judicial scrutiny that depend on the nature of the constitutional right being affected. Legislation that differentiates, for example, on the basis of race will be subject to the strictest scrutiny by the courts, and the government will carry a heavy burden to prove its case.[9]

> *Planning and land use regulation must comport with the requirements of the Fourteenth Amendment's due process clause, ensuring that procedures are fair and that the goals of planning and the means to accomplish those goals are reasonable.*

The Fifth Amendment applies to both the regulation and acquisition of private property. Under the Fifth Amendment, land use regulation must allow, with certain state-specific exceptions, reasonable economic use of land, and the Supreme Court has generally declined to second-guess legislative land use decisions. Where such decisions have been challenged on the grounds that they resulted in a temporary taking (one in which the landowner is deprived of use of the land for the temporary period in which the regulation is in effect), the Court has applied a balancing test that gauges the impact of the disputed land use control using a variety of factors, and the result has tended to favor local governments.[10] The Court has also given wide berth to local government use of the eminent domain power, upholding the use of this power in situations involving redevelopment and economic development.[11] Finally, as the First Amendment protects both free speech and religious activity, it may be implicated, for example, in cases involving sign regulation and the placement of news racks.[12]

### How communities plan

The authority for local governments to plan and regulate land use is delegated by state governments through enabling statutes or other mechanisms, such as statute constitutional amendments granting home rule power.

## The role of enabling legislation

Planning occurs through a variety of formal or relatively permanent legal structures, as well as through informal or temporary arrangements devised to solve a specific set of problems. These structures or arrangements exist to organize the work of planning; to fulfill legal requirements, such as the holding of public hearings on plans and development proposals; and to ensure citizen participation by providing people with opportunities to express their views on planning issues and influence the outcome of public policy decisions.

The formal legal structures are typically established through enabling legislation, a mechanism by which a state delegates its inherent police power authority, including the power to plan and to zone, to local government. Enabling legislation permits the local governments to do something, but in a certain way and through certain mechanisms. Sometimes, the local government will already have this power delegated directly to it through the state constitution (as in a municipal home rule provision) or through a statutory grant of power by the state legislature (also known as statutory or legislative home rule).

All states have planning and zoning enabling legislation. Such legislation will include definitions, a grant of authority, an organizational framework, a set of procedures, and often a set of duties that accompanies that delegation, as well as standards or criteria to guide plan making and land use administration. Municipal charters, which may have different procedures and institutional structures than state legislation, and are adopted under home rule authority or by action of the state legislature, will generally govern in lieu of state legislation. Some charters may simply require the municipality to follow the state statutes.

## Participants in the planning process

Planning typically engages a variety of formal participants apart from the general public. These participants include the planning commission, local elected officials, the chief administrative officer, the local planner, planning consultants, and the planning department.

---

**Pottawattamie County, Iowa, surveys residents on land use**

In 2003, residents of Pottawattamie County, Iowa (pop. 89,738), had the opportunity to use a survey to communicate their opinions on several county land issues to the county planning and zoning commission and the county board of supervisors. The county advertised the availability of the survey in newspapers and on its Web site, and the survey itself was available at county offices and in city clerks' offices in smaller communities, as well as on the county's Web site. Survey participants indicated their opinions on a range of land use issues, including housing developments, road improvements, and public facilities and services in rural areas. Because the survey was developed and tallied by a consulting firm as part of the firm's agreement with the county to help rewrite the county's land use plan, its costs mostly amounted to a few hundred dollars for advertising and mailing. The survey results were used to inform the county's rewriting of its land use plan.

***The planning commission***   The planning commission, the most common institutional structure for planning, was devised to represent a broad cross-section of community interests; interpret community values to professional planners; and act as a buffer between planners, local political interests, and the governing board. Composed of seven to nine members appointed by the chief elected official or legislative body, the planning commission advises the governing body on planning issues. Given strong leadership, planning commissions tend to work well in small to medium-sized communities (generally, those with populations of less than 75,000), particularly those where the commissioners have a good working relationship with elected officials.

***Elected officials***   The early twentieth-century government reform movement that gave rise to modern American city planning—along with the council-manager form of government and the civil service system—minimized the role of elected officials in planning. Elected officials, in theory, were to refer controversial issues to semiautonomous boards such as the planning commission for clear-headed, nonpartisan advice. Only the planning commission had the authority to undertake planning, adopt a plan, and, in many cities, employ a professional planning staff. Shut out of the planning process, elected officials often ignored the commission's advice.

Today elected officials, particularly in high-growth, environmentally aware communities, have begun to assert their right to a role in planning. Because they decide whether to adopt the policies, levy the taxes, and allocate the funds that help determine the community's future, their understanding and support are necessary if planning is not to become little more than an academic exercise. When elected officials have a role in formulating planning policies, they work harder to implement them. In some communities, one or two elected officials sit on the planning commission as representatives of the legislative body, breaking down the wall of formality that is sometimes erected between the two and strengthening the influence of practical politics on the advice of the commission.

***The chief administrative officer***   In many small communities without a staff planner, the chief administrative officer (CAO)—usually the county, city, or village administrator—is the de facto planning officer. As the individual in the position to command and direct the organization's resources, the CAO may facilitate the work of consultants and citizen task forces and may even administer development regulations. In any case, he or she must establish an atmosphere conducive to effective planning. Without the support of the CAO, planning will typically flounder and fail, regardless of the talents of all the people involved in the planning effort.

***The planner***   Many smaller communities employ a single planner, whose job is to prepare plans and studies, administer regulations, and staff boards and commissions. Today most planners have graduate or undergraduate degrees in city and regional planning from accredited planning programs. Others may be trained in architecture, landscape architecture, engineering, or related social sciences such as geography and urban studies. Many professional planners are members of the American Institute of Certified Planners (AICP), an affiliate of the American Planning Association that conducts testing and issues professional credentials. Planners certified by AICP have met requirements for education and experience, have passed a rigorous examination, and are subject to AICP's "Code of Ethics and Professional Conduct."

Although the attributes needed by a professional planner depend on the community for which the planner works, a planner should have a generalist's background and be technically competent. The modern planner, as the introduction to this chapter implies, must be able to function in a politically turbulent environment. Consequently, a nondogmatic personality, the ability to listen and accommodate, an appreciation for democracy (and its foibles), and sensitivity to a variety of diverse viewpoints are desirable traits.

*The planning consultant*   Although many communities have a full-time planner, many others find it more feasible to retain a private planning consultant whose services are confined to a specific assignment. A consultant can bring a new perspective or dimension to the local planning process.

The community should first formulate a clear concept of why it wants a consulting service. Typically, the community will distribute a request for proposals spelling out the tasks required and the product expected. When choosing a consultant, officials should carefully explore the credentials and experience of each candidate to ensure a good fit; a consultant should never be engaged solely on the basis of the least expensive bid. A regular reporting system should be established to keep the community aware of progress. The reporting system also helps put the community on notice that it must fulfill its commitments—reviewing work in a timely way, scheduling public meetings, providing necessary data, and paying the consultant—in order to benefit from the contract.

*The planning department*   In medium-sized and larger governments, planning is accomplished through a planning department staffed by professional planners, clerical personnel, drafters, graphic artists, computer specialists, and planning interns. Usually headed by a professionally trained planner, the planning department comes under the direction of the city or county administrator. Alternatively, the planning department may be a division of a larger department whose functions may include engineering and code enforcement; it may be part of the office of management and budget; or it may be included in the office of community and economic development. In some communities, planning will be separated from land use administration (permit processing), which may be combined with building and other code enforcement.

## Regional planning, especially for transportation

In some areas of the country, planning for an entire region, which may embrace a number of municipalities and counties, is conducted by a regional agency—for instance, a council of governments, an economic development district, or a special planning district. Sometimes special regional planning commissions composed of appointed representatives of municipalities and county governments are established to perform planning for more than one city and the unincorporated area of a county. This structure, which is particularly popular in Kentucky, Ohio, and Tennessee, is especially appropriate where there are a number of small communities that cannot afford the services of a full-time professional planning staff. Under this arrangement, the planning staff works for the regional planning commission, which assumes responsibility for planning for its member communities. The agency's activities are funded through assessments of member communities as well as through consulting fees and government grants.

In addition to undertaking regional planning, regional commissions also provide local planning assistance, serve as depositories for census and other important planning data, and undertake regional studies that can serve as important references for local planning efforts. They frequently prepare regional plans for specific functional areas, such as parks, sanitation, and economic development.

Transportation planning in the United States is a special case. As noted above, under federal law, states must design a metropolitan planning organization (MPO) for each region in order to receive funds for transportation projects in that region. The MPO is responsible for formulating a long-range transportation plan and a transportation improvement program—a short-range listing of projects that are to be supported with federal, state, and local monies. In some metropolitan areas, such as Boston and San Francisco, the MPO is separate from the regional planning agency; in others, such as Cleveland and Denver, the functions are combined.

## Advocacy planning: Nonprofit organizations in metropolitan areas

Advocacy planning, popularized by the late planner and attorney Paul Davidoff, envisions a style of planning in which a planner, representing a client's interests, presents "specific substantive solutions" to planning problems as alternatives to the official plans of government agencies.[13] Advocacy planning operates outside rather than inside government to influence its actions, although some planners may function as "guerrillas" within a local government bureaucracy to advocate alternative or unconventional and presumably progressive views not shared by the bureaucracy.

Many metropolitan areas have nonprofit groups that function in an advocacy role for better planning. For example, a local downtown business group that feels that the local planning department's work is unsatisfactory or that the department is unreceptive to its views might hire an outside firm to do a plan for the central business district. For the same reason, neighborhood and civic groups, developers and home builders, or low-income groups, believing that the government has not done enough for affordable housing, may develop their own plans. Davidoff argued that advocacy planning would improve the quality of official plans because of the competitive nature of the advocacy planning process.

## The instruments of planning

The basic documents for planning in cities and counties include the comprehensive plan, the zoning ordinance and map, the subdivision regulations, the official map, and the capital budget and capital improvements programs.

### The comprehensive plan

The comprehensive (or master) plan is a local government's statement of goals, objectives, and policies to guide public and private development within its planning jurisdiction. In order to reflect the changing times and values of a community, the comprehensive plan must be current. Thus, it should be modified and brought up-to-date on a regular basis, typically at five-year intervals, and it should be consulted as new public facility, zoning, and subdivision issues develop. The comprehensive plan is prepared under the supervision of the planning commission, which recommends action on it; it is then adopted by the legislative body, although this part of the process may vary depending on state legislation. Elements of a typical comprehensive plan are shown in the sidebar on page 140.

The first element in any plan should be an elaboration of the community's goals and objectives. These are usually developed through the visioning process, in which the members of the governing board, the planning commission, or both determine goals for the community for various future periods (five years, ten years, twenty years ahead) and develop strategies to achieve those goals. Goals and objectives should be based in part on information derived from various studies. Only after goals and objectives are established can planning move ahead.

### Elements of a comprehensive plan

An economic study that inventories the amount, type, intensity, and general location of commercial and industrial development, drawing on census and other public data. It usually examines the study area in the context of trends affecting the region in which the community is located, and it includes a projection of economic activity in terms of jobs.

A demographic study involving analysis of the population by age, education level, income, and employment characteristics that includes a forecast of population changes over the next ten to twenty years.

An assessment of the natural physical environment—geology, soils, climate, vegetation, ground and surface water—including the constraints the environment represents to development.

Planning goals, objectives, and policies, which sometimes take the form of a "vision statement"—the formal expression that depicts in words and images what the local government is striving to become and that serves as the starting point for the creation and implementation of the local comprehensive plan.

A land use element used in administering the zoning ordinance and in locating future major public and private facilities.

A transportation element that addresses the need for roads, bikeways, pedestrian facilities, mass transit, and aviation facilities. A component of this element is a major thoroughfare plan to be used in the review of subdivision plats and in preparation of street improvement programs. The plan contains standards for a hierarchy of streets (principal and minor arterials, collectors, local streets).

A community facilities element showing the need and potential locations for schools; parks and open spaces; libraries; municipal buildings; water, sewer, and other utility systems; and landfills.

A housing element that surveys the condition of the housing stock in the community and assesses the housing needs of persons residing or likely to reside there, particularly those of low and moderate income. A housing element may propose programs that ensure the availability of affordable housing and reduce barriers to it. The element may be a Comprehensive Housing Assistance Strategy (also known as the "Consolidated Plan"), a requirement for the receipt of federal Community Development Block Grant funds.

Other specific subplans or elements needed by the community, such as an economic development plan; a fiscal plan; a plan for the downtown area; a redevelopment plan; a plan to protect critical and sensitive areas such as aquifers, wetlands, or habitats; and a historic preservation plan.

An implementation framework identifying programs and projects to be carried out, their cost, and phasing.

The typical comprehensive plan includes projections of land uses—commercial, residential, industrial, and other categories—based on economic and population growth. The plan distributes these land uses to areas within the community, and these allocations are illustrated on a plan map, which shows the network of thoroughfares and all existing and proposed public facilities (see Figure 6–2 for an example of a future land use map). More complex plans may establish hierarchies of uses that gradually increase in size or intensity (e.g., neighborhood commercial versus regional shopping centers). Residential land uses may be shown in different densities (dwelling units per net acre). Industrial land uses may be subdivided into light industrial areas for research and warehousing and heavy industrial districts for manufacturing. Plans may also show agricultural preserves, which demarcate prime agricultural land and special resource protection areas such as wetlands.

## The zoning ordinance and map

The comprehensive plan is translated into regulation through the zoning map and ordinance. The map divides the community into use districts or zones (see Figure 6–3). The zoning ordinance regulates activities within these zones by controlling the type of use; building height; minimum lot area; front-, rear-, and side-yard setbacks; off-street parking; maximum lot coverage; landscaping; signage; and related considerations (see Figure 6–4).

---

### Best practices in online zoning ordinances

"The ultimate goal of an online ordinance is to answer questions from developers and citizens efficiently and easily–24 hours a day. An easily navigable ordinance is central to achieving these goals, but designers must first create a user-friendly way to get citizens from a community's homepage to the ordinance. ... Whatever the path, finding the code should be logical and intuitive, and site designers should strive for simplicity by shortening the number of clicks along the way....

"Well-designed codes should always use hyperlink cross-referencing, which makes the research process infinitely easier than using a bound paper copy...."

The following represent examples of current practices in online zoning ordinances:

Cumberland, Maryland (pop. 20,915)
ci.cumberland.md.us/dept/commdev/zoningtoc/zoningtoc.html
Simple and direct, easy to read and navigate.

Durham, North Carolina (pop. 204,845)
ci.durham.nc.us/departments/planning/zoneord/
An exemplary example of cross-referencing.

Portland, Oregon (pop. 533,427)
portlandonline.com/planning/index.cfm?c=31612
A well-designed pdf code.

Source: Excerpted from Barry Bain, "Putting the Zoning Ordinance Online: Why and How," *Zoning News* (August 2001), 1-3. Copyright (c) American Planning Association. Reprinted with permission.

**Figure 6-2  A future land use map from a comprehensive plan for Delaware, Ohio**

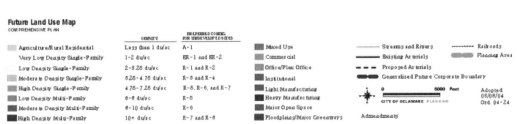

Source: City of Delaware, Ohio, delawareohio.net/assets/File/planning/compplan/compplandraft4/delcompplan11x17.pdf.

**Figure 6-3  Excerpt from a zoning map for Oxford, Ohio**

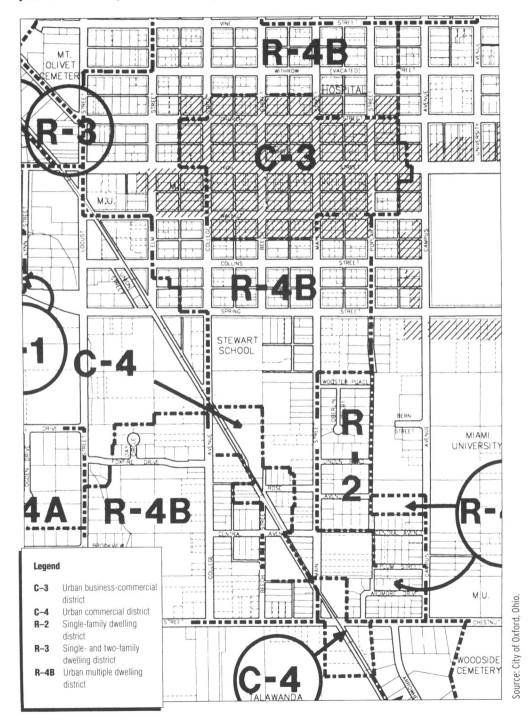

Legend

C–3  Urban business-commercial district
C–4  Urban commercial district
R–2  Single-family dwelling district
R–3  Single- and two-family dwelling district
R–4B  Urban multiple dwelling district

## Figure 6-4  Basic components of a zoning ordinance

| Section | Description | Examples |
|---|---|---|
| Zoning maps | Maps showing zoning district boundaries | Separate map book or pocket map |
| Definitions | Definitions of terms used throughout the zoning ordinance | "Dwelling unit," "structure," "lot," "yard" |
| General provisions | The operational rules and provisions applicable to the entire zoning ordinance | Title; purpose; authority; applicability of zoning ordinance; establishment of zoning districts; rules of interpretation |
| Zoning district regulations | All zoning district and overlay district regulations | Permitted and conditionally permitted uses in agricultural, residential, commercial, industrial, and floodplain overlay districts; parking |
| Special development standards | Specific development standards applicable to all uses and districts | Signs, nonconforming uses and structures, home occupations, recycling facilities, bed-and-breakfast inns |
| Administration and enforcement | Procedural requirements for all administrative and legislative reviews, appeals, enforcement, and penalties | Site plan review, architectural review, zoning ordinance amendments and rezonings, filings of appeals, enforcement and revocation of permits and penalties |

Source: Stuart Meck, Paul Wack, and Michelle J. Zimet, "Zoning and Subdivision Regulations," in *The Practice of Local Government Planning*, 3rd ed., ed. Charles J. Hoch, Linda C. Dalton, and Frank S. So (Washington, D.C.: ICMA, 2000), 349.

When a zoning change is requested, local government officials examine the comprehensive plan to determine whether the proposed change is consistent with the plan.

The comprehensive plan is prospective and general, providing guidance in establishing use districts and setting standards for those districts. In contrast, the zoning map and ordinance are current and specific, detailing the kinds of uses to which the property can be put in the present and the requirements that must be satisfied. Together, the map and ordinance constitute the law and can be changed only through legislative amendments.

### Map and text amendments

The zoning ordinance is amended in either of two ways. Changes in the boundaries or application of use districts are done through map amendments. For example, the establishment of a commercial district where there was a residential district would be a map amendment. Local governments also amend the ordinance through changes in the text. A text amendment would, for example, create a use district that would encourage the location of townhouses and establish standards and criteria for such uses. It would, however, take a map amendment or rezoning to actually designate land for townhouses at a specific location.

Petitions from property owners for site-specific modifications of the zoning regulations are typically referred to a local board of zoning appeals or adjustment—an administrative body usually composed of five persons (although in some communities, this function is handled by a zoning hearing examiner). Such bodies are authorized to grant variances—minor departures from the strict and literal interpretation of zoning regulations—for an individual property, and to hear disputes over the interpretation of the ordinance. Such variances are usually considered when enforcement of the zoning code would cause unnecessary hardship or practical difficulty. An example of a variance might be a reduction of a rear-yard setback requirement when a lot is pie-shaped and the stipulated requirement would leave insufficient depth. Each such request may need a special review to determine whether it would be compatible with the surrounding area, whether its impact can be accommodated, or whether the approving body wishes to impose conditions on the variance.

## Conditional uses

Conditional uses are uses that are only permitted in certain zoning districts upon application and upon a finding (usually by the planning commission or board of zoning appeals and sometimes by the legislative body) that certain criteria are met. (A public hearing with public notice is also required before findings can be made.) For example, electric utility substations and drive-in restaurants are often approved through conditional use permits. The local government may impose additional reasonable requirements, such as landscaping to ensure compatibility with the surrounding area. In contrast with a variance, which is a relaxation of a specific development standard, such as a setback or parking requirement, a conditional use deals with the approval of the entire use and, typically, a site plan for the use.

## Planned unit developments

A planned unit development (PUD) ordinance is another technique for altering the application of the zoning ordinance to a large tract of land under development. PUD regulations may permit relaxation of the zoning standards for a district, allow mixed uses (single- and multifamily housing, residential and commercial development), and provide flexibility in the placement of buildings in exchange for the preparation of an overall plan for the property. Under a PUD, the approved plan establishes standards for the uses of the property and the location of the uses on the site. A PUD can improve site design, preserve amenities such as open space through clustering of buildings, and lower street and utility costs through reduced frontages.

## Incentive zoning

Incentive zoning is a technique that has received renewed attention as communities aim to inculcate smart growth principles into planning and development processes. In this system, specific incentives or bonuses are granted to a developer on condition that certain physical, social, or cultural benefits or amenities will be provided to the community. One such bonus might be a waiver of specific regulatory requirements or fees, such as parking standards or

### Code reform in Milwaukee, Wisconsin

In light of concerns about deteriorating downtowns, developer complaints, and other growth issues, many local governments are taking a new look at their codes. Code reform can be quite a challenge, however. For example, in Milwaukee, Wisconsin (pop. 578,887), the zoning code originally enacted in 1920 had been modified so frequently that it became poorly organized and difficult to decipher. The code caused unnecessary nonconformities, discouraged investment, and effectively took large numbers of properties out of the market. Approximately 700 to 800 cases went to the board of zoning appeals every year, the average review took about twenty-eight weeks, and the planning department heard complaints not just from developers but also from neighborhood residents who felt that the code was not adequately protecting community character.

Updating the zoning code took more than four years. All changes proposed had to meet at least one of three rules: make the code easier to understand and use, cause fewer cases to go to the board of appeals, and clearly result in enhanced protection of a neighborhood's character. Specific actions to implement these principles included

- Using illustrations and tables where none previously had been used

- Shrinking the code from twenty-five to ten sections

- Creating a computerized, online ordinance, with links to a geographic information system (GIS) map to identify each parcel

- Writing design standards where none existed before

- Making parking requirements easier to meet

- Setting signage standards.

Source: Dan Emerine, "Smart Growth and Code Reform" (Washington, D.C.: ICMA, 2005), 3-4, at icma.org/main/ld.asp?ldid=19341& hsid=1&tpid=8.

impact fees, as an incentive for a developer to provide various amenities. Typically, however, a bonus is provided in the form of added permissible density to a development project to encourage, for example, the construction of affordable, housing, the construction of public plazas, or the donation of open space on the site. Added permissible density is provided by increasing the allowable floor area of a project above what is permitted in the zoning ordinance, or by increasing the allowable number of dwelling units in a residential development by reducing the minimum lot area per dwelling unit. Additionally, setback, height, and bulk standards are relaxed to accommodate the added density or, in the case of affordable housing, to reduce development costs. When incentive zoning is used to encourage more affordable housing, it may also be termed "inclusionary zoning."

## Form-based zoning

Some communities have been experimenting with form-based zoning, also known as form-based codes, as an alternative to conventional zoning ordinances. Form-based zoning operates on the theory that design controls can resolve many conflicts between land uses. The emphasis is on highly prescriptive zones regulating building type and orientation, but with the determination of use largely left to the building owner or occupant. In a form-based ordinance, the design controls include window and door treatments, building envelope standards, building frontage requirements, façade coverage, and façade element design. Form-based zoning regulations apply these elements to differentiate districts by building form and building-street relationships. A limitation of form-based zoning, however, is that it tends to minimize very real differences between types of uses—for example, the more intensive use of a building for medical offices versus the less intensive use of a building for insurance offices. Consequently, most form-based ordinances are a hybrid of design controls and use regulations.[14]

## Subdivision regulations and review

All states have laws that require that whenever the owner of a tract of land within a city or county divides that land into two or more parts in order to create additional lots for sale or lease—and when the development will involve the creation and dedication of streets, alleys, and other improvements to public use—the owner must prepare a subdivision plat. This plat, or plan of the division of land, must be reviewed, approved, and filed in accordance with the procedures established by state law and local regulations. This is typically a two-part process: first, a preliminary plan is drawn up in which the general concept of the subdivision is approved; next, a final engineered plat is produced, ready for recording as a legal document. In situations where only a few lots are created and where no new streets are dedicated, an abbreviated procedure, called a lot split or a minor subdivision, is employed.

Subdivision design should be consistent with general land use and thoroughfare plans (see discussion of the official map in the next section). Major roads proposed in the thoroughfare plan should be reflected in the plat, and local streets should be integrated with the major street system. The plat design should ensure adequate water, sewer, and stormwater facilities, as well as lot configurations that provide well-drained, buildable sites. Once constructed, the street pattern, lot design, and public facilities are relatively permanent. Even more than the restrictions imposed by the zoning ordinance, these elements determine the land use pattern and shape the character of an entire area.

> *Subdivision design should be consistent with general land use and thoroughfare plans.*

Each community should have an ordinance containing regulations governing subdivisions. In such an ordinance, the community sets its standards for site design; for streets, sidewalks, utilities, and storm drainage; and for payments by the developer to help provide schools, parks, arterial streets, and other needed services (see discussion of impact fees in the section on "Growth Management," pages 149–150).

The community's planning and engineering staffs should ensure compliance with the subdivision standards. This can be done by conducting site visits while the preliminary and final subdivision plats are being reviewed and approved, and holding inspections while streets, utility lines, and other features of the new development are being constructed. Local governments usually require the posting of a performance bond to ensure that required improvements are constructed, and of a maintenance bond to ensure that the improvements hold up through at least one year of use.[15]

## Official map

The official map is a plat of an area that has been adopted by the local legislative body. Implementing the general recommendations of the major thoroughfare plan, it gives precise locations for existing and planned streets and may also show sites for other public facilities. The official map reserves an area for streets but does not actually open a street or result in the taking of property for a street.

Some official maps are quite detailed, showing a full hierarchy of streets, public drainage basins, proposed future park sites, and related improvements. Others may show only major streets. The official map may control the location of streets in new subdivisions, show street locations and existing or prospective street widths, and fix the point from which front-yard setbacks for new buildings are to be measured, relating them to the zoning ordinance.

In a number of states, a proposed subdivision must be disapproved if it does not comply with the official map. Some statutes or local ordinances provide that no building permit may be issued for a building or structure that is intended for land set aside on an official map for a street. The official map is not, however, as widely used as zoning or subdivision regulations; this is in part because not all states authorize it and because of the technical and political difficulty in designating the specific location of public improvements well in advance.

## The capital budget and the capital improvement program

Plans for acquiring new public facilities described in the comprehensive plan are made in the capital improvement program (CIP). The CIP is a five- to six-year schedule of capital projects. Included are major, nonrecurring expenditures for municipal buildings, civic centers, fire stations, parks, playgrounds, street construction or reconstruction, sewage plants, waterlines, and swimming pools. Costs associated with such improvements include architectural and engineering fees and expenditures for land acquisition, construction, and related furnishings and equipment.

Each year, the planning department (or sometimes the public works department) prepares a new CIP. Often working with the finance director and the chief executive, planners request proposals from all operating departments, evaluate the proposals, determine the government's ability to pay for new projects, and then organize the projects into a schedule. The local planning commission may review the CIP and forward its recommendations to the governing body. If the governing body approves the plan for the first year of the CIP, the plan is adopted as the capital budget for the forthcoming fiscal year, along with the annual operating budget. Public hearings may be part of the CIP process as well.

## Relationship of regulations and projects to the comprehensive plan

Some states have very specific standards that require local governments to approve rezonings and other development proposals, zoning text changes (e.g., changes in use, density, and intensity), subdivisions, and capital projects only if these decisions carry out or are consistent with written and mapped policies in the comprehensive plan. Other states are less rigorous with respect to the relationship between these decisions and the comprehensive plan. However, if a development decision is challenged in court, the nature of that relationship will certainly be at issue. Consequently, when a local government does make a development decision, it should examine the plan and determine how that decision relates to it. It is also important that the plan be kept up-to-date so that it accurately reflects current trends and development issues in the community.

## Current issues

A number of issues continue to shape the practice of planning in cities and counties. Several of these issues are summarized here.

### The environmental movement

Beginning in the early 1970s, the federal and state governments passed new laws protecting water, land, and air. The environmental movement affected local planning as well, bringing increased recognition of the interrelated impacts of development decisions on air, water, land, and flora and fauna. The impact of the environmental movement has meant that land is now valued as a *resource*—part of a complex ecosystem—as well as a *commodity*.

As a consequence of environmentalism, plan making routinely takes into account the resource dimension of land use and the limitations of certain types of land for development. Modern plans identify the location and extent of wetlands, natural habitats, aquifers, prime farmland, and areas presenting natural hazards such as earthquakes, landslides, and flooding. Geographic information systems are used to map and assess such areas in order to formulate regulatory programs.

### Growth management

Growth management efforts began in communities that were experiencing rapid rates of growth, particularly in residential development. Feeling themselves overwhelmed by the pace of change and believing that their infrastructure would be overtaxed unless proactive steps were taken, these communities began to devise land use and public facilities systems that controlled not only the type and location of development, but also the rate at which development could occur.

A number of techniques are used to manage growth. One such technique is an adequate *public facilities ordinance*, a type of land development regulation that ties or conditions development approvals to the availability and adequacy of public facilities. The purpose is to ensure that the local government's public facilities have sufficient available capacity to serve development at a predetermined level of service (LOS). A development is determined to be in compliance with the ordinance if its impacts do not exceed the ability of public facilities to accommodate them at the specified LOS. If the proposed development cannot be supported by the existing system at the required service level, the developer must either install or pay for the required infrastructure improvements until the local government provides the needed public facilities. In some parts of the country, such as Florida, such ordinances are called "concurrency management ordinances" because they require public facilities concurrent with a development's impact.

Another technique, as used in such communities as Petaluma, California, is a *building permit allocation system*, in which only a certain number of building permits are awarded

---

### Cooperative Web site in Washington State

Eight municipalities and one county government in the state of Washington have joined to produce and support a cooperative Web site called MyBuildingPermit.com. The cities of Bellevue, Bothell, Issaquah, Kenmore, Kirkland, Mercer Island, Sammamish, and Snoqualmie (all located on or close to the eastern shore of Puget Sound, across from Seattle) and Snohomish County allow permit applicants to log on to a central site to apply for, pay for, and receive electrical, low voltage, mechanical, plumbing, and reroofing permits from each of the jurisdictions. The site also provides permit research, tracking of permit application status, inspection checklists, construction tip sheets, links to building resources and contacts, and schedules of upcoming events and seminars.

Source: L. Edward Purcell, "Streamlining Development and Building Permitting," *IQ Report* no. 2 (2005), 10.

---

in a city in a given year. This number depends on the local government's ability to accommodate new development and on trends in the regional land market.

A third growth management technique is a *development impact fee*, which is defined as any fee or charge assessed by the local government upon or against new development or its owners in order to recover whatever local government expenditures have been necessitated by the new development. A development impact fee is typically used for transportation, parks and recreation, or utility improvements. Before enacting such a fee, the local government must conduct a study that shows how the fee relates to the cost of meeting the needs created by new development, and it must periodically revisit and evaluate the fee to ensure that it is sufficient. Once the fee is collected, the local government must spend it on the public improvements needed by the new development, which are scheduled through the CIP.

A related growth management technique is a *transfer of development rights* (TDR) program, in which a landowner agrees to yield of some or all of the right to develop or use a parcel of land in exchange for the right to develop or use another parcel of land, or another portion of the same parcel of land, more intensively. In TDR programs, a local government or regional organization that wishes to preserve land in an undeveloped or less developed condition may do so without payment of cash compensation if it is willing to accept higher densities or more intensive uses elsewhere. TDR is used, for example, to preserve environmentally sensitive land or historic buildings by removing the pressure to develop the property. A persistent problem in TDR programs is deciding where the transferred development rights are to be located. Alternately, a local government or nonprofit organization may decide to use a purchase of development rights, in which the property owner permanently gives up these rights for money, regardless of what local land use restrictions say about use, density, or intensity.

## Smart growth

In the mid to late 1990s, the "smart growth" movement emerged as a reaction to what many believed were undesirable features of contemporary urban development. These features included unlimited outward and leapfrog expansion of low-density development; conversion of open space and environmentally sensitive lands; lack of choice among

**Smart growth for schools in Littleton, New Hampshire**

Smart growth advocates argue that the location of schools is an important driver of community development. To preserve the role of its in-town high school as a town focal point, the small town of Littleton, New Hampshire (pop. 6,139), decided to renovate the school instead of building in a new location. As a result, many students can still walk to school, and the school can continue to use nearby civic amenities, including athletic fields and parks. The decision was part of a larger effort to recruit businesses and employees to the town and coincided with other substantial investment in the downtown.

Source: Council of Educational Facility Planners International and U.S. Environmental Protection Agency, *Schools for Successful Communities: An Element of Smart Growth* (Scottsdale, Ariz.: Council of Educational Facility Planners International, September 2004), 38-39, at epa.gov/smartgrowth/pdf/SmartGrowth_schools_Pub.pdf.

housing types and neighborhood configurations; worsening traffic congestion and air pollution caused by a more intensive use of automobiles for ground travel; segregation of land uses rather than a mixture of uses that would reduce the need for transit by unifying trip purposes and encouraging pedestrian travel; costly requirements to expand infrastructure rather than repairing infrastructure already in place; and failure to redevelop older existing neighborhoods.

The smart growth movement—a loosely affiliated group of environmentalists, planners, architects, governmental and nongovernmental officials, and real estate developers—has pushed for planning and land development that incorporate principles of action to reverse these unwanted trends. The principles, as stated by land economist Anthony Downs, include the following:

- Limiting outward extension of new development in order to make settlements more compact and to preserve open spaces. One device to address this problem is an urban growth area, which restricts the outward expansion of cities while establishing minimum density and intensity standards to which new development must conform.

- Providing for more mixed uses and pedestrian-friendly layouts both to minimize the use of cars on short trips and to increase walking and thereby promote physical activity and better health.

- Loading the public costs of new development onto its consumers via impact fees, rather than having those costs paid by the community in general.

- Emphasizing public transit to reduce the use of private vehicles.

- Revitalizing older neighborhoods.

- Creating more affordable housing.

- Streamlining development project approvals.[16]

## New urbanism

Related to smart growth is new urbanism, championed by the Chicago-based Congress for the New Urbanism, which embraces many of the same ideas as smart growth but also seeks to incorporate early American town forms and urban design themes into what is termed *traditional neighborhood development* (TND). Urban design features found in TNDs include front porches, rear alleys, grid streets, zero lot lines, ground-level retail areas, and town squares. Dominant influences in particular are buildings that are brought forward on the site and have a vertical rather than horizontal orientation, and the street grid and town squares, which often serve as an axial organizing element. The street grid allows multiple paths through the development, reducing congestion by distributing vehicular traffic and providing opportunities for increased pedestrian contact.

## Affordable housing and exclusionary zoning practices

In many communities, finding affordable housing for either rent or purchase has become harder. Increased development costs, scarcity of properly zoned land, high costs of borrowing, and requirements for adequate supporting community facilities have all contributed to a slow-to-expand housing supply and the shrinking availability of affordable housing. (This topic is treated in depth in Chapter 8, "Community Development.")

Exclusionary zoning is a common problem in some parts of the country. It may be motivated by a desire to exclude people of certain races, religions, ethnicities, or low- and moderate-income groups; a desire to maintain a certain type of community character (rural, or upper-income estate residential); fiscal objectives (allowing only land uses that "pay for themselves"); or some combination of motives. However, the illegitimate motives (those that focus on race, religion, income, or ethnicity) are usually masked behind the more polite variety.

The practice of exclusionary zoning is enforced through requirements that make the construction of affordable housing difficult if not impossible to achieve—either by prohibiting it or by imposing additional regulatory costs that are unjustified by conventional health or safety criteria. Exclusionary techniques include requiring extraordinarily large lot sizes (one- to five-acre minimums) or large lot widths (escalating the cost of streets and water and sewer extensions); prohibiting multifamily dwellings and mobile homes; limiting the number of bedrooms in apartments (to restrict the size of families with children); and refusing to zone adequate land for higher-density single- and multifamily housing.

Tactics to dislodge exclusionary zoning include litigation by developers and by low- and moderate-income advocacy groups, state overrides of local zoning decisions (see below), state mandates for local housing planning, and state requirements to ensure a balance between land available for jobs and land available for housing. Another technique, used chiefly in Oregon, is for the state or regional planning agency to establish minimum, rather than maximum, densities and to require local governments to set aside a minimum of twenty years' supply of buildable land—land that is provided with urban services and no environmental constraints.

A number of states, such as California, Florida, and New Jersey, now require local comprehensive plans to address the long-range need for housing for existing and prospective residents of a community and particularly for low- and moderate-income persons. In 1985, New Jersey established the Council on Affordable Housing (COAH), whose responsibility is to oversee housing planning for the entire state. COAH set numerical goals for the rehabilitation (for the year 2000) and new unit construction (1987–1999) for low- and moderate-income housing; these initial obligations were still in effect as of 2004. In addition, as a result of rules adopted in 2004, municipalities must now plan for affordable housing using a "growth share" calculation, which represents one affordable dwelling unit for every eight market-rate units built, and one affordable unit for every twenty-five jobs created, as measured by the square feet for new or expanded nonresidential construction for the period 2000–2014. Together these three components constitute the municipal affordable housing obligation in New Jersey. Municipalities are expected to take reasonable steps to ensure that land is available for the construction of the number of low- and moderate-income units proposed under a state-approved housing plan that satisfies these goals.

Massachusetts enacted a state statute in 1969 that established a streamlined procedure for developers of state or federally subsidized housing to obtain a single development permit from a local zoning board of appeals (ZBA). The comprehensive permit is in lieu of a separate application to various local boards. Applicants may appeal a ZBA decision to the state-level three-member housing appeals committee, which may reverse denials of comprehensive permits, or may modify or reject conditions imposed that make an affordable housing project economically infeasible. Local governments whose affordable housing stock exceeds 10 percent of the housing in the municipality are immune from appeals. Similar laws are in effect in Connecticut, Illinois, and Rhode Island. Some communities, such as Sacramento, California; eastern portions of King County (Seattle), Washington; Columbus/Franklin County, Ohio; and Montgomery County (Dayton), Ohio, have established housing trust funds that provide various types of subsidies to affordable housing projects.[17]

Using linkage fees, some communities are requiring developers of market-rate housing and office, industrial, and commercial space to contribute funds to build or help rehabilitate affordable housing. Another technique is permit streamlining, in which bona fide affordable housing projects are placed on a fast track for permit approvals, or development approval procedures are simplified to shorten approval times for all types of projects.

## Conclusion

Planning in the future will bear little resemblance to planning during the last half of the twentieth century. The focus will no longer be simply on conventional land use, the desire to promote growth, and attempts to accommodate the automobile. Instead, planning will face a whole new set of challenges: it will need to

- Seek land use patterns that reinforce a sense of community through greater attention to design
- Be concerned with the adequacy and availability of housing for all income groups
- Be sensitive to environmental as well as economic concerns
- Focus on managing growth in order to achieve diverse community goals more effectively.

The processes of planning will also change. As citizens become more active and involved in government, they will target the planning process for special attention, seeking proactively to shape community goals and development strategies. Planners will have to become more sensitive to citizen activists, whether those citizens want to change land use patterns or simply complain about their neighbor's building code violations.

The planners of the future, more than ever before, will have to be good listeners, good communicators, and good at the political task of building community consensus. Planners must come to realize that citizen involvement—whether through public hearings, participation on special task forces, or advocacy planning—often leads to better plans and plan implementation. Community plans are improved by the debate that accompanies the clash of widely diverse views about community goals and how to achieve them. At the same time, planners themselves must actively ensure that planning leads to a more just and equitable society, one in which all members, not just those who are skilled at the tactics of citizen advocacy, have an opportunity to participate in the good life that is the promise of America.

---

**Questions to ask if you manage a small community**

At what rate is the community growing?

Have members of the planning commission and board of zoning appeals received training?

When was the last time the comprehensive plan, zoning ordinance, and subdivision regulations were revisited and updated?

Is there a professional staff? What is their workload?

Does the community regularly prepare a capital budget and capital improvement program?

Does the housing mix reflect the needs of the larger region surrounding the community? Is there a mix of housing types, for-sale and rental units, and affordable housing?

Does the community have any environmentally sensitive land or land subject to natural hazards?

Is there good communication between the legislative body, the planning commission, and the board of zoning appeals?

---

**Sources of help**

Even though it draws its values and aspirations about current and emerging community issues from the general public, planning is not a job for amateurs. Citizens, local government administrators, and even professional planners often need outside help. Important sources of planning assistance for cities and counties include

- Regional planning commissions, councils of governments, and state agencies with community assistance programs

- Statewide associations of cities and counties

- State universities with community assistance or governmental services centers (which are often linked to graduate and undergraduate programs in public administration or in city and regional planning)

- National professional groups, such as ICMA and the American Planning Association (including its state chapters), and advocacy groups, such as the Congress for the New Urbanism.

# Endnotes

1 The above discussion is abstracted from Elizabeth Hollander et al., "General Development Plans," in *The Practice of Local Government Planning*, 2nd ed., ed. Frank S. So and Judith Getzels (Washington, D.C.: International City/County Management Association, 1988), 70–71.

2 Stuart Meck, gen. ed., *Growing Smart Legislative Guidebook: Model Statutes for Planning and the Management of Change*, 2002 ed. (Chicago: American Planning Association, January 2002), 7-6 to 7-7.

3 See, generally, Laurence Conway Gerckens, "Historical Development of American City Planning," in *The Practice of Local Government Planning* (see note 1), 20–59.

4 Jon A. Peterson, *The Birth of City Planning in the United States: 1840–1917* (Baltimore, Md.: Johns Hopkins University Press, 2003).

5 The above discussion is abstracted from Stuart Meck, "Notes on Planning Statute Reform: Guideposts for the Road Ahead," in *Planning Reform in the New Century*, ed. Daniel R. Mandelker (Chicago: Planners Press, 2005), 40–41.

6 *Village of Euclid v. Ambler Realty Co.*, 272 U.S. 365 (1926).

7 *Nectow v. City of Cambridge*, 277 U.S. 183 (1928).

8 Daniel R. Mandelker, *Land Use Law*, 5th ed. (Newark, N.J.: Lexis/Nexis, 2003), §§ 2.39–2.41.

9 *Id.*, §§ 2.44–2.45.

10 *Penn. Cent. Transp. Co. v. City of New York*, 438 U.S. 104 (1978), *rehearing denied* 439 U.S. 883 (1978) (balancing test to be applied in evaluating regulatory takings claims); compare with *Lucas v. South Carolina Coastal Council*, 5005 U.S. 1003 (1982) (per se taking where regulations completely deprive an owner of all economically beneficial use of property); and *Loretto v. Teleprompter Manhattan CATV Corp.*, 458 U.S. 419 (1982) (per se taking where government requires an owner to suffer a permanent physical invasion of her property). See the discussion of these cases in *Lingle v. Chevron*, 125 S.Ct. 2074 (2005) (holding that the formula inquiring whether government regulation of private property "substantially advances" legitimate state interests prescribes inquiry into the nature of due process and is not an appropriate test for determining whether the regulation results in a Fifth Amendment taking).

11 *Berman v. Parker*, 348 U.S. 26 (1954); *Kelo v. City of New London*, 125 S.Ct. 2655 (2005).

12 *Metromedia, Inc. v. City of San Diego*, 453 U.S. 490 (1981); *Members of City Council v. Taxpayers for Vincent*, 466 U.S. 789 (1984); *Lakewood v. Plain Dealer Publishing, Inc.*, 486 U.S. 750 (1988).

13 Paul Davidoff, "Advocacy and Pluralism in Planning," in *A Reader in Planning Theory*, ed. Andreas Faludi (Oxford, England: Pergamon, 1973), 283.

14 Joel Russell, "Putting New Urbanism to Work," in Congress for the New Urbanism, *Codifying New Urbanism: How to Reform Municipal Land Development Regulations*, Planning Advisory Service Report No. 526 (Chicago: American Planning Association, 2004), 36; S. Mark White, "Classifying and Defining Uses and Building Forms: Land-Use Coding for Zoning Regulations," *Zoning Practice* (September 2005), 2.

15 The above discussion is abstracted from Stuart Meck, "Subdivision Control: A Primer for Planning Commissioners," *The Commissioner* (Fall 1996/Winter 1997), 4–6.

16 This discussion is abstracted from Anthony Downs, "Smart Growth: Why We Discuss It More Than We Do It," *Journal of the American Planning Association* 71, no. 4 (Autumn 2005): 368.

17 Stuart Meck, Rebecca Retzlaff, and James Schwab, *Regional Approaches to Affordable Housing*, Planning Advisory Report No. 513/514 (Chicago: American Planning Association, 2003), chaps. 4–6.

# 7

# Economic Development

## Donald T. Iannone

Local governments are major players in economic development. Many cities, towns, villages, boroughs, and counties across America offer economic development services and financial assistance (including business incentives) that help local businesses and spur job development. A number of jurisdictions also partner with and provide funding and leadership to private sector economic development groups serving businesses and citizens within their boundaries.[1]

This chapter first provides an overview of economic development and explains its importance to local government. It then describes the major goals, policies, strategies, and programs of economic development. Finally, it offers practical advice on how local government managers can plan, introduce, and manage successful economic development programs and initiatives.

## Key concerns for local government

Economic development is a critically important issue for local governments in communities of all sizes in both urban and rural areas for three reasons:

1. Community residents need high-quality jobs and the incomes that go with them to support themselves and their families.

2. The health of local economies significantly affects local government operations in various ways, not the least of which is the ability to generate local tax revenues to pay for local services.

3. Businesses, as important economic resources in communities, need help from local governments, chambers of commerce, private development groups, workforce training organizations, educational institutions, and other resource groups to remain competitive in today's fast-changing economy.

In short, economic development is an essential requirement in building high-quality communities where citizens live, work, and play. Communities cannot grow without a sound economic foundation. By playing a role in economic development, local government officials help to secure this foundation.

**Local government's role in economic development**

**Developing opportunities:** Local governments work in partnership with other groups to develop new businesses, create jobs, and generate incomes and tax revenues.

**Informing and advocating:** Local governments work to inform local citizens and businesses about opportunities and strategies to advance themselves financially and economically. In addition, local government officials may at times play an advocacy role in advancing economic development interests within the local community. Without advocacy, economic development can get lost among the multitude of community priorities.

**Protecting against threats:** Local governments work to protect the public interest against harmful side effects of major business and economic changes, such as business closings and corporate and industry restructuring.

## The local government role

The local government's role in economic development is to positively motivate private individuals and businesses to develop economic opportunities that are consistent with a community's character and values. In attempting to contribute to economic development, local governments should avoid usurping the role of the private marketplace or undertaking actions that discourage meaningful private economic initiatives. At the same time, when necessary, they must be ready to prevent private economic initiatives that are harmful to the larger public interest—for example, business activities that degrade the natural environment and pose a threat to public health.

Local government managers are often confronted with tough choices about whether and how to act with regard to economic development projects. While analytic tools such as cost-benefit analysis and scenario planning can help inform and support local decision making, there are no simple templates that managers can use to extract the right answers for any given situation. Experience, sound judgment, adherence to preestablished guiding principles, and willingness to work toward a community consensus concerning economic development priorities are all necessary if managers are to make the right decision about their local government's role in the economic development arena.

Local government managers must be prepared to use all available information to make the best economic decisions for the overall good of their communities. Planning and research are vital to this effort. For example, in large as well as small cities, it is not unusual for the business community and other groups to pressure the manager to help fund public facilities to house convention, tourism, entertainment, or sporting events. However, a 2005 Brookings Institution report warns that the convention center business, while an attractive economic target for many cities, is highly competitive, is peaking from a growth standpoint, and could be headed toward a "shakeout" with too many centers chasing too little business.[2] This is a case in which the local government manager must be ready to look beyond an overly optimistic economic impact study, which may be riddled with erroneous assumptions about future demand, and instead project alternative growth paths for the local convention industry.[3]

## Coordination and collaboration

Recognizing the importance of economic development, many local governments have stepped up their efforts to coordinate and collaborate with private sector organizations and other public sector partners. Coordination is important to avoid unnecessary duplication of effort: given serious fiscal constraints, local governments cannot afford to waste their resources on superfluous activities. Collaboration with other economic groups is needed to better focus their economic development activities on meeting the growing competition for businesses and jobs, and on ensuring that development occurs in a way that is consistent with community values and resources.

Strategic economic development collaborations among local governments are growing in number, occurring on various levels, and involving numerous stakeholders. Most of these collaborative activities take one of five forms:[4]

- Interdepartmental cooperation within a local government (e.g., departments of economic development, community development, planning, finance, public works, and other units working together)
- City-county government collaboration (within a single county)
- Local government–private sector collaboration
- Collaboration among the local government, the private sector, and local schools
- Collaboration among local governments on regional (i.e., across several counties) economic development initiatives.

These collaborations usually focus on

- Existing business retention and expansion
- New business recruitment
- New business formation and entrepreneurship
- Tourism and travel development (including convention center activities)
- Marketing and promotion
- Workforce development
- Economic development incentives
- Downtown development/revitalization
- Large-scale real estate development projects.[5]

Local governmental entities also collaborate on industry cluster development, international trade development, technological innovation, educational reform and development, retention and attraction of young talent, and the linkage of economic development with arts and culture.

Two types of coordination and collaboration are especially important to local economic development: public-private partnerships, and regional cooperation.

***Public-private partnerships***   Many city and county government entities work in partnership with the business sector and educational institutions in their communities to promote and assist economic development. For example, well over a third of local governments surveyed in 2004 reported that public-private partnerships helped develop local economic development strategies.[6]

***Regional cooperation*** It is important that communities work with their regional economic development partners. Technically speaking, regions are the real economies in which local communities exist. Communities have economic bases, which are functioning parts of the intricate regional economy that surrounds and supports them. In recognition of this reality, an increasing number of regional economic development organizations have been created across the country. The Charlotte Regional Partnership (CRP), for example, represents sixteen counties in both North Carolina and South Carolina. Funded jointly by

## Partnerships

### The Fort Wayne–Allen County Economic Development Alliance

Realizing that their economic and community futures are closely intertwined, the city of Fort Wayne (pop. 223,341) and Allen County (pop. 344,006), Indiana, have undertaken a joint comprehensive plan that focuses a great deal of attention on economic development issues. The Fort Wayne–Allen County Economic Development Alliance (theallianceonline.com) receives funding from the city of Fort Wayne and from Allen County, along with the private sector. Both entities recognize that a shared plan will result in coordinated investments in infrastructure and other public services that are vital foundations for future economic growth. For more information about this joint city-county planning process, go to the Allen County-Fort Wayne Comprehensive Planning Web site at planyourcommunity.org.

### The Chain of Lakes Downtown Economic Enhancement Study in Michigan

The villages of Bellaire (pop. 1,146), Central Lake (pop. 988), and Ellsworth (pop. 466) and the city of East Jordan (pop. 2,338) in Michigan could not qualify for a community development block grant from the Michigan Economic Development Corporation as single jurisdictions. As a group, however, they succeeded in obtaining a $36,000 grant. Each community contributed an additional $5,000, and a consultant developed the Chain of Lakes Downtown Economic Enhancement Study. The study report provides suggestions for each community and for the region as a whole. The communities have begun implementing the suggestions, which include transportation improvements and joint sponsorship of events that will attract tourists.

### The Southwest California Economic Alliance

The cities of Lake Elsinore (pop. 40,985), Murrieta (pop. 92,993), and Temecula (pop. 93,923), California, have teamed up with Riverside County (pop. 1,953,330) to form the Southwest California Economic Alliance, which strives to generate interest among nonretail businesses all over the world in locating in the region. The cities pay annual fees of $25,000–$75,000, depending on their populations, and the county provides staff and office space. The alliance's $150,000 annual budget is spent on Web site development, marketing, and attendance at trade shows; the Web site provides extensive data, for free, to businesses that are interested in locating in the region. For example, businesses can pull up details on properties available within a certain zip code, as well as data on surrounding markets. Several businesses have relocated to the area, benefiting all the partners by providing jobs in the region. A job-hosting Web site was developed to increase the number of area jobs held by local residents.

Note: All populations shown are California Department of Finance estimates as of January 1, 2006.

---

### Economic development and the arts

Linking economic development and the arts is a new focus and one that is catching on in both the United States and many other countries. Santa Fe, New Mexico (pop. 70,631); Laguna Beach, California (pop. 24,127); Sedona, Arizona (pop. 11,220); and Boulder, Colorado (pop. 91,685), have strong reputations as centers for the arts. These cities have effectively capitalized on their artistic and cultural resources to stimulate local economic development.

By contrast, Paducah, Kentucky (pop. 25,575), did not have a national reputation as a center for the arts, but it has successfully used an arts strategy to improve its economic base. Until just a few years ago, Paducah's Lower Town neighborhood was a popular spot for drug dealers and slumlords. It had good housing stock built, but property values were going down and the average annual income of the area was less than $10,000. On the basis of a neighborhood plan developed with input from neighborhood residents, the city established the Artist Relocation Program, encouraging working artists from around to country to settle in Paducah. The program has brought new and increased tax revenues to all the taxing entities, created a more diversified economy, added a growing tourism base, provided cultural enrichment, and increased the city's intellectual and entrepreneurial capital for generations to come.

---

local governments and private businesses within the region, the partnership has helped these counties and the many communities within them to work collaboratively in promoting the region for new business investment. Through their connection with the CRP, small Charlotte-area communities such as Mount Holly and Weddington gain much greater exposure to new business investment prospects.

For regional economic development to be successful, communities and counties within a region must trust each other and agree to work together to serve the larger economic whole. The Greater Phoenix Economic Council (GPEC) represents the economic interests of communities large and small within the fast-growing Phoenix metropolitan area. Phoenix-area cities such as Avondale, Gilbert, Glendale, Mesa, and Scottsdale have had to learn to work together as a team to promote business and job development because the economic success of their individual communities is influenced by what happens to the overall region.

To support and benefit from regional economic development efforts like those in Charlotte and Phoenix, smaller communities can

- Agree to work in partnership with their neighbors sharing the same regional economy
- Work with their regional economic partners to define how to market their community most effectively as part of the larger economic region
- Provide funding support to their regional economic development organizations in exchange for marketing and other benefits
- Participate as members of their regional economic development organizations' leadership teams or boards of directors.

## Fiscal issues

The importance of fiscal issues has grown significantly in economic development during the past decade. At one time, local governments, like their private sector economic development partners, were focused almost exclusively on job development as the primary outcome of local economic development processes. Cities and counties are now much more concerned about how to pay for the residential, commercial, and industrial growth occurring within their borders. Increasingly, local governments are using development impact fees and other types of development fees as strategies to finance new development.

Since the 1980s, development impact fees have become an integral part of local government efforts to finance public infrastructure, and twenty-seven states have adopted impact fee enabling legislation.[7] A wide variety of professional organizations in development-related fields, including the Urban Land Institute, the Lincoln Institute for Land Policy, and the American Planning Association, have observed that a growing number of local governments are adopting the view that "growth should pay its own way." Experience has shown that this is easier said than done, but more and more local governments are working toward this goal. For example, Hernando and Sarasota Counties in Florida; Naperville, Illinois; and Rock Hill, South Carolina, use development impact fees to help fund the demand for water, sewer, highway, and educational services. Each of these areas is undergoing significant growth, and their public services could not be funded without the use of such fees.

Fiscal needs are forcing local governments to ask harder questions about the short- and long-term costs to communities of various types of growth. Local officials are also raising more questions about the costs and benefits of business incentives, a subject that is discussed in more detail later in this chapter. Sprawl is costly for communities. The alternative, smart growth, is no longer strictly about protecting environmental resources; it also embodies concerns about fiscal equity, or who bears the costs of new growth in local communities.[8] Smart growth policies that include fiscally sound growth strategies are important in both bad and good economic times. Bad economic times increase concerns about cost containment and avoidance. More favorable economic times encourage greater growth, requiring governmental entities to provide new infrastructure and increased public services to support new development.

## Evaluating local needs

No one-size-fits-all model for economic development exists. Therefore, every local government must evaluate its own economic development service needs and provide those services that are most important to overall economic and community development. For example, areas with mature industry bases must pay attention to retaining existing businesses and to helping those employers remain competitive. Public officials in rural communities with few existing employers must work hard to recruit new businesses to their areas to create jobs for residents.

The workforce development needs of industries vary considerably. Highly technical manufacturing industries require workers who can operate complex, computer-controlled machinery and equipment. Distribution and warehousing businesses employ workers who can operate material-handling equipment and drive trucks of various sizes. Software development companies require computer programmers and analysts. Call center and back-office operations need workers with well-developed communications skills and the ability to work directly with the general public. These are just a few illustrations of why local economic development service needs must be tailored to specific local requirements.

# Economic development challenges

Economic vitality is a top concern of America's city officials. According to the National League of Cities (NLC), most, if not all, local governments are concerned about how the economy is treating them and whether they are getting their "fair" share of economic development opportunities.[9] Many local elected officials responding to a 2005 NLC opinion survey identified the growing competition among jurisdictions as a top concern.[10] In another NLC report from 2005, a two-year scan of future challenges facing cities, economic development and economic vitality issues were identified as the second most important set of issues facing America's cities, right behind fiscal issues.[11] These issues are equally important to county governments.

Achieving local economic development objectives has grown much more complex and difficult since the early 1990s.[12] Various forces, including industry and market globalization trends, have increased competition among worldwide locations for economic development opportunities. Business and industry restructuring, rapid technological changes, and shifting demographics have added to this competition.[13] The effects of new international trade and increased reliance of major corporations on business supply sources in developing countries (offshore outsourcing), such as India and China, is a growing threat to jobs and the economic vitality of America's communities.[14] Local governments now operate in a high-skills, high-wage economy and must compete on the basis of brainpower and quality of labor resources in addition to cost of production and good weather.[15]

Beyond these larger global challenges, economic development today faces many local and state government hurdles, which are believed to reduce the ability of local economies to grow and develop. Five challenges stand out from the rest:

1. *Growing interjurisdictional rivalry*. Competition for economic development opportunities has grown more intense among communities within the same substate economic region as well as across states.

2. *State and local costs of doing business.* State and local business climate issues, including business tax policies, environmental regulations, workers' compensation policies and costs, and state and local development project review and approval processes, remain top concerns for businesses that are expanding and seeking to locate business facilities. A 2005 study by the Tax Foundation predicts that many states will reduce or even repeal their corporate income taxes to compete for new business investment, jobs, and other tax revenues and to boost declining corporate tax collections.[16]

3. *Lack of local coordination.* An equitable system of checks and balances must exist among departments within local governments; nevertheless, many business executives continue to report concerns about the inability of local governments to coordinate and integrate important development processes, procedures, and requirements that are spread across their planning, utility service, building, community development, and economic development departments. Initiatives such as fast-tracking programs that are designed to speed up the review and approval of development permits should not lower development quality standards in a community. Rather, they should reduce the time associated with these review and approval processes.

4. *Need for public infrastructure.* Tighter budgets have limited the ability of local governments to provide essential public infrastructure services that are the foundation for

**Connecting downtown to the office parks in El Segundo, California**

About 80,000 people work in the city of El Segundo, California (pop. 16,517), but many do not work downtown. To bring these workers downtown and encourage them to patronize local businesses, the city offers a free lunchtime shuttle that picks workers up from several large companies located about a mile from downtown. The service's three vans run for about two and a half hours every weekday, pick up passengers every nine minutes, and drop them off at several downtown locations. The city promotes the service through handouts and coupons, as well as through its well-informed van drivers, who can direct workers to businesses that will meet their needs.

most development projects. This is of particular concern for outlying rural communities hoping to accommodate the expansion of existing businesses as well as to attract new employers and jobs. To address this problem, some state and local governments have created new programs to fill funding "gaps" to help finance development-related infrastructure. Examples include the Missouri Department of Economic Development's Industrial Infrastructure Grant Program and California's Infrastructure and Economic Development Bank. Many communities in a growing number of states are making increased use of tax increment financing (TIF), which funds infrastructure improvements through a partnership between the local government and a private developer or company; expected growth in property tax revenues from a designated TIF district is used to finance the bonds that pay for improvements in that district. Columbus, Ohio, for example, used TIF to help fund infrastructure in two major mixed-use developments.

5. *Need for brownfields cleanup.* Many older communities have exhausted their supply of clean and developable sites for business and industry expansion. Without a new land supply, these communities will not grow. The pragmatic solution to this problem is brownfields redevelopment—the cleanup and redevelopment of underused, blighted, and environmentally contaminated sites and buildings. However, this solution poses a major challenge for many "built" communities as the financial costs of improving brownfields are significant and fiscal realities often limit what public agencies can do in this area.

These five issues alone suggest that local government leaders have much hard work ahead of them if they are to expand their economic bases. In the future, they will have to confront these issues with fewer financial and other resources. This argues for much greater innovation, creativity, and collaboration in advancing economic development. It also means that local governments and their development partners must limit the number of economic development priorities they can tackle at any one time.

## A sensible approach to economic development

While no universally accepted definition of *economic development* exists, most economic development experts agree on its top goal, which is to improve the economic well-being of a community and its residents. The economic well-being issue is one that deserves special attention from local managers because prosperity levels in a large number of communities are suffering as a result of industry and business globalization, heightened business productivity, and major technological changes. What's good for business competitiveness is not always good for community prosperity.

According to the Washington-based Economic Policy Institute (EPI), which regularly tracks economic well-being issues, wages for the bottom 10 percent of wage earners fell by 9.3 percent between 1979 and 1999.[17] This development caused public officials in many communities to refocus their economic development efforts on developing higher-paying jobs. EPI researchers noted, however, that figures have not improved since 1999, signaling a return to the 1980s widening of wage inequality. While some may argue that America remains the most prosperous nation in the world, the sobering reality is that more American communities than ever before are feeling the pain of stagnating and declining incomes.[18]

> *What's good for business competitiveness is not always good for community prosperity.*

A large part of the problem is that many employers are unable to create enough "good" jobs offering higher wages and acceptable employee benefits. Beyond this are several strategic factors that are seen as hampering the ability of local and state economic development organizations to increase the economic well-being of citizens:[19]

- Corporate and industry restructuring, especially in the manufacturing sector
- Business outsourcing to offshore service and manufacturing sources
- Local economic structure and declining industry mix
- State and local government factors shaping the local business climate
- Citizens' low levels of educational attainment.

The first two of these factors, corporate and industry restructuring and business outsourcing, are clearly business strategy issues; although local officials have little direct control over them, these strategies have a major bearing on whether new business investments occur within the community. The third factor, local economic structure, is a function of both local business factors and geographic area. For example, many local economies with large concentrations of old-line manufacturing plants are experiencing either slow growth or decline. Over the long haul, however, economic development groups can have some impact on a local economy's industry mix. The final two issues, state and local business climate and citizen educational attainment, are localized factors, on which state and local government officials can have a much greater impact over time.

However, myriad factors and issues shape a community's economic development potential, and it is often impossible to pull apart the influence of these various factors. Some of the major factors converging on a community and affecting its ability to grow its economic base are discussed in the following sections.

## Improving the climate for business

What can local government managers do to ensure that the proper attention is given to the right types of businesses and industries for developmental purposes? There are four practical steps that these officials might consider taking.

***Get the facts on who and what is growing***   One step would be to conduct or sponsor a study of local industry and business growth trends. This could include an analysis of which existing industries and major businesses are likely to be the strongest sources of future investment, employment, and tax revenue growth; future business retention and expansion efforts should then be focused on the industries and businesses with the brightest prospects—that is, those that will create the most economic development opportunities for the community.

This analysis should also identify those industries and firms that are likely to struggle with future growth or face other problems that would cripple their ability to generate additional jobs and create other local economic benefits. Efforts should be focused on helping these enterprises face their difficulties as well as on helping their workers adjust to expected employment dislocations. Experience shows that protracted and costly economic development assistance initiatives, including the provision of major financial incentive packages aimed at preventing inevitable business reductions and closings, are both economically unwise and unjustified. This is a difficult decision, but local government managers must work to create realistic expectations about future growth. Moreover, they have an obligation to ensure that taxpayer money is not needlessly thrown away on projects that will produce little or no economic benefit to the community. It takes leadership to resist political pressure and stand up and say no when a project is a bad use of local taxpayers' money.

> *Protracted and costly economic development assistance initiatives are both economically unwise and unjustified.*

It is important to remember that businesses, jobs, markets, tax bases, and other aspects of the economic development process are dynamic in nature; change is the only constant. Increasingly, local economies are being shaken by the larger forces described earlier, such as globalization and major technological shifts. Given these influences, the ability to predict the future is much more difficult. This argues for using new analytic methods such as scenario planning to better anticipate future change and economic possibilities.

***Define what works and how well***   Once an adequate understanding of the current and future growth potential of various local industries and companies exists, it is important to decide which economic development policies and strategies will have the greatest impact on identified problems and opportunities. This sounds simple, but it is not.

More empirical research is being conducted on the costs, benefits, and impacts of economic development policies and strategies, but there still is a less-than-perfect understanding of how these tools really work and what impact they have.[20] Unlike in scientific research experiments, many unknowns exist in an understanding of the nature and behavior of social, economic, and political systems commonly found in economic development.

Given this constraint, how do local managers proceed to the next step? First, it is important to realize that although many national professional associations and other organizations lay claim to knowing "what works in economic development," even the best examples of success or best practice are fraught with problems. Rather than jumping to adopt economic development policies and programs that have been used in other places

## Figure 7-1   Organizing for economic development

| Type | Mission | Tools | Special powers | Structure | Geographic scope |
|------|---------|-------|----------------|-----------|------------------|
| Community development departments | To carry out all duties of community and economic development | Planning, land assembly, regulation, financing, infrastructure, promotion and marketing, technical assistance | Pledge credit of municipality; eminent domain | Public | Municipality |
| Economic development industrial corporations (EDICs) | To do industrial development in areas of high unemployment and physical deterioration | Land assembly, planning, financing, infrastructure, promotion and marketing | Eminent domain | Quasi-public | Municipality or consolidated EDIC for more than one city or town |
| Development and industrial commissions | To promote and market industrial land | Promotion and marketing | None | Quasi-public | Municipality |
| Industrial development finance authorities | To issue tax-exempt bonds for industrial development | Land assembly, financing, infrastructure | None | Quasi-public | One municipality or two or more contiguous municipalities |
| Redevelopment authorities | To plan and implement urban renewal activities | Planning, land assembly, infrastructure, promotion and marketing, financing | Eminent domain | Quasi-public | Municipality |
| Local development corporations | To strengthen commercial and industrial sectors by revitalizing older downtown areas or assisting location of industry | Financing, land assembly, promotion and marketing | None | Quasi-public or private nonprofit or public-private partnership | Flexible: could be municipal or neighborhood |
| Chambers of commerce | To improve the commercial and industrial sectors | Technical assistance, promotion and marketing, land assembly, financing | None | Private, nonprofit | Flexible: county, municipal, or regional |
| Community development corporations | To improve general economic conditions | Technical assistance, land assembly, financing | None | Private, nonprofit | Flexible: neighborhood, citywide, or regional |
| Private, nonprofit development organizations | To develop industrial and commercial land | Financing, land assembly, infrastructure, technical assistance, promotion and marketing | None | Private, nonprofit | Flexible: neighborhood, citywide, or regional |

There is no single pattern of organization for economic development. Different approaches seem to work best in different communities: a few types of economic development organization are briefly described in the table above. No matter which form of organization is chosen, the sincere and effective cooperation of the public and private sectors is vitally important to a successful economic development program.

Source: Adapted from "Matrix of Organizational Characteristics" in *Organizing for Economic Development: Municipal and Regional Options* (Boston: Massachusetts Department of Housing and Community Development, August 1998), 22–23.

---

### Scenario planning

Scenario planning is exploring the future, not predicting it. Used by military strategists, corporate planners, and futurists for many years as an analytic tool to identify alternative paths that change may follow, scenario planning involves identifying trends and exploring the implications of projecting them forward, usually as high-, medium-, and low-probability forecasts. Scenario planning can be useful in local economic development as it can help public officials chart different ways in which their economy and major development projects might progress in the future. If these officials are aware of what *could* happen, they are more likely to be able to deal with what *will* happen. The town of Mooresville, North Carolina (pop. 20,488) has used scenario planning in its planning and economic development efforts, as has the Thomas Jefferson Planning District Commission in Charlottesville, Virginia (pop. 40,437), in regional planning efforts that have included economic development issues.

---

and are claimed to be successful, local officials should assume an experimental attitude and be willing to learn from the experience of others in this field as well as from their own programmatic efforts.

***Build long-term service relationships with businesses***   Providing responsive, high-quality services is of great importance for business growth. Economic development groups that build and maintain ongoing, results-oriented service relationships with companies are seen as more successful than those that engage businesses on an intermittent basis. Trust is vital in order for business executives and managers to feel comfortable in calling city hall or the county courthouse for help. They must believe that the community is genuinely interested in their future and that they will be treated fairly. Trust is also essential in order for local elected officials and managers to feel confident that, in exchange for the help they provide, businesses will care for their workers, be good corporate citizens, and do the best they can to grow within the community.

***Work at continuous improvement***   Communities that work at improving themselves on a continuous basis are much more likely to discover what works in helping businesses and workers gain and maintain a competitive edge. The adoption of service performance standards and quality improvement processes by local managers can improve the chances that their jurisdictions' economic development policies and programs are delivering the value that businesses (as well as the local government) need on an ongoing basis.

### Improving community competitiveness

Communities must work all the time to improve their competitiveness for economic development. Local public officials must set priorities in terms of which improvements will be made and how scarce investment resources will be used to make these investments. Top priorities for improving community competitiveness are funding local economic development improvements; strengthening the local workforce to compete for higher-quality jobs; improving the educational system to make it more responsive to labor market needs; strengthening the local entrepreneurial sector to foster home-grown businesses, and strengthening public and private leadership for economic development.

**Effective policies and strategies**

The following economic development actions seem most effective in retaining, expanding, growing, and attracting businesses:

- Providing a good overall environment for businesses, with reasonable operating costs and quality amenities, high-quality schools, affordable housing, reasonable government regulations, etc.

- Investing in training and development for both existing and new workers

- Providing performance-based financial and tax incentives that motivate businesses to invest locally and create new jobs

- Providing well-located, high-quality sites and buildings at reasonable cost

- Investing in quality public infrastructure to support business expansion

- Providing an environment where startup businesses have favorable access to growth resources, including financing, technology, and business expertise.

*Funding*   According to the ICMA *Economic Development 2004* survey, the majority of funding for local government economic development programs comes from local government revenue sources. Which sources are used most often? Eighty-eight percent of respondents said that the leading source of this funding is local revenues or general fund revenues. Other sources include tax increment financing (28 percent), state grants (25 percent), federal grants-in-aid (23 percent), and hotel/motel taxes (20 percent).[21] The latter source is used mostly to fund travel and tourism development and promotion activities.

*Workforce development*   Workforce development is a leading local economic development priority for large and small communities alike. According to corporate surveys conducted by *Area Development Magazine,* workforce availability has consistently been ranked as one of the top three corporate location decision factors for the past twenty years.[22] These surveys point to the need for better educated, more highly trained workers who are flexible in adjusting to ongoing workplace changes. Generally, the leading public sector funding sources for workforce development are the U.S. Department of Labor, through its Workforce Investment Act, and state governments, which provide money for customized job training under their economic development and employment training/ workforce development agencies.

*Educational improvement*   Educational improvement is another top priority for advancing economic development in U.S. communities. At the local level, many economic development organizations have added municipal and county school superintendents to local economic development boards to ensure that schools play a more active role in supporting their goals. In the private section, a growing number of employers are helping local schools revise their curricula to meet the needs of today's and tomorrow's workforces, and the Committee for Economic Development (CED) in New York City has been actively promoting education-business alliances at all levels. With the realization that much of a child's capacity for learning is shaped early in life, CED has also been giving greater attention to strengthening early childhood education.[23]

## Evaluating workforce development programs

A good workforce development program must find a balance in meeting the needs of its dual customer base: individuals and businesses. Individuals need training that supports their aspirations, and businesses need employees who serve their needs. An effective program will identify ways to support both customers. Business involvement in programs, therefore, is critical.

Retention rates should hold more weight than placement rates in an evaluation. Placement rates are only one part of the picture. The real test for training programs is how long individuals stay in the job.

### Quantitative measures

Number of individuals trained

Number of individuals placed

Retention rates (lengths of time individuals stay in a job)

Percentage of women and minorities assisted

Cost per person trained

Number of businesses hiring from the training program

Number of businesses that keep coming back for new hires

### Qualitative measures

Business involvement in design of training program (e.g., identifying skill standards)

Type and range of supportive services (e.g., retention services)

Stated project goals and the degree to which they have been achieved

Follow-up (does the program follow up with businesses and individuals to ensure that training is appropriate?)

Source: International Economic Development Council, "Economic Development Reference Guide," iedconline.org/index .php?p=Guide_Workforce.

*Entrepreneurship*    Entrepreneurship in communities is an increasingly important local economic development strategy. According to the ICMA *Economic Development 2004* survey, local governments play a role in this area by providing revolving loan funds to small companies (reported by 48 percent) and by funding and operating small business development centers (reported by 55 percent); they also fund and operate new business incubator facilities, provide microenterprise loans to new risky startup companies, help new startup companies compete for business contracts with other businesses and government agencies, and make matching improvement grants available.[24] The Kellogg Foundation, based in Battle Creek, Michigan, provides major support to entrepreneurial development efforts. This support has included grants to smaller communities, such as rural communities and counties in New Mexico, North Carolina, and Oregon, to support innovations in rural entrepreneurship.

***Leadership***   Finally, effective leadership is a critical success factor for economic development. Penn State University's Rural Leadership Development Program (RULE) has offered training in hundreds of smaller communities across Pennsylvania on how to provide better community and economic development leadership. The North Carolina Rural Economic Development Center offers similar leadership training services to smaller cities and towns in North Carolina. These are just two of many programs in place to help smaller communities build stronger community leadership for economic development.

## Incentives and incentive policies

A large number of local governments provide financial, tax, and nonfinancial (e.g., development permit fast-tracking services) incentives to encourage new business investment and job creation within their jurisdictions. ICMA's *Economic Development 2004* survey indicates that more than 72 percent of its respondents use business incentives to support and assist economic development. The most popular tools are assistance with zoning and development permits, infrastructure improvements, tax increment financing, and property tax abatements.[25]

> *Local elected officials [should] adopt a business incentive policy that creates the right expectations about how various tax, financial, and other incentive programs will be used.*

Flying by the seat of your pants is not a wise approach to awarding incentives to businesses expanding and locating in a community. All local economic development stakeholders lose credibility when incentive programs are used improperly. Local elected officials are especially subject to criticism when local incentive deals misfire. The best advice is to adopt a business incentive policy that creates the right expectations about how various tax, financial, and other incentive programs will be used. A written policy toward this end has a number of benefits, including providing for fairness (businesses react negatively when they believe that local government has given preferential treatment to one business or industry over another) and delineating how incentive agreements will be monitored and assessed in terms of compliance and performance. Such a policy helps local governments ensure that their scarce financial and tax resources are being used as effectively as possible to produce quality growth and employment opportunities for the community.

A formal incentive policy is one that exists in written form, has been adopted by legislative action, is used in making decisions about whether economic development projects are worthy of public investment, and is enforceable by law.[26] Formal incentive policies should be crafted carefully to avoid discouraging qualified companies from using the programs.

Local governments are making their incentive programs more performance based. Like other formal incentive programs, performance-based programs have guiding rules; companies using these programs are legally bound to meet the requirements of the incentive agreement; the programs must produce economic and financial benefits equal to or greater than their economic and financial costs; and development projects receiving incentives must contribute in a positive way to the community.[27]

More than 60 percent of local governments now require a performance agreement as a condition for a company to receive a business incentive.[28] In simple terms, a performance agreement is a legal document that binds the company receiving the incentive to meet the job development and facility investment requirements stated in the agreement.

There is no perfect economic development incentive policy that is suited to the needs of all communities. Every community must assess its own needs and develop an incentive policy that meets those needs. In general, business incentive policies should strike a balance between the need to guarantee business compliance and accountability, and the need to develop new economic opportunities within the community.

## Working with target industries and clusters

Many communities give special attention to those industries and industry clusters that they believe have special advantages for development. This long-standing practice in economic development is commonly referred to as "targeting."[30] Examples of industries or clusters that are often targeted include plastic products manufacturing, life sciences and biotechnology, motor vehicles and suppliers, precision manufacturing, medical equipment and supplies, and back-offices and call centers. Clusters may be quite specialized; for example, houseboat manufacturers were a target cluster in Kentucky.

Communities need to analyze their economies carefully to identify target industries or clusters; some of the questions to ask employers are shown in the sidebar on page 173. Once it has identified industry clusters to target, a community can implement a cluster strategy by

- Engaging companies to work together by identifying cluster "champions," common external threats, and common opportunities, and by offering incentives

- Developing education, training, and human resource strategies that support the targeted cluster

- Promoting entrepreneurship in the community, especially among employees within the target industry.[31]

Targeting encourages a focused approach to economic development that couples area strengths with industry opportunities; it helps community officials prioritize area improve-

---

### Target industries and industry clusters

A target industry is an industry group, usually defined by its Standard Industrial Classification (SIC) or North American Industrial Classification System (NAICS) Code, which has been selected by an economic development group for special attention. An industry cluster is a group of businesses and nonbusiness organizations (institutions) for whom membership within the cluster is an important element of each member firm's individual competitiveness. Binding the cluster together are buyer-supplier relationships, common technologies, similar buyers, shared distribution channels, and common labor pools. Much like target industries, clusters are selected for special development attention by economic development organizations.

## Identifying target industries or clusters

One way to identify target industries or clusters for economic development is to conduct a survey of the business community. Questions to ask include the following:

- What are your products, and where are your markets?
- How many employees do you have? How does that number compare with the numbers last year and the year before?
- What sets your main product or service apart from that of your competitors?
- What advantage do you gain from being located in your community or region?
- What are the major threats to your competitiveness?
- Are there any disadvantages to doing business in this region?
- Do you use any public sector services? Which ones? Are they well known and easily accessible?
- Do the people you deal with in government understand your industry?
- Are you part of any business, trade, or professional associations? Are these local, state, or national? Are you an active participant (i.e., do you attend more than one meeting a year)? How do you benefit from the organization?
- Where are you most likely to learn about industry developments and new technologies? From vendors? From other companies?
- How well do you know your peers in your industry? How often do you interact with them, and why?
- Do you ever partner with other companies on business matters? If yes, give examples.
- Do you have any problem finding qualified employees? Where are you most likely to find them?
- Do the nearby educational institutions do a good job of preparing workers?
- Do you train your employees? If not, who provides training services?

Source: Phil Psilos and Dan Broun, "Cluster-Based Economic Development," *IQ Report* 38, no. 1 (2006): 7.

ments needed to gain a competitive edge with the best development prospects; and it aligns economic development policies and strategies with future growth prospects. The disadvantages of targeting are that the community may pick the wrong industries to target or that the area's opportunities may change in the future. Also, local companies in those industries not targeted may resent the community favoring one industry group over another. Despite the considerable use of this practice, the effectiveness and long-term impacts of targeting are not well understood.

## Marketing communities

Marketing plays an important role in economic development. Economic development marketing activities tend to be aimed at business managers and their consultants and advisors, especially consulting firms involved in corporate site selection. The overall objective of these activities is to interest the decision makers in making an investment in a state or community.

Marketing encompasses a wide array of activities, including advertising, public relations, telephone and Web-based contacts, in-person sales visits with business managers, the use of testimonials from existing companies, relationship-based marketing, and many other actions. What marketing practices work best? According to the experts, the "facts" sell best. In other words, accurate and useful information about doing business in an area has the greatest value to business decision makers. Economic developers must use the Internet to provide this information, since the vast majority of business site selection professionals turn to the Web as their initial information source about geographic areas and what those areas have to offer from an economic development standpoint.[29]

In setting up a marketing program for economic development, it is important to remember that the biggest challenges will be converting leads into investment deals, competing for the attention of business decision makers and site consultants, and sustaining funding for the marketing program.

## Expected economic development outcomes

To the extent possible, local economic development stakeholders should agree on the outcomes expected from their local development effort. Some communities are better at doing this than others. Public and private sector economic developers tend to focus on different outcomes (see accompanying sidebar). For example, tax revenues, quality of life, and diversification may be more important to public sector officials than to private stakeholders.

Robin Roberts, executive vice president of the Greater Oklahoma City Chamber of Commerce, explains the difference in expectations by public and private development groups in this way:

> The outcomes expected by an economic development organization are most often related to the standards (performance measures) it is judged by, the legal form of organization, and its board make-up. Public organizations, while focused on job creation, tend to be measured by other criteria that are more directly important to the governmental body, such as tax revenues.

---

**Top five desired outcomes**

| Public sector economic developers | Private sector economic developers |
|---|---|
| 1. Job development | 1. Job development |
| 2. Tax revenue generation | 2. Payroll and income generation |
| 3. Area quality-of-life enhancement | 3. Business competitiveness |
| 4. Payroll and income generation | 4. Innovation and new products |
| 5. Economic diversification | 5. Business investment |

Source: ED Futures Economic Development Trends and Issues Scan, 2005.

Community development efforts give greater priority to "place making," or quality-of-life. Private sector-led development organizations, including chambers of commerce, will focus on job creation, but will also expect to see various business progress outcomes (innovation, market growth, etc.), because these are desired outcomes of their business leaders.[32]

## Advice to local government managers

Economic development will remain a major priority for local governments in the next few years. City and county managers will be asked to respond to their communities' leading economic challenges and opportunities in creative ways. The following eight points may help them in their response:

1. *Engender strategic collaboration.* The local government manager's leadership is essential in forging greater collaboration within the local government and with external public and private sector partners. *The community that does not work together cannot prosper.* Managers need to work on coordinating various economic development efforts within the community and create incentives for groups to work together. The starting point is ensuring that various local departments, including economic development, community development, and planning, are all working together. With that accomplished, managers can then work to coordinate the local government's economic development programs with those of external organizations.

2. *Create a leadership team.* Effective leadership should be in place for economic development. The leadership team, which should include representation from all essential stakeholders, including government, business, education, and citizens, should share a logical and professional approach to development and a vision for the community's economic future. The mayor and city manager can play a crucial role in reinforcing this shared vision and reminding the team about what it will take to achieve it. While commitments to a shared vision and plan are essential, local economic development leaders must also show flexibility when new unanticipated situations present themselves. Finally, leaders must be prepared to evaluate their performance regularly to ensure that they are getting the job done.

---

### Supporting small manufacturers in Grants Pass, Oregon

The city of Grants Pass, Oregon (pop. 26,087), has teamed up with a local community college and the nonprofit Oregon Manufacturing Extension Partnership (OMEP) to offer consulting services to small manufacturers at affordable rates. The city provides $5,000 a year to OMEP, which offers technical assistance to, on average, two small manufacturing companies a year to help them survive and grow in today's difficult economy. The community college coordinates the program, which helps the companies change the way they do business so that they can become more productive and competitive. Because of the economy, few other low-cost programs are available to small manufacturing companies, which sometimes operate inefficiently and need only some good guidance to turn themselves around. Manufacturing companies are eligible for the program if they are located in the greater Grants Pass area, and both companies currently being served were referred to the program by the city's economic development specialist.

3. *Rely on planning and research.* Economic development decisions need to be backed with planning and research tools and based on sound data and knowledge. Managers should insist that important decisions about local government's role in economic development projects be supported by the facts.

4. *Operate from a plan.* The local government manager should develop a plan or strategy to guide local economic development activities. In the absence of a plan, all choices appear equal, when in reality they are not. Given the rapid pace of change in the local, state, national, and global economies, economic development plans should be examined annually for updates.

5. *Adopt the right program mix.* Economic development programs should be chosen carefully and designed to meet local needs and priorities. The manager should avoid pursuing the "copycat" approach to economic development; if an established program does not exist to meet the community's needs, the manager should be ready to experiment with new ideas.

6. *Handle incentives with care.* Business incentives should be viewed as investments, not subsidies. Managers need to ask hard questions about the return on investment to the community. Incentive programs should be used to promote the right outcomes for the community, especially high-quality jobs, balanced growth, and coordinated action and investment by the public and private sectors.

7. *Monitor and measure performance.* Managers should adopt a performance-based approach to economic development that holds everyone accountable for results. Performance should be monitored on an ongoing basis and results checked often to ensure that programs are on track. If economic development programs are not working, managers need to be ready to make the necessary changes in policies, strategies, and programs to get desired results.

8. *Be creative.* Economic development success is predicated on a community's ability to learn and adapt over time. The global economy and technological change are creating new challenges every day for communities. A manager needs to accept that change is a constant, anticipate it, and get the jump on helping his or her community become better prepared for future challenges.

## Conclusion

The local government manager has a vitally important role to play in economic development. This role starts with getting the government's house in order by ensuring that various city departments—including economic development, community development, planning, public works, and finance—are in harmony about the community's economic development priorities and the means by which the local government can best contribute to them.

The next step for the manager is to ensure that the jurisdiction builds effective working relationships for economic development with other key levels of government (especially at the county and state levels), with the local business community (especially private economic development organizations), and with the educational sector (including both the K-12 system and local colleges and universities). These relationships will be key to ensuring that a coordinated and focused approach to economic development is followed.

Finally, it is crucial that the manager remember the human element. People are the beginning and end point in economic development. The ultimate test of a community's economic development success is whether its residents prosper financially from meaningful employment. If this perspective is firmly maintained, an economic development program will always concern itself with what is most important.

---

### Questions to ask if you manage a small community

Does your economic development program focus on the priorities that are most important to building a more prosperous community?

Does your economic development program rely on partnerships and strategic collaboration both within local government and with the community to accomplish its goals?

Does your jurisdiction follow a professional approach to economic development that transcends personal agendas in politics?

Is your jurisdiction's leadership and funding commitment to economic development sufficient to get the job done effectively?

Is your approach to economic development performance based on the premise that you can measure your program's effectiveness and impact on specific goals?

Is your economic development program designed to deal simultaneously with today's opportunities and challenges and with those that will shape your community's economic future?

---

### Competencies for managers in the field of community economic development

Ability to effectively manage an economic development program or department within the context of local government

Ability to work collaboratively with the business community and private sector, as well as with other local government departments, on economic development projects and priorities

Thorough knowledge of available local government incentives (financial, tax, and nonfinancial) to encourage new business investment and job creation

Familiarity with analytic tools, such as cost-benefit analysis, scenario planning, economic base analysis, business trend analysis, and workforce analysis, that can help inform and support local decision making

Knowledge of commercial and industrial real estate, and the ability to work on economic development projects involving real estate issues

Ability to achieve community consensus on economic development priorities

Ability to balance economic development with other community priorities, including environmental conservation

Proficiency at writing grants

Knowledge of and ability to implement diversification strategies appropriate for the community

## Endnotes

1 Two-thirds of the respondents to ICMA's *Economic Development 2004* survey indicated that local government has the primary responsibility for economic development in their community and that, on average, 79 percent of funding for local government economic development programs comes from local government sources (see survey results at icma.org/upload/bc/attach/{34A39D05-637E-4BA6-9D9F-BB9EEDD48AB7}ed2004web.pdf). In another 2004 survey of U.S. public and private development organizations, respondents reported receiving, on average, 54 percent of their total economic development budget from local government general fund sources ("2004 Survey of Local and Regional Economic Development Organizations," Natelson Company and McClure Consulting, Phoenix, Arizona, September 2004); for a copy of the survey findings, contact The Natelson Dale Group at natelsondale.com. From Donald T. Iannone and Associates' experience in consulting with many smaller rural communities and counties on economic development issues, local governments were found to provide 60–65 percent of the funding for local economic development programs.

2 Heywood Sanders, *Space Available: The Realities of Convention Centers as Economic Development Strategy*, Research Brief (Washington, D.C.: Brookings Institution, January 2005).

3 Much has been written about the use of scenario planning as a management and policy decision-making tool for organizations. To gain a working grasp of concepts and tools used in scenario planning, a good starting point is Mats Lindgren and Hans Bandhold, *Scenario Planning: The Link between Future and Strategy* (Hampshire, U.K., and New York: Palgrave McMillan, 2003).

4 *Economic Development Futures Journal (ED Futures), ED Futures* Survey of Economic Development Partnerships, March 2004.

5 Ibid.

6 Thomas S. Lyons and Steven G. Koven, "Economic Development and Public Policy at the Local Government Level," in *The Municipal Year Book 2006* (Washington, D.C.: ICMA, 2006), 14–15.

7 Clancy Mullen, "Impact Fee Surveys: The National Perspective" (paper presented at the National Impact Fee Roundtable, San Diego, California, 2003).

8 Bruce Katz, "Smart Growth Saves Money," *Detroit News,* April 13, 2003.

9 Interview with Dr. William Barnes, director of research, National League of Cities, October 2005.

10 National League of Cities (NLC), *The State of America's Cities 2005* (Washington, D.C.: NLC, 2005).

11 NLC, *The State of America's Cities 2005: The Annual Opinion Survey of Municipal Elected Officials Report on America's Cities* (Washington, D.C.: NLC, 2005), available at nlc.org/content/Files/RMPSoACrpt05.pdf.

12 George A. Erickcek and Hannah McKinney, "Small Cities Blues': Looking for Growth Factors in Small and Medium-Sized Cities," Upjohn Institute Staff Working Paper 04-100 (Kalamazoo, Mich.: W. E. Upjohn Institute for Employment Research, June 2004).

13 Ann R. Markusen and Virginia Carlson, "Deindustrialization in the American Midwest: Causes and Responses," in *Deindustrialization and Regional Economic Transformation: The Experience of the United States,* ed. Lloyd Rodwin and Hidehiko Sazanami (Boston: Unwin Hyman, 1989), 29–59.

14 Michael W. Klein, Scott Schuh, and Robert K. Triest, *Job Creation, Job Destruction, and International Competition* (Kalamazoo, Mich.: W. E. Upjohn Institute for Employment Research, 2003).

15 Interview with Rick Weddle, president and CEO, Research Triangle Park Foundation, Research Triangle Park, North Carolina, September 2005.

16 Chris Atkins, "A Twentieth Century Tax in the Twenty-First Century: Understanding State Corporate Tax Systems," Background Paper 49 (Washington, D.C.: Tax Foundation, September 2005).

17 Lawrence Mishel, Jared Bernstein, and Sylvia Allegretto, *The State of Working America 2004/2005* (Ithaca, N.Y.: Cornell University Press, 2005).

18 William W. Beach and Tim Kane, "Revised! Job Creation Better Than Ever," WebMemo 815 (Washington, D.C.: The Heritage Foundation, August 2005).

19 "Economic Well-Being Survey Report," *ED Futures* (September 2005).

20 For a discussion of the state of economic development research, see Ann Bowman, "Two Steps Forward, One Step Back: Uncertainty in Local Economic Development," *Economic Development Quarterly* 15, no. 4 (2001): 317–319, and Laura Reese and Raymond Rosenfeld, "Yes, But...: Questioning the Conventional Wisdom about Economic Development," *Economic Development Quarterly* 15, no. 4 (2001): 299–312.

21 ICMA *Economic Development 2004* survey.

22 "2005 Corporate Location Survey," *Area Development* magazine (December 2005).

23 Research and Policy Committee, *Preschool for All: Investing in a Productive and Just Society* (New York: Committee for Economic Development, 2002).

24 ICMA *Economic Development 2004* survey.

25 Ibid.

26 The *ED Futures* Economic Development Trends and Issues Scan in 2005 found that about 56 percent of respondents had these policies in place.

27 Interview with Jeffrey Finkle, executive director, International Economic Development Council, Washington, D.C., January 2006.

28 ICMA *Economic Development 2004* survey.

29 Development Counsellors International, *The Corporate View: Winning Strategies in the Economic Development Marketing* (New York: Development Counsellors International, 2005), available at dc-intl.com/index.cfm.

30 According to the *ED Futures* Scan, 61 percent of respondents said they use "targeting."

31 Phil Psilos and Dan Broun, "Cluster-Based Economic Development," *IQ Report* 38, no. 1 (2006): 12–15.

32 Interview with Robin Roberts, executive vice president, Greater Oklahoma City Chamber of Commerce, January 2006.

# 8

# Community Development and Affordable Housing

**Anita R. Brown-Graham and Jonathan Q. Morgan**

The nation's overall growth and prosperity depend on the economic and social vibrancy of its communities. The term *community development* refers to the idea that, in order for a community to be viable, its development choices must (1) be led by community residents; (2) be systematically linked to a community's infrastructure—physical, human, financial, natural, civic, and social; and (3) encourage local enterprises that serve the needs of residents, promote stable employment, and increase social equity.

Like economic development (see Chapter 7), community development focuses on creating opportunities for jobs, income, wealth, and business growth.[1] However, in contrast to traditional economic development, community development is concerned with questions of who shapes, creates, and benefits from development opportunities. Ideally, community development strategies seek to adhere to the "triple bottom line" of sustainable development: economic, social, and environmental responsibility.[2] In practice, however, many communities find it difficult to balance these often competing interests.

There is no universally accepted precise definition of community development; it may mean different things to different people in different contexts. The purpose of this chapter is to provide a comprehensive and holistic view of what community development is from multiple perspectives. No single community is likely to manifest all or even most of the aspects of community development discussed here. The intent is to provide the reader with exposure to the breadth of the field and to stimulate thinking about the possibilities for action in a local community.

The chapter first explores the theory and practice of community development and offers a framework for considering a variety of the field's activities. The second half focuses on a single community development activity: public sector efforts to increase the availability of decent, affordable housing to lower-income households.

## Community development in context

This chapter defines community development as the development of tangible community assets— physical, human, financial, natural, civic, and social—in geographically defined

## What is community development?

Community development focuses a great deal on ensuring that the physical infrastructure–water and sewer, utilities, housing, schools, public facilities–is in place to support economic growth and investment. However, "community development is not only about physical structures and their contents, but also involves leadership training and development. It includes building the social structures for governance and community involvement while facilitating citizen participation and input. Capacity building includes creating a critical mass of an involved, informed, and enthusiastic citizenry; giving a community the capacity to solve its problems and create a better quality of life."

Source: Robert W. Shively, *Economic Development for Small Communities: A Handbook for Economic Development Practitioners and Community Leaders* (Washington, D.C.: National Center for Small Communities, 2004), 9.

areas where residents share not only common space but also some common circumstances. The urban "community" is usually a neighborhood. In rural areas, "community" typically means a larger geographic area. A small rural county's residents might well consider the county to be the primary community.

Presumably, every community seeks to be viable. For some locations, however, the task is harder than it is for others. In many of the nation's communities, from urban inner cities to small rural towns, residents suffer from troublingly similar manifestations of economic, social, and physical distress. These communities are often characterized by high rates of poverty, joblessness, underemployment, school dropouts, poor health outcomes, and substandard housing. The lack of community vibrancy significantly affects residents' quality of life. Researchers have termed these effects the "geography of opportunity."[3] While the field is certainly not limited to distressed areas, community development tends to focus on these areas because of their need for comprehensive approaches to development.

The circumstance of distressed communities invariably calls for some activities that may be classified as economic development. As quality-of-life factors have become increasingly important to stimulating private investment and creating jobs and wealth, many experts have questioned whether any distinction lies between the two fields.[4] An apparent fundamental difference between community development and economic development is in how they each define success. The local economic development director may define success in terms of growth—more firms, more jobs, and a larger tax base—and may target business and industry. In contrast, the community development director focuses on providing the community infrastructure to support growth and on creating a

### Services and functions addressed by community development

| | |
|---|---|
| Community revitalization | Affordable housing |
| Job creation strategies | Strategic visioning |
| Sustainable development | Citizen participation |
| Physical infrastructure | |

**Figure 8-1  The components of community development**

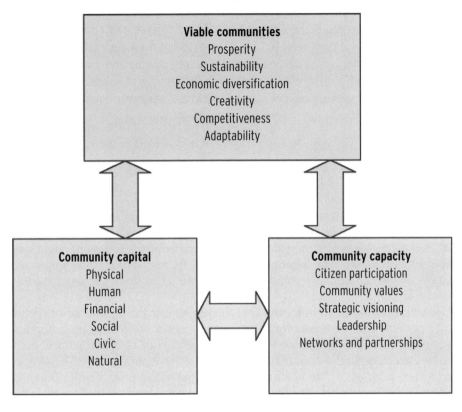

broad range of economic opportunities for residents. Encompassing more than economic development, community development is a multifaceted approach for addressing the various "building blocks" required to create viable communities capable of thriving in the new economy (see Figure 8–1).

## Types of community capital

Contemporary community development emphasizes capital or asset creation more than community needs and shortcomings. It emphasizes the importance of leveraging and building on community strengths and assets as a means of achieving economic self-sufficiency. Again, community capital may take many forms—physical, human, financial, natural, civic, and social—and it can be either individual or collective. Moreover, there is a strong relationship among the many forms of capital; they are not independent.

### Physical capital

Physical capital refers to built resources: buildings (including houses, retail stores, and factories) and infrastructure (including roads, water, sewer, and telecommunication).

---

**Identifying blight**

High vacancy rates

Inability to develop vacant or irregularly shaped lots

Unsafe building conditions

Aging, deteriorating, and poorly maintained buildings

Poor structure quality that requires significant improvements to buildings in order to ensure safe occupancy

Inadequate infrastructure (i.e., utilities, storm drainage, sewers, and streetlighting) to support development.

---

These resources are essential to attracting private investment to a community, and the implications of absent or inadequate physical capital can be far-reaching. For example, evidence exists of a link between the built environment in a community and public health.[5] Residents who live in a "walkable" neighborhood or have convenient access to health food grocers are more likely to engage in greater physical activity and have a healthier diet. By contrast, a physical environment filled with liquor stores and fast food restaurants with few venues for exercise and recreation tends to facilitate negative and unhealthy lifestyles.

Physical revitalization programs are common local government responses to the distressed physical environment that often characterizes lower-income neighborhoods. With state and federal help, first under the National Housing Act of 1949 and later under the Community Development Block Grant (CDBG) program inaugurated in 1974, local governments have tried to revitalize blighted areas through property acquisition, clearance, replanning, rehabilitation, or rebuilding. The CDBG program now serves as the largest grant source for community development, and much of the funding is used for the development of physical capital, particularly housing.

## Human capital

Human capital is the potential productivity of a community's residents and includes both hard (technical) skills and soft (nontechnical) skills, practical knowledge, and learned abilities. Education and formal training, on-the-job training, and family and nonfamily mentoring are sources for human capital development. The new workforce development paradigm is lifetime learning.

Two federal laws have raised the significance of human capital development—or "workforce development," as it is now more commonly called. As federal welfare reform sought to eliminate the long-term eligibility of employable applicants for welfare benefits, the 1996 Personal Responsibility and Work Opportunity Reconciliation Act (PRWORA) made job training and placement efforts for low-income people particularly important. People being moved from welfare to work require opportunities to develop needed skills. The Workforce Investment Act (WIA), passed in 1998, addresses the needs of three types of job seekers—adults, dislocated workers, and youth; and it provides each type with basic support services, including job search assistance, assessment and case management, and job training provided by local one-stop job centers. PRWORA has created an

---

**New Choices Workforce Development Program in North Carolina**

Roanoke Economic Development, Inc. (REDI), the nonprofit subsidiary of the Roanoke Electric Cooperative, in collaboration with many of the agencies that make up the Roanoke Chowan Partners for Progress (RCPP), has established the Roanoke Center to catalyze and support sustainable economic and community development in Roanoke Electric's five-county service area (Bertie, Gates, Halifax, Hertford, and Northampton Counties) in northeastern North Carolina. This is an economically disadvantaged region of the state, with above-average poverty and unemployment and below-average income levels. The Roanoke Center administers the New Choices Workforce Development Program, a three-year program that began in 2003 to provide training and employment-matching services.

New Choices draws together a group of partners that includes local governments, nonprofits, Roanoke-Chowan Hospital, Roanoke-Chowan Community College, Hertford County JobLink, and Gates County Cooperative Extension. The program provides training and services to low-skilled and/or inexperienced adult workers, and matches graduates with clinical job vacancies in the local health care industry, which is considered a priority growth sector of the regional economy. Through REDI's partners in this effort, participants receive job training and tuition support; soft skills and developmental training; financial assistance for child care, transportation, books, and supplies; individual counseling and case management; and an employment contract in health care or another workplace upon successful completion of the program.

---

unprecedented need for job training for poor people, many of whom live in economically distressed communities, and WIA has created a fresh approach to job training needs.

These shifts in federal workforce and social policy have given rise to a number of sectoral employment initiatives that attempt to provide disadvantaged workers with greater access to livable-wage jobs in a region's growing industry sectors.[6] These initiatives often focus on job training for a narrow set of entry-level occupations that might be most appropriate for less skilled people. One such initiative, Project Quest (Quality Employment Through Skills Training) in San Antonio, is a well-known example of a community-based partnership created to prepare disadvantaged workers for higher-wage employment opportunities.[7] The project attempts to meet the workforce needs of local employers primarily in health care, business services, and environmental technology industries by brokering training at community colleges for workers who have some skills and experience but remain stuck in low-wage jobs.

## Financial capital

Affordable credit, basic financial services, and investment of capital are critical to the health of communities, but private capital markets and traditional financial services often do not adequately meet the needs of low-income people, minorities, and small firms in distressed areas. The reasons for this are varied and include discrimination, suburbanization, and consolidation of the banking industry.[8]

As a responsive strategy, community development focuses on creating access to capital to purchase homes, start businesses, and provide community amenities. There are two basic approaches to increasing access to financial capital: (1) forcing the existing private market to make capital available and (2) creating alternatives to the private market to serve the specific needs of community residents.

The primary regulatory approach for increasing access to financial capital in underserved communities is implemented through the federal Community Reinvestment Act (CRA). The CRA was enacted in 1977 to prevent banks from engaging in the practice of "redlining," or refusing to make loans in low-income and/or minority areas. There is a growing consensus that the CRA has increased the availability of credit from commercial banks in disadvantaged communities.[9]

Community development tools that create new sources of capital beyond that available from banks include the New Markets Tax Credit program, community development financial institutions (CDFIs), microenterprise loan programs, and individual development accounts (IDAs).

*New Markets Tax Credit program*    The U.S. Congress passed the New Markets Tax Credit (NMTC) program as part of the federal Community Renewal Tax Relief Act of 2000. Designed to stimulate $15 billion of new investments over a ten-year period, the NMTC program allows taxpayers to receive a credit against their federal income taxes for supporting eligible community development entities (CDEs)—that is, those CDEs that invest in commercial and economic activities that will benefit low-income communities.[10]

*Community development financial institutions*    Community development financial institutions (CDFIs) have the primary mission of improving economic conditions for low-income individuals and communities; they do this by providing a range of financial products and services that often are not available from more mainstream lenders and financiers. With the establishment of the Community Development Financial Institutions Fund, administered by the U.S. Treasury Department, community-based organizations can apply to become certified CDFIs that are eligible to receive capital from the fund. Since its inception in 1994, the fund has provided a total of more than $400 million in direct funding to more than 250 CDFIs and has facilitated an additional $1 billion in CDFI-related investments from banks.[11]

*Microenterprise lending*    Microenterprise lending originated in Bangladesh in the later 1970s, when the Grameen Bank began making loans to groups of poor women villagers to finance small enterprises and self-employment ventures.[12] Variants of microenterprise development have subsequently emerged in the United States, with economic literacy training as the primary feature. By providing financial capital and business skills training to low-income people, microenterprise programs seek to accomplish both social policy and development goals and to promote economic self-reliance among the disadvantaged. A recent study of microenterprise development in the United States suggests that program participants realize noneconomic benefits, such as increased pride, self-esteem, and a sense of ownership, that outweigh tangible economic outcomes.[13]

*Individual development accounts*    Some states sponsor individual development accounts (IDAs), another asset-building strategy designed to increase access to financial capital and expand economic opportunities for low-income people. IDAs are matched savings accounts that provide a mechanism for poor people to save cash for buying a home, starting a business, or pursuing higher education and job training.[14] The public sector often provides the funds used to match the agreed-upon savings goals of program participants using a ratio of 1:1 up to 1:8.[15]

## Natural capital

A community's environmental and natural resources comprise an asset that has been referred to as the "ecology of place."[16] The many forms of natural and environmental capital include a community's aesthetic qualities, scenic resources, lakes, groundwater supply, cultural heritage, topography, plant life and vegetation, greenways, and wildlife habitats.[17]

Unbridled and haphazard growth can cause negative by-products, including traffic congestion, air pollution, crowded schools, and loss of open space. The recent interest in growth management reflects the need to find ways to grow that avoid these by-products and minimize the disruption of a community's natural ecology and quality of life (see Chapter 6). Communities use a variety of specific development strategies to balance economic growth with the physical and natural setting of place. These strategies include redeveloping abandoned or vacant urban properties, capitalizing on natural attributes, and focusing on green infrastructure.

*Redeveloping brownfields*   Brownfields are vacant or abandoned properties that have real or perceived contamination that prevents them from being redeveloped.[18] The assessment

---

### Federal and state brownfields programs

Several federal programs exist to facilitate the cleanup of contaminated sites and encourage their redevelopment and reuse. The two most actively involved federal agencies are the U.S. Environmental Protection Agency (EPA) and the U.S. Department of Housing and Urban Development (HUD). EPA's brownfields programs provide grants for site assessment, cleanup, and the creation of revolving loan funds, and they offer funding to address environmental problems affecting low-income and minority communities.[1] HUD's Brownfields Economic Development Initiative (BEDI) is intended to assist local governments in redeveloping brownfields properties so that they can be returned to productive economic use.[2] BEDI funds must be used to improve the viability of projects financed with Section 108 loan guarantee commitments through the Community Development Block Grant program. Other federal incentives that are available to support brownfields redevelopment include the federal Brownfields Tax Incentive, the New Markets Tax Credit program, the Low Income Housing Tax Credit program, the Historic Preservation Tax Credit program, and the CRA.

A majority of states have instituted voluntary cleanup programs, and nearly half offer various kinds of tax incentives to lower cleanup costs or to safeguard against increased property tax assessments until the site is fully prepared for redevelopment. State enterprise zone programs that target incentives to stimulate investment in distressed geographic areas often specify brownfields redevelopment as an eligible activity.

1   *Brownfields Federal Programs Guide* (Washington, D.C.: U.S. Environmental Protection Agency, 2005), at epa.gov/swerosps/bf/partners/2005_fpg.pdf.

2   For more information, go to hud.gov/offices/cpd/economicdevelopment/programs/bedi/.

---

### Brownfields redevelopment

Bridgeport, Connecticut (pop. 139,008), raised $4.4 million to clean up and convert Went Field—a site that had been contaminated by circus animals and both metals processing and printing industries—into a multiuse recreational park, pavilion, and amphitheater in the city's impoverished West End. The money came from a combination of municipal bond funds; community fund-raising; and grants from HUD, the National Park Service, and the state.

Clearwater, Florida (pop. 249,079), secured more than $500,000 from the state to clean up contamination from underground storage tanks on the site of a former gas station. The redeveloped site is now a health center that provides free services to poor and mostly minority residents of the North Greenwood community.

Fayetteville, North Carolina (pop. 129,928), generated funds through federal, state, and county grants and private contributions to build the $22.5 million Airborne and Special Operations Museum. The 6.6-acre site in a declining downtown location had been contaminated by gas stations and other former uses.

Source: U.S. Environmental Protection Agency, epa.gov/brownfields/success.htm.

---

and remediation costs associated with redeveloping a contaminated or polluted site can be prohibitive. The financial risks, together with the potential legal liability stemming from such projects, are a major barrier to redevelopment efforts. That brownfields are prevalent in many older, distressed, predominantly minority communities only hampers revitalization efforts. In this sense, brownfields redevelopment can create job opportunities for low-income residents while improving the natural environment and eliminating physical blight from the neighborhoods in which they live.

Local governments can help broker brownfields projects by coordinating resources across all levels of government and engaging the private sector. Successful examples of such projects are presented in the sidebar on brownfields redevelopment.

*Capitalizing on natural attributes*   While brownfields redevelopment is about converting problematic, contaminated, idle properties into productive reuse, other natural capital development strategies seek to maintain, preserve, and take fuller advantage of a community's environmental attributes, history, and character. Agritourism, heritage tourism, and ecotourism are all particularly well suited for smaller rural areas in which the natural environment is perhaps the greatest distinguishing feature. The challenge is to find ways to translate natural amenities and attributes into substantive economic outcomes (e.g., job creation) that do not jeopardize those same community features. For some communities, this may mean limiting land uses and making façade improvements in locations that serve as "gateways" or major entry points to a place in general or to particular amenities such as national or state parks.

*Building green infrastructure*   Natural capital development might also involve investing in "green infrastructure" projects that preserve and connect natural areas—greenways, waterways, wildlife habitats, parks, and open spaces—in ways that support a community's quality of life.[19]

---

### Green infrastructure planning in Kinston–Lenoir County, North Carolina

In the aftermath of Hurricanes Fran in 1996 and Floyd in 1999, both of which devastated eastern North Carolina, one community decided to take matters into its own hands with respect to planning for future storms. When parts of Kinston–Lenoir County, North Carolina (pop. 57,961), located within the floodplain of the Neuse River, suffered substantial flood damage from the two hurricanes, the city and county used Federal Emergency Management Agency funds to purchase several of the damaged properties in the floodplain area.

In 2001, the city and county enlisted the assistance of graduate students in the City and Regional Planning program at the University of North Carolina (UNC)-Chapel Hill to develop a "green infrastructure" plan for the Neuse River floodplain. The plan identifies suitable opportunities for restoring and maintaining existing natural resources; it also describes how converting flood buyout properties into a network of greenways, parks, and trails could create new types of green infrastructure to support various conservation and recreational purposes. In 2002, the students helped prepare a follow-up plan for the city and county that connects the community's green infrastructure features to specific economic development possibilities, including heritage tourism related to a lost Civil War battlefield site and the creation of an all-terrain vehicle park. In this way, Kinston–Lenoir County is using green infrastructure planning to mitigate the effects of future natural disasters by keeping development out of floodplain areas, to preserve the environment by creating natural flood and runoff buffers, and to enhance the quality of life by generating new economic and recreational opportunities.

Sources: Graduate Student Workshop, "Kinston-Lenoir County Green Infrastructure Plan for the Neuse River Floodplain" (Department of City and Regional Planning, UNC-Chapel Hill, 2001), and Graduate Student Workshop, "Linking Natural and Historic Assets: Green Infrastructure as Economic Development in Lenoir County, North Carolina" (Department of City and Regional Planning, UNC-Chapel Hill, 2002).

---

### Civic capital

Civic capital, or civic infrastructure, refers to "the capacity of individuals and organizations to work together effectively—mobilizing resources and directing them toward a common purpose."[20] The multifaceted challenges of community development require civic capital in the form of numerous actors—including federal, state, and local governments; nonprofits; and private entities—covering a range of issues, such as regional growth planning and management, local business development, and home ownership.

The federal government operates more than 100 programs through multiple federal agencies, and it spends billions of dollars annually on grants, loans, loan guarantees, and other types of assistance for community development. However, a large share of this assistance is administered through state and local governments and nonprofit organizations. Thus, it is usually those who lead institutions within a community who can most facilitate or impede community development through their attitudes toward change and experimentation.

Notably, community-based development organizations, particularly community development corporations (CDCs), have played an important role in developing civic capital. Because they are often formed by neighborhood residents and almost always have residents

---

### Community development corporations

The majority of the nation's 3,600 or more community development corporations (CDCs) focus primarily on housing production. In fact, the organizations boast a development and rehabilitation record of more than 550,000 housing units, nearly half of which were produced between 1994 and 1997. In addition to housing, CDCs engage in business enterprise development, commercial and industrial real estate development, and social programs. The increased prominence of these organizations presents challenges for local governments, which are being asked by the public to evaluate their own records on making low- and moderate-income communities better places to live. Many local governments have concluded that they are unable to build communities in the comprehensive way that is the trademark of CDCs and have thus entered into successful joint ventures with CDCs.

Sources: See Avis C. Vidal and W. Dennis Keating, "Community Development: Current Issues and Emerging Challenges," *Journal of Urban Affairs* 26 (June 2004): 125-137; and Anita Brown-Graham, "Thinking Globally, Acting Locally: Community-Based Development Organizations and Local Governments Transform Troubled Neighborhoods," *Popular Government* (Winter/Spring 1996): 2-18.

---

on their boards and as members, such organizations are considered to be credible voices for and accountable to the communities they serve. In addition to their roles in organizing the community, they are responsible for mediating between the community and external actors as well as for attracting resources and support from external organizations, such as foundations, financial institutions, corporations, and public agencies at all levels of government.

### Social capital

Social capital refers to relations or social networks among individuals, organizations, communities, and other social units that result in tangible economic benefits. Social networks can provide access to critical supports, such as child care and transportation, that people need in order to work. Moreover, when residents get plugged into economically diverse social networks, they can gain vital information about training, employment, and business opportunities that can translate into economic value. People in communities endowed with a rich stock of social networks are in a stronger position to develop the capacity to address the problems of poverty, rebuild their communities, and achieve a measure of control over their lives.[21]

### Building community capacity

No one form of community capital can stand alone as a strategy for developing low-income communities. Social capital, for example, acts to enhance other assets and help communities create responses to the circumstances that constrain them. Financial capacity, a trained workforce, an adequate physical infrastructure, and supportive public institutions and policies are needed to develop rich and poor communities alike. But most low-income communities severely lack several of these important assets and must develop some combination of them to take full advantage of development opportunities. The ability to successfully mobilize and leverage various types of community capital is tied to the concept of community capacity.

Community capacity is about the interaction of human capital, organizational resources, and social capital that can be leveraged to solve the collective problems and improve or maintain the well-being of the community.[22] This focus on process leads away from simple evaluations of the production of outputs, such as the number of jobs created or houses constructed, to more complicated considerations of how the community functions and makes decisions—that is, the community's ability to make public development choices in a way that involves a broad spectrum of interests, distinguishes between problems and symptoms, and identifies and implements solutions. In communities that work well, community capacity will be reinforced by robust levels of civic involvement, citizen participation, and organizational collaboration. In communities that work less well, leaders may need to facilitate interventions that both increase community capacity overall and achieve specific development outcomes.

Community capacity is exemplified by a set of core characteristics:

- A sense of community, reflected by the degree of connectedness among members and the recognition of shared circumstances, values, and vision. This sense of community allows people to come together in ways that support a common good.

- The level of commitment, or the responsibility that individuals, groups, or organizations take for what happens in the community. Level of commitment is reflected both in the existence of community members who see themselves as stakeholders in the collective well-being of the community and in the willingness of these members to participate actively in the stakeholder role.

- The ability of the community to address problems or pursue collective goals by translating its commitment into action. Such action may be planned or spontaneous, undertaken through formal or informal means.

- The level of access to economic, human, physical, and political resources within and beyond the community's boundaries. Communities with abundant capacity can garner resources and have some ability to influence policies that directly affect their development.

Community strategic visioning is one tool that communities increasingly use to build community capacity while developing a capital development strategy tailored to their unique assets and specific needs. Visioning initiatives incorporate broad stakeholder involvement, an assessment of the community's assets and weaknesses, an articulation of the community's values, an evaluation of current trends and issues affecting the community, a shared vision for the community's future among stakeholders, a specific action plan detailing the long- and short-term steps necessary to achieve that vision, and an ongoing appraisal of the success of the initiative. By focusing on both process and product, visioning processes help communities develop both capacity and capital.

## Creating affordable housing: A community development case in point

Creating affordable housing options is a primary strategy of community development. Housing is viewed by community developers as far more than shelter. By influencing property values, where one goes to school, access to jobs, level of community amenities available, and the social conditions of one's environment, housing often defines a household's economic opportunities.

## What is affordable housing?

The term *affordable housing* refers to physically adequate housing that is made available to those who, without some special intervention by the government or other providers of housing, could not afford to pay the minimal rent or the mortgage that would be available ordinarily in the private marketplace. A federal housing affordability standard defines affordable units as "units for which a family . . . would pay no more than 30 percent of their income."[1]

Although the rising costs of housing leave many upper-income persons struggling to afford the housing they desire,[2] affordable housing programs are those that typically target persons of low and moderate income. Some communities have affordable housing programs that are more accurately described as workforce housing. With housing costs in many areas increasingly exceeding the financial reach of many low- to moderate-wage workers, these communities focus on making housing affordable for the individuals in administrative, clerical, and service jobs, who account for about one-third of the nation's workforce.

1  According to the U.S. Department of Housing and Urban Development, housing is affordable when all housing costs (rent or mortgage, utilities, property taxes, and insurance) do not exceed 30 percent of total household income. This standard applies to any persons or households, regardless of their source or level of income.

2  See Charles G. Field, "Building Consensus for Affordable Housing," *Housing Policy Debate* 8, no. 4 (1997): 801-832.

CDCs and other private sector community developers regularly aim to create new and rehabilitated housing in areas ignored by home builders, realtors, lending institutions, and home insurers. By focusing on building both the physical capital of housing and the community's capacity to engage in this development activity, these community developers seek to respond to the visible and invisible vestiges of blight that often characterize distressed communities.

Affordable housing development requires significant subsidies, and those subsidies more often than not come from the public sector. However, the public sector rarely carries out these developments without the partnership of other actors.

Many local governments are actively engaged in creating affordable housing opportunities for those families that need it. In some fast-growing communities, teachers, firefighters, and other young families may lack the income or savings to buy, or sometimes even to rent, a home. These families often need only one-time or short-term housing subsidies. Other lower-income households require longer-term subsidy assistance to supplement their inadequate incomes. In some localities, families might need a broad range of housing choices, including mobile and manufactured housing. For other families, the eradication of discrimination in the private market would make available a host of housing opportunities.

Local governments possess no inherent powers to respond to these various circumstances. Whatever powers they possess must be granted to them by the state, even when all the funds that support housing activity come from the federal government.[23] Within the authority granted by state law, local government affordable housing support is usually intended either to increase or maintain the supply of affordable housing, or to make the cost of available housing affordable. The sidebar on page 193 offers various ways in which a local government's housing program can contribute to this effort.

### Techniques for providing affordable housing

Low-interest loan programs for housing rehabilitation for renter- and owner-occupied dwellings

Evaluation of local zoning codes for regulatory barriers; the waiving of development or impact fees for affordable housing developments

Subsidized site improvements—water and sewer lines and streets—to serve affordable developments

Streamlined development approvals to minimize construction delays

Inclusionary zoning, a form of incentive zoning, in which density bonuses are given for any residential housing development that sets aside a substantial percentage of units—10 to 25 percent or more—for low- and moderate-income households

Grants to very low income households for emergency housing repairs, such as the replacement of a furnace or the installation of additional insulation

Rehabilitation or construction of single-room occupancy housing

Construction of "granny flats"—accessory dwelling units for one or two persons, in connection with existing single-family homes

Establishment of nonprofit housing corporations that construct or rehabilitate affordable housing, often with monies from state-administered housing trust funds.

Source: Stuart Meck, FAICP, Senior Research Fellow, American Planning Association, Chicago, Illinois, and author of Chapter 6, "Planning," in this textbook.

## Increasing the supply of affordable housing

The supply of affordable housing can be increased in a number of ways: direct ownership and operation of low-income housing through public housing agencies; conservation of existing housing through the prevention or elimination of blight; homesteading; rent control; and the provision of new housing.

***Direct ownership and operation of housing through public housing agencies***  Under its public housing program, HUD gives grants to public housing agencies (PHAs) to finance the development of public housing, including the capital costs of construction, rehabilitation, or acquisition. HUD also pays operating subsidies to most PHAs to cover the shortfall between tenant rents and operating expenses. In this situation, the role of the city or county in providing assisted housing may be limited to working with the PHA in approving the project for federal assistance and site location, providing the municipal services spelled out in the cooperation agreement with the PHA, and providing an exemption to the PHA from local real estate taxes.

***Conservation and rehabilitation of existing housing***  By preventing or eliminating blight in neighborhoods and dealing with housing stock that presents a threat to the health, safety, and welfare of the community, local governments can conserve and make existing housing habitable. Toward this end, they have several tools at their disposal.

*General police powers*  The authority to regulate the use of land and the condition of existing housing comes from the police powers granted to local governments. These powers authorize local governments, by ordinance, to define and regulate or abate conditions that are detrimental to the health, safety, and welfare of citizens. By exercising their authority to abate nuisances; enforce health, sanitation, and safety regulations; regulate use and occupancy; condemn buildings and land; zone for the uses of land; and eliminate urban blight, local governments are able to conserve existing housing.[24]

*Minimum housing ordinances*  Local governments often use housing codes, more commonly known as minimum housing ordinances, to combat blight in existing neighborhoods. The tool allows a local government to require that a property owner rehabilitate his or her property without the benefit of any public financing.

The first housing codes in the country were enacted in the mid-nineteenth century by northeastern states, such as New York, as a response to the large concentrations of immigrant poor living within their communities. Housing codes did not become commonplace, however, until they were firmly entrenched in federal policy and funding opportunities. Examples of early federal support for housing codes include the Housing Act of 1949, which established and made funding available for urban renewal, and the Housing and Development Act of 1965,[25] which stipulated that in order to be eligible for federal housing subsidies, municipalities had to adopt a "workable plan" that included rehabilitation and conservation. As a justification for requiring the enactment of codes, federal agents made clear their belief that "the ultimate causation factor [for slum and blight] is the local government itself [that fails] to enforce effectively... adequate police power measures to control bad housing, improper environments and overcrowding."[26]

*Building codes*  The first known building code—found in the Code of Hammurabi (from the sixteenth-century B.C. Babylonian ruler)—specified that a builder should be slain if a house fell in and killed the head of the household. Today's builders do not have to lay their lives on the line, but they must comply with strict building construction standards intended to ensure the health and safety of occupants. These standards have evolved over time, and today we have building codes that cover structural matters, electrical work, plumbing, heating—every facet of residential, commercial, and industrial construction. While local governments are active in enforcing these comprehensive building codes, the code is actually a state regulation.

In a discussion of housing, it is important to remember that *building codes* regulate how new construction must be done, focusing on the *condition* of the structure (safety and electrical, plumbing, and heating systems). Given this focus, they may be distinguished from *minimum housing codes,* which focus on the *effect* of a structure on its inhabitants.

*Nuisance ordinances*  Many local governments rely on their police powers to enact nuisance ordinances that prevent one person's use of his or her land from harming neighbors. For example, nuisance lot ordinances typically set minimum standards to prevent housing lots from becoming overgrown or turning into repositories for unsightly and unhealthy collections of refuse. Similarly, junk car and abandoned car ordinances limit the ability to keep inoperable vehicles on a site.

**Homesteading**  State law may authorize local governments to attempt housing rehabilitation and neighborhood conservation through locally initiated homesteading programs.

Properties of little or no value that the locality acquires through abandonment, tax delinquency foreclosures, dedication, gift, or purchase may be conveyed to eligible families at nominal cost.[27] The families must then commit themselves to making the major repairs, rehabilitating the property so that it meets or exceeds minimum code standards, maintaining property insurance, and living in the dwelling for a specified number of years.

Urban homesteading programs are premised on the theory that previously unattractive units can be made available to qualified owners for little or no initial cost, with the result that parcels that have not been economically viable can come back on the market simply for the cost of rehabilitation borne by the new owners. One advantage of such programs is that the city avoids the time-consuming and expensive processes of either rehabilitating the building itself or forcing the property owner to do so.

***Rent control***  In some states, local governments have authority to set limits on the amount of rent that a private landlord may charge a tenant. In other states, local rent control is barred absent specified circumstances, such as where the local government owns the property or has entered into an agreement with the owner for the control of subsidized rental property, or has provided a public subsidy to the construction of the property.

## Inclusionary zoning

In recognizing that local zoning ordinances have broad extraterritorial impact, some courts and policy makers may determine that each community must provide its share of a region's affordable housing needs. This fair-share principle is often articulated as inclusionary zoning.

*Inclusionary zoning* and its correlative, *inclusionary housing,* are terms used to describe a wide variety of techniques that local governments use to link the construction of housing for low- and moderate-income citizens to the construction of housing for the marketplace. Under an inclusionary zoning program, affordable housing is built and integrated into more expensive housing developments, thereby becoming an integral part of the community's overall residential development. Simply put, inclusionary zoning encourages or requires developers, as a condition of permit approval, to include some portion of affordable housing in new market-rate housing developments. The principal objectives of inclusionary zoning are to increase the supply of affordable housing in a community and to do so in a manner that fosters greater economic and racial integration.[28]

## Restoration and rehabilitation of historic properties

Federal and state tax incentive programs for historic preservation encourage the rehabilitation and restoration of historic properties for both commercial and residential uses. The federal tax incentive program (as well as programs in many states) recognizes rental housing as a commercial use of historic properties, qualifying developers who convert designated historic structures into suitable rental housing for reductions in federal and state tax liability. These credits do not require that rental housing that is rehabilitated using the tax credit programs be occupied by individuals of specified income levels; however, many projects that do contain restrictions on tenant income are developed in conjunction with the federal low-income housing credit program, which *does* contain tenant income restrictions.

## Manufactured housing

Commonly referred to as trailers or mobile homes, manufactured housing has become a relatively low-cost alternative to conventional stick-built housing. It increasingly plays a major role in providing safe, affordable, and adequate housing not only for lower-income home buyers and renters, but also for those of higher economic status. Manufactured housing refers to a specific type of factory-built housing that has been constructed and manufactured in compliance with HUD's construction and safety standards.[29] Modular housing and other types of industrialized housing that are also factory built do not comply with these standards but must comply with state building codes. State law may limit a local government's ability to completely exclude manufactured housing within its jurisdiction.

## Making available housing affordable

Local governments may use rent subsidies, mortgage assistance, and financial literacy training to increase the ability of residents to afford housing in a community.

***Rent subsidies to low-income persons*** Many localities, either through a PHA or directly by the local government, administer federal rental certificate and voucher programs. In addition, state law sometimes authorizes a local government to use local funds to provide similar rental supplements. These kinds of direct assistance are sometimes collectively referred to as *housing allowances*.

Housing allowances are forms of economic assistance to low-income households who require help to pay rent for a dwelling unit that meets certain minimum physical standards. The most important advantage of housing vouchers and certificates is that they give a recipient household the freedom to choose the kind and location of housing that best meets its needs. In fact, research that analyzed the distribution of federal voucher recipients in the nation's fifty largest metropolitan areas concluded that virtually every census tract in these areas contains some voucher recipients.[30]

That is not to say, however, that rental voucher and certificate programs are without problems. Some families who receive a voucher may not be able to find a landlord willing to accept it. This is especially true in tight housing markets.

***Mortgage assistance to persons of low and moderate income*** Home ownership has long been a cherished part of the American housing ideal. Local governments often seek to facilitate residents' access to this ideal by providing down-payment assistance or second mortgages. A local government may reserve its program for area employees who otherwise could not afford to own a home—or may make the program available to any lower-income person seeking to buy a home—in the area.

---

### Affordable housing in Highland Park, Illinois

The city of Highland Park, Illinois (pop. 31,380), implemented four mechanisms to increase the city's affordable housing stock: establishment of a housing trust fund, inclusionary zoning, a community land trust, and promotion of employer-assisted housing. These efforts have significantly increased both the affordable housing stock in the community and the level of funding available for future affordable housing developments.

*Credit counseling and home ownership classes*   Local governments may directly offer or give financial assistance to a nonprofit organization that provides financial literacy programs for residents. The basic assumption behind this strategy is that if residents are adequately prepared to participate in private capital markets, the demand for affordable housing will drive an increase in the supply.

## Conclusion

A comprehensive approach to community development builds both community capital and the local capacity to be a place that is conducive to economic activity and desirable as a place to live, work, and play. The future of the field lies in its ability to operate at various scales of geography that range from the neighborhood level to broader multijurisdictional regions, where the regional perspective has the potential to achieve greater equity in development. Other challenges include

- Identifying regional solutions
- Strengthening connections to economic and workforce development
- Pooling funds from multiple sources
- Building the operational and managerial capacity of nonprofit community-based organizations.

Overall, however, is the enormous challenge of helping people and places better compete and prosper in a changing economy. This challenge points to a need to better align efforts to stimulate economic activity, educate and train workers, and build vibrant communities—a need that is reflected in a growing concern over the chasm separating economic, workforce, and community development.[31] Researchers and practitioners alike acknowledge that the implementation of public policies in these three areas is fragmented and disjointed. That these distinct policy areas seldom overlap impedes a more comprehensive approach to the challenge of community revitalization, particularly in disadvantaged, low-income communities. To build bridges across these policy areas will require the organizations operating within them to overcome differences in values, policy goals, and political motivations in working toward a common agenda.

---

### Questions to ask if you manage a small community

What does community development look like in your jurisdiction? To what extent is it distinguished from economic development, planning, and public works?

What local organizations are involved in community development? What role do nonprofit groups play in administering community development?

What community-based development organizations exist in your area?

How effectively does your local government engage community-based organizations?

How might your community benefit from a strategic visioning effort?

What local sources of funding are available for community development projects?

What external sources of funding are available for community development projects?

---

**Competencies for managers in the field of community development**

Ability to work with and manage contracts with nonprofit community-based organizations

Ability to provide facilitative leadership of diverse constituencies and interests spanning the public, private, and nonprofits sectors

Technical knowledge of housing policy, rules, and regulations

Technical knowledge of physical infrastructure policies and procedures

Familiarity with housing and real estate finance

Familiarity with the intergovernmental nature of community development programs

Appreciation for the value of citizen engagement and participation

Capacity to draw from multiple funding sources in implementing projects

Basic understanding of program performance measures and evaluation criteria

---

## Endnotes

1  Ron Shaffer, Steve Deller, and Dave Marcouiller, "Rethinking Economic Development," *Economic Development Quarterly* 20 (February 2006): 59–74.

2  See Scott Campbell, "Green Cities, Growing Cities, Just Cities: Urban Planning and the Contradictions of Sustainable Development," *Journal of the American Planning Association* 62, no. 3 (1996): 296–312.

3  Xavier de Souza Briggs, ed., *The Geography of Opportunity: Race and Housing Choice in Metropolitan America* (Washington, D.C.: Brookings Institution Press, 2005).

4  See Richard Florida, *The Rise of the Creative Class* (New York: Basic Books, 2002); David Salvensen and Henry Renski, *The Importance of Quality of Life in the Location Decisions of New Economy Firms* (Washington, D.C.: Economic Development Administration, 2002); Gary Paul Green, "Amenities and Community Economic Development: Strategies for Sustainability," *Journal of Regional Analysis and Policy* 31, no. 2 (2001): 61–76; Kilungu Nzaku and James O. Bukenya, "Examining the Relationship between Quality of Life Amenities and Economic Development in the Southeast USA," *Review of Urban and Regional Development Studies* 17, no. 2 (2005): 89–103; and John P. Blair, "Quality of Life and Economic Development Policy," *Economic Development Review* 16, no. 1 (1998), 50–54.

5  The Prevention Institute (preventioninstitute.org) has profiled eleven examples of predominantly low-income communities that have been transformed by changes in the physical environment, particularly in terms of health outcomes; see Manal J. Aboelata, *The Built Environment and Health: 11 Profiles of Neighborhood Transformation* (Oakland, Calif.: Prevention Institute, July 2004).

6  John Foster-Bey, "Bridging Communities: Making the Link between Regional Economies and Local Community Economic Development," *Stanford Law and Policy Review* 8 (Summer 1997): 25–45.

7  See Project Quest, questsa.com.

8  Lehn Benjamin, Julia Sass Rubin, and Sean Zielenbach, "Community Development Financial Institutions: Current Issues and Future Prospects," *Journal of Urban Affairs* 26, no. 2 (2004): 177–195. See also Melvin Oliver and Thomas Shapiro, *Black Wealth/White Wealth* (New York: Routledge, 1995); and Michael Stegman, *Savings for the Poor: The Hidden Benefits of Electronic Banking* (Washington, D.C.: Brookings Institution Press, 1999).

9  Allen J. Fishbein, "What's Next for CRA?" *Journal of Housing and Community Development* (July/August 2003): 18–22.

10  An eligible CDE is any domestic corporation or partnership that (1) has as its primary mission to serve or provide investment capital for low-income communities, (2) is accountable to residents of low-income communities by having them represented on governing or advisory boards, and (3) is certified by the U.S. Treasury Department as a CDE.

11  Benjamin, Rubin, and Zielenbach, "Community Development Financial Institutions," 177–178.

12  See David Bornstein, *The Price of a Dream: The Story of the Grameen Bank and the Idea That Is Helping the Poor Change Their Lives,* reprint ed. (Chicago: University of Chicago Press, 1997).

13  See Margaret A. Johnson, "An Overview of Basic Issues Facing Microenterprises in the United States," *Journal of Developmental Entrepreneurship* 3, no. 1 (1998): 5–21; Lisa J. Servon, "Microenterprise Programs in U.S. Inner Cities: Economic Development or Social Welfare?" *Economic Development Quarterly* 11, no. 2 (1997): 166–180; and Margaret Sherraden, Cynthia Sanders, and Michael Sherraden, *Kitchen Capitalism: Microenterprise in Low-Income Households* (Albany: State University of New York Press, 2004).

14  See Michael Sherraden, *Assets and the Poor: A New American Welfare Policy* (Armonk, N.Y.: M. E. Sharpe, 1991); and Thomas Shapiro and Edward Wolff, eds., *Assets for the Poor: The Benefits of Spreading Asset Ownership* (New York: Russell Sage Foundation, 2001).

15  William Rohe, Lucy Gorham, and Roberto Garcia, "Individual Development Accounts: Participants' Characteristics and Success," *Journal of Urban Affairs* 27, no. 5 (2005): 503–520.

16  Timothy Beatley and Kristy Manning, *The Ecology of Place: Planning for Environment, Economy, and Community* (Washington, D.C.: Island Press, 1997).

17  Gary Paul Green and Anna Haines, *Asset Building and Community Development* (Thousand Oaks, Calif.: Sage, 2002).

18  For a comprehensive examination of brownfields redevelopment, see Seth D. Kirshenberg, *Brownfields Redevelopment: A Guidebook for Local Governments and Communities,* 2nd ed. (Washington, D.C.: ICMA, 2001).

19  Mark Benedict and Edward McMahon, *Green Infrastructure: Smart Conservation for the 21st Century* (Washington, D.C.: Sprawl Watch Clearinghouse, 2001). See also Karen S. Williamson, *Growing with Green Infrastructure* (Doylestown, Pa.: Heritage Conservancy, 2003), 4, quoting the President's Council on Sustainable Development, *Towards a Sustainable America—Advancing Prosperity, Opportunity and a Healthy Environment for the 21st Century:* "Green infrastructure is defined as 'our nation's natural life support system—an interconnected network of protected land and water that supports native species, maintains natural ecological processes, sustains air and water resources and contributes to the health and quality of life for America's communities and people.'"

20  Robert Giloth and John DeWitt, "Mobilizing Civic Infrastructure: Foundation-Supported Job Generation," *National Civic Review* 84 (Summer/ Fall 1995): 196.

21  Mark R. Warren, J. Phillip Thompson, and Susan Saegert, "The Role of Social Capital in Combating Poverty," in *Social Capital and Poor Communities,* ed. Susan Saegert, J. Phillip Thompson, and Mark R. Warren (New York: Russell Sage Foundation, 2001).

22  Robert J. Chaskin et al., *Building Community Capacity* (New York: Aldine De Gruyter, 2001).

23  Since local governments have no inherent powers, they cannot participate in a federally funded program without a grant of state authority. To do so would subject them to a charge of *ultra vires* activity—activity that exceeds the scope of the powers delegated by the state. While the general legal principle—that local governments have only those powers given to them by the state—is universal, individual states may alter the state-local government relationship (see Chapter 2 of this volume).

24  See Eugene McQuillin, *Municipal Corporations,* vol. 7, 3rd ed., rev. 1981 and suppl. 1988, section 24.558.

25  Housing and Development Act of 1965, Public Law 89–117, 79 Stat. 451.

26  Samuel Bassett Abbott, "Housing Policy, Housing Codes and Tenant Remedies: An Integration," *Boston University Law Review* 56 (1976): 1, 40.

27  See Note, "Homesteading Urban America after *Moore v. Detroit:* The Constitutionality of Detroit's Nuisance Abatement Plan and Its Implications for Urban Homesteading Legislation," *Wayne Law Review* 34 (1988): 1609

28  See, generally, Anita R. Brown-Graham, ed., *Locally Initiated Inclusionary Zoning Programs: A Guide for Local Governments in North Carolina and Beyond* (Chapel Hill: School of Government, University of North Carolina, 2004).

29  Federal law sets construction standards for manufactured housing, and a city or county may not impose additional building or safety standards. This limited federal preemption does not prohibit local government regulation of the appearance of manufactured housing.

30  Deborah J. Devine et al., *Housing Choice Voucher Location Patterns: Implications for Participant and Neighborhood Welfare* (Washington, D.C.: U.S. Department of Housing and Urban Development, January 2003).

31  See Joan Fitzgerald and Nancey Green Leigh, *Economic Revitalization: Cases and Strategies for City and Suburb* (Thousand Oaks, Calif.: Sage, 2002); Herbert J. Rubin, "Economic Partnering with the Poor: Why Local Governments Should Work with Community-Based Development Organizations to Promote Economic Development," *International Journal of Public Administration* 23, no.9 (2000): 1679–1709; and Robert P. Giloth, "Learning from the Field: Economic Growth and Workforce Development in the 1990s," *Economic Development Quarterly* 14, no. 4 (2000): 340–359.

# Public Works

**Cathy R. Lazarus**

Public works is the business of planning, designing, building, operating, and maintaining the public infrastructure and services—roads, bridges, water and sewer systems, public buildings, street cleaning, solid-waste removal, and so on—that support health, safety, and quality of life in our cities and towns. Public infrastructure and services are delivered through capital project planning, creative financing, and extensive discourse between elected officials and their constituents, supported by the technical expertise of the administration, engineers, architects, and operations and maintenance professionals.

Public works departments vary in terms of organizational structure, range of services provided, methods of delivery (i.e., whether services are contracted out or provided by public employees), and financing. Anything owned, operated, or maintained in the public domain will likely fall under the purview of public works. Some of the common public works services are listed in the sidebar on page 202.

In most communities, public works is an array of programs and services provided by employees from many specialized technical backgrounds, including engineering, architecture, environmental sciences, building maintenance, construction, vehicle mechanics, solid-waste management, finance, utilities management, and real estate. Each area is a unique discipline with its own professional associations and licensing and registration requirements.

Given the broad diversity of programs under the public works umbrella, the goal of this chapter is not to focus on the "nuts and bolts" of providing public works services; rather, it is to emphasize the management and administrative strategies and principles that achieve the successful provision of quality services. The chapter discusses public works constituencies, management and personnel considerations, the regulatory and funding environment, infrastructure and capital project planning, service delivery and purchasing options, technology, core public works services, and utility and enterprise fund services.

## Public works constituencies

Unlike parks, libraries, transit, and public safety, public works has few consistently vocal political constituencies. Short of a natural disaster or emergency, people expect toilets to flush, streetlights to work, potholes to be filled, garbage to be taken away, clean drinking water to flow from their faucets, and public buildings to be clean and well maintained.

## Common public works services and functions

### Infrastructure and capital project planning

Capital budget

Capital improvement program (e.g., planning, budgeting, financing, construction, maintenance, replacement of public facilities and infrastructure)

Capital project design

Capital project delivery

### Technology

Computerized maintenance management system (CMMS)

Computerized equipment diagnostics and controls

Radio system

Supervisory control and data acquisition (SCADA) system

Geographic information system (GIS)

### Core public works services

Engineering and related functions

Land development engineering (e.g., plan review, permits, mapping, infrastructure design, telecommunications technology, surveying, utility locating)

Traffic engineering (e.g., signs, signals, calming techniques, bicycle and pedestrian facilities)

Transportation planning

Operations engineering (e.g., operating plans, regulatory permits, environmental studies, compliance and monitoring reports)

### Core public works services (continued)

Operations and maintenance

Equipment procurement and maintenance

Streets and related infrastructure (e.g., pavement maintenance, stormwater management, cleaning, signs, markings, snow removal, trees, parking meters)

Facility maintenance (custodial services, inspections, maintenance services)

Fleet management (vehicle procurement and maintenance)

Park maintenance

Airport services

Animal control

Real property management

Property acquisition

Easements

### Utility and enterprise fund services

Water (safety, distribution, service, treatment, conservation, alternative suppliers, meter readings)

Wastewater (collection, treatment, recycling)

Solid waste (collection, recycling, disposal, landfills)

Gas/electric billing

Gas/electric power distribution

Energy conservation

---

These are basic services that residents expect from their tax dollars and often take for granted. The general public also understands the need for public works projects and will tolerate the temporary disruption of services for a street resurfacing project or a water main replacement. For the most part, elected officials hear about public works only when something goes wrong, such as a broken water main or a burned-out streetlight.

Much of the public works domain is hidden from view. The general public does not see water or sewer mains, pumping stations, or heating and cooling systems in buildings. The design and implementation of capital projects usually attracts attention to public works only when residents believe that their property values or quality of life will be altered by a proposed project.

Because public works departments are responsible for the construction and maintenance of facilities and equipment, other "customer" public agency departments are frequent advocates for funding these services. For example, police and fire departments want well-maintained and reliable emergency vehicles. Firefighters rely on the water system to supply adequate pressure for fighting fires. Library and recreation administrators want facilities that present a positive image to their customers. School district administrators want to be sure that crosswalks, bike lanes, and safe routes to school are clearly marked and freshly painted.

> *In public works you know you're doing a good job when nobody thinks about you.*
>
> **–Jim Russell, retired assistant director of public works**

But without staunch citizen or business advocates, it is easy in times of constrained budgets for elected officials to shift funds from ongoing investment in infrastructure to more visible services and programs. Most people do not want to dwell on the "what-if" scenarios: what if there is not enough reservoir storage, what if the wastewater treatment plant is reaching capacity, what if the local landfill is polluting the groundwater, what if the senior center is found to be structurally unsafe? The solutions to these types of problems typically require large infusions of money, often at the expense of more popular public safety and recreational programs.

One of the challenges for city and county managers is to make sure that the community and its elected officials understand the importance of preventive maintenance and ongoing investment, both to extend the useful life of facilities and infrastructure and to avoid the public disruption associated with the breakdown of essential services. The responsibility of the manager is to develop the constituencies and strategies to provide sustained investment in maintenance and incremental improvement in community infrastructure systems.

So that public works has an equal priority with other critical services, the public works director and manager should ensure that the community has identified its capital needs for a five- to ten-year period and has a strategy to finance implementation. In older communities the priority may be the replacement of end-of-life infrastructure; in growing communities it may be a major expansion of infrastructure capacity.

## The public works organization

The broad mix of employee skills required to provide services makes public works a management adventure. No other local government department has a workforce ranging from entry-level maintenance employees to highly trained administrators and engineers. Achieving and sustaining a common organizational vision and sense of purpose with such a diverse work group is no easy task.

Employee recruitment and retention in public works is a growing problem, as it is for public service in general. Experienced engineers and utility operators are in great demand and are recruited heavily by private consulting firms; small cities often compete with

---

**Environmental management and employee development in Kent County, Delaware**

Kent County, Delaware's (pop. 143,968) wastewater agency has several operators who have been on staff for more than thirty years. The county estimates that one-third of its workforce, with decades of practical experience, will retire in the next five years. Therefore, an important component of the county's new environmental management system (EMS) is its focus on ensuring regular training, transfer of historical knowledge from longtime staff to new employees, and consistency in best management practices among all shifts. As part of this system, a part-time EMS intern shadowed employees conducting covered activities, asked questions about procedures, drafted operational controls and standard operating procedures, and truth-tested these controls and procedures with employees. In addition, Kent County has recorded critical processes and activities via flowcharts, work instructions, diagrams, and even photographs. All these efforts have given EMS team members an opportunity to learn the in's and out's of the organization's activities.

Source: Public Entity Environmental Management System Resource Center, EMS Case Studies in the Public Sector, "Kent County Department of Public Works, Wastewater Treatment Facility" (November 2005), at peercenter.net/ewebeditpro/items/073F8200.pdf, 22.

---

one another to attract experienced, certificated employees. Providing career ladders and training talented in-house employees for advancement is becoming critical to ensure an adequate workforce to sustain essential services.

Although public works functions rely on equipment, tools, parts, and materials, a department's greatest asset is a motivated, well-trained, and dedicated workforce. Many communities expect public works personnel to be available twenty-four hours a day and to be an integral part of emergency and disaster response efforts. To meet these expectations, employees must understand their roles and responsibilities, believe that their work makes a difference, and have the authority to make independent decisions in the field.

## The public works director

Historically, the public works director was a licensed civil engineer who also served as the city or county engineer, signing off on plans for public projects as well as for subdivision maps and other legal instruments associated with the land development process. In the last few years, however, many communities have recruited nonengineer public administrators as their public works directors.

The current-day public works director must be expert in many facets of local government. (In fact, many city managers came from the public works profession during the early years of the council-manager form of government.) A typical day can involve meeting early in the morning with maintenance crews, conferring with staff and consultants on a capital project design, working with a developer on conditions for a housing project, meeting with residents who are concerned about the design of a proposed park, and closing the day with a session of the city governing body.

Whether the director is an engineer, a planner, or a general administrator, he or she must be a strong leader with a thorough knowledge of the technical aspects of the public works profession and superior communication skills. When citizens believe that they are being misled or "sandbagged" with technical jargon, the decision-making process becomes prolonged and contentious. The director must be able to work closely with technical staff to determine how much detail is critical to decision making, and then take complex information and communicate it in clear, logical, and understandable terms to the public, city or county manager, and decision makers.

The director must also be able to work collaboratively with department employees. The workday experience of the frontline maintenance employee is very different from that of the office employee who deals with developers and consultants. A successful director understands the needs of all employees, having spent time at work sites and getting to know people individually.

> *The director must be able to take complex information and communicate it in clear, logical, and understandable terms to the public, city or county manager, and decision makers.*

The director must set forth behavioral norms for the workforce and clear expectations for timely customer service. For utility and maintenance functions, priority activities include ongoing safety training and the development of standard operating procedures (SOPs). For professional, technical, and administrative employees, adherence to schedules, timely project delivery, and budget management should be basic performance expectations. Every employee should understand the importance of a thorough, constructive, and timely annual performance review with his or her manager as well as of the annual performance goal-setting exercise, both of which contribute to a common understanding of work expectations between the employee and the manager.

Public works is an area where things will inevitably go wrong during the normal course of business; for example, a water main or gas line will break, or the pump on a fire engine will fail. The director should always expect the unexpected. The director also must let employees know that unavoidable mistakes will be excused, but that errors due to inattention or sloppy, unsafe work practices will not. Above all, operations and maintenance employees need to know that safety—both their own and that of their crewmembers—is always the highest priority.

### The manager/supervisor

As the bridge between the field personnel and the director, public works managers and supervisors hold the most strategic positions in the department. In many departments, managers and supervisors are former frontline maintenance employees who were promoted because they have good interpersonal skills, the respect of their co-workers, a good work ethic, and an understanding of customer service. Typically, these personnel are responsible for training their employees in maintenance procedures and safe work practices and for conducting the annual performance evaluation. They are the director's eyes and ears in the field and the first contact with citizens who have filed a work order or complaint. By closely directing fieldwork, the supervisor can identify emerging employee performance issues and intervene quickly before such issues become serious disciplinary problems.

**Succession planning in Westminster, Colorado**

The city of Westminster, Colorado (pop. 105,084), provides an award-winning employee training and development program for all employees, as well as a special emphasis program for employees who demonstrate exceptional skills and interest in professional growth. The city also provides growth opportunities for promising employees by periodically examining its departmental structures to ensure that city service needs are being met while allowing promising employees to fill those needs on a part-time or full-time basis. In addition, Westminster encourages employees to expand their work experience by serving on special committees, task forces, or supervisory and management task teams. The city provides funds and adjustable work schedules to employees seeking advanced college degrees and certification in both management and technical fields of employment. These programs are strongly supported by city management, the employee development and training staff, and the city council.

Source: Based on Ron Hellbusch, "Succession Management Planning," *APWA Reporter* (December 2004).

## Frontline employees/maintenance workers

The frontline operations and maintenance worker is the backbone of the public works department. Maintenance jobs, such as reading water and gas meters, painting red curbs to prohibit parking, mowing lawns, flushing water mains, and cleaning storm drains, are physically demanding, hazardous, repetitive, and often boring, yet they are absolutely essential to public health and safety. Maintenance employees are in the community daily as a visible presence of public service. In many communities, garbage day or street-sweeping day is an event for neighborhood children, who wait to see the vehicles go by and get a friendly wave from the driver.

Many entry-level maintenance jobs require minimal education and job experience. New hires are typically trained on the job by their supervisors and managers. Consequently, the first year of employment, or the "probationary year," is critical to ensure that the new hire establishes good working relationships with co-workers, comes to work on time, does not abuse sick leave, and understands technical and safety procedures. Some positions that involve driving large vehicles or operating heavy equipment may need special licenses or may fall under federal Department of Transportation random alcohol and drug testing requirements. New employees must understand these requirements as well as expectations regarding workplace violence and harassment.

Developing and motivating maintenance employees are important for sustaining public works services. Many of the jobs are "crew oriented" and provide a comfortable working environment for employees who do not like being singled out as individual performers. Recognizing crews for good attendance or a spotless safety record is a good motivational technique. Acknowledging individuals for obtaining certifications for water treatment, pesticide application, or pavement management is also appreciated. Some departments open up their maintenance yards to schools and the community to explain and demonstrate maintenance practices. However, the most powerful acknowledgment for frontline employees, as it is for any employee, is being told that they have done a good job. A "thank you" from the city manager or the director goes a long way in letting employees know that their work has value and meaning.

## Public works management considerations

Public works management issues include dissemination of organizational values and behavioral expectations, an understanding and awareness of occupational safety and health requirements, labor relations, emergency and standby response, and technical expertise.

*Organizational values*  Because many public works maintenance activities require teamwork, managers need to create a collaborative environment where all crewmates understands their jobs and what their management team and co-workers expect from them.

One way to promote this fundamental understanding is to establish a process by which employees develop a compendium of values that define how they want to be treated by their co-workers and crewmates. Typical values from public works employees include basic work attributes such as teamwork, support, honesty, trust, punctuality, and attention to safety. Once these basic principles are established, managers can intercede when an employee exhibits behaviors that violate group values.

Managers should give new hires a copy of the department values and explain what they mean and how they are used. Specific departmental values can also be incorporated into the annual personnel evaluation as goals to be worked on during the year. Once the concept of values is accepted by employees and incorporated into the culture of the department, the number of interpersonal disputes should decline over time.

*Occupational safety and health*  An awareness and understanding of occupational safety and health requirements is important at all levels of a public works department. Public works services are hazardous by nature. The highest number of work-related injuries is typically in the public safety (police, fire) and public works departments. Lost-time work injuries affect co-workers and productivity as well as being hard on the injured employee and his or her family. Thus, attention to workplace safety and training is crucial for the employer striving to keep the workforce healthy and productive.

> *Public works contracts, particularly those in the construction arena, should contain provisions requiring contractors to comply with all OSHA requirements appropriate to the job site and nature of construction.*

Attention to workplace safety and training is also the law. In some states, occupational safety and health requirements are governed by the federal Occupational Safety and Health Administration (OSHA). Other states have their own regulations that are more rigorous than those of the federal government. Because OSHA requirements apply not just to the public agency workforce, including hourly employees, but also to contractors working for the agency, public works contracts, particularly those in the construction arena, should contain provisions requiring contractors to comply with all OSHA requirements appropriate to the job site and nature of construction.

Federal and state OSHA guidelines typically mandate annual training for hazardous work functions, as well as annual medical monitoring of employees whose jobs require them to work around loud equipment or with hazardous materials. One of the primary functions of frontline supervisors is to identify areas where special training is needed

---

### Safety tailgates

Safety tailgates are routine, documented meetings in which the supervisor and crew meet to review accident prevention and safety procedures pertaining to their jobs. Tailgates can be run by the supervisor, safety officer, or crew members. Examples of tailgate topics that apply to most public works field operations include safe driving; traffic control; accident reporting; back injury prevention; frostbite or heat stress prevention; head, eye, and face protection; first-aid kits; vehicle and equipment inspection; storm patrol; radio protocol; and emergency response.

---

(e.g., for operation of a forklift or chain saw), and it is the responsibility of the director to ensure that such training is provided.

The cost associated with annual training requirements and medical monitoring can be expensive, but it is part of the basic cost of providing service. Some jurisdictions partner with one another to hire trainers, others rely on in-house trainers, and still others use computer or video-based training modules. Since refresher training is required annually, keeping the information fresh and new is often difficult.

In larger departments, responsibility for worker safety may rest with a safety officer. In smaller departments, it rests with managers and supervisors supported by a safety committee comprising a cross section of the department workforce. At the core of an effective program are training, up-to-date SOPs for hazardous work tasks (traffic control, power equipment operation, and confined space entry), and current Material Safety Data Sheets (MSDSs) for chemicals and other substances used during the course of work. These procedures and guidelines should be reviewed by employees at their safety tailgate meetings and stored in a prominent location or "safety center" in the workplace. Monthly work site, equipment, and vehicle inspections conducted by the manager/supervisor or safety committee are also essential for an effective program. A periodic safety audit by an outside risk manager is another method to ensure a safe workplace. A jurisdiction's insurance company, workmen's compensation provider, or professional associations may have risk management or industrial hygiene consultants available to conduct the audit.

When an employee is hurt on the job, managers and supervisors need to know how to respond. Workers' compensation procedures are usually developed by the risk management or human resource department and should be strictly adhered to when an injury occurs. Managers and supervisors should stay in touch with the injured employee if the nature of the injury will keep the employee off work for an extended period of time. The department should, when feasible, create temporary light-duty assignments for the injured worker so that he or she can return to the workplace as soon as medically possible.

*Labor relations*  Frontline, office professional, and administrative employees are often represented by unions. Whether unionized or not, however, departments should strictly follow the concept of progressive discipline (increasing the level of discipline with each new or repeated infraction, beginning with oral counseling and ending with termination).[1] Nonunionized jurisdictions that do not follow progressive discipline to ensure fair treatment of employees may soon have a union. Employees monitor management responses to disciplinary situations for consistency, confidentiality, and fairness.

Establishing open communication with employees selected by their co-workers to be union stewards or team leaders is an important way to resolve emerging workplace issues at the lowest level in the department. Substantial grievances or disciplinary actions emanating from a work group are important signals that communication and mutual respect are breaking down. When this happens, frequent meetings between the steward, manager, and director are critical to stabilizing the work group. With an open relationship, stewards and managers can work together to resolve employee concerns and craft effective disciplinary strategies to correct performance or behavioral problems.

*Emergency and standby response*   In an emergency, the public works director and/or other managers will be assigned to the city emergency operations center to coordinate response. Public works employees are an essential part of disaster response and are expected to report for work automatically as disaster service workers. In the immediate aftermath of a catastrophe, maintenance crews focus on supporting the public safety response and restoring essential services. Engineering staff play a more flexible role, ranging from supporting field operations to inspecting damaged buildings to determine if they are habitable. Up-to-date emergency response plans and emergency drills are essential for reinforcing emergency roles and responsibilities. Emergency plans should outline the role and callback status[2] for all employees and also anticipate prolonged emergencies in which rotating shifts will be essential to sustain service and the well-being of employees.

Many communities also want public works employees to be available to respond twenty-four hours a day to service calls for sewer blockages, water service problems, or downed tree limbs. To meet this demand, municipalities should establish standby or duty programs in which employees are paid a premium to be available after hours on a rotational basis and are paid overtime when they respond to a service call. Standby programs can be expensive, particularly if the jurisdiction has multiple programs for each public works discipline (sewer, streets, landfill maintenance or facilities, etc.) and if employees take home public vehicles to facilitate response. Employees assigned to standby programs are expected to work independently, have the technical skill to assess field problems accurately, and communicate effectively with the citizens calling for service.

*Technical expertise*   Staff in small departments rarely have the broad range of expertise to manage all aspects of the public works program. Technical consultants and contractors are often needed for specialized engineering services, environmental studies, regulatory testing, analysis, and reporting. Some departments keep environmental consultants and testing laboratories on retainer. With mandatory regulatory monitoring and reporting, it is helpful to work with a single consultant—to the extent permitted by the agency's contracting procedures—to ensure reporting continuity.

## The regulatory and funding environment

The continuing trend is for more regulation in areas pertaining to public health, environmental protection, and, since September 11, 2001, utility and infrastructure security. Over the past decade, stringent guidelines and requirements have been established for drinking water quality; stormwater discharge and treatment; and air emissions from landfills, equipment, and facilities. This growing bundle of regulations has increased the cost and complexity of local government operations because many regulations are beyond the expertise of local agency personnel and compliance requires assistance from specialized consultants and laboratories. Moreover, small agencies lack the resources to monitor the complex federal and state regulatory environment, and so they tend to rely on information and updates from professional associations and city and county associations.

Rarely is sufficient state or federal funding earmarked to help local agencies with the testing, monitoring, cleanup, and reporting required to attain regulatory compliance. In areas of infrastructure development where there is a long tradition of federal and state funding, such as transportation, available revenues have not kept pace with inflation. According to the San Francisco Bay Area Metropolitan Transportation Commission, the purchasing power of the federal excise tax on gasoline, which was 18.4 cents per gallon in 1996, will drop to 13.5 cents per gallon in 2009. The commission goes on to say:

> To make matters worse from a finance perspective, as automobile fuel efficiency improves (a good thing from an air quality perspective), the link between gas tax revenues and traffic congestion and roadway wear-and-tear will erode even further.[3]

Federal funds for investment in transportation and water and air quality management are often awarded at the state or regional level through associations of governments, metropolitan planning organizations, or air quality management districts. Funding needs for local public works are substantial, and federal and state grants often enable a community to implement priority projects. However, it is not always cost-effective to accept small grants of federal or state funds because of the associated procedural and record-keeping requirements. Federal funds used for local planning and design projects (e.g., trails, parks, and other public facilities) must follow federal National Environmental Policy Act protocols and federal contracting and accounting procedures. Sometimes project managers must hire special expertise to assist in formatting projects to meet these requirements. Thus, before submitting funding applications, the public works department should be sure that matching local funds are available and that there are staff and resources to deliver the project within the grant timelines and to meet all grant procedural requirements.

---

### APWA on public investment in infrastructure

The dismal funding and regulatory situation for public works is reflected in the guiding principles used to set the public policy priorities of the American Public Works Association (APWA):

- Support for adequate investment in public infrastructure
- Respect for local authority
- Reasonable regulations and protection from unfunded mandates
- Support for streamlining government oversight.

Specific APWA policy objectives call for increased federal investment in transportation, wastewater and water infrastructure, stormwater management, and homeland security, as well as the development of cost-effective ways to protect air quality.

Source: Jim Fahey, "Board Adopts APWA Advocacy Priorities for 2006," Washington Insight, *APWA Reporter* (November 2005): 4, at apwa.net/Publications/Reporter/ReporterOnline.

## Infrastructure and capital project planning

The development of strategies for the planning, financing, construction, maintenance, and replacement of public facilities and infrastructure is an important public works function. It is the responsibility of the city or county manager and public works director to advance the case for infrastructure maintenance because, short of a major breakdown or disaster, the public will not. Decisions to expand infrastructure and build new facilities should be made with a clear understanding of the cost of maintaining them over their anticipated life cycle.

At the core of capital facility planning is a community that understands and values the importance of sustained investment in infrastructure to extend its useful life. The rule of public sector maintenance is the same as that governing our cars and homes: it is cheaper to maintain than to replace. This is often a difficult tenet for elected officials to uphold when mundane maintenance projects such as a new boiler in town hall compete with more exciting projects like new community ball fields. But insufficient annual investment in assets and infrastructure sets the stage for unplanned emergency breakdowns that disrupt public services and generally cost more to correct because they must be done on an expedited basis.

*The rule of public sector maintenance is the same as that governing our cars and homes: it is cheaper to maintain than to replace.*

Infrastructure master plans enable a community to strategically program its investment in infrastructure replacement and expansion. Many communities now prepare and adopt water, sewer, storm drain, parks, and facility master plans on a ten-year cycle to better plan the timing and scope of both maintenance and major new capital investment. Unlike city or county general plans, public works master plans involve detailed engineering studies of the condition and capacity of existing infrastructure. A water system master plan, for example, will answer such important questions as, Are water pressures adequate throughout the service area? Is there sufficient reservoir storage? Are wells and pumping stations in need of rehabilitation? How much useful life remains in the water main network? Do major distribution trunk lines have sufficient capacity for projected demand? With this information, decision makers can establish priorities, funding strategies, and a master schedule for constructing the needed improvements. With adequate long-range planning, some communities may be able to make improvements on a pay-as-you-go basis through modest sustained increases in utility rates.

In many jurisdictions, well over half of the capital budget is allocated for annual investment in infrastructure maintenance. But such investment should be set at a funding level that can be maintained through rich and poor budget cycles. One technique for funding annual infrastructure investment is to establish the concept of "annual maintenance projects" in the capital improvement program or operating budget. Annual maintenance projects should be given a funding priority equivalent to that of health and safety and regulatory compliance. In times of economic downturn, elected officials should understand that full funding of annual maintenance projects has a higher priority over investment in new facilities. Once maintenance schedules are deferred for several years, it becomes harder and harder to catch up without a very large infusion of capital funds.

---

**Examples of annual maintenance projects**

| | |
|---|---|
| Street resurfacing | Street and parking lot slurry seal |
| Street lane line and legend repainting | Concrete sidewalk/curb repairs |
| Sidewalk replacement | Street tree replanting |
| Water main/service line replacement | Storm and sanitary sewer main replacement |
| Facility maintenance | |

---

## The capital improvement program

The adopted capital improvement program (CIP) establishes a community's roadmap for investment in facilities and infrastructure, typically for several years out. Like a master plan, it prioritizes projects and infrastructure needs but is adjusted annually through the budget process. It includes all the annual maintenance projects discussed previously, as well as one-time projects that can range from the preparation of specialized master plans or studies to the construction of new facilities and to major equipment purchases. Not all communities have a separate CIP, but those that do generally develop and adopt it parallel to the operating budget. Usually, only projects in the first year of the multiyear CIP are funded for implementation.

Preparation of the CIP can reside with either the finance or public works department, but in either case, the expertise of both is needed to develop a credible plan. The finance department frames the fiscal picture for the CIP, projecting available funds over the plan horizon, assessing the impact of proposed projects on fees and utility rates, and determining strategies to fund priority projects. Some common financing techniques for capital projects include pay-as-you-go, rate increases, interfund loans, certificates of participation, and bonds. Some states have very attractive low-interest revolving loan funds for local government capital investments.

The public works department defines the scope of the proposed projects and develops preliminary project cost estimates. Sometimes the proposed projects are in a very conceptual stage precluding the development of a realistic construction estimate. In such instances it is useful to break a project into separate design and construction projects spanning two or more years of the CIP because construction budgets can be more precisely estimated after the project design phase.

As part of the CIP adoption process, the governing board holds public hearings and then determines which projects will be funded over the span of the program. Some communities develop a set of funding policies or strategies to guide the funding deliberations and the placement of projects over the planning horizon.

## Capital project delivery options

Few small communities have the in-house expertise to design capital projects, so they rely on architectural and engineering consultants for project design. Public works engineers act as project managers, overseeing the design team to ensure that the project stays within budget, schedule, and scope. Professional consultants are typically hired through a request for proposal (RFP) process, in which interested firms submit proposals and the top firms are ranked after a presentation to an impartial selection committee. Some states preclude the ranking of consultants for professional services on the basis of price. While jurisdictions have different consultant selection requirements, the overarching objective is to ensure that the selection and award process is as impartial as possible.

One of the challenges of capital project delivery is to determine to what degree elected officials and the community should be involved in project design. When a project is anticipated to generate controversy or a high level of community interest, the city manager and public works director should decide on the appropriate level of public participation as well as of elected official involvement before the project begins. For every project there is a sensitive balance between the right of the public to participate and the need to design and construct a project efficiently within the available budget. A protracted design, review, and approval process delays construction, allowing inflation and other factors to affect the overall project cost. Including project constituencies in the early phases of design helps the design team understand what design features are important to future users and brings to light the concerns (noise, traffic, parking) of citizens. Constituent concerns should be thoroughly vetted and resolved before a project is brought to elected officials for environmental clearance or project approval. If opposition or design details cannot be fully resolved at the staff level, elected officials should be advised of this before the public meeting and presented with options for resolving areas of conflict.

After the governing board approves project design, the design team prepares detailed plans and specifications, a cost estimate, and a bid package for contractors to use in preparing construction bids. To avoid the appearance of political influence and impropriety, state

---

**Criteria for prioritizing capital improvement projects in Mountain View, California**

The capital improvement program (CIP) in Mountain View, California (pop. 69,276), sets forth the following criteria for prioritizing capital improvement projects:

- Reduced operating and maintenance costs
- Preservation of existing assets
- Health and safety
- Legal mandate
- Availability of outside funds
- Priority of governing board
- Citizen and/or neighborhood interest
- Implementation feasibility
- Conformance with adopted plan, goal, objectives, and policies
- Secondary benefits: impact on water or energy conservation, traffic
- Interjurisdictional effects/opportunity for joint project implementation.

Source: Adapted from the city of Mountain View, California, CIP.

> **Sustainable design in Austin, Texas**
>
> A growing number of communities are embracing green or sustainable building concepts for new projects, incorporating recycled or renewable materials to the extent feasible. Sustainable design includes an array of green options, from recycling demolition debris and reusing building sites to installing solar panels and products made from recycled materials. In Austin, Texas (pop. 690,252), a new 27,000-square-foot building that serves as a meeting place and support center to help people transition out of homelessness was designed to use a minimal amount of finished materials and form work. It employs a rainwater collection system to supplement the building's nonpotable water supply, a passive solar hot-water system to preheat water for showers, and a photovoltaic array to supplement the electrical system. Natural light and views reach more than 90 percent of the work spaces.
>
> Sources: U.S. Green Building Council, www.usgbc.org/, and the American Institute of Architects, aia.org/release_042505_cotegreen.

law or local ordinances strictly prescribe the bidding and contracting process and almost always require the construction contract to be awarded to the lowest responsible bidder.

Today, public sector contracting offers a variety of project delivery options in addition to the traditional design/bid/build. These options include

- *Multiple prime:* The city acts as general contractor issuing separate bid packages for the various building trades required for the project. Often a construction manager is part of the city team charged with managing the various subcontractors.

- *Design/build:* The public agency develops a set of performance documents that are bid by firms who design and construct the project. This method generally allows for faster project delivery but less design control than desired by many public entities, and it is used less often than other methods.

- *Construction management:* For complex building projects, some cities hire a construction manager, often a general contractor, to oversee the project design and construction and to represent the city's interest in working with the architect and contractor.[4]

Regardless of the preferred project delivery method, public works project managers must rigorously monitor the schedule and budget at all phases of the project. Cost overruns, inferior work, and construction delays can have major political repercussions, placing a heavy responsibility on the project management and construction inspection team.

## Service delivery and purchasing options

Historically, public works services were provided by city, county, or special district employees. However, with today's tight budgets and limited federal and state funding, local governments are devising new models of service delivery and equipment procurement.

### Partnerships

For smaller communities it is sometimes cost-effective to join together to provide services that benefit from economies of scale. These partnerships can take the form of contractual agreements or more structured joint powers authorities.[5] Unlike service contracts with private entities, in which charges are cost recovery plus profit, public agency agreements generally provide for cost recovery only.

Small communities often contract with one another for such basic nonemergency public works services as traffic and streetlight maintenance, street sweeping, and sewer/storm drain maintenance. These are the easiest and most flexible cooperative arrangements. For the jurisdiction selling the service, contractual arrangements allow expensive maintenance equipment such as boom trucks and sewer power flushers to be fully utilized, and the revenue from the neighboring community helps offset the costs of labor, equipment, and maintenance. For the jurisdiction buying the service, contractual arrangements avoid the additional costs of staffing, training, purchasing, and maintaining expensive specialized equipment. In entering into a service agreement, all parties should clearly define their service-level expectations and develop simple performance standards (e.g., streets in residential neighborhoods will be swept monthly, nighttime streetlight inspections shall occur twice a month) for easy contract administration.

More complex arrangements involve the development, construction, and operation of major service facilities, such as wastewater treatment plants, recycled water systems, sanitary landfills, and solid-waste resource recovery and transfer stations. In situations involving substantial capital investment and ongoing operations, the contractual arrangement between the parties can take several forms. In some partnerships one of the partners assumes responsibility for the construction, operation, and maintenance of the shared facility with ongoing oversight from partner agency staff. The managing partner is also responsible for the financial management of the shared infrastructure, including budget preparation and member agency invoices. Partnerships can also take the form of a joint powers authority (JPA), which is a quasi-governmental agency established to provide a specific service or array of services. A JPA generally has its own staff and a governing board of elected officials from the member jurisdictions, and it tends to function autonomously.

## Special service districts and parcel taxes

Many states authorize the formation of special service delivery or maintenance districts for public works services. Because there is great variation from state to state, it is difficult to generalize about the scope and legal structure of these entities. They are called service districts, benefit assessment districts, special assessment districts, or (in California) Mello-Roos districts. Most require an election either of voters or of property owners in the proposed service area. The revenue stream to fund the services can be an increment of the property tax rate or a flat parcel tax. Recent special assessment and parcel tax initiatives have fared better with voters when they have limited terms or require voter reauthorization in five or ten years and also have a very specific, clear purpose (e.g., build a new library, maintain or renovate parks, reconstruct levies or flood channels). Almost any service can be funded by these special districts, but they are commonly used for water, sewer, streetlighting, landscaping, street/sidewalk construction, and even cemetery maintenance.

## Privatization of public works services

Privatization of services is another viable service delivery option. Political and labor relations considerations aside, it is possible to privatize almost all public works services. Some communities have contracted with private water system operators or have even sold

**Top five service contract considerations**

In August 2005, *American City and County* published survey findings regarding public works contracting practices. Almost 400 communities responded to the survey. More than half of the responses were from communities with populations under 100,000.

**Why services are contracted**
Saves money
Professional management/expertise
Saves management time
Improves operations
Improves service quality

**Why services are not contracted**
Service quality will not improve
Operations will not improve
Too expensive
Displaces government employees
Inefficient

The top ten contracted services were road/bridge construction, 38 percent; solid-waste collection/disposal, 33 percent; pension fund services, 28 percent; grounds maintenance, 24 percent; building maintenance, 24 percent; information technology/computer services, 20 percent; traffic engineering, 16 percent; wastewater/sludge treatment, 14 percent; GIS services, 11 percent; and street cleaning and maintenance, 9 percent.

Source: Adapted from Bill Wolpin, "Hired Hands," *American City and County* (August 2005): 44-46.

their water systems to private companies. The cautionary note is that once a service has been contracted, it is expensive to hire employees, managers, and equipment to bring it back into the public domain.

Rarely are long-term contracts or franchises sole-sourced in the public sector. Service contractors are selected after an RFP process. Clear minimum performance expectations, contract terms, and cost criteria should be outlined in the RFP. Analysis of the submitted proposals should be based on quantitative and qualitative criteria and be as unbiased as possible. According to a national survey, the four top incentives offered by successful contractors were guaranteed performance, performance standards/metrics, revenue or cost sharing, and guaranteed employment of existing staff.[6]

## Equipment procurement

Public works maintenance operations depend on tools, materials, and equipment. For operational efficiency, the day-to-day "nuts and bolts" should be quick and easy to procure from local suppliers. Specialized equipment such as pumps and motors are sometimes sole-sourced or procured according to performance specifications developed by the department. Heavy equipment and vehicles (e.g., bulldozers, street sweepers) can be leased or purchased outright. Better pricing can be obtained by piggy-backing onto state contracts when possible or by joining with other local agencies to purchase multiple units.

## Technology and public works

Technology has revolutionized mapping and information systems, improved methods for planning and tracking maintenance activities, and automated manual functions to make them more efficient. However, not all technology pays for itself with offset savings in labor and materials. Before a public works department embarks on the design and installation of an expensive computerized system, the operational costs and benefits of the system should be clearly evaluated and understood. Strategies for operating, maintaining, and upgrading computer-based technology should also be considered up-front to ensure that the technology will be fully used.

## Computerized maintenance management systems

A computerized maintenance management system (CMMS) is a tool to track preventive maintenance schedules, work orders and service calls, productivity, parts inventories, and work quality. It replaces the vast stacks of binders with paperwork orders, maintenance histories, and maintenance schedules found in almost every public works department.

A growing number of systems in the marketplace have modules for virtually all public works activities. The features of the ideal CMMS depend on a department's needs and objectives. Small communities may find simple spreadsheets sufficient to capture preventive maintenance schedules while others want to track all diagnostic tasks performed as part of a work order. For example, one department may simply need to know that basic preventive maintenance (PM) was performed on a patrol car, on schedule, on a specific date. Another department may need not only to track that the PM was performed on schedule but also to capture the specific work performed (oil changed, breaks checked, windshield wiper replaced, faulty door lock replaced, etc.).

Before a department commits to a specific CMMS, employees who will use the system should have an opportunity to participate in a hands-on demonstration. It is important to contact agencies that are already using the product to see if they are satisfied with the system, the training, and the support provided by the vendor and whether there are pitfalls to avoid during installation and start-up.

## Computerized equipment diagnostics and controls

Today's vehicles, motors, pumps, generators, heating and cooling systems, and other specialized equipment come equipped with internal computers or programmable logic controllers. These advances allow intelligent programming that enables automatic or computer-based calibration and adjustment of fans, valves, and motor speeds—previously labor-intensive manual tasks.

## Supervisory control and data acquisition systems

A supervisory control and data acquisition (SCADA) system is typically used to automate the operations and monitoring of distribution-type networks such as water, gas, or electricity, enabling staff to monitor and operate the systems from a central location. A SCADA system collects real-time operating data from remotely located facilities and transmits the data to a central computer that sends commands back to regulate the operation of equipment. With heightened concern about the security of utility systems, SCADA technology is now used to monitor doors, locks, gates, reservoir hatches, and equipment at essential installations.

For example, a SCADA system will monitor the level of water in a reservoir, automatically open valves and turn on pumps when the tank needs to be refilled, and shut things down when the fill level is reached. The system will track water consumption, water pressure, disinfectant injection, fluoride levels, and other information to create a history of operating characteristics. If something goes wrong, the system will send an alarm to alert operators to the problem, which may be corrected remotely via the SCADA system. Some operators use laptop computers to monitor and calibrate the system from home after hours or on the weekend.

While the operating efficiency and energy- and labor-saving benefits from a SCADA system are considerable, maintaining system security can be difficult with multiple remote locations and operators. Monitoring system security and maintaining and updating software programs, sensors, and other hardware are beyond the scope of a small agency and thus are often contracted. It is important to ensure that the SCADA system architecture is well documented should there be a need to change vendors or bring system development and maintenance in-house.[7]

## Geographic information systems

A geographic information system (GIS) is a computer system combining layers of information that accurately describe the physical and infrastructure characteristics of an area or individual parcel of land. A GIS is based on aerial photographs or digitized maps, with map layers capturing data about environmental, property, road, utility, and aerial imagery down to the level of a street tree or fire hydrant (see Figure 9–1). With a mouse click, the user can identify land use characteristics of a property (address, elevation contours, zoning, Federal Emergency Management Agency flood zone, building footprint) and service infrastructure (water, sewer, street markings) supporting the land use. A powerful maintenance tool, a GIS enables crews to more accurately locate infrastructure in the field, and aids developers and engineers in designing and planning the replacement or expansion of infrastructure.

Although GIS systems are used by public safety personnel for emergency response as well as by planners, they are often incubated in the public works department and financed by the utility funds.

Several important operational and policy questions should be considered at the early stages of GIS implementation: Will the system be developed by a consultant or by in-house resources? Is a customized system needed? Who will maintain and update the GIS

---

### GIS-based asset management in Saco, Maine

The city of Saco, Maine (pop. 18,230), built a GIS-based asset management system to improve the city's financial position (under GASB 34—see Chapter 4), forge better relationships among departments, and emphasize long-term operations and maintenance goals. Finance and public works staff met several times with city council members to explain the potential benefits (e.g., maps, increased efficiencies, and improved bond ratings). An outside vendor contracted to create the asset management system, which provides the city with a comprehensive inventory, inspection, and management system for all its roadway, sewer, and stormwater infrastructure assets. Existing information from a recent inventory of the city sewer system infrastructure and a pavement condition survey was compiled, and data on the city's remaining infrastructure were collected from the field using handheld computers and wireless technology.

**Figure 9-1  GIS maps showing drainage, Pierce County, Washington**

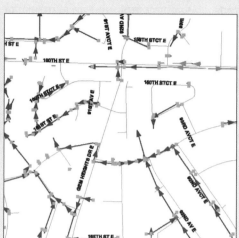

Portion of drainage project area with road coverage

Portion of drainage project area with orthophotos

These maps are part of the GPS Drainage Project being conducted by the Pierce County, Washington (pop. 753,787), public works and utilities road maintenance, water programs, and GIS departments. The project, which uses global positioning system (GPS) technology to collect the county's drainage infrastructure data, will identify and maintain Pierce County's drainage features, support the Endangered Species Act, and analyze spatial drainage data.

Source: David M. Grinstead, Pierce County, Washington (data), in *ESRI Map Book*, Vol. 20, available at esri.com/mapmuseum/ mapbook_gallery/volume20/state6.html.

layers? How secure should the system be? Should information from the system be considered public information or proprietary? Should there be open access to data pertaining to water systems and other sensitive infrastructure?

## Core public works services

Core public works services are the basic programs that are often taken for granted but are essential to allow cities to function and grow. As the sidebar on page 202 shows, the core public works services are engineering and the related functions of land development, traffic, transportation planning, and operations; operations and maintenance as they pertain to street and related infrastructure, facilities, and fleet management; and real property management.

### Engineering and related functions

Public works engineering functions fall into two broad areas: (1) project-based engineering, supporting land development and capital project implementation; and (2) operations engineering, supporting day-to-day operations, maintenance, and service delivery ranging from traffic signal timing to utility system operations. In small communities with limited resources, engineers may work across all functions. In larger communities engineers may be organized in specialized work units.

***Land development engineering***   Public works is generally responsible for the plan review, conditioning, and permitting of all construction and development activities in the public right-of-way as well as for the placement and size of public service infrastructure. The local engineer also signs off on subdivision maps, easements, encroachments, parcel maps, and other legal documents that require accurate property descriptions.

Much of this work is part of the land development process and requires close collaboration with the planning department; at times, however, the perspectives of the engineers and planners conflict. Public works tends to operate from the perspective of standardization of infrastructure ranging from street widths and the placement of water and sewer lines to the design and placement of garbage/recycling enclosures. These standard specifications are developed to facilitate service provision and maintenance over the useful life of the infrastructure as well as future replacement of the infrastructure.

*While infrastructure design requires flexibility to meet community standards for urban design and development, it should not compromise the quality of life and services that future residents will expect.*

Although planners often seek to create denser development patterns that conserve land, narrower street grids can be difficult for emergency vehicles, garbage trucks, and other maintenance equipment to maneuver. In townhouse or small-lot single-family developments, placing water or sewer lines through private backyards is a scenario for future problems if a pipe breaks or needs to be replaced. Engineers and planners need to understand that while infrastructure design requires flexibility to meet community standards for urban design and development, it should not compromise the quality of life and services that future residents will expect.

After projects are approved and in construction, public works is responsible for inspecting the public infrastructure to ensure that it meets standards and complies with project conditions. Some communities use performance bonds that require a two- or three-year maintenance period in which failures are either repaired by the developer or paid for through the bond.

Telecommunications technology and local governments' ability to franchise and regulate telecommunications services and infrastructure are complex areas of public policy at all levels of government. In its role as steward of the public right-of-way, public works is also involved in this developing regulatory environment. Many communities are dealing with the issue of multiple telecommunications companies wanting to install infrastructure in the public right-of-way. Construction of telecommunication facilities typically involves tearing up streets and sidewalks to install conduit and cable as well as above- and underground equipment vaults. Some streets simply do not have room to accommodate additional conduits and vaults.

In permitting these activities, public works needs to coordinate closely with legal counsel to ensure that the community is protected from costs associated with street and sidewalk repair and that telecom contractors are fully licensed to do the work. Some communities have adopted ordinances that restrict installations for a period of years after a street has been resurfaced.

Wireless (WiFi) technology also has public works implications to the extent that WiFi companies want to install equipment on publicly owned streetlights or utility poles.[8]

***Traffic engineering and transportation planning***    Traffic engineering is the design and operation of the street and highway system. It includes development of the standard profile for streets, sidewalks curbs, and related improvements. The traffic engineer conducts or reviews traffic studies to determine what impact new development will have on the capacity and operation of the existing street network. In most communities, the traffic engineer is responsible for approving the location of road markings (e.g., bike lanes, pedestrian crossings), signs, and on-street parking. The engineer is also responsible for conducting studies to determine if traffic signals, stop signs, and other types of traffic control are needed on a street.

Transportation planning activities can be found in either the public works or planning departments. Transportation planners fill the increasingly important function of representing the jurisdiction's interests with regional congestion management agencies and metropolitan planning organizations that disburse state and federal grant funds.

With limited funds for traffic improvements or the acquisition of private land and easements to widen streets, traffic engineers are turning to automated systems, such as computerized traffic controllers and synchronized traffic signals, that allow the existing street system to function more efficiently and safely.

> *Transportation planners represent the jurisdiction's interests with regional congestion management agencies and metropolitan planning organizations that disburse state and federal grant funds.*

Whereas accommodating nonvehicular travel needs used to be an afterthought, it is now a significant part of transportation planning. Walking and bicycling are now acknowledged as modes of transportation equivalent to motor vehicle travel. Many communities have adopted bicycle and pedestrian plans and established bicycle and pedestrian advisory committees. Dedicated bicycle/pedestrian pathways are being incorporated into residential projects, and some cities are designating bicycle boulevards to provide safe, crosstown routes for bicyclists. Many communities are employing methods to make intersections safer with pedestrian countdown signals, pedestrian flags, raised crosswalks, or crosswalks with pavement lights. And new commercial and industrial projects may be required to include bicycle parking, showers, and lockers for bicyclists.

Speeding, cut-through traffic, and safety are hotly debated and politicized neighborhood topics. A growing number of communities are adopting Neighborhood Traffic Management Programs (NTMPs), which establish a process for neighbors to vote on whether traffic calming is desirable on their streets and, if so, what type of traffic calming methods they prefer. Traffic calming techniques are a grab bag of relatively inexpensive improvements designed to slow traffic on neighborhood streets after a speed study confirms that a problem exists. These techniques include speed humps, turn restrictions, narrow median islands, traffic circles and islands, bulb-outs, and street closures. Stop signs are not considered a traffic calming method because their purpose is to regulate the right-of-way rather than to slow speed. A popular device is the automated flashing speed radar sign, which warns oncoming drivers of their speed.

In many communities the NTMP is initiated when affected residents submit a petition to the traffic engineer. The advantage of the program is that the residents directly affected by the problem have the opportunity to vote for the solution. After a neighborhood process, the desired traffic calming methods can be approved, administratively, by the manager, the elected body, or an appointed traffic commission.

*Operations engineering*   Part of the engineering function in small communities is to provide day-to-day support to operations and maintenance staff. This support can take the form of developing operating plans, obtaining regulatory permits, filing compliance and monitoring reports, and, in water operations, making decisions about operating pressures and parameters. In the case of a municipal landfill, the engineer rather than the maintenance crew is typically responsible for air and groundwater quality testing and reporting.

Engineers and maintenance professionals have different approaches to problem solving. Often the engineering solution seems impractical to the maintenance superintendent while the maintenance approach may not follow accepted engineering and design practices. In an effective public works department, both perspectives are given credence. A good collaborative relationship between engineers and maintenance staff sets the stage for efficient, cost-effective operations.

## Operations and maintenance

Maintenance of streets, fleet, and facilities is the public works service that is most dependent on discretionary, general fund revenues—the same funds that support police, fire, recreation, and other programs. Unlike water and wastewater systems maintenance, this service carries no ongoing utility or user charges to support it. Consequently, in an economic downturn, infrastructure and equipment maintenance is the public works service that is cut most severely. Because the deterioration of streets and sidewalks, vehicles, and buildings takes a few years to become visible, it is easy to defer preventive maintenance.

*Streets and related infrastructure*   Around the country, funding for local road maintenance comes from a variety of sources, such as state fuel taxes, vehicle license fees, and local sales tax initiatives that earmark funds for pothole repair or local construction and conveyance taxes. The biggest funding source is usually the local government's general fund or other discretionary revenue.

Pavement maintenance consists of sealing cracks, repairing potholes, and patching to prevent water from penetrating the street surface and accelerating the deterioration process (see Figure 9–2). These ongoing activities are supported by periodic street overlay projects (chip seal, slurry seal, or asphalt overlay). According to the San Francisco Bay Area Metropolitan Transportation Commission,

> Experience shows that delayed maintenance leads to even costlier rehabilitation.... If it costs $1 to keep a section of roadway pavement in good condition through timely maintenance, it will cost $5—five times as much—to restore the same roadway if it is allowed to deteriorate to the point where major rehabilitation or reconstruction is needed.[9]

Many communities use a pavement management system (PMS) to prioritize and strategically establish their maintenance overlay priorities. A PMS is a computerized software program that collects data regarding the condition of streets and develops a numerical condition rating according to a pavement condition index (PCI). The data are collected by field inspection that records information about cracking, bumps, failing utility trench repairs, and other street conditions. PMS rating systems range from 0 to 100, where 10 or lower means complete pavement failure and 100 means excellent condition. Communities will establish their desired PCI targets—generally 70–85 in the good to very good range. Streets with a PCI below the target level are prioritized for overlay or other major maintenance.

Sidewalks are typically installed when a neighborhood or subdivision is developed, and they have a long service life if they are maintained. Maintenance consists of grinding down elevated sections or ramping them to correct tripping hazards, and patching spots or repaving sections damaged by weather, tree roots, or heavy vehicular traffic on driveway approaches. Responsibility for replacing end-of-life sidewalks varies by community. Some local ordinances clearly assign sidewalk replacement as the property owner's responsibility, while other communities bear the cost entirely or share costs with the property owner. Cities and counties are responsible for putting in the intersection ramps to make them accessible in accordance with federal Americans with Disabilities Act (ADA) criteria.

Traffic signal and streetlight maintenance are related responsibilities and are either contracted or done with in-house staff. New light-emitting diode (LED) technologies have made traffic signals more energy efficient, and grants are available in some parts of the country to encourage the retrofit of existing installations. Additionally, many communities are installing battery backups to ensure that signals at critical intersections operate during power outages. ADA requirements also encourage the retrofit of existing signals to install audible pedestrian signals and pavement delineations at approaches to an intersection. Pedestrian countdown

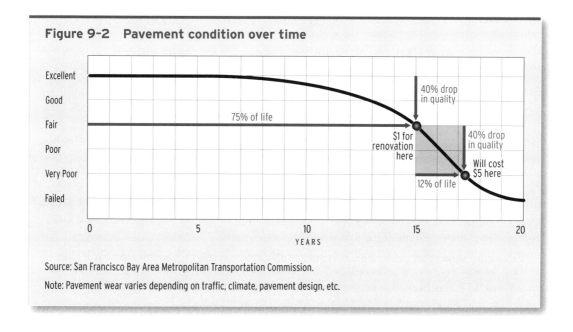

**Figure 9-2  Pavement condition over time**

Source: San Francisco Bay Area Metropolitan Transportation Commission.

Note: Pavement wear varies depending on traffic, climate, pavement design, etc.

signals and bicycle loop detectors are already widely available retrofits to improve nonmotorized travel around the community.

Because of federal and state requirements regarding stormwater management and treatment, street sweeping is taking on an important role in improving environmental quality in addition to the aesthetic appearance of communities. For example, routine sweeping is an important and relatively inexpensive way to collect dust and particles from brake linings, which are rich in copper and other heavy metals, and prevent them from washing into the storm drainage system and thereby polluting rivers, bays, and other surface waters.

Finally, street maintenance may include painting curbs and road markings, and fabricating and installing street signs.

*Facility maintenance*   Facility maintenance has two broad components: custodial services and maintenance services. Custodial services are often contracted. Custodial (cleaning) contracts stipulate the frequency with which facilities are serviced and include an allocation for less frequent activities, such as carpet cleaning and window washing.

Maintenance of public buildings can be wholly or partially contracted. Smaller jurisdictions may have a small facility maintenance workforce to take care of routine facility needs for plumbing, HVAC filter replacement, light ballast replacement, painting, and simple electrical and carpentry work. Major maintenance and repair of specialized equipment, such as elevators, fire station automatic roll-up doors, and roofs, are almost always contracted. A CMMS is particularly important to a facilities program where building condition, breakdown history, and preventive maintenance schedules form the basis of the capital investment program.

*Fleet management*   Fleet management is the procurement and maintenance of vehicles and large pieces of equipment. In-house mechanics, contractors, or a combination of the two maintain the public agency fleet. The fleet manager is responsible for establishing preventive maintenance schedules, purchasing tires and other parts, and determining when it is more cost-effective to replace rather than repair equipment. An equally important function is to work with other departments to develop specifications for purchasing or leasing vehicles and equipment. To the extent possible, specifications for sedans, light-duty trucks, patrol cars, and even fire engines should be standardized for ease of maintenance and to allow vehicles to be rotated among departments to ensure that they are fully used. Standardization also facilitates the purchase of multiple vehicles, which usually means a lower cost per vehicle.

Small jurisdictions can achieve economies of scale in vehicle purchases by collaborating with one another to develop joint vehicle bids. Some states, such as California, allow cities and counties to purchase patrol cars and other types of equipment off the state contract at substantial savings.

## Real property management

The sale, purchase, and lease of a public agency's real estate assets are sometimes located in the public works department because acquisition of property and easements for road rights-of-way and utilities are integral to the department's operations. In recent years, small jurisdictions have begun to use real estate assets more strategically by buying, selling, or leasing land to generate income to support municipal goals (e.g., park development, affordable housing) or to stimulate private development. Strategic joint use of property between agencies is a cost-effective method for helping agencies meet financial and operational objectives. For example, a California city and the local elementary school district recently entered into a partnership in which the city leased the middle school's playfields for ninety-nine years to construct a buried reservoir in exchange for the reconstruction, operation, and maintenance of the fields and athletic facilities over the lease term. An entrepreneurial approach to property management, to the extent permitted by state statute and local ordinance, is a way to enhance the community and generate an income stream for general government purposes.

## Utility and enterprise fund services

Water, wastewater, and solid-waste services are funded by user fees and charges rather than by general government revenues. Revenues and costs associated with these services are typically segregated from the general fund in accounts referred to as utility funds, enterprise funds, or special funds.

The public works and finance departments develop utility rate recommendations jointly. While there are many different types of rate structures, rates should be set at a level that supports operations, maintenance, and staffing; planned capital improvement projects; and debt service and that maintains a reserve for unforeseen needs or emergencies. Rates can be structured to achieve public policy goals such as encouraging water conservation, energy efficiency, or recycling.

Utility rates are set during the annual budget adoption process, and the issue can be politically charged. Sometimes it is helpful to compare recommended rates with rates charged in surrounding communities. If rates are higher than in neighboring communities for equivalent service and capital investment, it may be a red flag that the utility is not operating efficiently and may need to be reorganized. Elected officials need to know that the recommended rates are neither the highest nor the lowest among neighboring jurisdictions for the level of capital investment and service provided. Because small incremental rate increases avoid the uproar associated with sharp spikes, many communities project average costs and smooth rate increases over three or more years.

### Water

The delivery of a safe, abundant, secure, and affordable supply of water is one of the most fundamental public services, but it also entails one of the most complex and highly regulated service delivery systems. According to the American Public Works Association (APWA), there are more than 54,000 community drinking water systems in the United States, with an infrastructure network spanning more than 700,000 miles—more than four times longer than the National Highway System.[10]

The water system infrastructure consists of a distribution system that transports water from its source (groundwater or surface water) to homes and businesses for use. Along the way the water may be pumped, stored in reservoirs, chlorinated or chloraminated, and fluoridated before being transported through a system of water mains with connections to fire hydrants, through the water meter, and into homes and businesses. Most of the water system is publicly owned with the except for the water line running from the meter to a structure. This infrastructure requires ongoing maintenance and investment to ensure that mains, valves, saddles, and other connections are in good repair to minimize water main breaks.

---

### Issues affecting the water industry

A "State of the Industry Report 2005," published in the *American Water Works Association Journal,* identified the top five issues affecting the water industry:

- Regulatory factors (compliance, number of regulations)
- Business factors (funds to meet new regulations; financing of repairs, replacements, and upgrades)
- Source water supply (sufficiency of supply, source water protection, future supplies)
- Security (general security issues, terrorism)
- Water storage/infrastructure.

Source: Excerpted from Jon Runge and John Mann, "State of the Industry Report 2005: A Guide for Good Health," *American Water Works Association Journal* 97 (October 2005): 58–67, by permission. Copyright (c) 2005 American Water Works Association.

---

The complexity, cost, and risk associated with operating a water utility is causing some communities to question whether they want to stay in the water business. There are a growing number of private water providers around the country, and some communities have sold their entire water infrastructure to those providers; other have contracted with a neighboring jurisdiction or private company to operate the water system.

*Water safety*   The public health and safety of a community water system is the highest priority, and it requires ongoing vigilance and testing to ensure that water quality meets federal and state drinking water requirements. The federal Safe Drinking Water Act of 1974 empowered the U.S. Environmental Protection Agency (EPA) to establish national standards for drinking water safety and to oversee attainment of those standards. According to the American Water Works Association, the number of federally promulgated drinking water regulations has increased from approximately 20 in 1976 to almost 100 in the year 2000.[11] Meeting these requirements is a major challenge for all water systems, but it is especially difficult for smaller, rural systems, which lack the sophisticated testing and treatment capabilities needed to monitor regulated substances and ensure that they are below maximum contaminant levels.

Water retailers are required to annually provide all customers with a consumer confidence report on the quality of water delivered over the past year. The framework for the report is mandated by EPA and includes detailed findings about the level of regulated constituents such as lead, copper, and cryptosporidium as well as information about whether violations occurred during the reporting period. Some water retailers use the report to inform customers about major capital improvement projects or the importance of water conservation.

*Water supply*   Of equal priority is an adequate quantity of water to serve the community. Some communities are fortunate to be self-sufficient with an abundant supply of surface or groundwater. But with urbanization, many communities must purchase or import water from other agencies to meet consumption requirements. A related consideration is the assurance that water storage is sufficient for emergencies and firefighting as well as for daily needs. A water system master plan, discussed earlier, is the vehicle for a community to chart its long-term water supply and storage strategy.

*Conservation and alternative water supplies*   With the cost and scarcity of potable water, there is increasing pressure to find ways to reduce water consumption. Promoting conservation is one of the easiest strategies, and this can be accomplished by establishing a tiered conservation rate structure (the cost per unit of water increases with consumption above a baseline level) and providing incentives to install water-saving fixtures. Requiring low-flow toilets and fixtures as well as water-efficient landscaping in new developments are two ways to reduce consumption. Offering consumers rebates for installing low-flow showerheads, water-efficient clothes washers, and low-flow toilets is another. Some communities offer water consumption and landscape audits to residential and commercial customers to promote conservation.

Developing recycled/reclaimed water systems is an increasingly popular drought-proof method to offset potable water demand. Recycled water is highly treated wastewater (sewage) that can be used for a variety of purposes, including residential and freeway landscape irrigation, toilet flushing, food crop irrigation, and groundwater recharge. It is not used for drinking.

Cost and community acceptance are the two impediments to recycled water use. A recycled water system is expensive to construct because it is a parallel distribution system with a network of pipes that connect to irrigation systems and other reuse sites. Some communities have encountered strong opposition to recycled water projects out of concern about the quality and "aesthetics" of the product. However, in communities where the cost of potable water has increased significantly, recycled water is often seen as a cost-effective alternative water supply.

Desalination is a process in which salt is removed from ocean water or brackish water to make it suitable for drinking. Desalination technology has been used internationally, and projects are now being developed in the United States to supplement traditional water supplies. Federal and state grants are available to offset project costs.

## Wastewater

Like water, wastewater or sewage treatment is a basic service. Many small and rural communities still rely on private septic systems to process waste, but today more than 72 percent of the U.S. population is served by wastewater treatment facilities.[12] Wastewater flows from homes and businesses into the privately owned sewer lateral and into a system of increasingly larger public mains that transport it to the wastewater treatment facility.

---

### Recycled water in small California cities

In 2003 California cities used more than 545,000 acre feet, or 1.77 billion gallons, of recycled water. Small cities that have successfully introduced recycled water for landscape irrigation and habitat restoration include Calistoga, Ceres, Lodi, Los Banos, Palo Alto, Ridgecrest, Scotts Valley, Simi Valley, and Upland. Many other California cities and utility districts are successfully using recycled water for agricultural irrigation and to offset the demand for potable water in manufacturing processes.

Source: California State Water Resources Control Board, Office of Water Recycling, "2002 Statewide Recycled Water Survey," at waterboards.ca.gov/recycling/docs/wr2002survey_attc.pdf (accessed October 10, 2006).

Some systems are gravity operated; others require pumping or lift stations to transport the sewage to the treatment facility.

Maintenance of sewer mains is different from that of water mains. A water main break presents an immediate problem because customers lose water and the streets may flood; however, a sewer main break can go undetected for years because the effluent drains into the ground with no obvious affect on the customer. (In some areas of the country, leaking sewer mains affect the quality of surface water and groundwater.) On the other hand, sewer main blockage and backup into a home or business is an emergency that can cause substantial property damage and a potential damage claim against the public agency. Blockages can be caused by the intrusion of tree roots or grease and can be cleared by shooting high-pressure water into the line to clear the obstruction. To minimize liability, some jurisdictions are adopting sewer ordinances that require home owners to install two-way cleanouts; these fittings facilitate cleaning and backflow devices that prevent sewage from flowing backward into private lines. Today, the foundation of an effective sewer maintenance program is the video camera that enables sewer mains to be inspected on a rotating basis for blockages, cracks, failures, and capacity.

> *To minimize liability, some jurisdictions are adopting sewer ordinances that require home owners to install two-way cleanouts*

The regulatory environment for wastewater treatment is technical and complex. Regulations govern the discharge of treated effluent into surface waters as well as emissions from the incineration of by-products. For example, in areas where the concentration of mercury in surface water is a problem, programs must be developed with local dentists and medical laboratories to install systems that capture waste mercury and to recycle thermometers to ensure that the mercury does not enter surface waters through landfill or sewer systems. Treatment plants have in-house laboratories to monitor the chemical constituents in wastewater discharge. These plants are required to report detected violations to the regulatory permitting agency, and violations can result in monetary fines depending on severity.

The nature of advanced wastewater treatment processes and regulatory requirements makes it difficult for a small community to operate a wastewater treatment plant cost-effectively. Regional partnerships or special wastewater treatment districts are the operational models of choice for smaller jurisdictions. In some arrangements, each member jurisdiction has an ownership share of the plant capacity; in others, the plant is operated by a regional authority and the local agency contracts for service.

## Solid-waste collection, recycling, disposal, and the landfill

For solid-waste collection, recycling, and disposal, communities have a number of service models to choose from. For smaller communities, contracting some if not all of the solid-waste program is increasingly attractive because of the costs associated with the collection and separation of recyclable and hazardous materials, the difficulty in managing the sale of recycled materials, and the regulatory cost of operating a public landfill. Services can be privatized through a franchise agreement or contract. Communities can also join together through a JPA or other collaborative structure to provide service and achieve operational efficiencies and economies of scale.

The trend in solid-waste management is to divert as much material as possible from landfills. In California, for example, a minimum of 50 percent of the solid waste must be diverted from landfills through recycling and other diversion programs. Across the country, some communities are establishing the ambitious goal of zero waste and are developing aggressive recycling and diversion programs to achieve it. The APWA reports that in the United States, 28 percent of municipal solid waste is recovered and recycled or composted, 15 percent is burned at combustion facilities, and 57 percent is disposed of in landfills.[13]

The collection of solid waste and recyclables from the can or dumpster is the first step in the disposal process. In some communities the material is hauled directly to the recycling center and landfill; in others the material is first hauled to a materials recovery facility. At the facility, sorters separate out recyclable material, which is then crushed, baled, and shipped for reuse; green waste is turned into compost; and the material that cannot be reused is transported to a landfill or incinerated.

*Collection*   Solid-waste collection is typically a weekly service for single-family customers. Some communities have backyard pickup; others require property owners to place cans curbside for collection. Some communities provide garbage and recycling toters; others require the property owner to provide them. Recycling programs are more variable for materials that are collected weekly or less often. Denser apartment developments, restaurants, and commercial and industrial customers require more frequent service. Solid-waste staff need to work with these accounts to determine the appropriate bin size and frequency of collection as well as the increased challenges to recycling: space limitations may hamper the storage of recycling bins on-site, and multiple users may mean a greater chance of contaminating recyclables with garbage.

The cost of collection vehicles, fuel, and labor are a significant portion of the consumers' garbage bill. Garbage, green waste, and recyclable materials are collected with different trucks. Some jurisdictions are requiring solid-waste haulers to purchase vehicles fueled by liquid natural gas or other less polluting fuels when older, diesel-fueled vehicles are replaced. Air quality management districts in areas with poor air quality may require older trucks to be retrofitted with emission control equipment.

*Recycling*   The environmental benefits of recycling are well understood and accepted by the public. The issue is not whether to recycle but rather how and what to recycle. A major debate in the recycling community is whether the basic recyclable materials (cans,

**Marketing a new trash collection system in Lynchburg, Virginia**

When the city of Lynchburg, Virginia (pop. 66,973), stopped collecting trash manually and began using a semiautomated collection system, it developed a marketing and communications campaign to inform residents of why the new system was needed, what types of trash receptacles were available, and when their new pickup days would be. The campaign included bringing the new receptacles to public meetings, rewarding citizens for ordering their new receptacles, educating city employees, and creating an entertaining cartoon character, Bart the Cart, who appeared in television and print ads. The campaign was judged a success when the transition went smoothly.

plastics, glass, paper) should be commingled or separated. While commingling is easier for the customer, separated materials generally have a higher value in the recycled market-place. Green waste is always collected separately to facilitate composting. The adoption of local ordinances mandating the recycling of construction and demolition debris is emerging as an effective way to divert this material from the landfill and put it to beneficial use.

Hazardous materials such as paints and solvents, fluorescent lights, batteries, motor oil and other petroleum products, and e-waste (electronic devices such as cell phones, computers, and televisions) must be separated for special curbside handling. It is rarely cost-effective for smaller communities to develop individual programs to dispose of hazardous materials. Instead, effective service models are regional collection facilities where consumers make appointments to drop off hazardous materials or have them collected. The cost of regional drop-off or collection services can be funded by the member communities and incorporated into the garbage rate.

The disposal of e-waste has become a hotly debated public policy topic in recent years: much of the e-waste from this country is being shipped offshore to countries that do not have adequate regulations to protect the environment and worker health. A few retail establishments that sell electronic devices will collect them for recycling, sometimes charging a fee for handling and disposal. Although some states have adopted laws mandating retailers to accept e-waste for recycling, future regulatory changes and new requirements for city recycling programs can be expected.

The market for recycled materials is volatile, reacting to international demand and fluctuations in the economic cycle. Small communities are at a disadvantage in negotiating a favorable price for recycled materials because they do not offer the processor an economy of scale. Policy makers should not approach recycling from a cost-recovery basis but as a way to extend the life of the local landfill and as an environmentally appropriate thing to do.

**Disposal**   Disposing of solid waste in landfills is expensive, partly because of environmental regulations but also because the number of landfills in the United States is steadily declining—from 8,000 in 1988 to 2,300 in 1999, according to the APWA—although the capacity has remained relatively constant as the new landfills tend to be larger than older ones. And the declining number of landfills makes transportation of solid waste more costly because the material must be transported over increasingly longer distances. In 2004, 21.3 million tons of solid waste moved across state lines for disposal.[14]

**The landfill**   Historically, the garbage dump was perhaps the most undesirable public land use, conjuring images of piles of uncovered malodorous refuse, populated by scavenging birds, rats, and other disease vectors. Landfills were notorious for migrating methane gas into nearby homes and structures and for leaching toxic materials into groundwater. The image of the garbage dump still lingers in the public mind and is one of the reasons it is so difficult to locate and permit new landfills in this country.

However, the modern sanitary landfill bears little resemblance to its historical ancestor. It consists of a network of cells that have an impermeable liner and are sealed with a clay cap to keep the garbage in an anaerobic (without air) condition to facilitate its decomposition. In an operating landfill, the refuse is covered with dirt every day so that no garbage is exposed to the elements. The liquid produced by the decomposing garbage is called leachate and is extracted by a series of wells. Depending on its chemical constituents and local requirements, leachate can be discharged into the sanitary or storm sewer.

**Recycling a landfill in Mountain View, California**

Mountain View, California (pop. 69,276), has converted a 750-acre landfill on the shore of San Francisco Bay into a regional park that includes a 25,000-person capacity amphitheater, a sailing lake with a boathouse and restaurant, a links-style golf course, a driving range and pro shop, a kite-flying area, a banquet center and restaurant, and miles of trails. The park and restored wetlands are a wildlife refuge with habitat for burrowing owls and other protected species. Microturbines convert methane gas, a by-product of garbage decomposition, into electricity to power city infrastructure in the park. The city also sells methane gas to a private company to generate electricity.

Methane gas, a by-product of the decomposition process, is a greenhouse gas that remains in the atmosphere for about nine to fifteen years, and according to EPA, landfills are the largest human-related source of methane emissions in the United States.[15] Methane gas is also explosive. Landfills have an elaborate network of gas extraction wells that collect the gas and either flare it into the atmosphere or put it to use by converting it to electricity. Surface and groundwater emissions from landfills are rigorously regulated and monitored to protect public health and safety and to minimize environmental harm.

Maintaining a "healthy" and compliant landfill is an expensive and long-term commitment for a public agency. When a landfill reaches capacity, it is closed and enters the postclosure phase of its life cycle. This phase lasts as long as it takes for the solid waste to decompose—typically twenty to thirty years or more—during which time the gas and other environmental systems must remain in place. As the refuse decomposes, the surface of the landfill subsides, causing the clay cap to crack or water to pond on the surface. The clay cap must be maintained and monitored to ensure that it remains intact with no cracks that enable methane gas to vent into the air. Surface drainage must be maintained to protect the clay cap and prevent liquid intrusion into the landfill cell.

To extend the life of the landfill, some public and private operators are using a new technology that accelerates the decomposition process, thereby allowing the landfill cell to be reused. Unlike traditional landfill technology designed to keep the landfill cell free of liquids, the bioreactor process pumps liquid into the cell to accelerate decomposition. The objective is to extend the life of the landfill so that it can be reused for more garbage or for other purposes. Bioreactors can stabilize a landfill in five to ten years as opposed to the twenty or more years required for a traditional "dry tomb" landfill.

Despite the cost and negative perceptions associated with them, landfills can be turned into community jewels. Across the country, closed landfills have been reclaimed for parks and open space, golf courses, amphitheaters, and other beneficial uses.

## Conclusion

Today, public works is a broad mix of traditional maintenance practices and new technology that has revolutionized data collection and the way that fundamental services such as water, sewer, solid waste, and transportation are managed. Never before have local governments had so many service delivery models to choose from. But with these many options comes a similarly impressive array of challenges for public works departments:

- Attracting and retaining a competent workforce
- Navigating the complexity of the regulatory environment
- Coping with unfunded state and federal mandates
- Integrating technology into day-to-day operations
- Planning for and responding to emergencies
- Training strong maintenance supervisors
- Securing sustained funding for maintenance and infrastructure upgrades
- Developing a constituency for public works investment
- Balancing neighborhood interest with community-wide benefit
- Incorporating environmental principles into public projects
- Managing the budget impact of global price increases in petroleum products and other essential construction materials, such as steel and concrete.

These challenges can be met. Technological advancement notwithstanding, the unshakable core of a public works program is the dedication and judgment of the employees who have made public works their career choice. Public works is an area of public service in which a strong collaborative relationship between the city or county manager and public works director can truly make a difference in a community's quality of life.

---

**Questions to ask if you manage a small community**

Do my employees understand the community's customer service expectations and are they meeting them?

Do my employees understand how to interact with the public and contractors ethically?

Are we properly staffed and trained to respond in an emergency?

Do our maintenance programs and practices maximize our infrastructure investments?

Can our citizens feel proud of our facilities, vehicles, and infrastructure?

Do we comply with regulatory requirements?

Are we successful in recruiting and retaining talented, skilled employees?

Are we providing the right training, tools, equipment, and technology to empower employees to work safely, smartly, and efficiently?

Do we have the right balance between in-house expertise and consultants?

Are we seeking partnership opportunities with our neighbors to achieve economies of scale?

Would contracting services to a private or other public entity improve service delivery and efficiency?

Are we doing all we can to seek grants and other outside funding?

Does the capital improvement program adequately invest in infrastructure?

Do we seek optimum community participation in project planning and implementation?

Is the service ripe for establishing an enterprise fund with appropriate service charge?

Are we coordinating service delivery effectively within the department and with other departments?

---

**Competencies for managers in the field of public works**

Understanding of the technical aspects of and technological advancements in public works

Strong written and oral communication skills

Strong supervisory skills

Strong grant-writing skills

Knowledge of environmental regulations

Ability to act collaboratively and build consensus

Ability to think strategically and solve problems

Ability to think regionally as well as locally

Familiarity with public policy making

Knowledge of public sector contracting and purchasing

Proficiency at capital budgeting

---

## Endnotes

1 For more information on the subject of progressive discipline, see Joseph C. Palermo, "From Hiring to Firing: Managing the Risk of Difficult Employees," *IQ Report* 38, no. 5 (2006).

2 Callback status refers to whether employees are expected to report automatically to a particular location or assignment in an emergency or to contact their supervisors for instructions about where and when to report for duty.

3 Metropolitan Transportation Commission, *Mobility for the Next Generation—Transportation 2030 Plan for the San Francisco Bay Area,* final report (February 2005), 30, 31.

4 Brian Danley, "How Do I Get My Project Built?" *Harris Progress* (Harris Associates, Summer 2005): 3–4; Stephen B. Gordon, "Alternative Procurement Strategies for Construction," *IQ Report* 37, no. 6 (2005).

5 For more information on interlocal partnerships, see Scott Collins, "Interlocal Service-Sharing Agreements," *IQ Report* 38, no. 3 (2006).

6 Bill Wolpin, "Hired Hands," *American City and County* (August 2005): 44–46.

7 John Stubbart, "Does Automation Help Operations?" *Opflow* 31, no. 9 (September 2005): 6–7.

8 League of California Cities, "How the Telecommunications Revolution Will Affect Your City," *Western City* 81 (November 2005): 13–24.

9 Metropolitan Transportation Commission, *Mobility for the Next Generation,* 41.

10 American Public Works Association (APWA), "Facts about America's Public Infrastructure," at apwa.net/Advocacy/Infrastructure/.

11 Edward G. Means III, Nicole West, and Roger Patrick, "The Regulatory Horizon: Implications for Water Utilities," *American Water Works Association Journal* 97 (November 2005): 62.

12 U.S. Environmental Protection Agency, "Clean Watersheds Needs Survey (CWNS)," at epa.gov/owm/mtb/cwns/1996rtc/faqwfd.htm.

13 APWA, "Facts about America's Public Infrastructure."

14 Ibid.

15 U.S. Environmental Protection Agency, "Methane: Sources and Emissions," at epa.gov/methane/index.html.

# Public Parks and Recreation

Candace Goode Vick

Until the late 1800s, public park and recreation services were not considered a function of local government. Commercial recreation enterprises, religious organizations, private athletic clubs, nonprofit youth agencies, and special-interest groups provided opportunities for people to use their leisure time. The effects of urbanization, industrialization, and mass production launched the public parks and recreation movement. Large urban parks, playgrounds, and community centers were built in Chicago, New York, Philadelphia, and other large cities to address the social needs and improve the quality of life for all people. Early leaders felt that recreation programs and parks could help prevent delinquency and antisocial behavior, reduce stress, and improve the livability of communities. While public parks and recreation began as an urban phenomenon, today many small jurisdictions provide leisure services for their citizens. The public has grown to expect recreational facilities, opportunities, and services to be provided by local governments.

## The benefits of parks and recreation

The types of recreational opportunities and facilities have changed drastically since the creation of the sandlot playgrounds and the development of Central Park in 1853, but the benefits have remained the same. Physical activity helps adults and children fight obesity and other health problems, such as diabetes, coronary disease, and high blood pressure; it also increases good cholesterol, relieves insomnia, strengthens muscle tone, and improves self-esteem and confidence.[1] Building greenways and trails, locating parks close to homes, and improving access to parks are just three ways in which agencies can encourage active living and promote healthy lifestyles. And by establishing partnerships with corporations, school systems, land conservation agencies, and developers, communities can overcome some of the barriers to building smaller parks and multiuse paths, trails, and greenways.

Many parks and recreation departments are offering educational programs designed to help park users understand the health benefits of getting active. Beyond offering organized fitness classes, these programs encourage people to be active throughout the day.[2] Recreational programs, leagues, and classes help young and old alike develop the skills they need to participate in a wide range of social activities. Through sports, for example, children can develop motor skills, learn teamwork, and practice sportsmanship, while arts and cultural activities can help people develop their creativity and intellectual capacities.

---

**Creating small parks in Lakewood Township, New Jersey**

Lakewood Township, New Jersey (pop. 68,834), has focused on creating small parks. Over the past several years, it has build sixteen neighborhood playgrounds, some of which have been put on vacant lots owned by the city. The township has also partnered with the school district to build playgrounds on school grounds; these playgrounds are open to the community during non-school hours. In addition, developers are being asked to put playgrounds in new developments that are owned by the community.

---

**Promoting public life in Stroud Township and Bucks County, Pennsylvania**

Stroud Township (pop. 30,096) and Bucks County (pop. 621,342) in Pennsylvania organize "Community Days" as a way to create a sense of community, raise awareness of park areas and the environment, and help residents learn about recreational opportunities and government organizations. The entire community is involved in organizing and implementing the celebration. Local businesses provide sponsorship; local artists provide entertainment; and various local groups, such as Boy Scout troops, the Historic Society, environmental groups, garden clubs, and local government agencies, assist with the activities.

---

Parks can also provide a place where people can go to ease everyday stress and improve their mental health through contact with nature.

Parks, recreational services, and cultural activities also provide social benefits as they can help stimulate participation in public life and build social capital. One of the most significant amenities a city can offer is a public place where residents can meet to discuss important issues.[3] Recreational programs and facilities give residents an opportunity to come together to build trust, socialize, develop friendships, and become actively involved in their community, thereby improving their overall quality of life.

And local parks and recreation programs can contribute to the positive development of young people. By partnering with police departments, health departments, schools, and other youth-serving agencies, recreation staff can provide youth with safe places to play and socialize while helping to address numerous youth-at-risk issues, such as vandalism and gang activity.

Parks, open spaces, and recreational facilities and programs can be a significant factor in a community's economic development. Well-designed and easily accessible parks and recreational facilities, as well as carefully preserved open spaces, are among the selling points that communities use to attract business and residents.[4] Moreover, because homes located near a park or greenway often command higher sales prices than homes that are farther away, these amenities help improve real estate values. Taken together, these factors can help revitalize cities.

Communities are discovering that heritage tourism, festivals, and cultural and sporting events are also excellent ways to produce economic returns for the area, while local and regional parks and facilities can generate jobs and promote small business development. The Virginia Creeper Trail, for example, not only provides people with a way to be

**The National Police Athletic/Activities Leagues, Inc.**

The National Police Athletic/Activities Leagues, Inc. (PAL) is an excellent example of how local law enforcement agencies can work with community partners to sponsor youth athletic leagues and recreational programs in an effort to prevent juvenile crime and violence. PAL was started in 1910 by Capt. John Sweeney of the New York Police Department in an effort to create trust and understanding between police officers and community youth. Today there are 350 PAL member chapters in law enforcement agencies servicing more than 700 cities and 1,700 facilities.

Source: National Association of Police Athletic/Activities Leagues, Inc., "Police Athletic Leagues (PAL)," www.nationalpal.org/.

**The Virginia Creeper Trail**

The Virginia Creeper Trail is a thirty-five-mile rail trail located in rural southwestern Virginia. In the late 1970s, the towns of Abingdon (pop. 7,925) and Damascus (pop. 1,083) purchased the railroad right-of-way and developed a walking and biking trail. Since then, real estate values have increased for property adjacent to the trail, which has also become a vacation destination for people outside the local area. Today the area sports numerous inns and bed-and-breakfasts, four new bike and shuttle service shops, and three new outfitter businesses, in addition to other services.

Source: The Virginia Creeper Trail, vacreepertrail.com/index.html.

active and improve their health but also has stimulated small business development and enhanced tourism opportunities for communities in the region (see sidebar).

Protection of our natural environment is another important benefit of public parks, greenways, and open space. As communities continue to expand and develop, parks offer a way to preserve green space and protect wildlife habitats. They also act as natural sound barriers, help reduce heat island effects, and increase carbon uptake from trees and vegetation. In addition, proper park development can reduce nonpoint source pollution, contribute to aquifer recharge, mitigate floods and droughts, and provide for habitat diversity. A park system should therefore be considered an investment in keeping the living environment healthy.

In summary, public park and recreation services can play an important role in improving the quality of life for individuals, families, and communities. They are critical to the health and welfare of children, the quality of life for residents, the vitality of the local economy, and preservation of the natural environment. To ensure these benefits, local governments should plan for and administer public park and recreation services in accordance with the needs and interests of the people served as well as the resources available.[5]

## Organization of public parks and recreation

Local governments, school systems, and special districts are given legal authority by the state to provide park and recreation services for their citizens. Although the enabling legislation varies by state, it outlines how these services should be organized and authorizes such activities as the acquisition of property, the purchase and construction of facilities, the appropriation and expenditure of funds to provide services, and the establishment of supervised recreation.

## Organizational patterns

When a local government decides to provide park and recreation services, it must decide what type of managing authority would be best to use. In making that decision, it should consider

- Which options are available under the state's legislation
- Which managing authority will provide the best financial support
- Which organizational option is preferred by the public
- Which arrangement would be best given the facilities that are available.[6]

There are five primary alternatives to organizing public park and recreation services: a line department within the local government, a special park and/or recreation district, a joint department formed by two or more units of government, a contractual agreement with a private or public agency to provide services, and a line department within a school district.

*Line department within the local government*   The most common of the five approaches is a line department within the local government, usually administered by a director who reports to the local manager or elected officials. The mission and scope of the department will determine its title. Some local governments may elect to establish both a parks department and a recreation department while others may combine the services into one entity. The combined parks and recreation department has become the most prevalent organizational structure because it avoids potential conflicts between the functions, produces financial savings, reduces overlapping services, and provides a broader base for public support.

In times of budget cuts and right-sizing of local governments, park and recreation services have sometimes been reassigned to other divisions. For example, in some cities, park maintenance has been moved from the parks and recreation department to public works. But while the consolidation of similar services into one department is a viable alternative on paper, caution should be used. The public works staff must understand the demands for maintenance that recreational services and facilities generate. Recreational programs are often held in the late afternoon, evenings, and on weekends, requiring maintenance services to be available seven days a week. Excellent communication between the recreation and public works staff and a willingness to work together are essential for this organizational structure to work. The recreational function has also been placed within the human services or community services departments. Again communication, understanding of the recreation mission, and professional leadership are critical for success.

In some communities, rather than moving parks and recreation under other governmental departments, the local government has expanded the scope of the recreation department to include the administration of cultural resources, greenways, open spaces, libraries, historic sites, and civic centers. This added responsibility is usually reflected in the agency title by words that identify the addition service.[7]

***Special park and/or recreation district***   Some states use the special district approach to establish local park and recreation services. A special district functions as an independent governmental unit with the power to tax for services. Residents of an area must vote to approve the establishment of a special district.[8] While the director of the special district usually reports to an elected or judicially appointed policy-making board, the district is responsible for its own organization, personnel, fiscal matters, areas and facilities, and programs.

The major advantage of a special park district is that it does not have to compete with other government functions for resources; its sole focus is on providing quality park and recreation services. Moreover, special districts that serve multiple jurisdictions can maximize their financial and physical resources by minimizing the duplication of services. This organizational model is used extensively by communities in California, Colorado, Illinois, Michigan, Ohio, and Oregon.

***Joint provision***   As a third organizational approach, a local government may choose to enter into an agreement with another local government to provide recreation services for its residents. There are two variations on this approach. First, a local government can contract with an established parks and recreation department to provide specified recreation services. This option is most often used when a city lacks the financial resources to establish an independent department yet wants to provide parks and recreational opportunities for its residents.

Second, two or more cities can come together with a county to create a regional parks and recreation department. This option, which is a solution for communities with fewer than 20,000 residents and limited financial resources, allows several local agencies to combine their resources to provide services that would otherwise be impossible or too expensive to provide. It can also help communities avoid duplication of services and facilities and can require fewer administrative positions. The disadvantages of a regional department are the potential loss of local autonomy and the possible decrease in the participation of local citizens on advisory boards or in planning groups.

***Contractual provision with private agency***   The fourth organizational option is for the local government to contract with private or nonprofit organizations such as the YMCA, Boys and Girls Clubs, school districts, home owners associations, or athletic associations to provide park and recreation services for the public. As with the joint provision option, this approach most benefits a small community that lacks the resources to establish a full-time parks and recreation department on its own. A possible disadvantage is that residents often do not recognize that the services provided are sponsored by the local government (and their tax dollars) and thus might not support future expansion of public recreation or realize that the programs are available to all citizens.

When contracting with an outside agency, local officials are responsible for ensuring that services are rendered to all residents and not just to those who are members of the nonprofit organization. The contract for recreation services should include such items as

- Scope and nature of programs that the agency will offer to the entire community
- Duration of programs
- Financial responsibilities, including a policy for setting and collecting fees and charges
- Operation, maintenance, and ownership of existing facilities
- Establishment of a recreation advisory board

**A sample public-private recreational contract: Stokes County, North Carolina**

The following excerpt is from the recreational contract between the Stokes Family YMCA and Stokes County, North Carolina (pop. 45,848):

Responsibilities of the YMCA
The YMCA agrees to provide the following minimum services:

1. A Summer Youth Program shall be provided to the youth of Stokes County on an annual basis. This program shall be for the length of time specified each year in the Annual Budget. This program shall utilize school sites as well as YMCA facilities, including Camp Hanes.

2. A Baseball Camp shall be provided yearly to the youth of Stokes County. Other camps shall be provided based upon registration and participation. Examples of Camp offerings shall include but are not limited to soccer and tennis.

3. The YMCA shall retain all revenues generated by program offerings, except those fees generated from Moratock Park.

Responsibilities of the County of Stokes
The County of Stokes agrees to the following responsibilities:

1. The County shall maintain ownership of Moratock Park located in Danbury, North Carolina. Further, the County shall provide maintenance and repair services for Moratock Park up to and including grounds maintenance, facility maintenance, insurance and utility cost.

2. The County shall appoint a Parks and Recreation Advisory Committee to offer advisory assistance to the YMCA and the County in program offerings and program administration. The county shall at all times during the term of the Agreement maintain a minimum of one (1) YMCA representative or a designee thereof to serve as a voting member of the Parks and Recreation Advisory Committee.

- Length of term for the contract
- Provisions for terminating the contract.

*Line department within a school district* In addition to authorizing local governments and special districts to provide recreation services, states have also authorized school districts to provide athletics and community recreation or community education, which includes recreation education. The recreation services provided by school districts vary widely from a few organized classes in such activities as sewing, guitar, and aerobics to a full-time recreation department. These services are made available to all citizens of the school district, which can include multiple local governments. This model allows for the extended use of school facilities for recreation, maximizes local resources, and can reduce duplication of services and facilities.

## Parks and recreation citizen boards

No matter how a local government decides to provide park and recreation services, the formation of a parks and recreation citizen board or commission is essential. A board's

**School district recreation departments**

In South Orange County, California, the Saddleback Valley Unified School District's Department of Recreation and Community Services provides services for a ninety-five-square-mile area, which includes the cities of Aliso Viejo, Laguna Hills, Lake Forest, Mission Viejo, Rancho Santa Margarita, and Trabuco Canyon. In Sheboygan, Wisconsin (pop. 48,872), the Sheboygan Area Community Recreation Department, which has been in existence within the Sheboygan Area School District since 1927, serves the residents of Sheboygan and the surrounding area. The city of Sheboygan has a separate parks department, which operates and maintains nine parks and two community centers.

members can interpret the needs of the citizens, provide a bridge between the paid professional staff and local residents, and be advocates for both the public and the department. Board members can also help analyze resources, assist in long-range and master planning for facilities, determine desirable programs, make recommendations to elected officials, and recruit volunteers and community leaders. In communities that cannot hire professional recreation staff, the board can assist elected officials with the day-to-day operations and concerns of the parks and recreation programs. Whether members are appointed or elected, it is critical that the board membership be representative of the social, economic, and cultural groups of the community.

In most states, when parks and recreation boards are established for departments that are under the direction of a local government or school district, they are generally advisory policy-making bodies without taxing authority. However, in several states, such as Colorado, Illinois, and Missouri, the citizen boards for the special park and/or recreation districts are composed of elected members and are usually policy-making boards with taxing authority; as such, they have the legal authority to establish policies, adopt a budget, raise funds, hold title to property, and manage personnel.

## Scope of services

Each community decides on the scope of its park and recreation services on the basis of its residents' needs and interests; its character, financial resources, and traditions; its environmental features; its other available leisure opportunities, including those provided by the private sector, nonprofit organizations, and other government entities; the philosophy and interest of its leadership; and relevant state law, local ordinances, and administrative procedures.

Some departments will directly provide recreational services and facilities; other departments will facilitate or broker service delivery by allowing individuals, private agencies, and nonprofit organizations to use public facilities to provide those services. Little League Baseball and Pop Warner Football are usually provided through this mode: a private group organizes and operates the teams while games are played on publicly owned fields.

Parks and recreation departments can offer a wide variety of recreational programs, including cultural and performing arts, social recreation, athletics, outdoor recreation, therapeutic recreation, aquatics, literary activities, and volunteer services. Some departments are even including such services as public gardens, community festivals, high

**Promoting Leisure Activities for Youth (PLAY) in Virginia Beach, Virginia**

Collaborating with the Virginia Beach city schools; community services board; juvenile court services; public libraries; departments of police, public health, housing and neighborhood preservation, and social services; and other community agencies, the parks and recreation department in Virginia Beach, Virginia (pop. 438,415), was instrumental in developing the Promoting Leisure Activities for Youth (PLAY) team program. PLAY works to provide prevention programs that enable children and teens to learn positive behaviors, develop marketable skills and increase life skills, achieve goals and build self-esteem, and give back to the community. Programs include a mobile activity center that can be brought into targeted areas where children and teens lack access to transportation, a stress management course for teens, an educational camp designed to teach middle-school youth alternative approaches to resolving issues, a cheerleading program that incorporates community service projects and life skill sessions, and a regional girls' basketball league.

Source: Peter Witt and John L. Crompton, *Best Practices in Youth Development in Public Park and Recreation Settings* (Ashburn, Va.: Division of Professional Services, National Recreation and Park Association, 2002), 123-133.

adventure programs, health screenings, and dog parks. Some departments focus primarily on youth sports and summer playground programs; others offer a full spectrum of recreational programs for all ages and ability levels; and still others provide only those programs that are not offered by other leisure service agencies in the area. Some departments have the resources to provide an active park orientation and will develop an extensive system of ball fields, tennis courts, golf courses, community centers, greenways, and aquatic facilities; others may provide only limited park sites and facilities. Some communities not only build their own recreation facilities but contract with other agencies, such as a school system, to use their facilities for programs as well.

Citizen input into all aspects of parks and recreation planning is critical if a department is to meet the needs of the residents. Focus group meetings with relevant groups in the community, mail surveys, telephone surveys, Internet surveys, face-to-face interviews, and public meetings are the most frequently used methods to gather public input.

Although each department is unique, staff can meet the needs of their communities if they employ the following planning principles:

- Listen to the public and involve citizens in planning and conducting recreational programs whenever possible.

- Establish a mission and goals, stating program objectives clearly so that everyone knows what is to be done and how.

- Be flexible and explore alternatives, realizing that no one program or approach will be accepted by all.

- Market programs, keeping in mind the limits of the appeal and the extent of the demands of a given service or program.

- Provide sound leadership and adequate financial support, and have an appreciation for the forces such as local traditions that condition effective programming.

- Ensure that recreation is inclusive so that all citizens in the community have opportunities to experience leisure and play in a welcoming and accessible environment.[9]

**Public input survey in Washoe County, Nevada**

In 2005, the Department of Regional Parks and Open Space in Washoe County, Nevada (pop. 389,872), sent a survey out to residents to obtain information for use in planning its recreational programs and facilities. The information sought included the number of hours per week spent on recreational activities, both physical (e.g., running, hiking, playing a sport) and educational (e.g., going to museums, taking an art class, visiting a nature center); the frequency with which individuals and households visit county parks and open spaces; the level of satisfaction with the number and type of specific facilities and programs offered; and residents' relative priorities for future funding and projects. Residents were invited to complete the survey online or print it out, fill it in, and return it to any Washoe County Parks facility. To access the survey, go to washoecountyparks.com/survey_reports.php.

## Personnel

Regardless of the organizational structure chosen, professional leadership and the use of volunteers are two essential ingredients for the successful delivery of services.

### Professional staff

Parks and recreation department administrators and staff should be academically prepared and professionally trained. More than one hundred colleges and universities in the United States offer degrees in parks, recreation, and leisure services, and numerous community colleges offer an associate degree in some aspect of recreation. The National Recreation and Park Association (NRPA) sponsors the Certification for the Park and Recreation Professional Program. While certification is voluntary, professionals can become credentialed as Certified Park and Recreation Professionals and Certified Associate Park and Recreation Professionals, verifying that they have met the minimal requirements to practice in this capacity.[10] The National Therapeutic Recreation Certification Board provides certification for therapeutic recreation professionals. NRPA, various state park and recreation associations, and other recreation-related associations offer professional development opportunities through continuing education programs, conferences, and publications. In addition to park and recreation professionals, local governments need to hire professionals in the fields of turf management, horticulture, planning, physical education, child development, and technical information management.

### Volunteers

Without volunteers many special events, youth sport activities, and fund-raising opportunities would not be possible. Volunteers support professional staff efforts through their time, expertise, and donations. In addition to serving as citizen board members, volunteers can also undertake a wide variety of jobs, such as athletic coach, docent for historic sites and museums, and special events worker, as well as partner for individuals with disabilities, mentor for youth, and member of local park advisory groups.

A department should actively recruit, train, and reward volunteers for their service. In some cases, volunteers should be required to have appropriate certifications. For example, youth coaches can receive certification from the National Youth Coaches Association. In

---

**Adopt-A-Park in Elmhurst, Illinois**

The Elmhurst, Illinois (pop. 44,976), park district's Adopt-A-Park program provides an opportunity for citizens to become involved with their neighborhood parks by working hands-on to help keep the parks clean, attractive, and safe. The program is open to individuals, neighborhood associations, civic groups, religious organizations, service organizations, schools (groups and teams), businesses, and other community organizations. The adoption commitment begins on April 1 and concludes on December 31. When a group adopts a park, its members set up monthly work dates in which they pick up litter; report vandalism; make recommendations to improve the park's equipment, tree planting, and general maintenance; and keep an eye on the park. At the end of the adoption season, each group receives recognition in the park district's winter brochure.

Source: Elmhurst Park District, "Adopt-A-Park," epd.org/adopt-a-park/index.asp.

---

recent years, most public parks and recreation programs require background checks to be conducted on all volunteers, especially those who have direct contact with children.

## Recreational facilities

Traditional recreational facilities include playgrounds, athletic fields and courts, community centers, swimming pools, senior centers, picnic shelters, golf courses, trails, and public gardens. As recreational interests have diversified, local departments have also been building dog parks, skate and BMX (bicycle moto cross) parks, disc golf facilities, splash pools, climbing walls, and ropes courses. As previously noted, decisions about which recreational facilities to develop should take into account the community's interest and needs, financial resources, and traditions; opportunities provided by other area agencies; relevant state and local laws; and the philosophy and interest of the leadership.

Planning for parks and recreational facilities should begin at the community level. Comprehensive or strategic plans should establish the overall goals, objectives, and priorities for future park and recreation development from the broader community perspective. In the context of the comprehensive plan, a systemwide master plan should be drawn up to ensure that planned development will meet current and future needs.[11]

It is important for communities to make sure that they do not overextend their resources. Operational costs require a careful assessment of which programs and services a government should offer and which it should encourage others to provide. Capital development implies that additional monies will be spent on operations and maintenance. If money to operate and maintain current facilities is tight, it is probably not appropriate to add more facilities unless new sources of funding are generated.

Officials should also be aware that developing facilities may create greater demands for their use than anticipated. Providing a trail for bikers may stimulate interest in biking, but it may also bring into conflict different groups of citizens who previously did not interact. The walkers, bikers, and dog owners who use a multiuse trail may clash because they have different expectations of the recreational experience. To help reduce user conflicts, park managers must establish rules, educate users, and develop communication avenues among user groups.

People expect park areas to be safe, free from crime and other hazards. Because departments need to be concerned with employee and participant safety, risk management plans are a necessity. Playground safety is a major focus for many recreational, school, and day care programs. The National Playground Safety Institute conducted by NRPA and the National Program for Playground Safety provide training and certification programs for staff to learn how to design and maintain outdoor play spaces that are free from hazards. Proper design and maintenance of these spaces also help reduce vandalism.

Involvement of community and neighborhood groups in the operation of park spaces also helps build community pride and support for the park. Many parks and recreation departments find that they must have both a risk management plan and a public partnership plan in order to be successful.

## Funding

Local parks and recreation departments are primarily funded through general government revenues and user fees, but they do receive operating and capital improvement monies from other sources. Approximately 7–10 percent of local budgets is typically expended on recreational services; for the most part, this share comes from a combination of general revenues and special taxes whose proceeds are dedicated by law for parks and recreational use only. Capital development is supported by general tax revenues and bond issues, private philanthropy, and state-operated lotteries. General obligation bonds, revenue bonds, and certificates of participation have been used successfully to acquire parks, natural areas, and open space.

Because of limited federal, state, and local funding for parks and recreation, local departments are exploring alternative sources of funding for facilities and programs. User fees, land transfer fees, impact fees, landfill tipping fees, and occupancy tax revenues are all being used to expand programming, purchase parkland, and develop recreational facilities. Some departments have developed gift catalogs to allow people to purchase or donate needed items, such as benches or trees, to specific facilities and parks. Others have sold the naming rights to parks and facilities, sold advertising space in facilities, and established local foundations and trust funds to generate revenue to support and maintain facilities.

### Fees and charges

Revenue-producing facilities and programs are probably the most common methods for supplementing general fund appropriations. Some departments are even required to generate a specific percentage of their budget through user fees and charges. While most professionals believe that public recreation services are a public good and thus should be provided

---

### Fees and charges in recreation departments

Fees and charges are normally assessed for (1) specialized facilities (e.g., golf courses, swimming pools, and tennis courts) that require intensive maintenance; (2) programs requiring higher than average costs for material used; (3) rental of specialized equipment (e.g., cameras, golf clubs, and skis); (4) programs requiring instruction or personnel (e.g., a basketball league or a cake decorating class); (5) rental of a facility by an individual or group; and (6) use of facilities, programs, and services by nonresidents.

Source: James R. Sellers and Stephanie T. West, "Local Government Park and Recreation Services," in *Introduction to Leisure Services in North Carolina,* 5th ed., ed. Paul L. Gaskill (Dubuque, Iowa: Kendall/Hunt Publishing Company, 2006), 70.

free to local residents, many departments cannot offer the quality services needed without using some mix of fees and charges. Fees are often imposed for recreational classes and athletic programs, entrance to such facilities as swimming pools and skate parks, and rental of facilities for exclusive use. Departments should establish policies that outline the services for which fees and charges can be assessed and the mechanism that will be used to determine their amount. For example, some departments may decide to subsidize all youth athletic programs, to operate adult athletic programs on a break-even basis, and to manage specialized facilities such as a golf course to generate revenue. It is also very common for departments to establish differential fees for residents and nonresidents.[12]

Revenue can also be produced by contracting with vendors to provide such services as concessions, concerts, boat rentals, and outdoor adventure programs in exchange for either a percentage of the gross or a specified amount. The revenue may be controlled by the department or reverted to the local government's general fund.

While revenue-producing programs and facilities can allow departments to decrease their reliance on tax dollars, they can also cause inequities. Some people cannot afford to take advantage of these recreational programs, which means that they are no longer available to all. To deal with this problem, local governments use a range of strategies; among the most common are vouchers for low-income groups and public days—that is, specified days on which admission to pools, concerts, and museums is free. Another strategy is to solicit sponsors to underwrite programs, enabling a department to reduce its cost or to provide scholarships so that low-income groups can attend programs like summer camps or join athletic teams. Whatever strategies are used, policies must be established and staff time dedicated to managing the process. Ideally, recreation departments will establish an overall service that strikes a balance between programs that are funded through general government revenues and those that produce revenue.

## Cooperation with other organizations

In today's fiscal environment, innovative cooperation and partnerships with other organizations is another funding strategy that departments must explore. Partnerships with hospitals, fitness centers, health departments, nonprofit youth agencies such as 4-H and Boys Clubs, national organizations such NRPA, and local businesses can provide resources for new recreational programs and facilities.

The school-park concept is one kind of partnership that many communities have used to lower costs for facilities, reduce duplication of effort, and increase recreational opportunities for all residents. In this concept, a school and park are built immediately adjacent to one another, and each is designed to complement and expand the recreational opportunities for both students and the community. For example, an elementary school might be designed with recreational facilities such as a gym, auditorium, playground, and special classrooms that the recreation department could program for public use after school hours. The park might include facilities such as a swimming pool, soccer fields, a nature trail, and a track that the school officials could schedule for use during school hours. In this way, both organizations have access to facilities they might not have been able to offer without the partnership.

## Public-private partnerships

Public-private partnership agreements to build recreational facilities are also quite popular. Such partnerships have several advantages. For example, when a local government allows

---

**KaBOOM! A public-private partnership and community involvement**

An excellent example of a public-private partnership with community involvement is KaBOOM!, a nonprofit agency that helps communities create great places to play within walking distance for every child in America. To do this, the agency brings together businesses and communities to construct playgrounds, skate parks, sports fields, and ice rinks. In the last ten years, KaBOOM! has partnered with corporate sponsors, local governments, and citizen groups to help build 1,000 play environments. Funding partners include Home Depot, American Eagle, and Kimberly Clark. Case studies of projects can be found on the KaBOOM! Web site, kaboom.org/.

---

private developers to construct specialized facilities, such as water parks, amphitheaters, and ski runs, on public land, the public has access to additional recreational activities without the local government having to expend public funds for capital development. In such agreements, the developers pay rent or make an equivalent payment in kind (e.g., a reduced resident use fee for a specific time period or a series of free concerts). As another example, when a power company allows the public to use its watersheds and water areas for recreational purposes, the company is usually given tax credits or relieved of certain liabilities. The public relations value to the company is considerable, as is the value of the recreational resources to the public.

## State and federal funding

Federal funding available for public parks and recreational services is limited to the following sources:

- The Land and Water Conservation Fund, administered by the National Parks Service, provides limited funding for local and state governments to acquire parkland and develop outdoor recreational facilities.

- The Transportation Equity Act of 2005 (officially, the Safe, Accountable, Flexible, Efficient Transportation Equity Act: A Legacy for Users, or SAFETEA-LU), administered by the U.S. Department of Transportation, provides funding for pedestrian and bicycle trails, acquisition of scenic easements, historic preservation, and recreational use of abandoned railroad corridors.

- The U.S. Department of Health and Human Services offers grant programs to support senior citizens, public housing playgrounds, and community centers.

- The 21st Century Community Learning Centers, administered by the U.S. Department of Education, include recreational programs among the services that can be provided to reinforce and complement the regular academic program.

At the state level, funding opportunities for parks and recreation vary by state. Monies may be available to fund recreational programs that deal with juvenile delinquency, other youth-at-risk issues, cultural arts, trails, and healthy lifestyles. Some states, such as Florida, North Carolina, South Carolina, and Texas, have established grant programs that provide funding to local governments for the development of recreational facilities and the acquisition of parkland.

Clemson University, the University of Illinois, and West Virginia University have set up a rural recreation project designed to help small rural communities that lack the funds to establish recreational services develop such programs. Working with selected rural communities over multiple years, the project hires a full-time summer recreation director for each community. The director is responsible for planning and coordinating summer recreation programs with an emphasis on youth. Most of the rural recreational programs are designed to provide funding on a sliding scale so that, at the end of a specified period, the town can independently fund the program and continue providing the services to its residents with money from community resources and civic organizations as well as from the general fund.

## Management issues

Beyond the basic responsibilities of a parks and recreation department described above—organizing services to meet the needs of residents, providing facilities and programs in accordance with community need and interest, staffing, and funding—managers face many complex management issues. Three such issues are the increasing number of federal regulations, the need to ensure safety and security, and the challenges that come with a more diverse population.

### Increasing regulations

One of the responsibilities of the public parks and recreation professional is to provide quality services in an environment of increasing federal regulations. Occupational Safety and Health Administration standards for blood-borne pathogens, guidelines for playground safety, and the Americans with Disabilities Act of 1990 (ADA) are just a few of the regulations that affect program delivery, staffing, and facility design.

The ADA has increased local responsibility for providing recreational opportunities for individuals with disabilities and for eliminating physical and attitudinal barriers to access. The physical barriers are often easier to remove than the attitudinal barriers created by staff and participants. Some recreation professionals mistakenly assume that disabled people do not want to recreate with nondisabled people. Additionally, participants might be concerned about being in programs with disabled people because of misinformation about the disability and a lack of exposure to anyone with a disability. However, education, communication, and well-planned programs can help eliminate attitudinal barriers. With often slight modifications, standard recreational programs—summer camp, for example—can be made accessible to disabled individuals. But while recreational programs for special populations, such as those who are visually impaired, deaf, or mentally or physically disabled, are important, so too are recreational opportunities that are inclusive.

Since the mid-1990s, public playground safety has been a priority for parks and recreation departments. The U.S. Consumer Product Safety Commission developed playground safety guidelines to help communities build safe playgrounds, and two national programs—the aforementioned National Program for Playground Safety and the National Playground Safety Institute—were established to address safety issues. The focus on playground safety has forced many localities to replace old, hazardous playground equipment with safer equipment and to improve surfacing under the equipment in order to reduce the number of severe playground injuries. New and remodeled playgrounds are being designed, constructed, and maintained with safety as a top priority.

## Security

The continued risk of terrorist attacks and a rise in gang activity have increased the responsibility of public parks and recreation agencies for ensuring that participants have a safe and enjoyable experience at major sporting events, festivals, parks, and recreational facilities. Purchasing security equipment, hiring security guards to patrol events, hiring additional event staff to operate security gates, expanding risk management plans, and establishing emergency protocols have all added to the expense and complexity of hosting major sporting and recreational events.

Special events should have a written security plan that includes site or building plans and maps, a description of unique risk factors, coordination with other agencies, command post locations, communication plans, transportation arrangements, and emergency procedures.[13] Staff must be trained to recognize and report suspicious activities and should know how to respond in emergency situations. Departments must work with local law enforcement agencies or private security firms to increase the visibility and active presence of police and security guards at events, parks, and facilities. Electronic surveillance cameras and other equipment can enable staff to monitor areas and can enhance the detection of firearms and other dangerous weapons. Since September 11, 2001, it is commonplace to find security gates at athletic events, concerts, and other large events where people, backpacks, and baby strollers can be searched or screened for drugs, alcohol, firearms, and other dangerous weapons.

Design and maintenance can also play a role in creating a safe place for participants. Effective lighting, proper maintenance of facilities and natural areas, ingress and egress control, and quick removal of graffiti can help parks and recreation staff deter crime.

## Diversity

The rapid growth in ethnic populations in some communities has caused recreation service delivery problems. Where language and cultural barriers prevent recreational services from being accessible to all residents, some cities are giving employees bonuses if they are fluent in a second language. Some traditional recreational programs and facilities may not meet the needs of the new residents. Understanding the cultures, beliefs, and values of those who live in a community will help recreational professionals design programs that will remove barriers to participation.

Age is another dimension of community diversity that can cause service delivery problems. Baby boomers are becoming senior citizens. Many are retiring earlier, living longer, and staying more active than previous generations, and they expect recreational services to meet their needs. Their voting patterns can affect local decisions ranging from which

### A multigenerational park in Lewisburg, Pennsylvania

Lewisburg Area Recreation Park in Lewisburg, Pennsylvania (pop. 5,562), developed a multigenerational park as a way to promote active living and fitness for children, teenagers, adults, and senior citizens. Part of a $2.5 million renovation project on a twenty-two-acre site, the park includes a swimming pool, tennis courts, a basketball court, a seasonal ice skating rink, a skate park, playgrounds, climbing boulders, trails, and a senior walking path with seven wellness stations that provide a complete fitness program for active older adults.[14]

recreational facilities can be developed to which recreational programs should be funded. At the other end of the spectrum, children are still a major focus of many parks and recreation departments, which are being asked to increase programming efforts to help address youth-at-risk issues. Providing recreational programs and facilities that can meet the diverse leisure needs for all ages requires innovation and partnerships.

## Conclusion

Local government parks and recreation departments serve an extraordinarily vital function in communities today. By offering an opportunity for citizens of all ages to participate in a wealth of activities, both physical and educational, these departments help to promote a healthy lifestyle, provide at-risk youth with an alternative to gangs and vandalism, make museums and cultural events accessible to disadvantaged citizens, and enable seniors to remain physically and socially active. And by providing and maintaining open spaces and well-designed parks, they also help to revitalize communities.

At the same time, public parks and recreation professionals face a number of challenges to achieving their goals. Among these challenges are the need to

- Increase public recognition of the benefits of parks and recreation programs
- Find a balance between professional staff and volunteers
- Plan facilities and programs to meet community needs
- Find alternative sources of funding for programs and capital projects
- Form innovative partnerships with other agencies
- Comply with increasing federal regulations, such as the ADA

---

### Questions to ask if you manage a small community

Does your agency have a clear expression of purpose, such as a written mission statement? Does it have written goals and objectives, and does it annually report its accomplishments?

Is your agency involved in ongoing planning? Does it have a long-range master plan and is that plan part of a citywide comprehensive plan?

Does your agency promote citizen involvement? Does it have an active citizen advisory board?

Do all residents have equitable access to parks and recreational facilities and programs?

Does your agency have certified playground safety inspectors? Does it collect data on crime in parks? Can residents safely walk to parks?

Does your agency have a risk management plan?

Does your agency design parks and recreation programs to improve the quality of life for individuals, communities, and the environment? Does it advocate for the benefits of public parks and recreation?

Does your agency take a leadership role in joining with other area agencies to address community issues? Does it seek out partnerships to help financially support park and recreation programs?

Does your agency hire professionals to manage its facilities and programs? Is funding allocated for professional development?

- Accommodate an increasingly more diverse population
- Address the demands of security and risk management.

These challenges notwithstanding, public parks and recreation departments are successfully bringing community agencies together to design and fund services, programs, and facilities that can benefit everyone. In so doing, they are successfully addressing social issues and improving the quality of life for individuals, families, and communities.

---

**Competencies for managers in the field of parks and recreation**

An understanding of the economic, social, personal, and health benefits of parks and recreation and an ability to articulate those benefits to elected officials and citizens

Ability to hire, train, supervise, coach, and mentor full-time, part-time, and volunteer staff

Familiarity with potential funding sources, including grants, to expand and support programs

Willingness to seek advice from citizens when planning facilities and programs

Ability to network and build partnerships to provide programs, facilities, and financial support

Flexibility; the ability to implement changes to meet the needs of residents

Familiarity with up-to-date management and programming trends in parks and recreation

---

## Endnotes

1 Geoffrey Godbey, "Providing More for Older Adults," *Parks and Recreation* 40 (October 2005): 76–81.

2 National Recreation and Park Association (NRPA), "Parks and Health: How Public Parks and Recreation Contribute to a Healthy Lifestyle," CYB_Parks_Health_3.pdf (accessed June 1, 2006).

3 Don DeGraaf, Jill Lankford, and Sam Lankford, "A New Perspective on Urban Spaces: Urban Sprawl, New Urbanism, and the Role of the Park and Recreation Field," *Parks and Recreation* 40 (August 2005): 56–64.

4 NRPA, "Parks and Economic Development: Why Public Parks, Open Space and Greenways are Wise Investments" (June 1, 2005), at CYB_Econ_Benefits_5.pdf (accessed June 1, 2006).

5 Public parks and recreation departments can be accredited by the Commission for Accreditation of Parks and Recreation Agencies (CAPRA) sponsored by NRPA. For more information on CAPRA, go to nrpa.org/content/default.aspx?documentId = 1038.

6 Clayne R. Jenson, *Outdoor Recreation in America,* 5th ed. (Champaign, Ill.: Human Kinetics, 1995), 134.

7 Candace Goode Vick, "Parks and Recreation," in *City and County Government in North Carolina,* ed. David M. Lawrence (Chapel Hill, N.C.: School of Government, University of North Carolina at Chapel Hill, 2006).

8 Merry Moiseichik and Kimberly Bodey, "Legal Authority and Jurisdiction," in *Management of Park and Recreation Agencies,* 2nd ed., ed. Betty van der Smissen, Merry Moiseichik, and Vern J. Hartenberg (Ashburn, Va.: National Recreation and Park Association, 2005), 25–59.

9 Karla A. Henderson et al., *Introduction to Recreation and Leisure Services,* 8th ed. (State College, Pa.: Ventura Publishing, 2001), 207–208.

10 Vick, "Parks and Recreation."

11 For an example of a systemwide plan, see *The Five-Year Parks and Recreation Master Plan 2005–2009* for Butler, Indiana, available at butler.in.us/appointed_bodies/RecBd/2005FiveYearParkRecPlan.pdf (accessed September 19, 2006).

12 James R. Sellers and Nancy J. Gladwell, "Financial Management," in *Management of Park and Recreation Agencies* (see note 8), 493–535.

13 Charles M. Nelson, James A. Colley, and Dale Larsen, "Law Enforcement and Security," in *Management of Park and Recreation Agencies* (see note 8), 617–653.

14 Stacy St. Clair, "A Multigenerational Place to Play," *Recreation Management* (2006), available at recmanagement.com/facility_profiles.php?fid = 200602FP02 (accessed September 26, 2006).

# 11

# Health and Human Services

## Abraham David Benavides

Although under the New Deal and the Great Society, programs to help the poor and disadvantaged became part of the mission of the federal government, health and human service programs that serve the well-being of all citizens—including the poor, the old, the physically disabled, the subjects of ethnic and racial discrimination—have traditionally fallen under the purview of local government. Almost forty years ago, ICMA issued a policy statement asserting that it was the local government manager's responsibility to achieve social and economic justice for all citizens in the community.

Local governments provide a range of human service programs. Some of these programs are designed to confront community problems, public safety issues, private health matters, and social concerns that individual citizens are ill-equipped to address on their own—for example, alcoholism. The efforts of well-intentioned churches and nonprofits to tackle such problems are usually neither well coordinated nor comprehensive in scope, so local government must provide leadership, coordination, and oversight.

Still other human service programs, such as the elimination of architectural barriers to the physically disabled, have been instituted in response to state and federal mandates. Programs created by the federal government are typically intended to ensure nationally uniform standards. As a result, local governments have the responsibility for their implementation and administration but little or no authority for program design. Moreover, many of these mandates are unfunded, which presents even more of a challenge to local authorities.

Problems such as violence, poverty, unemployment, substance abuse, and AIDS (acquired immunodeficiency syndrome), which were once found mainly in large cities, are spreading to smaller communities in the suburbs and rural areas. Inevitably, there are differences of opinion regarding the best ways to deal with these problems. To reduce delinquency, for instance, some people want to increase the number of police, others want to start a drug education program, and still others want to provide youth with opportunities for employment or recreation. Administrators may have a difficult time convincing elected officials and the community that the long-term approach may be the more cost-effective response, but many communities are realizing that in order to avoid major, expensive, and disruptive problems later, it makes sense to invest now in preventive human services such as health education, child care, and counseling.

## Who is responsible for human services?

All levels of government share a responsibility for the welfare of the people. For the most part, the nature of that responsibility is a matter of either policy making or implementation.

### Federal and state responsibility

From the 1935 Aid to Families with Dependent Children to its 1996 successor, Temporary Assistance to Needy Families (TANF), the federal government has been dominant in setting national policy for families in relation to human services. The 1996 Personal Responsibility and Work Opportunity Reconciliation Act, which established TANF, gave states enormous discretion in how to allocate their block grant monies earmarked for human service issues. In exchange for a fixed amount from the federal government ($16.5 billion a year), states were given the latitude to design and run their own human service programs. Federal guidelines emphasized that states should be flexible and creative in how they use their monies, with the assumption that their innovations will meet the critical goals set forth in the TANF statutes. While this flexibility has created very different human service programs across the fifty states, most states use their county governments to deliver these vital services to their residents.

In 2001 the Office of Faith-Based and Community Initiatives (OFBCI) was created in the White House to support organizations that serve people in need, particularly at-risk youth, ex-offenders, the homeless and hungry, substance abusers, persons with HIV/AIDS, and welfare-to-work families. The executive order that established the OFBCI states that it will "provide policy and legal education to State, local, and community policymakers and public officials seeking ways to empower faith-based and other community organizations and to improve the opportunities, capacity, and expertise of such groups."[1]

### Local government responsibility

Although the federal and state governments serve an important policy-making role, it is the local government that deals one-on-one with individual citizens on a daily basis, and it is the local government that ultimately must cope with the human service issues unresolved by federal or state programs. It is therefore the responsibility of both counties and cities to evaluate the needs of the local community, carry out and monitor the policy directives of the state and federal governments, and merge the intent and values of policy with the needs and concerns of residents.

Local government's role in the provision of human services can be broken into three categories: (1) ensuring that local human service needs are met; (2) providing the necessary leadership and oversight for the community's human service effort; and (3) understanding how routine government operations affect human service concerns and consciously using those operations to minimize community problems.

*The role of cities*   Most cities have relied on county, state, and federal governments to provide human services. However, federal and state mandates (funded and unfunded), regulations, court orders, and laws—combined with limited federal and state resources and the growing magnitude of social ills—have forced local governments to address the human service needs of their communities. Some city governments have established a separate department of human services for this purpose. To the extent that a city or town can afford to employ experienced human service staff, that staff's direct participation in service delivery will likely improve the efficiency and effectiveness of the programs.

***The role of counties***   Counties are key partners in the design, implementation, and reform of the broad range of human service programs. Although the functions of county government vary widely among the states, almost every county administers and contributes financially to social service needs. Many county governments, for example, will levy taxes for community mental health programs and then give the tax proceeds, in the form of grants, to private, nonprofit mental health centers. In this way, the counties ensure the availability of community mental health services without assuming the responsibility for administering them. Many community-owned hospitals are also organized and operated as not-for-profit agencies.

***The role of nonprofits***   Many human service programs are provided by nonprofit agencies—private, nongovernmental corporations organized to provide a particular public service, usually with a special emphasis on serving those who cannot afford it. These agencies employ professional staff who are paid fixed salaries, while their boards of directors are made up of civic-minded individuals who usually serve without pay. Any year-end revenue balances are reinvested in service programs. Funding is derived from government and foundation grants, private fund raising, and fees for services delivered to those who can afford to pay for them.

## Intergovernmental cooperation

Multiagency cooperation helps to overcome the fragmentation that can hamper service delivery. When the project team comprises the top members of the participating organizations, coordination and cooperation usually flow downward through all affected units. For example, in a community effort to combat youth gang activity, representatives of law enforcement agencies, youth service agencies, and schools might establish a task force to address the problem.

Other activities can be implemented by marshaling existing community resources. To do a responsible job in the social sector, the local government need not offer a single program directly. If another agency can be persuaded to add drug counseling and alcohol treatment to its list of services, a major problem may be solved. If a school district can be persuaded to establish a child care center or if the human service coordinator can organize a group of volunteers to run such a center, the mission can be completed. Although there can be political barriers to cooperation and collaborators may have difficulty agreeing on goals and levels of commitment, the benefits certainly outweigh the costs.

## Community attitudes toward local government provision of human services

In some communities, there may be those who question the role of local government in providing human services. Some elected officials, for example, may believe that social problems should not be the responsibility of the local government but instead are best handled by the family, churches, other nonprofit organizations, or professional counselors. Cities, especially those faced with limited resources, may simply want to focus on the more tangible needs of the community, such as new streets, parking lots, or more police protection. And residents may be, at best, ambivalent about the issue as long as they receive the traditional services they expect from their local government (i.e., police, public works, roads, planning, and parks).

To gain their support, the local government manager needs to provide elected officials with objective information on (1) community needs; (2) resources, if any, that are currently being expended in the community to cope with those needs; (3) shortcomings of the status quo; and (4) alternative courses of action. Similarly, better communication can be used to generate community support. Mistrust or distaste for programs that are thought of as "welfare" can often be overcome when issues or problems are isolated or individual programs are examined. Thus, the manager's role becomes that of communicating the very specific nature of the problems confronting a number of residents, driving home the human aspect of human service programs.

> *Mistrust or distaste for programs that are thought of as "welfare" can often be overcome when issues or problems are isolated or individual programs are examined.*

Administrators can easily be preoccupied with the more visible and demanding challenges facing a community, such as infrastructure decay, rising crime rates, declining revenues, and the need for economic development. Where such problems exist, it is quite easy to become more concerned with the "big picture" issues than with those issues affecting a smaller, less vocal segment of the community. Managers must make a committed and sustained effort to champion human services if those services are to have a chance of succeeding. While they cannot be expected to correct the social ills of the community on their own, managers can be expected to take a leadership role in encouraging and helping community and elected officials to take on the challenge.

## Human service programs and concerns

The concerns with which communities are increasingly expected to deal are seemingly endless. Although there is no universally accepted list of local government programs that fall under the heading of human services, a representative group of such programs would include those concerned with

| | |
|---|---|
| Youth | Mental health issues |
| Elderly citizens | Physically disabled citizens |
| Housing | Health and public health, |
| Transportation | including alcohol and drug abuse |
| Employment, including | Consumer protection |
| child care issues | Poverty |

### Youth

If a community does not deal with youth problems through its social programs, it will eventually deal with worse problems through its law enforcement department. The traditional youth problems of vandalism, truancy, alcohol and drug involvement, teenage

## Alcohol abuse

According to a report from the U.S. Department of Health and Human Services, alcohol is the number one drug of choice among children and adolescents. A higher percentage of youth aged 12–20 use alcohol (29 percent) than use tobacco (23 percent) or illicit drugs (15 percent).[1] In 2002, about 2 million youth in this age bracket drank five or more drinks per occasion, five or more times a month. It has been noted that "in many ways, alcohol is the hidden health issue of the younger generation, obscured by the publicity given to tobacco, teenage pregnancy, and illegal drugs."[2] Although the prevalence of underage drinking has decreased since reaching its peak in the late 1970s, it still poses a major concern for local governments.

1   Substance Abuse and Mental Health Services Administration, *Results from the 2002 National Survey on Drug Use and Health: National Findings*, NHSDA Series H-22, DHHS Publication No. SMA 03-3836 (Rockville, Md.: Office of Applied Studies, National Clearinghouse for Alcohol and Drug Information, 2003); available at oas.samhsa.gov/NHSDA/2k2NSDUH/Results/2k2results.htm.

2   Susan G. Parker, "Reducing Youth Drinking: The 'A Matter of Degree' and 'Reducing Underage Drinking Through Coalitions' Program," in *To Improve Health and Health Care*, vol. 8, ed. Stephen L. Isaacs and James R. Knickman (San Francisco: Jossey-Bass, 2005), 47; a pdf of this report is available at rwjf.org/files/publications/books/2005/chapter_03.pdf, 1.

pregnancy, sexually transmitted diseases including AIDS, and gang violence, just to name a few, are issues that should not be ignored. Although some problems, such as teen pregnancy and drug use, have decreased over the years, others, such as alcohol consumption, have stabilized at distressingly high levels.

Employment programs have proven to be one of the most effective ways of assisting youth to avoid or overcome these problems. A school district may provide job training or tutorial programs; other community efforts might include recreational programs, halfway houses for runaways, and counseling for drug abuse or pregnancy. Some communities operate group homes and receiving homes for foster children, as well as therapeutic group homes to treat young people who otherwise would be placed in vocational schools. Some communities even identify children's needs in their strategic planning efforts.

The current social welfare system divides the problems of children and families into rigid and distinct categories that fail to reflect interrelated causes and effects. Services designed to correspond to discrete problems are administered by literally dozens of

## Hire-A-Youth in Glendora, California

Glendora, California (pop. 50,540), created the Hire-A-Youth (H.A.Y.) program to help teenagers and young adults find employment. The H.A.Y office accepts job orders for various types of work, such as housework, yard work, child care, food services, and clerical. Youth fill out employment cards and interview with the H.A.Y. department, which then puts their cards on file. After the interview, youth call in to inquire about employment opportunities and are given contact information for potential employers; it is their responsibility to contact the employers to discuss employment opportunities.

Source: City of Glendora, ci.glendora.ca.us/community_services/humanservices.html.

agencies and programs, each with its own particular focus, source of funding, guidelines, and accountability requirements. This lack of active cooperation among the different agencies in the community can stand in the way of meaningful and long-lasting solutions. A disjointed criminal justice system, in particular, will serve as a barrier to effective youth programs; working in isolation, police and probation departments may regard each other with suspicion, resentment, and even hostility, ultimately failing those youth who need help. But bringing such agencies together to work cooperatively to address the needs of those young people who are most at risk can yield substantial results.

Finally, unless at-risk youth receive effective intervention and young people struggling to avoid or overcome multiple problems receive adequate support and early treatment, they are unlikely to develop the basic skills they will need to survive in the job market. Virtually without exception, this failure will worsen their nonacademic problems and increase the demand placed on human services for more costly treatment and long-term financial subsidies.

## Elderly citizens

Persons born between 1946 and 1964 have been labeled by demographers and the media as "baby boomers." As this cohort of about 76 million begins to retire, their longer life span and unprecedented numbers will create challenges for all levels of government. Common needs of elderly citizens include transportation, housing, health care, nutrition, recreation, employment, and financial resources—all of which are typically greater among the elderly than among the population as a whole. Many local governments appoint a council on aging to give senior citizens a voice and to evaluate programs; others use existing organizational structures to achieve the same ends.

Examples of programs that can benefit the elderly include reduced transportation fares, housing programs, meals-on-wheels, consumer protection, guardianship services, counseling, recreation programs, and the elimination of barriers to those who are physically disabled. Another growing need is for adult day care services so that older and disabled citizens can remain at home and avoid more costly care options; such services also provide assistance and relief for the caregivers.

---

### Residential alternatives for elderly citizens in Catawba County, North Carolina

Catawba County, North Carolina (pop. 151,641), gives elderly and disabled individuals the option of remaining in their own homes or entering a nursing or rest home. Begun in 1984, the Community Alternative Program (CAP) sends a social worker and nurse to assess the feasibility of elderly residents remaining at home and to determine the in-home services that would be required. After the assessment, the agency either provides or contracts for the needed services. Medicaid reimburses the eligible population for the cost of those services as long as they do not exceed the actual costs of nursing home care. Since it began twenty years ago, the program has avoided millions of dollars in Medicaid payments—$1.5 million in fiscal year 2004-2005 alone. More than just a cost-effective program, CAP enables many elderly citizens to remain at home longer than would otherwise be possible.

Financial help and advice on implementing programs for the elderly are available through the federal government's Older Americans Act, social service block grants, Medicare, and Medicaid. Medicare, for instance, is a program for people over 65 years of age and for certain disabled individuals who qualify. In 2003 the Medicare program added the Medicare Prescription Drug Improvement and Modernization Act to defray substantial amounts of prescription drug costs for its beneficiaries. In the following year it made drug discount cards available, with estimated savings through discounts reaching between $1.4 and $1.8 billion. In 2006 the act enabled anyone on Medicare, regardless of income, health status, or drug usage, to enroll in a drug prescription plan. Enrollees are required to pay a premium, which they can either pay directly or have deducted from their social security checks.[2]

## Housing

Decent housing for all citizens has been a goal in the United States for over half a century. To achieve this objective, local government managers need to identify and tap into federal and state programs that best fit the community's needs. Such programs can include housing projects owned and operated by the government as well as rehabilitation and conservation programs, the latter of which seek to identify historic districts, revitalize older neighborhoods through an infusion of local resources, and secure Community Development Block Grant funds to promote renovation in selected neighborhoods. Local governments can also enlist the assistance of nonprofit organizations such as Habitat for Humanity to help provide suitable housing. For more on housing-related issues, see Chapter 8.

*Affordable housing*   Communities that wish to provide affordable housing should review their zoning ordinances and subdivision regulations and, if appropriate, make changes that will facilitate the development of land for this purpose. Flexible housing regulations

### Integrated approach to rehabilitation in Gaithersburg, Maryland

Gaithersburg, Maryland (pop. 57,698), owns and operates transitional housing for homeless addicts and alcoholics in recovery. The Wells/Robertson House provides housing for homeless men and women who have undergone alcohol or drug treatment or have received other professional counseling, and who want to break the cycle of homelessness. The city gets referrals for the facility from the department of social services, the county addiction rehabilitation program, and local shelters. Facility staff help residents learn how to be self-sufficient, working, and functioning members of society. The two-year program calls for the creation of a master plan for each individual, requiring residents to obtain a sponsor, attend a twelve-step meeting daily as well as meetings of Alcoholics Anonymous or Narcotics Anonymous, plan for work or school, pay rent, do chores around the house, complete specific activities, and attend classes and workshops to improve living skills. Case managers counsel residents and monitor their progress.

Source: City of Gaithersburg, gaithersburgmd.gov (under "City Services," click on "Homeless Assistance").

---

### Home rehabilitation loan program in Englewood, Colorado

Englewood, Colorado (pop. 32,350), established a program to preserve housing in existing neighborhoods and to help families finance major household repairs or improvements relating to health, safety, energy conservation, and handicap retrofitting. Any home owner who maintains a primary residence in Englewood and meets certain income requirements is eligible to apply for a loan. These loans can be used not only for repairs but also to assist people in the purchase of a home.

Source: City of Englewood, ci.englewood.co.us/home/index.asp?page=389.

---

that permit planned unit development, cluster housing, zero lot line development (in which homes are built close to each other, thereby making it possible to build smaller, affordable homes, protect environmentally sensitive areas, and promote open space), and the transfer of development rights will encourage developers to build housing for families with low to moderate incomes. Another way to promote development for this population is through inclusionary zoning: local governments can enact zoning regulations to require—or allow for voluntary compliance by—developers that are building a number of market-rate units to set aside a percentage of those units for low- and moderate-income households. Such ordinances also produce more economical housing for firefighters, police, nurses, teachers, and the elderly. Communities may also wish to review their building regulations. Although most regulations relating to safety and quality must be retained, it may be possible to adjust those that unnecessarily increase housing prices.

It is important to remember that citizens cannot make choices about housing if they are not informed. Therefore local governments, chambers of commerce, developers, and builders should distribute information to educate the public about available housing options.

*Tenant rights*   Low-income and undereducated people can be victims of unscrupulous landlords or of people who acquire investment property in good faith and then find that the costs of maintenance or rehabilitation exceed their rental income. Local government can help by providing educational programs concerning legal rights and covering such subjects as rent increases, evictions, leases, repairs, and common illegal practices. It can also teach tenants what to look for before renting and can provide home-management training. Whenever possible, tenants and landlords should be encouraged to resolve disputes voluntarily. Absentee landlords are a special problem, however, and efforts to hold owners responsible for the condition and safety of buildings is often the local government's responsibility. If the community operates a public housing authority, its employees must be sensitive to the problems of tenants.

### Transportation

It has become increasingly important for small communities, especially those in rural areas, to consider transportation as a necessary component in human service delivery. Although some areas require areawide mass transit, most communities can benefit from a more modest approach. Some operate bus lines; others subsidize private transportation firms that

**Meeting transportation needs in James City County, Virginia**

Recognizing that transportation problems prevent many social service clients from obtaining permanent full-time employment, James City County, Virginia (pop. 57,525), receives donated vehicles from private citizens, repairs them, and sells them for the price of the repair. The division of social services has a partnership with the Community Action Agency of James City County, which holds the title on the cars until they are paid off (monthly payments are made for a few years at around $30.00 a month). One of the stipulations in the Cars-for-Work program is that recipients must remain employed in order to keep the cars. Currently, about one car a month is being offered.

might otherwise go out of business. Reduced-fare programs are popular with senior citizens, university students, and youth, and a few communities have offered free bus service. Some communities without bus service have volunteer transportation programs that enable elderly and disabled residents to go shopping and to get to medical appointments.

## Employment

If a community's unemployment problems are severe, the chief administrator, working with the elected body, must make proactive efforts to increase employment opportunities. Such efforts may involve consulting an advisory committee of labor and government officials to stimulate ideas for job creation, using private sector training and placement services, or providing leadership in attracting and keeping businesses in the community (see Chapter 7 on economic development). With jobs and regular paychecks, people can begin to deal with their needs in terms of their own priorities, not those of a government program.

Although the official TANF welfare-to-work program ended in 2004, various acts of Congress have extended work opportunity tax credits for employers who hire individuals from several targeted groups. Eligible workers include economically disadvantaged youth, Vietnam veterans, and recipients of long-term family assistance. Tax credits give an added incentive to employers to hire individuals from these groups, which in turn benefits the local and national economies. Millions of people on public assistance have entered the workforce through programs that have tax credits associated with them.

*Job training*　Residents lacking employment skills can be hired, trained on the job, and later brought into regular, full-time employment. The local government can participate in job training programs supported by the state or federal government. However, even without state or federally funded programs, hiring and development goals can be set for poor or disadvantaged residents. The success of such efforts will require a commitment, not only from the administrator but also from elected officials and the staff of the organization.

*Child care*　In many families, both parents work outside the home, creating a need for child care. Adding to this need is the growing number of single-parent families. In the past, such problems as noise and traffic congestion led communities to view child care centers as undesirable and to enact zoning ordinances against them. Today, however, communities are rewriting zoning ordinances to allow child care centers, and some are operating centers of their own. Under federal prompting, some centers are also offering educational and cultural activities as well as custodial care.

## Mental health issues

Two aspects of mental health service provision have moved to the forefront. The first is the community mental health center. These facilities help citizens cope with a wide range of problems, from transient personal difficulties such as divorce and unemployment to long-term problems such as mental illness, alcoholism, drug dependence, and developmental disabilities. The centers may be run by the local government, by nonprofit agencies, by hospitals, or by a combination of service providers.

The second aspect is deinstitutionalization. The number of mentally ill and developmentally disabled people housed and treated in large, usually state-run, institutions has been significantly reduced. As these individuals are returned to their communities, those communities must assume responsibility for their well-being. Local governments have had to consider issues of housing, medical management, recreation, employment, and social contacts—all common needs for this population. Failure to meet these needs may contribute to both a rise in homelessness and the criminalization of the mentally ill, all at great cost to the local government.

Because deinstitutionalization appears to be an established, continuing policy, local government leaders would do well to plan for long-range solutions to the challenges it presents. They must be prepared to deal with community sentiments of the Not-in-My-Back-Yard (NIMBY) variety with regard to setting up group homes. They also must promote public education and cooperation among police departments, human service agencies, and hospitals. Cooperation among governments is important to ensure that the complete array of needed services is provided. The county government, for example, may be responsible for locating a mental health group home, but the site chosen may be within the city limits; the city's zoning regulations must therefore be followed.

## Physically disabled citizens

To ensure that people with disabilities have full access to civic life, Title II of the Americans with Disabilities Act (ADA) requires state and local governments to make their programs and services accessible to physically disabled citizens. This requirement encompasses more than just physical access to government facilities, programs, and events; it includes policy changes that governmental entities must make to ensure that all people with disabilities can take part in, and benefit from, the programs and services of state and local governments. While public entities that have fewer than fifty employees are not required to comply with limited sections of the regulations, no general exemption applies: all public entities, regardless of size, must comply with Title II's requirements.

The requirement does not, however, mean that cities and counties must take any action that would fundamentally alter the nature of the service, program, or activity in question, or pose undue financial and administrative burdens. In terms of the ADA's applicability to local governments, there are a few requirements that must be followed. These relate to program accessibility; historically significant facilities; curb ramps; effective communication; local laws, ordinances, and regulations; 911 systems; and law enforcement policies and procedures.

***Program accessibility*** Program accessibility means that people with disabilities will not encounter any physical barriers to city services, programs, and activities. For example, local governments should hold public meetings in accessible buildings and relocate services for disabled citizens to accessible levels or parts of buildings. In addition, all newly constructed city or county facilities must be fully accessible to people with disabilities.

***Historically significant facilities*** Historically significant facilities are those facilities or properties that are listed—or eligible to be listed—in the National Register of Historic Places, or those properties that are designated as historic under state or local law. While structural changes to these facilities need not be undertaken, cities and counties must consider alternatives to address the needs of physically disabled citizens, such as using audiovisual materials to depict the inaccessible portions of the facility.

***Curb ramps*** When streets and roads are newly built or altered, they must include ramps wherever there are curbs or other barriers to entry from a pedestrian walkway. Similarly, when new sidewalks or walkways are built or altered, they must contain curb ramps or sloped areas wherever they intersect with streets or roads.

***Effective communication*** To ensure that communications with all citizens are as effective as possible, cities and counties should provide appropriate auxiliary aids and services for people with disabilities (e.g., qualified interpreters; note takers; computer-aided transcription services; assistive listening systems; written materials, including large print and braille; audio recordings; and computer disks). These aids could be provided at such venues as council meetings, public hearings, work sessions, and special government meetings.

***Local laws, ordinances, and regulations*** Local governments are required to make reasonable modifications to policies, practices, or procedures to prevent discrimination on the basis of disability. For example, a municipal ordinance banning animals from city health clinics may need to be modified to allow a blind individual who uses a service animal to bring the animal to a mental health counseling session.

***911 systems*** Local governments that provide emergency telephone services must provide direct access to teletypewriter (TTY) and/or telecommunication devices for the deaf (TDD) calls. This means that emergency telephone services can directly receive calls from TTY and computer modem users without relying on state relay services or third parties.

***Law enforcement policies and procedures*** Law enforcement agencies should make reasonable modifications in policies and procedures unless such modifications would fundamentally alter the law enforcement practice. For example, where appropriate, officers should allow arrestees who are deaf to be handcuffed in front of their bodies so they can communicate with others and should allow detainees access to their medication.[3]

## Health and public health

Local government is playing an increasingly larger role in determining the response to a growing list of significant health concerns. Traditional areas of concern include prevention and control of communicable diseases; prevention and control of chronic diseases; injury prevention; alcohol and drug abuse; environmental health; and infant, child, and adolescent health.

### Integrated service provision in West Hollywood, California

Confronted with a disproportionate share of Los Angeles County's AIDS caseload, West Hollywood, California (pop. 36,732), provides a continuum of care through integration and coordination of a number of city-created or city-funded services, including medical care, counseling, transportation, and housing. The city works closely with the West Hollywood Homeless Organization to provide both emergency housing (housing for one week or less) and transitional housing, as well as health screening, case management, job training and placement, mental health and addiction recovery services, and meals. The city also supported the development of sixty-two apartment units designed to meet the needs of low-income, disabled persons. Preference goes to people with AIDS.

Health problems are especially prevalent among pregnant women, babies and small children, elderly citizens, and people with little access to health services because of poverty or isolation. These groups need the advocacy of a community public health program to help them attain and maintain good health. Moreover, about 45.8 million people in the United States, or 15.7 percent of the population, do not have health insurance.[4] This lack of health coverage places additional burdens on local government services.

*Prevention and control of communicable diseases*    Historically, local health departments have monitored the spread of communicable diseases and established primary intervention programs. These programs include spraying for mosquitoes to avoid the West Nile virus, testing for mad cow disease, and administering flu shots in hopes of avoiding widespread diseases such as the avian influenza H5N1 (bird flu). In addition, local governments have had to deal with substantial increases in other diseases—for instance, occurrences of AIDS and the human immunodeficiency virus (HIV). In order to avoid a pandemic, all levels of government must be ready to work with each other to prevent the spread of communicable diseases.

Increasingly, community health programs are assuming a leadership role in efforts to prevent disease. Because immunization for the young and the elderly is still the most effective way to prevent disease, local health programs provide immunization for such vaccine-preventable diseases as measles and polio; the goal of immunization programs is the total elimination of these diseases in the community, a goal recently achieved worldwide with smallpox. Local governments also need to promote health education programs that inform residents about available hepatitis tests, mammogram screenings, and other important health issues. Finally, local governments need to ensure the distribution of educational materials; a number of communities have partnered with local colleges and universities to fulfill this role.

*Prevention and control of chronic diseases*    The prevention and control of chronic conditions such as cancer, high blood pressure, and heart and lung diseases are also important concerns. With an increased understanding of their causes, public health workers have designed programs to reduce risk factors associated with these diseases. For example, many communities are emphasizing the importance of decreasing tobacco use and improving diets to prevent cancer. Local governments have taken the lead in offering smoking cessation programs and in passing city ordinances that restrict the use of tobacco in public places, workplaces, and certain restaurants and bars. Although these ordinances have sparked controversies, a majority of cities now have them for the purpose of promoting public health.

Because drunk driving and alcohol-related diseases are public health problems directly related to heavy alcohol consumption, many community programs promote the responsible use of alcohol. Many also promote adequate exercise and nutrition, and even provide dietary counseling.

***Injury prevention***   Communities involve themselves in injury prevention through education, regulation, and legislation. For example, a local prevention effort may stress the use seat belts, helmets, and protective clothing. Because traffic control, pedestrian habits, smoke alarms, and other factors may also affect rates of injury, police and fire departments often participate in injury prevention activities.

***Alcohol and drug abuse***   Treatment for alcohol-related conditions is taking an increasing percentage of health care funds, and alcohol is the single most frequently found human factor in fatal automobile accidents.

Although drug programs abound, few are unqualified successes, and enforcement of antidrug laws receives far more federal support than does education about or treatment of the problem. Still, some programs have been successful; for instance, former addicts have had a positive impact on prevention efforts with youth. Halfway houses and crisis centers are also effective.

Former addicts usually need help finding employment, which can help them establish the sense of personal worth essential to helping them keep "clean." Besides encouraging private sector employers to give jobs to former addicts, government can look at its own hiring practices.

***Environmental health problems***   Environmental health problems are caused by human exposure to a variety of dangerous contaminants. Exposure to toxic substances, such as pesticides on farmland or suburban lawns and solvents in the workplace, is a major public health problem. In some communities, lead-based paints, asbestos, radon, mold, and even radioactive wastes are cause for concern. Landfills, abandoned dumps, and underground fuel storage tanks can contaminate air and water; contaminated drinking water is a hazard of particular concern. Contamination can occur in many ways, including accidents, poor sewage treatment, agricultural practices, and inadequate care in disposing of toxic substances. Environmental sanitation and health are therefore key areas for local government action.

---

### Environmental health problems in Nashua, New Hampshire

The city of Nashua, New Hampshire (pop. 87,321), provides a Web site with regard to mold problems. While it does not conduct testing, the city strives to promote awareness and education. It has an entire page on its Web site that provides both information on how to avoid mold contamination and links to other resources that are even more informative (see ci.nashua.nh.us/content/51/86/289/320.aspx).

---

**Women's Wellness and Maternity Center in Monroe County, Tennessee**

To provide a safe, inexpensive alternative to delivering babies in distant hospitals, rural Monroe County, Tennessee (pop. 43,185), helps fund the Women's Wellness and Maternity Center. Certified midwives provide nutrition counseling and childbirth education, deliver babies, provide prenatal and postpartum care, and pay three visits to babies and mothers at home. The center delivers about 120 babies a year and allows an average stay of six to twelve hours in the center for uncomplicated deliveries. The county owns part of the building and provides the maintenance.

Source: Women's Wellness and Maternity Center, wellnessandmaternity.net.

---

*Infant, child, and adolescent health programs*   Many communities are stepping up their efforts to ensure adequate nutrition and a healthy start for young infants. In particular, the nutrition and health needs of the large number of children being raised in poverty must be addressed if proper growth and development are to occur.

Adolescent health is also of growing concern. Dissemination of adequate health care information on sexual behavior, the prevention of sexually transmitted diseases, birth control, pregnancy and birth, and parenting skills is extremely important. So, too, are education and treatment programs for substance abuse and mental health problems. The dramatic physical and emotional changes that occur during adolescence make young people especially vulnerable to emotional and behavioral disorders. According to the National Institute of Mental Health, an estimated one in ten children and adolescents in the United States suffers from mental illness severe enough to cause some level of impairment; sadly, only one in five of these children receives treatment.[5]

*The nutrition and health needs of the large number of children being raised in poverty must be addressed if proper growth and development are to occur.*

A related concern is teen suicide, the incidence of which has tripled since 1970. Suicide is currently the third leading cause of death for 15- to 24-year-olds, surpassed only by accidents and homicide.[6] Communities need to be aware of family-centered and community-based programs that can combat this problem.

Another illness that has reached epidemic porportions among children and adolescents is diabetes. More than 13,000 young people are diagnosed with diabetes every year.[7] As reported by the Palo Alto Medical Foundation, as many as 80 percent of U.S. youth may be overweight at the time of diagnosis.[8] The American Diabetes Association anticipates that as our society becomes more and more overweight and the levels of physical activity among our youth decline, the frequency of diabetes among the young is very likely to increase.

*Healthy communities*   Some local governments may want to follow the principles of a healthy communities program. In California, for instance, the Department of Health Services, with a grant from the Centers for Disease Control and Prevention, contracted

---

**Keeping children active in Santa Monica, California**

Childhood obesity is a point of growing concern in our society, and the city of Santa Monica, California (pop. 87,800), has taken a stance to confront it. With a focus on engaging children in physical activity, the city offers youth sports training and league play, after-school programs, enrichment classes (such as yoga and dance), swimming lessons, and aquatic fitness classes for youth. In addition, its Web page discusses the advantages of eating healthy and warns of some of the possible risks of childhood obesity. All of this is done in order to encourage a healthy lifestyle among children.

Source: City of Santa Monica, santa-monica.org/services/choc/272.htm.

---

**Principles of healthy communities**

**Access to care:** Ensure primary and specialty care for underserved populations, assess insurance coverage and eliminate barriers to access, remove disparities in care due to language and cultural differences, and make adequate transportation available.

**Chronic disease prevention and management:** Develop community-based approaches to create the conditions for good health and reverse the course of chronic disease.

**Collaborative strategies:** Generate effective partnerships based on these principles to achieve real advances in community health while strengthening the health care system.

**Measurement and evaluation:** Develop logic models, indicators, and assessments to help establish goals, understand outcomes, and communicate progress.

Source: Adapted from the mission statement of the Association for Community Health Improvement, communityhlth.org/communityhlth/about/mission.html.

---

with the Center for Civic Partnerships to create a resource for local governments. California Healthy Cities and Communities has the object of ensuring that every person in California can live a healthy, productive life in a clean, safe environment.

## Consumer protection

Although consumer protection is probably better handled by counties, larger cities, and higher levels of government, it can be pursued in smaller jurisdictions with just one or two investigators. Alternatives include contracting with a consumer protection council for watchdog services or entering into a cooperative program with other local governments. The office of the county attorney (usually called the district or state attorney general) should be a good source of aid.

## Poverty

The word *poverty* connotes a condition in which people have insufficient funds to meet basic needs. However, people living in poverty are likely to need more than money. Those in poverty often feel exploited and powerless and have a sense of failure and dependency. Unable to share in most social and material benefits, they feel alienated from the community.

The federal Personal Responsibility and Work Opportunity Reconciliation Act passed in 1996 dramatically changed the nation's welfare system into one that requires work in exchange for time-limited assistance. The law contained strong work requirements, a performance bonus to reward states for moving welfare recipients into jobs, state maintenance of effort requirements, comprehensive child support enforcement, and supports for families moving from welfare to work—including increased funding for child care and guaranteed medical coverage. Other provisions of the act included a five-year time limit, personal employability plans, job subsidies, performance bonuses to reward work, and state flexibility.

As noted earlier, the 1996 act established a block grant program, Temporary Assistance for Needy Families (TANF), to replace AID to Families with Dependent Children (AFDC), the cash assistance program that previously helped millions of poor families. Each state now receives a lump sum of federal money to run its own welfare and work programs.

Many positive developments seem to have occurred since the passage of the act. Welfare caseloads have dropped considerably, poverty has fallen among children and families, and many formerly unemployed individuals have joined the workforce. Nevertheless, some analysts caution that these developments hide many troubling concerns for millions of current and previous welfare recipients. The primary concern revolves around earning potential: some of these individuals are not working full-time or full-year, and most earn between $5.15 and $9.00 per hour—a wage inadequate to provide for a family. Although the poverty rate declined after the passage of the act, it has since increased, particularly among families headed by single mothers. For those families that were already poor, poverty in the last several years has deepened.[9]

*Living-wage laws provide that a company contracting with the city or county pay wages high enough to keep a family of four above the federal poverty line.*

These and other issues have given added momentum to the "living-wage movement," which seeks to establish wage floors above the federal $5.15-an-hour minimum. Living-wage laws provide that a company contracting with the city or county pay wages high enough to keep a family of four above the federal poverty line. One hundred cities (including Boston, Chicago, Detroit, Santa Fe, and the California cities of Los Angeles, Sonoma, and Ventura) and counties (including Broward and Palm Beach Counties, Florida; Westchester County, New York; Prince Georges County, Maryland; and Ingham County, Michigan) have passed such laws. The increased wages could be a step in the right direction; whether they will be enough to offset increases in inflation, however, is another question.

Finally, a number of cities have begun programs to help their residents claim the federal Earned Income Tax Credit (EITC). For most low-income taxpayers, their EITC exceeds their tax bill, thus making them eligible for a refund. A small investment from the city can bring thousands of dollars to local residents, who in turn will use the money to purchase local goods and services.

---

**Living-wage ordinances in Sonoma, California, and Durham County, North Carolina**

In 2004 the city of Sonoma, California (pop. 9,885), passed an ordinance mandating that covered employers pay a wage of $11.70 with health benefits, or $13.20 without health benefits, indexed annually to the consumer price index. The ordinance covers the city of Sonoma, companies with a city service contract worth at least $10,000, nonprofits with city contracts of at least $75,000, and companies receiving loans or economic assistance worth $100,000 or more. Covered employers must also provide twelve compensated days off, as well as ten uncompensated days off. Small businesses are exempt from the law.

In that same year, the Durham County Board of Commissioners in Durham County, North Carolina (pop. 242,582), passed an ordinance setting the county's living wage at 7.5 percent above the federal poverty level for a family of four. The ordinance applies to all employees of the county as well as to persons working on county service contracts, including contracts for temporary services.

Source: The Living Wage Resource Center, livingwagecampaign.org.

---

## Program planning

Two areas of knowledge are vital to the planning process: knowing who needs help but is not getting it, and knowing what human services *are* being provided in the community. Determining needs and inventorying resources are often done simultaneously as the first steps in planning human services. Subsequent steps may entail a strategic plan including a social base study, which is roughly equivalent to the economic base study that is normally part of a general land use plan, and a social impact statement. Involvement of elected officials in the planning process is also vital.

### Needs assessment

Numerous potential problems—too many to explore in detail here—await those trying to decide who needs what in human services. This is because *need* can be defined in many different ways. If someone says, "I need help," the person has an *expressed need.* Others have needs but do not say so. These are *perceived needs,* because the administrator believes that they may exist. If in providing a service an administrator must choose between two people with different needs, the administrator will draw conclusions about their *relative needs.* Evidence shows that needs grow or shrink depending on the availability of help. In other words, if people think they might get help, they will acknowledge the need for it, but if they do not expect help, they will not acknowledge the need. Needs, then, are somewhat elastic.

Determining needs can be a process that includes receiving or soliciting citizen input; assigning citizen task forces; observing needs identified by citizen groups, interest groups, and the media; and monitoring changing demographic and socioeconomic trends in the community. Need determination must also include close attention to state and federal requirements for what services must be provided, at what level, and to whom, including explicit minimum qualifications for clientele participation.

Several methods are available for quantifying needs—each useful, some time-consuming, others expensive, none foolproof. One method is to assess existing programs.

The data collected from the assessment often show trends, reveal user profiles, and demonstrate the capacity of existing programs to provide services and meet needs.

Another method is to carry out formal surveys. Although this method is usually expensive and time-consuming, there are shortcuts that do not affect the survey's ability to provide valuable information. These shortcuts include using the telephone and abbreviated question lists, and using volunteers or university students.

> *Whereas a good needs assessment is a valuable management tool,*
> *a poor one is probably worthless.*

When focusing on highly controversial needs, such as community housing for the mentally disabled, the expert opinions of community workers are sometimes useful; they are often voiced at the public hearing. Although it remains questionable whether the testimony at such hearings represents the community as a whole, the hearings do provide an opportunity to gather information from diverse sources. Hearings are especially effective if the community is alerted well beforehand of the opportunity to be heard.

Still another method of assessing needs is the focus group. This technique involves planned discussions among the people from whom information is desired. A group of community human service workers, for example, might be asked to spend a half-day in a focus group, in which it is given a predetermined number of questions to answer through group discussion. A convener, who knows what information is desired, can lead the discussions to keep participants on track and elicit the desired information. Discussions are recorded so that the information can be extracted later on. Focus groups should consist of representatives from the different categories of persons to be served (e.g., youth, single mothers, senior citizens, disabled individuals, unemployed workers), human service clientele, and/or professional human service workers and management.

Whereas a good needs assessment is a valuable management tool, a poor one is probably worthless. A needs assessment does not guarantee that the political process will respond to meet identified needs, but a well-planned process of assessing needs can help mobilize support for the political decisions that follow.

## Resource inventory

Once areas of need in the community are identified, the next step is to inventory existing public and private resources. The best place to start is with the local hospital and such local organizations as the United Crusade, United Givers, and United Way. These sources may already have completed studies on social indicators affecting the entire region and surveyed the agencies available to help. Such an inventory can provide a quick appraisal and immediately identify some of the worst problems and the best resources. Using information already compiled avoids needless duplication of effort. Some local governments might also want to create a human services information and referral-type system—a potential 211 for nonemergency calls.

If an inventory is to be conducted, it should include the resources of the local government, the federal Departments of Labor, Housing and Urban Development, and Health and Human Services; state departments of economic development, human resources, and planning; county welfare and health departments; and, in many cases, school districts.

Charitable and nonprofit agencies are another resource. Some types of public and charitable operations are workshops for disabled workers, residential treatment centers for children, adoption agencies, family counseling agencies, the Salvation Army, coordinating councils, urban coalitions, the Urban League, emergency relief organizations, Big Brothers and Big Sisters, halfway houses, hotlines, job counseling services, legal aid groups, rehabilitation centers, associations for disabled citizens, homemakers' services, and visiting nurses associations.[10] Several business organizations operate in the job training sector and offer consulting services to nonprofit agencies.

Churches also offer a large variety of social programs, either through local congregations or through centralized special-purpose organizations. As indicated in the introduction, additional support for this volunteer sector comes from the White House Office of Faith-Based and Community Initiatives, which was established to strengthen and expand the role of faith-based and community organizations in addressing the nation's social problems. As part of its mission, the office supplies information and training to such organizations to empower them to apply for federal social service grants.[11]

## Community strategic planning

Optimally, those concerned with planning human services should develop a plan that is integral to the community's general plan. This plan should also be flexible, frequently updated, and integrated with the plans of other governments, neighboring communities, and community action agencies. Minimally, the plan should push community leaders to think through social problems and their possible solutions.

Because the composition of the community's social structure can change rapidly, a social base study should be part of this plan. The study can be an extension of the needs assessment that is then combined with long-range goals. The study should contain specific types of quantifiable information, such as the numbers of unemployed people, individuals and families below the poverty level, and people over the age of sixty-five. The goals, too, should be quantifiable as well as realistic.

## Social impact statement

A social impact statement is another element of planning for human services. For some time, communities have prepared environmental impact reports on proposed public and private projects within their boundaries. Although too much red tape and too many bad procedures have been created in the name of good environmental planning, the concept of an impact study still has great validity. In the end, a community's impact study should not be three separate statements (environmental, economic, and social); rather, it should be one statement that analyzes and integrates all three facets, without artificial distinctions between social and physical programs. Such comprehensive impact studies are new and may not be done as well as they should be, but if communities are to become more humane and livable in the future, this method holds great promise.

Elaborate general plans with well-rehearsed social impact statements are not absolutely necessary to deal with social needs. If a major industry closes down within a month and puts 20 percent of the community's labor force out of work, there is not enough time to compose overly detailed statements or plans. However, communities that look ahead and approach their social programming on a systematic basis can do much to prevent future crises.

### Elected officials and the community

Sometimes, if no other government or charitable agency offers the service or if special circumstances demand community action, the best or only available strategy may be to have the government provide the service directly. In that case, involving elected officials in the planning process is an important step as it helps them decide how far the local government can go toward resolving the problem. For particularly difficult social problems, it may make more sense to appoint an ad hoc task force to make recommendations than to appoint a permanent human service commission.

In designing a new service delivery system, other communities that have provided or are providing the service should be consulted as their experience can be invaluable. The administrator should also try to involve members of the public and leaders of the various groups in the community. Local government officials will be more successful in planning effective human service programs if they listen to the wider community's ideas and concerns.

## Organization for service delivery

When organizing to provide a new human service function, there are two principal alternatives to consider: (1) attaching the function to the administrator's office or (2) creating a strategic alliance with a nonprofit provider of service. No single alternative is necessarily right in every situation.

### Service delivery as a function of the administrator's office

If the community is small, there are advantages to assigning human service personnel to the chief administrator's office. Such a move tells elected officials, the community, and staff that the administrator takes human service problems seriously and is not going to let them get buried in an existing department. This approach may be particularly beneficial if the services deal with minorities or others who feel they have been neglected or treated unfairly as it maximizes opportunities for communication between the people to be served and the local government. It also makes it easier for the central staff to compile needed information about other interrelated programs and to monitor information from diverse sources; in this way they can identify emerging problems and give local officials early warning before problems get out of hand.

If a community cannot afford staff to deal with particular human service needs, or if the problems do not warrant additional personnel, another approach is to form an interdepartmental task force, such as a social concerns committee. This approach enables the administrator to take the lead in educating management personnel about the social problems of the community, the resources available, and how staff may relate to those problems.

It often happens that an opportunity to improve human services presents itself through the regular operations of established government programs. For communities that want to implement human service programs but have few funds with which to do it, one option can be to design or redesign existing government policies to serve human service needs, including those policies concerned with hiring and training, establishing fees, investing funds, using regulatory powers, and generally setting the tone of the organization.

The local government administrator may play any of several roles—often simultaneously—in providing human service programs. Elected officials may exercise little oversight or may require the administrator to work in close concert with them. The roles played by the administrator, which include leader, goal setter, power broker, ambassador, advocate, and ombudsperson, depend heavily on the duties that elected officials assign or allow the administrator to have.

*Leader*   Although an administrator alone can do little to improve the quality of life for those in need, he or she can act as a leader in the process, conveying to elected officials, the community, and staff a sense of commitment and the importance of taking action. The administrator can provide the direction necessary to move from a human service need to a human service program and, finally, to a human service solution. As leader, an administrator can also set the tone for the whole organization. For example, if staff perceive that sensitivity to diversity is not important at the top, such sensitivity is not likely to permeate very far down into the organization. Similarly, if staff and citizens know that a decision maker is serious about listening, they are more likely to listen to the views of others. The administrative officer should also take the lead in ensuring that appropriate community groups, and especially minority groups, are consulted about pending policy and administrative decisions that affect them.

*Goal setter*   The administrator can play an important role in helping elected officials set goals. The administrator's function is not to tell the elected council the best course of action but to document needs, assess public interest, identify desirable goals, determine alternatives, and make policy and goal recommendations. The effort put forth by the administrator in fulfilling these functions can dictate the success or failure of the human service program.

*Power broker*   A county or city manager is often required to act as a power broker, especially in communities where many private and not-for-profit agencies share the task of providing human services. The more economically and ethnically diverse the community, the more divided it will be and the more conflict will mark government activities. To be caught amid competing interests is a dangerous position to be in. However, the skillful administrator, with the understanding and support of the elected officials, can maneuver within policy guidelines and arbitrate in the public interest, always seeking to use government influence to coordinate the efforts of diverse social service agencies toward the goal of ensuring adequate human services for the entire community.

*Ambassador*   When working out solutions to community problems, it is often necessary to establish strong working relationships with other government units, whether city, county, state, or federal. Although the role of ambassador may sometimes be filled by the mayor, county board chairperson, elected county executive, or manager, it often falls upon the administrator. In such cases, the administrator must act as liaison in dealing with those other government units as well as with social service agencies.

*Advocate*   As an advocate, the administrator identifies issues affecting those in need—the poor, the elderly, the young, and members of racial and ethnic minorities. Advocacy involves making officeholders and other administrators aware of problems and encouraging them to take action. This role grows in importance in communities that lack an individual, department, or committee assigned to represent these groups.

*Ombudsperson*   As ombudsperson, the administrator ensures that his or her own organization is fair and responsive to the needs of the community, especially those citizens who are poor or disadvantaged. This role involves presenting the interests of the community before other levels of government and, occasionally, before large corporations.

## Alternatives for service delivery

While a community may be deeply involved in the implementation of a human service program, it does not have to provide the service directly. Alternative service delivery approaches are discussed in depth in Chapter 15, but since these approaches are so common in the area of human services, a brief discussion is included here of three roles for the local government.

*Indirect provider*   Local governments can provide human services indirectly by subsidizing other organizations or agencies, cooperating with other communities or agencies, or contracting out. A local government may purchase services from a private organization, a nonprofit agency, or a charitable organization. It may, for example, contract with a local restaurant to provide a daily meal program for the elderly; secure volunteers to deliver meals-on-wheels to people who are confined to their homes because of illness or disability; pay a family service agency to provide counseling programs for dysfunctional families; or subsidize cab rides for the disabled.

Some communities use vouchers with which human service clients can secure services from their choice of private or nonprofit providers. This method is often used, for example, for the provision of day care services. Many communities subsidize organizations that will provide homeless shelters or food programs; others depend on volunteers to help them provide the service themselves.

Still another approach to indirect service provision is to join with other agencies. Mental health programs, drug counseling, and various youth programs are often managed on a regional basis. Major programs (e.g., housing and transportation) may have to be provided

---

### The Ben Gordon Center in DeKalb County, Illinois

The Ben Gordon Center in DeKalb County, Illinois (pop. 97,665), has provided community mental health services, including counseling and substance abuse treatment, since 1968. Through the following four decades, the center has expanded to provide services at four sites in addition to its main site in DeKalb. As it proclaims on its Web site, "Our mission is to provide behavioral healthcare services in a timely and affordable manner to the people we serve, in order to assist them in creating the highest quality of life possible." The center serves women, children, adolescents, couples, and families. With comprehensive coverage in the county, the center offers convenience for the client and cost-effective care for local government, corporate, and managed care buyers. The center's funds come from private fund raising; from federal, state, and local grants, including an annual grant from the county's mental health tax levy; and from fees charged for its services on an ability-to-pay basis.

Source: Ben Gordon Center, DeKalb, Illinois, bengordoncenter.org.

on this basis if they are to be effective on a metropolitan or broad scale. Sometimes a government can ensure the availability of a service by persuading a service provider from another area to open a branch office in the community, even if only for a few days a month.

Contracting out or privatization—as used in some circles—is not always cost-effective. Although there has been a movement toward this type of service delivery, a responsible degree of caution should be exercised to ensure that the most vulnerable in our society are not compromised.

*Catalyst*  A second alternative in service delivery is to act as a catalyst by encouraging existing governments, private organizations, or nonprofit agencies to supply services in a facility provided by the local government. Some communities have built or rented space to be shared by a variety of agencies that offer human services. Such space does not have to be expensive. Old houses, acquired as part of a site for a future public facility, often serve this purpose well.

*Coordinator*  If many public and private programs are already operating effectively in or near the community, the local government's role may be that of coordinator. This involves ongoing needs assessment, planning, and evaluating of existing programs to ensure that needed services are available. Most important, it means developing the level of inter-agency communication and cooperation required to secure a balanced, adequate program of service provision.

The human service coordinator must be just that—a coordinator, able to coordinate the work of various agencies in the human service field. As already noted, some of the local government's human service contribution can be made through regulatory programs, but enforcement should not be the sole function of any human service staff member. Much more can be accomplished through facilitation. Moreover, the community wastes talent and perhaps misses opportunities if the member is restricted to an enforcement role.

In such circumstances, the coordinator also performs a vital referral function. Although a helping agency exists to assist those in need, the person in need may be unaware of its availability or of his or her eligibility to use its services. Many local government workers have frequent contact with people who need help; such workers can be trained to identify those people and refer them to the appropriate agencies. Police officers, switchboard operators, and recreation staff are especially high on the list of those who can be trained

**Coordinated human services in the schools in Catawba County, North Carolina**

To combat the effects of many kinds of social problems evident in its public school children, Catawba County, North Carolina (pop. 151,641), has organized human service teams to work directly with the children in school settings. Each team consists of a social worker from the department of social services, a nurse from the public health department, and a psychologist from the mental health department. The teams are assigned to specific schools with the purpose of responding to social problems that interfere with the education process. These teams often function as a bridge between the schools and the families as well as provide ready access to other services. From the child's perspective, the teams function as providers, advocates, and brokers of services.

as referral agents. Any referrals are general in nature, and if confidential information will be shared, it is essential to secure the proper signed release forms.

The coordinator's primary stock-in-trade is the confidence he or she is able to engender in various client groups. If perceived as a law enforcement official, the coordinator will not be able to maintain this confidence. Thus, some administrators prefer to use the coordinator as mediator, facilitator, or broker between conflicting groups.

## Management concerns in the delivery of human services

Once human service needs have been identified and assessed, programs have been planned, and the delivery of services has been secured, several issues must be addressed in the management of the program. These issues include funding, public safety, citizen participation, diversity training, program evaluation, and the use of technology.

### Funding

Human services is an area of government in which there is never enough money in the budget; moreover, spending obligations go up in tough economic times, when government revenues are apt to decline. It is during bad economic times that the need and demand for human service programs becomes greatest. A manager may be required to become more creative, and sometimes entrepreneurial, in his or her approach to funding human service programs.

Tailoring tax policy to promote certain public policies is probably as old as imposing taxes. Such tailoring can be used to promote human welfare by easing the tax burden on those less able to pay. Some communities have reduced utility rates for elderly and low-income citizens; others have offered reduced bus fares or have deferred or reduced property taxes for such citizens. And in some communities, community-run swimming pools that charge admission offer free passes to children from low-income families.

Communities that do not have sufficient revenues to sustain existing human services or develop new programs can obtain needed funds by charging user fees for the new programs, for some existing programs, or for both. For example, elderly residents who pay part of the costs of such services as transportation or meals-on-wheels can provide an important source of revenue to help support these and other valuable services. Care must be used in designing programs that are dependent on user fees, however, as not all those who need the program may be able to afford the fee. Those with little or no ability to pay can be offered discounted or free services.

Programs to reduce taxes or fees can fail if they make recipients feel self-conscious about receiving special treatment. Communities must also be conscious of whatever legal requirements may be pertinent. Holding the line, cutting back, or reducing the incremental funding for existing services will usually free up resources for reallocation. The administrator who asks really tough questions about the budget and is willing to work to change long-held views may find a surprising amount of money for new social programs.

Having identified possible sources of funding, the administrator should then develop a separate budget for human service programs, taking into account proposed government expenditures as well as the spending of other public and private agencies in the community. The human service budget should be made part of the overall budget document, thereby institutionalizing the services.

**Community-oriented policing project in Southern Pines, North Carolina**

The police department in Southern Pines, North Carolina (pop. 11,881), confronted with major drug-related crime in an apartment complex, instituted a community- and problem-oriented policing policy. The department employed a community service officer to serve as a public contact, secured a grant to hire and equip two patrol officers to work in high-crime areas and receive special training in the community-oriented policing philosophy, and established a community center in a converted apartment in the complex. The center provides space for a police satellite office, making the police more accessible. It also offers a place for community functions and has established social programs for children and adults based on the expressed needs of the residents.

Support for the project came from local residents; local businesses, churches, and the United Way provided supplementary funding; and the apartment ownership supplied the apartment. The result has been a 70 percent drop in calls for police service in the area as well as a heightened sense of togetherness among residents of the apartment complex.

## Public safety

Good police work can prevent or at least minimize social problems; bad police work will aggravate them. Minority communities are often particularly sensitive to law enforcement procedures. A well-trained police force, emphasizing good rapport with all parts of the community, can prevent small problems from getting bigger. Sensitivity to different cultures and to the use of resources other than law enforcement to solve problems may not guarantee a peaceful community, but it will go a long way toward achieving social progress.

Fire department policy can also play a role in human services. In one Texas community, before the last pumper leaves the scene of a fire, firefighters advise the affected family that the Red Cross and other programs are available to provide them with assistance. Later the fire marshal contacts relevant agencies to advise them of the burnout and give them information about the family. This process helps to ensure that the family will have their needs met quickly, thereby lessening, to the extent possible, the impact of the trauma they have experienced.

## Citizen participation

Achieving success in most human service areas is difficult, if not impossible, without effective citizen participation. Public meetings and annual reports, the traditional means of communicating with citizens, do not begin to go far enough, especially in the field of human services. Ideally, local government leaders will communicate personally with various interest groups; however, if a group speaks a different language or has little experience in dealing with government, its members may be more comfortable talking through another member who acts as intermediary.

Some communities have umbrella human service bodies that oversee many programs—for example, youth commissions, senior citizen councils, and disability advisory committees. If such groups are staffed by human service workers who are involved in the

**Neighborhoods in Action in Orem, Utah**

Recognizing the need to involve its citizens more directly in its decision-making process, the city of Orem, Utah (pop. 89,713), has instituted a program known as Neighborhoods in Action. Within the program there are twenty neighborhood organizations, each of which has a committee that oversees quarterly planning, information sharing, and problem-solving meetings. Focusing on bringing solutions rather than problems to local government leaders, the program seeks to increase people's awareness of local government and sense of responsibility for their neighborhoods.

Source: City of Orem, orem.org/index.php?option=com_content&task=view&id=289&Itemid=267.

community, local government administrators can gain an invaluable, two-way conduit for communication with key community leaders.

Another way of encouraging participation in—and developing rapport with—interest groups is to provide leadership training for them. One manager described this process as "releasing the energies in the people," and reported how thrilling it was to watch individuals who once had little hope for progress begin to learn how to deal with their problems.

Some people may find it hard to believe that going to a government office can be a terrifying experience, but for many citizens that is often the case. Thus, it is helpful for local government officials and citizens to meet in familiar settings such as local schools, senior centers, a sheltered workshop, or a counseling center. Government leaders who hold meetings in such settings are typically pleased at the response.

### Diversity training

A training program in cultural diversity helps sensitize all local government employees to people from different racial, ethnic, or cultural backgrounds. It is important to remember that diversity training should be ongoing with all employees; attitudes and values are not changed in a single session, nor are old prejudices easily erased. But given regularly, such training will help employees understand and relate better to new employees and residents of the community who come from different backgrounds. With a growing Hispanic population, it is also essential that employees understand language and cultural differences within this community.

Diversity training is especially important for police officers, emergency service employees, human service workers, parks and recreation personnel, and those who are seen as authority figures. Such training does not guarantee the absence of conflict, but it can reduce the likelihood of a thoughtless remark or a careless action offending someone and possibly triggering an unfortunate incident.

### Program evaluation

Evaluating social service programs is often difficult, but it is not impossible. It can be approached in several different ways.

***Goal attainment***   Determining the success of a program in meeting its goals requires a clear understanding of those goals and objectives as well as a strategy to measure them.

For example, if the goal is to improve the nutrition of elderly residents who live alone, and if the number of hot meals they eat is directly related to good nutrition, a reasonable goal might be to deliver five hot meals a week to every elderly person living alone. Simple record keeping can provide the information needed to determine when that goal is met.

## Cultural diversity in the United States

In a recent press release from the U.S. Census Bureau, it was reported that the state of Texas had joined California, Hawaii, and New Mexico as a majority-minority state along with the District of Columbia. Five additional states–Arizona, Georgia, Maryland, Mississippi, and New York–were next in line with minority populations of about 40 percent.[1] The designation "majority-minority state" means that the majority of state residents are ethnic minorities and that Anglos are in the minority. Without a doubt, the demographic changes faced by the United States and its communities in the next few years will have a great impact on the social, political, and economic makeup of a number of local governments.

As the population of North America becomes increasingly diverse, all local government officials must demonstrate cultural sensitivity and awareness. Training in cultural diversity will help managers and department heads recognize and deal with racial prejudice within themselves and among employees. Behavior that can be seen as racially prejudiced or insulting cannot be tolerated. Employee training and stringent administration of nondiscrimination regulations are two of the best ways to deal with racism.

1  U.S. Census Bureau News, press release, March 23, 2006, available at census.gov/Press-Release/www/releases/archives/population/005514.html.

## Reaching out to immigrant communities

The rapid influx of immigrants to the United States, both legal and illegal, concerns state and local officials on a number of levels. Of prime concern is communication. Engendering a civic-minded populace requires official documents, ordinances, laws, and notices to be accessible in a number of languages.

Local governments need to make every effort to reach out to immigrant communities to understand their specific needs and service requirements. The International Hispanic Network, an association of Hispanic public administrators, has compiled a number of best practices from cities that are serving Hispanic communities.[1] The city of Santa Barbara, California, for instance, translates all city council meetings into Spanish. A number of cities have Hispanic cultural centers, and still others offer a variety of services from English-as-a-second-language courses and fiestas to outreach programs and bonuses for Spanish-speaking employees. Some cities have even created special positions, such as a community liaison to facilitate communication with immigrant communities. A number of cities on the West Coast also offer these types of services for immigrant Asian communities. In the coming years cities and counties will need to reach out to growing immigrant populations in order to avoid isolating an emergent segment of the population.

1  For additional information on the International Hispanic Network, go to internationalhispanicnetwork.org.

*Cost-effectiveness*   Determining the cost-effectiveness of a benefit requires attaching a dollar cost to that benefit, such as an hour of training provided, a referral made, or a hot meal delivered. Knowing the dollar cost per benefit may affect decisions about whether to maintain, increase, or cut back a program. For example, if the cost of delivering one hot meal a day to an elderly person is five dollars, it may be deemed too expensive even if it achieves the goal.

*Program support*   Still another way to evaluate a program is to measure public or consumer support for it through surveys or other methods. It is not unusual for a program to remain popular and strongly supported even if it exhibits poor cost-effectiveness and fails to meet its goals.

In the three approaches to evaluation just described (as well as others), much depends on the questions being asked. Too often, evaluation information is interesting but not timely or relevant. Given the complexity of human service programs and the difficulty of measuring their various dimensions, it is important to know who is going to use the evaluation information and for what purposes. The evaluation should then seek to determine whether a program is effective and its goals are being met. In the case of a failed program, the evaluation should elicit information about the efficacy of program design and the efficiency of implementation. A problem cannot be corrected if information is not kept on the costs of implementation.

Monitoring human service activities is often difficult because of the nature of those activities, inadequate means of measuring results, and uncertainty about what the goals should be. In addition, evaluation is too often performed by persons or agencies with vested interests in the program, which may hinder an unbiased evaluation.

## The use of technology

Although the use of technology in the human service field extends back many years, it is only in the last few years that various applications have had a tremendous impact on service delivery. From laptops and cell phones for caseworkers to geographic information

---

### The integration of laptops, GIS, and customer service

Imagine that a single mother without a car calls her caseworker in an effort to change day care providers. As they talk, the caseworker enters the mother's address into her laptop, generates an on-screen map centered on the mother's residence, and selects "child care" and "bus routes." In an instant the program overlays the map with child care icons and highlights the relevant bus routes. When the caseworker clicks on the icon for a specific child care provider, a small photo of the location pops up in the corner, along with a text box describing the hours of operation, the number of openings, contact names, and phone numbers. This information is relayed to the mother. If the conversation takes place during a face-to-face interview, the caseworker can print out a copy of the map and text and immediately hand it over to the client.

Source: Patrick Gaunt and Paul Smyth, "Mapping for Caseworkers," *PM* Magazine (June 2002): 24-26.

systems (GIS), disease mapping, and spatial analysis, technology has enabled the field to better integrate voluminous amounts of data. The benefits allow for the analysis of complex situations, better evaluation of program performance, the education of and communication with clientele, and the professional development of employees via Web-based systems.

## Summary

As this chapter has shown, the challenges to local government in the field of human services can seem quite overwhelming. Among the more prevalent issues are

- The increasing number of elderly citizens who require special services
- Prevention and control of communicable diseases
- Unfunded mandates from higher levels of government
- The ability to finance human services
- Issues related to youth, youth health, and youth employment
- Poverty and its impact on local government
- Housing affordability
- Compliance with the Americans with Disabilities Act.

Unquestionably, human service programs often involve enormous difficulties and complexities, but it is essential for the social health of the community that local governments provide or oversee them. In terms of simple expediency, administrators should choose the path of anticipation and prevention rather than the more expensive, more traumatic, and less satisfactory method of trying to react to a situation after it has reached serious or crisis proportions.

The role that communities may take in providing human services will ultimately be determined by elected officials. This reality, however, does not excuse local administrators—the chief administrative officer, department heads, and even middle managers—from concern for those in the community who need special help. The quality of life in the community cannot be sustained, regardless of the quality of public works, public safety, and leisure services, if the needs of those with special problems and challenges are not met.

Administrators should communicate the importance of meaningful human services to their governing bodies; superficial support will result only in disillusionment as the expectations of those in need are raised and then disappointed. Communities involved in human service programs need to commit themselves to long-range planning and follow through just as they do with public safety, public health, and other ongoing programs. Only then will the community reap the rewards of a successful effort.

### Questions to ask if you manage a small community

What are the responsibilities of the federal, state, and local governments?

How should citizen's human service needs be assessed and determined?

How can strategic planning aid in human service delivery?

What are some potential resources available for human service delivery within communities?

What are the administrator's roles in human service delivery?

How do intergovernmental relationships affect the delivery of human services?

What role do nonprofit agencies play in administering human services?

How can contracting out services affect human service delivery?

What are some of the major human service-related concerns that local governments must deal with?

What are some ways to encourage citizen participation with regards to the delivery of human services?

What are some ways to finance human services?

What are some approaches to evaluating social service programs?

### Competencies for managers in the field of human services

Appropriate knowledge of the role of local government in the delivery of human services

The talent to bring people together for a common goal

The capability to review programs and eliminate those that are not working

The skill to outsource the right services to the private and nonprofit sector

Proficiency in intergovernmental relations, cooperation, networking

An understanding of the field of human service

## ▓ Endnotes

1 Section 3, letter (g); complete text available at whitehouse.gov/news/releases/20010129-2.html.

2 For more information on the Medicare Prescription Drug Plan, go to medicare.gov.

3 For more information on how local governments can comply with ADA regulations, go to the Department of Justice's ADA home page at usdoj .gov/crt/ada/adahom1.htm.

4 U.S. Census Bureau News Release, August 30, 2005; available at census.gov/Press-Release/www/ releases/archives/income_wealth/005647.html.

5 National Institute of Mental Health, "Youth in a Difficult World," Publication No. 01-4587, updated February 17, 2006; available at nimh.nih.gov/ publicat/youthdif.cfm.

6 National Institute of Mental Health, "Suicide Facts and Statistics," posted April 9, 2004; available at nimh.nih.gov/suicideprevention/suifact.cfm.

7 American Diabetes Association, "Student's Rights," available at diabetes.org/for-parents-and-kids/ for-schools/students-rights.jsp.

8 Palo Alto Medical Foundation, pamf.org/diabetes/ human_toll.html.

9 See Heather Boushey, "The Effects of the Personal Responsibility and Work Opportunity Reconciliation Act on Working Families," testimony given before the Committee on Education and the Workforce of the U.S. House of Representatives on September 20, 2001.

10 As an example, the Tennessee Commission on Children and Youth has an excellent resource inventory for children services; see tennessee .gov/tccy/services.html.

11 For more information about the OFBCI, see whitehouse.gov/government/fbci/mission.html.

# 12

# *Emergency Management*

**Bob Hart**

Government efforts to cope with potential and actual disasters that disrupt communities are termed *emergency management.* The concept covers both emergencies and disasters, although the distinction between them is substantial. Emergencies are occurrences that can be handled adequately with community resources, as in the case of a fire, localized flooding, or an auto accident; disasters require outside assistance, as happens with a major flood or an earthquake. These events may be natural, or they may be the result of human acts—accidental or intentional.

Preparing for such dire occurrences is most effective when emergency management is an integral part of everyday local government operations. Because disasters and emergencies often give little advance notice, the most opportune time to plan for them is long before they happen.

The need for emergency preparedness may not be self-evident, and funding to ensure preparedness may not be readily allocated. Thus, it is vital that local government administrators take the initiative to establish an emergency management program as an ongoing community function. This chapter discusses the need for integrated emergency management, describes the activities involved, and briefly addresses related issues.

## Elements of emergency management

The emergency manager occupies a professional staff position. In this capacity, the manager serves as the local government's liaison on emergency preparedness issues; coordinates training programs and emergency management drills; coordinates planning efforts between the local government and other jurisdictions, nonprofits, and industries; assists departments with their emergency and mitigation plans; and administers the claims submittal process for federal and state reimbursement for costs incurred during emergency management operations. The tendency to place the emergency manager in the police or fire department should be resisted; instead, the emergency manager be situated within the organization, preferably in the city manager's office/department, to ensure organization-wide participation and influence.

For all emergency and disaster threats, there are four distinct facets of comprehensive emergency management: preparedness, mitigation, response, and recovery. Although in practice they overlap, each facet has its own aims while serving as a building block for the others.

- *Preparedness:* The planning, resource allocation, and training of individuals. This phase also includes disaster response exercises, which help people practice what to do if a disaster occurs.

- *Mitigation:* The assessment and prevention of threats of man-made or natural disasters in the community. Efforts may include different land use planning, improved building codes, and intelligence gathering.

- *Response:* Public donations, incident management, search and rescue operations, damage assessments, and handling of fatalities.

- *Recovery:* Cleanup, the reinstitution of public services, the rebuilding of public infrastructure, and all that is necessary to help restore civic life, including disaster assistance and crisis counseling.

All these areas demand high levels of coordination. Preparedness is improved by mutual-aid agreements and other forms of interjurisdictional planning. Mitigation is more effective when the entire community has been involved in hazard assessment. Response is stronger when key governmental units and private organizations have coordinated plans. Recovery is faster when tasks and responsibilities are allocated across the widest possible range of agencies and individuals.

Coordination channels resources in order to use them for the overall benefit of the community. The more complex a community's organization—that is, the more special districts, overlapping jurisdictions, and organizations with highly specialized responsibilities—the more important it is to ensure coordination. However, coordination is important to emergency managers in every community, regardless of the degree of organizational complexity.

## Federal programs

In the United States, the initial response to an emergency is expected to come from the local government, with support from the state. If the emergency overwhelms local and state resources, federal assistance is sought through established criteria and procedures. Other federal systems and initiatives have been established to help local governments prevent and/or prepare for disaster, to enhance regional response capability and capacity, and to coordinate federal disaster response.

### National Incident Management System

The National Incident Management System (NIMS) provides a flexible framework that helps government and private entities at all levels work together to prevent, respond to, and recover from incidents regardless of size, location, or complexity. Its flexibility extends to processes, procedures, and systems designed to improve interoperability.[1] Its components include command and management, preparedness, resource management, communications and information systems, supporting technologies, and ongoing management and maintenance.

NIMS standard incident management structures are based on three key organizational systems:

- The Incident Command System (ICS), which defines the operating characteristics, management components, and structure of incident management organizations throughout

---

### Emergency management accreditation and certification

The Emergency Management Accreditation Program (EMAP) is a voluntary accreditation process for local government emergency management programs. EMAP looks not just at the individual emergency management agency or department but at a jurisdiction's program or system of emergency management as a whole. It considers how emergency management integrates and coordinates all the players involved in planning, preparedness activities, and response (e.g., public health, transportation). For more information, go to emaponline.org/.

---

the life cycle of an incident. (A more extensive discussion of ICS begins on page 297 of this chapter.)

- The multiagency coordinating system, which defines operating characteristics, managing components, and the organizational structure of supporting entities.
- The public information system, which includes the processes, procedures, and systems for communicating timely and accurate information to the public during emergency operations.[2]

## Homeland security

The Federal Emergency Management Agency (FEMA) is one of five agencies consolidated into the Emergency Preparedness and Response directorate of the U.S. Department of Homeland Security (DHS). It is part of the effort to oversee domestic disaster preparedness training and coordinate government disaster response.

In 2002 DHS established a national warning system for advising the public and all levels of government of a possible risk from a terrorist attack. This color-coded warning system specifies five levels of possible terrorist threats confronting the nation—low (green), guarded (blue), elevated (yellow), high (orange), and severe (red)—and spells out various "protective measures" suited for each level. Police personnel are involved in many of these measures.

## Strategic National Stockpile

The Strategic National Stockpile (SNS), a program within the Centers for Disease Control and Prevention (CDC), has large quantities of medicine and medical supplies to protect the American public if there is a public health emergency (e.g., a terrorist attack, flu outbreak, earthquake) severe enough to cause local supplies to run out. Once federal and local authorities agree that the SNS is needed, medicines will be delivered to any state in the country within twelve hours. Each state has plans to receive and distribute SNS medicine and medical supplies to local communities as quickly as possible.

## Urban Area Security Initiative

The Urban Area Security Initiative (UASI) is designed to set a strategic direction for the enhancement of regional response capability and capacity. UASI's mission is to reduce area vulnerability and prevent terrorism and/or incidents involving weapons of mass destruction.

## Disaster preparedness

Damage to the physical and social environment can be reduced if potential problems and solutions have been identified, studied, and evaluated in advance.[3] This is the goal of preparedness planning.

Preparedness has three elements: the development of emergency operation plans, practice in putting the plans into effect, and public education. Plans must be kept up-to-date in order to meet changing conditions and requirements, and personnel must know and be trained to perform their jobs under highly stressful conditions.

### Hazard analysis

The first step in any emergency or disaster planning is to identify the risks. Risks are measured in terms of threats and vulnerability. A threat—whether natural, accidental, or intentional—is anything adversely affecting an asset; vulnerability is any weakness or flaw that can conceivably be exploited by a threat. The overall risk assessment process has three stages: (1) an assessment of the credibility and/or nonrandomness of the threat; (2) an assessment of vulnerability, which normally ranks the expected losses from impact; and (3) an analysis of risk, which usually integrates vulnerability ratings (e.g., the probability that an area might be flooded) with the impact or loss ratings (e.g., the extent of property damage that such flooding might incur, the estimated economic loss to the area, and the corresponding mitigation cost) to produce a matrix for the cost-benefit evaluation of various countermeasures. Once the hazard identification and analysis have been done, the emergency manager can begin to create community awareness of and support for mitigation efforts.[4]

Risks vary from location to location, and it is important to customize planning and preparedness for each location. Nevertheless, certain hazards—natural, technological, civil, and biological and chemical disasters—will always exist, and these can serve as starting points in any risk analysis:

- *Natural* disasters are those that occur naturally, such as earthquakes, volcanic eruptions, hurricanes, tornadoes, ice storms, floods, flash floods, landslides, wildfires, and insect infestations.
- *Technological* disasters are those associated with technological advances; examples include toxic spills; transportation accidents; and the structural failure of bridges, dams, power plants, and pipelines.
- *Civil* disasters are incidents primarily involving social unrest, although terrorist incidents as well as bombings, shootings, and hostage taking tend to be classified in this category.
- *Biological and chemical* disasters are the result of terrorist incidents involving bacterial pathogens, nerve gas, or a lethal plant toxin (e.g., ricin). Chemical terrorism acts require a response from police, fire, and emergency medical services. Biological agents require the involvement of the public health infrastructure and the CDC.

### Emergency management plan

Since it is impossible to plan for every contingency, an all-hazard emergency management plan (EMP) that focuses on fundamental principles should be in place. Detailed plans for specific emergencies or for special aspects of response should be addressed in "annexes" to the general plan that can be easily changed or updated (see accompanying sidebar). The general EMP must be as streamlined as possible, including only essential elements:

- *Context:* The legislative framework and participating organizations
- *Scenarios:* Hazard, vulnerability, risk, and impact
- *Emergency needs:* Search and rescue, medical care, public safety, food and shelter, and damage prevention and limitation
- *Available resources (structure, items, competencies):* Manpower (personnel), equipment, vehicles, and buildings and facilities
- *Resource utilization:* Application of resources to problems posed by the scenario; dissemination of the plan; and testing, revision, and use of the plan.

In general, each community should develop a comprehensive written emergency plan anticipating all possible hazards that pose a significant threat to the community. Most plans follow a common format based on FEMA guidelines. Recommended components of the written EMP are the basic plan, functional annexes in support of the basic plan, and hazard-specific appendixes in support of each functional annex.

---

**Emergency support function, support, and incident annexes to the emergency management plan**

| Emergency support function (ESF) annexes | Support annexes | Incident annexes |
| --- | --- | --- |
| ESF 1–Transportation | Financial Management | Biological Incident |
| ESF 2–Communications | International Coordination | Catastrophic Incident |
| ESF 3–Public Works and Engineering | Logistics Management | Cyber Incident |
| ESF 4–Firefighting | Private Sector Coordination | Food and Agriculture Incident |
| ESF 5–Emergency Management | Public Affairs | Nuclear/Radiological Incident |
| ESF 6–Mass Care, Housing, and Human Resources | Science and Technology | Oil and Hazardous Materials Incident |
| ESF 7–Resource Support | Tribal Relations | Terrorism Incident Law Enforcement and Investigation |
| ESF 8–Public Health and Medical Services | Volunteer and Donations Management | |
| ESF 9–Urban Search and Rescue | Worker Safety and Health | |
| ESF 10–Oil and Hazardous Materials Response | | |
| ESF 11–Agriculture and Natural Resources | | |
| ESF 12–Energy | | |
| ESF 13–Public Safety and Security | | |
| ESF 14–Long-Term Community Recovery and Mitigation | | |
| ESF 15–External Affairs | | |

## Emergency management training

Emergency management training is conducted by FEMA and state departments of emergency management. FEMA's training is done primarily through the Emergency Management Institute and the National Fire Academy, which primarily target fire service and emergency management officials.

Local training, when done, is done using FEMA or DHS material. However, any local training effort should take advantage of the programs and courses available through FEMA and state agencies, which publish schedules showing subjects, locations, and dates of training. The effort should also involve both the general population and emergency response agencies.

## Emergency management exercises

Once EMPs have been established and training has been provided, the plans should be exercised. A comprehensive, all-hazard, risk-based exercise program (a CEP, for comprehensive exercise program) will provide policy, guidance, and standards for scheduling, designing, developing, conducting, and evaluating emergency response exercises at all levels of government.

There are two ways to help ensure that the local government and other personnel know what to do when the EMP is implemented. First, when a unit responds to an ordinary emergency, such as a fire or a downed power line, the applicable annex should be activated (e.g., ESF 4 – Firefighting or ESF 12 – Energy). Each annex is an operating plan that outlines the specific actions to be taken in a particular situation. This approach makes the EMP, or at least its annexes, part of normal operations.

*A good exercise that is well evaluated will reveal inconsistencies in plans, highlight deficiencies in resources, and underscore the need for remedial training.*

Second, an emergency exercise is the best way for participants to learn their roles and for the emergency manager to test and evaluate the components of the plan. Exercises may include a mock response to simulated events, such as a tornado touchdown at a public school, an airplane crash at the airport, or an explosion at a local industrial site. A broad spectrum of exercise activity is necessary if functional emergency response and

---

### Emergency plans for businesses in Orlando, Florida

The Office of Emergency Management in Orlando, Florida (pop. 213,223), helps local businesses plan for potential disasters. When a business requests assistance in developing a plan, an emergency manager meets with the business's supervisory staff to help them identify goals; it then offers advice on establishing a business disaster planning team, developing a comprehensive emergency management plan, interacting with the city during a disaster, notifying employees, and planning for business continuity. The business then develops its own emergency plan, which it can use to train its employees.

recovery capability is to be realistically assessed. A good exercise that is well evaluated will reveal inconsistencies in plans, highlight deficiencies in resources, and underscore the need for remedial training.

Once exercises have been conducted, the EMP and its component policies, procedures, systems, and facilities should all be evaluated to assess disaster response capabilities and develop recommendations or identify corrective actions to improve these capabilities in the event of an actual emergency.

## Policies

Because the EMP cannot provide for every contingency, it is important to have policies in place well before an emergency happens.

***Personnel***   Local government job descriptions and personnel policies should reflect each employee's added responsibilities during an emergency or disaster. References need not be expansive or complicated. In Georgetown, Texas, for example, emergency management responsibilities are included in every job description. For example,

> Director of Planning and Development Services—Serves in extension of current duties as required for emergency management, particularly in the areas of mitigation, transportation, damage assessment, and recovery.[5]

In addition, Georgetown city personnel policy states that in the event of a natural or technological emergency or disaster, every employee has a role to perform and must be familiar with the city's emergency response plan. Moreover, normal working hours may be suspended, and employees may be required to work as necessary.

***Mutual aid***   Mutual aid is a plan whereby jurisdictions will share personnel and equipment when responding to emergencies. The mutual aid plan is based on the tenet that the requesting jurisdiction has made a full commitment of its resources before initiating the mutual aid request. This does not require that all resources actually be exhausted, but it does anticipate their full mobilization and commitment to the emergency.

The general policies and procedures guiding mutual aid include the following:

- Mutual aid will be requested and provided because it is needed to respond to an emergency, not because the local government anticipates that it will be reimbursed by state or federal disaster funds.

- Mutual aid between local jurisdictions will be for a specific, agreed-upon period of time for each local emergency response. Normally, seven days (minimum) to fourteen days (maximum) will be the standard commitment period.

- When mutual aid between jurisdictions involves the loan of individuals, such individuals will primarily be emergency management personnel—that is, public employees who, during disaster situations, are considered disaster service workers.

- Work-related injuries will be handled by the responding jurisdiction under workmen's compensation.

- In the case of extraordinary damage to a personal or local government vehicle during the performance of a specific emergency assignment, the cost of repairs will be covered by the requesting jurisdiction. Normal wear and tear is excluded.

- Under certain circumstances, mutual aid costs may be reimbursable. Individuals providing mutual aid will be responsible for maintaining their own logs, time sheets, travel claims, and other documentation necessary for reimbursement. This documentation will be submitted to their agencies. Associated costs incurred by the jurisdictions providing assistance may also be eligible for reimbursement.

- When a local government plans its regular training exercises, the mutual aid responding agency will assist in the overall planning and ensure that relationships, contact records, and practices are current.

*Interoperability for communications*   True radio interoperability requires first responders to be able to communicate not just within their units, but also across disciplines and jurisdictions. Reaching the goal of full communications interoperability requires the coordinated efforts of leadership at the local, state, and federal levels.[6] Thus, as a local government plans for radio interoperability, its officials should consider potential users in emergency circumstances, such as police (local and state), sheriff, fire, emergency medical services, hospital, public works, utilities, and animal control.

In 2004, DHS's SAFECOM program released the first national statement of requirements for wireless public safety communications and interoperability. The statement, which defines future interoperability requirements for crucial voice and data communications in day-to-day, task force, and mutual aid operations, is driving the development of interface standards. DHS has also developed the "Interoperability Continuum" as a tool kit for local leaders; the continuum illustrates how progress in communications interoperability can be measured at the local level.[7]

## Public education

To increase the public's awareness of possible disasters and of what should be done before, during, and after such events, any comprehensive EMP must include a public edu-

---

### Public education

The public education component of the emergency plan should include some or all of the following:

- Identification of who is responsible for generating and who is responsible for distributing official information about disasters in the local area

- An explanation about how the release of public information and access to it will be organized

- Guidelines and checklists for dealing with the media

- Forms and logs for record keeping

- Pre-scripted media releases and emergency public information messages.

The person who is to serve as public information officer in an emergency should keep an updated list of media contacts and have a good rapport with local journalists.

Source: *Guide for All-Hazard Emergency Operations Planning* (SLC 101), Attachment D, "Emergency Public Information" (Washington, D.C.: Federal Emergency Management Agency [FEMA], September 1996), 5-D-1.

---

### Citizen corps

The U.S. Department of Homeland Security encourages communities to establish a Citizen Corps to promote

- **Personal responsibility:** Developing a household preparedness plan and disaster supplies kits, observing home health and safety practices, implementing disaster mitigation measures, and participating in crime prevention and reporting

- **Training:** Taking classes in emergency preparedness, response capabilities, first aid, CPR, fire suppression, and search and rescue procedures

- **Volunteer service:** Engaging individuals in volunteer activities that support first responders, disaster relief groups, and community safety organizations. Everyone can do something to support local law enforcement, fire, emergency medical services, community public health efforts, and the four stages of emergency management: prevention, mitigation, response, and recovery.

The five national components of the Citizen Corps are the Neighborhood Watch program, the Community Emergency Response Team (CERT) program, Volunteers in Police Service (VIPS), the Medical Reserve Corps, and the Terrorism Information and Prevention System (TIPS).

Source: *Citizen Corps: A Guide for Local Officials* (Washington, D.C.: U.S. Department of Homeland Security, 2002).

---

### Disaster preparedness video in Arlington Heights, Illinois

The village of Arlington Heights, Illinois (pop. 74,620), has produced a one-hour video for the public on how to prepare for disasters. Using federal funding, Arlington Heights hired a professional production company to develop the video, which shows residents how to take care of themselves and their families in the event of a weather emergency or a terrorist event. The village shows the video on its cable channel and has distributed copies to local churches and community groups. Residents and businesses seeking to expand on the lessons covered in the video can sign up for a twenty-hour course on disaster preparedness taught by the village.

---

cation program. A good program not only disseminates educational material on individual and family preparedness but also takes the opportunity to learn from disasters that occur elsewhere in order to broaden local education efforts.

Successful education efforts include a component that targets children. Children are often the best means of conveying emergency management information to adults living in the households, especially those adults who do not read or speak the language in which the information is presented.

## Technology

In order to respond and take appropriate action during an actual emergency, it is critical to have the correct data at the right time displayed logically. Emergency personnel often need detailed information concerning pipelines, building layouts, electrical distribution, sewer systems, and so forth. A geographic information system (GIS) provides a mechanism to centralize and visually display critical information during an emergency. Dispatchers for police, fire, and emergency medical service units will use global positioning systems (GPS) vehicle tracking to determine which police car, fire truck, or ambulance is nearest to an emergency.

### Warning system

One of the most serious problems in disasters is not public panic, but the public's unwillingness to acknowledge and react to obvious signs of danger. For this reason, an essential responsibility of public officials is to get an effective warning to the public in a timely way. An all-hazard alerting system is an important part of emergency management planning. It should include notification of key public officials, mechanisms for warning the community at large, and provisions for alerting special populations, such as disabled or non-English-speaking residents.

To overcome the public's reluctance to act on reports of imminent danger, disaster warnings must be specific about the danger, about what to do, and about who is being warned, and they must also be issued through all possible mediums. In addition, they must be related to previous education efforts. In the event of rising water, for example, a warning should contain an estimate of the rise (e.g., 12 to 15 feet is expected), the area to be evacuated (e.g., south of Main Street, between Highland Avenue and Fortune Street), the route to follow in the evacuation, and the time at which the area must be cleared. If the message is not direct and explicit, residents tend to assume they are safe and will not react.

### Emergency management funding

Funding for emergency management is largely a local government effort, although some limited funding is available as pass-through funds from DHS and the states. The federal government stipulates that at least 80 percent of homeland security funds must go directly to local recipients to meet local priorities and needs. Local funding for emergency management is best used when spending is designed to achieve multiple objectives, such as mitigation, public information, and training.

## Disaster mitigation

Although nothing can stop a hurricane, a tornado, or an earthquake, it is possible to reduce their effects. For example, a community can build dikes to restrain floodwaters or enact building codes that require structures to be earthquake resistant. Hazard mitigation is defined as any sustained action taken to reduce or eliminate long-term risk to life and property.

However, mitigation efforts may be unpopular. People tend to think that disasters will not occur (or recur), and they may be unwilling to spend public or private money on mitigation. Thus, for the safety and well-being of their communities, local government officials should take an active role in promoting mitigation.

Mitigation planning has four steps: organizing resources, assessing risks, developing a mitigation plan, and implementing the plan and monitoring progress. FEMA has created a Hazard Mitigation Planning unit to promote and support the mitigation planning process and to provide guidance and resources to local communities. In addition, FEMA's "Disaster Resistant Communities" mitigation strategy is a model for reducing the impact and cost of disaster; according to this strategy, communities must

**Floodplain management**

Nearly 20,000 communities across the United States and its territories participate in the National Flood Insurance Program (NFIP) by adopting and enforcing floodplain management ordinances to reduce flood damage. In exchange, the NFIP makes federally backed flood insurance available to home owners, renters, and business owners in these communities. Buildings constructed in compliance with NFIP building standards suffer approximately 80 percent less damage annually than do those that are not built in compliance.

Source: *NFIP Floodplain Management Requirements: A Study Guide and Desk Reference for Local Officials* (Washington, D.C.: Federal Emergency Management Agency, 1998).

- Build a partnership of all elements within that can work together toward the common goal of saving lives and protecting property
- Undertake a program of risk identification so that they clearly know what types of threats they face and the magnitude of those threats
- Identify what they are going to do and establish a plan to mitigate against and prepare for identified threats
- Obtain support from all segments of their population to initiate these efforts.

Mitigation measures may be adopted either during preparedness planning for a potential disaster or during recovery from a past disaster. As hazards are identified during the first stage of development of an EMP, various options for dealing with those hazards emerge that make it possible to either prevent disasters or mitigate their harmful effects. Possible options might include preparing land use and management plans for hazardous areas (e.g., prohibiting development in the floodplain or residential development adjacent to an industrial complex), relocating buildings away from hazardous areas, strengthening building codes, and educating decision makers and the community about risks. Before undertaking a major public education campaign on mitigation, local officials must decide which option, or combination of options, to use. If citizens are involved in this decision, they will be more likely to support the proposed mitigation measures.

Disasters present an opportunity for dramatic change, for better or worse. It is important that public officials not be swept along by the seemingly overwhelming pressure to return to normal life as quickly as possible, but that they take advantage of public support to implement mitigation measures for the future. If changes are to be made, they must be made quickly. As each day passes and the memory of the disaster becomes less vivid, support for corrective action weakens. Therefore, redevelopment plans that include mitigation measures must be ready before disaster strikes.

## Disaster response

Response takes place immediately before, during, or directly after a disaster. The purpose of response is to minimize personal injury and property damage through functions such as warning, evacuation, search and rescue, and the provision of shelter and medical services.

## Emergency operations center

The response effort is directed by designated officials from the emergency operations center (EOC), which is the physical location where the information and resources to support emergency management activities are coordinated. The EOC has overall logistical responsibility for the incident (i.e., public communication, media relations, resource requests to outside agencies, and resource allocation).

In addition to the police, fire, and public works departments, a number of other agencies and organizations generally have representatives at the EOC.[8] For example, officials from utility companies and from the American Red Cross (ARC) or Salvation Army are normally present, as are representatives from emergency medical services if that function is not part of the fire department. Depending on the nature of the disaster, there may also be representatives from such organizations as the National Weather Service, FEMA, the U.S. Forest Service, and the U.S. Geological Survey.

*Functions*    The functions of the EOC are to

- Assess the disaster threat and coordinate organizational resources to counter it
- Make the broad policy decisions (e.g., to evacuate) that guide the overall community response to the disaster
- Manage operations
- Gather information
- Issue information to the public and the media
- Host visitors (e.g., state and federal officials or representatives from neighboring communities).

Responsibilities for specific functions are assigned: typically, every EOC has assigned employees for communications and for public information. Many EOCs also have assigned employees for damage assessment and for operations and resource planning. The local government manager takes the leadership role, relying on the emergency manager and department heads for advice. Elected officials, especially the mayor or county board chair, should be consulted when decisions are made; although they typically lack the experience needed to manage and coordinate the community's response teams, they can play a significant role as liaisons with the press and the public.

*Elements*    When planning to set up an EOC, the local government should consider the following elements:

- *Site location:* The EOC needs to occupy a location well connected in terms of telecommunications and roads. Insofar as possible, the site should be safe from hazards, and the building should be resistant to wind damage, water infiltration, earthquake shaking, or whatever potential hazards the plan has identified.
- *Communications:* The EOC must be adequately supplied with telephone, fax, Internet, and radio transmitter equipment and connections. The level of investment in these resources will obviously depend on available funds, the size of the emergency services to be directed, and the extent and population size of the area to be covered. Duplication in communications is important, especially in terms of having different means of send-

ing the same messages: damage or overloading can render some channels, especially telephone services, useless in emergencies.

- *Other equipment:* Other vital equipment for an EOC include computing equipment and software, complete with equipment for the large-scale communal display of data and maps, a GIS for the analysis of local site conditions, and emergency management and communications programs. Television and radio receivers provide news media treatment of evolving disasters. Because the messages that have been broadcast will often determine how the general public reacts to the disaster, it will be necessary to monitor these messages as well as the public's reactions to them.

- *Media-briefing facilities:* The EOC should have a conference room where information can be given to journalists and interviews can be conducted for radio and television. This room will require audiovisual equipment and other appropriate aids, such as a lectern and a backdrop with the agency's logo on it.

- *Other facilities:* At the least it is helpful to have a small committee room in which heads of emergency services, scientists, and political and community leaders can get together and confer on tactics as conditions change during emergencies.

- *Provisions:* Well-equipped EOCs have stocks of food and drink, limited cooking and sleeping facilities, and supplies of tools and protective clothing to accommodate EOC staff.

**Environment**   To appreciate the environment of an EOC, one must understand its four predominant characteristics: pressure to take action, limited and uncertain information, shifting priorities, and overlapping lines of authority and responsibility. Perhaps the most pervasive and formidable characteristic is pressure. The air is thick with pressure to take action in order to prevent or alleviate human suffering and physical destruction. This pressure is intensified by a shortage of time: during disasters, decisions often must be made quickly if they are to have any effect at all.

**Structure**   The structure of an EOC is designed to complement and support the Incident Command System (ICS). The ICS, which is at the specific site of the incident (and there can be multiple ICSs), exercises command over tactical matters, while the EOC exercises command over logistical matters, including the authority to make decision in crises. The EOC is the hub through which resources flow to the incident commander(s).

## Incident Command System

The ICS is an on-scene, all-hazard incident management system used by firefighters, hazardous materials teams, rescuers, and emergency medical teams.[9] NIMS has established the ICS as the standardized tactical incident organizational structure for the management of all incidents.

During any emergency that involves response personnel, only one person can be in command at a specific site. This person, the incident commander, must assess the situation and available resources, determine an appropriate action plan, monitor the plan's effectiveness, and continually modify the plan to meet the realities of the situation. The incident commander is assisted by several staff members, to whom he or she assigns responsibility for key activities.

When more than one jurisdiction or agency is responding to an incident, it is important to establish a unified command (UC).[10] A UC team overcomes much of the inefficiency and duplication of effort that can occur when agencies from different jurisdictions and different levels of government operate without a common system or organizational framework. In a UC structure, the individuals designated by their jurisdictional authorities jointly determine objectives, plans, and priorities and work together to execute them. NIMS provides guidelines to enable agencies with different legal, geographic, and functional responsibilities to coordinate, plan, and interact effectively.

*During any emergency that involves response personnel, only one person can be in command at a specific site.*

The on-site incident command point can be a vehicle, tent, or open-air table. In the event of multiple or large incidents, several command posts and incident commanders may be needed. Requests for supplies, equipment, or additional personnel should be routed by the incident commander from the command post to appropriate officials located in the EOC. Equipment, personnel, and other resources that are available but not yet needed are kept in designated staging area(s) with the assets under the control of the EOC.

It is critical that all local responders, as well as those coming into the affected area from other jurisdictions and states, know and use commonly established operational structures, terminology, policies, and procedures. The ability of responders from different jurisdictions and different disciplines to work together depends greatly on their ability to communicate with each other. Thus, a new requirement of NIMS is to use "plain English" rather than 10-codes (e.g., 10-4, 10-19, etc.).

## Sheltering and evacuation issues

When a disaster is imminent or in progress, local officials must decide whether to evacuate citizens. The potential risk to evacuees is a primary concern. The EOC commander must scrutinize the safety of the evacuees' destination as well as their route and should assess alternative protective measures (such as shelter within the community) before advising that evacuation be initiated. In such a case, it may even be necessary for the public to shelter-in-place—that is, to stay where they are rather than traveling to a shelter. Shelter-in-place means selecting a small, interior room with no or few windows and taking refuge there. It does not mean sealing off an entire home or office building.

Sheltering the population from peacetime radiological and hazardous materials, natural disasters, or the effects of nuclear weapons detonation requires trained personnel. Although the local government has the basic responsibility for the protection of life and property, the ARC has a congressionally mandated charter to undertake relief activities to mitigate human suffering caused by a disaster. A government/ARC team approach is necessary to facilitate the most efficient use of personnel and shelter-related resources.

A balanced combination of several methods must be used in a comprehensive shelter program. Normally, public schools, churches, government buildings, colleges and universities, and private buildings are designated as shelters. Should it become necessary to occupy emergency shelters, the primary mode of transportation is walking, supplemented by private vehicle.

**Community emergency response in Clearwater, Florida**

The fire and rescue department in Clearwater, Florida (pop. 249,079), created a community emergency response team (CERT) with more than 100 trained volunteer citizens. Clearwater maintains a comprehensive emergency management plan that includes coordination between the city and other units of government, including land use planning, stormwater planning, and transportation. Since evacuation is not always possible, a primary focus of the city's efforts is to educate citizens to be prepared to shelter in their homes for up to fifteen days without outside assistance.

When evacuation is called for, the police department usually serves as the lead organization. As such, it is responsible for planning the timing and conduct of the evacuation; it must also carefully coordinate with both the organizations that will provide shelter and those that will barricade or mark exit routes (normally public works personnel). The part of the emergency plan that deals with evacuation establishes procedures for choosing evacuation routes and maintaining the flow of vehicles.

The evaluation plan should also address the needs of special populations (e.g., residents who do not own vehicles; residents who own pets; disabled persons) and institutions such as schools, hospitals, nursing homes, and jails.

*Special-needs populations*   The emergency management plan should include an emergency evacuation assistance program, which is a registry of persons needing help when an emergency evacuation becomes necessary. Such a registry should include residents who require skilled nursing care or assistance with daily living, or who have life-saving medical equipment dependent on electricity. The plan should provide for generator-powered health care facilities that are open during emergencies. Trained employees and health care staff should be available to provide minimal health assistance not available at general population evacuation centers. The plan should also accommodate a caregiver, should the evacuee require one.

Some states require local emergency management offices to maintain lists of those individuals requiring special assistance who voluntarily register their names. However, many people with special requirements prefer to keep their circumstances private and seek assistance only when an emergency occurs. If the emergency manager has not prepared for this eventuality, last-minute calls may overwhelm the communication system and prevent these residents from obtaining the assistance they require.

EMPs should also contain provisions to assist citizens with disabilities (e.g., those citizens who are physically disabled, hearing impaired, or mentally disabled). The Americans with Disabilities Act has identified key elements that should be included in an EMP. For example, the shelter plan should provide for disabled individuals' need for structures and appliances that are accessible to them during their stay at the shelter. Warning and information systems should address the requirements of persons with impaired sight or hearing and those who cannot move freely, in addition to those who are medically dependent. Moreover, all warnings, information, and educational materials should be issued not only in English but also in any languages understood by a substantial portion of the population.

---

### Animal evacuation plan in Apple Valley, California

In 1999, during a major fire in the town of Apple Valley, California (pop. 65,156), many residents found it difficult to bring their animals with them when they evacuated. The city's emergency preparedness manager and animal control supervisor created an animal evacuation plan that was approved by the town council as an annex to the town's emergency management plan. Under the plan, thirty volunteers have been trained to assist in evacuating and caring for animals during emergencies. The plan also covers foster care, reuniting animals with owners, long-term medical care, and disposal when needed.

---

*Transportation*   Although most individuals will use their own transportation if they own a vehicle, the emergency management planners should determine the likelihood of individuals relying upon public transportation during the public education and consultation phase. Transportation may also be required for people needing assistance. Lift-gate buses and other specialized transportation should be available to pick those persons up and take them to their assigned facilities.

*Sex offenders*   Before any event occurs, emergency management officials must address the issue of having sex offenders report to public shelters. Many localities will no longer accept sex offenders, instead requiring them to report to designated jails or prisons or not report at all. Once a determination is made, public notice must be provided.

*Institutions*   When schools, hospitals, nursing homes, and jails are referenced and relied upon in the EMP, the local government should ensure that the institution's emergency plan is coordinated with the jurisdiction's EMP and that the institution is capable of delivering the service as contemplated.

*Animals*   Emergency management officials and animal care organizations should work together to define plans for the care of animals in disasters. Such plans should respect the concerns of both animal owners and persons who do not own animals or who have medical or psychological reasons to distance themselves from animals—for example, persons with allergies or phobias against animals. These reasons, along with food hygiene and other public health concerns, are primarily why animals are not allowed in human shelters.

## Emergency medical systems

A medical emergency has three phases:

1. *Impact*, when medical facilities are damaged and some medical personnel may be lost

2. *Emergency and isolation*, in which initial medical relief is administered solely by available local resources and manpower

3. *Stabilization and recovery*, which involves medical care of injured people; the recovery of the dead; the monitoring and control of communicable diseases; the care and health maintenance of displaced populations; and special care for infants, the handicapped, the sick, and the elderly.

Local governments can prepare for disease epidemics by establishing an epidemiological surveillance system. When bioterrorism strikes, this system should move into action within 24 hours to collect and interpret data, investigate apparent outbreaks, and provide medical care for confirmed emergencies.

Disasters place extensive and often unexpected demands on medical systems. The medical response plan should include, among other things, provisions for triage, traffic control, and alternative means of communication. Emergency medical services are discussed in Chapter 14.

## Public information

During a disaster, there is an enormous demand for information. Collaboration between the media and the authorities can help stop rumors, dispel myths, avoid confusion, inform and educate the public, and convey official information efficiently to general recipients.

Often a leading elected official acts as spokesperson during regularly scheduled press briefings. Under no circumstances should any spokesperson meet the press unprepared. Anticipating questions and formulating responses ahead of time is an effort that repays itself many times over. In addition, the spokesperson must remember that honesty is essential. Statements that normally would be routine and unimportant may assume new significance during a crisis. Unfounded speculation should be avoided. The simplest and safest response to a question for which there is no answer is the frank admission that the answer is not known. If a written press statement is issued, it should be reasonably neat and there should be a sufficient number of copies.

## Public services during disaster response

Local police, fire, and water departments as well as electricity, gas, and telephone service providers are critical in the initial response to an emergency or disaster. Police officers and firefighters serve in an extension of their regular duties, with particular emphasis on rescue and on-scene control. Firefighters require special training to handle incidents involving hazardous materials; this training must be coordinated with the overall EMP. Water departments help restore or maintain the water supply and prevent its contamination.

### Thunderstorm and tornado warnings in Edmond, Oklahoma

Because Oklahoma has more tornadoes than any other place in the world, the educational programs and warning systems within the emergency management plan in Edmond, Oklahoma (pop. 74,881), focus heavily on thunderstorm and tornado warnings. The city is geographically covered with outdoor warning systems. Indoor warning systems are available ("and a great gift idea") through a programmable weather alert radio and a link to Edmond's page on the National Weather Service's Web site (srh.noaa .gov). The programmable feature enables one to hear watches and warnings for a specific area rather than alarms from areas too far away to be of concern. The device is equipped with an internal battery backup so that service is available during power failures. Watches and warnings can also be picked up with an AM/FM clock radio.

Because power sources are essential to protecting and saving lives and property, widespread power failures require immediate attention, making coordination between power companies and government agencies paramount.[11]

Food and clothing, mass shelter, and counseling are crucial services often provided by organizations such as the ARC and Salvation Army. Special efforts are required to coordinate provision of these services to elderly, disabled, and non-English-speaking residents.

## Volunteers

Volunteers can be a tremendous asset to the local government during a disaster. Local officials should take advantage of existing skills and talents within the community by identifying and actively recruiting pharmacists, veterinarians, amateur radio operators, clergy, and others who can be trained for specific roles prior to an incident. However, to be effective, the volunteers must be familiar with citywide emergency plans and understand their place in the response phase.[12]

Inevitably, regardless of the opportunities for preplanned volunteer training, altruistic tendencies prompt many community members to offer their services spontaneously when disaster strikes. This phenomenon presents itself at every disaster, and emergency managers must be prepared to handle it effectively. A good plan must anticipate legal requirements for registration, screening, and training of spontaneous volunteers. It must provide for the care of these volunteers during their service to the community, and it must take responsibility for dealing with any aftereffects they may experience (e.g., by providing psychological counseling).

Agencies such as police, fire, public works, and emergency medical services work to provide immediate response in disasters. However, these organizations may not be able to meet immediate needs during an actual event because of heightened demands and disrupted communication and transportation systems. In order to better respond to disasters, a city or county can establish a community emergency response team (CERT). A CERT program educates residents about disaster preparedness for hazards that may affect their area and trains them in basic disaster response skills, such as fire safety.

The Neighborhood Watch Program is a highly successful effort that has been in existence for more than thirty years in cities and counties. It provides a unique infrastructure that brings together local officials, law enforcement, and citizens to protect communities. It can also serve as the basis for bringing neighborhood residents together to focus on disaster preparedness and terrorism awareness, evacuation drills and exercises, and the organization of group training.

## Mass fatalities

Every EMP should have a section on mass fatality management. By definition, a mass fatality incident is any situation in which there are more bodies than can be handled using existing local resources. The medical examiner/coroner is responsible for the recovery, identification, and disposition of mass fatality incident victims.[13] There are three major activities in a mass fatalities incident response: search and recovery, morgue operation, and family assistance.

***Search and recovery*** Urban search and rescue (USAR) involves the location, rescue (extrication), and initial medical stabilization of victims trapped in confined spaces.

Structural collapse is most often the cause of such situations, but victims may also be trapped in transportation accidents, mines, and collapsed trenches. Recovery starts after the search of an area is complete. Simply stated, search and recovery normally involves locating and removing bodies, body parts, and personal effects. Bodies and body parts must be treated with dignity and respect at all times. A good policy is to treat every site as a crime scene until the medical examiner/coroner says differently.

*Morgue operation*   The main purpose of a morgue is to determine the cause of death and identify victims. Postmortem records must be completed for every body and body part as they are processed. Personal effects, such as driver licenses found on the victim or statements of recognition, should be used as tentative rather than positive identification; positive identification is a responsibility of the medical examiner/coroner. After identification is established, the medical examiner can release the body and/or body parts in accordance with the desires of the victim's family.

Depending on the size and nature of the incident, the medical examiner/coroner will determine where to establish an incident morgue site. School gymnasiums should not be used, particularly when school is in session. The medical examiner/coroner should lay out the site, giving consideration to the physical condition of the victims, the number of victims, and the number of personnel needed to perform morgue functions. The operational areas can include areas for receiving, photography, X-ray, personal effects, anthropology, dental identification, fingerprinting, pathology, storage, shipping, and perhaps embalming.[14]

*Family assistance*   The family assistance center (FAC) is one of the most sensitive operations in a mass fatalities event. Its purposes are to provide relatives of victims with information and access to services they may need in the days ahead, to protect families from the media and curiosity seekers, and to allow investigators and the medical examiner/coroner access to families so that they can obtain needed information more easily.

An FAC should be established quickly, and the area selected should be secured in order to give the families privacy. Regular briefings will help keep the families informed. Meeting with the families on an individual basis early on makes it possible to start the process of collecting antemortem records for use in the morgue operations. Grief counselors should be available, and translators may be necessary when working with non-English-speaking families.

## Disaster recovery

Usually communities think of preparing for a disaster before its onset, and they consider response and recovery as activities that occur after the disaster. However, sometimes communities do respond before disaster happens. For example, in predictable events, such as slow-rise river flooding or most hurricanes, there is time to notify people of the impending danger, take some protective measures, and evacuate safely. Such precautions can lessen not only the need to respond further but also some elements of short-term recovery, such as utility restoration and debris clearance.

Traditional, postevent disaster recovery occurs in phases: short term and long term. Recovery begins immediately with efforts to restore essential services to the stricken area, and it continues until the community returns to normal. Along with utility restoration and search and rescue, essential elements of short-term recovery include damage assessment, debris clearance, public information, and the provision of food and shelter. An accessible location should be identified for a disaster application center, where disaster assistance services are provided. Sites where debris may be burned or disposed of must be identified and made to comply with U.S. Environmental Protection Agency guidelines.

> *Communities that are serious about disaster recovery tend to focus first on improving response activities before tackling the more advanced concepts involved with holistic recovery.*

How short-term recovery efforts proceed will affect how some longer-term decisions are made. Long-term recovery begins when a community starts to repair or replace roads, bridges, homes, and stores and begins to implement mitigation programs. It is also the period when holistic changes for the better, such as stronger building codes, revised land use and zoning designations, improved transportation corridors, and the replacement of "affordable housing" stock, are considered. Long-term recovery may continue for years until the entire disaster area has been completely redeveloped, either as it was in the past or for entirely new purposes that are less disaster sensitive.

If a local government fails to adequately respond to a disaster, its credibility suffers. This loss of credibility can become a barrier to implementing a holistic disaster recovery. Communities that are serious about disaster recovery tend to focus first on improving response activities (warning, evacuation, power restoration, debris management) before tackling the more advanced concepts involved with holistic recovery.

## Planning for disaster recovery

As soon as possible after a disaster, local officials must decide what they want to do and who is to participate in planning and implementing the recovery. They also must ensure that intergovernmental cooperation exists early in the postdisaster period and that cooperative efforts are implemented by both executive and administrative staff. Strong, capable leadership increases the likelihood of obtaining the resources necessary to repair damage in the community. Skill and predisaster public management experience, in addition to well-established predisaster interorganizational relationships, are essential for a satisfactory recovery.

Organizations may prepare briefing papers for local leaders in order to ensure that everyone is conveying the same message to the public and media. In the recovery phase, this means communicating the same desire for a course of action (e.g., a rebuilding strategy, changes in planning or building criteria, etc.).

Some local administrative mechanisms that are in place before a disaster become important in its aftermath; these mechanisms are land use controls, building codes, inspection and enforcement procedures, mutual aid pacts for public safety, public works activities, and contract agreements. Technical mechanisms include maps and detailed assessments of known hazards or zones. A community with a good record-keeping system in place will be better able to track disaster-related expenditures.

Ideally, disaster recovery processes should improve the community and make it a better, safer place for citizens. Disaster recovery should also include a review of ways to avoid future emergencies and to capitalize on opportunities to mitigate the effects of disasters that occur. Possible mitigation measures include elevating or relocating chronically flood-damaged homes away from flood hazard areas, and retrofitting buildings to make them resistant to earthquakes or strong winds.

## Damage assessment

Damage assessment is an appraisal or determination of the actual effects of an emergency or disaster on human, economic, and natural resources. Although a preliminary assessment is desirable and should be made as quickly as possible, a more accurate assessment should be compiled as soon as weather and other local conditions permit.

## Disaster assistance

When a disaster strikes, local authorities and individuals request help from private relief organizations and their state government. If these requests exceed the state's capabilities, the governor may ask the president to declare the location a "major disaster" area (see sidebar on page 306). The Stafford Disaster Relief and Emergency Assistance Act of 1988 provides the greatest single source of federal disaster assistance: the President's Disaster Relief Fund. In the event of a presidential declaration of a major disaster, this act requires FEMA to coordinate the disaster relief activities undertaken by various federal agencies. Local governments may also request technical assistance from FEMA in determining which federal agencies and volunteer organizations have disaster relief programs that can be of assistance.[15] FEMA can also help fund damage mitigation measures.

## Debris management

Debris management involves the removal, collection, and disposal of debris following a disaster. Such cleanup is essential in order to mitigate against any potential threat to the health, safety, and welfare of the affected citizens, expedite recovery efforts in the affected area, and address any threat of significant damage to improved public or private property.

The location and size of the area over which debris is dispersed directly affect the type of collection and disposal methods used to address the problem, the associated costs incurred, and the speed with which the problem can be addressed. A debris management program should be based on the waste management approach of reduction, reuse, reclamation, resources recovery, incineration, and land filling.

While the public works department is generally responsible for debris removal, it will work in conjunction with designated support agencies, utility companies, waste management firms, and trucking companies to facilitate debris clearance, collection, reduction, and disposal needs following a disaster. The department's range of authority is the public right-of-way; only when it is preapproved and deemed in the public interest will the public works department remove debris from private property. Private contractors also play a significant role in the debris removal, collection, reduction, and disposal process.[16]

## Psychological recovery

Traditionally, recovery procedures have focused on technical, economic, and administrative recovery. However, there must also be a focus on victims. Once basic safety has been

### State/federal disaster declarations

First response to a disaster is the job of local government's emergency services with help from nearby municipalities, the county, the state, and volunteer agencies. However, in the event of a major disaster (e.g., a hurricane, earthquake, flood, tornado, or major fire) that is clearly beyond the capacity of the state or local government to handle alone, the governor may request a declaration of emergency to obtain supplemental federal aid for search and rescue, electrical power, food, water, shelter, and other basic human needs. If the president warrants that a major disaster has occurred and approves the request, funding comes from the President's Disaster Relief Fund, which is managed by FEMA, and from the disaster aid programs of other participating federal agencies.

There are two types of emergency declarations:

1. A presidential **major disaster declaration,** which puts into motion long-term federal recovery programs, some of which are matched by state programs, to help disaster victims, businesses, and other public entities.

2. An **emergency declaration,** which is more limited in scope and does not include the long-term federal recovery programs of a major disaster declaration. Generally, federal assistance and funding are provided to meet a specific emergency need or to help prevent a major disaster from occurring.

In addition, there are two major categories of disaster aid:

1. **Individual assistance,** which is aid for damage to residences and businesses or for personal property losses. Individual disaster aid generally falls into such categories as disaster housing, disaster grants, low-interest disaster loans, and other disaster aid programs.

2. **Public assistance,** which is aid to state or local governments to pay part of the costs of rebuilding a community's damaged infrastructure. Generally, public assistance programs pay for 75 percent of the costs of approved projects, which may include debris removal, emergency protective measures, the restoration of public services, repair of damaged public property, loans needed by communities for essential government functions, and grants for public schools.

Source: FEMA, "The Disaster Process and Disaster Aid Programs," at fema.gov/hazard/dproc.shtm.

restored, victims who have lost their homes, loved ones, or livelihoods may experience overwhelming psychological reactions. To compound the problem, these reactions often occur when resources that were mobilized for the disaster are being withdrawn. A recovery plan that addresses both the physical and the psychological needs of citizens is likely to be much more successful than a disaster plan that focuses exclusively on technical, economic, and/or administrative recovery.[17]

Crisis counseling is a continuum of individual and group interventions that are designed to meet the specific needs of people experiencing different levels of impact. After a traumatic experience, the biggest human needs are the simplest: relocation to a safe place, any required medical assistance, accurate information, reassurance, and a chance to talk about feelings. By helping to meet these needs as soon as possible after the incident has occurred, crisis counseling services can facilitate a return to normal business activities and minimize the negative effects of a crisis on employees.[18]

## Preparing an effective crisis counseling plan

The following steps can be helpful in preparing an effective crisis counseling plan for your organization:

- **Define a "critical incident."** For instance, would the death of an employee's spouse qualify?

- **Evaluate your own resources.** Are any staff members experienced in trauma response, first aid, or personal counseling?

- **Establish a first responder team.** Include at least one manager and one human resource person. The team leader is authorized to call for assistance and make referrals. Create a written agreement to verify who will do each task.

- **Arrange training sessions for first responders.** Address the common reactions that first responders may have to the stress of the situation, as well as any longer-term effects (e.g., disturbed sleep or ongoing depression) that may indicate a need for referral to medical or mental health professionals. If possible, include the entire staff.

- **Identify and train representative(s) who will work with family and community members.** Ensure that the organization is ready and able to respond promptly to citizens in need.

- **Develop channels for crisis information and communication.** Compile and distribute to the entire staff a list of procedures and resources for use during or after any emergency. Include sources of assistance for anyone who might have ongoing problems in the months that follow.

- **Hold a detailed annual role play, simulating responses to an actual disaster.** Establish a place where everyone will be taken in the event of an emergency, designate the person who will bring them there, and run through the plan in advance of any emergency to be sure it meets its objectives. Have top management participate in order to simulate giving accurate, unfiltered information immediately after a crisis.

- **Be redundant.** Identify an alternate for each role to avoid adding confusion to disaster if someone is unavailable for an assigned responsibility.

After a crisis counseling plan has been developed, the final step is pinpointing its providers. Even if an organization's own human resource or employee assistance program (EAP) staff is qualified to deliver professional crisis counseling services, they may be very shaken by the catastrophe and not ready to lead a group. Prearrangements should be made for outside assistance, even if it is never needed.

## Legal issues

Should a disaster occur, the emergency manager must ensure that a legal framework is in place, particularly with respect to lines of authority; such a framework must allow authorities to make necessary decisions during disasters and to act on them. In addition to ordinances outlining decision making and responsibilities, it is also important to have fill-in-the-blank ordinances available for immediate approval by the governing body during the response and recovery phases.

In general, tort suits over alleged flaws in disaster response procedures have been dismissed. In many states, statutory protection is comprehensive. Even without statutory protection, however, each aspect of response is still likely to be immune from suit as either a "governmental function" or a "discretionary action." Only the most flagrant or obvious deviations from procedure or good practice have been found to be negligent.

### Donation management

After every major disaster, donations of goods from across the country overwhelm emergency workers. A predetermined plan for handling offers of goods can help facilitate the process of matching those donations with the people who need them. If social service agencies are willing to participate in the donation management program, items should be distributed among the agencies according to the types of items each agency normally handles.

A plan is also needed to ensure that donated funds are accounted for, spent on authorized expenditures, and directed to those most in need of assistance.

### Appreciation

During a disaster, people want to help. After a disaster, people want to be thanked for their help. It is important to hold a volunteer reception event several months after the disaster. All pretrained and spontaneous volunteers should receive certificates noting their dates of participation and the type of help they provided. Businesses that donated materials or labor should be recognized as well, as should agencies such as the ARC and Salvation Army for any help they rendered during the disaster.

## Conclusion

As the experience of Hurricane Katrina in New Orleans has shown, emergency management issues confronting local government officials can be daunting. And beyond natural disasters, emergency management plans must also be prepared to deal with homeland security issues and the threat of terrorism.

In brief, the emergency management challenges confronting local officials include

- *Preparedness planning and hazard mitigation:* As commercial and residential areas develop, underlying principles of the disaster-resistant communities program must be incorporated into local planning standards and development codes.

- *Public education and involvement:* Citizens must be a part of any planning and response effort. They need to know how they can respond within their own neighborhoods, what to look for in potential terrorism threats, and how to take care of themselves and their families in the critical first seventy-two hours after an emergency.

- *Evacuation and sheltering issues:* Because a lack of fuel, time, or noncongested routes can make large evacuations nearly impossible to accomplish, officials must ensure that sufficient supplies are on hand for the shelters and must be prepared to deal with differing cultures, lifestyles, special-needs populations, sex offenders, and animals within the shelters.

- *Communications maintenance and interoperability:* Local officials must plan for and acquire the proper equipment that will enable them to communicate with other responding agencies.

- *Maintenance of infrastructure and public services during and after a major disaster:* Local officials must ensure that the water supply remains available and uncontaminated, and that power failures are addressed and power restored as quickly as possible.

- *Disaster assistance for both short- and long-term recovery:* Because local governments are often ill-equipped to finance the recovery of their communities and cannot necessarily depend on reimbursement or state and federal aid, officials must have contingency plans for reimbursement and adequate reserves to finance governmental operations during the recovery phase and beyond.

Meeting these challenges requires extensive preparedness planning combined with outreach to the private sector, other public agencies, and individuals. For example, the chemical industry, through the Community Awareness and Emergency Response program,[19] is actively involved in emergency management planning. Local government officials should embrace this involvement in the manufacturing and transportation of chemicals. Similarly, the Federal Bureau of Investigation (FBI) has initiated InfraGard, a national information-sharing program between the FBI and the private sector. Local government officials must be involved in these local chapters as a part of their preparedness planning efforts.

Time must also be spent beforehand developing relationships with individuals and groups that the local government will depend on during the response and recovery phases of an emergency—for example, state emergency officials, officials from support agencies, hospital officials, and the ARC. Waiting until an event actually occurs to secure their involvement and coordinate response activities is too late.

In a related vein, a major event that affects a region, as opposed to an individual unit of government, may render mutual aid agreements meaningless. Should this event occur, the local government must have an appropriate contingency plan in place.

Organizational development efforts within an organization must be consistent with emergency response planning. Unless the structure for day-to-day operations is the same as that for disaster response and recovery, the organization will not be able to properly function at the level required during a response and recovery effort, nor will the public and elected leadership recognize the points of interaction during an actual event. Without this recognition, elected officials may not allow professionals to do their jobs and may even second-guess decisions or attempt politically to overturn them. Finally, staff members need to be well trained in the ICS process to ensure prompt and effective communication and coordination.

A long-simmering issue is one of communication between the medical and law enforcement communities. Physicians are often reluctant to breach patient confidentiality; as a result, when a patient is the focus of a law enforcement investigation in which chemical or biological agents are involved, law enforcement personnel may have difficulty obtaining all the information they need to ascertain the parameters or impact of the activity. Not wishing to compromise the ongoing investigation or unduly alarm the public, especially when evidence or information is not explicit enough to validate suspicions, they are thus reluctant to move forward. In such cases, the local government manager must be prepared to initiate discussion with both parties because without a resolution of this issue, local citizens can suffer.

Clearly, the challenges of emergency management are many, and when disaster strikes a community, much is at stake. Perhaps more than at any other time, this is when a local government manager's commitment to leadership and quality service delivery is vital to the health and well-being of the community.

## Questions to ask if you manage a small community

Do my employees know what to do in the event of an emergency?

Given our relatively small staff, is there sufficient redundancy to adequately respond to an extended emergency? If not, have we included staff assistance in our mutual aid agreements?

Can we expect our mutual aid agreements to be honored in the event of a regional or widespread disaster?

Have we sufficiently coordinated our emergency response plans with our school system, county, and hospital?

If our city or county orders an evacuation, what is the likelihood that citizens will comply by evacuating rather than staying, which will necessitate more shelters?

Have we sufficiently involved our citizens in emergency management planning?

Have we identified those businesses and industries that will be significantly affected in an emergency?

Is our organizational emergency response structure similar to the day-to-day operational structure?

Do our radios allow us to communicate with potential responders, especially the state police and area fire and emergency medical services personnel?

Have the manager and/or department heads developed relationships with organizations or agencies that they must work with or rely on in the event of an emergency?

Is our planning department actively involved in mitigation planning efforts?

Does the city or county maintain sufficient cash reserves to finance operations while waiting for reimbursement aid?

## Competencies for managers in the field of emergency management

Basic understanding of the four areas of emergency management: preparedness, mitigation, response, and recovery

Leadership and delegation skills

Ability to organize the staff around emergency management principles

Ability to influence elected officials to adopt policies and ordinances that increase the community's capacity to mitigate and respond to emergencies

Ability to help elected officials and employees understand the importance of and avenues of involvement for citizens during an emergency or disaster

Ability to assist department heads, elected officials, and line employees to understand their roles within the context of the larger picture

Strong working relationships with outside organizations to effectively align emergency response plans so as to eliminate redundant, conflicting, or overlapping practices

Ability to advocate effectively for the inclusion of emergency management in the daily operations of the local government

Ability to work with the media in educating the public and creating a sense of urgency based on emergencies that occur in other areas of the country

# Endnotes

1 *National Incident Management System* (Washington, D.C.: U.S. Department of Homeland Security [DHS], March 1, 2004), 1, available at nimsonline.com/docs/NIMS-90-web.pdf.

2 Ibid., 3.

3 Emergency Management Accreditation Program, emaponline.org.

4 *National Response Plan* (Washington, D.C.: DHS, December 2004), available at dhs.gov/xlibrary/assets/NRP_FullText.pdf.

5 City of Georgetown, Texas, georgetown.org.

6 Brenna Smith and Tom Tolman, "Can We Talk? Public Safety and the Interoperability Challenge," National Institute of Justice *Journal* (April 2000): 16–21.

7 *Interoperability Continuum: A Tool for Improving Public Safety Communications and Interoperability* (Washington, D.C.: DHS, 2004), available at safecomprogram.gov/NR/rdonlyres/54F0C2DE-FA70-48DD-A56E-3A72A8F35066/0/ContinuumBrochure.pdf.

8 *National Incident Management System*, 26–27.

9 Ibid., 7–26.

10 Ibid., 14.

11 David F. Gillespie, "Coordinating Community Resources," in *Emergency Management Principles and Practices*, ed. Thomas E. Drabek and Gerard J. Hoetmer (Washington, D.C.: ICMA 1991), 70–71.

12 Francis E. Winslow, "Caring for Workers and Spontaneous Volunteers: A Local Government Perspective," in *The Second Annual International Emergency Management Conference Proceedings*, San Francisco, Calif., March 17–19, 1992 (Needham, Mass.: The Interface Group, 1992), 84.

13 Ray L. Blakeney, "Providing Relief to Families after a Mass Fatality: Roles of the Medical Examiner's Office and the Family Assistance Center," in *OVC Bulletin* (Washington, D.C.: Office of Victims of Crime, Office of Justice Programs, U.S. Department of Justice, November 2002).

14 Tom Ralph, "Mass Fatality Management: What Industry Teams Should Know," *Disaster Resource Guide* (Santa Ana, Calif., 2006), available at disaster-resource.com/articles/00bibli1.shtml.

15 *Disaster Assistance Programs: Digest of Federal Disaster Assistance Programs*, DAP-21 (Washington, D.C.: Federal Emergency Management Agency [FEMA], 1989).

16 *Public Assistance Debris Management Guide*, FEMA 325 (Washington, D.C.: FEMA, 1989).

17 Patrick Prince and Ann T. Phelps, "Disaster-Proofing Your People: Caring for the Psychological Needs of Employees," in *The Second Annual International Emergency Management Conference Proceedings* (see note 13), 204.

18 See National Mental Health Information Center, Center for Mental Health Services, at mentalhealth.samhsa.gov/cmhs/emergencyservices.

19 For more information on Community Awareness and Emergency Response, go to caer-mp.org.

# Police Services

**Gary Cordner**

Police agencies are substantially different from other local government agencies for the simple reason that police officers have more power, authority, and discretion than other local government workers. Police officers (including sheriff deputies and other law enforcement officers) occasionally make life and death decisions; they regularly make decisions about whether to restrict or revoke the freedom of citizens and other residents of their communities. They make these decisions on behalf of the government, the legal system, and the people. Most importantly, they have discretion in making these decisions, which means that they choose whether to use force and how much to use; whether to intervene in people's lives; and whether to arrest, cite, or release a crime suspect or disorderly person. On top of that, individual police officers make most of these incredibly important decisions in the field, under time pressure, alone, with little or no direct supervision.

This description of police work identifies the central challenge of police management: getting police officers to make the best possible decisions about the use of force and authority in the context of danger. Certainly, police managers face many other challenges not unlike those that confront all local government managers, such as fiscal management, implementation of modern technology, selection and retention of quality personnel, communication with and motivation of employees, public relations, and quality improvement. But the police manager is also responsible for an agency that deploys armed and powerful agents into the community twenty-four hours a day, 365 days a year. Even when police chiefs and sheriffs are at home sleeping or away on vacation, their employees are in the field making important, and sometimes momentous, discretionary decisions.

Another feature of policing that introduces complications for local government management is the legal status of police officers. Unlike most other government employees, police are bound *by law* to behave in certain ways. For example, state law may require them to make arrests whenever they have probable cause to believe that a suspect has committed a domestic assault. Statutory or case law requires them to obtain search warrants before looking for evidence or contraband in certain situations and to advise suspects of their right to remain silent. Constitutional law affects their handling of protestors and demonstrations. A judge may order them to carry out some action or to desist from some practice. In some respects, then, police officers are governed by the law and the legal system as well as by police managers, local government managers, or locally elected officials.

**Police services and functions**

| | |
|---|---|
| Preventive patrol | Community policing |
| Traffic safety | Problem-oriented policing |
| Rapid response | Homeland security |
| Criminal investigation | |

One further complication associated with policing is that police also work for the people. Of course, in some sense all government employees work for the people, but the nature of police work tends to place police officers into more frequent and intensive contact with community residents and community leaders than might be true for a town's or county's clerks, personnel specialists, public works employees, or even firefighters. Especially under community policing, the police are expected to work directly with the community residents and leaders to identify and resolve crime and disorder problems. Local government managers and political leaders are sometimes integrated within this process, but street-level police officers often find themselves helping communities address problems related to graffiti, trash removal, abandoned cars, and building code violations even more than drugs and burglaries. Officers are sometimes thrust into the role of ombudsman or point person for "their community," becoming in essence the community's representative to the rest of local government. This role sometimes creates conflict with other local government agencies and political leaders.

These defining features of police work—power, authority, discretion, special legal status, direct contact with the public—complicate police management in communities large and small. Police executives in smaller communities have fewer subordinates, fewer serious crimes, fewer major incidents to deal with, and less overall organizational complexity to manage than chiefs and sheriffs in larger jurisdictions, but the fundamental challenges they face in directing and controlling the exercise of police power and ensuring the delivery of quality police services are the same.

Police work and police administration have changed dramatically in the past thirty years. Technology has evolved and has had profound effects on policing. Levels of training, education, and professional expertise have greatly improved. Research has helped tremendously in identifying traditional practices that were not as effective as previously thought, leading to significant changes in police programs and strategies. In addition, police organizations have become much more open to outside input and scrutiny. Yet there is no shortage of both new and continuing issues, such as the use of excessive force, the hiring of women and minorities, racial profiling, terrorism, and homeland security.

## Variations in U.S. policing

Policing in the United States is primarily a responsibility of local government. Of the country's 800,000 full-time sworn law enforcement officers, 55 percent are local while another 21 percent work for sheriffs.[1] In general, the remaining 24 percent of officers are accounted for by the federal government and by special-purpose jurisdictions (e.g., universities and transportation authorities).

## Traffic operations

An important aspect of police operations is the traffic function. Police departments promote traffic safety through enforcement, public education, and recommendations for improved traffic engineering. They also direct traffic to help people and vehicles get where they are going more safely and expeditiously, and they investigate traffic accidents in order to document the facts and determine causes.

Because the traffic function accounts for a significant portion of police-public contacts, it can have a major impact on police-community relations, especially in smaller communities. When officers are less busy with crime, disorder, and calls for service, they have more time for proactive work, including traffic enforcement. It is important for police managers to exercise direction and control over officers so that traffic safety is maximized without resorting to oppressive or arbitrary levels of traffic enforcement.

Local police agencies are predominantly small organizations. Of local police departments, more than half have fewer than ten full-time sworn officers, and three-quarters have fewer than twenty-five.[2] Even so, much of the research and literature about policing, including police administration textbooks, is focused on large police departments.

With a few exceptions around the country, police chiefs are appointed officials while sheriffs are elected. The appointing authority for police chiefs varies among mayors, county executives, councils, police commissions, and local government managers. Sheriffs, although generally elected and therefore largely independent, usually must negotiate with county executives and county councils for at least a portion of their budgets. The duties of the sheriff's office also differ significantly from those of the police department, with more emphasis on court security, transportation of prisoners, jail operation, civil process (serving and enforcing various writs and court orders), and, in some cases, collection of taxes and fees. These nonpolice duties comprise the bulk of services provided by some sheriff departments, although other sheriff departments provide substantial police services (patrol, investigations, etc.) as well.

*Policing in the United States is primarily a responsibility of local government.*

The structure of policing varies around the United States. For example, sheriff departments play a very significant role in policing throughout the West, Midwest, and South but almost no role at all in the Northeast. State police agencies provide a major share of the police services in a few states (e.g., Delaware and Vermont) but little beyond highway patrol in others. Large county police departments (as distinct from sheriff departments) are found in a few states, particularly Maryland, New York, and Virginia, but are nearly unheard of elsewhere. North and South Dakota have the most fragmented police systems (the most police agencies per population), while California and Hawaii have the least fragmented systems.

Levels of police employment also vary around the country and by size of jurisdiction. Data from the Federal Bureau of Investigation (FBI) show that for cities of all sizes, the Northeast averaged 2.7 full-time sworn law enforcement officers per 1,000 population in

2005 compared with 1.7 in the West. Nationally, the smallest and largest cities had the highest levels of police employment: cities under 10,000 in population had 3.3 officers per 1,000 while cities over 250,000 had 2.8 officers per thousand. Cities with populations in the four separate size categories between 10,000 and 250,000 all averaged below 2.0 officers per 1,000.[3]

## Police operations

Police use the term *operations* to refer to activities undertaken in direct service to the public. Traditionally, the three main components of police operations have been patrolling, responding to calls, and investigating. One hundred years ago, preventive patrol was mainly undertaken on foot, but during the twentieth century almost all patrolling shifted to patrol cars so that officers could cover larger geographic areas and respond more quickly to emergencies and crimes. Starting in the 1980s, though, foot patrol began making a comeback along with bicycle patrol, horse patrol, and other alternatives to patrol cars.

Responding to calls became an increasingly important police activity with the proliferation of telephones in homes and businesses, the development of two-way police radios, and the implementation of 911 telephone systems and computer-aided dispatching. Reducing response time to calls from the public became one of the primary objectives of professional police departments, influencing budget requests, police officer schedules, and the design of patrol beat boundaries. Most police departments have reported an ever-increasing number of calls to be handled over the past twenty years, even during periods when the amount and rate of reported crime were down. This increase in call handling often translates into more workload for patrol officers, which then leaves less time for patrolling, investigating, and other activities.

Police investigations usually begin after a crime has been committed and reported. These reactive investigations are typically initiated by the patrol officers who respond to the crime report. Continuing or follow-up investigations of serious crimes are then conducted by detectives (if the agency is large enough to have any). Less serious crimes may or may not get follow-up investigations by patrol officers or detectives.

Research in the 1970s and 1980s found each of these primary operational components of policing—patrolling, responding to calls, and investigating—to be less effective than previously believed (see accompanying sidebar). A basic awareness of the findings of this important research is essential for understanding such modern-day developments as directed patrol, hot spots, community policing, and problem-oriented policing, all of which are discussed further on.

## Modern police strategies

Before describing the three main policing strategies in use today, it is important to articulate the goals or purposes that a police department is supposed to achieve. This is particularly crucial because of the tendency to focus on just one police goal—crime control—to the exclusion of the others. But in fact communities count on their police to work toward accomplishing several interrelated yet distinct ends:[4]

- *Reducing serious crime and making public spaces safe.* This goal is tantamount to protecting life and property.

## Research leads to new policing methods

The 1974 Kansas City Preventive Patrol Experiment demonstrated that varying the levels of routine motorized patrolling among no cars, one car, and two or three cars per beat for an entire year had no effect on crime, fear of crime, citizen satisfaction, arrests, accidents, or anything else that was measured. In fact, residents and businesses in the fifteen study beats did not even notice the yearlong changes in levels of motorized patrolling.[1]

A national study of reactive criminal investigation found that

- Only 20 percent of reported serious crimes are ever solved
- When cases are solved it is usually because of victims and witnesses rather than detectives
- Most detective work is bureaucratic and clerical in nature
- Few crimes are solved by physical evidence and/or forensic science.[2]

A study of rapid response to reported serious crimes in three cities found that police made response-related arrests in only 2.9 percent of responses. The main reasons were that

- Seventy-five percent of crimes were not discovered by victims or witnesses until after the fact
- Even when crimes were discovered in progress, victims and witnesses waited four to five minutes on average before calling the police.[3]

The cumulative impact of these findings was to motivate police planners and executives to look for alternative methods of policing. The result is a new understanding about police effectiveness.

1   George Kelling et al., *The Kansas City Preventive Patrol Experiment: Summary Report* (Washington, D.C.: Police Foundation, 1974).

2   Peter W. Greenwood and Joan Petersilia, *The Criminal Investigation Process,* Volume I: *Summary and Policy Implications* (Santa Monica, Calif.: Rand Corporation, 1975).

3   William Spelman and Dale K. Brown, *Calling the Police: Citizen Reporting of Serious Crime* (Washington, D.C.: Police Executive Research Forum, 1981).

- *Holding offenders accountable.* Helping society and the criminal justice system hold offenders accountable (by solving crimes and arresting suspects) reflects basic notions about justice: people should not get away with crime.
- *Making people feel secure.* Fear of crime wreaks havoc on communities and on residents' quality of life.
- *Enhancing trust and confidence in the police, and protecting the legitimacy of the police institution.* Police in a free society must be respectable and trustworthy in order to operate with the consent of the governed; if police are not trusted, citizens will not report crimes, serve as witnesses, or provide assistance in other ways that are essential to police effectiveness.
- *Using force and authority fairly, effectively, and efficiently.* The police must be wise and judicious in using the force and authority granted to them by the people; if they are not, they are clearly not performing their function effectively.

- *Using resources fairly, effectively, and efficiently.* The police have a responsibility to use the public's money wisely. If they waste or misuse that money, they are being inefficient as well as giving their communities less protection, security, and justice than they could with the resources available. This would be not only ineffective but also unethical.

The studies cited in the sidebar on page 317 demonstrated rather convincingly that 1970s-era police operational strategies were not sufficient to achieve the important goals and purposes of policing. Police departments today that still rely on motorized preventive patrol, rapid response, and reactive follow-up investigations as their primary methods for reducing crime, holding offenders accountable, making public places safe, making people feel secure, and enhancing trust and confidence in the police are not using their resources as efficiently and effectively as they should.[5]

## Strategic policing

One alternative is strategic policing, which aims primarily at improving performance in reducing crime and holding offenders accountable. In the patrol arena, strategic policing incorporates more focused tactics, such as directed patrol, saturation patrol, crackdowns, and hot spots policing (see accompanying sidebar). Call-driven 911 policing has been replaced by differential responses, in which immediate rapid response is reserved for in-progress situations while other calls are handled through delayed response, telephone reporting, nonsworn personnel, referral to outside agencies, and various other methods. Traditional criminal investigations have been refined through the use of solvability factors, case screening, an enhanced role for patrol officers in investigations, and major crime teams and task forces.

---

### Targeted patrol

Strategic policing emphasizes targeted rather than routine or diffuse patrol. In general, patrols are focused on specific locations, offenses, or offenders rather than merely being spread throughout the jurisdiction. A few of the most common varieties of strategic policing are

- **Directed patrol:** Patrol officers assigned to beats are given specific assignments to carry out during their free patrol time. These assignments are usually based on up-to-date crime analysis (e.g., recent incidents that have occurred during evening hours involved thefts of visible, easy-to-carry items from within unlocked vehicles, so patrol the area around Fourth and Vine looking for thefts from vehicles).

- **Saturation patrol:** Multiple officers are assigned to an area to provide a saturation level of patrolling in order to deter offenses from occurring or to provide sufficient police presence for strict enforcement.

- **Crackdowns:** Patrol officers are instructed to focus their attention on a specific location or a specific set of offenses (e.g., public drinking) and to implement strict enforcement.

- **Hot spots policing:** Patrols and/or specialized units are assigned to specific locations (e.g., a city block, an intersection, a small neighborhood, a shopping area) following an analysis of calls for service and/or reported crimes. These units are instructed to address the types of calls or crimes most common in the hot spots using enforcement, deterrence, problem solving, situational prevention, or other techniques.

One of the most celebrated manifestations of strategic policing has been COMPSTAT, a system developed in the New York City police department primarily to establish command accountability in such a large agency.[6] Headquarters staff use up-to-date crime data and crime maps in order to hold area commanders (in this case, precinct captains) accountable for identifying and responding to current crime problems. Instead of merely spreading their officers around the community and waiting for calls and crimes to happen, commanders are encouraged to use their resources strategically to address immediate problems. Many police departments large and small have adopted some form of COMPSTAT over the last few years.

The latest development in strategic policing is intelligence-led policing. This approach seems to have had several sources: COMPSTAT; the growing availability of crime analysis, crime mapping, data mining, and similar tools; nationwide implementation of intelligence-led policing in England and Australia (insofar as developments in police strategy in other countries sometimes affect U.S. policing);[7] and renewed police emphasis on intelligence collection and analysis in the aftermath of the terrorist attacks of September 11, 2001. Intelligence-led policing, perhaps better termed "information-led policing," calls for all police resources to be deployed and directed on a continuous, real-time basis according to careful analysis of the latest intelligence and other data. It is a much more command-directed and demanding approach to police management than the traditional approach of assigning each officer to a beat and reminding him or her to "be careful out there."

The evidence in support of strategic policing is fairly strong.[8] When police patrols and other resources are carefully targeted at hot spots and similar problems, crime is typically reduced. To some extent this may result in the displacement of crime to locations that are not being targeted, but it usually represents real reductions in that police efforts targeted at one location often lead to crime reductions in other locations as well. Policing that is targeted and focused seems clearly superior to that which is nontargeted, all other things being equal. COMPSTAT and intelligence-led policing, though, have not been adequately evaluated in their own rights to determine what additional benefits they provide, if any.

## Community-oriented policing

A second strategic alternative for police departments is community-oriented policing (COP). This strategy was developed primarily to enhance the public's trust and confidence in the police and make community residents feel more safe and secure. After twenty years of experimentation, there is little doubt about the effectiveness of COP on those two criteria, but debates continue about whether the strategy is effective in reducing crime and about whether it uses police resources efficiently.

The immediate precursor to COP was the rediscovery of foot patrol in the 1980s, thanks to the development of small, portable police radios that allowed officers to become independent of their patrol cars without losing voice communications with headquarters. Early studies were widely interpreted as demonstrating that, whether or not foot patrol decreased crime, at least it made citizens feel safer and led to improvements in police-community relations.[9]

More and more police departments began using foot patrol as a central component of their operational strategy rather than as a novelty or an accommodation to downtown business interests. If full-time foot patrol was not practical, alternatives such as bicycle patrol, "stop, walk, and talk," and "positive interaction patrol" (i.e., encouraging patrol officers to take advantage of every reactive or proactive opportunity for positive interactions with motorists, complainants, and ordinary members of the public encountered in schools, shopping centers, and neighborhoods) were implemented to make officers more accessible to citizens and to increase police-public contact. Crime prevention programs became increasingly reliant on community involvement, as in Neighborhood Watch, citizen patrols, and Crime Stoppers programs. Police departments began making greater use of civilians and volunteers in various aspects of policing and made permanent geographic assignments an important element of patrol deployment. This all came to be called "community-oriented policing," and it entailed a substantial change in police thinking involving increased citizen involvement, engagement, partnerships, and the tailoring of policing to neighborhood needs and preferences.[10]

---

### Community policing in Arlington County, Virginia

"As a police chief making my first attempt to implement community policing, I can recall the rolling of the eyes and the crossed arms over chests of doubting and unconvinced officers.... A decade later, the bulk of my patrol force in Arlington County had known no other strategy than community policing. Yes, they still like to respond rapidly to emergency calls. Yes, they still enjoy the thrill of a good 'pinch.' But police officers, managers, and chief executives all understand their responsibilities. The development of trust-based partnerships in neighborhoods, the critical importance of problem solving, and collaborative problem identification remain central components of crime control efforts."

Source: Edward A. Flynn, "Community Policing Is Good Policing, Both Today and Tomorrow," in *Community Policing: The Past, Present, and Future*, eds. Lorie Fridell and Mary Ann Wycoff (Washington, D.C.: Annie E. Casey Foundation and Police Executive Research Forum, 2004), 35, available at policeforum.org/upload/CommunityPolicingReduced_570119206_12292005152352.pdf. Additional information about community policing programs, training, and funding is available from the Office of Community Oriented Policing Services, U.S. Department of Justice, at cops.usdoj.gov/.

---

### The "Broken Windows" theory of crime control

Why the difference between motorized patrol and foot patrol? In what has come to be known as the "Broken Windows" theory, foot patrol officers seem to pay more attention to disorderly behavior and minor offenses than do motor patrol officers. Also, they are in a better position to manage their beats, understand what constitutes threatening or inappropriate behavior, observe it, and correct it. Foot patrol officers are likely to pay more attention to derelicts, petty thieves, disorderly persons, vagrants, panhandlers, noisy juveniles, and street people who, although not committing serious crimes, cause concern and fear among many citizens. Failure to control even the most minor disorderly activities on the street contributes to neighborhood fears. Foot patrol officers have more opportunity than motor patrol officers to control street disorder and reassure ordinary citizens that the streets, sidewalks, and other public spaces are safe to use.

Source: The "Broken Windows" theory was introduced by James Q. Wilson and George L. Kelling in "Broken Windows: The Police and Neighborhood Safety," *The Atlantic Monthly* (March 1982): 29–38.

---

### Volunteers in the Billings, Montana, police department

About seventy-five volunteers perform a wide range of services for the Billings, Montana (pop. 98,721), police department. The volunteers contact victims of vandalism, theft, and cold property crimes, and then write up police reports, saving police officers the need to go out on calls. Because the crime prevention program makes up only 50 percent of an officer's time, volunteers provide virtually all of the staffing, including that needed for research, program design, and administration. Volunteers also developed a computer program that collects information on all transactions from pawnshops and matches this with information from the police database. As a result, victims are getting their property back, and the program is spreading regionally. Those interested in volunteering must complete an application, provide three references, undergo a criminal-records check, and participate in an interview. The department relies on more experienced volunteers to mentor those who are new to the department.

---

Community policing got a tremendous boost from the federal government during the 1990s. Approximately $9 billion was appropriated by Congress and distributed by the Office of Community Oriented Policing Services to state and local jurisdictions around the country to hire, train, and equip 100,000 additional police officers to do COP. (Federal funds covered 75 percent of the cost of a new officer for the first three years of employment.)[11] After a decade of generous funding and sustained national attention, research on the effectiveness of COP has discovered some officer resistance to working closely with citizens but promising effects on public satisfaction, fear, disorder, and crime.[12]

Many smaller agencies adopted the COP strategy in the 1990s if for no other reason than to obtain federal funds. However, there should be less need for COP in small places where community relations are already positive and fear of crime is not elevated; moreover, some of the specific components of COP (e.g., ministations, formal community surveying, organizational decentralization, and citizen patrols) may not make much sense in the smallest jurisdictions. But some small police agencies emphasize motorized patrol and rapid response, and consequently they do not develop the kinds of intimate community knowledge and close relationships with the public that should come naturally to police departments in smaller jurisdictions. Thus, while it is probably true that a special strategy to develop good community relations is not necessary in most smaller places, it cannot be taken for granted, and COP may well be a wise strategic choice for some small agencies.[13]

### Problem-oriented policing

The third major contemporary strategy that was developed in the wake of the traditional model is problem-oriented policing (POP).[14] This approach puts more emphasis on reducing crime and making public spaces safe than on the other criteria of police effectiveness. Importantly, POP emphasizes that police should use a range of innovative and creative techniques to achieve those goals. This distinguishes it from both the traditional approach and the more contemporary strategic policing approach, each of which focuses on the goal of crime reduction but tends to rely almost exclusively on one technique: enforcement of the criminal law.

POP posits that police should focus more attention on *problems*, as opposed to *incidents*. Problems are defined as collections of incidents related in some way (e.g., if they occur at the same location) or as underlying conditions that give rise to incidents, crimes, disorder, and other substantive community issues that people expect the police to handle. By focusing more on problems than on incidents, police can address causes rather than mere symptoms and thus have a greater impact. The public health analogy, with its emphasis on prevention and a proactive approach, is often used to illustrate this difference. It also reminds us that even with a strong public health approach, people still get sick and need medical attention; similarly, even if POP successfully prevents some problems and reduces the overall demand for reactive policing, police still need to respond to calls and make arrests.

> *POP emphasizes that police should use a range of innovative and creative techniques to reduce crime and increase safety.*

One of the fundamental tenets of POP is that law enforcement—that is, using the criminal law—should be understood as one *means* of policing, rather than as the end or goal of policing. This is much more than a subtle shift in terminology. It emphasizes that police pursue large and critically important societal goals—controlling crime, protecting people, and reducing fear—and that in every instance, they should choose those lawful and ethical means that yield the most efficient and effective achievement of those ends. Sometimes this may involve law enforcement, and sometimes it may not. Thus, the terms *policing* and *law enforcement* are not synonymous, and law enforcement is not the only, or even necessarily the principal, technique of policing.

In place of overreliance on the criminal law, POP recommends a range of tailored responses, including

- Mobilizing the community
- Engaging specific stakeholders
- Providing information to people
- Changing the physical environment
- Using civil law and other regulatory authority
- Referring problems to more appropriate agencies.

The POP process uses a rational and analytical approach to problem solving, which is best known in police circles as the SARA model (*s*canning, *a*nalysis, *r*esponse, *a*ssessment).[15] According to this approach, police should continually scan their areas of responsibility, drawing on a variety of informational sources, in order to identify problems. Next, they should carefully analyze those problems to verify, describe, and explain them. Only after this analysis stage should police turn their attention to responses, and when they do, they should identify and consider a wide range of responses before narrowing their focus down to the most promising alternatives. Finally, after implementing these responses, they should carefully assess the impact in order to determine whether they need to try something else and also to document lessons learned for the benefit of future problem-solving efforts.

Countless individual case studies have been completed with fairly convincing evidence that the targeted problems were substantially reduced.[16] As with COP, though, implemen-

---

**Problem-oriented policing**

A very useful product of the problem-oriented policing movement has been a series of guidebooks (thirty-five at present and growing), some titles of which are *Speeding in Residential Areas, Disorder at Budget Motels, Street Racing, Bullying in Schools, Drug Dealing in Privately Owned Apartment Complexes, Assaults in and Around Bars,* and *Robbery of Automated Teller Machines.* Each of these guidebooks summarizes the key features of the problem, the research about it, ways to analyze the problem locally, police and nonpolice responses to it, and what has been learned about the effectiveness of different responses. The guidebooks, available free at popcenter.org, are short, practical, and full of great ideas for handling specific problems.

---

tation is a big challenge. While it is relatively easy to get a few analytically inclined officers to take a problem-oriented approach to the occasional big problem in a community, it is much more difficult to get all patrol officers, detectives, and other employees to consistently take this approach to their everyday work instead of the more traditional incident-oriented approach.[17] The most consistent criticism of POP as practiced is that analysis is often cursory or nonexistent. Some observers have also been disappointed that POP responses often emphasize enforcement and other conventional police practices. One careful study, however, found that most POP examples use multiple responses (five on average) and that enforcement is often used to supplement more innovative responses rather than as the main response.[18] Evaluations of the impact and effectiveness of POP have been generally positive, indicating reduced crime and disorder and increased public safety, although most such evaluations have used rather weak research designs.[19]

## Police administration

The range of functions and responsibilities associated with managing local police services is broad. Police administration entails planning, decision making, leading, and managing. This is equally true whether the police agency is small or large, rural or suburban or urban.

### Choosing an operational strategy

One of the key responsibilities of police administration is choosing the agency's operational strategy and then working to implement it. Before the 1980s there was nearly complete consensus that police departments had to provide continuous motorized patrol throughout their jurisdictions, respond immediately to every call as it came in, and assign every reported crime to a detective for in-depth follow-up investigation. Now that other strategies are available, the choice of an operational strategy is the most important decision that police executives must make.[20]

Where resources are limited, the police executive should avoid relying entirely on motorized preventive patrol, rapid response, and detective investigations; at the very least, these practices should be more directed and targeted, taking elements from strategic policing. Preferably, police departments should emphasize community-oriented and problem-oriented practices that have demonstrably better effects on crime, safety, feelings of security, and public trust and confidence in the police. Most importantly, police departments should tailor their strategies to the particular needs of their communities.

## Managing discretion

Another key responsibility of police administration, mentioned at the outset of the chapter, is structuring and guiding the discretion exercised by individual police officers.[21] Regardless of whether a department adopts traditional policing, strategic policing, community-oriented policing, or problem-oriented policing, its officers will be called upon to make discretionary decisions in the field about whether to intervene, how to intervene, whether to cite or arrest, whether to use force, and how much force to use. Strategic policing creates some additional challenges because officers are typically instructed to intervene more often, stopping more

---

### Techniques for managing discretion

Police departments employ a range of techniques to guide decision making and the use of discretion by police officers. Among these techniques, police departments

- Recruit and select employees carefully, emphasizing maturity, judgment, discipline, and willingness to follow direction.
- Give officers extensive basic training. This training tends to emphasize job-related knowledge and technical skills, but the best police training also aims to teach decision making and problem solving.
- Require officers to undergo field training after completion of their academy training. In addition to teaching new officers how to make good decisions in the field, field training monitors their initial performance to weed out probationary officers who do not make good decisions.
- Promulgate policies that are aimed at guiding officers' decision making. These policies usually emphasize factors to be considered in a situation, legal considerations, any actions that are either mandatory or prohibited, the department's preferred response in specific circumstances, and the overarching purpose or goal of police action in the situation.
- Develop organizational cultures that promote good decision making. They often have mission statements, statements of values, and codes of conduct that remind officers what the department stands for, what it cares about, and what it regards as good police work.
- Are organized so that officers have supervisors and commanders. At a minimum, these management personnel are responsible for reviewing officers' decisions after the fact. When feasible, they provide direct supervision and command over decisions in real time.

In addition to these techniques, larger police departments have internal affairs units that investigate allegations of illegal, unethical, or simply inappropriate decision making by officers. Some communities also have external bodies (civilian review boards, police auditors, ombudsmen, etc.) that review police officer decisions. And police officer decisions that result in citations or arrests are also reviewed within the legal system, first by prosecutors and then by judges and juries.

cars and more people, checking out more suspicious behaviors and situations, and using formal sanctions to address irritating problems of disorder and incivility. COP and POP create different challenges because officers are encouraged to work more intimately with the public, tailor enforcement and problem solving to the specific needs of different neighborhoods, and implement creative and innovative responses. These latter two strategies typically promote the concept of empowering police officers to be creative problem solvers, an approach that inevitably grants officers more discretion.

Despite an impressive menu of techniques for guiding police decision making (see accompanying sidebar), managing police officer discretion is still a huge challenge for any police department. First, it is hard to make good decisions. Officers usually work alone, facing uncertainty and danger; citizens often make conflicting demands on them; and some decisions need to be split-second, requiring tough choices to be made. Second, the police organization does not always know whether good or bad decisions are being made. Many decisions by police officers have low visibility, and unless an arrest is made, a supervisor may never even know about the officer's actions. Third, it cannot always be assumed that officers are trying to make decisions in accordance with the organization's wishes. Approved organizational values often run counter to the values of the dominant police culture, which sometimes emphasizes officer safety over everything else, police solidarity, a cynical view of the public, and little tolerance for questions or demands from citizens, not to mention indifference or hostility toward cultural diversity. It is also common for police officers to hold their managers and politicians in disdain for not understanding or appreciating the realities of police work on the street.

## Leadership

Police executives have both internal and external constituencies, a fact that greatly complicates their situation.[22] Beyond being expected to lead their organizations—a daunting challenge as described above—they also have to satisfy local government managers, political leaders, the community, interest groups, the media, and the legal system. These external constituencies often make demands that are at odds with the perceived interests and worldviews of street-level police officers. In particular, a major concern of these external groups is that the police executive demonstrate effective control over police officers, preventing abuses of power and authority against the public. Thus, the police executive has to walk a tightrope, not leaning too far toward favoring either "the troops" or groups outside the department.[23]

Another important feature of a police executive's responsibilities is public leadership. The public looks to police chiefs, sheriffs, and other law enforcement leaders for leadership on issues related to crime, disorder, and justice. Today's police executives are usually trained and educated for this role, although conflicts may still arise occasionally with local government managers and elected officials since crime control is inevitably a contentious political issue.

## Managing resources

Aspects of resource management that are unique to the police department include department structure, staffing requirements, personnel training, the use of information technology, and issues of consolidation.

---

### Interagency cooperation in Wisconsin

The Wisconsin counties of Dodge (pop. 88,103), Jefferson (pop. 79,328), Kenosha (pop. 160,544), Racine (pop. 195,708), and Walworth (pop. 99,844) joined forces in 2005 to form the Southeast Area Drug Operations Group (SEADOG) to increase the efficiency and effectiveness of each county's drug unit activities. A regional task force comprising the counties' sheriffs or drug board directors meets quarterly to oversee administrative issues. Task force supervisors for each county meet electronically or by teleconference at least once a week to share information and coordinate the employment of undercover agents and equipment.

---

*Structure*   Police departments have traditionally used bureaucratic and quasi-military organizational structures that emphasize hierarchy, chain of command, and position titles such as sergeant, lieutenant, captain, and commander. At the same time, though, the lowest rung on the sworn ladder is the police *officer,* in recognition of the power, authority, and discretion exercised at the bottom of the hierarchy. For this reason police departments have sometimes been called symbolic bureaucracies. They are also often punitive bureaucracies, emphasizing the threat of punishment for rule violations, probably because of the reality that low-level employees have so much power and discretion.

Decentralization and flattening of the hierarchy have been common refrains in police administration over the past decade, as they have in other types of public and private organizations. Many police departments have eliminated one or two levels of management in order to make their operations leaner and more responsive. Decentralization generally means delegating more authority to district commanders and other unit commanders; in larger police agencies, it may also include shifting specialists, such as detectives, from headquarters to districts in order to place them and their commanders closer to neighborhoods and community leaders. Under COP, decentralization often involves delegating more authority and responsibility to area commanders, neighborhood teams, and/or individual beat officers.

> *A better approach in small agencies is to rely on generalist/ specialists: that is, every officer is a patrol officer who also has developed special knowledge and skills in selected areas to be used when needed.*

Structure presents a particular challenge for small police agencies. If the agency or community wants a supervisor on duty around the clock, extra sergeants are needed. The agency or community may want specialists, such as detectives or Drug Abuse Resistance Education (DARE) officers. Members of the department probably also desire promotion and/or special assignments, which creates additional pressure for vertical and horizontal differentiation. Thus, a better approach in small agencies is to rely on generalist/specialists: that is, every officer is a patrol officer who also has developed special knowledge and skills in selected areas to be used when needed. Officers are treated as professionals, expected to perform as such, and held to the highest standards, thereby reducing the need for in-person supervision. Staffing levels are kept to the minimum needed, so that limited funds are spread across fewer personnel; this allows salaries to be higher, thus helping the small agency attract and retain the best available people.

***Staffing***   A recurring issue for police agencies and their communities is the proper level of police staffing. The most common approach is to use the national average of 2.3 sworn officers per 1,000 population.[24] A town of 20,000 residents, then, might use forty-six officers as a benchmark for its staffing needs. This benchmark could be deceiving, however, because the national average for towns of that size is actually 1.9 officers per thousand, which would translate to thirty-eight officers. Police departments arguing for more officers sometimes neglect to use cities of comparable size when citing these national averages.

More importantly, every jurisdiction has differing policing needs, so it is best not to use national staffing averages for anything more than a rough guide. Towns, cities, and counties differ in demographics, tourism, residential versus business composition, density of liquor establishments and other sources of entertainment, and other factors that affect crime, disorder, and policing. A better approach is to measure the actual demand for police service in the jurisdiction, as reflected in the number of calls, reports, incidents, arrests, and other activities, and then translate that into staffing needs. This requires good data about calls for service and police activity, but the techniques for transforming such data into staffing requirements have been well developed within police administration for many years.[25]

> *A community's current data about police activity are partially a function of what police officers choose to do, individually or as part of a particular policing strategy.*

Even this analytical approach is inadequate, however. A community's current data about police activity are partially a function of what police officers choose to do, individually or as part of a particular policing strategy. That is, some of the data are self-fulfilling. If officers follow a zero-tolerance policy toward minor offenses, for example, the data will swell with incidents, reports, and arrests, which will suggest the need for more officers. Or conversely, if officers engage in underpolicing, the data may suggest that the community has few problems and does not need many police, which may not be true.

A larger and more proper question to ask is what level of police services does the community want and need, and how many officers are required to provide that level of service? In other words, to some extent the question about police staffing levels is a political question—not just because it comes down to tax dollars or because political leaders ultimately make the decision, but because it really involves what a community needs and desires. Some communities want a police officer standing in front of each elementary school in the morning and afternoon, while others do not (or are not willing to cover the cost). Some citizens want a police officer to come to the house to take a report when a bicycle is stolen, while others are satisfied to file their reports by telephone. Some small towns want twenty-four-hour police coverage, which necessitates at least five officers, and probably six or seven (depending on the amount of time lost to holidays, vacations, military leave, and training); others are willing to accept partial coverage, relying on the sheriff's department or the state police at other times. The questions posed above are not scientific questions, nor are they primarily professional questions that can be answered by following modern police administration practices. Rather, they are political and financial questions.

---

**The school resource officer in Oskaloosa, Iowa**

The city of Oskaloosa, Iowa (pop. 11,026), school resource officer spends virtually all of his working hours in the city's elementary, middle, and high schools building relationships with children, teachers, and parents. He currently teaches weekly Drug Abuse Resistance Education (DARE) classes to children in the second and fifth grades. He also gives presentations to students in government and physical education classes about such issues as alcohol use, and he spends time with the students during breakfast and lunch. The officer is called in on all criminal investigations involving school property as well as on all truancies. Sometimes students or school counselors report problems to the officer that he then addresses or refers to the appropriate agency. A grant from the U.S. Department of Justice supports this officer's work, although the police department and school district will take over funding in the program's fourth year.

---

*Personnel issues*   A fundamental approach to improving and professionalizing policing has been training. State minimum training standards vary across the United States, but nearly every police officer has completed a basic or recruit academy of ten weeks or longer that included skills training (firearms, driving, arrest techniques), criminal law, criminal procedure, accident investigation, criminal investigation, and related topics. Most academies also cover police ethics and cultural diversity, and many use modern instructional methods such as adult learning principles and problem-based learning.

Police training does not end with the recruit academy. Ideally, academy graduates enter a field training stage during which they are paired with a field training officer (FTO) who grades their performance for three to six months to verify that the probationers are ready to work alone. Also, police officers need refresher and update training during their careers as well as specialized training for new assignments. Police departments use training as the vehicle for the continuing education of police officers. This creates a particular challenge for small agencies. The training itself may be costly, and staffing problems arise while officers are away at training. The tendency in some small agencies is to cut corners on training, but this solution is shortsighted as it ultimately reduces the quality of service provided and increases liability risks.

> *Police departments use training as the vehicle for the continuing education of police officers.*

Three contentious personnel issues in police administration are higher education, minority hiring, and physical fitness testing. Probably no more than about one-third of current police officers have bachelor's degrees (although many more officers have at least some college credits). The evidence relating education to improved performance is generally inconclusive.[26] Perhaps the strongest arguments in favor of higher education for police relate to representativeness and professional status.[27] In a society in which most high school graduates go on to college, police would lose ground and would not mirror their communities if they did not recruit on university campuses.

Almost all police officers were male and white into the 1960s, but since that time a variety of equal opportunity, affirmative action, and targeted recruiting initiatives have significantly changed the composition of law enforcement personnel in the United States. As of 2005, 11.6 percent of sworn officers were women.[28] As of 2000, in local departments with 100 or more officers, 15 percent of sworn officers were African American and 11 percent were Hispanic.[29] However, many individual police departments still have difficulty achieving a workforce as diverse as their communities.

At one time, height and weight standards for police employment created significant roadblocks to minority hiring (especially of women and Asian Americans), but such requirements have been largely eliminated. One remaining requirement that often stymies female applicants is physical fitness testing,[30] but women and small men have proved over the past thirty years that they can perform police work successfully. Police work involves much more talking, listening, looking, and writing than extreme physical exertion. Some agencies use no fitness tests at all in their hiring process, some use separate physical fitness standards for male and female applicants, and some use one standard regardless of sex. A case can be made for any of these approaches. The latter approach, however, typically creates adverse impact, with women failing at two or three times the rate of men.[31] If this approach is used, the agency should expect criticism and be prepared to prove, in a court of law if necessary, that its testing process is job related and necessary.

*Information technology*   Police officers expect to have reliable voice communication with headquarters and with each other, whether they are in patrol cars or on foot. The main issue with respect to voice communication is interoperability—that is, the capacity to talk via radio to field units in other police departments, to the fire department, to ambulances, etc. This kind of interoperability is useful on a routine basis and essential in emergencies. Most police agencies do not have complete interoperability. Technological solutions are quickly being developed and implemented, but it will take longer to overcome human and bureaucratic obstacles, such as getting police agencies to agree on equipment standards and radio frequencies, and getting policies and procedures in place to regulate the situation when numerous agencies are tied together on one radio channel.

Police agencies have moved rapidly to implement wireless data systems. With handheld devices and computers in patrol cars, officers can query databases directly, use text messaging and e-mail to communicate with headquarters and other field units, and complete and submit reports electronically.

Most police agencies use some type of computerized records management system (RMS), and larger ones also use computer-aided dispatch (CAD) systems to aid dispatchers and to capture information on calls for service for later analysis. As part of their CAD, RMS, or separate databases, most departments also keep electronic files on arrests, citations, field interrogations, investigations, evidence, recovered property, equipment inventory, training records, and numerous other operational and administrative matters.

Technology acquisition and management pose special challenges for police executives:

- Major information technology systems are complex and expensive.

- Most software for police use is adapted from other sectors, including the military, and may not deliver as expected.

- Technical support and upgrades may not be available because the market is fragmented and vendors come and go.

- As seen during recent major disasters, voice and data systems can crash when power systems and cell and radio towers go down and wireless systems are overwhelmed.

***Consolidation***   In response to the extremely fragmented nature of U.S. law enforcement, critics and reformers have long argued for consolidation. Over time, many police consolidations have occurred in urban areas (e.g., Charlotte and Mecklenberg County, North Carolina) and in more rural areas (Versailles and Woodford County, Kentucky). Also, around the country one can find numerous instances of towns contracting with sheriff's departments or state police for police service in lieu of forming or continuing their own independent police agencies. There are still more than 12,000 local law enforcement agencies in the country, though, with additional start-ups every year. Despite the advantages to be gained from consolidating or contracting (which usually include reduced cost, greater access to specialized services, and more flexible staffing), most local jurisdictions prefer to have their own police department with their own police chief. This is because local agencies are presumed to be more responsive to the needs of local people and because town officials have the opportunity to hire (and fire) their own police chief, which they cannot do if they are served by the sheriff's department or state police.

A different type of consolidation is to combine police and fire into a public safety agency. But only a few jurisdictions have implemented the full public safety concept, with personnel cross-trained as police officers, firefighters, and paramedics. One reason for this is training. Each of the three disciplines—police, fire, and emergency medical services—has significant entry-level and continuing training requirements. Employees with all three designations were often in training as much as on the job. Also, the three disciplines sometimes attract different types of people, making it difficult to find and retain employees who are interested and competent in all three areas. Many jurisdictions use a partial public safety approach, such as giving police officers some basic training in fire suppression and first aid or placing separate police, fire, and ambulance services within a public safety bureau so that they all have the same overall director; however, only a few communities use the public safety concept in its most robust form.

## Key policy issues

Written policies and procedures have proliferated in police departments over the last two to three decades in response to new social and political issues, the evolution of administrative and employment law, civil liability concerns, and the impact of law enforcement agency accreditation (see accompanying sidebar). Smaller agencies, in particular, have come to realize that they too need policies governing police officer decision making; although they may have fewer officers, they make the same kinds of important discretionary decisions as officers in larger departments. Three of the most significant policy issues are use of force, pursuit driving, and domestic violence.

### Use of force

The authority to use force against the public is one of the defining elements of policing, but it is important to recognize that police officers do not use force very often. The most complete national survey of the public indicated that officers used or threatened to use force in about 1.5 percent of public contacts.[32] Most of these instances involved pushing, shoving, or other low-level threats or shows of force. About one in seven people against whom police used force claimed to have suffered some type of injury. In other words, about two in every one thousand police-public contacts resulted in an injury.

## Accreditation

For most of American police history, there were few if any national standards that a local government manager, elected official, or ordinary citizen could use to determine whether his or her police department was operating in a modern, professional manner. That situation began to change in 1979 with the creation of the Commission on Accreditation for Law Enforcement Agencies (CALEA). CALEA eventually established a set of accreditation standards (446 at present) for police agencies and a process of self-study and external review leading to accreditation recognition. As of 2005, about 5 percent of all law enforcement agencies (900 departments) representing about 25 percent of the country's sworn officers were in some stage of the CALEA accreditation process.

Although the majority of U.S. police agencies have not chosen to pursue national accreditation, CALEA has had an extended impact in two ways. First, its accreditation standards are widely used as a best-practices reference by police executives and other local government managers and policy makers. Second, some states have chosen to establish state-level law enforcement agency accreditation programs, sometimes because of philosophical opposition to national accreditation and sometimes to provide a scaled-down and less expensive alternative. In either case, these state-level programs have often adopted some of the same standards as CALEA, and have had the same objective of encouraging fragmented and localized police agencies to recognize and adopt some minimum standards related to police operations and administration.

Source: For more information on the accreditation process, go to calea.org.

Police policies and training emphasize that officers should always use the least amount of force necessary to accomplish lawful purposes. Most police agencies use some version of a force continuum; the continuum articulates levels of force, beginning with presence and voice and continuing through several intermediate levels to deadly force. It specifies the appropriate police response given the nature of the situation and the actions of the suspect, and it instructs officers about the use of retreat and cover when applicable. Of course, good police tactics are designed to avoid placing officers in precarious situations (such as in front of or behind vehicles occupied by suspects) that increase the level of danger and the likelihood that officers will have to resort to deadly force for their own protection.

Police officers today usually have access to one or more less-lethal weapons, including batons, pepper spray, and conducted energy devices (Tasers). When used properly, each of these weapons can be effective both in subduing violent suspects and in reducing the need to use deadly force. Police agencies must provide initial and continuing training, clear policies and procedures, supervision, and administrative review in order to ensure that these weapons are used properly and no more often than necessary. Less-lethal weapons can cause injury and even death in rare situations. Police use or abuse of such weapons can generate public controversy, especially when that use is captured on video and replayed on television. There also seems to be a tendency for police officers to resort to new less-lethal weapons more often than they should, skipping lower levels of the force continuum such as command voice and soft hands (guiding, holding, or restraining without striking).

---

**The law and deadly force**

Police use of deadly force was significantly restricted by the 1985 U.S. Supreme Court decision *Tennessee v. Garner* (471 U.S. 1). The effect of that case was to strike down the so-called fleeing felon doctrine derived from common law. The court ruled that police can use deadly force only against someone who is posing a significant threat of death or serious physical injury to the officer or others and not merely for the purpose of capturing an escapee or a fleeing suspect. Since that 1985 case, many states have refined their statutes regarding police authority to use force, and police departments have promulgated policies that clarify when their officers are authorized to use deadly force.

---

## Pursuit driving

Research, tragic crashes resulting in deaths and injuries to police officers and others, and lawsuits against officers and their superiors have led to the development of formal policies that govern police emergency driving of all types, including pursuit driving.[33] Policies still differ, though. Some police departments nearly prohibit high-speed pursuits except when the fleeing person is known to have committed a serious violent crime, while other departments allow officers to use their judgment based on several factors, including the nature of the suspected offense, traffic conditions, weather, and the type of roadway involved (e.g., residential street versus highway).

In most departments, regardless of the flexibility or rigidity of the policy, supervisors are now required to carefully monitor pursuits over the police radio and regulate vehicle speed, the number of police units involved, and the length of the chase. This exerts a degree of management control over the situation instead of leaving all decisions in the hands of an officer who is already driving fast and feeling the rush of adrenalin. In small agencies, however, there may be many times when no supervisor is on duty, in which case the entire decision-making responsibility falls on the officer engaged in the pursuit. This feature of small departments makes it even more essential to have a clear and firm policy in place to guide officer decision making and behavior associated with pursuits and other high-speed driving situations.

## Domestic violence

Police departments have not typically promulgated formal written policies that structure police discretion with respect to specific types of crime and disorder; for example, few agencies have formal policies on disorderly conduct, open-air drug markets, or school truancy. Rather, it has been traditional to allow officers to decide how to handle these types of matters according to situational considerations. The main exception is domestic violence. Starting in the mid 1980s, research suggested that arrest was the most effective response to domestic assault. Victims' groups began pressuring police and criminal justice agencies to take domestic violence more seriously, and many states revised their statutes to allow police to make warrantless arrests for spousal misdemeanor assault. It was also common for new statutes to require police reporting of domestic violence, to require responding officers to protect victims, and even to make arrest mandatory.

In reaction to these changes, as well as to the threat of civil liability for failing to protect domestic violence victims, departments have issued formal policies designed to guide officers in their handling of domestic violence cases. Such policies state the department's overarching goal of protecting victims, specify actions that officers must take (e.g., offering to transport the victim to a shelter), and outline considerations to be weighed when making any discretionary decisions. Some agency policies require arrest whenever probable cause is established, while others indicate that arrest is the preferred response. In the latter case, the policies often require officers to articulate their reasons for *not* making an arrest whenever that route is chosen.

## Homeland security

Among the immediate consequences of the new homeland security mission for local police are new training requirements, an enhanced focus on identifying and protecting critical infrastructure, increased interaction with federal law enforcement and intelligence agencies, and equipment procurement for handling weapons of mass destruction, including chemical, biological, radiological, nuclear, and explosive materials.[34] Local police chiefs clearly have taken on several major new responsibilities, although everyday police work in local departments has not really been greatly affected thus far. This may change, however, if terrorist incidents increase and become a more imminent threat in places outside New York, Washington, D.C., and Los Angeles.

The delineation of specific responsibilities for homeland security is still evolving, but a few important local police responsibilities can be identified:

- Local police should be directly involved in vulnerability assessments for their communities. They need to be knowledgeable about their community's risks and vulnerabilities, including those associated with the private sector, in order to carry out preparation, prevention, and response duties.

- Local police should be directly involved in emergency planning for their communities. Plans and procedures for emergency management and incident command must be worked out in advance with other local, county, state, and federal officials to resolve issues about who is in charge and who is responsible.

- It is particularly important that (1) local police, fire, and emergency medical services work out protocols and practice them, (2) mutual aid agreements are established among neighboring jurisdictions (see sidebar on page 334), and (3) local government managers and elected officials know their critical incident roles and responsibilities.

- Local police should be thoroughly trained in homeland security and antiterrorism tactics.

- Local police should be linked to their region's Joint Terrorism Task Force led by the Federal Bureau of Investigation.

- Local police should fully participate in their state's intelligence fusion center. Intelligence fusion centers are designed to analyze statewide crime and terrorism data, produce actionable intelligence and analytical products, and serve as the link between local and federal law enforcement and intelligence agencies.

- Local police should cultivate community support to maximize the likelihood that residents will report suspicious terrorism-related behavior. At the same time, local police

---

**A mutual aid pact for police in Massachusetts and Connecticut**

The towns of Brimfield (pop. 3,639), Holland (pop. 2,536), Sturbridge (pop. 8,860), and Wales (pop. 1,821), Massachusetts, and Union, Connecticut (pop. 744), have established a mutual aid pact. Most of these towns have part-time police departments and generally have only one, or sometimes two, officers on duty at night. When police officers in these towns require backup, they can call one of the other towns and receive additional assistance rapidly. The towns have agreed to help each other out at no cost to the towns needing assistance. The arrangement has worked well, and the towns have called on each other several times, primarily for motor vehicle accidents and domestic situations.

---

should provide public education and leadership in the community to minimize hysteria and discrimination based on race, ethnicity, religion, and country of origin.

- Local police should look for opportunities to reduce the public's fear of terrorism. Because of the nature of terrorism and its specific objective of causing terror, local police can play an important antiterrorism role by helping reassure the public that the local community and the nation are vigilant, prepared, and determined.

Of particular importance for local jurisdictions are the costs associated with their new homeland security–related roles and responsibilities. Federal funding has become available to purchase some needed equipment and to cover the costs associated with some training, but many aspects of the new homeland security mission have been experienced as unfunded mandates at the local level, especially for small and medium-sized local jurisdictions.

## Policing trends

Several important long-term trends in policing and police administration should be recognized: civilianization, privatization, federalization, militarization, and globalization. These trends have already affected the delivery of police services in local communities, and they have the potential for having even greater impact in the future.

### Civilianization

Police departments have been gradually increasing their employment of civilians—that is, nonsworn personnel—for many years. Today, most departments use civilian employees whenever the duties of a position do not require a badge and a gun. Nationally, in 2005, more than 30 percent of all police department employees were civilians.[35] Besides administrative duties, some departments are now using civilians to take police reports (in person or over the telephone), conduct investigations, and collect physical evidence at crime scenes.

There are at least two strong motivations behind civilianization. One is financial: civilians are usually paid less, have less generous retirement plans, need less equipment, and are subject to less mandatory training than sworn officers. The other motivation is diversification of the police workforce. Employment of women, minorities, older citizens, and people with disabilities is often more successful in civilian positions than it is in sworn positions. Civilian police employees also help diversify the police culture because they tend to be not quite so caught up in the ethos and worldview of street police officers.

## Privatization

Private policing is not new. In fact, private police preceded the formation of public police in England, and private detectives such as the Pinkertons provided most criminal investigation in the United States throughout much of the 1800s. Nevertheless, Americans are accustomed to thinking about the police as a public agency. But the public role played by the police may be shrinking in the face of privatization. Over the past thirty years, the government's traditional monopoly over police services has diminished. Today in the United States there are three times more private security agents than public police officers.[36]

Within this context, an important change has occurred in the use of physical space. The latter half of the twentieth century witnessed the rise of mass private property—facilities and properties that are privately owned but freely used by the public. These include shopping malls, college and school campuses, residential communities, high-rise condominiums, banks, commercial facilities, and recreational complexes. Private security specialists have become the most likely form of policing for these kinds of facilities. Along similar lines, another modern phenomenon is the gated community, which is separated from surrounding areas by tall walls and gates staffed by security guards.

A related trend is for local police to privatize or outsource specific functions. For example, at one time police departments would escort business owners to the bank to make large deposits, but today police are more likely to refer businesses to armored car companies. Similarly, many police now refer "keys locked in car" complainants to locksmiths rather than trying to gain entry themselves. Years ago both business and residential burglar alarms were wired right into police stations; today they are usually wired into alarm services companies. The latest trend is for police to refuse to even respond to burglar alarms until it is verified that a crime has occurred. The motivation for this is the cost and burden of false alarms, which typically comprise over 90 percent of alarm activations.[37] When police stop responding to burglar alarms, the alternative is for security firms to respond—another example of privatization.

## Federalization

A strong trend throughout the second half of the twentieth century, and one that seems to be gaining increased momentum, is the federalization of crime control and law enforcement. In recent years the U.S. Congress has passed more and more federal criminal laws that give wider jurisdiction to federal prosecutors and investigators. Many crimes today, especially those involving guns or drugs, can be investigated and prosecuted federally as well as by state and local law enforcement. Most recently, the nation's heightened concerns about international terrorism and weapons of mass destruction have led to an even greater tendency to rely on federal laws and federal law enforcement.

## Militarization

Traditionally, the regular military has been very restricted in its role in crime control and policing within the U.S. borders. (The National Guard and Coast Guard are somewhat less restricted.) Military police have always had jurisdiction on military bases and over military personnel, of course, but otherwise, the military has generally been used only for law enforcement or order maintenance duties in serious emergencies, such as natural disasters or mass civil disorder, when martial law is declared. These limitations on the domestic police role of the military were enacted in the Posse Comitatus Act of 1878.

However, military involvement in domestic law enforcement seems to have increased over the last ten to twenty years, most commonly in conjunction with the war on drugs and more recently following the terrorist attacks of September 11, 2001. Since then, it has become common to see military personnel guarding airports, train stations, and other critical facilities, and there have been calls for military participation in other types of counterterrorism efforts. In some citizens' minds it is a fairly easy and comforting segue from Army special forces chasing terrorists in Afghanistan to Army units chasing terrorists in New York or California. For other citizens, though, the specter of U.S. soldiers patrolling the streets or knocking on doors in the middle of the night is frightening and antithetical to the American way of life.

## Globalization

Developments in business, finance, trade, travel, communications, and computers have made the world a smaller place over the last decade or two. It is far more likely now than twenty years ago that a local criminal investigation might involve international transactions as well as foreign individuals who might have traveled to the local jurisdiction or played their roles (as witnesses, victims, or suspects) from afar. Many traditional crimes can have international features today, such as drug distribution and theft. Crimes committed with computers, including fraud, theft, vandalism, and hacking, know no boundaries. Then there are the newer crimes (or perhaps crimes that are simply getting more attention today), such as human trafficking of women and children and illegal smuggling of immigrants, weapons, and even nuclear material. The term "transnational crime" has been coined to describe the increasingly international nature of crime.

Another aspect of globalization that has affected American policing has been the participation of local and state police in international policing missions in such places as Haiti, Bosnia, and Kosovo.[38] As the United States, the United Nations, the European Union, and other bodies have accepted peacekeeping roles in war-torn countries around the world, it has become evident that a key element in the restoration of order and civil society is effective policing. Many American police officers have now had the experience of serving in such international missions, and many American police departments now see that part of their responsibility is to support the development of more professional and democratic policing in other countries. This is a relatively new awareness for American police, and it contributes to their sense of being part of a global police community.

It is difficult to predict all the future ramifications that this trend toward globalization will have for policing. Clearly, though, international issues and considerations that were once thought to be irrelevant for local American policing have become relevant and even significant. This trend can only continue.

## Challenges

Managing police services involves some challenges familiar to all public managers, including those related to planning, budgeting, human resources, communicating with and motivating employees, and adapting modern technology. Yet police executives also have some significant challenges that are unique to police agencies:

- Managing the discretionary decision making and behavior of police officers, who have power, authority, and weapons and are deployed 24/365 all over the jurisdiction

- Designing the police agency's alternatives to traditional police strategy (i.e., preventive patrol, rapid response, and follow-up investigation) based on strategic policing, community policing, and problem-oriented policing; and overcoming a resistance to change in order to implement the alternative strategies, especially those that affect traditional values associated with officer autonomy and the primacy of law enforcement and crime fighting

- Managing resources and activities in order to maximize the achievement of multiple separate and distinct goals (including but not limited to reducing crime)

- Carrying out the mission of homeland security despite unclear parameters and implications and in accordance with a greater emphasis on increased interagency cooperation, information sharing, intelligence analysis, and vulnerability assessment

- Adapting to important long-term trends affecting police management, such as civilianization, privatization, federalization, militarization, and globalization, which all add uncertainty to the task of managing police services in local communities.

Police managers today tend to be as well versed in the latest management and leadership practices as are other local government managers, thanks to tremendous strides in police professionalization since the 1960s. Nevertheless, the peculiar nature of the police business and the dynamic nature of crime, disorder, and terrorism guarantee that police services will continue to be one of the most controversial and challenging aspects of local government management.

---

### Questions to ask if you manage police services in a small community

Does the police department meet the state's minimum training requirements for police officers?

Does the police department have written policies on use of force, pursuit driving, domestic violence, processing of drugs and other contraband, handling of prisoners (including women and juveniles), and other high-risk situations?

Does the police department meet state and national standards for accreditation?

What is the police department's operational strategy?

What is the public's perception of the police department?

Is the police department able to attract and retain quality personnel?

Is the police chief a leader in the community?

Is the police chief an effective manager of the police department?

Is the police department obtaining its fair share of state and federal funding to help support its operations and implement new programs?

Is the police department operating within its budget, including overtime expenses?

**Competencies for managers in the field of police services**

Knowledge of operational police work, usually obtained through experience as a police officer

Knowledge of police strategies, especially community-oriented policing and problem-oriented policing

Knowledge of police administration techniques for guiding police use of discretion

Knowledge of legal considerations pertinent to police work and police administration

Familiarity with and participation in professional police associations

High ethical standards

Effective oral and written communication skills

Ability to balance competing demands of political leaders, police employees, and the community

## Endnotes

1 "Law Enforcement Statistics," available at ojp.usdoj.gov/bjs/lawenf.htm#summary.

2 Brian A. Reaves and Matthew J. Hickman, *Census of State and Local Law Enforcement Agencies, 2000* (Washington, D.C.: Bureau of Justice Statistics, 2002), 3, at ojp.usdoj.gov/bjs/pub/pdf/csllea00.pdf.

3 Federal Bureau of Investigation, *Crime in the United States: 2005* (Washington, D.C.: U.S. Department of Justice, 2006), Table 71, at fbi.gov/ucr/05cius/data/table_71.html.

4 Mark H. Moore et al., *Recognizing Value in Policing: The Challenge of Measuring Police Performance* (Washington, D.C.: Police Executive Research Forum, 2002).

5 Malcolm Sparrow, Mark H. Moore, and David M. Kennedy, *Beyond 911: A New Era for Policing* (New York: Basic Books, 1990).

6 Eli B. Silverman, *NYPD Battles Crime: Innovative Strategies in Policing* (Boston, Mass.: Northeastern University Press, 1999).

7 Jerry H. Ratcliffe, ed., *Strategic Thinking in Criminal Intelligence* (Leichhardt, NSW, Australia: The Federation Press, 2004).

8 Wesley Skogan and Kathleen Frydl, eds., *Fairness and Effectiveness in Policing: The Evidence* (Washington, D.C.: National Research Council, 2004).

9 Police Foundation, *The Newark Foot Patrol Experiment* (Washington, D.C.: Police Foundation, 1981); Robert C. Trojanowicz, *An Evaluation of the Neighborhood Foot Patrol Program in Flint, Michigan* (East Lansing: Michigan State University, 1982).

10 Lorie Fridell and Mary Ann Wycoff, eds., *Community Policing: The Past, Present, and Future* (Washington, D.C.: Annie E. Casey Foundation and Police Executive Research Forum, 2004).

11 Jeffrey A. Roth et al., eds., *National Evaluation of the COPS Program: Title I of the 1994 Crime Act* (Washington, D.C.: National Institute of Justice, U.S. Department of Justice, 2000), 1.

12 Skogan and Frydl, *Fairness and Effectiveness;* Anthony M. Pate et al., *Reducing Fear of Crime in Houston and Newark: A Summary Report* (Washington, D.C.: Police Foundation, 1986); Wesley G. Skogan and Lynn Steiner, *Community Policing in Chicago, Year Ten: An Evaluation of Chicago's Alternative Policing Strategy* (Chicago: Illinois Criminal Justice Information Authority, 2004).

13 Quint C. Thurman and Edmund F. McGarrell, eds., *Community Policing in a Rural Setting*, 2nd ed. (Cincinnati, Ohio: Anderson Publishing Company, 2003).

14 Herman Goldstein, *Problem-Oriented Policing* (New York: McGraw-Hill, 1990).

15 John E. Eck and William Spelman, *Problem-Solving: Problem-Oriented Policing in Newport News* (Washington, D.C.: Police Executive Research Forum, 1987).

16 These are available online at popcenter.org.

17 Gary Cordner and Elizabeth Perkins Biebel, "Problem-Oriented Policing in Practice," *Criminology & Public Policy* 4 (May 2005): 155–180.

18 Michael S. Scott, *Problem-Oriented Policing: Reflections on the First 20 Years* (Washington, D.C.: Office of Community-Oriented Policing Services, 2000).

19 Skogan and Frydl, *Fairness and Effectiveness.*

20 Mark H. Moore and Darrel W. Stephens, *Beyond Command and Control: The Strategic Management of Police Departments* (Washington, D.C.: Police Executive Research Forum, 1991); Mark H. Moore and Robert C. Trojanowicz, "Corporate Strategies for Policing," in *Perspectives on Policing* No. 6. (Washington, D.C.: National Institute of Justice, 1988).

21 Herman Goldstein, *Policing a Free Society* (Cambridge, Mass.: Ballinger, 1977).

22 Gary W. Cordner, Kathryn E. Scarborough, and Robert Sheehan, *Police Administration*, 5th ed. (Cincinnati, Ohio: Anderson Publishing/ LexisNexis, 2004), 179–208.

23 Renford Reese, *Leadership in the LAPD: Walking the Tightrope* (Durham, N.C.: Carolina Academic Press, 2005).

24 Federal Bureau of Investigation, *Crime in the United States: 2005*, Table 71.

25 Margaret J. Levine and Thomas McEwen, *Patrol Deployment* (Washington, D.C.: National Institute of Justice, U.S. Department of Justice, 1985).

26 David W. Hayeslip Jr., "Higher Education and Police Performance Revisited: The Evidence Examined through Meta-Analysis," *American Journal of Police* 8, no. 2 (1989): 49–62; Robert E. Worden, "A Badge and a Baccalaureate: Policies, Hypotheses, and Further Evidence," *Justice Quarterly* 7 (September 1990): 565–592.

27 Charles B. Saunders Jr., *Upgrading the American Police: Education and Training for Better Law Enforcement* (Washington, D.C.: Brookings Institution, 1970).

28 Federal Bureau of Investigation, *Crime in the United States: 2005*, Table 74, at fbi.gov/ucr/ 05cius/data/table_74.html.

29 Brian A. Reaves and Matthew Hickman, *Law Enforcement Management and Administrative Statistics, 2000: Data for Individual State and Local Agencies with 100 or More Officers* (Washington, D.C.: Bureau of Justice Statistics, 2004), Table C, at ojp.usdoj.gov/bjs/pub/pdf/lemas00.pdf.

30 Kimberly A. Lonsway, "Tearing Down the Wall: Problems with Consistency, Validity, and Adverse Impact of Physical Agility Testing in Police Selection," *Police Quarterly* 6, no. 3 (2003): 237–277.

31 In Kentucky, for example, men have a 77 percent pass rate and women have a 33 percent pass rate on the state-administered Peace Officer Professional Standards physical fitness test taken by more than 5,000 police candidates as of April 2006: see Kentucky Law Enforcement Council, *Second Quarter Meeting* (Richmond: Kentucky Law Enforcement Council, 2006).

32 Matthew R. Durose, Erica L. Schmitt, and Patrick A. Langan, *Contacts between Police and the Public: Findings from the 2002 National Survey* (Washington, D.C.: Bureau of Justice Assistance, U.S. Department of Justice, 2005), v, at ojp.usdoj .gov/bjs/pub/pdf/cpp02.pdf.

33 Geoffrey P. Alpert et al., *Police Pursuits: What We Know* (Washington, D.C.: Police Executive Research Forum, 2000).

34 Chad Foster and Gary Cordner, *The Impact of Terrorism on State Law Enforcement: Adjusting to New Roles and Changing Conditions* (Lexington, Ky.: Council of State Governments, 2005).

35 Federal Bureau of Investigation, *Crime in the United States: 2005*, Table 75, at fbi.gov/ucr/ 05cius/data/table_75.html.

36 David Bayley and Clifford Shearing, "The Future of Policing," in *The Criminal Justice System: Politics and Policies*, 7th ed., ed. George Cole and Mark Gertz (Belmont, Calif.: West/Wadsworth Publishing, 1998), 150–167.

37 Rana Sampson, *False Burglar Alarms*, Problem-Oriented Guides for Police No. 5 (Washington, D.C.: Office of Community-Oriented Policing Services, 2001), at popcenter.org/Problems/ problem-false-alarms.htm.

38 Robert Perito, *The American Experience with Police in Peacekeeping Operations* (Clementsport, Nova Scotia: Canadian Peacekeeping Press, 2002).

# 14

# Fire and Other Emergency Services

## John W. Swain

Fire departments were originally created to suppress fires. In the popular imagination, fearless firefighters slide down station poles, race to fires, chop down doors, and dash into burning buildings to save lives. But today's fire departments do even more. Because of their success in reducing and coping with fire dangers and their traditional role in ensuring public safety, in addition to budgets constraints in local government, fire departments now provide services in the areas of fire prevention, hazardous materials (HAZMAT) incidents, rescue, emergency medical treatment, and emergency management (discussed in Chapter 12).

These expanded services are a natural outgrowth of the traditional role of fire departments. Involvement with hazardous materials evolved from concern about the dangerous properties of some burning materials (e.g., poisonous fumes emitted by burning plastics) and about the potential for fires at locations where highly flammable, explosive, or poisonous materials are stored. Rescue work has become a function of fire departments because of their ability to provide equipment and personnel as well as their lifesaving tradition. Similarly, emergency medical service (EMS) is a logical extension of their role as fire personnel move beyond giving first aid at fire scenes to providing medical services in other situations, particularly vehicle accidents and cardiac failures. These service areas are discussed in this chapter, as is emergency management and the technical and administrative aspects of fire and other emergency services, because they are all part of the vital role that fire departments play in the community.

Fire department services essentially involve "fire and life safety," which necessarily entail managing risks to life and property. All policy and operational decisions about those services represent choices regarding risk: what levels of risk are acceptable, what ways to deal with risk are best, and what resources should be expended to do so. Policy makers decide the acceptable levels of risk and allocation of resources. Although more resources reduce risks, not all risks can be alleviated, and other services require resources as well. Fire departments make the operational decisions, choosing which risks to focus on and managing their operations in light of those risks to the public and themselves. Some risk to personnel is justified in lifesaving activities, much less risk is acceptable to protect property, and no exceptional risk is acceptable unless life or property is involved.

---

**Public safety and health services provided by fire departments**

| | |
|---|---|
| Baby-sitter training | Fire station as safe haven for children |
| Blood pressure and glaucoma screening | HAZMAT disposal |
| Car seat safety check | Immunization program |
| Chimney inspection | Juvenile fire-setter program |
| Courtesy home inspection | Sandbags |
| CPR and first-aid classes | Smoke detector program (e.g., testing and battery |
| Explorer/cadet program | replacement) |
| Fire extinguisher training | Wellness training |
| Fire safety training | |

---

## Prevention

Good fire departments work hard to prevent emergencies and to mitigate those that arise. Many emergency events can be eliminated or mitigated by judicious local government actions, including code provisions, code enforcement, and public education. Prevention work requires coordination with planning, building, zoning, code enforcement, health, police, and other departments; with operators of schools, hospitals, factories, and commercial buildings; and with the general public.

### Code provisions

Codes are laws and regulations that require or prohibit certain kinds of action. Most code provisions relevant to fire departments concern fire safety. Some deal with hazardous materials and processes. Relatively few code provisions deal specifically with EMS, rescue, or emergency management issues.

*Fire safety*   Many useful substances are combustible, flammable, or explosive. Often the most dangerous substances, such as gasoline, are among the most useful. When such substances are placed in proximity to heat, flames, or controlled explosions (such as those in a home furnace), unintended fires may result, harming people and property. Fire prevention codes contain measures that lessen the possibility and severity of fires by reducing fire hazards, making buildings fire resistant, and facilitating the quick and safe evacuation of people from burning structures. Some states have a statewide code, and some prohibit local codes. Some states allow localities to supplement statewide codes, and some simply authorize local governments to pass their own codes.

Most state and local codes are based on model codes. Model codes reflect a wide range of experience and provide authoritative interpretation and explanation of standards for building construction, electrical wiring, heat sources, hazardous materials and processes, public assemblies, fire exits, and fire protection and suppression equipment. The leading sources of model codes are the National Fire Protection Association (NFPA) and the International Code Congress.

Because fire prevention provisions are often incorporated in building codes, fire departments need to coordinate code development and revision efforts with the departments primarily responsible for building codes. Building codes concerning new construction materials and methods require constant monitoring. Provisions dealing with electrical wiring, heat sources, and fire-resistant construction features are particularly important.

Many codes require smoke detectors and automatic on-site sprinkler or standpipe systems in larger and taller buildings and those posing greater hazards (e.g., theaters, schools, and hospitals). Smoke detectors signal dangerous conditions by emitting an alarm. Smoke detectors that sound an alarm within a structure are the simplest, most cost-effective, and most important fire safety devices because they are intended to signal people while there is still time to escape. A more sophisticated detector system can signal off-site fire suppression units.

Required on-site suppression systems may be effective because most fires start out small, and smaller fires can be controlled or extinguished with much less difficulty than larger ones. People in the building may be able to suppress small fires themselves with fire extinguishers or with internal standpipe systems that are fitted with hoses and nozzles ($1^1/_2$-inch couplings and hoses) for use by building residents. Larger internal or external standpipe systems can be used by trained personnel who bring their own $2^1/_2$-inch couplings and hoses. Fires activate automatic sprinkler systems.

Fire safety codes may also require signed fire exits that facilitate escape as well as provisions to ensure that large groups of people can be safely evacuated in the event of fire.

Some provisions that are initially or principally oriented toward fire safety also contribute to safety in nonfire emergencies. Examples include provisions dealing with safety inspections, permits, assembly, exits, warning and water systems, fire lanes, and emergency vehicles.

*Hazardous materials and processes*   Provisions concerning hazardous materials and processes appear in fire codes and elsewhere. In addition to explosive and flammable materials, many other materials and processes pose great dangers. Hazardous materials that are not a fire risk range from the obvious to the obscure: for example, acids, biocides, radioactive wastes, and heavy metals. Provisions regulating hazardous materials and processes

### Sprinklers

Since local governments started requiring automatic sprinklers for buildings intended for public assembly and particularly vulnerable populations (e.g., theaters, schools, hospitals, and high-rise buildings), they have gradually expanded the types of locations targeted. Despite significant opposition from building owners and builders, advocates of automatic sprinklers continue to gain approval for the wider use of automatic sprinklers in new and existing buildings: for new buildings, proponents call for sprinklers in new residential housing, particularly single-family dwellings; for existing structures, they call for the retrofitting of high-rise buildings. Scottsdale, Arizona (pop. 226,013), and Prince Georges County, Maryland (pop. 846,123), adopted ordinances requiring automatic sprinklers in all new residential construction. Their experience appears to be quite positive, with fewer lives lost and less property damage for structures with automatic sprinklers.

prohibit some and regulate others; generally, requirements grow in proportion to population or risk. The requirements may involve location (zoning), structural features (ventilation), or compliance with specific procedures (e.g., license, permit, and inspection).

*Other provisions* Code provisions related to EMS, rescue, and emergency management tend to be relatively narrow in focus. EMS-related provisions include regulations about having, maintaining, and using automatic external defibrillators in public places in cases of cardiac arrest. Rescue-related provisions generally concern avoidance of rescue situations through prohibitions or requirements, such as prohibitions against rock climbing or swimming in dangerous waters. Emergency management–related provisions may prohibit people from being in disaster-prone areas (e.g., flood zones) and may impose fines for failure to comply with directives.

## Code enforcement

Effective prevention depends on code enforcement, which requires the local government to conduct inspections and make code compliance a prerequisite for permits (e.g., for building, occupancy, zoning, and health) and licenses (e.g., liquor and business) (see Figure 14-1). Fire departments should keep other departments apprised of both code provisions and enforcement problems so that personnel from those departments can learn to spot fire code violations and issue citations for them. (Similarly, fire departments should assist other departments in code development and enforcement.)

When a code violation is discovered, usually through an inspection, the building owner, manager, or occupant is issued an order to correct the violation. A first violation usually results in a warning. After a suitable period to correct a violation, another inspection is conducted; if the violation has not been corrected, a penalty—a fine, a denial of the right to use the affected structure, or a jail sentence—is generally imposed.

Some inspectors enforce codes reluctantly because they want to maintain the good will of the building owners and managers. City and county managers can help by reinforcing the importance of the enforcement process with inspectors. Sometimes a review of that process can lead to simplified procedures and better management support as well as to more vigorous enforcement.

## Public education

Prevention education teaches the public how to guard against hazards and react appropriately in emergency situations. Fire prevention efforts, especially those associated

### Figure 14-1 Benefits of permits, inspections, and investigations

| Permits | Inspections | Investigations |
|---|---|---|
| Prohibition of unsafe activities | Limitation of unsafe activities | Incident preplanning |
| Identification of potentially dangerous situations | Incident preplanning | Arson prosecution and prevention |
| Revenue | Public education | |
| | Site familiarization | |

---

### Cooking with the Fire Department in Old Town, Maine

Cooking with the Fire Department is a joint program of the public library and the fire department in Old Town, Maine (pop. 7,792), designed to teach kitchen safety. Children sign up at the library, and library staff accompany them to the fire department. All available firefighters on that shift (usually six people), as well as the lieutenant and chief, work with the children to plan, shop for, prepare, and eat a meal. While the meal is cooking, the firefighters discuss safety in the kitchen. The library and the fire department split the food bill, which is the main cost of the program.

---

with smoke detectors and building codes, reduce deaths, injuries, and property losses. Although not as dramatic, such prevention activities may be ultimately more effective than the most urgent emergency responses. The NFPA's *Learn Not to Burn®* curriculum, which teaches twenty-two fire safety behaviors, has been particularly effective in teaching children how to react to fire dangers.

Although fire departments tend to stress fire safety education, they also provide training in first aid and CPR, and information about particular medical conditions. Instruction about water and wilderness safety reduces the need for those kinds of rescues. Fire departments also educate about alert and warning systems and response plans (e.g., evacuations from around nuclear power plants).

## Emergency response

Fire departments must always be ready to respond to emergencies: a quick response can make the difference between a routine success and a major catastrophe. Although this section emphasizes what is needed when responding to a fire emergency, the discussion generally applies to calls for other types of service as well.

### Information

Preparing to respond to emergencies requires information about predictable problems, response techniques, and location. Relevant information should be observed, recorded, and analyzed systematically.

*Predictable problems*   Each jurisdiction has specific problems. The information most obviously needed deals with the kinds of problems that might be encountered (e.g., the kinds of fire that occur, the most significant fire hazards, the kinds of hazardous materials present, the most common medical emergencies, and the most likely rescue and emergency management calls).

The precise mix of problems plays a part in determining the location of stations, the choice of equipment, and personnel decisions, especially those concerning staffing levels and the content of and schedules for training. The staffing level—the number of persons on duty or readily available—is especially critical for fire suppression because differences in staffing levels affect the extent to which fires can be extinguished by initial response teams. For

---

*Learn Not to Burn®* is a registered trademark of the National Fire Protection Association (NFPA), Quincy, MA 02269.

example, the Occupational Safety and Health Administration requires that before any firefighters enter a burning building, no fewer than two firefighters must be available to go in and two more must be available to remain outside, which means that unless the fire is endangering an occupant, three firefighters have to await a fourth before anyone enters a burning structure.[1]

*Response techniques*   Specific knowledge needed for emergency response includes techniques of fire suppression, methods for handling the specific hazardous materials a department might encounter, rescue procedures, appropriate treatment in cases of medical emergencies, and responsibilities in emergency management situations. For fires, efforts to enhance human safety involve putting fires out and ventilating buildings to lessen fumes; opening, keeping open, and cooling building exits; and searching for building occupants. The sidebar below outlines the fire suppression activities at a working fire (a fire that is growing and threatening lives and property).

Two other important response technique subjects are the National Incident Management System (NIMS) and incident preplanning The federal government requires that emergency service entities conform to the requirements of NIMS as a precondition for federal preparedness assistance funding. At the core of NIMS is the Incident Command System (ICS), which determines who is in charge at the scene of an emergency. Many fire departments had developed their own incident command systems before the federal government adopted NIMS. As long as the system is consistent with the NIMS ICS guidelines, a department can continue using its own.

As the term implies, incident preplanning entails making plans in advance either for specific types of recurring incidents or for special incident situations. In the first case, this process involves analyzing and deciding on response technique choices so that responders

---

### Fire suppression activities at a working fire

While their order may vary, the following activities describe what must be done to combat a working fire:

1. Advance initial attack hose lines to the most critical positions in order to confine the fire or protect the occupant.

2. Provide lighting (at night).

3. Raise ladders for rescue, attack, and ventilation crews.

4. Rescue occupants who are unable to escape on their own.

5. Advance backup attack lines and lay lines to supply sprinkler and standpipe systems and heavy-stream appliances.

6. Operate pumping apparatus to supply water.

7. Enter fire structure and immediately threatened buildings, forcibly if necessary, first to ventilate, attack, and rescue and later to open the structure to search for hidden fire.

8. Provide first aid to those injuried.

9. Perform salvage operations to prevent needless water and smoke damage.

can be appropriately trained. Evaluation of response techniques leads back to preplanning. In the second case, the process involves looking at unusual situations that require additional information or different responses from fire department personnel; such situations might include evacuation of nursing homes and hospitals or of an unusual building, or any other unusual element that might affect emergency response. For example, responders to automobile accidents should be prepared to deal with high-voltage batteries and wires in hybrid vehicles.

*Location*   Information regarding the location of an emergency situation includes physical dimensions, buildings, transportation routes, and surface features (e.g., ravines or forest). Fire departments use maps (paper or electronic) to display location information, analyze fire problems, navigate when responding to calls, and choose station locations. Many departments use geographic information systems (GIS) to organize digital information by physical location and to produce maps that show dimensions and spatial relationships. GIS can operate on computers mounted on vehicles, be carried by personnel, or be centrally located with information conveyed to field personnel.

Because emergency situations worsen as time passes (e.g., fires get more dangerous and damaging, and medical problems become more life-threatening), the location of fire stations is also a crucial factor. Thus, criteria used for choosing where to locate a station include travel times to probable incident sites as well as acceptable service levels and costs. Figures 14–2 and 14–3 indicate the importance of time for fire and medical emergencies at crashes.

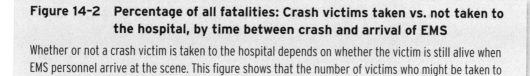

**Figure 14-2   Percentage of all fatalities: Crash victims taken vs. not taken to the hospital, by time between crash and arrival of EMS**

Whether or not a crash victim is taken to the hospital depends on whether the victim is still alive when EMS personnel arrive at the scene. This figure shows that the number of victims who might be taken to the hospital decreases with time.

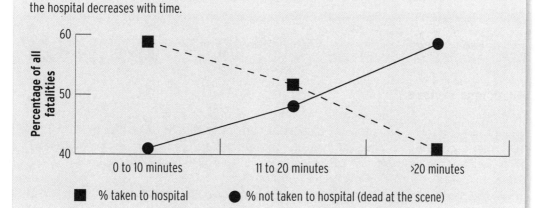

Source: Based on National Highway Traffic Safety Administration, *CIREN Program Report 2002* (Washington, D.C.: 2002), available at www-nrd.nhtsa.dot.gov/departments/nrd-50/ciren/networkreport/fore.html (accessed November 17, 2006).

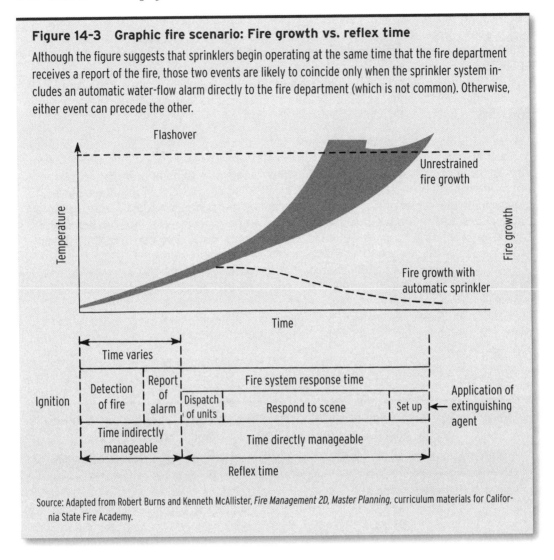

**Figure 14-3   Graphic fire scenario: Fire growth vs. reflex time**

Although the figure suggests that sprinklers begin operating at the same time that the fire department receives a report of the fire, those two events are likely to coincide only when the sprinkler system includes an automatic water-flow alarm directly to the fire department (which is not common). Otherwise, either event can precede the other.

Source: Adapted from Robert Burns and Kenneth McAllister, *Fire Management 2D, Master Planning,* curriculum materials for California State Fire Academy.

## Readiness reviews

Line personnel test and maintain departmental equipment and carry out review activities under the supervision of managers. Inspections and tests should always be made when major items are delivered; regular inspections and tests ensure the highest possible level of readiness when emergencies arise. Readiness reviews also cover employees, including their physical fitness and knowledge of procedures.

Managerial reviews look for potential changes that would affect fire departments, such as the construction of new buildings, the different use of a particular building, and the creation of new fire hazards. For instance, newly developed subdivisions may require another fire station, a redistribution of equipment, and more personnel; new high-rise buildings may require aerial equipment. Managers can track such changes by regularly reviewing the records of the planning department as well as by observing events in the community. Through regular reviews, the emergency problems of the jurisdiction as a whole can be seen in perspective.

### Departmental performance evaluation

Evaluation of departmental performance is another essential part of planning the activities involved in recurring emergency services. Systematic evaluation of fire department performance using the kinds of information listed in the sidebar below can provide insights into strengths, problems, and possible improvement strategies. One key performance indicator is response time to emergencies, particularly fire and EMS calls.

Fire department activities should be organized primarily to respond to common problems. Therefore, departments should regularly and systematically record and evaluate their work by organizing data on the causes of emergencies as well as on the responses. Observed patterns and relationships generally provide more useful information for decision making than single cases or totals; unique events, such as a single large arson fire, distort statistics. Certain relationships may be apparent, such as between locations and response times, whereas other issues (e.g., a large number of fires in a given area) may require further analysis.

Information on departmental performance is useful not only to prepare for emergency responses but also to plan prevention strategies. Current information on inspections and occurrences of emergencies can lead to changes in inspection patterns, code provisions, and code enforcement.

## Personnel

Fire department staffing involves a number of factors, including frequency of emergency calls, budgetary considerations, population density, and availability of qualified personnel who have the requisite technical skills and knowledge.

---

### Information needed for performance evaluation

To perform a systematic evaluation of the fire department's performance in response to a particular emergency incident, the following information should be gathered:

- Type of service performed (fire, EMS, HAZMAT, rescue, or emergency management)
- Location of incident
- Time of day
- Location of fire station
- Apparatus (i.e., vehicles and equipment) and personnel deployed
- Response time
- Description of emergency situation
- Losses: death, injuries, and property
- Cause(s) of losses
- Special problems or circumstances.

## Staffing requirements

Staffing requirements for firefighting are easily underestimated. Staffing one position around the clock means 168 hours of availability each week. The number of full-time personnel required to cover one position ranges from a minimum of three (working 56 hours a week) to more than four (working fewer than 42 hours a week). The 1985 amendments to the Fair Labor Standards Act require that firefighters be paid overtime for hours worked in excess of an average of 53 a week—that is, for more than a maximum of 212 hours in a twenty-eight-day work period.

> *Firefighters emphasize staffing as a safety and an employment issue, and local officials emphasize it as a financial issue.*

When a full-time person is unavailable for firefighting because of illness, vacation, or off-site training, a department has to replace that person or accept a lower level of staffing. Administration and other assignments take personnel time. Moreover, the use of part-time or volunteer personnel increases the number of people who must be trained and managed.

A typical full-time staffed fire department dispatches a minimum of three people to a building fire; firefighters prefer a minimum of four people. Paid firefighters and local government officials disagree regularly about the adequacy of fire department staffing. Firefighters emphasize staffing as a safety and an employment issue, and local officials emphasize it as a financial issue.

## Types of personnel

Fire departments invest considerable time in recruiting, testing, and selecting personnel. In addition to the physical and mental abilities and interests on which they are evaluated, applicants must have or develop and maintain competencies in technical knowledge and skills. Training, planning, and management efforts also take time. Personnel work varies for the various types of personnel.

Departments use one or more of three types of personnel: full-time paid employees, volunteers, and part-time paid employees. Many local governments have combinations of two or three types. The three types differ in availability and scheduling, pay and benefits, levels of qualification and training, and the difficulties they present for managers.

*Full-time employees*   Full-time employees devote their careers to the fire service. Typically, they work a forty- to fifty-six-hour workweek, taking responsibility for training, fire prevention, and equipment maintenance as well as for fire suppression and other emergency response duties. Of the three types of personnel, full-time employees are the most available, easiest to schedule, and most costly with respect to pay and benefits. They are also the most qualified initially, as they are selected from a pool of applicants on the basis of qualifications and may have prior experience or training as part-timers or volunteers, and they are the ones most easily required to take training. Finally, full-time employees are the easiest to manage because they are fewer in number and their livelihoods depend on complying with their organizational superiors.

*Volunteers*   Volunteers are part-time personnel primarily used on an on-call basis. Many people view fire service work, most commonly firefighting, as a community service activity.

And in recent years, particularly in metropolitan areas, many volunteers see this service as the first rung of a full-time fire department career. The major reasons for employing volunteer personnel are the low cost for local governments—typically, volunteers either are not paid or are paid only a nominal sum either per call or per year—and the desire of the volunteers to be involved in community life. Among the three personnel types, volunteers are the least costly with respect to pay and benefits; however, they are also the least available, hardest to schedule, least qualified initially, and least easily required to take training.

A major difficulty with volunteers is their lack of availability, especially during daytime hours. Experts suggest that it takes three volunteers on a departmental roster to ensure that one will respond to any given alarm. Thus, to be assured of ten respondents, a department needs thirty active volunteers. This ratio can be reduced by arrangements that ensure volunteer availability; for example, some fire departments require their volunteers to take duty hours in a station, and some rely on volunteers for evening, weekend, and holiday hours but use employees from other local government departments to respond to emergency calls during the business day.

Other difficulties with volunteers include deploying them to activities other than fire suppression. Increasing service demands (resulting from a growth in population, housing, and commercial and industrial developments) make volunteer service more dangerous than it once was; among the dangers are taller buildings, AIDS, hazardous materials, and threats posed by terrorists. These situations, as well as the more complicated responses they call for, require increased skills and capabilities, and it is difficult to make volunteers undergo the necessary training. Finally, because there are so many of them, volunteers create more work for managers.

***Part-time employees*** Local governments employ part-time employees most often to supplement one of the other two personnel types. Part-time employees are paid only for the time that they work. They may be full-time employees in other departments of a local government who leave those duties to respond to emergency calls, or they may be individuals who work only a limited number of hours for a fire department. Part-time employees are somewhat in between full-time employees and volunteer personnel with respect to scheduling, qualifications, and training; most importantly, they cost less than full-time employees but have greater availability than volunteers.

## Qualifications and training

Required qualifications and level of training increase from volunteers to part-time employees to full-time personnel. Many states and local fire departments require that firefighters be certified as meeting specific qualifications. Those qualifications typically include knowledge (e.g., of the physics of fires), skills (e.g., in fire suppression), and physical abilities (e.g., to lift certain amounts of dead weight).

Emergency calls require rapid, effective responses. Any time wasted in getting organized and deciding upon a course of action worsens the problem. Responses should be instinctive, honed through comprehensive, intensive, time-consuming, continuous, and often expensive training. Training involves the acquisition of knowledge and development of skills through drills. Basic knowledge provides the foundation; drills develop the instinctive responses required. Drills with equipment, actual structures, and lifelike situations are indispensable. Some training may include observation of actual emergency responses.

**Volunteer training areas**

| | | |
|---|---|---|
| Aerial operations | General orders review | Rescue |
| Apparatus driving | Hazardous materials | Ropes and knots |
| Apparatus familiarization | High rise | Safety |
| Building construction/preplans | Hose | Salvage and overhaul |
| Cardiopulmonary resuscitation | Incident management systems | Self-contained breathing apparatus |
| Communications | Installed fire protection systems | |
| Disaster training | Ladders | Small tools |
| Emergency medical training | Live fire training | Tactics and strategy |
| Engineer's training | Mutual aid drills | Technical rescue |
| Equipment and station maintenance | Nonwater operations | Terrorism |
| | Nozzles and appliances | Truck company operations |
| Fire behavior | Officer training | Vehicle extrication |
| Fire prevention and inspection | Orientation | Ventilation |
| Fire streams | Physical fitness | Water rescue |
| Forcible entry | Pump and hose testing | Water supply |

Subjects covered in a fire suppression training program include orientation, communication, street and hydrant location, emergency vehicle riding and driving, fire preplanning (visiting a site to determine, for example, where to position trucks, hoses, and ladders should a fire occur there), rescue procedures, equipment, tools, first aid, overhauling (making sure that no fire remains), and salvage. Drills include vehicle runs; ladder placement; building ventilation; rescues; hookup, line laying, and water application; foam application; and fire preplanning.

## Firefighting resources

Firefighting has been greatly improved since the days when colonists shouted "Fire!" and gathered on foot, formed lines, and passed leather buckets of water hand to hand from a well to a blazing building. Shouts and leather buckets have been replaced by communication systems, water distribution systems, vehicles, equipment, and maps showing property locations and access routes.

## Communication systems

Communication systems link alarms, dispatch centers, vehicles, traffic signals, and personnel. Alarms may be oral communications stemming from human detection of emergencies, or they may be signals triggered by automatic systems that detect fire conditions. Dispatch centers receive alarms, send out vehicles, and maintain contact with emergency personnel, vehicles, and sites. Departments employ communication devices to control traf-

**A fire academy in Sugar Land, Texas**

The Sugar Land, Texas (pop. 75,754), fire department has teamed up with Wharton County Junior College to create the Sugar Land Fire Academy. More than forty students enroll every semester to become eligible to test for state certification, and almost all of them pass the test. The department provides training space, fire apparatus, and firefighters as instructors, so students receive instruction in firefighting practices; gain hands-on experience in rescue and suppression activities, self-contained breathing apparatus orientation, and techniques for rescuing disoriented firefighters; and are introduced to the core values of the Sugar Land fire department (customer service, creative problem solving, and teamwork). The academy enables students to see what fire service is really like before they decide whether to become firefighters. At the same time, it provides the city with a first look at potential hires, who then require as little as one week of orientation. In addition, the firefighters find that teaching others sharpens their own skills.

fic signals; this allows for quicker response times while increasing safety for firefighters and the public.

Permanent centers may use dedicated telephone lines to receive calls from the public; communications between a dispatch center and personnel at the emergency scene, as well as among personnel at the scene, occur on specific radio frequencies. Personnel at the scene also operate equipment, such as robots or nozzles, by remote control. Some departments equip firefighters with personal alert safety systems, which can be used to locate and communicate with individuals carrying a device and to warn others when a person stops moving.

Computer-aided dispatch (CAD) software, as well as the increasing capacities and declining size and cost of wireless communication devices, promises great benefits for fire department operations. CAD software, which relies on GIS to assist in dispatching, provides relevant information to dispatchers and can actually determine which available unit to send in response to a call, thereby decreasing the time it takes to dispatch a unit. CAD software can also be used to record call-related information: it processes information generated automatically or in response to input from dispatchers or firefighters.

> *Departments employ communication devices to control traffic signals; this allows for quicker response times while increasing safety for firefighters and the public.*

Automated CAD information may be based on a global positioning system (GPS). For example, a telephone call to a dispatch center may generate a screen display of the call's point of origin, along with the response units that are closest in travel time and a travel route for the driver of a fire vehicle. Dispatch centers may communicate instructions orally or with relatively few keystrokes. Location-specific information may be sent to responders orally or through a digital information device (a wireless-enabled mobile computer or data device); such information may include area photographs, building plans, and sources of water. In turn, mobile response personnel can communicate information back to dispatch centers and other locations. Having GPS on response vehicles that are equipped with wireless communications to a dispatch center allows the center to maintain constantly updated information on the availability and location of those units. CAD may display scripts or checklists for dispatchers to deal with calls.

Fire department digital and voice communication systems need to be reliable, especially in extremely harsh conditions. Communication among different organizations (interoperability) is also crucial. A particularly positive development for reliability is the development of network communication systems in which each communication device serves to relay messages for any other device in that network. Such systems avoid the "weak link" problem associated with the limitations or failure of one or a few pieces of equipment in a traditional centralized system. Progress is being made in making emergency communication equipment interoperable. Devices operating on the same radio frequencies appear to be coming available for all emergency services.

## Water distribution systems

Water is the least expensive, most widely used fire extinguishing agent. Firefighters can obtain water from community water systems, stationary or flowing bodies of water, and vehicle tanks. However, they can start fighting fires sooner and more effectively if water is readily available at the fire than if they have to bring it in.

Most local governments make sure that their water delivery services provide an adequate volume of water for fire emergencies. Communities that have full-time firefighters usually meet NFPA Standard 1710, which specifies minimum water requirements of an uninterrupted supply of 400 gallons per minute for thirty minutes and two water handlines collectively delivering 300 gallons per minute. Volunteer-staffed departments rely on a standard from ISO (the Insurance Services Organization), a company that supplies information to the insurance industry. Water supply constitutes 40 percent of the ISO Public Protection Classification rating system, which goes up from 10 to 1. For a community to be rated 8 or above, the minimum water supply must be 250 gallons a minute for two hours.

## Vehicles, equipment, and supplies

Vehicles and equipment for fire suppression vary widely. The most basic unit, which is found in various sizes, is a "triple combination" pumper with a pump, hoses and nozzles, a tank for water or another extinguishing agent, and a limited complement of ladders. Although they were once relatively rare, quints have become more common (e.g., all stations in St. Louis, Missouri, have a quint); in addition to the triple combination elements, quints carry more ground ladders and an aerial device, such as a ladder, platform, ladder with platform, and aerial nozzle. Other basic equipment carried on fire vehicles includes specialized hand tools (axes), specialty equipment (for rescue, ventilation, and salvage), and personal safety equipment (protective clothing, self-contained breathing apparatus, and personal alert safety systems). Basic supplies carried include water, foam, and compressed air.

Departmental vehicle, equipment, and supply requirements vary depending on their services, problems, and organizational and personnel arrangements. For instance, some departments send minipumpers as a first-response unit to structural fires because these vehicles can be operated by two people; this allows for a quicker initial response even though another fire apparatus is required to supply everything needed to deal with such fires. Minipumpers are small versions of the triple combination pumper used for first responses, especially responses to brush, grass, trash, and car fires. Some jurisdictions use water-tank vehicles, grass- or brush-fire vehicles, or single-pumper vehicles to pump water from a water supply to a triple combination pumper. Minipumper and crash-fire rescue units are common specialty units. Crash-fire rescue units at airports carry foam to prevent or extinguish aviation-fuel fires.

Rural-oriented departments are more likely to have tanker and off-road vehicles. More urbanized departments are more likely to use boats and the highest-reaching equipment. Some large-city departments operate helicopters with heating-sensing devices.

## Emergency medical service

If fire departments were named for the type of service call they receive most often, many would be called EMS departments. EMS typically has several different and overlapping aspects: recognition of medical emergencies; response, dispatch, and communication; personnel; medical care; vehicles, equipment, and supplies; and patient transportation. Collectively, these are called prehospital services because EMS care is assumed to result in hospitalization.

Local elected officials decide whether to provide EMS and to what extent. However, once a decision to provide the service is made, local officials have less control over EMS operations than they do over other government services. EMS is fundamentally a medical service; the criteria for operational decisions are medical ones; and the final arbiters of medical decisions are doctors and state regulators, not fire chiefs, managers, or governing bodies. EMS managers pay a great deal of attention to state regulations, which typically cover training and licensing of service providers, physician supervision of services, procedures, and ambulances.

In deciding to provide EMS, local elected officials must be aware that EMS demands are likely to exceed initial estimates. However, cutting EMS levels or budgets, even during times of severe fiscal stress, can be politically unpopular and therefore difficult.

### Recognition of medical emergencies

With doctors' house calls relegated to history, laypersons now diagnose most medical emergencies. Along with many organizations, fire departments facilitate EMS by educating the public to recognize and cope with medical emergencies. Disseminating information about the signs of heart attack and stroke as well as providing training in first aid and CPR exemplify such efforts.

### Response, dispatch, and communications

Response and dispatch, often through 911 systems, involve screening calls to determine the nature of a medical emergency and may include the provision of medical advice prior to the arrival of medically trained personnel. Dispatchers advise against harmful procedures and give detailed directions that may save lives.

EMS communication systems vary. The simplest system involves a call center that can respond to telephone calls, dispatch staffed vehicles, and communicate with vehicles. Additional links include those to hospitals and specialized personnel.

## EMS personnel

Personnel matters especially relevant to EMS include training, staffing levels, and work assignments. As in other emergency service areas, personnel are the most important resource.

*Training*    Although state requirements vary, emergency personnel typically acquire one of four general levels of medical training for public safety operations:

- *First aid or first responder:* Training that is typically required of all public safety personnel.

- *Emergency medical technician–basic (EMT-B):* Training for basic life support (BLS), the minimum level of training required to provide EMS. This level, which requires a minimum of 81 hours and usually more than 100 hours, focuses on maintaining breathing, administering CPR, and treating trauma.

- *Emergency medical technician–intermediate (EMT-I):* Training that includes some medical techniques in the category of advanced life support (ALS)—for example, intravenous (IV) therapy and initial cardiac drug therapy.

- *Emergency medical technician–paramedic (EMT-P):* Training for ALS. The EMT-P qualification requires 800 hours or more of training, which covers many types of medical difficulties and involves more invasive medical practices, such as drug administration.

The number of personnel trained at each level determines the kind and amount of medical response available at each level.

*Staffing levels and work assignments*    The number of EMTs needed to staff an EMS operation depends on the number of response vehicles, the actual or anticipated number of calls, and the variety of work assignments given to EMTs. When EMTs also have fire suppression responsibilities, a department needs more of them to maintain a specific EMS response capability. Although staff used exclusively as EMTs may be less costly than people trained to be both firefighters *and* EMTs, this option lessens the integration of the EMS mission into the fire department's mission and of the EMTs themselves into the fire department. It also limits EMTs' career options.

## Medical care

Physicians supervise EMS operations, and paramedics and EMT-I's work under a physician's medical license. Emergency aspects of situations dictate the kind of medical care that EMTs provide. Medical care starts with an assessment of a situation. The most obvious concern is the victim's condition. However, rescue considerations may complicate treatment. Generally, EMTs operate using the maxim, "First, do no harm." In medical emergencies, a decision must be made very quickly to act or to transport a patient to more qualified medical personnel and locations with more treatment options.

BLS measures are noninvasive, essentially done on the surface of the patient's body. These measures typically include keeping airways open for breathing, assisting breathing, stopping bleeding, treating shock, immobilizing broken bones, moving patients, and assisting in childbirth. ALS measures include invasive procedures, such as using specialized airways, defibrillation, IV therapy, drugs, and other medications. These measures involve the practice of medicine on the street, so to speak, but the medicine is delivered by highly trained technicians who practice on the street only because that is where their patients need assistance.

Although supervising physicians bear formal responsibility for the quality of medical care, fire departments should evaluate their medical responses for the sake of quality assurance and improvement. The logic of evaluation and iterative incident preplanning applies to all fire department services and not just to their response to fires.

### Vehicles, equipment, and supplies

EMS vehicles, equipment, and supplies vary according to the EMS service strategies. Fire departments use a variety of vehicles, both fire apparatus and specialized vehicles (e.g., on-road, off-road, boats, aircraft), to transport EMS personnel, equipment, and supplies. Fire apparatus can respond to more scenes—and to some scenes more rapidly—than can specialized EMS vehicles because of their greater numbers and locations; however, they usually carry less medical equipment than ambulances and do not transport patients. Specialized EMS vehicles carry more equipment, and some may be used to transport patients, but they may be fewer in number and may respond less rapidly than fire apparatus.

EMS equipment and supplies are similar to those found at medical facilities except that some equipment is specialized to transmit data to doctors, deal with moving patients, take up less space, or deal with field conditions. Stretchers and backboards facilitate moving injured patients safely; IV fluid warmers heat fluids to be infused into patients.

### Patient transportation

If EMS vehicles do not transport patients in emergency situations, some sort of arrangement with one or more emergency ambulance services is necessary. If EMS does include emergency ambulance service, the question becomes whether to provide nonemergency ambulance service between hospitals, nursing homes, and residences and how much to charge. Fees can provide supplemental revenue. When ambulances transport nonemergency patients, fire departments may need more ambulances and personnel to maintain the same level of emergency response capability.

### Hazardous materials, rescue, and emergency management

Fire departments often respond to HAZMAT and rescue incidents and other emergency situations with fire protection and EMS personnel and vehicles. However, these incidents may raise concerns with regard to information and personnel, and may perhaps require specialized vehicles, equipment, and supplies. Decision makers must consider whether they want to train and equip the fire department to respond to the full range of possible emergencies.

### Specialized information

Fire departments have to gather and process information ranging from the general to the specific in order to prepare for likely emergencies, such as dealing with poisonous gases, extricating people from wrecked automobiles, and evacuating people. More specialized information is needed to deal with emergencies that might have wider-ranging consequences (e.g., situations involving unusual chemicals, subterranean caves, mudslides, avalanches, or a nuclear power plant). Because geography plays a leading role in determining likely or important emergencies, local governments can benefit from working intergovernmentally to gather and share specialized information.

Certain risks, especially transported hazardous materials, can easily be overlooked, so fire departments should be creative in gathering information to protect their populations and personnel. Beyond making use of such sources as intergovernmental organizations, fire departments might create a list of places to find more information, take advantage of the efforts of larger jusrisdictions, and simply remain observant. For example, U.S. Department of Transportation regulations for railroads and trucking firms include a system of placards for identifying hazardous materials being transported; they also require that records be kept so that those shipments can be identified when they pass through a locality. Through a local government organization, the fire department could gather information from larger local governments looking for hazardous shipments at local truck stops and destinations along the same transportation routes. It could also develop a list of appropriate twenty-four-hour emergency telephone numbers for railroads and trucking firms known to transport hazardous materials.

## Specialized personnel issues

Specialized knowledge and skills are needed to respond to some emergencies, such as rescue operations conducted with ropes. When a department's leadership decides that the department will respond in such situations, someone has to gather the requisite information and someone has to have or develop the requisite skills. Acquiring skilled personnel, training existing personnel in new skills, and maintaining personnel readiness—especially over extended periods of time when there are few or no calls for service—can be challenging. Primarily, such readiness requires regular training and exercises—particularly serious, meaningful, extensive, and realistic exercises that require displays of skills.

## Specialized vehicles, equipment, and supplies

The vehicles, equipment, and supplies that are used in a particular emergency situation are most often dictated by the type of emergency situation at hand.

*Hazardous materials*   HAZMAT calls are answered with fire apparatus in many cases. Common specialized vehicles for HAZMAT incidents include trucks and trailers to carry equipment, including flatbed trailers to carry earthmoving equipment. Every emergency response vehicle should be equipped with the U.S. Department of Transportation Chart 12 (transportation placard guide for hazardous materials) and the Emergency Reponse Guide from the department's Pipeline and Hazardous Materials Safety Administration.

General equipment for dealing with hazardous materials includes binoculars for viewing labels and placards at a safe distance; personal protection gear (garments, goggles, and breathing apparatus); lighting; and earthmoving equipment (usually hand shovels) for damming or channeling hazardous liquids. Specialized equipment includes patching and pumping devices; various kinds of decontamination equipment ranging from a basic kit composed of a five-gallon bucket, sponge, and liquid soap to an enclosed shower system to a water purification system; and a chemical information database. HAZMAT supplies include decontamination washes, absorbent and packaging materials, and disposable personal protective gear.

*Rescue*   For rescue work, fire apparatus or EMS vehicles may be used. Specialized vehicles include trucks to carry equipment and off-road vehicles to transport people, equipment, and supplies. Geography tends to determine the less common off-road vehicles (e.g., snowmobiles, motorcycles, amphibious vehicles, aircraft, and boats). Common rescue equipment includes ropes, winches, lighting, and air compressors and hydraulic tools for cutting and spreading metal. Specialized equipment includes pneumatic shoring and support struts for trench entry, air supply systems, and swift-water rescue equipment. Supplies for rescue work include food, water, and medical treatments appropriate to the likely problem (e.g., trauma, breathing, dehydration, frostbite, and sunburn).

*Emergency management*   For emergency management, fire departments use fire apparatus and whatever other vehicles they have. Equipment includes large-scale maps, pumps, warning systems, communication systems, remote video cameras, listening devices, and barricades to manage traffic. Specialized equipment includes various chemical, biological, and radiological sensing devices. Common supplies include food and water. Specialized supplies include various biological agents (e.g., antidotes for exposure to certain diseases or chemicals).

## Policy issues

Initially, firefighters were volunteers who formed a social organization at the center of community life to suppress fires. Changing conditions and circumstances now place more demands on fire departments, and most (although not all) departments have added fire prevention, EMS, hazardous materials, rescue, and emergency management services to the task of fire suppression. Entailed in any decisions about new fire department services are such related policy issues as how to organize and staff existing and new services, how to cooperate with neighboring jurisdictions, and how to ensure that sufficient personnel are available and trained to meet the demand for new services.

### Organizing for service provision and delivery

Local communities decide how to organize in order to secure funding or resources to provide and deliver services. Fire department services can be provided and delivered through general-purpose local governments, fire protection district governments, nonprofit fire departments, private companies, and individual self-reliance (self-service). The primary sources of funding are taxation for government provision; donations, including labor, for nonprofit provision; and fees for private provision. Additionally, governments and nonprofit organizations fund fire services with grants and fees. Local governments may find, however, that they are the only providers interested in or capable of funding new or expanded fire department services.

Service delivery in many cases is handled by the same organization that provides the service, but some local governments that provide the service choose to fund other organizations, either fully or partially, to deliver the services. For example, many local governments provide funding for volunteer fire departments. The major reason that some local governments choose not to deliver services they fund is that other organizations

---

**Private sector fire protection in Scottsdale, Arizona**

Rural/Metro Corporation in Scottsdale, Arizona (pop. 226,013), pioneered private sector fire protection services in 1951. Private companies, following the example of Rural/Metro, use innovative personnel practices, manufacture some of their own equipment, and take advantage of technological advances. Historically, private ambulance firms delivered emergency medical services, but many withdrew from the market because of the cost of complying with increased governmental regulations.

---

**Interlocal cooperation in Illinois**

The Flossmoor Volunteer Fire Department in Flossmore, Illinois (pop. 9,390), shares a backup ambulance with the village fire departments in Hazel Crest (pop. 14,415) and Homewood (pop. 18,917), a joint dispatch center with those two villages and the village of Glenwood (pop. 8,663), a public education van with Hazel Crest, and a communications van with the village of Matteson (pop. 15,675).

---

can deliver those services at less cost. In addition, other organizations may have greater access to funding, more limited liability exposure, or an operational scale advantage (i.e., adding to an existing operation tends to cost less than starting a new one, and larger operations have cost advantages for capital items). Nonprofit organizations, for example, are likely to have much lower labor costs and may have operational scale advantages. Private companies may also have scale advantages, but even without those advantages, some of them have been able to operate fire department services at lower costs than equivalent-size local governments operations would entail.

### Intergovernmental relations

Intergovernmental cooperation offers opportunities to improve services without increasing expenditures. The most widely used method is the mutual aid pact, through which neighboring fire departments pledge assistance to one another in emergency responses and all parties increase their capacity without significant new expenditures. Other areas of interlocal cooperation are joint training facilities and exercises, joint dispatch facilities, joint purchasing, and information sharing.

Cooperative agreements are now covering wider areas as fire departments move further into emergency management. Natural disasters and potential terrorist attacks have encouraged the formation of statewide pacts and the creation of the federal National Response Plan, which is designed to integrate domestic responses into emergency incidents. Some departments have sent personnel hundreds of miles to participate in emergency responses.

The federal and state governments affect local fire departments through their regulations and assistance. Regulations address such things as working hours, occupational safety, the handling of and reporting on hazardous materials (including items contaminated by infectious diseases), radio frequencies, and required vehicle lighting. Assistance can take the form of funding, emergency responses, training, investigation, and information.

## Personnel policies

Successful organizations require effective personnel policies. This principle applies to an even greater degree in a fire department because personnel affect life safety. Personnel policies should ensure that recruitment, appointment, dismissal, probation, and grievance procedures for all personnel are appropriate. Such policies can also ensure that volunteer firefighters are screened and selected on the basis of task-related qualifications and not on social or political criteria, and that they are given adequate training to deal with the increased service demands of today's fire departments.

*Recruitment*    Programs that increase community awareness of and support for a volunteer department enhance volunteer recruitment. Researchers agree that the primary motivations for voluntary service are

- A sense of duty—to provide service and to help others
- An opportunity to gain experience and learn new skills
- Social satisfaction from interacting with other volunteers
- Community commitment.

Therefore, recruitment efforts should highlight the opportunities to fulfill such needs through the volunteer fire service.

In addition to psychological motivations, other incentives may be needed to ensure the sustained service of volunteers. Incentive programs should emphasize service and career potential rather than monetary gain, although monetary compensation, including retirement benefits, is a strong incentive. Other incentives include

- Training
- Formal awards and recognition
- Insurance coverage, especially while on duty
- Letters of recommendation for future employment
- Reimbursement for out-of-pocket expenses
- Structured advancement opportunities for more responsibilities
- Active participation in department planning and goal setting.

---

### Senior fire volunteer program in San Marcos, California

Senior citizens aged 55 and older who volunteer for the San Marcos, California (pop. 73,487), fire department perform a range of services, allowing firefighters to focus on responding to emergencies. Most seniors work about ten hours a week and share responsibility for being available twenty-four hours a day to respond to emergencies. During a fire, these volunteers set up shelter, retrieve equipment, provide food and drink, and refill oxygen tanks for firefighters' breathing apparatus. The city spends about $100 per volunteer per year for uniforms and supplies. Seniors who are accepted spend one week in a mini training academy, with classes taught by firefighters and managers.

*Training*   As noted previously, one problem with volunteer firefighters is the difficulty in getting them to take the necessary training. However, appropriate training is essential to ensure the safety of the volunteers and the successful performance of their responsibilities, and therefore it must be mandatory. Personnel policies should establish clear guidelines for training and specify the consequences for failing to adhere to training requirements.

## Legally independent departments and local governments

Some fire departments operate legally and independently as nonprofit organizations or special-district governments with few ties to the municipal or county governments. In such cases, a municipality or county cannot safely assume that the department will be able to meet all of the community's emergency service needs. Municipalities and counties should ascertain what emergency services are provided by the department and whether those services are adequate. They can then choose to supply the missing services, offer assistance, or supplant the inadequate independent department. Even where relatively independent fire departments are technically under the authority of a general-purpose local government, the local government policy makers should concern themselves with fire department services as if the department were legally independent, examine the extent and adequacy of services provided, and act if changes are warranted.

> *A municipality or county may be able to work cooperatively with an independent fire department so long as it recognizes the department's legal independence as a precursor to effective cooperation.*

The legal independence of a fire department means that a general-purpose local government cannot directly exercise control over it. Nevertheless, a municipality or county may be able to work cooperatively with an independent fire department so long as it recognizes the department's legal independence as a precursor to effective cooperation. A positive working relationship can improve the capacity of the department to serve the public and enable it to offer a wider array of emergency services. Independent volunteer departments can provide services at a relatively low cost, while general-purpose local governments usually have greater access to funding, including borrowing, and have employees who can augment the volunteer department's services. In addition, local governments can control traffic at and around emergency situations, freely share relevant information (e.g., road closures), and involve the independent fire departments in land development decision making. In most cases, local governments also have greater regulatory authority (such as over land use, traffic, etc.). In some states, only general-purpose local governments can access workmen's compensation programs.

Local governments can also provide a variety of services to an independent department, with or without compensation, that the department would otherwise have to produce for itself. Administrative services—for example, capital budgeting, annual budgeting, purchasing procedures, centralized purchasing, computer dispatching, recordkeeping, grants planning and administration, and personnel management—loom large in this regard, but other services such as maintenance could also be useful. General-purpose local governments can also recognize the service of volunteers to their communities.

A volunteer department that selects its own chief and perpetuates itself by choosing new members as the old ones leave may develop into a closed organization that does not cooperate with the general-purpose local government. It also may not concern itself beyond fire suppression; may not give sufficient attention to training; and may resist cooperation with local governments in code enforcement, prevention, and the provision of other services. Engaging in conflict with legally independent departments would likely produce negative political and financial consequences, and local residents would probably not be well served in such situations. Therefore, cooperation appears to be the best way to secure an integrated service delivery relationship with a legally independent department.

## Management issues

Fire department managers face a variety of management issues that vitally affect the quality of service. Among other things, these include personnel issues and concerns, such as staffing and labor relations; management styles and leadership; innovation and change; and master planning.

### Personnel issues and concerns

Personnel issues in the fire department are wide-ranging and can, in some instances, be especially sensitive.

*Staffing*   Many factors affect fire department personnel choices. Lower costs and greater community involvement make the use of volunteers desirable. However, with increased service demands requiring more effort devoted to prevention, training, and administrative tasks, as well as the fact that volunteers are less available than other fire department personnel to deal with the increase in calls, departments are finding that exclusive reliance on volunteers is more difficult.

Moreover, the number of volunteers in fire departments has decreased as people have become more transient, less interested in fire departments as social institutions, and more often employed outside their community of residence. Options available to a department with a declining number of volunteers include increasing recruitment efforts, increasing benefits to volunteers, putting more reliance on paid personnel, decreasing services, and contracting with other organizations.

*Scheduling*   Scheduling is an issue for fire departments because they always must be ready to respond at any hour of any day. The difficulty of scheduling for 168 hours a week is compounded by minimum staffing requirements, training time, different personnel types, and specialized work assignments. Also, fire departments with full-time firefighters often confront questions relating to the length of shifts. Some departments use shifts based on twenty-four-hour periods; others use shifts from eight to fourteen hours in length. The shorter shifts promise greater productivity, but many employees prefer the longer shifts, which leave them with more free time and greater opportunities for part-time employment.

*Labor relations*   Fire department personnel spend many hours in each other's company and face danger together, which bonds them into a close-knit group. Together, they often

**Working together in Mesa, Arizona**

The Mesa, Arizona (pop. 442,780), fire department is noted for its Relationship-by-Objectives program, which aims to foster good working relationships between management and labor in that department. Labor and management personnel meet and discuss problems together, and work toward solutions that take into account the varying perspectives involved. The openness of communication and the positive orientation appeal to both sides.

resist change and may collectively resist management directives. Perhaps as a result, full-time fire department personnel have become the most highly unionized and militant local government employees. This fact has serious implications for matters involving union recognition, collective bargaining, and contract implementation, which are discussed in Chapter 5.

In many places, fire department managers—and sometimes even the fire chief—are union members. Departmental cohesiveness favors this arrangement, but the need for managers to participate in formal labor relations and collective bargaining makes union membership for managers undesirable.

As cohesive groups, fire department personnel often act forcefully in local politics, especially when fire department matters are at issue. People become emotional over public safety issues in any case, and a unified fire department group can mobilize political forces in a fashion matched only by law enforcement groups. Local managers have learned that technical decisions may become political issues.

*Management development* Fire departments should encourage the development of increasingly sophisticated management abilities by designating appropriate positions as management positions, selecting and promoting officers to these positions on the basis of managerial ability and education, and providing those officers with continuing management education and training. Increasingly, modern fire department managers (chief, captain, and lieutenant) earn public administration degrees to complement line fire service experience. Fire department managers can also develop their managerial capacity by aggressively seeking out information on trends, issues, and technologies that relate to the fire service and by thinking through how newly acquired information can be applied within their departments.

## Dual management styles and leadership

Choosing a fire chief is an especially important decision. Managers in the fire department have to be leaders who have the respect and trust of those they must send into hazardous situations. They increase their capacity for leadership by using dual management styles.

In emergency situations, fire department managers command personnel with the expectation of complete and willing compliance: they direct personnel to do what needs to be done. Therefore, they must prove worthy of command by demonstrating good judgment. In nonemergency situations, however, they must use a much more participative management approach, seeking and listening to opinions from subordinates, answering questions, and explaining management decisions. This style serves various purposes: managers gain information and insights from subordinates and clear up potentially dangerous misunderstandings. Participative practices also help develop subordinate personnel by exposing them to managers' concerns and thought processes.

Although the two styles differ, they both contribute to managers' ability to exercise leadership. Command management in emergency situations becomes habitual for managers and their subordinates through repetition in training and real emergencies. Participative management enables managers to display their knowledge and reasoning ability.

## Innovation and change

Fire departments have a proud history and strong public support, both of which can lessen their inclination to innovate. Yet in a world of constant change, innovation is a key to improving service quality. Managing change requires being aware of the advantages and costs of change, choosing from among change alternatives, seeking the active cooperation of those who will be implementing change, and supervising change. Any significant change may create difficulties that need to be overcome.

*Technology*   At one time, fire personnel resisted horse-drawn and motorized fire engines, and even windshields, but today they are generally receptive to new technology. Any resistance to technological advances now comes primarily from local officials who are reluctant to spend money on equipment. Fire department managers must demonstrate that new technology will improve service.

*Personnel*   Fire departments may add new kinds of personnel to handle new tasks, such as EMS and fire prevention, or may supplement existing personnel with another personnel type. Such changes typically evoke much stronger reactions than expected. Fire department personnel also tend to resist organizational innovations, such as using alternative service providers, contracting for services with other entities, combining police and fire services into public safety departments, partially or completely consolidating fire protection services among adjacent or overlapping jurisdictions, and creating specialized organizational subdivisions. Managers need to pay close attention to negative reactions in order to avoid adverse impacts on performance. To minimize the potential for resistance when making personnel changes, policy makers and managers should explain the situation to their current personnel in a participatory fashion.

*Interdepartmental cooperation*   An especially difficult area of change is interdepartment cooperation. Historically, fire departments have acted relatively independently, even when part of a local government. Now, even if independent, their service concerns overlap with those of local government departments. Fire departments need to work with law enforcement officials on emergency management operations; with planning departments on development decisions; with code development and inspection departments on prevention efforts; with public works departments on the use of heavy equipment; and with relevant central departments on legal, personnel, and financial matters.

*Volunteer departments*   Despite a general decline in the number of volunteers since the 1980s, the quality of volunteer fire departments over the years and the economies they afford strongly favor their continuation. Still, policy makers for volunteer departments should consider changes, such as a more broadly defined mission. Because volunteer departments historically saw their role exclusively as fighting fires, some departments today neglect fire prevention, inspections, and code enforcement. Some critics suggest that pay on a per-call basis makes firefighting more attractive than fire prevention. To take on a broader view of their mission, then, volunteer departments should work on all aspects of fire safety and consider adding other services. Further changes to consider would be increased attention to personnel concerns, such as training in these other areas, and stronger relations with general-purpose local governments.

## Master planning

Master planning for fire department services means systematically deciding about service provision, related costs, and levels of risk. These decisions should be made explicitly with public involvement because they involve public safety. In addition to public involvement, master planning involves information analysis, a study of alternatives, and decision making. Final approval of fire department master plans rests with the governing body. Implementation of master plans requires attention to details. Fire departments should also review and revise their master plans periodically to ensure that the plans continue to meet public needs.

The master plan should not rely on the community's ISO rating. Some fire departments point to those ratings as tangible measurements of fire department quality in order to justify spending more money. However, as the ISO itself strongly asserts in its "Public Protection Classification" brochure:

> Comments, surveys and criteria are intended only for use in determining a property insurance classification. They are not intended for purposes of life safety or property loss prevention.

## The manager's role

With the expanding role of today's fire departments into the range of emergency services, managers face a number of challenges:

- Ensuring adequate attention to prevention work
- Fostering interdepartmental, intergovernmental, and interorganizational cooperation
- Maintaining readiness
- Addressing personnel issues (e.g., staffing, training, and labor relations)
- Avoiding unnecessary politicization of issues
- Sustaining the focus on planning and evaluation for incidents
- Encouraging leadership/management development.

In dealing with these challenges, managers can probably work most productively with fire departments by facilitating decisions about services (choices, levels, quality, and resource allocation), including fire department personnel in the policy process, and assisting with intergovernmental and interdepartmental relations. First, managers should make sure that questions concerning whether to start or stop a service, whether to increase or decrease service levels, whether service quality is adequate, and how much resources to devote are being seriously addressed. For service quality, prevention should be specifically examined. Second, managers should strive to ensure that fire department concerns and personnel are routinely addressed in their governments' policy processes. Too often, fire departments are figuratively and literally distant from policy processes. Finally, managers can assist fire departments in navigating intergovernmental and interdepartmental relations from their central government position.

---

**Questions to ask if you manage fire and other emergency services in a small community**

Are our emergency services done as well as we can afford and desire?

Should we add more service areas?

Can we work with other jurisdictions or organizations to upgrade our emergency services?

Are we current with the National Incident Management System (NIMS)?

Are we doing sufficient prevention work?

---

**Competencies for managers in the field of fire and other emergency services**

Knowledge of service areas for prevention and response: fire protection, EMS, hazardous materials and processes, rescue, and emergency management

Knowledge of management techniques (e.g., planning and evaluation)

Skill in performing specific service activities in the service areas

Leadership

---

## Endnotes

1   Steven C. Carter and Lyle J. Sumek, "Leadership Strategies for the Political Process," in *Managing Fire and Rescue Services*, ed. Dennis Compton and John Granito (Washington, D.C.: ICMA, 2002), 70.

# 15

# Service Delivery Alternatives

## Gordon P. Whitaker

Decisions to provide a public service include two steps: (1) choosing which outcomes government officials want to provide to the public and (2) choosing how to produce those outcomes. The first step articulates the public purpose or objective for government action—the "whereas" section of an ordinance. What public benefit is the government trying to create? The second step tells what the government intends to do to achieve that objective—the "therefore" section. What tool or technique does the government plan to use to produce the desired outcome? Which service delivery alternative will the government use?

## Alternative tools for delivering services

Local governments use a variety of service delivery alternatives to accomplish public objectives. Among the most important alternatives are

- Production of services
- Provision of incentives and sanctions to shape private behavior
- Purchase of services
- Grants of money or in-kind subsidies for others' service delivery
- Franchises for service delivery
- Partnerships with other governments or private organizations for services.[1]

The first two alternatives—government production of services directly and government incentives and sanctions to encourage the private production of public services—have been addressed in other chapters of this book. These are the tools that local governments have traditionally used to deliver most services. During the last decades of the twentieth century, however, the other four alternatives—service purchases, grants, franchises, and partnerships—came to be used with increasing frequency. This chapter focuses on these less traditional tools for service delivery.

### Purchasing services

Local governments have always purchased land, supplies, and equipment to produce services in-house. The focus of this chapter is not on government procurement to support government production of services; rather, it is on government's purchase of services that others deliver to the public—for example, a county paying another local government to provide job training for the county's residents, a city contracting with private companies to tow illegally parked cars from its streets, or a local government buying shelter services for homeless people from a nonprofit organization.

Governments typically purchase services in order to save money or to obtain higher quality than would be possible with in-house production. When there is an active market for the service and a variety of potential vendors (as is the case with vehicle towing and day care services, for example), competition among producers for a government purchase contract can drive costs down and encourage better service. Cost savings can also be passed on to a government purchaser when a producer can take advantage of economies of scale; producing more allows the producer to spread the fixed costs of capital and expertise over a larger number of units of service and thereby reduce per unit costs. The costs of a large commercial solid-waste packer truck, for example, are largely the same whether the truck empties a few collection boxes a day or operates at full capacity. When small local governments must invest in expensive equipment or staff expertise that they cannot use to capacity, their fixed cost per unit of service is unnecessarily high.

Local governments also purchase services to have greater flexibility in adding or discontinuing the service. If producing a service requires large capital investments or specialized personnel, purchasing the service allows the government to provide it without making those capital or staffing commitments.

> *When there is an active market for the service and a variety of potential vendors, competition among producers for a government purchase contract can drive costs down and encourage better service.*

At the same time, however, government officials often face more challenges in purchasing services than in buying materials and equipment. One common challenge is the lack of a competitive market for many public services, especially in rural or remote locations. Another is that government officials may find it difficult to measure the quality of the services being delivered (and even the quantity for many public services). Purchasing services places more control over service delivery with the vendor.

Some local governments buy services from other local governments. Instead of setting up their own bus service, for example, some municipalities contract with another local government to provide bus service within their jurisdictions. An ICMA survey of local government alternative service arrangements across the United States provides an overview of these practices in 2002.[2] As Table 15–1 shows, local governments contract with other governments for a wide range of services. Because some of these services (e.g., health care and transit services) have high operating costs for specialized personnel or high entry costs for capital goods regardless of the number of people served, contracting with another local government enables the government that is purchasing the service to obtain that service at lower cost than it would incur by producing the service in-house. Another sort of service that governments buy from other local governments—for example, jails—involves the use of government's coercive powers.

**Table 15-1  Public services most commonly purchased from other local governments in 2002**

| Service | No. of survey respondents reporting that they provide the service | Percentage of local governments purchasing the service from another local government |
|---|---|---|
| Job training programs | 261 | 48 |
| Mental health/retardation programs/facilities | 201 | 45 |
| Public health programs | 350 | 45 |
| Hospital operations/management | 67 | 43 |
| Alcohol and drug treatment programs | 256 | 38 |
| Welfare programs | 219 | 38 |
| Child welfare programs | 248 | 38 |
| Bus/transit operations/maintenance | 258 | 35 |
| Prisons/jails | 457 | 32 |
| Paratransit operations/maintenance | 240 | 32 |

Source: Mildred Warner and Amir Hefetz, "Pragmatism over Politics: Alternative Service Delivery in Local Government, 1992-2002," in *The Municipal Year Book 2004* (Washington, D.C.: ICMA, 2004), Table 2/3.

Private companies compete for local government service contracts in a number of fields. As Table 15–2 shows, purchases from for-profit companies are generally for services for which there are also private customers—for example, vehicle towing and storage, solid-waste collection, utilities, and tree trimming. These also tend to be "packagable" services that can be bought and sold in easily measured units. For these reasons, there are more likely to be active markets and competition among potential vendors and/or available "benchmark" prices for these services than for many of the services that local governments buy from other governments.

Local governments also purchase services from nonprofit organizations; most commonly these would include cultural, health, and human services (see Table 15–3 on page 373). Many of the services that governments buy from nonprofits do not attract competition from businesses because there is too little margin for profit. In fact, nonprofits often rely on volunteer labor and use private donations to subsidize the services that governments buy. While some nonprofits are large-scale producers (e.g., hospitals), most are small producers with strong ties to the local community they serve and to a pool of donors and volunteers. Gifts of money and time mean that nonprofits are often able to offer such services as homeless shelters, day care facilities, job training programs, substance abuse treatment, and cultural/arts programs at prices below those that for-profit businesses would need to charge to cover their production costs.

**Table 15-2  Public services most commonly purchased from for-profit companies in 2002**

| Service | No. of survey respondents reporting that they provide the service | Percentage of local governments purchasing the service from for-profit companies |
|---|---|---|
| Vehicle towing and storage | 473 | 80 |
| Commercial solid-waste collection | 408 | 43 |
| Gas utility operations/management | 113 | 43 |
| Residential solid-waste collection | 620 | 39 |
| Tree trimming/planting | 904 | 38 |
| Disposal of hazardous materials | 399 | 38 |
| Solid-waste disposal | 504 | 38 |
| Day care facilities | 124 | 38 |
| Street repair | 971 | 35 |
| Disposal of sludge | 559 | 31 |

Source: Mildred Warner and Amir Hefetz, "Pragmatism over Politics: Alternative Service Delivery in Local Government, 1992–2002," in *The Municipal Year Book 2004* (Washington, D.C.: ICMA, 2004), Table 2/3.

Note: Services purchased to support governmental service production were eliminated from this list: legal services (56%), emergency vehicle maintenance (40%), heavy equipment maintenance (37%), and other vehicle maintenance (36%).

## Grants to subsidize services

Local governments provide grants to help pay for public service programs that nonprofit organizations plan and carry out. Grants are typically less specific than purchase contracts about the activities that the producer is going to conduct or the amount of service that it will produce; instead, grants generally support programs with more broadly defined outcomes or impacts.[3] For example, rather than buying meals for fifty clients per day, a government may make a grant to support a program that feeds the elderly but does not specify exactly how many meals it will serve. In awarding a grant to a nonprofit, a local government expects the public service mission and values of the nonprofit to lead its leaders to apply the funds toward the intended public purpose.

The contrast with purchases is important: "POS [purchase of service] contracting is more coercive than grants, since service contracts hold the contractor to account for serving the government's objectives, whereas grants are far more responsive to the recipients' objectives."[4] In addition to providing grants of money, many local governments also subsidize nonprofits' production of public services by providing staff assistance, office space, and/or equipment to the organization producing the service.

**Table 15-3  Public services most commonly purchased from nonprofit organizations in 2002**

| Service | No. of survey respondents reporting that they provide the service | Percentage of local governments purchasing the service from nonprofit organizations |
|---|---|---|
| Homeless shelters | 124 | 15 |
| Cultural and arts programs | 417 | 13 |
| Museum operations | 290 | 12 |
| Alcohol and drug treatment programs | 256 | 12 |
| Day care facilities | 124 | 11 |
| Mental health/retardation programs/facilities | 201 | 10 |
| Child welfare programs | 248 | 10 |
| Programs for the elderly | 614 | 8 |
| Paratransit operations/maintenance | 240 | 7 |
| Job training programs | 261 | 7 |

Source: Mildred Warner and Amir Hefetz, "Pragmatism over Politics: Alternative Service Delivery in Local Government, 1992-2002," in *The Municipal Year Book 2004* (Washington, D.C.: ICMA, 2004), Table 2/3.

According to ICMA's 2002 survey of alternative service delivery choices, local governments are most likely to provide grants to programs for special populations (the ill, the homeless, the elderly, children) and for cultural enrichment (Table 15–4). Although the survey did not ask about economic development activities, local governments also often subsidize chambers of commerce and other nonprofits to support economic development in their communities. For example, a North Carolina study found that 18 percent of the nonprofits receiving grant funding from cities and 8 percent of those funded by counties produce economic development services.[5]

*In awarding a grant to a nonprofit, a local government expects the public service mission and values of the nonprofit to lead its leaders to apply the funds toward the intended public purpose.*

The North Carolina data also suggest that local government grants to nonprofits may be considerably more common than the ICMA data show. For example, the North Carolina study found that 79 percent of the cities and 95 percent of the counties reported budgeting funds for grants to nonprofits, and that 63 percent of both cities and counties reported providing in-kind support to nonprofits.[6]

**Table 15-4  Public services most commonly subsidized by local governments in 2002**

| Service | No. of survey respondents reporting that they provide the service | Percentage of local governments subsidizing the service |
|---|---|---|
| Homeless shelters | 124 | 15 |
| Cultural and arts programs | 417 | 13 |
| Museum operations | 290 | 12 |
| Alcohol and drug treatment programs | 256 | 12 |
| Day care facilities | 124 | 11 |
| Mental health/retardation programs/facilities | 201 | 10 |
| Child welfare programs | 248 | 10 |
| Programs for the elderly | 614 | 8 |
| Paratransit operations/maintenance | 240 | 7 |
| Job training programs | 261 | 7 |

Source: Mildred Warner and Amir Hefetz, "Pragmatism over Politics: Alternative Service Delivery in Local Government, 1992-2002," in *The Municipal Year Book 2004* (Washington, D.C.: ICMA, 2004), Table 2/4.

## Franchises for service delivery

Some local governments arrange for public services by granting franchises that allow businesses special access to sell their services within the jurisdiction. Franchise agreements often include permission for the business to use public property or rights-of-way. Franchises also usually restrict competition from other potential vendors of the service and regulate service quality, set charges to customers, or establish other conditions of service delivery in the public interest. In return for access to customers in their jurisdiction, local governments typically receive fees from the businesses they franchise. Unlike service purchases or grants, franchises thus produce revenue for local governments rather than entailing government expenditures.

Local governments typically use franchises to provide services that users can pay for directly—for example, solid-waste collection and disposal, utilities, or similar services that are easily packaged and can be withheld from those who do not pay (Table 15–5). In some cases, such as solid-waste collection, local governments may require residents or businesses to purchase the service. In other cases, such as airports or golf courses, only those customers who choose to use the service pay for it. Typically, however, the franchise agreement limits rates that the business can charge for the service. This is to ensure that the service is available at a price that is widely affordable, government officials having determined a public interest in the service being provided to the community.[7]

**Table 15-5   Public services most often delivered under local government franchise in 2002**

| Service | No. of survey respondents reporting that they provide the service | Percentage of local governments franchising the service |
|---|---|---|
| Commercial solid-waste collection | 408 | 20 |
| Gas utility operations/management | 113 | 20 |
| Residential solid-waste collection | 620 | 16 |
| Electric utility operations/management | 172 | 11 |
| Solid-waste disposal | 504 | 10 |
| Vehicle towing and storage | 473 | 6 |
| Airport operations | 302 | 4 |
| Disposal of hazardous materials | 399 | 4 |
| Recreation facilities operations/maintenance | 940 | 3 |
| Homeless shelters | 124 | 3 |

Source: Mildred Warner and Amir Hefetz, "Pragmatism over Politics: Alternative Service Delivery in Local Government, 1992-2002," in *The Municipal Year Book 2004* (Washington, D.C.: ICMA, 2004), Table 2/4.

## Partnering for services

In partnering for services, local governments cooperate with for-profit businesses, non-profit organizations, or other governments to plan services, coordinate services with or through other organizations, or carry out programs jointly. For example, a local government may work with other entities to develop a common plan for economic development. If partnering is limited to planning, each of the partners independently chooses whether and how to implement its part of the plan. Typical ways in which local governments coordinate service delivery are mutual aid agreements among police departments and shared dispatchers for city and volunteer fire departments and rescue squads. Joint programs in which the partners work together may include carrying out a community festival or implementing an economic development plan. Several local governments may partner even with each other to set up a special authority to operate an airport, provide public utility services, or undertake other regional ventures.

In a 2003 ICMA survey on reinventing government, 71% of responding municipalities indicated that they had recommended funding for partnering with businesses or nonprofits during the preceding five years. Moreover, two-thirds of those recommendations for partnering were always funded, and two-thirds of those funded were always implemented, according to the survey.[8] And counties may partner more than cities.

## Public-private partnership in Santa Clarita, California

Through partnering, Santa Clarita, California (pop. 168,353), was able to build a needed highway and new school and also develop a business park with the potential for 10,000 new jobs.

In 2000, a small group of local leaders (including the city manager, the high school superintendent, and the business park developer) undertook what would become a multimillion-dollar, multiyear public works project enlisting ninety entities, including private industry, government, utilities, and nonprofits. The project had three parts:

1. Golden Valley Road, a three-mile-long roadway to provide access to the planned business park and school

2. Golden Valley High School, a brand-new facility with a capacity for 2,600 students

3. Centre Pointe, the east side's first major business park, which would create 10,000 new jobs.

The construction schedule was dictated by the school district's need for the new school, which would be inaccessible without the roadway. Thus, to take advantage of economies of scale and to eliminate conflicts, the two projects were combined.

An interim funding agreement between the city and the school district allowed the plans to progress. Once the agreement was finalized but before construction started, a "partnership workshop" was held with all ninety stakeholders. Following that, thirty-four members of the project team (representatives of the three major projects and their contractors) met to identify goals, discuss issues that needed resolution, and develop a code of ethics. This partnership became the cornerstone for problem solving and teamwork in the ensuing months.

April 2002 saw the grand opening of Golden Valley Road. The following December, ground was broken for the high school, which opened in August 2004. As for Centre Pointe, nearly all of its available lots had been purchased by summer 2006.

As a result of their collaborative efforts, the city, the school district, and the developer saved at least $4 million because the road, high school, and business park were graded and constructed within the same time frame in the most efficient, cost-effective manner possible.

Source: "Program Excellence Award for Outstanding Partnerships: Public-Private Partnerships," 2005 ICMA Annual Awards Section, *PM* Magazine (September 2005): 28.

## A public-private partnership for recreation in James City County, Virginia

The parks and recreation division of James City County, Virginia (pop. 57,525), in partnership with the Williamsburg Soccer Club (WSC), offers the Grove Community Partnership Program, an outreach program for at-risk youth. The program has three main objectives: to provide free professional instruction in an area of the county that has few positive recreational sports activities for children, to foster an interest in soccer in the community, and to help the WSC identify athletes who show promise as soccer players and want to progress in the sport.

Source: Excerpted from NACo Model County Programs, listed at www.naco.org/.

---

### Intergovernmental cooperation in Dowagiac, Michigan

Dowagiac (pop. 5,955) is the only city in rural Cass County, Michigan. In 2003, the city joined with Cass County, Southwestern Michigan College, Borgess-Lee Memorial Hospital, and five companies to undertake a connectivity plan for high-speed Internet access for the entire community. The plan was to identify the level of service available to citizens and to make recommendations on how to improve it. The city provided funding, participation on the planning team, and meeting space for the public hearing about the final report.

Two years later the city partnered with the school district in a joint development agreement to install a robust "dark-fiber" loop in the community to connect all school district facilities and some city-owned facilities. As of 2006, Dowagiac was looking to identify potential private partners that would like to lease excess fiber capacity from the city for use in WiFi and other technologies, and it was evaluating future municipal opportunities to use the fiber—for example, for remote meter readings.

Source: "Program Excellence Award for Outstanding Partnerships: Intergovernmental Cooperation," 2005 ICMA Annual Awards Section, *PM* Magazine (September 2005): 23.

---

## Deciding when to use which alternative

Several considerations are relevant when deciding which tool to select for delivering a service:

- What potential producers are available?
- How "packageable" is the service?
- How important is equal access to the service?
- What principle of funding equity do government officials want to apply to the service?
- How much control do local government officials want to exercise over service production, quality, and quantity?

The following sections show how each consideration applies to each of the various types of alternative service delivery.

### Potential producers

One consideration in deciding on alternative service delivery is the availability of alternative producers. How many alternative producers are there? What can each offer? What does each expect from the local government? What is the history of their relationship with government?

Local government officials often choose to purchase services because they hope that competition among would-be vendors will drive down the cost and increase the quality of the services they purchase. Franchises are sometimes awarded on the basis of competitive bids for the same reason. But purchasing services or awarding franchises does not automatically produce competition. While numerous producers exist for many public services in most parts of the country, other places may have few or no prospective vendors or franchisees. And unless there are several organizations interested in bidding, competition is unlikely. In some cases, a local government may stimulate competition by inviting its own

**Competitive services policy in Arlington, Texas**

Arlington, Texas (pop. 362,805), requires every city department to periodically review all its services to ensure the highest quality at the lowest cost. For each service it delivers, each department must decide which of the following actions is most appropriate: elimination, retention, reengineering, collaboration with other jurisdictions, transfer of control to an outside entity, outsourcing, or managed competition. The department presents its findings to a competitive services steering committee that includes the deputy city manager, finance director, and human resource director.

internal service department to bid on the service. If the government does not have that production capacity already, however, it may be unwilling to set up its own department simply to compete with outside suppliers.

Key characteristics of the alternative service producer are also important considerations, especially in the absence of competition. A government that is purchasing services in a noncompetitive market must rely heavily on the vendor's trustworthiness, public service motivation, and effective management for efficient service delivery. What basis do government officials have for trusting the vendor to deliver high-quality services while keeping prices low? What is the vendor's record of service? What are the vendor's management practices? Those same organizational characteristics are important for a government's grantees and partners.

## Service "packageability"

Some public services can be readily "packaged"—divided into units for distribution to the people who use them. For example, water can be measured in cubic feet, parking spaces can be rented by the minute, and admission to a swimming pool can be allotted in person-visits. But other services are not so easily divisible. Flood control reduces the risk of catastrophe for entire communities all at once rather than just building by building. Well-maintained public parks extend aesthetic and health benefits to the entire community. Many public services have some aspects that are more packageable and some that are less so.

The purchase of packageable services is usually easier to arrange and manage because officials can know how much service they are buying. Nonpackageable services are more difficult to purchase because they cannot be directly measured. Instead of specifying the level of fire protection or park maintenance to be produced, for example, purchase agreements for nonpackageable services have to focus on the resources the vendor is to provide or the production activities the vendor is to conduct. (Thus, if a local government buys fire protection from another government or from a nonprofit fire department, typically the payment is for the purchase of equipment or for a commitment to respond to all fires in the buyer's jurisdiction, rather than for the department's responses to a set number of fires.) Similarly, franchises work best for packageable services that consumers can buy directly from the franchise holder.

Because grants support the work of the grantee and are often less specific in terms of the results to be produced or the activities to be performed, packageablity is usually less of an issue for this alternative. Partnerships can involve both packageable and nonpackageable services.

## Accessibility

Sometimes public officials want to ensure equal access to a service, regardless of the user's ability to pay. In this case, franchises do not work well because the franchise holder expects users to pay for whatever services they receive. Governments can, of course, subsidize the cost of a franchise service with payments to the franchise holder, but this can become a cumbersome procedure. In contrast, when a local government purchases services, provides grant support for services, or partners for services, it can make service availability a condition of the purchase, grant, or partnership agreement regardless of the service user's ability to pay.

## Funding equity

Public officials use a variety of principles to determine who should pay for public services. For some services—typically those whose benefits are largely nonpackageable—officials determine that the public at large should pay. They then use a variety of taxes to allocate the tax burden according to some mixture of equal taxes for all, equal tax rates for all, or tax rates based on ability to pay. For services that are packageable, public officials often decide that they should be paid for by those who use them—for example, through user fees for water or other utilities.

Of course, it is also possible to mix the two types of funding for a single service. Thus, bus riders may pay a fare to cover part of the cost of bus service, while the public at large pays the rest of the cost through tax levies. Franchises are well suited for fee-for-use funding. Service purchases, grants, and partnership activities may lend themselves to either public-at-large or user funding.

## Control over service production, quality, and quantity

A government can have the greatest control over service production, quality, and quantity when the services are produced by its own employees. This is a major reason given by those who argue that law enforcement and other "intrinsically governmental" services—those involving the use of coercive power—should be produced by government agencies. A government can also retain considerable control when it purchases services: as buyer, it can specify not only the quality and quantity of service to be rendered, but also particular conditions for production, such as those regarding employment practices. If the vendor accepts those conditions as terms of the purchase agreement, they become binding on the vendor.

Typically, when government uses an alternative to direct production, officials have decided that they do not want or need to exercise direct control over service production. With each of the four alternative service delivery tools discussed here, another organization hires and supervises the personnel who implement the service and is responsible for the operational decisions about what to do and how to do it.

Grants in particular tend to be used for situations in which the government wants to support another organization's production of the service rather than assume responsibility for producing the service itself. Franchises also involve very little government control of service production, quality, or quantity; however, as with purchases, franchise agreements can contain terms that specify some aspects of production—for example, hours of operation or frequency of service delivery. Because partnering involves a wide range of shared responsibility among the partners, governments may retain considerable control over some aspects of service delivery, especially in cases where government agencies are coordinating or implementing services jointly with other organizations.

## Management challenges

Using an alternative to direct service production does not end local government managers' responsibilities for delivery of that service. Although these managers do not have direct oversight of production and delivery of the service, they play a key role in making arrangements with alternative service producers; monitoring service delivery; evaluating the services delivered; and recommending whether to continue, alter, or end the arrangements.

### Identifying alternative producers

Identifying and selecting prospective service producers involves a number of steps, which vary, depending on the type of service delivery alternative that has been chosen.

When purchasing a service, government managers typically draw up specifications for the service they want to buy. A similar process is sometimes used in awarding franchises. The specifications (often called a request for proposal, or RFP) can provide considerable detail about the quality and quantity of service being sought. They may also include the service conditions that producers must meet. These specifications are then provided to prospective vendors through a solicitation for bids. Even when competitive bidding for services is not required by law, many local governments advertise for bids to encourage competition and thereby motivate vendors to cut production costs and increase service quality.

If there are several bidders, government officials must assess the bids in light of the criteria provided in the solicitation as well as in terms of price. Which bid will best provide the service being sought for the lowest cost to government? It may be that the local government's own department is able to outbid private companies for the service contract, in which case the competition from the private market can have the same positive cost and quality impacts on "in-house" service production.

> *Even when competitive bidding for services is not required by law, many local governments advertise for bids to encourage competition.*

To assess service quality, officials with expertise in the service area usually help select the winning bid. However, there may be legal restrictions on the selection of the winning bid; for example, the local government may be required to select the "lowest responsible bid" or to choose a minority or local vendor.

Before awarding grants, a local government may issue a request for grant proposals, also sometimes called an RFP. Typically, a request for grant proposals is less specific than a bid solicitation about the details of the services to be produced. Instead, it invites applicants for government funding to submit proposals that describe the public services or benefits that would result from their work. As with bid solicitations, grant RFPs may also include conditions that the government requires grantees to meet. Grant proposals may be evaluated through a process similar to that used to evaluate bids; however, the comparisons across proposals are often more difficult to make because there is no common set of service specifications in the RFP. In addition, grantees are often selected through less formal ways. In some cases, if the local government has maintained a long-established relationship with a nonprofit service producer, no RFP is issued. And sometimes elected members of the governing board recommend nonprofit agencies for local government grants.[9]

Identification of potential service delivery partners is usually informal. Conversations among officials from various local governments or between government officials and business or nonprofit leaders often generate opportunities for a local government to collaborate in planning services, coordinating service delivery, or carrying out services jointly with others. City and county managers who are active in their communities get to know other civic leaders and identify partnership opportunities.

## Contracting for service

After an alternative service producer is selected, negotiations are often required to work out the details of the purchase, grant, franchise, or partner relationship.

Service purchase contracts typically specify what service activities the vendor will provide, how many clients will be served, other measures of service process or output, other conditions to be met by the vendor, the terms of payment by the government for the service, and the duration of the agreement. In "performance contracting," the emphasis is on the results that the vendor will achieve rather than on the activities the vendor will conduct.

Grant award contracts may describe the services the grantee will produce under the grant, operating or reporting conditions the grantee agrees to meet, and terms of payment of the grant. In many cases, local governments may not require grantees to enter into formal contracts. In such cases, however, the government often specifies a set of conditions that the grantee accepts along with the funding.

Franchise agreements typically include the privileges being granted to the franchisee, conditions of service delivery and charges to customers, terms of payment by the franchisee to the government, and the duration of the franchise.

Partnership agreements vary considerably from informal understandings to quite detailed legal documents, but in all cases they should allocate responsibilities among the parties. A shared understanding of what the government and its alternative service

---

**Living-wage requirement for contractors in Brookline, Massachusetts**

The citizens of Brookline, Massachusetts (pop. 55,590), amended the town's living-wage bylaws in May 2005 to cover employees of contractors working on contracts for the town. Coverage of contractors is to be phased in over three years: in 2006, the bylaws were extended to contractors holding contracts of $25,000 or more; in 2007, they will extend to contracts of $10,000 or more; and in 2008, to contracts of $5,000 or more.

producers expect from each other can guide those who carry out the work and can provide criteria for evaluating the success of the relationship.

Negotiating and signing a contract are only the first steps in managing the relationship. Carrying out the agreement, evaluating how it is working, and revising the relationship as needed are also key to ensuring the accountability of both the government and the alternative service producer. Whether it produces the services itself or obtains them from an alternative producer, the local government is accountable to its constituents for both the public services it provides and the public funds it spends. The alternative service producer must also be accountable in order for the government to fulfill its public responsibility.

## Establishing accountability[10]

Accountability concerns fulfilling expectations. Sometimes accountability is defined as being held to answer for the failure to meet expectations, but that situation is really a failure of accountability. People want expectations to be met. Only when expectations are not met do people seek someone to blame. Successfully accountable relationships are those in which expectations are met and there is no blame to be assigned.

Accountability processes can be established with answers to the following questions:

1. Who is expected to carry out which actions and for whom?

2. Who can invoke or alter these expectations?

3. Who should provide what information to whom about how responsibilities are carried out?

4. Who should use what information to decide about the future of the relationship?

In *hierarchical accountability,* one party (e.g., the local government) creates the answers to those questions and the other (e.g., the service provider) accepts the process they create. At the extreme, the government simply sends the other party (e.g., a landscape firm) a contract that sets out the terms of the relationship and expects a signed copy to be returned. The communication about expectations and responsibility is decidedly one-way: from the government to the vendor.

*Mutual accountability* is different: both parties decide together on accountability processes, and both parties follow them. The relationship begins with a conversation in which both parties negotiate and agree upon the terms of the relationship. Communication is two-way, ongoing, and reciprocal.

In practice, most accountability relationships fall between these two poles. The two ends of the continuum are valuable to think about, however, because these very different ways of setting expectations establish different relationships between the parties. Either may be appropriate depending on the service context. If the government knows exactly what it needs to buy to get the outcome it wants (e.g., a set number of blocks to be repaved in a certain way with specific materials), hierarchical accountability can work well.

Often, however, governments and their alternative service producers can produce better results if they explore ways to address public problems together. They are not sure which specific activities will be successful, so their agreements are worded in terms of general services or outcomes—for example, improving the economy of a district or enriching the community's cultural life. In such cases, service quality may also be difficult to measure, and the parties may need to work together over time to discover what works and to build

---

### Mutual accountability in Charlotte, North Carolina

What activities are appropriate for a nonprofit economic development organization to take to revitalize a down-at-the-heels business district? And how should it be held accountable for its activities? Like other local governments, Charlotte, North Carolina (pop. 610,949), faced this challenge. . . .

City officials in Charlotte partnered with nonprofit personnel and local property owners to assess the nonprofit organization's effectiveness in using funding from a special tax district to revitalize the area. A joint government-nonprofit review team collected information from local residents, from local businesses, and from nonprofit and city records. Team members deliberated on the meaning of this information and what it indicated about how best to continue improving economic development in the area.

What is important about this example is the partnership's relative success in achieving objectives and outcomes, in a relationship guided by the mutual accountability model. While the data suggested that the nonprofit had achieved only seven of the twelve initiatives it had undertaken, the assessed value of property in the district went up 20 percent from 2000 to 2002, compared with about 4 percent citywide. After several months of study, the cross-sector team unanimously recommended changes in the nonprofit's operations, raised city funding for the nonprofit's work, and continued interaction between the nonprofit and the city.

Source: Gordon Whitaker, Margaret Henderson, and Lydian Altman-Sauer, "Collaboration Calls for Mutual Accountability," *PM Magazine* 86 (December 2004): 17, summarizing Maureen Berner and Matt Bronson, "Program Evaluation in Local Governments: Building Consensus through Collaboration," *Popular Government* 68 (Winter 2003): 32-34.

---

trust in each other. Mutual accountability is appropriate when the parties need to share responsibility for defining, refining, monitoring, or revising the terms of their agreement.

Mutual accountability is not an all-or-nothing approach. It can involve a decision to join together to start a new project, to collaborate in collecting data about the performance of an ongoing project, or to work with each other in reviewing a project and deciding what's next. Using the model of mutual accountability, the challenge for community partners is to move beyond the limited buyer/seller relationship that is often embodied in local government contracts and toward real collaboration—ongoing, shared responsibility for improving public services.

## Monitoring the relationship

Regardless of which type of accountability local government officials want to develop, simply having a signed contract will not ensure it. An important challenge for local government managers is keeping track of what is happening under the contract. Are both parties meeting their responsibilities in fulfilling its terms? What services are being provided to the public? Do those services address public needs as intended? What changes need to be made either under the current contract or in any future contract to best serve the public?

Specifying what data an alternative service producer should collect and report to the local government is important for accountability. Local governments may also have to help nonprofit grant recipients develop the capacity to complete the required reports: some nonprofit organizations focus so many of their limited resources on producing

---

**Criteria for public works contracts in Monmouth, Illinois**

Under severe fiscal stress, the city of Monmouth, Illinois (pop. 9,198), decided to contract out all its public works services: water and wastewater, garbage collection, street maintenance, and billing. Monmouth officials established three criteria for each contract agreement:

1. Savings had to be significant, defined as more than 10 percent.

2. Service quality had to be increased; for example, technological upgrades and computerization had to be implemented.

3. Public employees would not be laid off (i.e., workforce reduction could occur only through attrition); wages and benefits had to be comparable to the city's; and good-faith bargaining with the union was to be continued.

Source: Adapted from Cynthia Jackson-Elmoore, "Privatization: Strategies for Success," *IQ Report* 36 (July 2004): 9.

---

services that they have little time (or much expertise) for administration.

Local government staff also must devote time and attention to monitoring the contract. Often this means more than reading reports provided by the service producer, although these reports may well include key performance measures, particularly in the case of performance contracting. Government officials may need to conduct on-site inspections and get feedback from service recipients or other independent sources of information about the producer's activities and how those activities affect the public. Keeping in touch with managers of outside service producers allows local government staff to seek clarification, raise concerns, and discuss new issues that arise in the course of service delivery. Conversations between local officials and the people responsible for service production provide opportunities for both parties to learn more about how the public is being served and how it might be served better.[11]

> *An important challenge for local government managers is keeping track of what is happening under the contract.*

In addition to collecting appropriate quantitative and qualitative data about services, monitoring involves interpreting those data to evaluate how well services are being delivered and how well they address the local government's public policy objectives. This is another demand on the time and attention of local government staff.

Monitoring service delivery is not just a government responsibility. The alternative service producer also needs to be monitoring its work and the results of that work. Sometimes, as already noted, the parties work together to develop and interpret information about how well the service is being delivered and how both the service and the relationship might be improved (see sidebar above).

## Resuming in-house production

Although alternative arrangements for delivering public services have been embraced as ways to cut costs and improve services, those benefits are by no means assured. Indeed,

---

**When local governments resume service production and delivery**

In Savannah, Georgia, a nonprofit fire protection company, South Side Fire, was charging more and providing lower-quality service than the city's own crews could provide. The Southside had experienced more commercial development, and the nonprofit fire crews, used to working in a more residential setting, could not keep pace.

Independence, Iowa, contracted back in hospital laundry services because the contractor charged on a weight basis when the laundry was wet, not dry, and refused to handle patients' personal clothing.

In Fort Collins, Colorado, and Charlotte, North Carolina, privatization of paratransit service for the elderly was plagued with problems of service quality—lack of courtesy on the part of drivers, problems with employee retention, and unreliable service.

In Whittier, California, the city ended a five-year contract for its public bus service because of similar quality concerns and higher costs due to higher accident rates and costs of repairs.

Source: Mildred Warner, with Michael Ballard and Amir Hefetz, "Contracting Back In: When Privatization Fails," in *The Municipal Year Book 2003* (Washington, D.C.: ICMA, 2003), 34-35.

---

many local governments have resumed in-house production of services because of problems with alternative producers' service costs or quality (see sidebar above).

## Conclusion

Effective use of service purchases, grants, franchises, and partnerships requires a different set of skills from managing in-house service production, but it is no less dependent on management involvement. Responsibility for day-to-day oversight is replaced by responsibility for identifying trends and negotiating changes. Instead of focusing on the selection of key personnel and the development of internal management practices, a local government manager needs to focus on building and monitoring relationships as well as services.

In addition, each of the service delivery alternatives brings with it its own set of challenges for the local government manager. For service purchases:

- No competition among vendors means no market incentives to keep costs down and quality high.
- Purchasing services in a noncompetitive market necessitates almost complete reliance on the vendor's trustworthiness, public service motivation, and effective management.
- Service quality and even quantity are difficult to measure for many public services.
- Monitoring activities under the contract requires the time and attention of local government managers and staff.

For grants:

- All the challenges that apply to service purchases.
- Nonprofit organizations often have little time and expertise for administration.
- Local governing board members sometimes make funding decisions as a way to reward supporters rather than on the basis of public policy priorities.

For franchises:

- Because the large companies that typically seek local government franchises may have more expertise with these agreements and more resources than the government, the local government often must combine efforts or seek special counsel in concluding franchise agreements.

For partnering:

- Unless the parties agree on expectations and responsibilities, it may be difficult to sustain a partnership over time and produce results.

- Establishing and formalizing each party's expectations and responsibilities requires time and skill in collaboration and group problem solving.

- As with purchasing services, partners often must rely heavily on each other's trustworthiness, public service motivation, and effective management to sustain their working relationship.

Few local governments are likely to rely entirely on alternative tools for delivering their public services or entirely on in-house service production. Instead, managers today need to hone both internal management and external relationship skills. But when alternatives offer better ways to serve the public, local government managers need the knowledge and skills to purchase services, make grants, award franchises, and build partnerships, as well as the capacity to monitor and evaluate those relationships. In small jurisdictions, the manager may be directly involved in all these activities. In larger jurisdictions, various aspects of alternative service delivery may be assigned to specialized personnel. Dividing responsibilities can help staff develop special skills, of course, but the manager should make sure that the team responsible for alternative service delivery arrangements focuses on services being delivered to citizens as well as on the administrative details of contract specification and reporting.

## Questions to ask if you manage a small community

If your community is already using an alternative service producer:

- What kind of information do we have about how well services are being delivered through this arrangement?
- How might we get more useful information or make better use of it in evaluating this arrangement?
- What other arrangements might give us better service for the same cost or the same service for less cost? (Be sure to include the costs of monitoring and revising the service delivery arrangement, as well as what would be paid to a vendor or grantee.)

If you are considering alternatives to existing in-house production of a service:

- What alternative producers are available in our area?
- Given the characteristics of the service and of potential alternative producers, how appropriate are purchase, grant, franchise, and partnering as options for us?
- What improvements in service quality or quantity can we reasonably anticipate from an alternative producer?
- What cost savings (including the costs of creating, monitoring, and revising the service delivery arrangement, as well as what would be paid to a vendor or grantee) can we reasonably anticipate?

If you are considering how to produce a new service for your community:

- What capacity do we have with existing departments and personnel to produce the service in-house?
- What alternative producers are available in our area?
- Given the characteristics of the service and of potential alternative producers, how appropriate are purchase, grant, franchise, and partnering as options for us?
- Is there an alternative producer who has already demonstrated the capacity to produce the service well and at a reasonable cost?
- How would the cost for in-house production of the service (including the costs of creating, monitoring, and revising the service delivery arrangement, as well as what would be paid to a vendor or grantee) compare with the cost of alternative production?

## Competencies for managers responsible for service delivery

Ability to clarify service goals and objectives

Proficiency in writing bid specifications and requests for proposals

Skill in building relationships across organizations

Ability to assess the capacity and trustworthiness of other organizations

Skill in negotiating agreements and revisions to them

Ability to assemble and interpret quantitative and qualitative data from diverse sources

## Endnotes

1 Lester Salamon has identified fourteen "tools of government,"of which six are listed here. See Lester Salamon, ed., *The Tools of Government: A Guide to the New Governance* (New York: Oxford University Press, 2002).

2 Mildred Warner and Amir Hefetz, "Pragmatism over Politics: Alternative Service Delivery in Local Government, 1992–2002," in *The Municipal Year Book 2004* (Washington, D.C.: ICMA, 2004), 8–16.

3 Government grant awards also often involve a contract between the government and the grant recipient. Thus, it is important to distinguish purchase-of-service contracts from grant contracts. While some authors refer to service purchases simply as "contracts," the term *contract* refers most precisely to the agreement entered into between the parties regarding their relationship, whether that relationship is buyer-seller or grantor-grantee.

4 Ruth Hoogland deHoog and Lester M. Salamon, "Purchase-of-Service Contracting," in *The Tools of Government: A Guide to the New Governance* (see note 1), 322.

5 Gordon P. Whitaker and Rosalind Day, "How Local Governments Work with Nonprofit Organizations in North Carolina," *Popular Government* 66 (Winter 2001): 28. In comparison, 35 percent of the nonprofits that cities funded provided human services, as did 40 percent of the nonprofits that counties funded. Additionally, 31 percent of the city-funded nonprofits and 15 percent of the county-funded nonprofits provided recreation, arts, or culture services.

6 Whitaker and Day, "How Local Governments Work," 26.

7 Local governments' authority to franchise electronic communications became the subject of intense state and federal legislative debate early in the twenty-first century and remains uncertain as of this writing.

8 Richard Kearney, "Reinventing Government and Battling Budget Crises," in *The Municipal Year Book 2005* (Washington, D.C.: ICMA, 2005), 29–31.

9 For example, in North Carolina less than 40 percent of the cities and only 60 percent of the counties reported receiving written proposals from the nonprofits they funded. In at least 60 percent of those same cities and counties, local elected officials recommended which nonprofits to fund; see Whitaker and Day, "How Local Governments Work," Table 5.

10 This section draws on Gordon P. Whitaker, Frayda S. Bluestein, Anita R. Brown-Graham, Lydian Altman-Sauer, and Margaret Henderson, "Accountability in Local Government–Nonprofit Relationships," *IQ Report* 35 (May 2003).

11 See, for example, Sergio Fernandez and Hal G. Rainey, "Local Government Contract Management and Performance Survey: A Report," in *The Municipal Year Book 2005* (Washington, D.C.: ICMA, 2005), 1–8.

# A Manager's Toolbox

William C. Rivenbark

The rumor is already making its way through town hall. The town manager is going to introduce a new management initiative at the next town council meeting. After completing his first year on the job, the town manager is now ready to implement continuous process improvement—a management tool that requires employees to serve on productivity teams, to identify processes that need improvement, to analyze the processes and make recommendations for improvement, and to monitor the results.

One employee tentatively suggests that the payroll process should be the first on the list. Another suggests that continuous process improvement is nothing more than the latest "flavor of the month." The conversation ends when a seasoned employee recommends the "wait-it-out" posture: he thinks the initiative will simply go away when the manager moves to his next job, and he cites the conflict between the manager and two elected officials over downtown development.

So why should local managers understand management tools like continuous process improvement, given the reality that these initiatives do come and go in local government? One reason is that management tools remain fundamentally similar over time. Performance budgeting, which is based on the notion that allocation decisions are shaped in part by the outputs, outcomes, and efficiencies of service delivery, is currently receiving a lot of attention in local government. However, performance budgeting can be traced back to the late 1940s and early 1950s as a management tool in local government.

Another reason is that a management tool's impact on local government often lasts long after it has given way to the next management reform. Management-by-objectives was popular in the early 1970s; however, the process of establishing quantifiable objectives to track outcomes of service delivery is now commonly used in local government. And there is a third reason why local officials should have a working knowledge of the management tools often found in a manager's toolbox: it's their job as leaders to promote the use of these tools in order to help the organization respond positively to change in its environment.

This chapter presents the management tools of strategic planning, performance measurement, performance budgeting, benchmarking, and program evaluation. All five tools are becoming professional norms in local government. They are commonly found in jurisdictions of all sizes and are encouraged by professional organizations such as ICMA, the Government Finance Officers Association (GFOA), and the American Society for Public Administration (ASPA).[1] They also form the foundation for an organizational culture shift to results-based management.

The purpose of this chapter is to discuss why each tool is useful and to present successful examples of how counties and municipalities have embraced these tools, encouraging managers and department heads to consider their use for maximizing limited public resources. It does not attempt to provide a comprehensive treatment of each tool; the professional and academic literature contains an abundant amount of information in that regard. This chapter concludes with a discussion of the success factors for results-based management.

## Strategic planning

There is an important reason why the town manager waited a year before introducing continuous process improvement. When he was hired, the town had no long-term goals to guide the overall direction of the organization. The manager scheduled a town council retreat after six months on the job and hired an outside facilitator to conduct a strategic planning session with council members and department heads. One of the long-term goals they identified was the provision of efficient and effective services. This new goal provided the necessary context for continuous process improvement.

Strategic planning is becoming a professional norm in local government; however, an agreed-upon definition for strategic planning has never been established. Strategic planning, broadly understood, represents a structured and coordinated approach for developing organizational direction that includes a vision, a mission statement, core values, and long-term goals. Some argue that strategic planning is more than developing direction; rather, it represents an effort to (1) solve community problems with stakeholder involvement and (2) build consensus around courses of action to accomplish long-term goals, including the establishment of measures and targets for monitoring organizational and community outcomes. Strategic planning also is an effective tool for prioritizing strategic initiatives and provides guidance on how to invest organizational resources.

> *Strategic planning, broadly understood, represents a structured and coordinated approach for developing organizational direction.*

Each local government must build the strategic planning process in accordance with its current situation and desired outcomes. Some organizations use a one-day retreat where elected officials and senior managers identify a handful of long-term goals to help guide the allocation of organizational resources. Other organizations use a very rigorous process, including a hired facilitator and the involvement of all stakeholders, to develop vision and mission statements, core values, long-term goals, quantifiable objectives, and performance measures. These more rigorous processes are often preceded by an environmental scan that requires the community to identify its *s*trengths, *w*eaknesses, *o*pportunities, and *t*hreats (SWOT).

Regardless of how it is conducted, strategic planning represents an important management tool in local government as demonstrated in part by the number of organizations

### Benefits of strategic planning

In an environment that has been shaped through the years by policy, statute, and tradition, properly conducted strategic planning can lead to many benefits. Regardless of why programs were originally created or what they were designed to achieve, a thoughtful planning process will

- Accelerate an agency's ability to solve identified issues and challenges
- Encourage creativity and innovation
- Ensure a more efficient use of resources
- Develop a greater degree of cooperation and collaboration
- Create a sense of team and mutual understanding
- Reduce confusion about roles, responsibilities, and accountability
- Serve as the basis for evaluating employee and program performance
- Tie the budget to program performance
- Serve as the basis for funding requests and the allocation process
- Clarify and showcase an agency's intent and use of funds.

Given this range of benefits, the ability to plan strategically could easily be the most importance legacy a public official could leave. Most managers and supervisors have been captured by the operational aspect of their work and focus on task completion. What about the final result? What impact will those managers have on the employees they supervise? Will those employees learn and grow and become creative, insightful planners who can also analyze, strategize, and implement quality programs? The planning process embodies more than the simple tasks of establishing a mission, creating a vision, and agreeing on general agency or program goals. By teaching the process to all employees, an organization can develop a culture of strategic thinkers who consistently seek measured improvement.

Source: John Luthy, "Strategic Planning: A Guide for Public Managers," *IQ Report* 34, no. 8 (2002): 5.

that have embraced it.[2] Survey research published in 2003 found that approximately 50 percent of municipalities with populations of 2,500 and above used strategic planning to establish organizational goals.[3]

Proactive organizational stakeholders do not participate in strategic planning processes simply to produce documents that sit on shelves and collect dust, which is a common criticism of this management tool. They invest time in strategic planning to collectively determine how the organization should move forward and invest its limited resources. They also embrace strategic planning to take advantage of the benefits listed in the accompanying sidebar, which includes the observation that the ability to plan strategically is potentially the most important legacy of public officials.

Two organizations that have been successful in using strategic planning are the cities of Scottsdale, Arizona, and Saco, Maine. Scottsdale provides a model for how to connect long-term goals to the annual budget process. Saco provides a model for developing strategies and attaining goals.

## Scottsdale, Arizona

Scottsdale, Arizona (pop. 226,013), begins its budget process with an assessment of needs and financial capacity. This phase includes citizen input, evaluation of infrastructure needs, financial trend analysis, and revenue forecasting. In the second phase of the process, the city council holds a retreat in order to review the information gathered in the first phase, review the organization's long-term goals (see accompanying sidebar), and establish and prioritize strategic directives. These long-term goals and *prioritized* strategic directives set the stage for making decisions during the remaining phases of the budget preparation and adoption process.

Several aspects of the strategic planning process in Scottsdale are considered "best practice." First, council members review the organizational goals annually in preparation for the budget process. This annual review ensures that the strategic plan becomes a "living" organizational document. Second, the organizational goals are reviewed within the context of financial trend analysis. Research has demonstrated that a feasibility assessment of proposed strategies, which includes affordability, is a success factor for strategic

---

### Organizational goals in Scottsdale, Arizona

Listed below are the broad goals of Scottsdale's mayor and city council

### Goal A: Neighborhoods

Enhance and protect a diverse, family-oriented community where neighborhoods are safe, protected from adverse impacts, and well maintained.

### Goal B: Preservation

Preserve the character and environment of Scottsdale.

### Goal C: Transportation

Provide for the safe, efficient, and affordable movement of people and goods.

### Goal D: Economy

Position Scottsdale for short- and long-term economic prosperity by stabilizing, promoting, strengthening, stimulating, expanding, and diversifying our economic resources.

### Goal E: Fiscal and resource management

Ensure that Scottsdale is fiscally responsible and fair in its management of taxpayer money and city assets, and coordinates land use and infrastructure planning within the context of financial demands and available resources.

### Goal F: Open and responsive government

Make government accessible, responsive, and accountable so that pragmatic decisions reflect community input and expectations.

Source: City of Scottsdale, Arizona, *Adopted FY 2004-2005 Budget*, vol. 1, *Budget Summary*.

planning.[4] In other words, an organization does not fund goals; it funds strategies to accomplish goals, and those strategies are based in part on the organization's ability to afford them. Finally, citizen input is an actual goal within the strategic plan (as shown in sidebar). Citizen input in Scottsdale is obtained from citizen surveys, public budget forums held throughout the city, and e-mails welcomed from citizens on the city's Web site.

## Saco, Maine

A strategic planning committee was formed in January 2003 to develop a strategic plan for the city of Saco, Maine (pop. 18,230). With input from various stakeholders, the committee created a strategic plan that contained nine organizational goals, covering such areas as downtown revitalization, growth management, environmental challenges, technology innovations, fiscal capacity, and public safety.

Two areas of the plan are considered best practice. First, the plan is aligned with the organization's performance measurement system shown in Figure 16–1. This creates a management system in which performance measures are used to track the progress toward goals and objectives at both the organization-wide and programmatic levels.

Second, departments develop specific strategies to advance one or more of the organizational goals, including key milestones with existing resources and key milestones with additional funding for strategy implementation. For example, one strategy for the environmental goal is to expand the city's recycling program. Key milestones toward this goal with existing organizational resources involve meetings with industrial and commercial accounts and citizen tours of the recycling center and transfer station. Key milestones

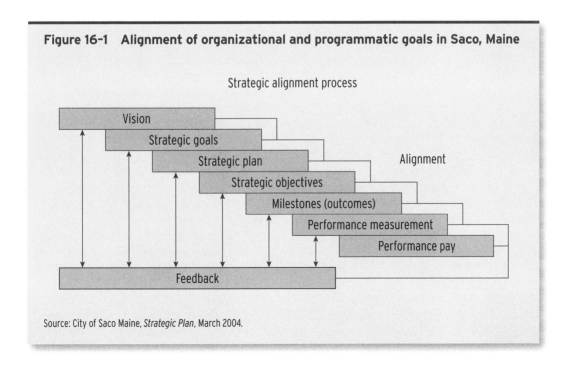

**Figure 16-1   Alignment of organizational and programmatic goals in Saco, Maine**

Strategic alignment process

Vision
Strategic goals
Strategic plan
Strategic objectives
Milestones (outcomes)
Performance measurement
Performance pay

Alignment

Feedback

Source: City of Saco Maine, *Strategic Plan*, March 2004.

with additional funding include the use of public-access television and the distribution of informational packets to customers. Performance measures are then used to track the success of these strategies. The setout rate (i.e., the percentage of households that set out recyclables for collection), for example, is an excellent measure by which to monitor the effectiveness of household recycling programs.

## Performance measurement

The town manager introduced his continuous process improvement initiative at the town council meeting and appointed the first productivity team to study the payroll process: the grapevine had informed him that the number of replacement checks being written was an ongoing problem for the finance department. The productivity team quickly determined that the outcome measure of number of replacement checks as a percentage of total payroll checks and the efficiency measure of cost per payroll check were not being tracked on a monthly or annual basis. The outcome measure was critical to determining both the severity of the problem and the subsequent effectiveness of the solution adopted. The efficiency measure was needed for analyzing the cost of alternative payroll processes.

After the productivity team struggled to collect and analyze performance and cost data for the previous two years, the first recommendation on its evaluation report was that the town should consider the adoption of a performance measurement system.

> *Well-managed performance measurement systems are critical for accurately and systematically demonstrating operational accountability in local government.*

Performance measurement is one of the most important tools in a manager's toolbox. Quantitative measures provide the necessary gauge for monitoring the performance of service delivery and for supporting the utility of other management tools. Just as it has long been understood that well-managed financial management systems are critical for accurately and systematically demonstrating financial accountability in local government, the profession now agrees that well-managed performance measurement systems are critical for accurately and systematically demonstrating operational accountability in local government.

The push for performance measurement in local government can be traced to the turn of the twentieth century with the work of the New York Bureau of Municipal Research.[5] Clarence E. Ridley and Herbert A. Simon promoted the standardization of performance measurement techniques during the 1930s through their work with ICMA.[6] More recent approaches to performance measurement in local government have been developed by Harry P. Hatry, David N. Ammons, and others.[7] By the beginning of the twenty-first century, more than a third of all municipalities with populations over 2,500 and at least a third of all counties with populations over 50,000 were engaged in performance measurement to some degree.[8]

A performance measurement system begins with the adoption of mission statements for individual local government programs and with a sustainable commitment from management. In other words, program managers must understand why specific services are provided and how those services support the long-term goals of the organization. Guided by the program's mission statement, the next step is to identify service delivery goals. These goals, which represent in broad terms what the program seeks to achieve, provide the basis for identifying quantifiable objectives, stating what the program expects to accomplish in specific and time-bound, measurable terms.

Quantifiable objectives provide the framework for creating output, outcome, and efficiency measures. *Output measures* (workload) report on the quantity of services provided (the number of checks written), while *outcome measures* (effectiveness) report on the quality of services (the percentage of checks correctly written). *Efficiency measures* report on the relationship between inputs and outputs, with cost per output and outputs per full-time equivalent (FTE) position representing common efficiency measures in local government (e.g., cost per check written, or number of checks written per payroll FTE).

Another example of this process can be shown with the program of police patrol. The mission of police patrol is to maintain an active presence in the community. A service delivery goal in response to this mission statement is to respond to dispatched calls in an efficient and effective manner. The quantifiable objective that flows from the service delivery goal is to respond to 90 percent of dispatched calls within five minutes or less during FY 2006–2007. Three measures can be identified from this objective, which together provide excellent quantifiable information on the performance of service delivery. The output measure is the number of dispatched calls. The efficiency measure is the cost per dispatched call. The outcome measure is the percentage of calls responded to within five minutes.

A process that begins with a program mission statement increases the likelihood that programs will move beyond simply tracking output measures. It helps program managers identify measures of efficiency and outcome, which are extremely important for service improvement. Reliance on output (workload) measures alone limits the utility of performance measurement; local governments are more likely to use performance measures for service improvement when they track and analyze the variances in efficiency and outcome measures.[9]

## Fairfax County, Virginia

Fairfax County, Virginia (pop. 1,006,529), is nationally known for its performance measurement system.[10] The county promotes performance measurement because this tool strengthens accountability, communicates results of programs and services, creates an environment for continuous process improvement, and provides information for making sound decisions.

The use of consistent, well-defined terms and processes is the reason why Fairfax County's performance measurement system is considered a best practice. The county has adopted a four-step methodology for creating good performance measures:

1. Review and evaluate existing agency mission and cost center goals

2. Identify service areas

3. Define service area objectives

4. Identify indicators that measure progress on objectives.

In addition, it promotes the accuracy and reliability of its performance measures by providing directions on how to collect both quantitative and qualitative data. It even provides in-house guidance on how to conduct surveys for reporting on measures of customer satisfaction. Figure 16–2 shows the performance measures of the Fairfax County Public

**Figure 16-2   Performance measures for the Fairfax County Public Library**

| Indicator | Prior year actuals | | | | Current estimate | Future estimate |
|---|---|---|---|---|---|---|
| | FY 2002 Actual | FY 2003 Actual | FY 2004 Estimate | FY 2004 Actual | FY 2005 | FY 2006 |
| **Output** | | | | | | |
| Library visits | 5,349,847 | 5,261,448 | 5,210,000 | 5,283,497 | 5,285,500 | 5,285,800 |
| Registered cardholders | 561,221 | 630,102 | 630,000 | 704,879 | 719,000 | 733,400 |
| Library Internet Web site page views | 5,791,001 | 7,568,996 | 7,947,445 | 10,854,528 | 11,620,000 | 12,200,000 |
| Library Internet Web site user visits | 1,763,323 | 2,132,493 | 2,196,467 | 2,512,234 | 2,690,000 | 2,824,000 |
| **Efficiency ($)** | | | | | | |
| Cost per capita | 25.53 | 26.55 | 26.29 | 25.39 | 26.36 | 26.80 |
| Cost per visit | 4.87 | 5.20 | 5.27 | 5.01 | 5.28 | 5.47 |
| Cost per registered cardholder | 46.39 | 43.39 | 43.62 | 37.59 | 38.84 | 39.44 |
| **Service quality** | | | | | | |
| Library visits per capita | 5.24 | 5.11 | 4.98 | 5.06 | 4.99 | 4.90 |
| New registrations added annually | 75,452 | 75,137 | 75,000 | 62,542 | 63,000 | 63,000 |
| Percentage change in registrations as percentage of population (%) | (22.9) | 0.6 | (1.5) | 6.4 | 0.3 | 0.1 |
| Percentage of customers (visitors) to the library's Web site who are satisfied with the information found (%) | NA | 98 | 91 | 98 | 92 | 93 |
| **Outcome (%)** | | | | | | |
| Customer satisfaction | NA | NA | 90 | 99 | 91 | 92 |
| Registered users as percentage of population | 55 | 61 | 60 | 68 | 68 | 68 |
| Percentage change in library Web site page views | 195 | 31 | 5 | 43 | 7 | 5 |

Source: Fairfax County, Virginia, *Fiscal Year 2006 Adopted Budget Plan*, vol. 1.

Library and illustrates the benefits of using a standardized process to create a meaningful collection of output, outcome, and efficiency measures.

Program managers often resist performance measures because of concern about unfavorable results, but this is exactly why programs need a *collection* of good measures to provide feedback on the multiple dimensions of service delivery. Fairfax County uses library visits per capita as a proxy measure for service quality. Library visits per capita, as shown in Figure 16-2, have gradually decreased since FY 2002. The figure also shows that the decline is expected to continue in FY 2005 and FY 2006. However, the customer satisfaction rating is extremely high at 99 percent. What is driving this seeming contradiction is that actual library visits are giving way to electronic library visits. As a result, the collection of measures shown in Figure 16-2 provides program managers and elected officials with the necessary performance trends to make informed decisions regarding library services in Fairfax County.

## Newberg, Oregon

As is clear from data on the widespread use of performance measurement (see endnote 8), small as well as large organizations are building the capacity to measure their performance of service delivery. The city of Newberg, Oregon (pop. 20,681), has established a performance measurement system that includes goals, objectives, and a collection of performance measures for each departmental function. Figure 16-3 presents the two program goals and the specific performance measures tracked by the building inspections function, which is

---

**Figure 16-3   Performance measures for the building division, Newberg, Oregon**

*Program goals for 2005-2006*

1.  Continue to provide excellent customer service, accurate and timely plan reviews, and thorough inspections.
2.  Fund the building division operations with permit fees.

| Indicators | 2003-2004 Actual | 2004-2005 Estimated actual | 2005-2006 Projected |
|---|---|---|---|
| No. building permits issued | 422 | 480 | 550 |
| No. plumbing permits issued | 369 | 325 | 450 |
| No. mechanical permits issued | 406 | 400 | 500 |
| No. plan reviews | 672 | 1,000 | 1,100 |
| No. inspections | 8,143 | 9,000 | 10,000 |
| Total revenue collected | $1,052,156 | $906,000 | $912,000 |
| Average time to complete plan review and issue permits (days) | 28 | 28 | 28 |

Source: City of Newberg, Oregon, *FY 2005-2006 Annual Budget.*

part of the planning and building department. Newberg has established five output measures and one outcome measure for the building inspections service delivery goal. It also tracks the amount of revenue collected in response to the second program goal of funding the departmental function with permit fees.

As do many smaller organizations, Newberg relies heavily on output measures. The next step for Newberg is to incorporate more efficiency and outcome measures into its performance measurement system, thereby increasing the likelihood that performance measures will be used for service improvement. Two possible efficiency measures for the building inspections function would be cost per building inspection and building inspections per building inspector FTE. Two possible outcome measures would be percentage of building inspections completed within one day of request and percentage of building inspections that are reinspections.

## Performance budgeting

The town manager agreed with the productivity team's recommendation that the town adopt performance measurement. Not only would performance measurement help support continuous process improvement, but it would also support the manager's goal of performance budgeting. In other words, the manager wanted to move beyond the incremental adjustment of the current year's budget in preparing the proposed budget for the following fiscal year. He wanted to create an environment where budget requests can be evaluated on identified levels of service performance.

Local managers, professional organizations, consultants, and academicians promote performance budgeting as a management tool for making allocation decisions on the basis of the performance of service delivery. But what is performance budgeting? For this discussion, performance budgeting means making accurate and reliable performance information part of budget development, implementation, and evaluation, and there are numerous approaches to ensuring that performance is part of the allocation process. Outcome-based budgeting, for example, as described in Osborne and Hutchinson's *The Price of Government,* focuses almost exclusively on outcomes and provides a methodology for allocating resources to accomplish them.[11]

> *Performance budgeting means making accurate and reliable performance information part of budget development, implementation, and evaluation.*

While research has demonstrated that performance budgeting is increasingly becoming a professional norm in local government,[12] several misconceptions about it have hindered its success. A misconception that almost guarantees failure is that performance budgeting originates in the budget office, beginning with a memo from the budget officer to department heads that performance measures must accompany next year's budget requests. Performance budgeting can begin only in departments and programs where well-managed performance measurement systems are already used to support ongoing management decisions. In other words, if an organization waits to collect and use performance measures for justifying budget requests, it has waited too long.

A second misconception about performance budgeting is that performance is the sole factor for making allocation decisions. Every effort should be made in a performance budgeting environment to use performance results and performance targets to shape allocation decisions. Other factors, however, including political considerations and fiscal constraints, will always exert some influence over allocation decisions in local government.

A third misconception is that performance budgeting eliminates the need for line-item budgeting, which suggests that performance budgeting is a stand-alone budgeting technique. But this is unrealistic in that a line-item budget forms the organization's chart of accounts and reconciles with the financial management system. There also is a political dimension to line-item budgeting. Governing boards are often more comfortable with line-item budgets given their desire to review specific line items such as travel, office equipment and furniture, and training.

A final misconception is that presentation of performance measures in the budget document represents performance budgeting. While performance measures should be included in the budget document for operational accountability and for the GFOA's Distinguished Budget Presentation Awards Program (see sidebar on page 76), true performance budgeting includes performance information in budget requests and considers this information during budget workshops.[13]

### Concord, North Carolina

The city of Concord, North Carolina (pop. 61,092), uses an annual budget process that meets the criteria for performance budgeting. Before moving toward a performance budgeting environment, senior leaders invested the necessary resources to develop a well-managed performance measurement system for their organization. The system developed for the communications department, as shown in Figure 16–4, includes a mission statement, performance goals and objectives, and a collection of workload, efficiency, and effectiveness indicators. Critical aspects of this system are that trend data are being tracked for the performance measures and that targets (objectives) have been established for the coming fiscal year, setting the stage for resource allocation and resource management.

*Ongoing strategic development is critical to the success of performance budgeting.*

Other important components of the system, as shown in Figure 16–5, are the department's accomplishments for FY 2004–2005 and the budget highlights and changes for FY 2005–2006. This information is taken from the communications department's annual work plan, which contains strategies on how to maintain and improve the performance of service delivery. Ongoing strategic development is critical to the success of performance budgeting.

The city implemented the budget development calendar shown in Figure 16–6 to ensure that performance, as based on the goals and objectives of each organizational unit, is part of the annual budget process for making allocation decisions. The city operates on a fiscal year beginning July 1, which is mandated by state law in North Carolina.

---

**Figure 16-4 Communications department budget in Concord, North Carolina: Mission statement, past performance, goals, and objectives**

**Mission:**

The Communications Department exists to provide, through partnerships with other departments, a high level of customer service to citizens in their time of need by quickly and efficiently handling calls and providing information to responding departments.

**FY 2004-2005 accomplishments:**

- Integration of computer-aided dispatch system with new police and fire records management systems.
- Implementation of part-time employees to provide more effective coverage during busy hours.

**FY 2005-2006 budget highlights/changes:**

- Continued replacement of aging computer workstations and servers.

**Performance goals and objectives:**

*Goal:* To provide efficient and effective handling of emergency calls dispatched to police and fire units in order to reduce potential life-threatening injuries and damage to property.

*Objective:* To maintain the cost per 911 call answered at less than $12.00.

*Objective:* To maintain the seconds from ring to answer response time of less than 5 seconds.

*Objective:* To maintain the percentage of calls answered within 3 rings to equal to or greater than 99%.

*Objective:* To maintain the percentage of emergency calls dispatched within 60 seconds to equal to or greater than 95%.

Source: City of Concord, North Carolina, *FY 2005-2006 Approved Annual Operating Budget.*

---

One of the first steps in the budget development calendar occurs in January and involves training on budget data entry and development of performance goals and objectives. While ongoing training is key to the success of well-managed performance measurement systems, Concord is one of the few localities that have embraced systematic training sessions on results-based management. Budget packages are then distributed to departments for completion in February. As shown in Figure 16–6, there are two due dates for completing the budget packages. Updated goals and objectives must be submitted several days before proposed budget requests are due from the departments.

This sequence of information represents an important step in successfully implementing performance budgeting. Budget requests are made after the desired levels of performance for efficient and effective service delivery have been established. More specifically, financial resources are requested in accordance with the desired level of performance rather than as (automatic) incremental adjustments to line-item budgets. To draw on a concept of reinventing government, managers and department heads must stop "rowing the boat" by simply providing services and must start "steering it" toward desired levels of results.[14] They can do this by using the budget process to influence performance.

**Figure 16-5   Communications department budget in Concord, North Carolina: Budget summary and performance summary**

**Budget summary**

| | 2002-2003 Actual expenditures | 2003-2004 Actual expenditures | 2004-2005 Council approved* | 2004-2005 Actual expenditures** | 2005-2006 Manager recommended | 2005-2006 Council approved |
|---|---|---|---|---|---|---|
| Personnel services ($) | 746,793 | 778,747 | 892,278 | 808,549 | 879,089 | *879,089 |
| Operations | 84,785 | 92,502 | 50,289 | 43,937 | 69,892 | 69,892 |
| Capital outlay | – | – | – | – | – | – |
| Debt service | 79,372 | 19,604 | – | – | – | – |
| Cost allocation | 146 | 125 | – | – | – | – |
| Total ($) | 911,096 | 890,978 | 942,567 | 852,486 | 948,981 | 948,981 |

*as amended
**unaudited

| | | | | | | |
|---|---|---|---|---|---|---|
| Authorized FTE | 24.50 | 20.50 | 20.50 | 20.50 | 20.94 | 20.94 |

Note: FTE reduction in FY 03-04 due to breaking out the Radio Shop into its own cost center.

**Performance summary**

| | 2003-2004 Measure actual | 2004-2005 Measure actual | 2005-2006 Measure objective |
|---|---|---|---|
| Workload indicators | | | |
| Total calls answered | 153,214 | 147,420 | 155,000 |
| Total calls dispatched | 82,151 | 88,082 | 94,000 |
| Efficiency indicators | | | |
| Cost per 911 call answered ($) | 12.00 | NA | < 12.00 |
| Effectiveness indicators | | | |
| Average no. seconds from ring to answer | 3.3 | 3.8 | < 5 |
| % of calls answered within 3 rings (18 seconds) | 99.8 | 99.5 | > 99 |
| % of emergency calls dispatched within 60 seconds | 98.1 | 96.5 | > 95 |

Source: City of Concord, North Carolina, *FY 2005-2006 Approved Annual Operating Budget*.

# Figure 16-6 Budget development calendar for Concord, North Carolina

| TASK | START DATE | DUE DATE(S) | JULY | AUG | SEPT | OCT | NOV | DEC | JAN | FEB | MARCH | APRIL | MAY | JUNE |
|---|---|---|---|---|---|---|---|---|---|---|---|---|---|---|
| Budget Process Improvement Team conducts annual review | 8/19/04 | 8/19/04 | | | | | | | | | | | | |
| Mgt. & Budget Team discuss process and calendar | 10/13/04 | 10/13/04 | | | | | | | | | | | | |
| CIP forms distributed | 11/15/04 | 12/23/04 | | | | | | | | | | | | |
| Training on budget data entry and development of performance goals & objectives | 1/05 TBD | 1/05 TBD | | | | | | | | | | | | |
| Budget Packets distributed to Internal Service Dept Directors; **goals/objectives due 1/21/05; budget $$ request due 2/4/05** | 1/3/05 | 1/21/05 2/4/05 | | | | | | | | | | | | |
| Finance Dir estimates revenues | 1/05 | 4/05 | | | | | | | | | | | | |
| Council and Community service level goals and objectives established at Mayor & City Council | 1/27/05 | 1/28/05 | | | | | | | | | | | | |
| State of the City Address by City Manager | 2/11/05 | 2/11/05 | | | | | | | | | | | | |
| Budget packets distributed to Dept Directors; **goals / objectives due 2/18/05; budget $$ requests due 3/4/05** | 1/31/05 | 2/18/05 3/4/05 | | | | | | | | | | | | |
| External agency budget requests accepted and hearing before Mayor & City Council | 2/4/05 | 3/4/05; 04/12/05 (hearing) | | | | | | | | | | | | |
| Internal Service budget reviews | 2/11/05 | 2/18/05 | | | | | | | | | | | | |
| Budget requests analyzed and reviewed with Dept Directors | 3/7/05 | 4/15/05 | | | | | | | | | | | | |
| City Manager's recommended budget compiled and presented to Mayor & City Council | 4/17/05 | 5/26/05 | | | | | | | | | | | | |
| Budget available for public viewing at City Clerk's Office | 5/26/05 | | | | | | | | | | | | | |
| Mayor & City Council review budget and performance objectives | 5/26/05 | 6/9/05 | | | | | | | | | | | | |
| Public Hearing conducted; budget adopted by City Council | 6/9/05 (hearing) | 6/9/05 | | | | | | | | | | | | |
| Evaluation of budget process | 7/25/05 | 8/19/05 | | | | | | | | | | | | |

Legend:
City Mgt., Budget Staff, Dept Directors & Staff
Budget Staff, Department Directors
Mayor, City Council, City Mgt., Dept. Directors, Budget Staff
External Agencies, Budget Staff, City Manager, Mayor & City Council
City Mgt. & Budget Staff
Budget Staff
Internal Service Departments
Budget Staff, Dept Dir. & Staff
Mayor & City Council
Department Directors

Source: City of Concord, North Carolina, *FY 2005–2006 Approved Annual Operating Budget.*

## Benchmarking

The town manager continued his review of the evaluation report submitted by the productivity team charged with improving the payroll process. The second recommendation in the report involved the efficiency measure of cost per payroll check. After comparing the town's efficiency data with that of other towns, the productivity team recommended the purchase of new software that a neighboring municipality used to greatly reduce the cost of its biweekly payroll process. The software also had increased the accuracy of that municipality's payroll data. What the productivity team members did not realize is that they had engaged in informal benchmarking.

The most common form of benchmarking in local government is a comparison of performance statistics. Local managers compare their own program's performance information with that of other departments and programs.[15] Informal benchmarking is common: many department heads and programs managers contact their counterparts in other jurisdictions to obtain comparative performance and cost data. The problem with informal benchmarking is the lack of controls over definitions and data to ensure "apples to apples" comparisons. The need for common definitions and comparable data is a major reason why formal benchmarking initiatives are growing in popularity.

Two nationally known benchmarking initiatives that use the methodology of "comparison of performance statistics as benchmarks" are ICMA's Comparative Performance Measurement (CPM) program and the North Carolina Benchmarking Project.[16] ICMA's program collects, cleans, and compares the performance results from more than 150 counties and municipalities across the United States using standardized measures. Figure 16–7 shows solid waste comparative data taken from the CPM's FY 2004 data report. North Carolina's project represents a regional benchmarking effort, which collects, cleans, and compares the performance results from sixteen municipalities within the state.

Although only a limited number of jurisdictions participate in formal benchmarking initiatives like the one managed by ICMA, the current interest in identifying best practices in local government is placing more emphasis on comparative statistics. Local officials join formal benchmarking initiatives to gain the power of comparative information. Internal trend data provide excellent information for tracking and analyzing performance results on the basis of current operational configurations and routines. Benchmarking data allow jurisdictions to place their performance results within the context of comparative statistics.

---

### Winston-Salem and the North Carolina Benchmarking Project

Winston-Salem, North Carolina (pop. 193,755), had tracked internal performance measures for residential refuse collection for some time. The city used a private hauler to service approximately 6,500 households, while in-house staff serviced the remainder. After Winston-Salem joined the North Carolina Benchmarking Project, the comparative data revealed that there was additional service capacity within the city's internal operations of residential refuse collection. The city decided to discontinue the private contract and absorb the 6,500 households into its existing internal staffing and equipment levels, which resulted in an annual savings of approximately $395,000.

Source: Ann Jones, "Winston-Salem's Participation in the North Carolina Performance Measurement Project," *Government Finance Review* 13 (August 1997): 35-36.

**Figure 16-7** **Operating and maintenance expenditures for refuse collection per refuse collection account, FY 2002–FY 2004, various cities**

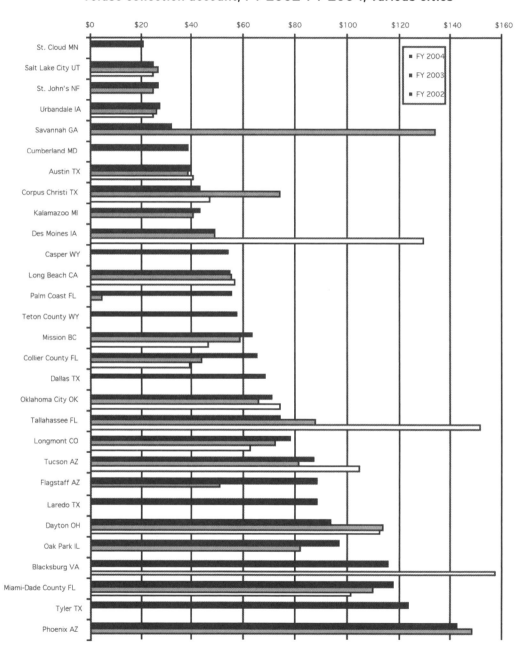

Source: Center for Performance Measurement, *Comparative Performance Measurement: FY 2004 Data Report* (Washington, D.C.: ICMA, 2005), 537.

## Program evaluation

Program evaluation—the periodic, regular evaluation of programs and services with the goal of improving performance—is on the way to becoming a professional norm in local government. These systematic reviews can take the form of management studies, special projects, or other forms of analysis. Research appears to show that program evaluation is one of the most common management tools in local government. One study found that more than 70 percent of municipalities with populations between 25,000 and 1,000,000 used program evaluation either citywide or within selected areas, making program evaluation the most prevalent among the fourteen tools studied.[17]

However, given the differences in how program evaluation is likely to be defined, caution is advised when interpreting survey research. Among local managers, the definition tends to be fairly broad. Among social scientists, however, program evaluation has a narrower meaning that includes the use of specific techniques and methodologies to systematically investigate the effectiveness of social programs.[18]

> *Program evaluation is on the way to becoming a professional norm in local government.*

There are numerous examples of program evaluation as broadly defined in local government. It is common for managers and department heads to analyze the community impact from recreational and social programs, or the possibility of privatizing solid-waste services, adding new law enforcement officers, or cross-training selected personnel such as building inspectors and foster care workers. A common obstacle to program evaluation in local government, however, is a lack of trained staff members with the time to conduct periodic evaluations. A strategy for overcoming this hurdle and identifying possible strategies for service improvement is to hire graduate interns from neighboring academic institutions to conduct evaluation projects.[19]

### Greensboro, North Carolina

The city of Greensboro, North Carolina (pop. 231,962), is committed to program evaluation. In fact, the mission statement of the budget and evaluation department is to lead the organization in making informed and ultimately successful decisions in resource allocation, program evaluation, financial management, and long-range financial and management planning. Budget staff members conduct periodic management studies, which have included studies on user fees, organizational development and communication, part-time benefits, a leaf collection program, and drainage improvements. The results of these studies are posted on the department's Web site for citizen review and are used to inform resource allocation decisions.[20]

An April 2004 management study conducted by budget staff members examined the current staffing level of the patrol function in the city's police department. The study found that Greensboro was below the average for sworn officers per 1,000 residents and was above the average for response time per high-priority calls when compared against selected benchmarking partners. (In other words, Greensboro had relatively fewer sworn officers and responded relatively more slowly than police departments in comparable jurisdictions.) A workload analysis also produced a patrol availability factor of 6.6 percent, which represents the percentage of time available for proactive patrol. In response to the management study and the organizational goal of public safety, Greensboro approved an additional thirty-two sworn officers for its police department. It should be noted that in this instance, strategic planning, performance measurement, performance budgeting, benchmarking, and program evaluation were all instrumental in making the final staffing decision.

## Success factors with management tools

The management tools presented in this chapter carry some risk of being perceived as the latest "flavor of the month." It is important for the manager to relate them to the goal of transforming the organizational culture into a results-based management environment. While no one strategy guarantees success, certain factors can enhance the successful adoption and implementation of management tools.

Not surprisingly, the foremost success factor is leadership throughout the organization. But an organizational culture shift to results-based management requires leadership from areas beyond the city or county manager's office. Board members are critical in this culture shift: they must use the new management tools to help them make policy decisions and to communicate those decisions to the public. Program managers also must embrace results-based management for making daily management decisions. Leadership from board members and program managers is vital if line employees are to see the value in changing their approach to service delivery. It also ensures that the culture shift will continue even when turnover occurs in the manager's office.

*An organizational culture shift to results-based management requires leadership from areas beyond the manager's office.*

Success factors for results-based management also include information, capacity, and incentive.[21] Information is needed to show the current condition of the organization (i.e., to measure performance) and to determine where it is going (i.e., to identify feasible long-term goals). However, most local governments need to improve systematic training for the collecting and reporting of accurate and reliable performance data. Capacity refers to the organization's ability to use performance information, which is often linked to time, education, training, and technical assistance. Unfortunately, analytical capacity is often cited as a barrier to results-based management in local government. After information and capacity are in place, employees need incentive to act on the information and to use their capacity. Some counties and municipalities have implemented recognition and bonus programs as motivation for service improvement.

Technology that helps local managers expand the utility of management tools is another success factor. Technology, for example, that facilitates the collection, cleaning, and reporting of accurate and reliable performance data improves a local government's ability to manage effective performance measurement systems. The numerous tools found in basic spreadsheet packages allow analysts to graph measures over time for trend analysis and to look for cause-and-effect relationships with correlations and scatter plots.

Finally, introducing any of these tools requires change, or innovation, and any change can be difficult to make in an organization. The accompanying sidebar outlines some

**Managing innovation**

Innovation starts with recognition of the advantages of change, the barriers to change, and the positive forces supporting change. The advantages of change include better services and lower costs. The barriers include resistance to change, whether expressed through lack of cooperation or political action, and the reluctance of managers and elected officials to support change or allow new expenditures. Positive forces include persons, information, and arguments that serve to overcome resistance to change. Managed innovation proceeds as follows:

1. Recognize the need for change

2. Identify, explore, and evaluate alternatives

3. Select one alternative and present the need for and benefits of the change(s) to those who must cooperate for implementation

4. Plan innovation implementation with those most affected and include explanations, demonstrations, training, tests, and the evaluation process.

Resistance to change is almost universal. Making careful choices not only enhances the prospects for a successful change but also increases the possibility for future innovations. Success in implementing innovations helps melt resistance and activates positive forces for future innovations. Securing early involvement of those likely to be affected by change is crucial. Those seeking change should expect frequent frustrations.

Source: John W. Swain, "Fire and Emergency Medical Services," in *Managing Small Cities and Counties: A Practical Guide,* ed. James M. Banovetz, Drew A. Dolan, and John W. Swain (Washington, D.C.: ICMA, 1994), 234-235.

common themes for introducing and leading change, which also apply to the implementation of continuous process improvement.

## Conclusion

The town manager decided to approve four of the five recommendations offered by the productivity team for improving the organization's payroll process. The results were immediate. The number of replacement checks being written and the cost of payroll decreased substantially in less than one year. Reasons for the success came from very specific implementation guidelines for the recommendations and from the organization-wide training for all individuals involved in the payroll data-entry process. To recognize the employees who served on the payroll productivity team, the town manager wrote an article for the town's quarterly newsletter on the success of the town's first continuous process improvement project.

This chapter has presented five management tools—strategic planning, performance measurement, performance budgeting, benchmarking, and program evaluation—whose use is becoming the professional norm in local government. It should be obvious that these tools work together and are not mutually exclusive for maximizing limited resources in local government. They build on and reinforce each other to inform sound management decisions:

- Strategic planning provides the road map for organizational direction.

- Performance measurement monitors the performance of service delivery.

- Performance budgeting ensures that performance information is part of the budget development, implementation, and evaluation phases.

- Benchmarking compares the performance results from one organization with the performance results from other organizations in search of best practices.

- Program evaluation provides an environment in which to periodically review the twin objectives of public administration—the efficiency and effectiveness of governmental programs—and to feed that information back to the strategic planning process.

While the management tools presented in this chapter are not a panacea for solving problems in local government, they do assist local managers with making decisions on the basis of the goals and results of an organization. The alternative is to make decisions from a reactionary posture, which hinders the long-term development of any organization. In summary, management tools are designed to help local managers with reinvention—*the fundamental transformation of public systems and organizations to create dramatic increases in their effectiveness, efficiency, adaptability, and capacity to innovate.*[22]

## Endnotes

1  Other organizations also promote these management tools, including the Governmental Accounting Standards Board (GASB) and the Association of Government Accountants (AGA).

2  We must proceed with caution when relying on survey research to demonstrate the prevalence of management tools in local government, being careful to take into account how survey questions are structured and how local managers interpret them.

3  William C. Rivenbark, "Strategic Planning and the Budget Process," *Government Finance Review* 19 (October 2003): 22–27.

4  Theodore H. Poister and Gregory Streib, "Elements of Strategic Planning and Management in Municipal Government: Status after Two Decades," *Public Administration Review* 65 (January/February 2005): 45–56.

5  Daniel W. Williams, "Measuring Government in the Early Twentieth Century," *Public Administration Review* 63 (November/December 2003): 643–659.

6  Clarence E. Ridley and Herbert A. Simon, "Technique of Appraising Standards," *Public Management* 19 (February 1937): 46–49.

7  Harry P. Hatry, *Performance Measurement* (Washington, D.C.: Urban Institute Press, 1999), and David N. Ammons, *Municipal Benchmarks*, 2nd ed. (Thousand Oaks, Calif.: Sage, 2001).

8  Theodore H. Poister and Gregory Streib, "Performance Measurement in Municipal Government: Assessing the State of the Practice," *Public Administration Review* 59 (July/August 1999): 325–335; Evan Berman and XiaoHu Wang, "Performance Measurement in U.S. Counties: Capacity for Reform," *Public Administration Review* 60 (September/October 2000), 409–420; and William C. Rivenbark and Janet M. Kelly, "Management Innovation in Smaller Municipal Government," *State and Local Government Review* 35 (Fall 2003): 196–205.

9  David N. Ammons and William C. Rivenbark, "Using Benchmark Data to Improve Services: Local Impact of a Municipal Performance Comparison Project," presented at the annual meeting of the Southeastern Conference on Public Administration, Little Rock, Arkansas, October 2005.

10  The information on Fairfax County's performance measurement system is from the following sources, all of which were prepared by the county's Performance Measurement Team and published in 2005, and are available at co.fairfax.va.us under the Department of Management and Budget: *Manual for Performance Measurement*, 9th ed.; *Manual for Data Collection and for Performance Measurement;* and *Manual for Surveying for Customer Satisfaction.*

11  David Osborne and Peter Hutchinson, *The Price of Government* (New York: Basic Books, 2004).

12  XiaoHu Wang, "Assessing Performance Measurement Impact: A Study of U.S. Local Governments," *Public Performance & Management Review* 26 (September 2002): 26–43.

13  William C. Rivenbark, "Defining Performance Budgeting for Local Government," *Popular Government* 69 (Winter 2004): 27–36.

14  David Osborne and Ted Gaebler, *Reinventing Government* (New York: Penguin Group, 1992).

15  David N. Ammons, "Benchmarking as a Performance Management Tool: Experiences among Municipalities in North Carolina," *Journal of Public Budgeting, Accounting & Financial Management* 12 (Spring 2000): 106–124.

16  For information on the ICMA Comparative Performance Measurement program, see icma.org. For information on the North Carolina Benchmarking Project, see ncbenchmarking.unc.edu. There are also other projects around the county that collect and report comparative performance statistics.

17  Theodore H. Poister and Gregory Streib, "Municipal Management Tools from 1976 to 1993: An Overview and Update," *Public Productivity & Management Review* 18 (Winter 1994): 115–125.

18  Another evaluation tool found in local government is performance auditing. For a discussion on the differences between performance auditing and program evaluation, see Dwight F. Davis, "Do You Want a Performance Audit or Program Evaluation?" *Public Administration Review* 50 (January/February 1990): 35–41.

19  For information on ICMA's internship guidelines, see icma.org/nextgen.

20  For more information on program evaluation for the city of Greensboro, see ci.greensboro.nc.us/budget.

21  James E. Swiss, "A Framework for Assessing Incentives in Results-Based Management," *Public Administration Review* 65 (September/October 2005): 592–602.

22  David Osborne and Peter Plastrik, *Banishing Bureaucracy* (New York: Addison-Wesley, 1997).

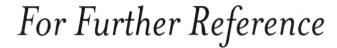

# For Further Reference

## Chapter 1: Meeting the Challenge of Change

*Organizations and Web sites*

American Society for Public Administration (ASPA), aspanet.org

National Academy of Public Administration (NAPA), napawash.org

National Association of Counties (NACo), naco.org

National League of Cities (NLC), nlc.org

U.S. Conference of Mayors (USCM), usmayors.org

## Chapter 2: The Legal Foundations of Local Government

*Publications and journals*

Baker, Lynn A., and Clayton P. Gillette. *Local Government Law: Cases and Materials.* 3rd ed. New York: Foundation Press, 2004.

Berman, David R. *State and Local Politics.* Armonk, N.Y.: M. E. Sharpe, 2000.

McCarthy, David, Jr., and Laurie Reynolds. *Local Government Law in a Nutshell.* 5th ed. St. Paul, Minn.: West Group, 2003.

Smith, Ken. "Working with the Municipal Attorney." *Current Municipal Problems* 31, no. 4 (2004–2005): 448.

## Chapter 3: The Clerk

*Publications and journals*

Cohen, Sheldon S. "The Paperless Council." *IQ Report* 34 (October 2002).

Freeman, Robert, Mark R. W. LeMahieu, Jason Sanders, David O. Stephens, and Julian L. Mims III, eds. *Electronic Records Management.* Washington, D.C.: ICMA, 2006.

Mims, Julian L., III. *Records Management: A Practical Guide for Cities and Counties.* Washington, D.C.: ICMA, 1996.

*Organizations and Web sites*

International Association of Clerks, Recorders, Election Officials and Treasurers (IACREOT), iacreot.com

International Institute of Municipal Clerks (IIMC), iimc.com

Municipal Code Corporation (MCC), municode.com

## Chapter 4: Budgeting and Financial Management

*Publications and journals*

Aronson, J. Richard, and Eli Schwartz, eds. *Management Policies in Local Government Finance.* 5th ed. Washington, D.C.: ICMA, 2004.

Benest, Frank. *Marketing Your Budget: Creative Ways to Engage Citizens.* Washington, D.C.: ICMA, 1997.

Bland, Robert L. *A Revenue Guide for Local Government.* 2nd ed. Washington, D.C.: ICMA, 2005.

Bland, Robert L., and Irene Rubin. *Budgeting: A Guide for Local Governments.* Washington, D.C.: ICMA, 1997.

Ebdon, Carol, and Aimee Franklin. "Searching for a Role for Citizens in the Budget Process." *Public Budgeting & Finance* 24 (Spring 2004): 32–49.

Epstein, Paul, James Fountain, Wilson Campbell, Terry Patton, and Kimberly Keaton. *Government Service Efforts and Accomplishments Performance Reports: A Guide to Understanding.* Norwalk, Conn.: Governmental Accounting Standards Board, 2005. Available at store.yahoo.com/gasbpubs/publications-user-guides.html.

Gauthier, Stephen J. *Evaluating Internal Controls: A Local Manager's Guide.* Chicago: Government Finance Officers Association (GFOA), 1996.

_____. *Governmental Accounting, Auditing, and Financial Reporting: Using the GASB 34 Model.* Chicago: GFOA, 2005.

Government Finance Officers Association. *An Introduction to Treasury Management Practices.* Chicago: GFOA, 1998.

Greifer, Nicholas, ed. *Banking Services: A Guide for Governments.* Chicago: GFOA, 2004.

Joseph, James C. *Debt Issuance and Management: A Guide for Smaller Governments.* Chicago: GFOA, 1994.

Lee, Robert D., Jr., Ronald W. Johnson, and Philip G. Joyce. *Public Budgeting Systems.* 7th ed. Sudbury, Mass.: Jones and Bartlett, 2004.

Marlowe, Justin. "The Budget as a Communication Tool." *IQ Report* 37, no. 4 (2005).

Nollenberger, Karl, Sanford Groves, and Maureen Godsey Valente. *Evaluating Financial Condition: A Handbook for Local Government.* Washington, D.C.: ICMA, 2003.

Reed, B. J., and John W. Swain. *Public Finance Administration.* 2nd ed. Thousand Oaks, Calif.: Sage, 1996.

Vogt, A. John. *Capital Budgeting and Finance: A Guide for Local Governments.* Washington, D.C.: ICMA, 2004.

*Organizations and Web sites*

Government Finance Officers Association GFOA), gfoa.org

Governmental Accounting Standards Board (GASB), gasb.org

## Chapter 5: Human Resource Management

*Publications and journals*

*American Review of Public Administration,* arp.sagepub.com.

Condrey, Stephen, ed. *Handbook of Human Resource Management in Government.* 2nd ed. San Francisco: Jossey-Bass, 2005.

Condrey, Stephen, and Robert Maranto, eds. *Radical Reform of the Civil Service.* Lanham, Md.: Lexington Books, 2001.

Dresang, Dennis. *Public Personnel Management and Public Policy.* 4th ed. New York: Longman, 2001.

Hatry, Harry P., Philip S. Schaenman, Donald M. Fisk, John R. Hall Jr., and Louise Snyder. *How Effective Are Your Community Services? Procedures for Performance Measurement.* 3rd ed. Washington, D.C.: ICMA, 2006.

Hays, Steven, and Richard Kearney, eds. *Public Personnel Administration: Problems and Prospects.* Englewood Cliffs, N.J.: Prentice Hall, 2003.

Kellough, J. Edward, and Lloyd G. Nigro. *Civil Service Reform in the States: Personnel Politics and Policy at the Subnational Level.* Albany: State University of New York Press, 2006.

Nigro, Lloyd G., Felix A. Nigro, and J. Edward Kellough. *The New Public Personnel Administration.* 6th ed. Wadsworth Publishing, 2006.

*Public Administration Review,* aspanet.org/scriptcontent/index_par.cfm.

*Public Personnel Management,* ipma-hr.org/content.cfm?pageid = 110.

Pynes, Joan. *Human Resources Management for Public and Nonprofit Organizations.* San Francisco: Jossey-Bass, 2005.

*Review of Public Personnel Administration,* roppa.org.

Riccucci, Norma. *Managing Diversity in Public Sector Workforces.* Boulder, Colo.: Westview Press, 2002.

_____. *Public Personnel Management: Current Concerns, Future Challenges.* Longman, 2005.

*Organizations and Web sites*

Academy of Human Resource Development (AHRD), ahrd.org

Academy of Management (AOM), aomonline.org

American Society for Public Administration (ASPA), aspanet.org

American Society for Training and Development (ASTD), astd.org

Center for Performance Measurement (CPM), icma.org/main/bc.asp?bcid = 107&hsid = 1&ssid1 = 50&ssid2 = 220&ssid3 = 297&t = 0.

Conference of Minority Public Administrators (COMPA), natcompa.org

HR.com

HR Internet Guide, hr-guide.com

Human Resource Planning Society (HRPS), hrps.org

International Association for Human Resource Information (IHRIM), ihrim.org

International Public Management Association for Human Resources, ipma-hr.org

National Association of State Personnel Executives, naspe.net

Office of Personnel Management (OPM), opm.gov

Society for Human Resource Management (SHRM), shrm.org

## Chapter 6: Planning

### Publications and journals

American Planning Association. *Planning and Urban Design Standards.* New York: John Wiley, 2006.

Anderson, Larz T. *Guidelines for Preparing Urban Plans.* Chicago: Planners Press, 1995.

_____. *Planning the Built Environment.* Chicago: Planners Press, 2005.

Baer, William C. "General Plan Evaluation Criteria: An Approach to Making Better Plans." *Journal of the American Planning Association* 63, no. 3 (1997): 329–344.

Daniels, Tom, and Katherine Daniels. *The Environmental Planning Handbook for Sustainable Communities and Regions.* Chicago: Planners Press, 2003.

Hoch, Charles, Frank S. So, and Linda C. Dalton, eds. *The Practice of Local Planning.* 3rd ed. Washington, D.C.: ICMA, 2000.

ICMA and the Smart Growth Network. *Getting to Smart Growth: 100 Policies for Implementation.* Washington, D.C.: ICMA, 2003. Available at bookstore.icma.org/obs/showdetl.cfm?&DID = 7&Product_ID = 958&CATID = 4.

_____. *Getting to Smart Growth II: 100 More Policies for Implementation.* Washington, D.C.: ICMA, 2003. Available at bookstore.icma.org/obs/showdetl.cfm?&DID = 7&Product_ID = 1041&CATID = 4.

Kaiser, Edward J., David R. Godschalk, and F. Stuart Chapin Jr. *Urban Land Use Planning.* 4th ed. Urbana: University of Illinois Press, 1995.

Kent, T. J., Jr. *The Urban General Plan.* Chicago: Planners Press, 1990.

Lerable, Charles. *Preparing a Conventional Zoning Ordinance.* Planning Advisory Service Report no. 460. Chicago: American Planning Association, 1995.

Listokin, David, and Carole Walker. *The Subdivision and Site Plan Handbook.* New Brunswick, N.J.: Center for Urban Policy Research, Rutgers University, 1989.

Mandelker, Daniel R. *Land Use Law.* 5th ed. Newark, N.J.: Lexis/Nexis, 2003.

McLean, Mary, and Kenneth Voytek. *Understanding Your Economy: Using Analysis to Guide Local Strategic Planning.* Chicago: Planners Press, 1992.

Meck, Stuart, ed. *The Growing Smart Legislative Guidebook: Model Statutes for Planning and the Management of Change.* Chicago: American Planning Association, 2002.

Nelson, Arthur C. *Planner's Estimating Guide: Projecting Land-Use and Facility Needs.* Chicago: Planners Press, 2004.

Purcell, L. Edward. "Streamlining Development and Building Permitting." *IQ Report* 37, no. 2 (2005).

Singer, Molly. *Small Spaces, Special Places: Coordination of Rural Brownfields Development.* Washington, D.C.: ICMA, 2001. Available free at icma.org/main/ld.asp?from = search&ldid = 16497&hsid = 1.

*Organizations and Web sites*

American Planning Association (APA), planning.org

Congress for the New Urbanism (CNU), cnu.org

Municipal Research and Service Center (MRSC) of Washington, mrsc.org

New Jersey Council on Affordable Housing, nj.gov/dca/coah

Oregon Department of Land Conservation and Development, lcd.state.or.us

Smart Growth Network (SGN), smartgrowth.org

U.S. Environmental Protection Agency (EPA), www.epa.gov

U.S. Department of Housing and Urban Development (HUD), hud.gov

## Chapter 7: Economic Development

*Publications and journals*

Banovetz, James. M., ed. *Managing Local Economic Development: Cases in Decision Making.* Washington, D.C.: ICMA, 2004.

Bingham, Richard D., and Robert Mier. *Theories of Local Economic Development.* Thousand Oaks, Calif.: Sage, 1993.

Blakely, Edward J., and Ted K. Bradshaw. *Planning Local Economic Development.* Thousand Oaks, Calif.: Sage, 2002.

Cohen-Rosenthal, Edward, and Judy Musnikow. *Eco-Industry Strategies.* Sheffield, United Kingdom: Greenleaf Publishing, 2003.

Corporation for Enterprise Development. *2004 Development Report for the States.* Washington, D.C., 2004. Available at cfed.org/focus.m?parentid = 31&siteid = 1099&id = 1099.

Cortright, Joseph, and Heike Mayer. "Increasingly Rank: The Use and Misuse of Rankings in Economic Development." *Economic Development Quarterly* 18, no. 1 (2004): 34–39.

Davis, Richard, and Robert J. Parsons. "Marketing for Economic Development." *IQ Report* 35, no. 2 (2003).

*Economic Development Futures Journal (ED Futures),* don-iannone.com/edfutures

*Economic Development Quarterly,* edq.sagepub.com.

Erickcek, George A. "Preparing a Local Fiscal Benefit-Cost Analysis." *IQ Report* 37, no. 3 (2005).

Feldman, Maryann P., and Johanna L. Francis. "Homegrown Solutions: Fostering Cluster Formation." *Economic Development Quarterly* 18, no. 2 (2004): 127–137.

Harper, David A. *Foundations of Entrepreneurship and Economic Development.* New York and London: Routledge, 2003.

Iannone, Donald, T. *Creating Leadership Advantage for Economic Development.* Amazon .com Publishing, 2006. Also available at don-iannone.com.

Iannone, Donald, and Daryl McKee. *Marketing Communities in the Information Age.* Chicago: American Economic Development Council, 1999. Available at iedconline.org.

ICMA. "Economic Development 2004" survey. Available at icma.org/upload/bc/attach/ {34A39D05-637E-4BA6-9D9F-BB9EEDD48AB7}ed2004web.pdf.

Immergluck, Dan. "Building Power, Losing Power: The Rise and Fall of a Prominent Community Economic Development Coalition." *Economic Development Quarterly* 19, no. 3 (2005): 211–224.

Koo, Jun. "How to Analyze the Regional Economy with Occupation Data." *Economic Development Quarterly* 19, no. 4 (2005): 356–372.

Koven, Steven G., and Thomas S. Lyons. Economic *Development: Strategies for State and Local Practice.* Washington, D.C.: ICMA, 2003.

Lyons, Thomas, and Steven G. Koven. "Economic Development and Public Policy at the Local Government Level." In *The Municipal Year Book 2006,* 11–18. Washington, D.C.: ICMA, 2006.

McGrath, John M., and Ronald Vickroy. "A Research Approach for Tracking Local Economic Conditions in Small-Town America." *Economic Development Quarterly* 17, no. 3 (2003): 255–263.

Mondello, Michael J., and Patrick Rishe. "Comparative Economic Impact Analyses: Differences across Cities, Events, and Demographics." *Economic Development Quarterly* 18, no. 4 (2004): 331–342.

Poole, Kenneth E., George A. Erickcek, Donald T. Iannone, Nancy McCrea, and Pofen Salem. *Evaluating Business Development Incentives.* Washington, D.C.: National Association of State Development Agencies, 1999.

Psilos, Phil, and Dan Broun. "Cluster-Based Economic Development." *IQ Report* 38, no. 1 (2006).

Schaeffer, Peter V., and Scott Loveridge. *Small Town and Rural Economic Development.* Westport, Conn.: Praeger/Greenwood, 2000.

Seidman, Karl F. *Economic Development Finance.* Thousand Oaks, Calif.: Sage, 2004.

### Organizations and Web sites

American Planning Association, Economic Development Division, planning.org/economic

CoreNet Global, www2.corenetglobal.org/home/index.vsp

Economic Development Administration (EDA), commerce.gov/eda

Economic Development Directory, ecodevdirectory.com/

Industrial Asset Management Council (IAMC), iamc.org/index.shtml

International Economic Development Council (IEDC), iedconline.org

National Development Council (NDC), nationaldevelopmentcouncil.org

## Chapter 8: Community Development and Affordable Housing

### Publications and journals

Garmise, Shari. *People and the Competitive Advantage of Place: Building a Workforce for the 21st Century.* Armonk, N.Y.: M. E. Sharpe, 2006.

Green, Gary Paul, and Anna Haines. *Asset Building and Community Development.* Thousand Oaks, Calif.: Sage, 2002.

Harrison, Bennett, and Marcus Weiss. *Workforce Development Networks: Community-Based Organizations and Regional Alliances.* Thousand Oaks, Calif.: Sage, 1998.

Hatry, Harry P., Philip S. Schaenman, Donald M. Fisk, John R. Hall Jr., and Louise Snyder. *How Effective Are Your Community Services? Procedures for Performance Measurement.* 3rd ed. Washington, D.C.: ICMA, 2006.

*"Why Not in Our Community?" Removing Barriers to Affordable Housing.* Washington, D.C.: Office of Policy Development and Research, U.S. Department of Housing and Urban Development, 2005. Available at huduser.org/publications/affhsg/whynotourComm.html.

### Organizations and Web sites

Center for Neighborhood Technology (CNT), cnt.org

Center for Performance Measurement (CPM)
　　　See listing under Chapter 5 above.

Coalition of Community Development Financial Institutions (CDFI Coalition), cdfi.org

Corporation for Enterprise Development (CFED), cfed.org

KnowledgePlex®, knowledgeplex.org

Local Initiatives Support Corporation (LISC), liscnet.org

National Affordable Housing Training Institite, nahti.org

National Association for County Community and Economic Development (NACCED), nacced.org

National Association of Housing and Redevelopment Officials (NAHRO), nahro.org

National Community Development Association (NCDA), ncdaonline.org

National Congress for Community Economic Development (NCCED), ncced.org

National Housing Conference (NHC), nhc.org

National Housing Institute (NHI), nhi.org

Urban Land Institute (ULI), uli.org

U.S. Department of Housing and Urban Development (HUD), hud.gov

## Chapter 9: Public Works

### Publications and journals

American Public Works Association (APWA). *Leadership in the New Age of Public Works with John Luthy.* CD-ROM. Washington, D.C.: APWA, 2004.

————, Leadership and Management Committee. *Building on the Basics: Core Competencies in Public Works.* Washington, D.C.: APWA, 2006.

Ammons, David N., Erin S. Norfleet, and Brian T. Coble. *Performance Measures and Benchmarks in Local Government Facilities Maintenance.* Washington, D.C.: ICMA, 2002.

Gordon, Stephen B. "Alternative Procurement Strategies for Construction." *IQ Report* 37, no. 6 (2005).

Green, Wyatt. "Stormwater Management." *IQ Report* 33, no. 10 (2001).

Hatry, Harry P., Philip S. Schaenman, Donald M. Fisk, John R. Hall Jr., and Louise Snyder. *How Effective Are Your Community Services? Procedures for Performance Measurement.* 3rd ed. Washington, D.C.: ICMA, 2006.

*Information Technology in Local Government: A Practical Guide for Managers.* Washington, D.C.: ICMA, 2001.

Luthy, John. "The Great Escape: How Retirement, Recruitment, and Retention Are Impacting the Field of Public Works." *Tech Transfer Newsletter* (Spring 2005). Available at techtransfer.berkeley.edu/newsletter/05-2/escape.php?print = t.

Vogt, A. John. *Capital Budgeting and Finance: A Guide for Local Governments.* Washington, D.C.: ICMA, 2004.

Walsh, Mary, and Beverly Salas. "Sustainable Energy: Power Solutions for Local Governments." *IQ Report* 33, no. 4 (2001).

Whiteman, Kathryn. "Green Building." *IQ Report* 35, no. 12 (2003).

### *Organizations and Web sites*

Air & Waste Management Association (A&WMA), awma.org

American Public Works Association (APWA), apwa.net

American Water Works Association (AWWA), awwa.org

Center for Performance Measurement (CPM)
    See listing under Chapter 5 above.

Landfill Methane Outreach Program (LMOP), epa.gov/landfill/index.htm

Local Government Environmental Assistance Network (LGEAN), lgean.org

  The Environmental Liability Outreach Web Template (lgean.org/html/elo_template_ intro.cfm)

Methane to Markets, methanetomarkets.org

National Association of Clean Water Agencies, nacwa.org

Public Entity EMS Resource (PEER) Center, peercenter.net

Solid Waste Association of North America (SWANA), swana.org

Stormwater Manager's Resource Center (SMRC), stormwatercenter.net

Water Environment Federation (WEF), wef.org

U.S. Environmental Protection Agency (EPA), epa.gov

U.S. Green Building Council (USGBC), usgbc.org

## Chapter 10: Public Parks and Recreation

### *Publications and journals*

Arnold, Margaret, Linda Heyne, and James Busser. *Problem Solving Tools and Techniques for Park and Recreation Administrators.* 4th ed. Champaign, Ill.: Sagamore, 2005.

Crompton, John L. *Financing and Acquiring Park and Recreation Resources.* Champaign, Ill.: Human Kinetics, 1999.

_____. *The Proximate Principal: The Impact of Park, Open Space and Water Features on Residential Property Values and the Property Taxbase.* Ashburn, Va.: National Recreation and Park Association (NRPA), 2004.

Degraff, Donald G., Debra J. Jordan, and Kathy DeGraff. *Programming for Parks, and Recreation, and Leisure Services: A Servant Leadership Approach.* 2nd ed. College Station, Pa.: Venture, 2005.

Edginton, Christopher R., Susan D. Hudson, and Samual V. Lankford. *Managing Recreation, Parks and Leisure Services: An Introduction.* Champaign, Ill.: Sagamore, 2001.

Edginton, Christopher R., Susan D. Hudson, and Kathleen G. Scholl. *Leadership for Recreation, Parks and Leisure Services.* 3rd ed. Champaign, Ill.: Sagamore, 2005.

Fogg, George F. *A Site Design and Management Process.* Ashburn, Va.: NRPA, 2000.

Hatry, Harry P., Philip S. Schaenman, Donald M. Fisk, John R. Hall Jr., and Louise Snyder. *How Effective Are Your Community Services? Procedures for Performance Measurement.* 3rd ed. Washington, D.C.: ICMA, 2006.

Henderson, Karla A., and M. D. Bialeschki. *Evaluating Leisure Services: Making Enlightened Decisions.* 2nd ed. College Station, Pa.: Venture, 2002.

Hultsman, John, Richard L. Cottrell, and Wendy Hultsman. *Planning Parks for People.* 2nd ed. College Station, Pa.: Venture, 1998.

Kutska, Kenneth S., Kevin J. Huffman, and Antonio Malkusak. *Playground Safety Is No Accident.* 3rd ed. Ashburn, Va.: NRPA, 2002.

Mertes, James D., and James R. Hall. *Park, Recreation, Open Space, and Greenways Guidelines.* Ashburn, Va.: NRPA, 1995.

Moon, M. Sherril. *Making School and Community Recreation for Everyone: Places and Ways to Integrate.* Baltimore, Md.: Paul H. Brookes, 1994.

Rossman, J. Robert, and Barbara E. Schlatter. *Recreation Programming: Design Leisure Experiences.* 4th ed. Champaign, Ill.: Sagamore, 2003.

Van der Smissen, Betty, Merry Moiseichik, and Vern J. Hartenburg. *Management of Park and Recreation Agencies.* 2nd ed. Ashburn, Va.: NRPA, 2005.

Witt, Peter, and Linda L. Caldwell. *Recreation and Youth Development.* State College, Pa.: Venture, 2005.

Witt, Peter, and John L. Crompton. *Best Practices in Youth Development in Public Park and Recreation Settings.* Ashburn, Va.: NRPA, 2002.

### Organizations and Web sites

Active Network, theactivenetwork.com

American with Disabilities Act (ADA), usdoj.gov/crt/ada/adahom1.htm

Bureau of Recreation and Conservation, Pennsylvania, dcnr.state.pa.us/info/ataglance/fsbrc.aspx

Center for Performance Measurement (CPM)
    See listing under Chapter 5 above.

Consumer Product Safety Commission (CPSC), cpsc.gov

Municipal Research and Services Center (MRSC) of Washington State, mrsc.org/Subjects/Parks/parks.aspx

National Alliance for Youth Sports (NAYS), nays.org

National Program for Playground Safety (NPPS), uni.edu/playground

National Recreation and Park Association (NRPA), nrpa.org

Office of Juvenile Justice and Delinquency Prevention (OJJDP), ojjdp.ncjrs.org

Parks and Recreation Technical Assistance Service, Tennessee, state.tn.us/environment/ recreation/park&rec.shtml

Project for Public Spaces (PPS), pps.org/info/aboutpps/?referrer = pps_navbar

Recreation Resources Service (RRS), North Carolina State University, natural-resources .ncsu.edu/rrs

Trust for Public Land (TPL), tpl.org

## Chapter 11: Health and Human Services

*Publications and journals*

Bluford, John, and Deborah Chase. "Hennepin County's Success with a Public HMO." *PM Magazine* 77 (March 1995): 9–13.

Brody, Ralph. *Effectively Managing Human Service Organizations.* Thousand Oaks, Calif.: Sage, 2005.

Brown, Alan. "Achieving Better Results with Limited Resources." *PM Magazine* 86 (August 2004): 16–19.

Crimando, William, and T. F. Riggar. *Community Resources: A Guide for Human Service Workers.* Long Grove, Ill.: Waveland Press, 2005.

Dorman, Rebekah L., and Jeremy P. Shapiro. *Preventing Burnout in Your Staff and Yourself: A Survival Guide for Human Services Supervisors.* Washington, D.C.: CWLA Press, 2004.

Folta, Jennifer, and John Scanlon. "Community Health Care Reform: Introducing the 100%/0 Campaign." *PM Magazine* 86 (April 2004): 26–28.

Gaunt, Patrick, and Paul Smyth. "Mapping for Caseworkers." *PM Magazine* 84 (June 2002): 24–26.

Hajer, Marilyn, and Mary Walsh. "Coping with Community Trauma." *PM Magazine* 87 (May 2005): 8–11.

Hornik, Robert C., ed. *Public Health Communication.* Mahwah, N.J.: Lawrence Erlbaum Associates, 2002.

Isaacs, Stephen L., and James R. Knickman, eds. *To Improve Health and Health Care.* Vol. 8. San Francisco: Jossey-Bass, 2005.

Kahn, William A. *Holding Fast: The Struggle to Create Resilient Caregiving Organizations.* Hove, East Sussex, Canada, and New York: Brunner-Routledge, 2005.

Ketchum, Stacie. "Health Care: Is It a Local Issue?" *PM Magazine* 83 (August 2001): 6–12.

Maheswaran, Ravi, and Massimo Craglia, eds. *GIS in Public Health Practice.* Boca Raton, Fla.: CRC Press, 2004.

Manning, Susan Schissler. *Ethical Leadership in Human Services: A Multi-Dimensional Approach.* Boston: Allyn and Bacon, 2003.

Pantazis, Cynthia. "Welfare Reform: One Year Later." *PM Magazine* 79 (November 1997): 10–15.

Parsons, Robert, H. Bruce Higley, Vicki Wallock Okerlund, Clark Thorstensen, and Howard Gray. "Assessing the Needs of Our Elders." *PM Magazine* 77 (February 1995): 14–16.

Payne, Ruby K. *A Framework for Understanding Poverty.* Rev. ed. Highlands, Tex.: RFT Publishing, 1998.

Rice, Kathy. "Health Services: Client-Based or Population-Based?" *PM* Magazine 86 (January/February 2004): 24–26.

Wuthnow, Robert. *Saving America? Faith-Based Services and the Future of Civil Society.* Princeton, N.J.: Princeton University Press, 2004.

### Organizations and Web sites

American Diabetes Association, diabetes.org

American Public Human Services Association (APHSA), aphsa.org

Centers for Disease Control and Prevention (CDC), cdc.gov

HandsNet (Human Services and Community Development), handsnet.org

Living Wage Resource Center, livingwagecampaign.org

National Association of Counties (NACo), naco.org

National Association of Regional Councils (NARC), narc.org

National Civic League (NCL), ncl.org

National League of Cities (NLC), nlc.org

National Organization for Human Services (NOHS), nohse.com

U.S. Census Bureau, census.gov

U.S. Conference of Mayors (USCM), usmayors.org

U.S. Department of Health and Human Services (DHHS), hhs.gov

World Health Organization (WHO), who.int/en

## Chapter 12: Emergency Management

### Publications and journals

Gordon, James A. *Comprehensive Emergency Management for Local Governments: Demystifying Emergency Planning.* Brookfield, Conn.: Rothstein Associates Inc., 2002.

Haddock, George, and Jane Bullock. *Introduction to Emergency Management.* 2nd ed. Burlington, Mass.: Butterworth-Heinemann Homeland Security, 2005.

Hatry, Harry P., Philip S. Schaenman, Donald M. Fisk, John R. Hall Jr., and Louise Snyder. *How Effective Are Your Community Services? Procedures for Performance Measurement.* 3rd ed. Washington, D.C.: ICMA, 2006.

Molino, Louis N., Sr. *Emergency Incident Management Systems: Fundamentals and Applications.* Hoboken, N.J.: John Wiley & Sons, 2006.

Waugh, William, and Gerard J. Hoetmer. *EM: Principles and Practice for Local Government.* 2nd ed. Washington, D.C.: ICMA, 2007.

### Organizations and Web sites

Building Owners and Managers Association International (BOMAI), boma.org

Center for Performance Measurement (CPM)
    See listing under Chapter 5 above.

Community Awareness and Emergency Response (CAER), caer-mp.org

Emergency Management Accreditation Program (EMAP), emaponline.org

Emergency Management Institute (EMI), training.fema.gov/emiweb

Emergency Management Issues Special Interest Group (EMI SIG), orau.gov/emi

Federal Emergency Management Agency (FEMA), fema.gov

InfraGard, infragard.net

Innovation Groups (IG), ig.org

International Association of Emergency Managers (IAEM), iaem.com

International Association of Fire Chiefs (IAFC), iafc.org

National Fire Protection Association (NFPA), nfpa.org

National Hurricane Conference, hurricanemeeting.com

Public Entity Risk Institute (PERI), riskinstitute.org

Public Risk Management Association (PRIMA), primacentral.org

Ready.gov

Transportation Community Awareness and Emergency Response (TRANSCAER), transcaer.org

U.S. Computer Emergency Readiness Team (US-CERT), us-cert.gov

U.S. Department of Homeland Security (DHS), dhs.gov

## Chapter 13: Police Services

### *Publications and journals*

Alpert, Geoffrey P., Dennis Jay Kenney, Roger G. Dunham, and William C. Smith. *Police Pursuits: What We Know.* Washington, D.C.: Police Executive Research Forum (PERF), 2000.

Cordner, Gary W., Kathryn E. Scarborough, and Robert Sheehan. *Police Administration.* 5th ed. Cincinnati, Ohio: Anderson Publishing/LexisNexis, 2004.

Ederheimer, Joshua A., and Lorie A. Fridell, eds. *Chief Concerns: Exploring the Challenges of Police Use of Force.* Washington, D.C.: PERF, 2005.

Fridell, Lorie, Robert Lunney, Drew Diamond, and Bruce Kubu. *Racially Biased Policing: A Principled Response.* Washington, D.C.: PERF, 2001.

Fridell, Lorie, and Mary Ann Wycoff, eds. *Community Policing: The Past, Present, and Future.* Washington, D.C.: Annie E. Casey Foundation and PERF, 2004.

Fyfe, James J., Jack R. Greene, William F. Walsh, O. W. Wilson, and Roy C. McLaren. *Police Administration.* 5th ed. New York: McGraw-Hill, 1997.

Geller, William A., ed. *Police Leadership in America: Crisis and Opportunity.* New York: Praeger, 1985.

Geller, William A., and Darrel W. Stephens. *Local Government Police Management.* 4th ed. Washington, D.C.: ICMA, 2003.

Goldstein, Herman. *Policing A Free Society.* Cambridge, Mass.: Ballinger, 1977.

_____. *Problem-Oriented Policing.* New York: McGraw-Hill, 1990.

Harris, David A. *Good Cops: The Case for Preventive Policing.* New York: The New Press, 2005.

Hatry, Harry P., Philip S. Schaenman, Donald M. Fisk, John R. Hall Jr., and Louise Snyder. *How Effective Are Your Community Services? Procedures for Performance Measurement.* 3rd ed. Washington, D.C.: ICMA, 2006.

ICMA/PERF. *Selecting a Police Chief: A Handbook for Local Government.* Washington, D.C.: ICMA, 1999.

Jones, Glenn R. "Police and Fire Physical Fitness." *IQ Report* 36, no. 1 (2004).

Moore, Mark, and Darrel W. Stephens. *Beyond Command and Control: The Strategic Management of Police Departments.* Washington, D.C.: PERF, 1991.

Moore, Mark with David Thacher, Andrea Dodge, and Tobias Moore. *Recognizing Value in Policing: The Challenge of Measuring Police Performance.* Washington, D.C.: PERF, 2002.

Office of Community Oriented Policing Services. *Law Enforcement Tech Guide: How to Plan, Purchase, and Manage Technology (Successfully!).* Available at cops.usdoj.gov/default.asp?Item = 512.

Romesburg, William H. *Law Enforcement Tech Guide for Small and Rural Police Agencies: A Guide for Executives, Managers, and Technologists.* Sacramento, Calif.: The Search Group, 2005. Available at cops.usdoj.gov/mime/open.pdf?Item = 1619.

Skogan, Wesley, and Kathleen Frydl, eds. *Fairness and Effectiveness in Policing: The Evidence.* Washington, D.C.: National Research Council, 2004.

Sparrow, Malcolm, Mark H. Moore, and David M. Kennedy. *Beyond 911: A New Era for Policing.* New York: Basic Books, 1990.

"Use of Force/Pursuits—Policies and Practices." Statement on the Web site of the Tallahassee, Florida, police department. Available at talgov.com/tpd/force.cfm.

### Organizations and Web sites

Center for Performance Measurement (CPM)
    See listing under Chapter 5 above.

Center for Problem-Oriented Policing (POP Center), popcenter.org

Commission on Accreditation for Law Enforcement Agencies (CALEA), calea.org

International Association of Chiefs of Police (IACP), theiacp.org

National Association of Women Law Enforcement Executives (NAWLEE), nawlee.com

National Law Enforcement and Corrections Technology Center (NLECTC), nlectc.org

National Organization of Black Law Enforcement Executives (NOBLE), noblenational.org

National Sheriffs Association (NSA), sheriffs.org

Office of Community Oriented Policing Services (COPS Office), cops.usdoj.gov

Police Executive Research Forum (PERF), www.policeforum.org

## Chapter 14: Fire and Other Emergency Services

### Publications and journals

American Academy of Orthopaedic Surgeons. *Emergency Care and Transportation of the Sick and Injured.* 8th ed. Boston: Jones and Bartlett, 2002.

Baker, Charles J. *Firefighter's Handbook of Hazardous Materials*. 7th ed. Boston: Jones and Bartlett, 2006.

Benest, Frank, and Ruben Grijalva. "Enhancing the Manager/Fire Chief Relationship." *PM* Magazine (January/February 2002): 6–9.

Benoit, John, and Kenneth B. Perkins. "Managing Conflict in Combination Fire Departments." *IQ Service Report* 32, no. 7 (2000).

Buckman, John M., III. *Chief Fire Officer's Desk Reference.* Boston: Jones and Bartlett, 2006.

Clay, Franklin. "Managers and the Volunteer Fire Service: Sharing the Common Ground." *PM* Magazine 80 (July 1998).

Collins, Larry. *Technical Rescue Operations*. Vol. 1, *Planning, Training, and Command*. Tulsa, Okla.: Fire Engineering Books, 2004.

Compton, Dennis, and John Granito, eds. *Managing Fire and Rescue Services.* Washington, D.C.: ICMA, 2002.

Cote, Arthur E. *Fire Protection Handbook.* 19th ed. Vols. 1 and 2. Quincy, Mass.: National Fire Protection Association, 2003.

Hatry, Harry P., Philip S. Schaenman, Donald M. Fisk, John R. Hall Jr., and Louise Snyder. *How Effective Are Your Community Services? Procedures for Performance Measurement.* 3rd ed. Washington, D.C.: ICMA, 2006.

Sanders, Mick J. *Mosby's Paramedic's Textbook*. 3rd ed. St. Louis: C. V. Mosby, 2005.

### Organizations and Web sites

Center for Performance Measurement (CPM)
      See listing under Chapter 5 above.

Emergency Management Institute (EMI), training.fema.gov/emiweb

Federal Emergency Management Agency (FEMA), fema.gov

Firefighter Close Calls.com, firefighterclosecalls.com

International Association of Fire Chiefs (IAFC), iafc.org

International Association of Fire Fighters (IAFF), iaff.org

National Fire Fighter Near-Miss Reporting System, firefighternearmiss.com/home.do

National Fire Protection Association (NFPA), nfpa.org

National Highway Traffic Safety Administration (NHSTA), nhtsa.dot.gov/

Pipeline and Hazardous Materials Safety Administration (PHMSA), phmsa.dot.gov

U.S. Department of Homeland Security (DHS), dhs.gov

U.S. Fire Administration (USFA), usfa.fema.gov

Volunteer & Combination Officers Section (VCOS), vcos.org

## Chapter 15: Service Delivery Alternatives

### Publications and journals

Ammons, David N., ed. *Accountability for Performance: Measurement and Monitoring in Local Government*. Washington, D.C.: ICMA, 1995.

Argranoff, Robert. "Managing Collaborative Performance: Changing the Boundaries of the State?" *Public Performance & Management Review* 29 (September 2005): 18–45.

Argranoff, Robert, and Michael McGuire. *Collaborative Public Management: New Strategies for Local Government.* Washington, D.C.: Georgetown University Press, 2003.

Behn, Robert D. *Rethinking Democratic Accountability.* Washington, D.C.: Brookings Institution Press, 2001.

Behn, Robert D., and Peter A. Kant. "Strategies for Avoiding the Pitfalls of Performance Contracting." *Public Productivity & Management Review* 22 (April 1999): 470–489.

Berry, Frances Stokes, and Ralph S. Brower. "Intergovernmental and Intersectoral Management: Weaving Networking, Contracting Out, and Management Roles into Third Party Government." *Public Performance & Management Review* 29 (September 2005): 7–17.

Bryson, John M., and Barbara C. Crosby. *Leadership for the Common Good: Tackling Public Problems in a Shared-Power World.* San Francisco: Jossey-Bass, 1992.

Cooper, Phillip J. *Governing by Contract: Challenges and Opportunities for Public Managers.* Washington, D.C.: CQ Press, 2003.

Feldman, Barry M. "Reinventing Local Government: Beyond Rhetoric to Action." In *The Municipal Year Book 1999,* 20–24. Washington, D.C.: ICMA, 1999.

Harney, Donald F. *Service Contracting: A Local Government Guide.* Washington, D.C.: ICMA, 1992.

Kubisch, Anne C., Patricia Auspos, Prudence Brown, Robert Chaskin, Karen Fulbright-Anderson, and Ralph Hamilton. *Voices from the Field II: Reflections on Comprehensive Community Change.* Washington, D.C.: Aspen Institute, 2002.

Linden, Russell M. *Working across Boundaries: Making Collaboration Work in Government and Nonprofit Organizations.* San Francisco: Jossey-Bass, 2002.

Luke, Jeffrey S. *Catalytic Leadership: Strategies for an Interconnected World.* San Francisco: Jossey-Bass, 1998.

Morley, Elaine. "Local Government Use of Alternative Service Delivery Approaches." In *The Municipal Year Book 1999,* 34–44. Washington, D.C.: ICMA, 1999.

Padovani, Emanuele, and David Young. "Managing High-Risk Outsourcing." *PM* Magazine 88 (January/February 2006): 29–32.

"Program Excellence Award for Outstanding Partnerships: Intergovernmental Cooperation." 2005 ICMA Annual Awards Section. *PM* Magazine (September 2005): 23.

"Program Excellence Award for Outstanding Partnerships: Public-Private Partnerships." 2005 ICMA Annual Awards Section. *PM* Magazine (September 2005): 28.

Salamon, Lester M., ed. *The Tools of Government: A Guide to the New Governance.* New York: Oxford University Press, 2002.

Warner, Mildred, and Amir Hefetz. "Pragmatism over Politics: Alternative Service Delivery in Local Government, 1992–2002." In *The Municipal Year Book 2004,* 8–16. Washington, D.C.: ICMA, 2004.

Warner, Mildred, Amir Hefetz, and Michael Ballard. "Contracting Back In: When Privatization Fails." In *The Municipal Year Book 2003,* 32–38. Washington, D.C.: ICMA, 2003.

Whitaker, Gordon P., Frayda S. Bluestein, Anita R. Brown-Graham, Lydian Altman-Sauer, and Margaret Henderson. "Accountability in Local Government–Nonprofit Relationships." *IQ Report* 35, no. 5 (2003).

Whitaker, Gordon P., and Rosalind Day. "How Local Governments Work with Nonprofit Organizations in North Carolina." *Popular Government* 66 (Winter 2001): 25–32.

Whitaker, Gordon, Margaret Henderson, and Lydian Altman-Sauer. "Collaboration Calls for Mutual Accountability." *PM* Magazine 86 (December 2004): 16–20.

## Chapter 16: A Manager's Toolbox

*Publications and journals*

Ammons, David N., ed. *Accountability for Performance: Measurement and Monitoring in Local Government.* Washington, D.C.: ICMA, 1995.

_____. *Municipal Benchmarks: Assessing Local Performance and Establishing Community Standards.* 2nd ed. Thousand Oaks, Calif.: Sage, 2001.

_____. *Tools for Decision Making: A Practical Guide for Local Government.* Washington, D.C.: CQ Press.

Bryson, John M. *Strategic Planning for Public and Nonprofit Organizations*. 3rd ed. San Francisco: Jossey-Bass, 2004.

Coplin, William D., and Carol Dwyer. *Does Your Government Measure Up? Basic Tools for Local Officials and Citizens.* Syracuse, N.Y.: Maxwell School of Government, 2000.

Fountain, James, Wilson Campbell, Terry Patton, Paul Epstein, and Mandi Cohn. *Reporting Performance Information: Suggested Criteria for Effective Communication.* Norwalk, Conn.: Governmental Accounting Standards Board, 2003.

Gordon, Gerald L. *Strategic Planning for Local Government.* 2nd ed. Washington, D.C.: ICMA, 2005.

Guajardo, Salomon A., and Rosemary McDonnell. *An Elected Official's Guide to Performance Measurement.* Chicago: Government Finance Officers Association, 2000.

Hatry, Harry P. *Performance Measurement.* Washington, D.C.: The Urban Institute Press, 1999.

Hatry, Harry P., James R. Fountain, Jonathan M. Sullivan, and Lorraine Kremer, eds. *Service Efforts and Accomplishments Reporting: Its Time Has Come.* Norwalk, Conn.: Governmental Accounting Standards Board, 1990.

Hatry, Harry P., Philip S. Schaenman, Donald M. Fisk, John R. Hall Jr., and Louise Snyder. *How Effective Are Your Community Services? Procedures for Performance Measurement.* 3rd ed. Washington, D.C.: ICMA, 2006.

Kelly, Janet M., and William C. Rivenbark. *Performance Budgeting for State and Local Government.* Armonk, N.Y.: M. E. Sharpe, 2003.

Miller, Gerald J., W. Bartley Hildreth, and Jack Rabin. *Performance-Based Budgeting.* Boulder, Colo.: Westview Press, 2001.

Osborne, David, and Ted Gaebler. *Reinventing Government.* New York: Penguin Group, 1992.

Osborne, David, and Peter Hutchinson. *The Price of Government.* New York: Basic Books, 2004.

Rivenbark, William C. *A Guide to the North Carolina Local Government Performance Measurement Project.* Chapel Hill, N.C.: Institute of Government, 2001.

### Organizations and Web sites

Association of Government Accountants (AGA), agacgfm.org

Governmental Accounting Standards Board (GASB), gasb.org

North Carolina Benchmarking Project, ncbenchmarking.unc.edu

# About the Authors

**Susan Lipman Austin** (Editor) is a project director with the School of Government's Master of Public Administration Program at the University of North Carolina at Chapel Hill. She is also a member of the Institute of Government's Public Leadership Team, working primarily with municipal and county elected and appointed officials. She worked for fourteen years in the private sector as a retail manager and buyer. Immediately prior to joining the institute she was a Governor's Fellow in the NC Department of Environment and Natural Resources—Onsite Wastewater Section. Ms. Austin has an MPA from UNC Chapel Hill.

**Abraham David Benavides** (Chapter 11) is an assistant professor in the Department of Public Administration at the University of North Texas. He specializes in local government, human resources, diversity issues, and local government best practices for the Hispanic community. Dr. Benavides has published in the journal *State and Local Government Review*. He serves as president of the North Texas Chapter of the American Society for Public Administration; as a civil service commissioner for the city of Denton, Texas; and as a board member for a local nonprofit organization that sponsors a preschool for teaching at-risk children in Denton. Before entering academia, Dr. Benavides worked for county government in Ohio. He received his PhD from Cleveland State University.

**David R. Berman** (Chapter 2) is a senior research fellow at the Morrison Institute for Public Policy and a professor emeritus of political science at Arizona State University. His research has been supported by numerous grants and contracts, and along with being a regular contributor to ICMA's *Municipal Year Book*, he has produced seven books and more than sixty published papers, book chapters, or referred articles dealing with state and local government, politics, and public policy. Professor Berman has served as a consultant for the U.S. Advisory Commission on Intergovernmental Relations and on the executive committees of the American Political Science Association's Federalism and Intergovernmental Section and of the American Society for Public Administration's Section on Intergovernmental Administration and Management.

**Anita R. Brown-Graham** (Chapter 8) is a professor of public law and government in the School of Government at the University of North Carolina at Chapel Hill, where she specializes in affordable housing, economic and community development, and public liability. She conducts training and has written books and articles focused on developing the economic base of distressed communities. Professor Brown-Graham currently serves on the boards of several development organizations and foundations. Before joining the School of Government's faculty in 1994, she served as law clerk to the Honorable William B. Shubb in the eastern district of California and as a business litigation counsel in a Sacramento, California, law firm. She received her undergraduate degree from Louisiana State University and, after attending graduate school at LSU, earned a law degree from the University of North Carolina at Chapel Hill.

**Gary Cordner** (Chapter 13) is a professor of police studies at Eastern Kentucky University, where he also serves as director of the International Justice & Safety Institute and director of the Regional Community Policing Institute. He is past-president of the Academy of Criminal Justice Sciences and past-editor of *Police Quarterly* and the *American Journal of Police*. He is co-author of the books *Planning in Criminal Justice Organizations and Systems*, *Police Administration*, and *Police & Society,* and co-editor of four police anthologies. His articles have appeared in such journals as *Criminology & Public Policy*, *Criminology*, *Journal of Criminal Justice*, *Police Studies*, and *Journal of Police Science and Administration*. Professor Cordner has served on the Lexington/Fayette Civil Service Commission, the Kentucky Criminal Justice Council, and the Kentucky Law Enforcement Council. He also served as a police officer and police chief in the state of Maryland. He earned his PhD at Michigan State University.

**Drew A. Dolan** (Chapter 3) is an associate professor in the Department of Public Administration and Policy Analysis at Southern Illinois University–Edwardsville, where he also serves as director of the MPA program. He has consulted with and conducted research on units of local government for more than twenty years; most recently he has been conducting research on the relationships between local governments and nonprofit organizations. He has published numerous articles, technical reports, and chapters, and had co-edited the previous volume of this text. He has an MPA and a PhD from Northern Illinois University.

**Candace Goode Vick** (Chapter 10) is an associate professor and undergraduate coordinator in the Department of Parks, Recreation and Tourism Management at North Carolina State University. Her areas of interest include program evaluation and youth development. Dr. Goode Vick previously served as NC State's director of the Recreation Resources Service, where she worked with local governments, nonprofit agencies, and private citizens to improve the quality of the parks and recreational opportunities throughout North Carolina. She has published articles in the *Journal of Park and Recreation Administration, SPRE Annual on Education,* and the *Recreation Research Review.* Dr. Goode Vick received her doctorate of recreation from Indiana University.

**Bob Hart** (Chapter 12) is president of The Innovation Groups (IG), a nonprofit organization dedicated to assisting local governments to be innovative and creative in their service delivery and policy development. He joined IG after having served as city manager of five Texas cities: Georgetown, Huntsville, Pampa, Sweetwater, and Sundown. Mr. Hart has been active in the field of emergency management as an instructor at the Emergency Management Institute in Emmitsburg, Maryland, as a speaker at the UN Environmental Conference on Awareness and Preparedness for Emergencies at the Local Level, and as an author of articles concerning emergency management in such publications *PM* Magazine and *The International Journal on Mass Disasters and Emergencies*. He served on the advisory committee for the Natural Hazards Research and Applications Information Center, University of Colorado, to develop the *Holistic Disaster Recovery Handbook*. He holds a BS degree from Baylor University and an MPA from the University of North Texas.

**Donald T. Iannone** (Chapter 7) is a thirty-year veteran of the economic development field. He has run his own economic development strategy consulting firm, Donald T. Iannone & Associates, since 1986. Previously, Mr. Iannone directed the Economic Development Center at Cleveland State University and was director of business development for the Greater Cleveland Growth Association. His firm has worked on more than 250 economic development projects in forty-one states and thirteen countries. He is the author of numerous academic and professional articles, book chapters, monographs, and other publications. He publishes the *Economic Development Futures Journal,* which tracks economic development trends and issues nationally and internationally.

**Cathy R. Lazarus** (Chapter 9) is the director of public works for the city of Mountain View, California. Before joining Mountain View ten years ago, Ms. Lazarus worked for Santa Clara County, California, in a variety of capacities, including strategic issues manager, deputy parks director, administrative services manager for general services, and risk management director. She is a member of the American Public Works Association, American Water Works Association, and Tau Beta Pi, the National Engineering Honor Society. Ms. Lazarus has a BA in environmental planning from Stanford University and a master of city planning from the Harvard Graduate School of Design

**Stuart Meck** (Chapter 6), FAICP, is director of the Center for Government Services in the Edward J. Bloustein School of Planning and Public Policy at Rutgers, the State University of New Jersey, in New Brunswick. Mr. Meck is a former national president of the American Planning Association (APA), has thirty-four years of experience as a professional planner and public administrator, and has written widely on planning and land use controls. He was the principal investigator for the APA's Growing Smart project, which developed a new generation of model planning and zoning enabling legislation for the United States. He is a licensed professional planner in New Jersey and a registered professional community planner in Michigan, as well as a Fellow of the American Institute of Certified Planners. He holds a BA and an MA in journalism, a master of city planning from Ohio State University, and an MBA from Wright State University.

**Jonathan Q. Morgan** (Chapter 8) is an assistant professor of public administration and government in the School of Government at the University of North Carolina at Chapel Hill. He specializes in state, local, and regional economic development. Dr. Morgan serves as course director for the annual Basic Economic Development Course at UNC-CH. Prior to joining the School of Government in 2003, he worked for Regional Technology Strategies, Inc., an economic and workforce development consulting firm located in

Carrboro–Chapel Hill. He has also served as director of economic policy and research for the North Carolina Department of Commerce, and research and policy director for the North Carolina Institute of Minority Economic Development. He holds a BA in economics from the University of Virginia, an MPA from Clark Atlanta University, and a PhD in public administration from North Carolina State University.

**William C. Rivenbark** (Chapter 16) is an associate professor in the School of Government at the University of North Carolina at Chapel Hill. He specializes in local government administration, focusing primarily on performance and financial management. He is the coauthor of *Performance Budgeting for State and Local Government* (M. E. Sharpe, 2003) and has published numerous articles in academic and professional journals. Dr. Rivenbark also has worked in local government in various management positions. He earned his BS from Auburn University, his MPA from Auburn University at Montgomery, and his PhD from Mississippi State University.

**Carl W. Stenberg** (Editor and Chapter 1) is a professor of public administration and government and director of the MPA program at the School of Government at the University of North Carolina at Chapel Hill. Previously, he served as dean, Yale Gordon College of Liberal Arts, University of Baltimore; director, Weldon Cooper Center for Public Service, University of Virginia; executive director, Council of State Governments; and assistant director, U.S. Advisory Commission on Intergovernmental Relations. He is former feature editor of the *Public Administration Review* and co-author of *America's Future Work Force*. He is a Fellow and past chair of the board of directors of the National Academy of Public Administration and past president of the American Society for Public Administration. His teaching and research interests include intergovernmental administration, leadership, regionalism, and strategic planning. Dr. Stenberg received his BA from Allegheny College and his MPA and PhD from the State University of New York at Albany.

**Gregory Streib** (Chapter 5) is a professor at the Andrew Young School of Policy Studies at Georgia State University, where he also serves as chair of the Department of Public Administration and Urban Studies. He specializes in public management and applied research methods. His research has addressed a variety of public management topics, including strategic planning, pay-for-performance, health care cost reduction, performance measurement, reinventing government, and the implementation of e-governance initiatives. Dr. Streib received his PhD from Northern Illinois University.

**John W. Swain** (Chapters 4 and 14) is a professor of public administration and director of the Institute for Public Policy and Administration in the College of Business and Public Administration at Governors State University. His research and writing interests include public budgeting and financial management and public administration. He co-edited the previous volume of this text. Dr. Swain was the first coordinator of the Secretariat of the Illinois City Management Association. He received a BA from the University of New Hampshire and MA and PhD degrees from Northern Illinois University.

**Gordon P. Whitaker** (Chapter 15) is a professor of public administration and government in the School of Government at the University of North Carolina at Chapel Hill. He currently directs the school's Public Intersection Project, focusing on cross-sector collaboration to address public problems. His research and writing interests include local government organization and management, alternative public service delivery arrangements (including nonprofit agencies), citizen participation, civic education, and professional education for public service. Professor Whitaker's research has been supported by grants from the National Science Foundation, the National Institute of Justice, the North Carolina Governor's Crime Commission, and the Jesse Ball duPont Fund. His teaching includes courses in performance evaluation, organization theory, public management and leadership, and local government. In 1997 he received ICMA's Award for Local Government Education for his work in civic education. Professor Whitaker earned his PhD in political science from Indiana University.

# *Index*

# Supplementary Material Online

Items can be accessed at http://bookstore.icma.org/Supplement_to_Managing_Local_Government_Services_W37.cfm

## Chapter 1: Meeting the Challenge of Change

"The City in the Regional Mosaic," by Nelson Wikstrom, in *The Future of Local Government Administration* (with response by James Keene) (ICMA, 2002).

"Structuring Local Government Units and Relationships," by Carl W. Stenberg, in *The Future of Local Government in Michigan: Symposium Proceedings,* ed. Joe Ohren (Michigan Municipal League Foundation, 2000).

"Moving Local Government GIS from the Tactical to the Practical," by William J. McGill, in *The GIS Guide for Local Government Officials,* ed. Cory Fleming (ESRI Press, 2005).

"My First Week as a City Manager . . . or What They Never Taught Me in 'Next Generation' School," by Linda Kelly, *PM* Magazine (May 2006).

"ISEEK Spotlight: Kandis Hanson," *PM* Magazine (January/February 2006).

"Continued Citizen Involvement Proves Effective," by Kelli Behr and Sergeant Richard King, *PM* Magazine (August 2005).

## Chapter 2: The Legal Foundations of Local Government

Ken Smith, "Working with the Municipal Attorney," *Alabama Municipal Journal* (April 2005).

"Managing Legal Services," *MIS Report* 27 (ICMA, December 1995), excerpt.

## Chapter 3: The Clerk

"Establishing a Records Management Program," Chapter 1 from *Records Management: A Practical Guide for Cities and Counties* (ICMA, 1996).

## Chapter 4: Budgeting and Financial Management

Job description for finance director (Monroe, Ohio)

Job description for budget director (Ormond Beach, Florida)

Appendix B, "Financial Policy Statements," *Evaluating Financial Condition: A Handbook for Local Government* (ICMA, 2003).

Sample fee schedules:

Wilmette, Illinois All

Hickory, North Carolina All

Emeryville, California Planning and building

Georgetown, Texas Development Services

For a list of all ICMA publications related to budgeting/financial management, go to the finance and budgeting topic on the main ICMA Web site, icma.org.

## Chapter 5: Human Resource Management

Job description for HR director (Allegan County, Michigan)

"Case Study: Who Is Doing the Department-Head Hiring Anyway?" *PM* Magazine (December 2005).

"Eagan, Minnesota: Growth with Grace," by Christine Smith, *PM* Magazine (December 2005).

"Developing a Competitive Pay Structure," Fox Lawson & Associates LLC.

Excerpt from *Public Sector's Guide to Skill-Based Pay System Development and Implementation,* by Rollie O. Waters (Waters Consulting Group, 2006).

"Workforce Development Planning Guide," Washoe County, Nevada (April 2005).

For a list of all ICMA publications related to personnel/human resources, go to the personnel/human resources topic on the main ICMA Web site, icma.org.

## Chapter 6: Planning

Job description for planning director (Gaithersburg, Maryland)

Two case studies from "Streamlining Development and Building Permitting," *IQ Report* 37 no. 2 (2005).

"Where We Live: The Impact of How Communities Grow," by Myrt Webb and Melinda Anderson, *PM* Magazine (September 2005).

For a list of all ICMA publications related to planning, go to the planning and zoning topic on the main ICMA Web site, icma .org, and to smartgrowth.org.

## Chapter 7: Economic Development

"Is Gambling a Good Economic Development Bet?" from Chapter 3 of *Economic Development: Strategies for State and Local Practice,* by Steven G. Koven and Thomas S. Lyons (ICMA, 2003).

Job description for economic development director, Silver City–Grant County Economic Development Corporation (New Mexico)

"Large Format [Big Box] Impact Study," from Bozeman, Montana

"Nothing Concentrates the Mind Like the Threat of Death," from *Managing Local Economic Development: Cases in Decision Making,* ed. James M. Banovetz (ICMA, 2004).

"Connections Matter: Using Networks for Economic Development," by Camille Cates Barnett and Oscar Rodríguez, *PM* Magazine (March 2006).

"Historic Train Depot Breathing New Life into One Small Town," by Jill FitzSimmons, *PM* Magazine (June 2006).

For a list of all ICMA publications related to economic development, go to the community and economic development topic on the main ICMA Web site, icma.org.

## Chapter 8: Community Development and Affordable Housing

Job description for community development director (Mountain View, California)

"There Are Good Ways to Take Care of Nuisance Abatement," by Donnie Tuck, *PM* (April 2006).

"Inclusionary Zoning: A Key Tool in the Search for Workable Affordable Housing Programs," by David Rusk, *PM* (April 2006).

"Consensus Building: Keys to Success," *IQ Report* 36 (October 2004).

For a list of all ICMA publications related to economic development, go to the community and economic development topic on the main ICMA Web site, icma.org.

## Chapter 9: Public Works

Job description for public works director (West Jordan, Utah)

"Fleet Reduction and Culture Change: 10 Steps to Success," by Jeffrey Friedman and Robert Fox, *PM* Magazine (August 2005).

"Green Building," *IQ Report* 35 (December 2003).

Public Works Citizen Survey (Douglas County, Colorado)

Climate Protection Plan (Cambridge, Massachusetts)

"Landfill Methane Recovery and Use Opportunities," from Methane to Markets Web site

For a list of all ICMA publications related to public works, go to the public works and environment topics on the main ICMA Web site, icma.org.

## Chapter 10: Public Parks and Recreation

Job description for parks and recreation director (Ames, Iowa)

Department of Regional Parks and Open Space, 2005 Master Plan Update Public Input Survey (Washoe County, Nevada)

Five Year Parks and Recreation Master Plan (Butler, Indiana)

For a list of all ICMA publications related to parks and recreation, go to the parks and recreation topic on the main ICMA Web site, icma.org.

## Chapter 11: Health and Human Services

Job description for director of human services (Phoenix, Arizona)

"Health Services: Client-Based or Population-Based?" by Kathy Rice, *PM* (January/February 2004).

"Health Care: Is It a Local Issue?" by Stacey Ketchum, *PM* Magazine (August 2001).

Resource List: Sustainable Planning for Aging in Place (ICMA, 2006).

Active Living Strategies—Amherst, Massachusetts, Case Study (ICMA, 2006).

For a list of all ICMA publications related to health and human services, go to the human services and the active and healthy living topics on the main ICMA Web site, icma.org.

## Chapter 12: Emergency Management

Job description for director of emergency management (Boulder, Colorado)

Emergency Operations Plan and appendices (Cranston, Rhode Island)

"After the Rescue Workers Go Home," by Cory Fleming, *PM* Magazine (May 2006).

"Emergency Operations Plan Self-Assessment," CityScan (May 2006).

For a list of all ICMA publications related to emergency management, go to the public safety topic on the main ICMA Web site, icma.org.

## Chapter 13: Police Services

Job description for police chief (Redmond, Oregon)

"Successful Police-Chief Mentoring: Implications from the Subculture," by Terry Eisenberg, *PM* Magazine (December 2005).

"A Comprehensive Approach to Reducing Demand for Services," by Michael Matulavich, *The Police Chief* (IACP, April 2006).

For a list of all ICMA publications related to police services, go to the public safety topic on the main ICMA Web site, icma .org.

## Chapter 14: Fire and Other Emergency Services

Job description for fire chief (Homewood, Illinois)

"Enhancing the Manager/Fire Chief Relationship," by Frank Benest and Ruben Grijalva, *PM* Magazine (January/February 2002).

"CFOD, the Next Step in Professional Development for the Fire Service," by Tom Harmer, *PM* Magazine (October 2005).

"Collaborative Response," by Dave Hanneman, *Fire Chief* (March 2006).

For a list of all ICMA publications related to fire services, go to the public safety topic on the main ICMA Web site, icma.org.

## Chapter 15: Service Delivery Alternatives

Administrative Internal Control Questionnaire, for evaluating non-profit contractors (Miami-Dade County, Florida)

"Shared Services Report" (Eau Claire, Wisconsin)

"Managing High-Risk Outsourcing," by Emanuele Padovani and David Young, *PM* Magazine (January/February 2006).

Guidelines for Alternative Service Delivery (Charlotte, North Carolina)

Guidelines for Services Contracting

Departmental Guide to Privatization and Competition Projects

Guide to Competitive Bidding and Optimization

For a list of all ICMA publications related to alternative service delivery, go to the management topic on the main ICMA Web site, icma.org.

## Chapter 16: A Manager's Toolbox

Appendix C, "Environmental Scan—Winston-Salem, North Carolina," from *Strategic Planning for Local Government,* 2nd edition (ICMA, 2005).

Chapter 14, "Implementation Suggestions," from *How Effective Are Your Community Services?* (ICMA, 2006).

"Developing and Sustaining Political Will to Use Performance Measurement," by Ray Patchett, *PM* Magazine (June 2006).

"Performance Budgeting: Dover's First-Time Strategic Approach," by Janet Kelly and Anthony DePrima, *PM* Magazine (November 2004).

For a list of all ICMA publications related to management, go to the management and performance measurement topics on the main ICMA Web site, icma.org.

## Photo Credits

Cover photos:
1. City of Longview, WA
2. iStockphoto.com
3. iStockphoto.com

| 1 | 2 | 3 |
|---|---|---|

Photo pages:
1. City of Lynnwood, WA
2. City of Longview, WA
3. iStockphoto.com
4. City of Longview, WA
5. iStockphoto.com
6. City of Lynnwood, WA
7. City of Chanhassen, MN
8. City of Lynnwood, WA
9. Sedgwick County, KS, photo by Tony Guiliano
10. City of Longview, WA
11. PhotoSpin.com
12. iStockphoto.com
13. iStockphoto.com
14. Sedgwick County, KS, photo by Tony Guiliano
15. City of Lynnwood, WA
16. PhotoSpin.com

| 1 | 2 | 3 | 4 |
|---|---|---|---|
| 5 | 6 | 7 | 8 |
| 9 | 10 | 11 | 12 |
| 13 | 14 | 15 | 16 |

**Managing Local Government Services**
A Practical Guide

Design and layout: Charles E. Mountain
Text type: Slimbach, Interstate

Printer: Batson Printing, Benton Harbor, MI